WORDS
IN
COMMON

WORDS IN COMMON

ESSAYS ON LANGUAGE, CULTURE, AND SOCIETY

Edited by
Gillian Thomas
Saint Mary's University, Halifax

 **ADDISON-WESLEY**

An imprint of Addison Wesley Longman Ltd.

Don Mills, Ontario • Reading, Massachusetts • Harlow, England
Melbourne, Australia • Amsterdam, The Netherlands • Bonn, Germany

Publisher: Brian Henderson
Managing Editor: Linda Scott
Editor: Pamela Erlichman
Cover Design: Anthony Leung
Cover Image: Copyright © Corel Corporation
Page Design and Layout: Heidy Lawrance Associates
Production Coordinator: Alexandra Odulak
Manufacturing Coordinator: Sharon Latta Paterson

The credits on page ix are an extension of this copyright page. The publishers will gladly receive information enabling them to rectify any errors in references or credits.

Canadian Cataloguing in Publication Data

Main entry under title:

Words in common : essays on language, culture, and society

ISBN 0-201-61374-3

1. English language — Rhetoric. 2. College readers. I. Thomas, Gillian, 1944–

PE1417.W672 1999   808'.0427   C99-930395-3

ISBN 0-201-61374-3

Printed and bound in Canada.

D E - DPC - 03

CONTENTS

PREFACE

The title of this text, *Words in Common*, reflects the situation in which we find ourselves, whether as teachers or as students, in a class on English composition. We arrive with widely differing personal histories and backgrounds in language practice. "English was never my best subject," is a familiar student complaint. Others grew up with a mother tongue other than English and find English idiom and structures literally alien. Most students are apt to assume that their teacher's own "mother tongue" is the formal prose of the academic essay. Yet probably hardly any of us grew up in homes where everyday language bore much resemblance to the way we later learned to write (or speak) as academics.

The selection of readings which follows assumes a common project — the task of developing ways of using the conventions of formal English prose to become a flexible and clear medium of expression. The selection has also been made with the assumption that we learn to write well, not by focusing on rhetorical devices and then inventing subjects to hone their use, but by first, as Kurt Vonnegut advises in "How to Write with Style," finding "a subject you care about." Consequently, the subjects covered in this text are all ones that nearly everyone in the classroom will have experienced directly in some form.

The selection of readings also recognizes that our notions of what is acceptable in formal writing is undergoing considerable change. Many of us, both teachers and students, have been told in the past to avoid the first person singular in formal writing. For some, "I" has become the forbidden word in any writing intended for public view. This once-firm rule is now routinely and deliberately broken in most popular and much academic writing. The established notion of what constitutes a formal "essay" has undergone radical shifts in recent years, allowing for more personal and, arguably, more honest expression. As Graham Good wrote in *The Observing Self: Rediscovering the Essay* (1988), "The essay is an act of personal witness. The essay is at once the *in*scription of a self and the *de*scription of an object."

Some of the essays selected for *Words in Common* adhere to traditional models of academic style and approach, for example Hugh Brody's "Language in the Arctic," Susan Ehrlich's "Linguistics in Action" or David Noble's "Digital Diploma Mills." Others, such as Nicole Nolan's "Isn't It Ironic?" are more journalistic in nature or, like Marie Annharte Baker's "Borrowing Enemy Language," owe more to the writer's style of speech than to the conventions of formal prose. Whatever the level of formality, all of the selections have been made with the intention of provoking readers to think, discuss and write.

In Plato's *Phaedrus*, Socrates compares written words unfavourably with speech, saying that written words are a static one-way form of communication, that they "seem to talk to you as though they were intelligent, but if you ask them anything about what they say, from a desire to be instructed, they go on telling you just the same thing forever." This is true only if one sees reading as a passive act to which the reader brings nothing but submission to the authority of the words on the page. The readings in *Words in Common* are presented, not primarily as models for students to follow, but as elements in a changing dialogue. The texts speak to each other, not only as they do in the formally paired essays such as those by Orwell and Fawcett, Amiel and Salutin and the two on "Dumpster Diving," but also as they comment on each other both within and across subject headings. Both the selections themselves and the framing apparatus of introductions and questions in *Words in Common* encourage students to be critical and active readers and to "talk back" to the texts both verbally and in writing.

ACKNOWLEDGEMENTS

A number of friends and colleagues have contributed greatly to this book. I would particularly like to thank Linda Burnett, Renee Hulan, Wendy Katz, and Terry Whalen at Saint Mary's, and Bruce Wark at the King's College School of Journalism for their suggestions and encouragement. Reviewers from a number of universities and colleges across the country offered useful recommendations at an early stage of the project, and I would especially like to thank Sharon Smulders of Mount Royal College for her painstaking and astute advice. At Addison Wesley Longman, Brian Henederson, Peter Luke, and Linda Scott were helpful in the several different stages of the project. Andrea Patterson was immensely resourceful and efficient in locating material and helping prepare the manuscript for publication. Throughout the project I relied constantly on the unfailing good judgement and support of Donna Smyth.

Gillian Thomas

CREDITS

Chapter 1

Richard Wright, "Discovering Books," from *Black Boy*, Harper and Row, 1945.

Alberto Manguel, "Forbidden Reading." Extracted from *A History of Reading* by Alberto Manguel. Copyright © 1996. Reprinted by permission of Knopf Canada.

Nick Smith, "Mediations on Meditation," from *Adbusters Quarterly*, (Autumn 1997), pp. 38-40. Reprinted by permission of Adbusters Media Foundation.

Margaret Atwood, "Nine Beginnings," from *The Writer on Her Work*, ed. Janet Sternburg, Virago, 1992. Copyright by Margaret Atwood. Reprinted by permission of the author.

Kurt Vonnegut, "How to Write with Style," from *Exploring Language*, ed. Gary Goshgarian, published by HarperCollins *Publishers Ltd.*

Chapter 2

Hugh Brody, "Language in the Arctic," from *Living Arctic: Hunters of the Canadian North* by Hugh Brody. © 1987, published by Douglas & McIntyre. Reprinted by permission of the publisher.

Marie Annharte Baker, "Borrowing Enemy Language: A First Nation Woman's Use of English." Copyright © 1993 by the author. Originally published in *West Coast Line*, vol. 10 (27/1) Spring 1993, pp. 59-66. Reprinted by permission of the author.

Eva Hoffman, "Lost in Translation," from *Lost in Translation: Life in a New Language* by Eva Hoffman. Published by E. P. Dutton, 1989.

Himani Bannerji, "The Sound Barrier: Translating Ourselves in Language and Experience," from *Language in Her Eye: Writing and Gender*, ed. Libby Scheir, Sarah Sheard, and Eleanor Wachtel, 1990. Copyright by Himani Bannerji. Reprinted by permission of the author.

David Carpenter, "Nom de Plume," from *Writing Home: Selected Essays*, by David Carpenter, published by Fifth House Publishers, 1994. Copyright © 1994 by David Carpenter. Reprinted by permission of the author.

Chapter 3

Casey Miller and Kate Swift, "One Small Step for Genkind," from the *New York Times Magazine*, April 16 1972. Copyright by Casey Miller and Kate Swift.

Deborah Tannen, "'I'll Explain It to You': Lecturing and Listening," from *You Just Don't Understand: Women and Men in Conversation* by Deborah Tannen, published by William and Morrow Co., 1990.

Deborah Cameron, "Rethinking Language and Gender Studies," from *Language and Gender: Interdisciplinary Perspectives*, ed. Sara Mills, published by Longman, 1995.

Jan Morris, "Travelling Writer," from *The Writer on Her Work*, ed. Janet Sternburg, Virago, 1992. Copyright by Jan Morris.

Susan Ehrlich, "Linguistics in Action," from *Changing Methods: Feminists Transforming Practice*, ed. Sandra Burt and Loraine Code, published by Broadview Press, 1995. Originally titled "Critical Linguistics as Feminist Methodology." Copyright by Susan Ehrlich. Reprinted by permission of the author and Broadview Press.

Emily Martin, "The Egg and the Sperm: How Science Has Constructed a Romance Based on Stereotypical Male-Female Roles," from *Signs* 16:3 (1991) 485-501. Copyright © 1991 University of Chicago Press. Reprinted by permission of the publisher.

Chapter 4

Thomas Friedmann, "Heard Any Good Jews Lately?" from *Speaking of Words*, ed. James MacKillop and Donna Woolfolk Cross. Published by Holt Rinehart and Winston, 1982. Copyright by Thomas Friedmann.

Gloria Naylor, "The Meanings of a Word," from *Language Awareness*, ed. Paul Escholz, Alfred Rosa, and Virginia Clark, published by St. Martin's Press, 1974. Copyright by Gloria Naylor.

Rachel Giese, "Hating the Hate-Crime Bill," from *This Magazine*, November 1995. Copyright by Rachel Giese.

Lynn Crosbie, "Last Words: A Memoir," from *This Magazine*, October 1996. Copyright by Lynn Crosbie. Reprinted by permission of the author.

Chapter 5

John Sopinka, "In My Opinion," from *University Affairs*, April 1994. Copyright by John Sopinka.

Allan C. Hutchinson, "Like Lunches, Speech Is Never Free," from *University Affairs*, June-July 1994, p. 12. Copyright by Allan C. Hutchinson.

Kimberley Noble, "Bound and Gagged," from *Canadian Forum*, January 1993. Copyright by Kimberley Noble.

Margaret Atwood, "Pornography," from *Chatelaine*, 56: 61 118 1983. Copyright by Margaret Atwood. Reprinted by permission of the author.

Chapter 6

George Orwell, "Politics and the English Language." Copyright © George Orwell, 1946. Reprinted by permission of Mark Hamilton as the Literary Executor of the Estate of the Late Sonia Brownell Orwell and Martin Secker & Warburg Ltd.

Brian Fawcett, "Politics and the English Language 1991," from *Unusual Circumstances, Interesting Times, and Other Impolite Interventions* by Brian Fawcett, published by New Star Books, 1991. Reprinted by permission of the publisher.

Barbara Amiel, "Backstage Mozambique: A Flagrant Violation of Rights," from *Maclean's*, January 19 1981. Reprinted by permission of Maclean's.

Rick Salutin, "The Mozambique Caper," from *Marginal Notes: Challenges to the Mainstream* by Rick Salutin, published by Lester and Orpen Dennys, 1984.

Chapter 7

Frank M. Coleman, "Big Lie in Marlboro Country," from *Adbusters Quarterly*, Summer 1994, pp. 83-86. Reprinted by permission of Adbusters Media Foundation.

Phil Ryan, "Compromising Partnerships," from *Canadian Forum*, July-August 1998, pp. 14-19. Copyright by Phil Ryan.

Nicole Nolan, "Isn't It Ironic?" from *This Magazine*, November-December 1996, pp. 23-25. Copyright by Nicole Nolan.

Chapter 8

Marshall McLuhan, "Television: The Timid Giant," from *Understanding Media* by Marshall McLuhan, 1964. Reprinted by permission of the Canadian Speakers' and Writers' Service.

Maude Barlow and James Winter, "The Horse's Mouth," from *Canadian Forum*, November 1997, pp. 20-22.

Linda Grant, "We're Losing the Plot," from the *Manchester Guardian Weekly*, June 21 1998, p. 29.

Andrew Cash, "Pump Up the Volume," from *This Magazine*, December-January 1996, pp. 16-19. Reprinted by permission of the author.

Michael Posner, "Art by Committee," from *Globe and Mail*, May 25, 1998, p. A6.

Chapter 9

Randal Marlin, "Where There's Smoke," from *Canadian Forum*, May 1998, pp. 11-13. Copyright by Randal Marlin. Reprinted by permission of the author.

seeKorum, "Adventures in the Number Trade," from *This Magazine*, June-July 1993, pp. 26-28.

John Goddard, "A Real Whopper," from *Saturday Night*, May 1996, pp. 46-54, 64.

Peter Robertson, "More than Meets the Eye," from *Archivaria*, vol. 1, no. 2 (1976): 33-43. Copyright by Peter Robertson. Reprinted by permission of the author. Photos courtesy of National Archives of Canada, C85885, C70696, PA648.

Thomas King, "How I Spent My Summer Vacation: History, Story, and the Cant of Authenticity." © 1988 Dead Dog Café Productions Inc. Reprinted by permission of the author.

Chapter 10

Joyce Nelson, "The Temple of Fashion." Reprinted with permission from *Sign Crimes/ Road Kill: From Mediascape to Landscape* by Joyce Nelson. Published by Between the Lines Inc., Toronto. © Joyce Nelson, 1992.

Dan Robins, "Third World Chic," from *This Magazine*, June 1994, pp. 23-24. Copyright by Dan Robins.

McKenzie Wark, "The Postmodern Pair," from *New Internationalist*, June 1998. Reprinted with permission from *New Internationalist*.

Lars Eighner, "Dumpster Diving: The Fine Art of Scavenging," from *Harper's Magazine*, December 1991, vol. 283, no. 1699.

Cory Doctorow, "Dumpster Diving." © 1997 Cory Doctorow, originally published in *Wired Magazine*, September 1997. Reprinted by permission of the author.

Chapter 11

Ursula M. Franklin C.C. FRSC, "All Is Not Well in the House of Technology." Appeared in *Transactions of the Royal Society of Canada*, Series VI, VII, VIII. 1997, p. 23-33. Reprinted by permission of the author.

Wayne Ellwood, "Seduced by Technology," from *New Internationalist*, December 1996. Reprinted with permission from *New Internationalist*.

David F. Noble, "Digital Diploma Mills: The Automation of Higher Education." Copyright by David F. Noble.

Tony Leighton, "The New Nature," from *Equinox* 1994. Copyright by Tony Leighton.

Robert Fulford, "The Ideology of the Book," from *Queen's Quarterly*, 101/3, Winter 1994. Copyright by Robert Fulford. Reprinted by permission of the author.

R. Murray Schafer, "Dub: Defending the Value of the Original in an Age of Duplicates," from *Canadian Forum*, November 1994. Copyright by R. Murray Schafer.

Chapter 12

Stephen Overbury, "Spinning Facts into Fiction," from *How To Research Almost Anything: A Canadian Guide for Students, Consumers, and Business*, by Stephen Overbury and Susanna Buenaventura, published by McGraw-Hill Ryerson, 1998.

Mark Jordan, "Ten Internet Myths," from *Emergency Librarian*, November-December 1997. Copyright by Mark Jordan. Reprinted with permission of *Teacher: Librarian: The Journal for School Library Professionals*.

Joyce Thomson, "Scholarly Surfing: Smart Strategies for Internet Research." Copyright by Joyce Thomson. Reprinted by permission of the author.

CHAPTER 1

READING & WRITING

We speak of "reading and writing" in a single breath as if they were twin activities. However, their relationship is a complicated one. Reading as a skill precedes writing. Most of us learned to read long before the marks we made on the page amounted to anything very coherent. It is also true that few people become effective writers without first being good readers. What is meant by a "good reader," however, is open to many interpretations. Some schools and public libraries reward children with pizzas or other prizes for the number of books read during a summer vacation, thus implying that reading is a necessary but irksome skill.

The three essays that treat the subject of reading in this chapter present a very different view. Both Richard Wright and Alberto Manguel describe situations in which access to books is severely restricted. Wright, growing up black in the segregated Southern U.S., has to use subterfuge to borrow books from the public library and then finds his inner world profoundly disrupted by the books he reads. Alberto Manguel outlines some of the ways in which restrictions on reading are used as a means of social and political control. In a contrasting essay, Nick Smith sees reading as one of a range of activities that tend to distract him from meditation. In their different ways each of these essays dwells on reading as a highly private activity. However it is worth pointing out that it is only in recent times that reading has come to be seen as an exclusively private act.

Before compulsory education was widespread, books were largely the property of the wealthy and most people only experienced books by being read to. "Reading" for centuries meant reading aloud. It has been suggested that even the literate in medieval times found it difficult to read silently and mumbled words under their breath, or at least moved their lips while reading. In 1198 Hugh of Saint Victor described, in the Latin which then served as the shared language of the educated, the three possible types of reading, "I can read aloud to you, you can read aloud to me, and I can read contemplatively to myself." Nearly seven centuries later, English novelist Jane Austen writes of her father reading Cowper's poems aloud to the family every morning, of her dissatisfaction with her brother's choice of Scott's *Marmion* for family reading every night, and of her more enjoyable candlelit readings with her sister. Some of us were lucky enough to have books read aloud to us as children, but for the most part, our adult experience of reading is now what Hugh of Saint Victor referred to as "silent contemplation of the text."

Writing, by contrast, however lonely an activity it almost always feels, inevitably has a public dimension. At the back of any writer's mind, even for someone writing a seemingly private diary, is some sense of an audience, sometimes ghostly, sometimes clear-cut and defined. Perhaps because of this element of performance, a certain mystique is attached to the notion of "a writer." Those who become known for their published writings often find themselves beset by questions that seem to them to have little to do with the hard work of writing. Margaret Atwood's response, "Nine Beginnings," to an editor's question "Why do you write?" shows some of this testiness about finding the occupation of writer set apart from other kinds of work. The truth, as Vonnegut suggests in his pithy "How to Write with Style," is much more mundane. The business of making "thousands of little marks on paper" is a "tough job," and is only ever worthwhile when the writer cares about the subject.

Anyone who writes is a writer, who first of all works at being a "good reader." Read on.

Richard Wright (1906-1960)

Born on a Mississippi plantation, Wright had his education interrupted by his family's poverty and the threat of violence from hostile whites. After successfully completing high school, he moved to Chicago where he wrote a first novel which remained unpublished till after his death. Following the publication of his two best-selling memoirs, Native Son *(1940) and* Black Boy *(1945), Wright moved permanently to Europe, partly because of the racism he continued to encounter in the U.S. and partly because he was hounded for the communist views he had held during the period of the Great Depression.*

This selection from Wright's autobiographical Black Boy *refers to a time when racial segregation was legally sanctioned and enforced in the southern U.S. Wright's illicit access to the public library and his reading of "deep stuff" is regarded with intense suspicion by the whites he knows. While the books he reads open up "new avenues of feeling and seeing," they also create "a vast sense of distance" between Wright's inner self and the world in which he lives.*

DISCOVERING BOOKS

1 One morning I arrived early at work and went into the bank lobby where the Negro porter was mopping. I stood at a counter and picked up the Memphis *Commercial Appeal* and began my free reading of the press. I came finally to the editorial page and saw an article dealing with one H. L. Mencken. I knew by hearsay that he was the editor of the *American Mercury*, but aside from that I knew nothing about him. The article was a furious denunciation of Mencken, concluding with one, hot, short sentence: Mencken is a fool.

2 I wondered what on earth this Mencken had done to call down upon him the scorn of the South. The only people I had ever heard denounced in the South were Negroes, and this man was not a Negro. Then what ideas did Mencken hold that made a newspaper like the *Commercial Appeal* castigate him publicly? Undoubtedly he must be advocating ideas that the South did not like. Were there, then, people other than Negroes who criticized the South? I knew that during the Civil War the South had hated northern whites, but I had not encountered such hate during my life. Knowing no more of Mencken than I did at that moment, I felt a vague sympathy for him. Had not the South, which had assigned me the role of a nonman, cast at him its hardest words?

3 Now, how could I find out about this Mencken? There was a huge library near the riverfront, but I knew that Negroes were not allowed to patronize its shelves any more than they were the parks and playgrounds of the city. I had gone into the library several times to get books for the white men on the job. Which of them would now help me to get books? And how could I read them without causing concern to the white men with whom I worked? I had so far been successful in hiding my thoughts and feelings from them, but I knew that I would create hostility if I went about this business of reading in a clumsy way.

4 I weighed the personalities of the men on the job. There was Don, a Jew; but I distrusted him. His position was not much better than mine and I knew that he

was uneasy and insecure; he had always treated me in an offhand, bantering way that barely concealed his contempt. I was afraid to ask him to help me to get books; his frantic desire to demonstrate a racial solidarity with the whites against Negroes might make him betray me.

5   Then how about the boss? No, he was a Baptist and I had the suspicion that he would not be quite able to comprehend why a black boy would want to read Mencken. There were other white men on the job whose attitudes showed clearly that they were Kluxers or sympathizers, and they were out of the question.

6   There remained only one man whose attitude did not fit into an anti-Negro category, for I had heard the white men refer to him as a "Pope lover." He was an Irish Catholic and was hated by the white Southerners. I knew that he read books, because I had got him volumes from the library several times. Since he, too, was an object of hatred, I felt that he might refuse me but would hardly betray me. I hesitated, weighing and balancing the imponderable realities.

7   One morning I paused before the Catholic fellow's desk.
"I want to ask you a favor," I whispered to him.
"What is it?"

10   "I want to read. I can't get books from the library. I wonder if you'd let me use your card?"
He looked at me suspiciously.
"My card is full most of the time," he said.
"I see," I said and waited, posing my question silently.
"You're not trying to get me into trouble, are you, boy?" he asked, staring at me.

15   "Oh, no, sir."
"What book do you want?"
"A book by H. L. Mencken."
"Which one?"
"I don't know. Has he written more than one?"

20   "He has written several."
"I didn't know that."
"What makes you want to read Mencken?"
"Oh, I just saw his name in the newspaper," I said.
"It's good of you to want to read," he said. "But you ought to read the right things."

25   I said nothing. Would he want to supervise my reading?
"Let me think," he said. "I'll figure out something."
I turned from him and he called me back. He stared at me quizzically.
"Richard, don't mention this to the other white men," he said.
"I understand," I said. "I won't say a word."

30   A few days later he called me to him.
"I've got a card in my wife's name," he said. "Here's mine."
"Thank you, sir."
"Do you think you can manage it?"
"I'll manage fine," I said.

35   "If they suspect you, you'll get in trouble," he said.
"I'll write the same kind of notes to the library that you wrote when you sent me for books," I told him. "I'll sign your name."

37   He laughed.
      "Go ahead. Let me see what you get," he said.
39   That afternoon I addressed myself to forging a note. Now, what were the
names of books written by H. L. Mencken? I did not know any of them. I finally
wrote what I thought would be a foolproof note: *Dear Madam: Will you please let
this nigger boy* — I used the word "nigger" to make the librarian feel that I could
not possibly be the author of the note — *have some books by H. L. Mencken?* I
forged the white man's name.
40   I entered the library as I had always done when on errands for whites, but I
felt that I would somehow slip up and betray myself. I doffed my hat, stood a
respectful distance from the desk, looked as unbookish as possible, and waited for
the white patrons to be taken care of. When the desk was clear of people, I still
waited. The white librarian looked at me.
      "What do you want, boy?"
      As though I did not possess the power of speech, I stepped forward and simply
handed her the forged note, not parting my lips.
      "What books by Mencken does he want?" she asked.
      "I don't know, ma'am," I said, avoiding her eyes.
45   "Who gave you this card?"
      "Mr. Falk," I said.
      "Where is he?"
      "He's at work, at the M —— Optical Company," I said. "I've been in here for
him before."
      "I remember," the woman said. "But he never wrote notes like this."
50   Oh, God, she's suspicious. Perhaps she would not let me have the books? If
she had turned her back at that moment, I would have ducked out the door and
never gone back. Then I thought of a bold idea.
      "You can call him up, ma'am," I said, my heart pounding.
      "You're not using these books, are you?" she asked pointedly.
      "Oh, no, ma'am. I can't read."
      "I don't know what he wants by Mencken," she said under her breath.
55   I knew now that I had won; she was thinking of other things and the race
question had gone out of her mind. She went to the shelves. Once or twice she
looked over her shoulder at me, as though she was still doubtful. Finally she came
forward with two books in her hand.
56   "I'm sending him two books," she said. "But tell Mr. Falk to come in next
time, or send me the names of the books he wants. I don't know what he wants
to read."
57   I said nothing. She stamped the card and handed me the books. Not daring
to glance at them, I went out of the library, fearing that the woman would call
me back for further questioning. A block away from the library I opened one of
the books and read a title: *A Book of Prefaces.* I was nearing my nineteenth birthday and I did not know how to pronounce the word *preface.* I thumbed the pages
and saw strange words and strange names. I shook my head, disappointed. I
looked at the other book; it was called *Prejudices.* I knew what that word meant;
I had heard it all my life. And right off I was on guard against Mencken's books.
Why would a man want to call a book *Prejudices?* The word was so stained with

all my memories of racial hate that I could not conceive of anybody using it for a title. Perhaps I had made a mistake about Mencken? A man who had prejudices must be wrong.

58 When I showed the books to Mr. Falk, he looked at me and frowned. "That librarian might telephone you," I warned him.

60 "That's all right," he said. "But when you're through reading those books, I want you to tell me what you get out of them."

61 That night in my rented room, while letting the hot water run over my can of pork and beans in the sink, I opened *A Book of Prefaces* and began to read. I was jarred and shocked by the style, the clear, clean, sweeping sentences. Why did he write like that? And how did one write like that? I pictured the man as a raging demon, slashing with his pen, consumed with hate, denouncing everything American, extolling everything European or German, laughing at the weaknesses of people, mocking God, authority. What was this? I stood up, trying to realize what reality lay behind the meaning of the words. ... Yes, this man was fighting, fighting with words. He was using words as a weapon, using them as one would use a club. Could words be weapons? Well, yes, for here they were. Then, maybe, perhaps, I could use them as a weapon? No. It frightened me. I read on and what amazed me was not what he said, but how on earth anybody had the courage to say it.

62 Occasionally I glanced up to reassure myself that I was alone in the room. Who were these men about whom Mencken was talking so passionately? Who was Anatole France? Joseph Conrad? Sinclair Lewis, Sherwood Anderson, Dostoevski, George Moore, Gustave Flaubert, Maupassant, Tolstoy, Frank Harris, Mark Twain, Thomas Hardy, Arnold Bennett, Stephen Crane, Zola, Norris, Gorky, Bergson, Ibsen, Balzac, Bernard Shaw, Dumas, Poe, Thomas Mann, O. Henry, Dreiser, H. G. Wells, Gogol, T. S. Eliot, Gide, Baudelaire, Edgar Lee Masters, Stendhal, Turgenev, Huneker, Nietzsche, and scores of others? Were these men real? Did they exist or had they existed? And how did one pronounce their names?

63 I ran across many words whose meanings I did not know, and I either looked them up in a dictionary or, before I had a chance to do that, encountered the word in a context that made its meaning clear. But what strange world was this? I concluded the book with the conviction that I had somehow overlooked something terribly important in life. I had once tried to write, had once reveled in feeling, had let my crude imagination roam, but the impulse to dream had been slowly beaten out of me by experience. Now it surged up again and I hungered for books, new ways of looking and seeing. It was not a matter of believing or disbelieving what I read, but of feeling something new, of being affected by something that made the look of the world different.

64 As dawn broke I ate my pork and beans, feeling dopey, sleepy. I went to work, but the mood of the book would not die; it lingered, coloring everything I saw, heard, did. I now felt that I knew what the white men were feeling. Merely because I had read a book that had spoken of how they lived and thought, I identified myself with that book. I felt vaguely guilty. Would I, filled with bookish notions, act in a manner that would make the whites dislike me?

65 I forged more notes and my trips to the library became more frequent. Reading grew into a passion. My first serious novel was Sinclair Lewis's *Main Street*. It made me see my boss, Mr. Gerald, and identify him as an American type. I

would smile when I saw him lugging his golf bags into the office. I had always felt a vast distance separating me from the boss, and now I felt closer to him, though still distant. I felt now that I knew him, that I could feel the very limits of his narrow life. And this had happened because I had read a novel about a mythical man called George F. Babbitt.

66   The plots and stories in the novels did not interest me so much as the point of view revealed. I gave myself over to each novel without reserve, without trying to criticize it; it was enough for me to see and feel something different. And for me, everything was something different. Reading was like a drug, a dope. The novels created moods in which I lived for days. But I could not conquer my sense of guilt, my feeling that the white men around me knew that I was changing, that I had begun to regard them differently.

67   Whenever I brought a book to the job, I wrapped it in newspaper — a habit that was to persist for years in other cities and under other circumstances. But some of the white men pried into my packages when I was absent and they questioned me.

"Boy, what are you reading those books for?"

"Oh, I don't know, sir."

70   "That's deep stuff you're reading, boy."

"I'm just killing time, sir."

"You'll addle your brains if you don't watch out."

73   I read Dreiser's *Jennie Gerhardt* and *Sister Carrie* and they revived in me a vivid sense of my mother's suffering; I was overwhelmed, I grew silent, wondering about the life around me. It would have been impossible for me to have told anyone what I derived from these novels, for it was nothing less than a sense of life itself. All my life had shaped me for the realism, the naturalism of the modern novel, and I could not read enough of them.

74   Steeped in new moods and ideas, I bought a ream of paper and tried to write; but nothing would come, or what did come was flat beyond telling. I discovered that more than desire and feeling were necessary to write and I dropped the idea. Yet I still wondered how it was possible to know people sufficiently to write about them? Could I ever learn about life and people? To me, with my vast ignorance, my Jim Crow station in life, it seemed a task impossible of achievement. I now knew what being a Negro meant. I could endure the hunger. I had learned to live with hate. But to feel that there were feelings denied me, that the very breath of life itself was beyond my reach, that more than anything else hurt, wounded me. I had a new hunger.

75   In buoying me up, reading also cast me down, made me see what was possible, what I had missed. My tension returned, new, terrible, bitter, surging, almost too great to be contained. I no longer felt that the world about me was hostile, killing; I *knew* it. A million times I asked myself what I could do to save myself, and there were no answers. I seemed forever condemned, ringed by walls.

76   I did not discuss my reading with Mr. Falk, who had lent me his library card; it would have meant talking about myself and that would have been too painful. I smiled each day, fighting desperately to maintain my old behavior, to keep my disposition seemingly sunny. But some of the white men discerned that I had begun to brood.

77   "Wake up there, boy!" Mr. Olin said one day.

"Sir!" I answered for the lack of a better word.

"You act like you've stolen something," he said.

80   I laughed in the way I knew he expected me to laugh, but I resolved to be more conscious of myself, to watch my every act, to guard and hide the new knowledge that was dawning within me.

81   If I went north, would it be possible for me to build a new life then? But how could a man build a life upon vague, unformed yearnings? I wanted to write and I did not even know the English language. I bought English grammars and found them dull. I felt that I was getting a better sense of the language from novels than grammars. I read hard, discarding a writer as soon as I felt that I had grasped his point of view. At night the printed page stood before my eyes in sleep.

Mrs. Moss, my landlady, asked me one Sunday morning:

"Son, what is this you keep on reading?"

"Oh, nothing. Just novels."

85   "What you get out of 'em?"

"I'm just killing time," I said.

"I hope you know your own mind," she said in a tone which implied that she doubted if I had a mind.

88   I knew of no Negroes who read the books I liked and I wondered if any Negroes ever thought of them. I knew that there were Negro doctors, lawyers, newspapermen, but I never saw any of them. When I read a Negro newspaper I never caught the faintest echo of my preoccupation in its pages. I felt trapped and occasionally, for a few days, I would stop reading. But a vague hunger would come over me for books, books that opened up new avenues of feeling and seeing, and again I would forge another note to the white librarian. Again I would read and wonder as only the naive and unlettered can read and wonder, feeling that I carried a secret, criminal burden about with me each day.

89   That winter my mother and brother came and we set up housekeeping, buying furniture on the installment plan, being cheated and yet knowing no way to avoid it. I began to eat warm food and to my surprise found the regular meals enabled me to read faster. I may have lived through many illnesses and survived them, never suspecting that I was ill. My brother obtained a job and we began to save toward the trip north, plotting our time, setting tentative dates for departure. I told none of the white men on the job that I was planning to go north; I knew that the moment they felt I was thinking of the North they would change toward me. It would have made them feel that I did not like the life I was living, and because my life was completely conditioned by what they said or did, it would have been tantamount to challenging them.

90   I could calculate my chances for life in the South as a Negro fairly clearly now.

91   I could fight the southern whites by organizing with other Negroes, as my grandfather had done. But I knew that I could never win that way; there were many whites and there were but few blacks. They were strong and we were weak. Outright black rebellion could never win. if I fought openly I would die and I did not want to die. News of lynchings were frequent.

92   I could submit and live the life of a genial slave, but that was impossible. All of my life had shaped me to live by my own feelings and thoughts. I could make

up to Bess and marry her and inherit the house. But that, too, would be the life of a slave; if I did that, I would crush to death something within me, and I would hate myself as much as I knew the whites already hated those who had submitted. Neither could I ever willingly present myself to be kicked, as Shorty had done. I would rather have died than do that.

93   I could drain off my restlessness by fighting with Shorty and Harrison. I had seen many Negroes solve the problem of being black by transferring their hatred of themselves to others with a black skin and fighting them. I would have to be cold to do that, and I was not cold and I could never be.

94   I could, of course, forget what I had read, thrust the whites out of my mind, forget them; and find release from anxiety and longing in sex and alcohol. But the memory of how my father had conducted himself made that course repugnant. If I did not want others to violate my life, how could I voluntarily violate it myself?

95   I had no hope whatever of being a professional man. Not only had I been so conditioned that I did not desire it, but the fulfillment of such an ambition was beyond my capabilities. Well-to-do Negroes lived in a world that was almost as alien to me as the world inhabited by whites.

96   What, then, was there? I held my life in my mind, in my consciousness each day, feeling at times that I would stumble and drop it, spill it forever. My reading had created a vast sense of distance between me and the world in which I lived and tried to make a living, and that sense of distance was increasing each day. My days and nights were one long, quiet, continuously contained dream of terror, tension, and anxiety. I wondered how long I could bear it.

Topics for consideration:

1. The young Wright develops a number of strategies for living in a racist world. What are they and how effective do they seem to be?

2. Why does Mencken appear to have such an influence on Wright? Are there drawbacks to Wright's adulation of Mencken?

3. Wright approaches his reading from the position of an outsider. Does this correspond to any aspect of your own educational experience? Can there be advantages to being an outsider?

Further reading:

H.L. Mencken, *Prejudices*, ed. James T. Farrell (1958)

Russell C. Brignano, *Richard Wright: An Introduction to the Man and his Works* (1970)

Alberto Manguel (1948-

Born in Argentina, Alberto Manguel emigrated to Canada in 1982, becoming a Canadian citizen three years later. He has achieved an international reputation as a prolific writer, anthologist and translator. Among his more recent works are Meanwhile, In Another Part of the Forest *(1994),* The Gates of Paradise *(1993) and* A History of Reading *(1996) from which the following selection is taken.*

Manguel uses examples ranging over several centuries and continents to show ways in which restriction of literacy and censorship of books has served as a means of social and political control. He describes the activities of the fanatical American censor Anthony Comstock and reflects on Comstock's position as reader with the implication that the career of Comstock and other censors is not so far removed from the role of the ordinary reader "who makes up readings."

FORBIDDEN READING

1   In 1660, Charles II of England, known to his subjects as the Merrie Monarch for his love of pleasure and loathing of business, decreed that the Council for Foreign Plantations should instruct natives, servants and slaves of the British colonies in the precepts of Christianity. Dr. Johnson, who from the vantage point of the following century admired the king, said that "he had the merit of endeavouring to do what he thought was for the salvation of the souls of his subjects, till he lost a great empire."[1] The historian Macaulay,[2] who from a distance of two centuries did not, argued that for Charles "the love of God, the love of country, the love of family, the love of friends, were phrases of the same sort, delicate and convenient synonyms for the love of self."[3]

2   It isn't clear why Charles issued this decree in the first year of his reign, except that he imagined it to be a way of laying out new grounds for religious tolerance, which Parliament opposed. Charles, who in spite of his pro-Catholic tendencies proclaimed himself loyal to the Protestant faith, believed (as far as he believed anything) that, as Luther had taught, the salvation of the soul depended on each individual's ability to read God's word for himself or herself.[4] But British slave-owners were not convinced. They feared the very idea of a "literate black population" who might find dangerous revolutionary ideas in books. They did not believe those who argued that a literacy restricted to the Bible would strengthen the bonds of society; they realized that if slaves could read the Bible, they could also read abolitionist tracts, and that even in the Scriptures the slaves might find inflammatory notions of revolt and freedom.[5] The opposition to Charles's decree was strongest in the American colonies, and strongest of all in South Carolina, where, a century later, strict laws were proclaimed forbidding all blacks, whether slaves or free men, to be taught to read. These laws were in effect until well into the mid-nineteenth century.

3   For centuries, Afro-American slaves learned to read against extraordinary odds, risking their lives in a process that, because of the difficulties set in their way, sometimes took several years. The accounts of their learning are many and

heroic. Ninety-year-old Belle Myers Carothers — interviewed by the Federal Writers' Project, a commission set up in the 1930s to record, among other things, the personal narratives of former slaves — recalled that she had learned her letters while looking after the plantation owner's baby, who was playing with alphabet blocks. The owner, seeing what she was doing, kicked her with his boots. Myers persisted, secretly studying the child's letters as well as a few words in a speller she had found. One day, she said, "I found a hymn book ... and spelled out 'When I Can Read My Title Clear'. I was so happy when I saw that I could really read, that I ran around telling all the other slaves."[6] Leonard Black's master once found him with a book and whipped him so severely "that he overcame my thirst for knowledge, and I relinquished its pursuit until after I absconded".[7] Doc Daniel Dowdy recalled that "the first time you was caught trying to read or write you was whipped with a cow-hide, the next time with a cat-o-nine-tails and the third time they cut the first joint off your forefinger."[8] Throughout the South, it was common for plantation owners to hang any slave who tried to teach the others how to spell.[9]

4   Under these circumstances, slaves who wanted to be literate were forced to find devious methods of learning, either from other slaves or from sympathetic white teachers, or by inventing devices that allowed them to study unobserved. The American writer Frederick Douglass, who was born into slavery and became one of the most eloquent abolitionists of his day, as well as founder of several political journals, recalled in his autobiography: "The frequent hearing of my mistress reading the Bible aloud ... awakened my curiosity in respect to this *mystery* of reading, and roused in me the desire to learn. Up to this time I had known nothing whatever of this wonderful art, and my ignorance and inexperience of what it could do for me, as well as my confidence in my mistress, emboldened me to ask her to teach me to read. ... In an incredibly short time, by her kind assistance, I had mastered the alphabet and could spell words of three or four letters. ... [My master] forbade her to give me any further instruction ... [but] the determination which he expressed to keep me in ignorance only rendered me the more resolute to seek intelligence. In learning to read, therefore, I am not sure that I do not owe quite as much to the opposition of my master as to the kindly assistance of my amiable mistress."[10] Thomas Johnson, a slave who later became a well-known missionary preacher in England, explained that he had learned to read by studying the letters in a Bible he had stolen. Since his master read aloud a chapter from the New Testament every night, Johnson would coax him to read the same chapter over and over, until he knew it by heart and was able to find the same words on the printed page. Also, when the master's son was studying, Johnson would suggest that the boy read part of his lesson out loud. "Lor's over me," Johnson would say to encourage him, "read that again," which the boy often did, believing that Johnson was admiring his performance. Through repetition, he learned enough to be able to read the newspapers by the time the Civil War broke out, and later set up a school of his own to teach others to read.[11]

5   Learning to read was, for slaves, not an immediate passport to freedom but rather a way of gaining access to one of the powerful instruments of their oppressors: the book. The slave-owners (like dictators, tyrants, absolute monarchs and other illicit holders of power) were strong believers in the power of the written

word. They knew, far better than some readers, that reading is a strength that requires barely a few first words to become overwhelming. Someone able to read one sentence is able to read all; more important, that reader has now the possibility of reflecting upon the sentence, of acting upon it, of giving it a meaning. "You can play dumb with a sentence," said the Austrian playwright Peter Handke. "Assert yourself with the sentence against other sentences. Name everything that gets in your way and move it out of the way. Familiarize yourself with all objects. Make all objects into a sentence with the sentence. You can make all objects into your sentence. With this sentence, all objects belong to you. With this sentence, all objects are yours."[12] For all these reasons, reading had to be forbidden.

6   As centuries of dictators have known, an illiterate crowd is easiest to rule; since the craft of reading cannot be untaught once it has been acquired, the second-best recourse is to limit its scope. Therefore, like no other human creation, books have been the bane of dictatorships. Absolute power requires that all reading be official reading; instead of whole libraries of opinions, the ruler's word should suffice. Books, wrote Voltaire in a satirical pamphlet called "Concerning the Horrible Danger of Reading", "dissipate ignorance, the custodian and safeguard of well-policed states".[13] Censorship, therefore, in some form or another, is the corollary of all power, and the history of reading is lit by a seemingly endless line of censors' bonfires, from the earliest papyrus scrolls to the books of our time. The works of Protagoras were burned in 411 BC in Athens. In the year 213 BC the Chinese emperor Shih Huang-ti tried to put an end to reading by burning all the books in his realm. In 168 BC, the Jewish Library in Jerusalem was deliberately destroyed during the Maccabean uprising. In the first century AD, Augustus exiled the poets Cornelius Gallus and Ovid and banned their works. The emperor Caligula ordered that all books by Homer, Virgil and Livy be burned (but his edict was not carried out). In 303, Diocletian condemned all Christian books to the fire. And these were only the beginning. The young Goethe, witnessing the burning of a book in Frankfurt, felt that he was attending an execution. "To see an inanimate object being punished," he wrote, "is in and of itself something truly terrible."[14] The illusion cherished by those who burn books is that, in doing so, they are able to cancel history and abolish the past. On May 10, 1933, in Berlin, as the cameras rolled, propaganda minister Paul Joseph Goebbels spoke during the burning of more than twenty thousand books, in front of a cheering crowd of more than one hundred thousand people: "Tonight you do well to throw in the fire these obscenities from the past. This is a powerful, huge and symbolic action that will tell the entire world that the old spirit is dead. From these ashes will rise the phoenix of the new spirit." A twelve-year-old boy, Hans Pauker, later head of the Leo Baeck Institute for Jewish Studies in London, was present at the burning, and recalled that, as the books were thrown into the flames, speeches were made to add solemnity to the occasion.[15] "Against the exaggeration of unconscious urges based on destructive analysis of the psyche, for the nobility of the human soul, I commit to the flames the works of Sigmund Freud," one of the censors would declaim before burning Freud's books. Steinbeck, Marx, Zola, Hemingway, Einstein, Proust, H.G. Wells, Heinrich and Thomas Mann, Jack London, Bertolt Brecht and hundreds of others received the homage of similar epitaphs.

• • •

7   In 1872, a little over two centuries after Charles II's optimistic decree, Anthony Comstock — a descendant of the old colonialists who had objected to their sovereign's educating urges — founded in New York the Society for the Suppression of Vice, the first effective censorship board in the United States. All things considered, Comstock would have preferred that reading had never been invented ("Our father Adam could not read in Paradise," he once affirmed), but since it had, he was determined to regulate its use. Comstock saw himself as a reader's reader, who knew what was good literature and what was bad, and did everything in his power to impose his views on others. "As for me," he wrote in his journal a year before the society's founding, "I am resolved that I will not in God's strength yield to other people's opinion but will if I feel and believe I am right stand firm. Jesus was never moved from the path of duty, however hard, by public opinion. Why should I be?"[16]

8   Anthony Comstock was born in New Canaan, Connecticut, on March 7, 1844. He was a hefty man, and in the course of his censoring career he many times used his size to defeat his opponents physically. One of his contemporaries described him in these terms: "Standing about five feet in his shoes, he carries his two hundred and ten pounds of muscle and bone so well that you would judge him to weigh not over a hundred and eighty. His Atlas shoulders of enormous girth, surmounted by a bull-like neck, are in keeping with a biceps and a calf of exceptional size and iron solidarity. His legs are short, and remind one somewhat of tree trunks."[17]

9   Comstock was in his twenties when he arrived in New York with $3.45 in his pocket. He found a job as a dry-goods salesman and was soon able to save the $500 necessary to buy a little house in Brooklyn. A few years later, he met the daughter of a Presbyterian minister, ten years his elder, and married her. In New York, Comstock discovered much that he found objectionable. In 1868, after a friend told him how he had been "led astray and corrupted and diseased" by a certain book (the title of this powerful work has not come down to us), Comstock bought a copy at the store and then, accompanied by a policeman, had the shopkeeper arrested and the stock seized. The success of his first raid was such that he decided to continue, regularly causing the arrest of small publishers and printers of titillating material.

10   With the assistance of friends in the YMCA, who supplied him with $8,500, Comstock was able to set up the society for which he became famous. Two years before his death, he told an interviewer in New York, "In the forty-one years I have been here, I have convicted persons enough to fill a passenger train of sixty-one coaches, sixty coaches containing sixty passengers each and the sixty-first almost full. I have destroyed 160 tons of obscene literature."[18]

11   Comstock's fervour was also responsible for at least fifteen suicides. After he had a former Irish surgeon, William Haynes, thrown in prison "for publishing 165 different kinds of lewd literature", Haynes killed himself. Shortly afterwards, Comstock was about to catch the Brooklyn ferry (he later recalled) when "a Voice" told him to proceed to Haynes's house. He arrived as the widow was unloading the printing-plates of the forbidden books from a delivery wagon. With great agility Comstock leapt onto the wagoner's seat and rushed the wagon to the YMCA, where the plates were destroyed.[19]

12   What books did Comstock read? He was an unwitting follower of Oscar Wilde's facetious advice: "I never read a book I must review; it prejudices you so." Sometimes, however, he dipped into the books before destroying them, and was aghast at what he read. He found the literature of France and Italy "little better than histories of brothels and prostitutes in these lust-crazed nations. How often are found in these villainous stories, heroines, lovely, excellent, cultivated, wealthy, and charming in every way, who have for their lovers married men; or, after marriage, lovers flock about the charming young wife, enjoying privileges belonging only to the husband!" Even the classics were not above reproach. "Take, for instance, a well-known book written by Boccaccio," he wrote in his book, *Traps for the Young*. The book was so filthy that he would do anything "to prevent this, like a wild beast, from breaking loose and destroying the youth of the country."[20] Balzac, Rabelais, Walt Whitman, Bernard Shaw and Tolstoy were among his victims. Comstock's everyday reading was, he said, the Bible.

13   Comstock's methods were savage but superficial. He lacked the perception and patience of more sophisticated censors, who will mine a text with excruciating care in search of buried messages. In 1981, for instance, the military junta led by General Pinochet banned *Don Quixote* in Chile, because the general believed (quite rightly) that it contained a plea for individual freedom and an attack on conventional authority.

14   Comstock's censoring limited itself to placing suspect works, in a rage of abuse, on a catalogue of the damned. His access to books was also limited; he could only chase them as they appeared in public, by which time many had escaped into the hands of eager readers. The Catholic Church was far ahead of him. In 1559, the Sacred Congregation of the Roman Inquisition had published the first *Index of Forbidden Books* — a list of books that the Church considered dangerous to the faith and morals of Roman Catholics. The *Index*, which included books censored in advance of publication as well as immoral books already published, was never intended as a complete catalogue of all the books banned by the Church. When it was abandoned in June 1966, however, it contained — among hundreds of theological works — hundreds of others by secular writers from Voltaire and Diderot to Colette and Graham Greene. No doubt Comstock would have found such a list useful.

15   "Art is not above morals. Morals stand first," Comstock wrote. "Law ranks next as the defender of public morals. Art only comes in conflict with the law when its tendency is obscene, lewd or indecent." This led the *New York World* to ask, in an editorial, "Has it really been determined that there is nothing wholesome in art unless it has clothes on?"[21] Comstock's definition of immoral art, like that of all censors, begs the question. Comstock died in 1915. Two years later, the American essayist H.L. Mencken defined Comstock's crusade as "the new Puritanism", ... "not ascetic but militant. Its aim is not to lift up saints but to knock down sinners."[22]

16   Comstock's conviction was that what he called "immoral literature" perverted the minds of the young, who should busy themselves with higher spiritual matters. This concern is ancient, and not exclusive to the West. In fifteenth-century China, a collection of tales from the Ming Dynasty known as *Stories Old and New* was so successful that it had to be placed in the Chinese index so as not to distract

young scholars from the study of Confucius.[23] In the Western world, a milder form of this obsession has expressed itself in a general fear of fiction — at least since the days of Plato, who banned poets from his ideal republic. The mother of the English writer Edmund Gosse would allow no novels of any kind, religious or secular, to enter the house. As a very small child, in the early 1800s, she had amused herself and her brothers by reading and making up stories, until her Calvinist governess found out and lectured her severely, telling her that her pleasures were wicked. "From that time forth," wrote Mrs. Gosse in her diary, "I considered that to invent a story of any kind was a sin." But "the longing to invent stories grew with violence; everything I heard or read became food for my distemper. The simplicity of truth was not sufficient for me; I must needs embroider imagination upon it, and the folly, vanity and wickedness which disgraced my heart are more than I am able to express. Even now, tho' watched, prayed and striven against, this is still the sin that most easily besets me. It has hindered my prayers and prevented my improvement, and therefore has humbled me very much."[24] This she wrote at the age of twenty-nine.

17   In this belief she brought up her son. "Never in all my early childhood, did anyone address to me the affecting preamble, 'Once upon a time!' I was told about missionaries, but never about pirates; I was familiar with humming-birds, but I had never heard of fairies," Gosse remembered. "They desired to make me truthful; the tendency was to make me positive and sceptical. Had they wrapped me in the soft folds of supernatural fancy, my mind might have been longer content to follow their traditions in an unquestioning spirit."[25] The parents who took the Hawkins County Public Schools to court in Tennessee in 1980 had obviously not read Gosse's claim. They argued that an entire elementary school series, which included *Cinderella*, *Goldilocks* and *The Wizard of Oz*, violated their fundamentalist religious beliefs.[26]

18   Authoritarian readers who prevent others from learning to read, fanatical readers who decide what can and what cannot be read, stoical readers who refuse to read for pleasure and demand only the retelling of facts that they themselves hold to be true: all these attempt to limit the reader's vast and diverse powers. But censors can also work in different ways, without need of fire or courts of law. They can reinterpret books to render them serviceable only to themselves, for the sake of justifying their autocratic rights.

19   In 1976, when I was in my fifth year of high school, a military coup took place in Argentina, led by General Jorge Rafael Videla. What followed was a wave of human-rights abuses such as the country had never seen before. The army's excuse was that it was fighting a war against terrorists; as General Videla defined it, "a terrorist is not just someone with a gun or bomb, but also someone who spreads ideas that are contrary to Western and Christian civilization."[27] Among the thousands kidnapped and tortured was a priest, Father Orlando Virgilio Yorio. One day, Father Yorio's interrogator told him that his reading of the Gospel was false. "You interpreted Christ's doctrine in too literal a way," said the man. "Christ spoke of the poor, but when he spoke of the poor he spoke of the poor in spirit and you interpreted this in a literal way and went to live, literally, with poor people. In Argentina those who are poor in spirit are the rich and in the future you must spend your time helping the rich, who are those who really need spiritual help."[28]

20 Thus, not all the reader's powers are enlightening. The same act that can bring a text into being, draw out its revelations, multiply its meanings, mirror in it the past, the present and the possibilities of the future, can also destroy or attempt to destroy the living page. Every reader makes up readings, which is not the same as lying; but every reader can also lie, wilfully declaring the text subservient to a doctrine, to an arbitrary law, to a private advantage, to the rights of slave-owners or the authority of tyrants.

Notes:

1. James Boswell, *The Life of Samuel Johnson*, ed. John Wain (London, 1973).

2. T.B. Macaulay, *The History of England*, 5 vols. (London, 1849–61).

3. Charles was nevertheless viewed as a worthy king by most of his subjects, who believed that his small vices corrected his greater ones. John Aubrey tells of a certain Arise Evans who "had a fungous Nose, and said it was revealed to him, that the King's Hand would Cure him: And at the first coming of King Charles II into St. James's Park, he kiss'd the King's Hand, and rubbed his Nose with it; which disturbed the King, but Cured him": John Aubrey, *Miscellanies*, in *Three Prose Works*, ed. John Buchanan-Brown (Oxford, 1972).

4. Antonia Fraser, *Royal Charles: Charles II and the Restoration* (London, 1979).

5. Janet Duitsman Cornelius, *When I Can Read My Title Clear: Literacy, Slavery, and Religion in the Antebellum South* (Columbia, S.C., 1991).

6. Quoted ibid.

7. Ibid.

8. Ibid.

9. Ibid.

10. Frederick Douglass, *The Life and Times of Frederick Douglass* (Hartford, Conn., 1881).

11. Quoted in Duitsman Cornelius, *When I Can Read My Title Clear*.

12. Peter Handke, *Kaspar* (Frankfurt-am-Main, 1967).

13. Voltaire, "De l'Horrible Danger de la Lecture," in *Mémoires, Suivis de Mélanges divers et precédés de "Voltaire Démiurge" par Paul Souday* (Paris, 1927).

14. Johann Wolfgang von Goethe, *Dichtung und Wahrheit* (Stuttgart, 1986), IV: I.

15. Margaret Horsfield, "The Burning Books" on "Ideas," CBC Radio Toronto, broadcast Apr. 23, 1990.

16. Quoted in Heywood Broun & Margaret Leech, *Anthony Comstock: Roundsman of the Lord* (New York, 1927).

17. Charles Gallaudet Trumbull, *Anthony Comstock, Fighter* (New York, 1913).

18. Quoted in Broun & Leech, *Anthony Comstock*.

19. Ibid.

20. Ibid.

21. Ibid.

22. H.L. Mencken, "Puritanism as a Literary Force," in *A Book of Prefaces* (New York, 1917).

23. Jacques Dars, Introduction to *En Mouchant la chandelle* (Paris, 1986).

24. Edmund Gosse, *Father and Son* (London, 1907).

25. Ibid.

26. Joan DelFattore, *What Johnny Shouldn't Read: Textbook Censorship in America* (New Haven & London, 1992).

27. Quoted from *The Times* of London, Jan. 4, 1978, reprinted in Nick Caistor's Foreword to *Nunca Más: A Report by Argentina's National Commission on Disappeared People* (London, 1986).

28. In *Nunca Más*.

Topics for consideration:

1. What connection do you see between the prohibitions of Afro-American slaves learning to read and the later experiences of Richard Wright in the Memphis Public Library described in "Discovering Books"?

2. Manguel collects a large number of examples of censorship of different kinds. Are there any distinctions to be made between the different examples that he uses? For example, were Comstock's activities equivalent to the Nazi book-burning to which Manguel refers?

3. Compare Manguel's approach to the subject of censorship with Margaret Atwood's in "Pornography" in the "Forbidden Words" chapter of this book.

Further reading:

Ray Bradbury, *Fahrenheit 451* (1967). Science fiction writer Bradbury imagines a future world where all books are forbidden and can only be preserved by dedicated dissidents committing them to memory.

Nick Smith

Nick Smith teaches English in an East Vancouver high school and has spent several years studying Buddhism.

Writers tend to regard nearly all forms of reading as "a good thing." In this piece Nick Smith takes the approach that reading, like listening to a personal stereo, is a distraction from the concentrated mindfulness that is regarded in Buddhism as the ideal mental state.

MEDIATIONS ON MEDITATION

1   As Sylvia shuffled to bed, I put on a borrowed Charlie Haden CD, settled into her still-warm futon spot and browsed the CD liner notes before burying myself in a back issue of the Village Voice. Perhaps it was all of the ads for electronic goods in the Voice, or the slow rhythm of Haden's plucked percussive crawl stirring emotion within, but I began wondering why I must always have the stereo on and fill every free moment reading. I pride myself on never watching television, but if questioned on my listening habits, I'd do little better than use several shades of hypocrisy to paint myself into a corner. Like the ex-smoker who binges on bacon puffs, had I merely chucked the channel changer in favor of the CD carousel? Although I recognized these as important points, I didn't begin chipping away at them until several months and half a world had flown past me.

2   In the fall of 1994, after two months of cycling in southeast Asia, my wife and I pedaled into Wat Suan Mokh, a Buddhist monastery in Southern Thailand. As a couple, we had no problems staying in segregated dorms, especially since we knew that come the 10 day silent retreat, we'd both be sleeping alone in concrete cells. For the week before the retreat began we managed to arise at four each morning for meditation. I spent my days reading about Buddhism, listening to my personal stereo while lying on a straw mat by the lotus pond and engaging in fiery debates on the finer points of Buddhism over instant coffee rich with condensed milk at an open thatched cafe just outside the monastery gates. In the evenings, after a silent supper of hot soy milk and bananas, most of us would convene in the meditation hall for a talk on the Buddha's teachings. Afterwards we'd walk carefully back through the forest, watching for pit vipers and cobras with our flashlights, before retiring to our wooden bunks, where I'd fall asleep under a mosquito net to the latest bootleg tapes from Bangkok blaring through my headphones.

3   The day that the retreat was to begin, over one hundred Westerners gathered in the library to hear the abbot's preparatory talk. He told us, in heavily accented English, that in addition to no meat, alcohol, drugs (including nicotine and caffeine) and sex, we were not to speak, read, write, or listen to music. A German fellow asked for the abbot's position on charades, a language in which all backpackers in Thailand are fluent. He replied that although charades and gesturing are forbidden, smiling is encouraged. The abbot then went on to explain that the reason for reducing the amount of stimuli to which we are exposed is to allow the turbid waters of our minds to settle. Only in this way can we begin to perceive

what is happening in our minds, and thus come to know ourselves. As he said this, my diaphragm began to tighten, the tension spread to my chest, then groin. I realized then that my fear wasn't, as I'd assumed, of boredom, but of the Self I'd been smothering under sounds, images and streams of black and white symbols. Yet this realization was only an initial step on what has come to be such a long journey.

4   For 10 days we sat, stood and walked in meditation. Together, we ate in silence on the cement floor. At first, like many others, I avoided my Self by daydreaming. By the beginning of the third day, I found the determination to pay attention to my breath for one second. It took all day. By day four, I progressed to three seconds, then five. During free time I washed myself and my clothes, made my bed and swept my cell. Then I would sit on the concrete bed and not read, not write, nor listen to music. My travel guide to Vietnam, brimming with words and pictures, whispered teasingly from my backpack, causing a struggle within my brain — like attending to a child having a tantrum in church. I wanted to write a letter in order to communicate to someone what I was experiencing. Soon I realized that my desire was to remove myself by describing the moment rather than living in it.

5   By the end of the session, the spin cycle in my skull was slowing. For a few post-retreat days at the monastery I began to become aware of subtle changes within the delicate ecology of my mind, but within a week we were in the city, once again drinking coffee to the thump of cheap boom boxes while skimming copious quantities of marginal magazines. Yet through experiencing stillness, I retained an awareness of why to slow down.

6   Perhaps even more important was learning how to slow down, by using mindfulness, which means performing just one activity at a time while really paying attention to what you are doing. This is a form of meditation in motion. It's an effective practice for those who want to be able to control the amount of information seeping through their sense organs.

7   So now, back at home, rather than reading and listening to music while eating, I pay attention to the taste of what I am chewing, putting my spoon down between bites. While washing dishes I feel the warmth of the water on my hands, smell the soap and pay attention to the task of doing a good job. I avoid driving as much as possible, but when I must make short trips around town, I drive without the radio on. When I hit a traffic light, rather than thumping the steering wheel with the heel of my hand, I use the break to pay attention to my breathing.

8   I have chosen not to replace my personal stereo, which was stolen in India. These devices are justifiable for those who work nights at monotonous jobs, but their very portability means that they have been made to use while the listener is doing something else — multi-tasking by design. I used to love riding my bike wired for sound; jumping off curbs and speeding down hills to the sloppy beat of grunge or bouncing on my pedals on a sunny day to some poppy folk. Now, when cycling, I pay attention to what I'm doing, and especially to traffic. It's not only safer, but saner. As well, when walking, or riding the bus, I find that earphones disconnect me from everyone else around me. When was the last time you struck up a conversation with someone wearing headphones? Now, while walking, rather than listening to pop songs, I pay attention to my footfalls. Being

mindful of how they synchronize with my breathing stills my mind, while focusing it upon the act of walking. I find this to be a good exercise for screening out billboards and ads on buses, bus stops and clothing.

9   I once made a point of keeping reading material near the phone and would refer to it if my ear was being talked off or if I was put on hold. Now I endeavor to really listen to what my caller is saying, even if it's Dad droning about the boat he's thinking of buying. And when put on hold, I take the opportunity to bring my attention to my breath and slow down. I've never owned a cordless or cell phone, lumping them in with personal cassette players. They are designed for the purpose of doing too many things at once.

10   I still read too much, but with increasing selectivity. I no longer secretly peruse flyers which come in the mailbox, or catalogues which come crashing, uninvited on my doorstep. Aside from our city's independent weekly, I no longer read newspapers. Before reading anything, I first ask if it has the potential to, in any way, enrich my life. I no longer feel obligated to be informed for the sake of being informed. I function quite well in ignorance of the latest murders in distant towns I've never heard of before. Even if I'm in a doctor's waiting room, or waiting for a friend at a cafe, I resist the urge to browse through a publication which doesn't meet my life enrichment criteria. Instead, I take the opportunity to breathe into my tired muscles and feel them relax one at a time.

11   Perhaps the most important idea which I took back with me was the practice of retreat and the realization of its necessity. Now, working full time, I don't have 10 days to devote at whim, but I can manage to take small retreats each day to deal with the mental overload associated with modern, urban life. I begin each morning by performing 20 minutes of stretching and yoga. I focus on my breath, my alignment and muscles and gently pull myself back from mental indulgences into what I'll do today or what happened yesterday. Some evenings I'll take a candle-lit bath with aromatic oils. While sitting in the hot water, I strive to still my mind. When eating dinner, Sylvia and I let the machine answer the phone, treating this time together as sacred.

12   I've stopped allowing myself to read and listen to music at the same time. I'll sit, late at night, alone, and really listen to a good jazz album, hearing subtleties that those who do housework to music will never hear. Often I'll dance on my own, sometimes with the headphones on, and let the notes penetrate to the marrow of my bones. And sometimes I'll just sit, saying nothing, doing nothing and thinking nothing.

Topics for consideration:

1. In this essay Smith describes a number of ways he once used to distract himself from living fully in the moment and coming to know himself. How does his description compare with the ways you use television, radio, recorded music or reading? Which of these would be the most difficult to give up?

2. Smith describes the ten-day silent retreat he and his wife took at a Buddhist monastery in Thailand and the ways in which he now tries "to take small

retreats each day to deal with the mental overload associated with modern urban life." What do you think would be the most effective way of taking such "retreats"?

3. Can any of the activities, such as reading or listening to music, that Smith regards as "distractions" help rather than hinder the process of allowing "the turbid waters of our minds to settle"?

Further reading:

Natalie Goldberg, *Writing Down the Bones* (1986). This best-selling guide for writers offers advice on how to use various forms of writing as a way to still what Buddhists refer to as the "monkey mind."

Lawrence LeShan, *How to Meditate* (1984)

Margaret Atwood (1939-

One of Canada's foremost literary figures, Atwood has established an international reputation for her fiction and poetry. She was awarded the Governor General's Award for her collection of poetry The Circle Game *(1964) and for her novel* The Handmaid's Tale *(1985), as well as the 1996 Giller Prize for* Alias Grace.

"Nine Beginnings" was originally published in The Writer on Her Work *(1981) edited by Janet Sternberg. "I hate writing about my writing," is Atwood's first irritable response to the editor's request for an essay in answer to the question, "Why do you write?" Nonetheless the piece proceeds to explore not only "what goes on around the edges of writing," but also the process of writing itself.*

NINE BEGINNINGS

1. WHY DO YOU WRITE?

1   I've begun this piece nine times. I've junked each beginning.

2   I hate writing about my writing. I almost never do it. Why am I doing it now? Because I said I would. I got a letter. I wrote back *no*. Then I was at a party and the same person was there. It's harder to refuse in person. Saying *yes* had something to do with being nice, as women are taught to be, and something to do with being helpful, which we are also taught. Being helpful to women, giving a pint of blood. With not claiming the sacred prerogatives, the touch-me-not self-protectiveness of the artist, with not being selfish. With conciliation, with doing your bit, with appeasement. I was well brought up. I have trouble ignoring social obligations. Saying you'll write about your writing is a social obligation. It's not an obligation to the writing.

2. WHY DO YOU WRITE?

3   I've junked each of nine beginnings. They seemed beside the point. Too assertive, too pedagogical, too frivolous or belligerent, too falsely wise. As if I had some special self-revelation that would encourage others, or some special knowledge to impart, some pithy saying that would act like a talisman for the driven, the obsessed. But I have no such talismans. If I did, I would not continue, myself, to be so driven and obsessed.

3. WHY DO YOU WRITE?

4   I hate writing about my writing because I have nothing to say about it. I have nothing to say about it because I can't remember what goes on when I'm doing it. That time is like small pieces cut out of my brain. It's not time I myself have lived. I can remember the details of the rooms and places where I've written, the circumstances, the other things I did before and after, but not the process itself.

Writing about writing requires self-consciousness; writing itself requires the abdication of it.

4. WHY DO YOU WRITE?

5   There are a lot of things that can be said about what goes on around the edges of writing. Certain ideas you may have, certain motivations, grand designs that don't get carried out. I can talk about bad reviews, about sexist reactions to my writing, about making an idiot of myself on television shows. I can talk about books that failed, that never got finished, and about why they failed. The one that had too many characters, the one that had too many layers of time, red herrings that diverted me when what I really wanted to get at was something else, a certain corner of the visual world, a certain voice, an inarticulate landscape.

6   I can talk about the difficulties that women encounter as writers. For instance, if you're a woman writer, sometime, somewhere, you will be asked: *Do you think of yourself as a writer first, or as a woman first?* Look out. Whoever asks this hates and fears both writing and women.

7   Many of us, in my generation at least, ran into teachers or male writers or other defensive jerks who told us women could not really write because they couldn't be truck drivers or Marines and therefore didn't understand the seamier side of life, which included sex with women. We were told we wrote like house-wives, or else we were treated like honorary men, as if to be a good writer was to suppress the female.

8   Such pronouncements used to be made as if they were the simple truth. Now they're questioned. Some things have changed for the better, but not all. There's a lack of self-confidence that gets instilled very early in many young girls, before writing is even seen as a possibility. You need a certain amount of nerve to be a writer, an almost physical nerve, the kind you need to walk a log across a river. The horse throws you and you get back on the horse. I learned to swim by being dropped into the water. You need to know you can sink, and survive it. Girls should be allowed to play in the mud. They should be released from the obligations of perfection. Some of your writing, at least, should be as evanescent as play.

9   A ratio of failures is built into the process of writing. The waste-basket has evolved for a reason. Think of it as the altar of the Muse Oblivion, to whom you sacrifice your botched first drafts, the tokens of your human imperfection. She is the tenth Muse, the one without whom none of the others can function. The gift she offers you is the freedom of the second chance. Or as many chances as you'll take.

5. WHY DO YOU WRITE?

10   In the mid-eighties I began a sporadic journal. Today I went back through it, looking for something I could dig out and fob off as pertinent, instead of writing this piece about writing. But it was useless. There was nothing in it about the actual composition of anything I've written over the past six years. Instead there are exhortations to myself to get up earlier, to walk more, to resist lures and distractions. *Drink more water*, I find. *Go to bed earlier.* There were lists of how many

pages I'd written per day, how many I'd retyped, how many yet to go. Other than that, there was nothing but descriptions of rooms, accounts of what we'd cooked and/or eaten and with whom, letters written and received, notable sayings of children, birds and animals seen, the weather. What came up in the garden. Illnesses, my own and those of others. Deaths, births. Nothing about writing.

11   *January 1, 1984. Blakeney, England. As of today, I have about 130 pp. of the novel done and its just beginning to take shape & reach the point at which I feel that it exists and can be finished and may be worth it. I work in the bedroom of the big house, and here, in the sitting room, with the wood fire in the fireplace and the coke fire in the dilapidated Raeburn in the kitchen. As usual I'm too cold, which is better than being too hot — today is grey, warm for the time of year, damp. If I got up earlier maybe I would work more, but I might just spend more time procrastinating — as now.*

12   And so on.

6. WHY DO YOU WRITE?

13   You learn to write by reading and writing, writing and reading. As a craft it's acquired through the apprentice system, but you choose your own teachers. Sometimes they're alive, sometimes dead.

14   As a vocation, it involves the laying on of hands. You receive your vocation and in your turn you must pass it on. Perhaps you will do this only through your work, perhaps in other ways. Either way, you're part of a community, the community of writers, the community of storytellers that stretches back through time to the beginning of human society.

15   As for the particular human society to which you yourself belong — sometimes you'll feel you're speaking for it, sometimes — when it's taken an unjust form — against it, or for that other community, the community of the oppressed, the exploited, the voiceless. Either way, the pressures on you will be intense; in other countries, perhaps fatal. But even here — speak "for women," or for any other group which is feeling the boot, and there will be many at hand, both for and against, to tell you to shut up, or to say what they want you to say, or to say it a different way. Or to save them. The billboard awaits you, but if you succumb to its temptations you'll end up two-dimensional.

16   Tell what is yours to tell. Let others tell what is theirs.

7. WHY DO YOU WRITE?

17   Why are we so addicted to causality? *Why do you write?* (Treatise by child psychologist, mapping your formative traumas. Conversely: palm-reading, astrology and genetic studies, pointing to the stars, fate, heredity.) *Why do you write?* (That is, why not do something useful instead?) If you were a doctor, you could tell some acceptable moral tale about how you put Band-Aids on your cats as a child, how you've always longed to cure suffering. No one can argue with that. But writing? What is it *for?*

18   Some possible answers: *Why does the sun shine? In the face of the absurdity of modern society, why do anything else? Because I'm a writer. Because I want to discover the patterns in the chaos of time. Because I must. Because someone has to bear witness. Why*

do you read? (This last is tricky: maybe they don't.) *Because I wish to forge in the smithy of my soul the uncreated conscience of my race. Because I wish to make an axe to break the frozen sea within.* (These have been used, but they're good.)

19   If at a loss, perfect the shrug. Or say: *It's better than working in a bank.* Or say: *For fun.* If you say this, you won't be believed, or else you'll he dismissed as trivial. Either way, you'll have avoided the question.

8. WHY DO YOU WRITE?

20   Not long ago, in the course of clearing some of the excess paper out of my work-room, I opened a filing cabinet drawer I hadn't looked into for years. In it was a bundle of loose sheets, folded, creased, and grubby, tied up with leftover string. It consisted of things I'd written in the late fifties, in high school and the early years of university. There were scrawled, inky poems, about snow, despair, and the Hungarian Revolution. There were short stories dealing with girls who'd had to get married, and dispirited, mousy-haired high-school English teachers — to end up as either was at that time my vision of Hell — typed finger-by-finger on an ancient machine that made all the letters half-red.

21   There I am, then, back in grade twelve, going through the writers' magazines after I'd finished my French Composition homework, typing out my lugubrious poems and my grit-filled stories. (I was big on grit. I had an eye for lawn-litter and dog turds on sidewalks. In these stories it was usually snowing damply, or rain-ing; at the very least there was slush. If it was summer, the heat and humidity were always wiltingly high and my characters had sweat marks under their arms; if it was spring, wet clay stuck to their feet. Though some would say all this was just normal Toronto weather.)

22   In the top right-hand corners of some of these, my seventeen-year-old self had typed, "First North American Rights Only." I was not sure what "First North American Rights" were; I put it in because the writing magazines said you should. I was at that time an aficionado of writing magazines, having no one else to turn to for professional advice.

23   If I were an archeologist, digging through the layers of old paper that mark the eras in my life as a writer, I'd have found, at the lowest or Stone Age level — say around ages five to seven — a few poems and stories, unremarkable precur-sors of all my frenetic later scribbling. (Many children write at that age, just as many children draw. The strange thing is that so few of them go on to become writers or painters.) After that there's a great blank. For eight years, I simply didn't write. Then, suddenly, and with no missing links in between, there's a wad of manuscripts. One week I wasn't a writer, the next I was.

24   Who did I think I was, to be able to get away with this? What did I think I was doing? How did I get that way? To these questions I still have no answers.

9. WHY DO YOU WRITE?

25   There's the blank page, and the thing that obsesses you. There's the story that wants to take you over and there's your resistance to it. There's your longing to get out of this, this servitude, to play hooky, to do anything else: wash the laundry,

see a movie. There are words and their inertias, their biases, their insufficiencies, their glories. There are the risks you take and your loss of nerve, and the help that comes when you're least expecting it. There's the laborious revision, the scrawled-over, crumpled-up pages that drift across the floor like spilled litter. There's the one sentence you know you will save.

26   Next day there's the blank page. You give yourself up to it like a sleepwalker. Something goes on that you can't remember afterwards. You look at what you've done. It's hopeless.

27   You begin again. It never gets any easier.

Topics for consideration:

1. Atwood calls her piece "Nine Beginnings" and provides nine different answers to the question "Why do you write?" Do you think these answers are really the "beginnings" that she tells us she has "junked"?

2. Some of the answers Atwood offers are samples of responses she gives to deflect the annoying question, "Why do you write?" Others offer some insight into her life as a writer. Based on what she tells us in this essay, why does Atwood write?

Further reading:

http://www.web.net/owtoad   Margaret Atwood's home page provides information about the writer and her work. This page also contains a complete listing of Atwood's novels, books of poetry and short fiction.

Kurt Vonnegut (1922-

Kurt Vonnegut's novels combine humour, fantasy and sometimes bitter satire. His experience in the U.S. Air Force during the firebombing of Dresden is recalled in his novel Slaughterhouse Five *(1969). Other novels that have gained a wide popular audience include* Player Piano *(1952),* Cat's Cradle *(1963) and* Breakfast of Champions *(1973). More recently he has published* Timequake *(1993), part memoir, part rescued novel, "a book that didn't want to be written," which he claims will be his last.*

Originally published as an advertisement sponsored by the International Paper Company, Vonnegut's advice can be applied to many forms of writing. The "style" that Vonnegut advocates is not mere decoration but what most readily communicates to the reader the writer's involvement with the subject.

HOW TO WRITE WITH STYLE

1 Newspaper reporters and technical writers are trained to reveal almost nothing about themselves in their writings. This makes them freaks in the world of writers, since almost all of the other ink-stained wretches in that world reveal a lot about themselves to readers. We call these revelations, accidental and intentional, elements of style.

2 These revelations tell us as readers what sort of person it is with whom we are spending time. Does the writer sound ignorant or informed, stupid or bright, crooked or honest, humorless or playful — ? And on and on.

3 Why should you examine your writing style with the idea of improving it? Do so as a mark of respect for your readers, whatever you're writing. If you scribble your thoughts any which way, your readers will surely feel that you care nothing about them. They will mark you down as an egomaniac or a chowderhead — or worse, they will stop reading you.

4 The most damning revelation you can make about yourself is that you do not know what is interesting and what is not. Don't you yourself like or dislike writers mainly for what they choose to show you or make you think about? Did you ever admire an empty-headed writer for his or her mastery of the language? No.

5 So your own winning style must begin with ideas in your head.

1. FIND A SUBJECT YOU CARE ABOUT

6 Find a subject you care about and which you in your heart feel others should care about. It is this genuine caring, and not your games with language, which will be the most compelling and seductive element in your style.

7 I am not urging you to write a novel, by the way — although I would not be sorry if you wrote one, provided you genuinely cared about something. A petition to the mayor about a pothole in front of your house or a love letter to the girl next door will do.

2. DO NOT RAMBLE, THOUGH

8 I won't ramble on about that.

3. KEEP IT SIMPLE

9 As for your use of language: Remember that two great masters of language, William Shakespeare and James Joyce, wrote sentences which were almost childlike when their subjects were most profound. "To be or not to be?" asks Shakespeare's Hamlet. The longest word is three letters long. Joyce, when he was frisky, could put together a sentence as intricate and as glittering as a necklace for Cleopatra, but my favorite sentence in his short story "Eveline" is this one: "She was tired." At that point in the story, no other words could break the heart of a reader as those three words do.

10 Simplicity of language is not only reputable, but perhaps even sacred. The *Bible* opens with a sentence well within the writing skills of a lively fourteen-year-old: "In the beginning God created the heaven and the earth."

4. HAVE THE GUTS TO CUT

11 It may be that you, too, are capable of making necklaces for Cleopatra, so to speak. But your eloquence should be the servant of the ideas in your head. Your rule might be this: If a sentence, no matter how excellent, does not illuminate your subject in some new and useful way, scratch it out.

5. SOUND LIKE YOURSELF

12 The writing style which is most natural for you is bound to echo the speech you heard when a child. English was the novelist Joseph Conrad's third language, and much that seems piquant in his use of English was no doubt colored by his first language, which was Polish. And lucky indeed is the writer who has grown up in Ireland, for the English spoken there is so amusing and musical. I myself grew up in Indianapolis, where common speech sounds like a band saw cutting galvanized tin, and employs a vocabulary as unornamental as a monkey wrench.

13 In some of the more remote hollows of Appalachia, children still grow up hearing songs and locutions of Elizabethan times. Yes, and many Americans grow up hearing a language other than English, or an English dialect a majority of Americans cannot understand.

14 All these varieties of speech are beautiful, just as the varieties of butterflies are beautiful. No matter what your first language, you should treasure it all your life. If it happens not to be standard English, and if it shows itself when you write standard English, the result is usually delightful, like a very pretty girl with one eye that is green and one that is blue.

15 I myself find that I trust my own writing most, and others seem to trust it most, too, when I sound most like a person from Indianapolis, which is what I am. What alternatives do I have? The one most vehemently recommended by

teachers has no doubt been pressed on you, as well: to write like cultivated Englishmen of a century or more ago.

6. SAY WHAT YOU MEAN TO SAY

16   I used to be exasperated by such teachers, but am no more. I understand now that all those antique essays and stories with which I was to compare my own work were not magnificent for their datedness or foreignness, but for saying precisely what their authors meant them to say. My teachers wished me to write accurately, always selecting the most effective words, and relating the words to one another unambiguously, rigidly, like parts of a machine. The teachers did not want to turn me into an Englishman after all. They hoped that I would become understandable — and therefore understood. And there went my dream of doing with words what Pablo Picasso did with paint or what any number of jazz idols did with music. If I broke all the rules of punctuation, had words mean whatever I wanted them to mean, and strung them together higgledy-piggledy, I would simply not be understood. So you, too, had better avoid Picasso-style or jazz-style writing, if you have something worth saying and wish to be understood.

17   ✴ Readers want our pages to look very much like pages they have seen before. Why? This is because they themselves have a tough job to do, and they need all the help they can get from us.

7. PITY THE READERS

18   They have to identify thousands of little marks on paper, and make sense of them immediately. They have to *read*, an art so difficult that most people don't really master it even after having studied it all through grade school and high school — twelve long years.

19   So this discussion must finally acknowledge that our stylistic options as writers are neither numerous nor glamorous, since our readers are bound to be such imperfect artists. Our audience requires us to be sympathetic and patient teachers, even willing to simplify and clarify — whereas we would rather soar high above the crowd, singing like nightingales.

20   That is the bad news. The good news is that we Americans are governed under a unique Constitution, which allows us to write whatever we please without fear of punishment. So the most meaningful aspect of our styles, which is what we choose to write about, is utterly unlimited.

8. FOR REALLY DETAILED ADVICE

21   For a discussion of literary style in a narrower sense, in a more technical sense, I commend to your attention *The Elements of Style*, by William Strunk, Jr., and E.B. White (Macmillan, 1979). E.B. White is, of course, one of the most admirable literary stylists this country has so far produced.

22   You should realize, too, that no one would care how well or badly Mr. White expressed himself, if he did not have perfectly enchanting things to say.

Topics for consideration:

1. The writers Vonnegut holds up for admiration — Shakespeare, James Joyce, Joseph Conrad, the seventeenth-century translators of the Bible — are almost universally admired and not likely to be challenged as "masters of language." Using Vonnegut's criteria, which of the essays in this book could serve as models of good style and which ignore one or more of his standards?

2. Does Vonnegut's advice match or clash with the instruction about writing you've so far received?

Further reading:

William Zinsser, *On Writing Well* (6th edition, 1998)

William Strunk and E.B. White, *The Elements of Style* (3rd edition, 1995)

CHAPTER 2

LANGUAGE & CULTURE

Consider the expression "mother tongue." Our first experience of language is intimately and intensely at the level of the body and rooted to our most primary attachment. No wonder then that when that mother tongue seems threatened we react at a visceral level. In Canada, anglophones who resent official bilingualism complain about French "being shoved down our throats." Francophones describe the experience of being prevented from speaking their own language as one of being "choked." No wonder too that former students' accounts of the Indian Residential School system so often recall teachers seizing children by their throats in an effort to stifle aboriginal languages.

Most people are also well aware that language mirrors culture. The often-repeated though not very accurate assertion that the Inuit language has fourteen words for snow underlines this widespread recognition. However, Inuktitut not only provides a rich vocabulary for weather conditions, but more importantly, as Hugh Brody's writing reminds us, has a plentiful range of expressions that provide precise descriptions of social interactions and states of mind for which there are no English equivalents.

What happens, then, when languages disappear and the capacity to name a whole range of phenomena vanishes? Aboriginal languages, systematically suppressed by colonialist policies, are now further eroded by the homogenizing effects of television and the electronic media. Amid the efforts being made to preserve aboriginal languages, many First Nations people and most First Nations writers find themselves having to, in Marie Annharte Baker's words, "borrow enemy language."

Our mother tongue shapes our vision of the world and structures our responses to it. Eva Hoffman's autobiographical account of finding herself "lost in translation" recalls the pain and alienation of being unable to match her perceptions with English, the "new language" in which she is forced to live.

Brody, Baker and Hoffman all deal with the subject of spoken language. Himani Bannerji and David Carpenter consider the task of the writer who must use an "other" language. Bannerji wrestles with the problems "of the integrity of language and experience." How can she write of a world experienced in Bengali in English? To what extent can her account be intelligible to English readers ignorant of the language and culture that has formed her?

33

David Carpenter, on the other hand, in an often amusing account, tells of his struggles as a translator trying to make use of his newly acquired French. Yet his account too returns to the many ways in which language reaches to the core of personal identity.

Hugh Brody (1943-

Writer and film director Hugh Brody has worked with and written about native peoples in Canada's North and West. He wrote and directed the NFB films Time Immemorial *(1991) and* The Washing of Tears *(1994). He is also the author of* The People's Land *(1975),* Maps and Dreams *(1981) and, with Michael Ignatieff,* Nineteen Nineteen *(1985). This selection is reprinted from his book,* Living Arctic: Hunters of the Canadian North *(1987).*

Hugh Brody delineates some of the most notable features of Inuktitut in comparison with English. He challenges some of the preconceptions readers may have about aboriginal languages and notes the many forces that contribute to the erosion of Northern peoples' languages.

LANGUAGE IN THE ARCTIC

1   *Inuk* is the Eskimo word for a person. There are two plural forms: *inuuk*, two persons, and *inuit*, three or more persons. *Inuit* is the people's own word for themselves, and is usually (though rather misleadingly) translated as human beings or the real people. *Inuktitut* is the Inuit word for the language, and is made up of the root *inuk*, a person, with the affix *titut*, in the manner of.

2   This seemingly simple word has its own cultural implications. Inuit use it to mean how they speak; it also refers to the way in which they do things. A person can talk, hunt, walk, eat, sleep, raise children, dance and even smile *inuktitut*. Everything the Inuit do is revealed in their manner of doing it. A distinct identity is bound up as much in the details of everyday behaviour as in the use of language.

3   Inuktitut has no genders, no specific grammatical endings that distinguish between he, she and it. These can, of course, be signalled in pronouns, but their absence from nouns and verb forms suggests the equality of human beings. Not even Inuktitut personal names are gender-specific: there is no such thing as a boy's as opposed to a girl's name.

4   On the other hand, Inuktitut makes a multitude of precise distinctions when it comes to descriptions of space. There, above your eye level and visible; there, below your eye level and not visible; there, above your eye level and not visible; there, close to you and visible; these here; those there. A complete list of all the exact terms for locating objects in space would be extremely long.

5   Aboriginally, Inuktitut had no words for thank you, hello or goodbye. Such expressions imply a mixture of posturing and intrusiveness that are at odds with northern hunters' ideals of interpersonal behaviour. Newcomers to the far north are often taken aback by the way in which Inuit men and women visit and leave one another's houses without any spoken formality. In fact, this reveals insistence upon and recognition of the right to do as you wish without repeatedly implicating others. Under pressure from newcomers' customs, Inuktitut had to find an equivalent for the routine English 'How are you?' or 'How do you do?' The word *quanuippit?* is the most widespread result. It means 'What has gone wrong for

you?' For the Inuit, the need to ask the question must be based on some evidence of difficulty.[1]

6   There are two ways in Inuktitut of saying perhaps. One of these, *imaqa*, in effect means probably not. The other, the infix *-qu-*, means probably. Inuit rarely make statements of any importance — especially about hunting and their movements — without employing one or other of these expressions. Persons raised with European planning and certainties have great difficulty in interpreting these uses of perhaps. But the two ways of expressing the possible speak volumes about hunters' consciousness.

7   The addition of infixes or affixes to root words is the basis of Inuktitut structure. It is a highly agglutinative language: whole sentences can be formed by building a series of affixes on to one root. For example, the Inuit can say 'he was not allowed to hunt for caribou' with a single word, *tuttusiurqujaulaungituq*.[2] For those interested in sounding this correctly it is important to know that *q* is used for a short, guttural *k*; try beginning 'cow' at the back of the throat. There are two other sounds in some eastern Arctic dialects that present problems for Europeans: a fricative *l*, familiar to anyone who has tried to pronounce Welsh names that begin with *ll*, and a rounded *r* sound that is like trying to pronounce *r* and *j* at the same time, as if trying to say 'regent' without the first *e*. Apart from these unfamiliar consonants, English speakers can easily learn to pronounce Inuktitut. Inuit themselves sometimes observe that French and German speakers have little difficulty with Inuktitut sounds.[3]

8   A feature of Inuktitut is its regularity. There are virtually no exceptions to its rules. The combination of precise agglutination with these clear logical principles means that Inuktitut has a remarkable capacity to deal with new notions and terms. So long as an imported expression or loan word is given an Inuktitut ending, it can be declined, conjugated and modified within the Inuktitut system.

9   Modern Inuktitut dialects reveal some incorporation of other languages. In Labrador, for example, where German-speaking Moravian missionaries were the first newcomers to influence the language, many Inuktitut loan words are obviously from the German. These include the words for week (*wurik* from *Woche*), year (*jaarik* from *Jahr*), the way of telling the time and some numbers (*ainsili, tsu-*

---

1. Athapaskans have borrowed *marsai* from the French *merci* for thank you.

2. This breaks down as: *tuttu* — caribou; *siur* — hunt for; *qu* — instruct, permit; *jau* — indicates passive mode; *lau* — indicates past tense; *ngi* — not the case that; *tuq* — he, she, it.
   The most important rule for the building of long sentence-like words is that each affix modifies everything that precedes it. This is much the same as the use of brackets in mathematics or formal logic: in an Inuktitut word in which a root x is modified by a, d and j and so is constructed $xadj$, the mathematical notation expressing the logical relation between the items would be: $j(d[a\{x\}])$, i.e. j modifies all that lies between the round brackets, d modifies all that lies between the square brackets and a all between the curly brackets, namely x, the root. Thus, in the example about not being allowed to hunt caribou, the negative, *ngi*, modifies the sum of the expression that precedes it, and not just the *lau*, the past tense indicator. It follows that the pronoun or person is usually the final element.

3. Algonquian presents few pronunciation difficulties to Europeans, whereas Athapaskan, from the point of view of both pronunciation and grammar, is extremely challenging to speakers of European languages. The Athapaskanist James Kari has said that it requires as much as ten years to develop a working facility in any Athapaskan language.

vailik, turai from *ein, zwei, drei*). In these cases, the Labrador Inuit adopted German forms for words that already existed in Inuktitut, and modern Labrador Inuit use both forms. In other cases, where new things required new words, German loan words were adapted to fit the Labrador dialect. An example of this is *kartupalak*, potato, from the German *Kartoffel*. In most dialects, this kind of borrowing is from English, so we find *tii* (tea), *kaapi* (coffee) and *palauga* (flour). The elaborate possibilities for agglutination also mean that Inuktitut terms can be combined to make new words. Modern Inuktitut abounds with such new expressions. Many go back to early contact with newcomers, but others are of recent origin. Older words include:

niaquujak (resembles a head)	bread
qianattuq (causes tears)	onion
naitingujarvik (time that resembles taboo-observance)	Sunday
kiinaujak (resembles a face)	money
imuksiutik (thing for milk)	cow
kuviasukvik (happiness occasion or place)	Christmas

Newer words include:	
nunakuurutik (device for going by land)	car
qangatasuuk (persistently soars)	aeroplane
irqiasulaaktigijutik (device that makes you curly)	hair curler
mamaksautik (thing that makes tasty)	perfume (Ungava)
	ketchup (N. Baffin)
ujaraksiurvik (place for looking for rock)	mine
uksualuk (great, extreme blubber)	petrol/oil
uksualungniartik (one who attends to great blubber)	oil company
inulirijik (one who fixes up people)	northern administrator
aijuksakturlirijik (one who fixes up ones who may be in difficulty)	welfare officer/ social worker

10   The languages of northern hunters are rich and precise. Never having relied on written texts, great care is taken when speaking to ensure that exact meaning is understood. As is the case in all oral cultures, conventions that guide the way in which people listen are no less rigorous than those that shape speaking styles. Someone who is telling a story or reflecting upon events can take it for granted that he or she will not be interrupted. As a result, the spoken language is slow, exploratory, often somewhat discursive and almost completely lacking the equivalent of English *ers* and *ums*. Also, anyone coming from a European-speaking tradition cannot help being struck by the way in which northern hunters speak without using gestures to emphasize or reflect their meanings and moods. Language is relied upon to do the real work.

11   A feature of all three language groups is their lack of generic terms. In Inuktitut, for example, there is no word for seal or fish. A speaker must identify particular species. Similarly, Athapaskan languages have no word for grouse; a hunter must indicate which of the several kinds of grouse he or she is talking about.

12   Specificity of language is a useful indicator of what language loss can mean. Under Euro-Canadian influence, modern Inuit use the work *iqaluk*, sea-going arctic char, to mean fish. Similarly, many northern Athapaskans use chicken to mean all species of grouse. Thus, when speaking English Dunne-za will refer to chicken, but in their own language will distinguish between spruce, ruffed and sharp-tailed grouse (*chi'djo, chicha* and *chis'konste*). Many white northerners use *natiq*, ringed seal, to mean seal. And when speaking English Inuit refer to seals, whereas in Inuktitut they speak of ringed seal, harp seal, bearded seal or harbour seal (*natiq, kairulik, ujjuk* or *qasigiak*). Presumably, a Dunne-za who speaks only English may see only chicken instead of the various species of grouse. Loss of language can constitute not only a reduction in knowledge but an impoverishment of the observed — of experience itself.

13   Tribal peoples' languages are often said to be primitive. In fact, the grammar of isolated languages tends to be richer than that of languages which have experienced outside linguistic influences. Encounters between grammars often result in grammatical simplification. For example, in Inuktitut there are two plural forms, a dual and a three-or-more. Inuit who speak English, however, and are familiar with the simpler division into singular and plural, tend to abandon the Inuktitut dual form. And we have already seen that richness of vocabulary can be eroded by innovative simplification.

14   A more persistent, popular charge against aboriginal languages is that they are paramountly concrete, that they cannot cope with abstract ideas and that peoples who speak them are not able to participate in debates about the future of their lands and society. In fact, Inuktitut can create abstractions with great ease. The infix *na*, when inserted after either verb or noun forms, establishes a disposition or an 'ism' rather like the German affix *-keit*. Thus, in Inuktitut *anniatuq* means it hurts; *anniarnattuq* means painful. That is a simple and translatable abstraction. But, using the same infix, the word for wearing a shirt, *uvinurutuq*, can be turned into an abstract concept, *uvinurunattuq*, whose meaning is hard to render in English. It is something like a tendency towards or disposition for shirts. The difficulty of translation here, however, in no way reflects a problem for Inuktitut speakers; for them, the abstraction generated by the *na* would be automatically intelligible. If some terms are not to be found in Inuktitut, it is because they have so far not been coined. 'Relativism' is no harder to render in Inuktitut than 'kangaroo': neither has, but both could become, part of the language.

15   Inuit received an orthography, adapted by missionaries from a writing system used to translate the Bible among northern Algonquian peoples in the late nineteenth century. This, the Inuit script, is a syllabic orthography, easy to learn but very imprecise and therefore usable only by persons who are more or less fluent in the language. Nevertheless, syllabics spread fast across the eastern Canadian Arctic, where isolated communities learned it from neighbours to the south. Some Inuit, therefore, were literate before any white missionaries reached them. In Greenland, a Roman orthography was used for the Greenlandic Eskimo during the early days of Danish administration. And in Siberia, first a Cyrillic and then a Roman orthography was developed in the 1920s for Yuit, the eastern Siberian Eskimoan group. But in the Canadian Arctic, the only writings available to Inuit in the 1960s were parts of the Bible, a book of common

prayer and a small number of government leaflets explaining various social welfare programmes.

16   In fact, colonial agencies — with the possible exception of missions — have imposed English upon peoples across the north. Those who have learned the aboriginal languages have usually done so to effect changes that would make the people more like themselves. And, in recent times, most Southerners who move to the north would never think that they could or should learn an indigenous language. Instead, the working assumption of new agencies has been that, with time and effort, all northern people will come to speak English. Attitude to local languages is a major indicator of how cultures view one another. In Canada this is reflected in the limited nature of available written materials. Comparison with other countries is also revealing. In Greenland, nineteenth-century literature — including such classics as *Jane Eyre* — was translated into Greenlandic Eskimo. In 1966 fifty-eight books, totalling over 56,000 copies, were available in Siberian Eskimo. The Siberian books included a mathematics textbook of high-school level.

17   The Siberian and Greenlandic evidence shows that Arctic languages are not limited or limiting in ways that would justify their displacement by English. The Canadian slowness to provide written materials, therefore, is a result of larger, broadly political forces. English was seen by many as the language of civilization, and by others as the facilitator of administration. Nonetheless, northern hunting peoples themselves have sought to retain their languages, and in many cases adapted them to new purposes. The Dene of the Mackenzie Valley, when negotiating their first land-claim proposals, insisted on bringing a group of elders, speakers exclusively of Athapaskan, to participate in and advise at all negotiating sessions. More recently, the Northwest Territories government became an elected instead of a delegated administration, as a result of which the Inuit and Dene found themselves in a position of majority control. They immediately implemented a thoroughgoing translation programme, both in the Council Chamber and across the Northwest Territories as a whole. They also pursued a policy of education in aboriginal languages for the first three grades of schooling in Dene villages in the Northwest Territories.

18   Programmes of this kind have shown that even northern Athapaskan languages can be written and take their place among modern literatures and in school curricula. With at least forty consonants, nine vowels and three tones (high, low and rising pitch), these would seem to defy simplified European orthography and language abilities. But writing systems have been devised in Alaska, Yukon and the Northwest Territories. In the 1980s, books have been published and used in schools. At Rae Edzo in the western Arctic, a Dene teacher discovered that Dene children learned to write more quickly if taught to do so in their own language. The limitations placed upon northern languages, therefore, are a feature of outside pressures; the languages themselves have the same possibilities as all others — in the north, for which they are finely tuned and superbly expressive, far more so. In fact, Inuktitut continues to be the first language for some 80 per cent of all Inuit homes. Among Naskapi the percentage who speak their own language is even higher. Among Athapaskans and Cree it is smaller and varies considerably from region to region. But in virtually every northern community, there is a strong reliance upon the native language.

19   Nonetheless, all northern languages are under great pressure. Most schooling continues to be in English. In Arctic Quebec, a small number of villages have
French schools. Training local persons to be teachers and the use of classroom
assistants who speak to children in their own languages play their part in the
northern educational programme. But it is a small part. To match northern to
southern curricula remains the objective of Canadian educational policy. This
leaves little space within northern schooling for the special circumstances of the
Subarctic and Arctic regions. The strengths, knowledge and confidence that
depend upon fluency in one's own language are still at risk.

Topics for consideration:

1. What differences between Inuit and the dominant Canadian culture are suggested by the differences in language that Brody notes at the beginning of
   this selection?

2. Brody notes that Inuktitut has no expression for greeting or parting. What
   are the typical words and expressions for these that you hear or use in everyday life? Which of these are specific to your particular group or region?

3. How would you compare Brody's attitude to aboriginal languages with that
   of Marie Annharte Baker in "Borrowing Enemy Language"?

Further reading:

Mark Abley, "Outrunning the Sun: The Loss of Native Languages," *Brick: A
Literary Journal*, Number 58, Winter 1998

Marie Annharte Baker (1942-

Marie Annharte Baker was born to Saulteaux and Irish parents and raised in Winnipeg. She has described herself as a cultural worker who "wants to produce films, plays and books that celebrate cultural survival after five hundred years of resistance to settler lit(ter) (not litera-ture)." Her published poetry includes Being on the Moon *(1990) and* Coyote Columbus Cafe *(1994). She now lives in Regina where she is a co-founder of the Regina Aboriginal Writers Group.*

Originally given as a talk, "Borrowing Enemy Language" exposes the relationship between First Nations peoples and the English language. The scope of her talk ranges over the way in which English has acted as a tool of colonialism, influencing native peoples' lives but also colonizing their minds and of her distrust of language originating in group therapy or bureaucracy.

BORROWING ENEMY LANGUAGE:
A FIRST NATION WOMAN'S USE OF ENGLISH

1   If an elder apologizes for speaking in a "borrowed language," I take it to mean more than a simple announcement that the speech will *not* be made in an Indigenous language. While standard English is spoken in Native homes and workplaces, foreign spiel like bureaucratese is also heard around the kitchen table to communicate family matters. Even the most personal thoughts or intimate experiences may be articulated in the strange lingo of cultural outsiders. Some conversations are laced with words borrowed from A.A. meetings, government-sponsored conferences, educational workshops, and from a mere glancing through handouts or manuals.

2   My anger rises at the shaming mention of the loss of fluency in a mother tongue or the scolding talk that seems directed at a speaker who has not retained an Indigenous language or dialect — as if being a dispossessed person with fragments of culture, history, and land base was not enough tragedy. Now, I agree with apologies directed to ancestral spirits who preside at Indian ceremonies and gatherings. If a speaker concludes a prayer with "All my relations," it is to include preceding generations and even those yet to be born. The ancestor's language was not English. Even while some of us use English, attendant with its limited foreign meanings, the innate understandings might go beyond language. Maybe we actually do speak from the heart.

3   Native people frequently say that English is impersonal or, if used in translation, it fails to carry the spirit of what was said. The frequent repetition of the word "I" in English discourse gives the subject so much importance, and distances him or her from the humble listener. The colonial context of the replacement of English for First Nations languages in our communities results from a 500-year history of European occupation and attempted cultural domination. When the colonizers or settlers approached everything Native, natural, or necessary for

North American survival as an enemy, English became an "Enemy Language." To "civilize" or "educate" was to take over a people's unique communication system.

4   As Indigenous peoples specify the relationship of Indigenous writing to the past and present destruction of both the environment and their lives, we should expect only tales of victimization and loss of culture. Especially when referring to the loss of Indigenous languages, the increased so-called literacy in the English language seems to bolster the idea of a "borrowed language" — one forced upon Indigenous peoples the world over. The death and mutilation of our peoples' spirits and bodies accompanied the teaching of English. Even today's educators want to hear "civilized" speech or the correct grammar and pronunciation of English words. One might recount horror stories of Native writers and educators who think their own people deficient in language skills because of a resistance to learn and use English the way it is taught in schools, where it is taught as a colonizer's language to communicate the words and symbols of the dominant society.

5   Thinking about English as the enemy's language is more than reversing the trend to overvalue English proficiency. The occasion to share experiences about subverting the English language is for me not just a discussion on First Nations' vernacular use in writing. I glibly mention that I "massacre" English when I write. Of course, I need to explain that I am deliberate about poetic language in my writing. Academic snobbery or cultural arrogance has adversely affected our ability to use catchy phrases. Anyone who gives an interesting talk is given accolades. The vulgarity of everyday expression is sacrificed for the deadness of scholarly language. Yet the ways to wring multiple meanings out of words still occur. The underclass English vocabulary is a source for my borrowing of language. "Sally Ann" was the way the Salvation Army was named in the neighborhood I grew up in. To help me "invent" or borrow English use for poetry, I listen to poor people speaking. As middle-class English starts to resemble more and more a computer language, and becomes an international business language, conversational English might just improve. Used by Indigenous peoples around the world to communicate, English may borrow from their struggle to maintain both land and cultural bases. I'm not suggesting further appropriation of ideas by ripping words and expressions out of a cultural context. I think borrowing does happen especially when reciprocity actually does happen.

6   Some of my poetry will appear in an anthology of Native North American women's writing, edited by Joy Harjo, called *Reinventing the Enemy's Language*. With more First Nations women writing in English, we must learn more about the kind of enemy that English literature pretends to be, or actually continues to be as its more oppressive forms are still promoted. Again, the history of Indigenous people in North, Central, and South America written in English texts may be inadequate. Translations of Indigenous thoughts on decolonization might eventually eliminate the practice of appropriating cultural icons and symbols described in English.

7   When I speak of English as the enemy's language, I see the enemy as being *within* the individual person — within one's own language use and how one is programmed to look at things. Those who see only the enemy outside are, fortunately, foolish, because it's more difficult to detect the enemy within. A second

language, or even one's first or mother tongue, might be the hiding place for a racist ideology. I do think of myself as a "word warrior" because I have a fight with words that demean my experience as an Indigenous person. I fight racist ideology or the ideas of white supremacy. Then again, I jokingly refer to myself as a "word slut." I find writing for me is a way to be sane in this society. I make sense of my world through writing. If a writer does not question imposed language, then, to me, this writer is only passing on oppression to the reader or listener — we are hearing the "colonized Native" voice. The fight for land and language against the loss of our past generations has to be the priority for our survival. One very identifiable enemy to our survival is that shame that our people were not "civilized," and that our people used language differently than Europeans or other newcomers to this country. The shame of having been a holocaust survivor is what I hear and read of the "colonized Native" voice that has become even more popularized in Canadian literary circles. "White guilt" has been effectively manipulated by some Native writers, especially when no attempt is being made to advance one's idea. Why not just reflect the "white people's ways"?

8   Sometimes, I meet Native people who seem to have a type of historical amnesia. I heard a Métis man who dismissed me as a writer because in his good old student days, John Donne's poetry was his particular expertise. I didn't perform the intellectual duel by saying that I'd read his favorite poet and even liked the old Anglican churchman. My own counter-plan was to immediately defend Indigenous writing. He put down not only our present efforts for recognition of Native writers, but also our significant oral traditional literary contributions. He might also have been sexist, so his attack on Native writing might have been directed against me personally, because I am a woman writer. He thought that with the credentials of a privileged white male, he might destroy my "illusion" of being a writer. I could have whipped out a booklist to show him his ignorance of the literature of his own people, but all I had was wit in my arsenal of word weapons. So instead, I gave him a "smart answer," or a riddle. I told him, "Well, to me, a pictograph is a novel." I realize many others might see a picture scratched on a rock or cave as being ritually painted. I was talking holy text, and my impromptu defence that a pictograph might actually generate more writing than one novel probably struck him as pure cheek. As an Ojibway writer who stands in awe of the pictographs and petroglyphs of the Great Lakes region, the mysterious meanings of our ancestors' writings are still a mystery to be deciphered. I believe prophecies for our coming age have been left for us. Even for those of us who speak or write in a borrowed language — we have been left with symbols many of us "educated" Natives would be limited to understand. Our "whiteman's education" doesn't have a contingency plan for understanding the complexity of our own tribal teachings.

9   I venerate and respect all writing forms that are non-English. If I didn't win that dispute on the importance of Native writing and reclaiming our history and identity, then I simply reaffirmed what I find to be challenging about writing in English. I am always searching for a simplicity and clarity in diction because English is an ultimate liar's language. I've heard Ojibwe speakers say it is easy to distort truth or reality in English. Harder to lie in an Indigenous language, some say.

10   Jimmie Durham, a Cherokee artist, has stated his position that Indigenous people shouldn't "educate the oppressor" because anything said or written in English will be used against us. Check any court record for quotes by anthropologists or other Indian experts. Sometimes, the words of our own elders are twisted out of context to support our so-called "non-occupation" of the environment. Obviously, our words will be used by "the enemy." Governments will want to take our land because too many of us speak English and are not "as Indian" or culturally pure as we are expected to be. I believe that is why some of our Ojibway people did not learn to speak English at all. I do appreciate why they don't want to use English: they prefer to speak their own Indigenous language because English is *not* superior.

11   The Ojibway language has now an achieved status of being a "sacred" language. It is a preferred spoken language at ceremonies. English, if used, is of minor importance. Speaking an Indigenous language is the better way of honoring the earth and the language of one's relatives. Our people know we respect this earth, or Turtle Island, through our words. Poetic narratives are prayers that engage the spirits of both audience and environment.

12   Maybe the visual artists who depict traditional icons and symbols realize the almost routine "appropriation" of their representations by other artists. While some artists condone stealing ideas from each other, when they steal images from Indian people, they talk the rhetoric of "cultural borrowing," or reciprocal exchange. It's almost as if the oppressor says "speak to me in English about your exotic culture," and then he or she publishes the literary or documentary exclusive impressionistic evidence — for cultural superiority. With all the rip-offs in the art world, no wonder Native artists have made such strong statements to protect their works from the copying or trivializing of indigenous cultural materials and intellectual property.

13   Language retention is crucial for Indigenous cultural survival and representation. The lament about the loss of languages is pretty loud to the ears. The frightening prediction is that by the year 2000, only four Indigenous languages might be spoken. Whenever I get down in attitude about those statistics, I look at a map that depicts the geographic distribution of Ojibwe speakers. The picture is far from being limited to tiny and endangered populations in North America. The Ojibwe peoples' land base is about one-third of the continent. What I see is not a few dots to suggest reserves or communities around the Great Lakes. With the history of our migrations from coast to coast, we have spread out across the land. We have a language that is fairly consistent with the extension of our Ojibwe trading networks. The Caribbean and American Black writers refer to an African diaspora; Ojibwe speakers and those others from the Algonkian linguistic group also form large, distinct populations. Names such as Ojibway, Chippewa, Sauk and Fox, Menominee, Cheyenne, Blackfoot appear in the historical or anthropological travelogues or documents. Yes, it is true that our language is threatened, but I also hear many stories of how our people speak Ojibwe to their children. If the dire prediction — that only a few languages of a total of more than 300 will survive — comes true, I think it will because of the attacks on our land and population bases. I don't think it will be because the colonizer lucks out. The adaptability of Ojibwe speakers and their travels across this land have given

us variation and incredible diversity. We were nations within nations. Our Ojibwe writers form probably the largest group of Native American or Native Canadian writers published in English. They write in Ojibwe, or may also display the current influence or infatuation with post-modernists and post-colonists. The Ojibwe language will survive because of our flexibility. England has been called the nation of shopkeepers, and English was used to develop an empire based on the slavery and the impoverishment of other Indigenous nations. Our Anishinabe nations also had a history of trading and were argonauts of the inland watersystems of the continent. Have canoe, will travel.

14   If the future means that you will have to listen up to Ojibwe writers published in their language of choice, I refer you to the text on our language, *Anishinababemodaa* or *Becoming a Successful Ojibwe Eavesdropper*. English has already borrowed many words from this language, such as "mooz" for moose, "mashkiig" for muskeg. Our language names rivers like the Mississippi, or cities like Winnipeg. Our word "doodem" is the source for totem. This book notes that fluent speakers always seem to be laughing heartily when speaking the language. It's impossible to be "too serious," and the language itself is picturesque. I particularly like the description that the Anishinabeg are a skeptical people: "We have so many words that mean 'maybe' ... many ways ... of saying 'I don't know'." When a speaker wasn't there to see the event he or she is describing, there is a word — "iinsan" — that is inserted into the sentence to indicate the uncertainty of relating information. Ojibwe speakers are still developing their terminology today and modernizing the language. They continue to make up words for things like "computer" or "insurance policy." The word for helicopter when written is huge, and sprawls halfway across the page:

Gaa-gizhibaayaagoseg ishpaasijigan

15   Language retention is a passing on of the culture through the imagery of words. It is not enough to have the outer trappings of being Indian or Native, such as braids or beads. I claim my identity though my motherline. My mother was fluent in the language and spoke to me in it when I was a child. I identify as an Anishinabe because of the way I was treated by my mother and relatives. I don't take the racial designations to be as important. Some people even prefer *terms* for themselves and not *names*. I think terms such as "Aboriginal," "Métis," or even "First Nations" do not tell as much as the name of a people. In addition to the legal designations or anthropological terms applied to Anishinabeg, there are the many distinct names for the various bands, clans, or family groups that lived across the country. I am usually approached to identify myself racially because I am a mixed blood person. My father is a Celtic-cross, or comes from a Celtic confusion of Irish, Scottish, and English crofter origins.

16   Cree writers have spoken about their language as being full of fun. I find that the speaking of English for some First Nations people presents moments of amusement. English has a strict idea that syntax is everything: for the sentence to have meaning, there is an order of separate words to be followed. We do certainly make different inferences. An example is me talking with my son, when he told me "Mom, I'm thinking of becoming celibate." I responded by saying "Well, don't think too much about it" — meaning I didn't want him to torture himself with thoughts of lust. The "thinking celibate" has an ambiguous meaning. The

words don't always describe the activity or behavior, yet we are expected to believe the speaker's intent.

17   Sometimes I find A.A. talk particularly horrible. We are forced to hear about everyone being "healed" or being in a state of "recovery." So much emotion or action is glossed over when someone refuses to give any detail of experience by saying simply that they are "healing." It's become so cliché that it is a type of code that silences the actual telling about a survivor's experience. We cannot find the words for genocide or holocaust because we are a "shame-based" culture. Other questionable phrases or buzz words such as "trickster," "shaman," "traditional," "two spirit," "windigo," and "contrary"/"heyoka" are tossed around in conversations. Even upon meeting another Indigenous person these days, one is obliged to listen to the recounting of clan names. While the common ancestry of tribal histories, or that of bands, has been replaced with the designation of First Nations, we still seem to know so little about actual differences among our own people. We are always lumped together. And, we are always pulling ourselves away from the generic terms that supposedly name us. Like if you claim to be an Aboriginal, then maybe you won't fit into Métis criteria. If you are non-status Indian, you might fit into one or both. We are inundated with these words. We also have logos like peace pipes, feathers, or other icons to represent us, whether or not our own ancestors or relatives engaged in these particular cultural practices. So much pretentiousness is exhibited by people's ability to manipulate these symbols to be "politically correct." Whenever I hear the word "shaman" I get apprehensive, because I think that whoever is using that word might be referring to a variety of performance art, or a New Age cult conversion, or even the equivalent of the English word "doctor." For me, I begin to distrust such speakers and their "loose" language. And I cannot always rely on other Native writers or readers to understand the disadvantage of using other people's names for us.

18   English has been the language used by what I call "settler lit." I sometimes include all of Canadian literature in my own loose terminology. It's not Can Lit but "settler lit" to me. What I think of as Canadian literature and the inclusion of Native writings is a creation of a non-settler literature, or a decolonized approach to Indigenous literature, especially when people are writing about their history and their relationship to land. I think that what I call "settler lit" is literature that promotes the false identities or re-vision of the past.

19   I found this postcard in Victoria which says "Poverty in an age of affluence is being unable to write, and having others write about you." I find this explanation of the informant relationship similar to the one forced upon some Native writers. Native people have to suffer informant roles when movies, books, or plays are being written. When this type of cultural representation and its products are criticized, then the critics must bear the stigma of being called "reverse racists." They are seen to be intolerant of the white corrective procedures of producing a literature about us but not written by us.

20   English is the language that I've used in order to become a published writer. I might have tried other media or art forms to express my ideas rather than books. In that way, maybe words would not have been a focus of my work. Politics and community organizing were fascinating alternatives to writing poetry for me. I don't feel that it is my job entirely to fix "settler lit" or to apologize for the

racist sexism that I experience with publishers and other writers. Or is it sexist racism? I hope that after 500 years of colonizer literature some of us will pursue a deconstruction of this mentality. In Ward Churchill's book, *Fantasies of the Master Race: Literature, Cinema, and the Colonization of American Indians*, are to be found analyses of the Euro-domination of our cultural and art forms. He's done a good job at starting us on our way toward understanding how cultural appropriation and racism are linked. Here he uses Vine Deloria's words:

> Underneath all the conflicting images of the Indian one fundamental truth emerges: the white man knows he is alien and he knows that North America is Indian — and he will never let go of the Indian image because he thinks that by some clever manipulation he can achieve an authenticity which can never be his.

21 I should add "hers," to include the many feminist or other women writers that have persisted in using their English commands as weapons against us to gain authenticity. Access to publishing doesn't always have to involve the paternalistic stance, or the pity, or the condescending approach to the study of Indigenous literature. I find now that all writers have a responsibility for cleaning up language use and if we understand that English may be used as an Enemy language by some, we might even have 500 years left to do the job of cleaning up the pollution of thought it has wrought. We don't have to keep on blindly repeating the folly of settler lit, or settler lit(ter).

Topics for consideration:

1. Baker ends her talk with the accusation that whites manipulate "the Indian image" in order to achieve an authenticity that they can never possess. How justified is this?

2. What is the distinction that Baker makes between Canadian literature and "settler lit(ter)"?

Further reading:

Daniel David Moses and Terry Goldie, eds., *An Anthology of Native Literature in English* (1992)

Joseph Bruchac, ed., *Returning the Gift: Poetry and Prose from the First North American Native Writers' Festival* (1992)

Isabelle Knockwood, *Out of the Depths* (1992). An account of loss of language and culture in the Residential School system.

http://www.nunanet.com/~nic/wwwvl-Aboriginal.html   World Wide Web's Virtual Library on Aboriginal Studies.

Eva Hoffman (1945-

Eva Hoffman was born in Cracow, Poland, and emigrated to Canada with her family at the age of fourteen. She now lives in New York and is an editor of the New York Times Book Review. *Her best known work, from which the following selection is taken, is her autobiography,* Lost in Translation: A Life in a New Language *(1989).*

These excerpts from Hoffman's autobiography recreate the experience of a forced transition from Polish to English. Hoffman vividly recalls her sense of loss as Polish becomes unusable as her inner language and becomes instead "a dead language, the language of the untranslatable past." Eventually she lives in a "verbal blur," unable to match her perceptions of the world around her with words that fit. Nonetheless, by the time she reaches high school, her mother is already criticizing her for being "too English."

LOST IN TRANSLATION

1 By the time we've reached Vancouver, there are very few people left on the train. My mother has dressed my sister and me in our best outfits — identical navy blue dresses with sailor collars and gray coats handmade of good gabardine. My parents' faces reflect anticipation and anxiety. "Get off the train on the right foot," my mother tells us. "For luck in the new life."

2 I look out of the train window with a heavy heart. Where have I been brought to? As the train approaches the station, I see what is indeed a bit of nowhere. It's a drizzly day, and the platform is nearly empty. Everything is the color of slate. From this bleakness, two figures approach us — a nondescript middle-aged man and woman — and after making sure that we are the right people, the arrivals from the other side of the world, they hug us; but I don't feel much warmth in their half-embarrassed embrace. "You should kneel down and kiss the ground," the man tells my parents. "You're lucky to be here." My parents' faces fill with a kind of naïve hope. Perhaps everything will be well after all. They need signs, portents, at this hour.

3 Then we all get into an enormous car — yes, this is America — and drive into the city that is to be our home.

• • •

4 "Shut up, shuddup," the children around us are shouting, and it's the first word in English that I understand from its dramatic context. My sister and I stand in the schoolyard clutching each other, while kids all around us are running about, pummeling each other, and screaming like whirling dervishes. Both the boys and the girls look sharp and aggressive to me — the girls all have bright lipstick on, their hair sticks up and out like witches' fury, and their skirts are held up and out by stiff, wiry crinolines. I can't imagine wanting to talk their harsh-sounding language.

5 We've been brought to this school by Mr. Rosenberg, who, two days after our arrival, tells us he'll take us to classes that are provided by the government to teach English to newcomers. This morning, in the rinky-dink wooden barracks where the classes are held, we've acquired new names. All it takes is a brief

conference between Mr. Rosenberg and the teacher, a kindly looking woman who tries to give us reassuring glances, but who has seen too many people come and go to get sentimental about a name. Mine — "Ewa" — is easy to change into its near equivalent in English, "Eva." My sister's name "Alina" — poses more of a problem, but after a moment's thought, Mr. Rosenberg and the teacher decide that "Elaine" is close enough. My sister and I hang our heads wordlessly under this careless baptism. The teacher then introduces us to the class, mispronouncing our last name — "Wydra" — in a way we've never heard before. We make our way to a bench at the back of the room; nothing much has happened, except a small, seismic mental shift. The twist in our names takes them a tiny distance from us — but it's a gap into which the infinite hobgoblin of abstraction enters. Our Polish names didn't refer to us; they were as surely us as our eyes or hands. These new appellations, which we ourselves can't yet pronounce, are not us. They are identification tags, disembodied signs pointing to objects that happen to be my sister and myself. We walk to our seats, into a roomful of unknown faces, with names that make us strangers to ourselves.

6   When the school day is over, the teacher hands us a file card on which she has written, "I'm a newcomer. I'm lost. I live at 1785 Granville Street. Will you kindly show me how to get there? Thank you." We wander the streets for several hours, zigzagging back and forth through seemingly identical suburban avenues, showing this deaf-mute sign to the few people we see, until we eventually recognize the Rosenbergs' house. We're greeted by our quietly hysterical mother and Mrs. Rosenberg, who, in a ritual she has probably learned from television, puts out two glasses of milk on her red Formica counter. The milk, homogenized, and too cold from the fridge, bears little resemblance to the liquid we used to drink called by the same name.

7   Every day I learn new words, new expressions. I pick them up from school exercises, from conversations, from the books I take out of Vancouver's well-lit, cheerful public library. There are some turns of phrase to which I develop strange allergies. "You're welcome," for example, strikes me as gaucherie, and I can hardly bring myself to say it — I suppose because it implies that there's something to be thanked for, which in Polish would be impolite. The very places where language is at its most conventional, where it should be most taken for granted, are the places where I feel the prick of artifice.

8   Then there are words to which I take an equally irrational liking, for their sound, or just because I'm pleased to have deduced their meaning. Mainly they're words I learn from books, like "enigmatic" or "insolent" — words that have only a literary value, that exist only as signs on the page.

9   But mostly, the problem is that the signifier has become severed from the signified. The words I learn now don't stand for things in the same unquestioned way they did in my native tongue. "River" in Polish was a vital sound, energized with the essence of riverhood, of my rivers, of my being immersed in rivers. "River" in English is cold — a word without an aura. It has no accumulated associations for me, and it does not give off the radiating haze of connotation. It does not evoke.

10   The process, alas, works in reverse as well. When I see a river now, it is not shaped, assimilated by the word that accommodates it to the psyche — a word that

makes a body of water a river rather than an uncontained element. The river before me remains a thing, absolutely other, absolutely unbending to the grasp of my mind.

11   When my friend Penny tells me that she's envious, or happy, or disappointed, I try laboriously to translate not from English to Polish but from the word back to its source, the feeling from which it springs. Already, in that moment of strain, spontaneity of response is lost. And anyway, the translation doesn't work. I don't know how Penny feels when she talks about envy. The word hangs in a Platonic stratosphere, a vague prototype of all envy, so large, so all-encompassing that it might crush me — as might disappointment or happiness.

12   I am becoming a living avatar of structuralist wisdom; I cannot help knowing that words are just themselves. But it's a terrible knowledge, without any of the consolations that wisdom usually brings. It does not mean that I'm free to play with words at my wont; anyway, words in their naked state are surely among the least satisfactory play objects. No, this radical disjoining between word and thing is a desiccating alchemy, draining the world not only of significance but of its colors, striations, nuances — its very existence. It is the loss of a living connection.

13   The worst losses come at night. As I lie down in a strange bed in a strange house — my mother is a sort of housekeeper here, to the aging Jewish man who has taken us in in return for her services — I wait for that spontaneous flow of inner language which used to be my nighttime talk with myself, my way of informing the ego where the id had been. Nothing comes. Polish, in a short time, has atrophied, shriveled from sheer uselessness. Its words don't apply to my new experiences; they're not coeval with any of the objects, or faces, or the very air I breathe in the daytime. In English, words have not penetrated to those layers of my psyche from which a private conversation could proceed. This interval before sleep used to be the time when my mind became both receptive and alert, when images and words rose up to consciousness, reiterating what had happened during the day, adding the day's experiences to those already stored there, spinning out the thread of my personal story.

14   Now, this picture-and-word show is gone; the thread has been snapped. I have no interior language, and without it, interior images — those images through which we assimilate the external world, through which we take it in, love it, make it our own — become blurred too. My mother and I met a Canadian family who live down the block today. They were working in their garden and engaged us in a conversation of the "Nice weather we're having, isn't it?" variety, which culminated in their inviting us into their house. They sat stiffly on their couch, smiled in the long pauses between the conversation, and seemed at a loss for what to ask. Now my mind gropes for some description of them, but nothing fits. They're a different species from anyone I've met in Poland, and Polish words slip off of them without sticking. English words don't hook on to anything. I try, deliberately, to come up with a few. Are these people pleasant or dull? Kindly or silly? The words float in an uncertain space. They come up from a part of my brain in which labels may be manufactured but which has no connection to my instincts, quick reactions, knowledge. Even the simplest adjectives sow confusion in my mind; English kindliness has a whole system of morality behind it, a system that makes "kindness" an entirely positive virtue. Polish kindness has the

tiniest element of irony. Besides, I'm beginning to feel the tug of prohibition, in English, against uncharitable words. In Polish, you can call someone an idiot without particularly harsh feelings and with the zest of a strong judgment. Yes, in Polish these people might tend toward "silly" and "dull" — but I force myself toward "kindly" and "pleasant." The cultural unconscious is beginning to exercise its subliminal influence.

15   The verbal blur covers these people's faces, their gestures with a sort of fog. I can't translate them into my mind's eye. The small event, instead of being added to the mosaic of consciousness and memory, falls through some black hole, and I fall with it. What has happened to me in this new world? I don't know. I don't see what I've seen, don't comprehend what's in front of me. I'm not filled with language anymore, and I have only a memory of fullness to anguish me with the knowledge that, in this dark and empty state, I don't really exist.

• • •

16   For my birthday, Penny gives me a diary, complete with a little lock and key to keep what I write from the eyes of all intruders. It is that little lock — the visible symbol of the privacy in which the diary is meant to exist — that creates my dilemma. If I am indeed to write something entirely for myself, in what language do I write? Several times, I open the diary and close it again. I can't decide. Writing in Polish at this point would be a little like resorting to Latin or ancient Greek — an eccentric thing to do in a diary, in which you're supposed to set down your most immediate experiences and unpremeditated thoughts in the most unmediated language. Polish is becoming a dead language, the language of the untranslatable past. But writing for nobody's eyes in English? That's like doing a school exercise, or performing in front of yourself, a slightly perverse act of self-voyeurism.

17   Because I have to choose something, I finally choose English. If I'm to write about the present, I have to write in the language of the present, even if it's not the language of the self. As a result, the diary becomes surely one of the more impersonal exercises of that sort produced by an adolescent girl. These are no sentimental effusions of rejected love, eruptions of familial anger, or consoling broodings about death. English is not the language of such emotions. Instead, I set down my reflections on the ugliness of wrestling; on the elegance of Mozart, and on how Dostoyevsky puts me in mind of El Greco. I write down Thoughts.

18   There is a certain pathos to this naïve snobbery, for the diary is an earnest attempt to create a part of my persona that I imagine I would have grown into in Polish. In the solitude of this most private act, I write, in my public language, in order to update what might have been my other self. The diary is about me and not about me at all. But on one level, it allows me to make the first jump. I learn English through writing, and, in turn, writing gives me a written self. Refracted through the double distance of English and writing, this self — my English self — becomes oddly objective; more than anything, it perceives. It exists more easily in the abstract sphere of thoughts and observations than in the world. For a while, this impersonal self, this cultural negative capability, becomes the truest thing about me. When I write, I have a real existence that is proper to the activity of writing — an existence that takes place midway between me and the sphere of artifice, art, pure language. This language is beginning to invent another

me. However, I discover something odd. It seems that when I write (or, for that matter, think) in English, I am unable to use the word "I." I do not go as far as the schizophrenic "she" — but I am driven, as by a compulsion, to the double, the Siamese-twin "you."

19   My voice is doing funny things. It does not seem to emerge from the same parts of my body as before. It comes out from somewhere in my throat, tight, thin, and mat — a voice without the modulations, dips, and rises that it had before, when it went from my stomach all the way through my head. There is, of course, the constraint and the self-consciousness of an accent that I hear but cannot control. Some of my high school peers accuse me of putting it on in order to appear more "interesting." In fact, I'd do anything to get rid of it, and when I'm alone, I practice sounds for which my speech organs have no intuitions, such as "th" (I do this by putting my tongue between my teeth) and "a," which is longer and more open in Polish (by shaping my mouth into a sort of arrested grin). It is simple words like "cat" or "tap" that give me the most trouble, because they have no context of other syllables, and so people often misunderstand them. Whenever I can, I do awkward little swerves to avoid them, or pause and try to say them very clearly. Still, when people — like salesladies — hear me speak without being prepared to listen carefully, they often don't understand me the first time around. "Girls' shoes," I say, and the "girls'" comes out as a sort of scramble. "Girls' shoes," I repeat, willing the syllable to form itself properly, and the saleslady usually smiles nicely, and sends my mother and me to the right part of the store. I say "Thank you" with a sweet smile, feeling as if I'm both claiming an unfair special privilege and being unfairly patronized.

20   It's as important to me to speak well as to play a piece of music without mistakes. Hearing English distorted grates on me like chalk screeching on a blackboard, like all things botched and badly done, like all forms of gracelessness. The odd thing is that I know what is correct, fluent, good, long before I can execute it. The English spoken by our Polish acquaintances strikes me as jagged and thick, and I know that I shouldn't imitate it. I'm turned off by the intonations I hear on the TV sitcoms — by the expectation of laughter, like a dog's tail wagging in supplication, built into the actors' pauses, and by the curtailed, cutoff rhythms. I like the way Penny speaks, with an easy flow and a pleasure in giving words a fleshly fullness; I like what I hear in some movies; and once the Old Vic comes to Vancouver to perform *Macbeth*, and though I can hardly understand the particular words, I am riveted by the tones of sureness and command that mold the actors' speech into such majestic periods.

21   Sociolinguists might say that I receive these language messages as class signals, that I associate the sounds of correctness with the social status of the speaker. In part, this is undoubtedly true. The class-linked notion that I transfer wholesale from Poland is that belonging to a "better" class of people is absolutely dependent on speaking a "better" language. And in my situation especially, I know that language will be a crucial instrument, that I can overcome the stigma of my marginality, the weight of presumption against me, only if the reassuringly right sounds come out of my mouth.

22   Yes, speech is a class signifier. But I think that in hearing these varieties of speech around me, I'm sensitized to something else as well — something that is

a matter of aesthetics, and even of psychological health. Apparently, skilled chefs can tell whether a dish from some foreign cuisine is well cooked even if they have never tasted it and don't know the genre of cooking it belongs to. There seem to be some deep-structure qualities — consistency, proportions of ingredients, smoothness of blending — that indicate culinary achievement to these educated eaters' taste buds. So each language has its own distinctive music, and even if one doesn't know its separate components, one can pretty quickly recognize the propriety of the patterns in which the components are put together, their harmonies and discords. Perhaps the crucial element that strikes the ear in listening to living speech is the degree of the speaker's self-assurance and control.

23   As I listen to people speaking that foreign tongue, English, I can hear when they stumble or repeat the same phrases too many times, when their sentences trail off aimlessly — or, on the contrary, when their phrases have vigor and roundness, when they have the space and the breath to give a flourish at the end of a sentence, or make just the right pause before coming to a dramatic point. I can tell, in other words, the degree of their ease or disease, the extent of authority that shapes the rhythms of their speech. That authority — in whatever dialect, in whatever variant of the mainstream language — seems to me to be something we all desire. It's not that we all want to speak the King's English, but whether we speak Appalachian or Harlem English, or Cockney, or Jamaican Creole, we want to be at home in our tongue. We want to be able to give voice accurately and fully to ourselves and our sense of the world. John Fowles, in one of his stories in *The Ebony Tower*, has a young man cruelly violate an elderly writer and his manuscripts because the legacy of language has not been passed on to the youthful vandal properly. This seems to me an entirely credible premise. Linguistic dispossession is a sufficient motive for violence, for it is close to the dispossession of one's self. Blind rage, helpless rage is rage that has no words — rage that overwhelms one with darkness. And if one is perpetually without words, if one exists in the entropy of inarticulateness, that condition itself is bound to be an enraging frustration. In my New York apartment, I listen almost nightly to fights that erupt like brushfire on the street below — and in their escalating fury of repetitious phrases ("Don't do this to me, man, you fucking bastard, I'll fucking kill you"), I hear not the pleasures of macho toughness but an infuriated beating against wordlessness, against the incapacity to make oneself understood, seen. Anger can be borne — it can even be satisfying — if it can gather into words and explode in a storm, or a rapier-sharp attack. But without this means of ventilation, it only turns back inward, building and swirling like a head of steam — building to an impotent, murderous rage. If all therapy is speaking therapy — a talking cure — then perhaps all neurosis is a speech dis-ease.

• • •

24   But being "an immigrant," I begin to learn, is considered a sort of location in itself — and sometimes a highly advantageous one at that. In uneventful Vancouver, I'm enough of a curiosity that I too enjoy the fifteen minutes of fame so often accorded to Eastern European exotics before they are replaced by a new batch. The local newspaper takes me up as a sort of pet, printing my picture when I give a concert at the Jewish Community Center and soliciting my views when I come back from a bus trip to the United Nations, on which I've been sent

after winning a speech contest. They want to know my opinions of the various cities I've been in, and I have no hesitation about offering them. "New York is the real capital of the United States," I readily opine. "Washington just has the government. It doesn't have the excitement." I take such attention blithely for granted, so I'm not too bowled over when a local radio Pontificator, after meeting me in a group of high school students, tells me he would like to hear my opinion on anything at all; for this purpose, he'll lend me one of the fifteen-minute spots that bring him fame with weekly regularity. At this point in my initiation into the English language, I have an active vocabulary of about six hundred words, but it doesn't occur to me that I should mince any of them. I want to tell Canadians about how boring they are. "Canada is the dullest country in the world," I write in the notes for my speech, "because it is the most conformist." People may pretend to have liberal beliefs, I go on, but really they are an unadventurous lot who never dare to sidestep bourgeois conventions. With the hauteur that can only spring from fourteen-year-old innocence, I take these observations to be self-evident, because they are mine. And it doesn't occur to me, of course, that my audience might be offended at being read such stern lessons; after all, I'm simply telling the truth.

25   I never hear myself in this performance, because I don't know how to find the radio station on which this bit of cultural commentary is being broadcast. But I'm told by someone who hears the program that my host had some very flattering things to say about my little diatribe. Apparently, Vancouverites, as most people, like to see themselves held up in an askew mirror — perhaps any mirror, for that matter. As for me, it is my first lesson in the advantages of an oblique vision — and in the sharp pleasure of turning anger into argument.

• • •

26   My mother says I'm becoming "English." This hurts me, because I know she means I'm becoming cold. I'm no colder than I've ever been, but I'm learning to be less demonstrative. I learn this from a teacher who, after contemplating the gesticulations with which I help myself describe the digestive system of a frog, tells me to "Sit on my hands and then try talking." I learn my new reserve from people who take a step back when we talk, because I'm standing too close, crowding them. Cultural distances are different, I later learn in a sociology class, but I know it already. I learn restraint from Penny, who looks offended when I shake her by the arm in excitement, as if my gesture had been one of aggression instead of friendliness. I learn it from a girl who pulls away when I hook my arm through hers as we walk down the street — this movement of friendly intimacy is an embarrassment to her.

27   I learn also that certain kinds of truth are impolite. One shouldn't criticize the person one is with, at least not directly. You shouldn't say, "You are wrong about that" — though you may say, "On the other hand, there is that to consider." You shouldn't say, "This doesn't look good on you," though you may say, "I like you better in that other outfit." I learn to tone down my sharpness, to do a more careful conversational minuet.

28   Perhaps my mother is right, after all; perhaps I'm becoming colder. After a while, emotion follows action, response grows warmer or cooler according to gesture. I'm more careful about what I say, how loud I laugh, whether I give vent

behaviour ton down , affect by envt

to grief. The storminess of emotion prevailing in our family is in excess of the normal here, and the unwritten rules for the normal have their osmotic effect.

29   Because I'm not heard, I feel I'm not seen. My words often seem to baffle others. They are inappropriate, or forced, or just plain incomprehensible. People look at me with puzzlement; they mumble something in response — something that doesn't hit home. Anyway, the back and forth of conversation is different here. People often don't answer each other. But the mat look in their eyes as they listen to me cancels my face, flattens my features. The mobility of my face comes from the mobility of the words coming to the surface and the feelings that drive them. Its vividness is sparked by the locking of an answering gaze, by the quickness of understanding. But now I can't feel how my face lights up from inside; I don't receive from others the reflected movement of its expressions, its living speech. People look past me as we speak. What do I look like, here? Imperceptible, I think; impalpable, neutral, faceless. *ppl not from culture , not as expressive need copy on one hand want to be like them but losing something she like*

Topics for consideration:

1. Hoffman has chosen to use the present tense to describe both the experiences of her early life in Vancouver and her present-day life in New York. Why do you think she made this choice? What difference would it make if she used the past tense when writing about her childhood?

2. Hoffman not only learns a new language but also is compelled to live entirely in that language before knowing it. Have you ever been in a situation of forced immersion of this kind? How did your experience resemble or differ from Hoffman's?

3. Throughout these excerpts Hoffman refers to ways in which language differences are attached to larger cultural differences. How do these compare with the distinctions David Carpenter makes between French and English in "Nom de Plume"?

Himani Bannerji (1942-

Himani Bannerji was educated in Calcutta where she taught until moving to Canada in 1969. She has published poetry and essays and edited Returning the Gaze: Essays on Racism, Feminism and Politics *(1993). She now teaches at York University.*

Starting with an epigraph from the Mahabharata, Himani Bannerji begins her essay with a piece combining "memories, textual allusions, cultural signs and symbols," and then asks the reader "Does it speak to you?" So begins her investigation of the complicated interrelation of Bengali and English in her life, where, from the beginning, English was associated with "duty," colonialism and the public world, while Bengali was literally her "mother tongue."

THE SOUND BARRIER: TRANSLATING OURSELVES IN LANGUAGE AND EXPERIENCE

IN THE FIRST CIRCLE

1 Maharaja [the great king] Yayati, after many years of tending his subjects as befitted the conduct prescribed by Dharma [religion], became senile due to the curse of Sukracharya. Deprived of pleasure by that old age that destroys beauty [appearance], he said to [his] sons: 'O sons! I wish to dally with young women by means of your youth. Help me in this matter.' Hearing this Devayani's eldest son Yadu said, 'Command us, great lord, how it is that we may render you assistance with our youth.' Yayati said, 'You [should] take my [senility] decay of old age, I will [take] your youth and use it to enjoy the material world [what I own] ... one of you [should] assume my emaciated body and rule the country [while] I take the young body [of the one who has taken on the old age] and gratify my lust [for the world].'
                                                            — Adi Purba, *The Mahabharata*, Chapter 75

2 It is evening. I am afraid. The sun's rays are weak. That red crucible partly sunk in the clouds is only a dim reflection of itself, not a source of light or life. The plains stretch far into the distance behind me. The human dwellings, the villages and cities are far away and hidden by the rising mist and fog from the swamps where only reeds rustle in the wind and waterbirds cry disconsolately. Beside me, the little grassy glade that I stand in, is a forest — ghana, swapada-shankula — dense and full of dangerous beasts of prey. The overhanging foliage has the appearance of clouds which hold and nourish a damp darkness. The giant trunks of the trees have grown so close together that the forest is both a prison and a fort. No footpaths are visible since the undergrowth denies the possibility of making an inroad. Standing at this juncture, between the swamp and this forest, with darkness fast coming upon me, I am overcome with fear. What shall I do? Where shall I turn? I can neither go forward nor return thence from whence under the

bright noon sun I began my unmapped wanderings. — Pathik, tumi Ki path Harayachho? Traveller, have you lost your way?

3   Miraculously, she stands beside me, risen from the ground it seems, immaculate, serene, fearless because renouncing and always in the quest for truth, dressed in orange, the colour of wandering mendicants — Kapalkundala of my childhood, the female ascetic, well versed in life and death. Her ghanakunchita Keshandam — long dark curly hair — cascades down her back, framing her face, as the nimbus monsoon clouds surround the full moon, her forehead, broad and generous, her gaze mild yet compelling, serene and unselfconscious. Extending her hand, taking mine in a firm but gentle grasp, she spoke to me. — Bha kariona. Druta chalo. Ratri Haiya ashitechhe. Jhhar ashite pare. Don't fear. Let us move quickly. The night approaches and a storm may arise.

4   Where? I said to her, O apparition from childhood, from behind the closed doors of homes destroyed, vanished, a long time ago, child of Bankim, vernacular spirit, where shall I hide? Where is my refuge, my shelter? Kothay jaibo? This forest is a fearful maze, populated with unknown, unnamed dangers. Where is there for me to go?

5   She gently pulled me towards her, while walking nimbly into the forest. In the gathering darkness I noticed that her feet were faintly luminous and suspended above the ground. Keeping her great head poised, her gaze fixed at the gnarled entrance and tremendously muscular arms of the forest, she uttered repeatedly. — Bhayang nasti. There is nothing to fear. Aisho. Come.

6   It is then that I noticed she had decorated her body with human bones. A necklace of skulls hung around her neck. She had made an ornament out of death — and wore it, fearless in her conviction and knowledge of life.

7   Where shall we go? I asked, where hide and seek shelter for the night? What will nourish us and quench our thirst? — Woman's body is both the source of uncleanliness and life, she said. So have the sages spoken. Let us go into that gate, that body, she said, to ascertain the verity of their famed masculine, Brahmin intellect and pronouncements. Let us, O daughter of woman, enter into your mother's womb, the disputed region itself, where for many months you sat in abject meditation and waiting, nourished by the essence of her life. The tree yoni — the female genitalia, the womb, the jewel at the heart of the lotus, the manipadma itself, shall be our first place of descent for the night. There we will be protected by her, who first woke you from the inert life of sole matter — and yet was herself all body. That was her first incarnation for you and your own.

8   But to enter into this darkness even deeper could be dangerous, I replied. It is not greater immanence, but transcendence that we seek. Our need is to move away from, rise above, this forest, the night. This horrific darkness that makes my body inert and that clouds my reason.

9   But her inexorable movement never ceased. We had advanced within the edge of the forest in no time. Holding me by the hand firmly Kapalkundala had borne me by her own strength. Moving as in a dream we covered what seemed many leagues. At last the movement ceased. — We have arrived, she said, here is the zone of the body. We enter now.

10   It is then that I noticed that the storm I had anticipated had arrived. I felt the swirling wind. It was in fact a great whirlwind. Around and around it went — a tunnel, a spiral, a vortex, with a ring of fire at its mouth. I rotated blindly within its circular motion — rose and fell. The folds of flesh around me expanded and contracted with a great force. Up and down, out and in, light and darkness, had lost all their distinctions. I went into a headlong flight, only Kapalkundala's hold on my wrist was as sinewy and unrelenting as the umbilical cord. Sometimes I heard or felt the deep reverberations of her laughter. She was amused with my fear. Finally I heard her say, open your eyes, open them as wide as you can and look around you, see who you can find, where you are. We have reached Ananda Math — The Temple of Joy.

11   Opening my eyes, as the darkness drifted away from my vision, I saw — Mother.

12   Ma ja chhillen, ja hoiachhen, ja hoiben. Mother as she was, as she has become, and as she will be.

13   The storm had ceased, A wonderful calm prevailed. We were in a cave, and it was suffused with light as though underwater whose source was unknown to me. There were three shrines next to each other, in three niches, holding three idols, images. Mata kumari — balika — Mother, a girl, a young nubile virgin, arrested in the act of play, body poised for motion, for flight. Mata, sangihini o garbhini — mother, a woman, crushed beneath the weight of a male figure, with one hand over her abdomen protecting the life within.

14   Mata, briddha o ekakini, mother, old and alone, a shrunken form, blind with a hand outstretched seeking pity, curled in a foetal position.

15   Pranum Kara. Bow down, prostrate yourself in front of her, said the female ascetic, herself doing the same. Her voice held the sound of clouds on the verge of rain. Her ascetic's serene eyes were filled with tears, they silently spilled on to her bosom. Thus we stood for a long time gazing at mother in her incarnations. Finally I gave voice to my thought.

16   Your renunciation is not complete, Kapalkundala, I said. You still cry. The world — its beauty and pain — still move you. You still have not succeeded in giving up an attraction for the mysteries it holds.

17   The Sannyasini, the woman mendicant, standing at the door of the world with her begging bowl made of a skull, looked at me sadly. — You don't understand, she said, I never did give up the world, the world was taken from me. And yet I hold onto what of it I can. What it will give me.

18   And what is that you hold on to, Kapalkundala, I asked her, through your severe intellections and meditations? — Compassion, she said. And since compassion cannot exist without a regard for truth and memory I seek after them as well.

19   Compassion for whom? I asked. — For mother and thus for you and for me. Through both involuntary responses and studied practices I hope to find my salvation.

20   Glancing at mother's incarnations, feeling my body tear at me in three ways, I begged her — make me your disciple. Please show me the way.

21   She gave me no answer. Standing as still as the icons that confronted us, wrapped in her pain and meditations, she drove me to distraction and supplications.

The violence of my own tears and anguish woke me and I heard a wail as I opened my eyes. I was born.

BREAKING THE CIRCLE: WRITING AND READING A FRAGMENT

22 Reader, you have just finished reading a piece put together by me from fragments of language, memories, textual allusions, cultural signs and symbols. It is clearly an attempt to retrieve, represent and document something. But what sort of text is it? Does it speak to you? And what does it say? You see, on the verge of writing, having written, I am still uncertain about the communicative aspect of it. I must reach out to you beyond the authorial convention, break the boundaries of narration, its progression and symmetry, and speak to you directly: in a letter, which you will answer to the author in you. And you, as much as I, will have to get engaged not only in reflections about memories and writing, but about writing in English as Asian women in Canada.

23 And I would like to know whether you, as much as I, feel the same restlessness, eagerness, worry and uncertainty about expression and communication that make me want to say it all and be mute at the same time. Are you also haunted by this feeling, that as an Asian woman, what you will say about yourself, selves, about *ourselves*, will end up sounding stillborn, distant, artificial and abstract — in short, not quite authentic to you or us? Are you also trying to capture alive, and instead finding yourself caught up in a massive translation project of experiences, languages, cultures, accents and nuances? Are you also struggling with the realization that you are self-alienated in the very act of self-expression?

24 At times you tell yourself or others tell you, that if you were a better writer, with something really worthwhile to say, with greater clarity and depth, you would not have this problem. Maybe then you would not turn away from your own articulations as the sound hits the air, or a thought hits the page. A real writer — a better writer. But upon careful consideration I have decided to dismiss this view of things. It is not skill, depth of feeling, wealth of experience or attentiveness to details — in short a command over content and form — that would help me to overcome this problem of alienation, produced by acts of self-translation, a permanent mediator's and interpreter's role. A look at much of the writings on history and culture produced by Asian writers in English reveals that the problem goes beyond that of conceptualization and skill to that of sensibilities, to the way one relates to the world, is one's own self. Literature, in particular, is an area suffering from this tone of translatedness.

25 It appears that we Asian immigrants coming from ancient cultures, languages and literature, all largely produced in non-Christian and pre-capitalist or semi-feudal (albeit colonial) terrains, have a particularly difficult time in locating ourselves centre stage in the 'new world' of cultural production. Our voices are mostly absent, or if present, often out of place with the rest of the expressive enterprises. A singular disinterest about us or the societies we come from, thus who we are substantively not circumstantially, is matched equally by the perverted orientalist interest in us (the East as a mystic state of mind to the West) and our own discomfort with finding a cultural-linguistic expression or form which will minimally do justice to our selves and formations. And this has not to do with language

facility, or ability to comprehend, negotiate or navigate the murky waters of a racist imperialist 'new world.'

26   Even for those of us who are fluent in English or our children who grew up in Canada, the problem is a pressing one. To the extent that these children are products of our homes, modulated by our everyday life inflections (though not well-versed in the languages we bring with us), they suffer from the possibility of 'etherization.' This is done by the historical separation of our worlds, understood in the context of values and practices produced by colonialism, imperialism and immediately palpable racism. All telling, then, self-expression and self-reification get more and more closely integrated. There is a fissure that cannot even begin to be fathomed between us, those with our non-Anglo Western sociocultural (often non-Christian) ambience, and others with all of these legacies. I mention religion only to enforce the view that it is a part of a totality of cultural sign and meaning systems, rather than something apart and thus easily abstracted or extrapolated.

27   In fact, the very vibrancy and substantiveness of the sociocultural world we come from work against us in our diasporic existence. They locate us beyond the binaries of 'self and other,' Black and white. It is not as though our self identities began the day we stepped on this soil! But, conversely, our 'etherization' becomes much easier as we do carry different sign or meaning systems which are genuinely unrelated to Western capitalist emotional, moral and social references. And this notwithstanding our colonial experience. The beyond-and-aboveness to Westernization and white man's presence, thousands of years of complex class and cultural formations (such as specialized intellectual and priestly or warrior classes: Brahmins in India, Mandarins in China, or Samurai in Japan to name a few), and struggles, with scripts, texts, and codifications, all make us an easy target of 'etherization.' The shadow of 'the East,' 'the Orient,' overhangs how we are heard, and the fact of having to express ourselves now in languages and cultures that have nothing in common with us continue to bedevil our attempts at working expressively and communicatively with our experiences and sensibilities.

28   I have been conscious of these problems, particularly of the integrity of language and experience, ever since I have been living in Canada and trying to write creatively in English. Speaking and being heard have often involved insuperable difficulties in conveying associations, assonances and nuances. But the problem takes on an acute form with experiences which take place elsewhere both in time and space — for example, in this text — in childhood, in Bengal. They are experiences in another language, involving a person who was not culturally touched by Westernization or urbanization, namely my mother. I wanted to write something about her, which also implies about us. I was repeatedly muted and repelled by the task on many counts. First there was the difficulty of handling the material itself.

29   Writing about one's own mother. Who can really re-present, hold in words, a relationship so primordial, with all its ebb and flow, do justice to it — in words? Probably true of all relationship to a degree, relationship with one's parents, which is implied in one's description of them, remains the most ineffable. Suggest, evoke, recall, narrate, the whole remains greater than the sum of its parts. The task is further complicated by the rhythm of time, growth and decline. After all she and

I — mother and child — grew and changed together and away, I growing older and she, old. She was at my inception, from my first day to my present. I witnessed her life and related to her from then to her death. We overlapped for awhile — overtaken however by aging, disease, decay, senility, silence and the shrillness of pain, and the ordinariness and irrevocability of death. As we moved in time our perceptions of each other changed kaleidoscopically. I cannot even recall my child's vision of her, because I cannot become that child again. She was another person, I cannot recapture her feelings and views of the world; though of course in some particular way she has been mutated, fused and transformed into my present self, each 'then and there' perhaps contributing to each 'here and now.'

30   Death adds a further twist to it. A living relationship is simultaneously fluid and focused and anchored in an actual person. But death fractures it into memories and associations, feelings that float about looking for a real person and interactions, but finding only spurious, associative points of reference. It is a strangely alienating moment in one's life when 'mother' is no longer an appellation which evokes a response, but is transformed into an abstraction, a knowledge involving a social structure called 'the family,' its directly emotive content now consigned to 'once upon a time.' After her death it is possible to find one's mother not only in personal memory, but in associations other than human, such as nature, and of course in a myriad of social and cultural gestures and rituals. A season or a festival becomes saturated with her memories and associations. For me the autumnal festival of the mother goddess Durga, the goddess of power with ten weaponed hands, only serves to remind me of my humble, domestic mother, who infused this festival with faith, whose world was the world of Hinduism filled with gifts, food, fasting and taboos. All this — life and death — are difficult to capture, for anyone anywhere since life is always more than any expression of living it. But the very attempt to do so is infinitely more frustrating for those who have to speak/write in a language in which the experience did not originate, whose genius is alien and antithetical to one's own.

31   Life, I am convinced, does not allow for a separation between form and content. It happens to us in and through the language in which it actually happens. The words, their meanings — shared and personal — their nuances are a substantial and *material* part of our reality. In another language, I am another person, my life another life. When I speak of my life in India, my mother or others there, I have a distinct feeling of splintering off from my own self, or the actual life that is lived, and producing an account, description, narrative — what have you — which distinctly smacks of anthropology and contributes at times to the paraphernalia of Orientalism. The racist-colonial context always exerts a pressure of utmost reification, objectification of self and others.

32   The importance of language and culture in the narrative and the integrity is even more concretely demonstrated to me when speaking in India about racism experienced by me in Canada (and other places in the West). Though less sharply alienating, being ex-colonials and experiencing racism and colonialism on our own soil and abroad, there is still a difficulty in conveying the feel of things, the contribution of exact words, tone, look, etc., in producing the fury and humiliation of a racist treatment. How can a Toronto white bank teller's silent but eloquent

look of contempt from a pair of eyes lurking in her quasi-Madonna (is that it?) hairdo be conveyed to a Bengali speaking, Bengali audience of Calcutta? How can the terror of skinheads — their bodies, voices, clothes or shaved heads — be adequately, connotatively expressed to a society where they are totally alien forms, where a shaved head, for example, signifies penance or a ritual for the loss of parents, or the benign-ness of *bhakticult*, a cult of devotion and love?

33   If we now go back to the text I have produced, in a relatively direct and uncensored manner, as though in Bengali, we can perhaps see how it expresses a sensibility alien to English and the postmodern literary world that we inhabit. I need to struggle not at the level of images and language alone, but at the levels of tonality and genre as well. It is a text with holes for the Western reader. It needs extensive footnotes, glossaries, comments, etc. — otherwise it has gaps in meaning, missing edges. It is only relatively complete for those who share my history or other noncapitalist and feudal histories — a world where epics and so-called classics are a part of the everyday life and faith of the people. They may decide that it does not work as a literary piece, but will not need many footnotes to the tone, emotions, conceptualization, references and textual allusions which create this mosaic.

34   Let us thus begin to footnote. This device that drags a text beyond its immediate narrative confines — might offer on the one hand the danger of objectification, of producing introductory anthropology, on the other, conversely, might rescue the text from being an Orientalist, i.e., an objectified experience and expression. To begin at the beginning — the epigraph from the Indian classical epic, *The Mahabharata* — what is it doing here in this piece? An obvious explanation is that like all epigraphs it establishes a 'theme.' It expresses my relationship with my mother and even a generalization about parent-child and age-youth relations. What we see in the episode of King Yayati and his son Puru is a trade of lives, youth and age, an aging person's ruthless desire to renew his own decaying life, even at the cost of the child's and finally a young person's internalization of an aging life. A knowledge of this legend necessitates a knowledge of this epic. Now, Western scholars of classical Indian literature would know this text, but how many are they in number? I could not take these allusions or their sign system for granted as I could, for example, the Bible, or even references to the peripheries of classical Greek literature. To do so is common practice in the West; to do what I have done is perceived as somewhat artificial, erudite, a little snobbish perhaps. Yet the commonness of such an evocation is obvious to those who see our cultures as forms of living, not museum pieces. Its presence in this text signifies not a detour into the classics, but an involuntary gesture to my mother's and my grandmother's world — in fact, to myself as a child. This is what it feels like from the inside:

35   It's afternoon — long, yellow, warm and humid. The green shutters with their paint fading behind the black painted rusty iron bars are closed to stop the hot air from coming in. The red cement floor has been freshly mopped and now cooled by the fan that comes a long way down from high ceilings, where shadows have gathered. Somewhere a crow is cawing and I can hear the clang and chimes of brass pots as they are being washed at the tube well. I am lying on the floor on a rush mat, listlessly. I am eight, I don't go to school yet, they have

captured me, and will force me to be here until the afternoon is over because they don't want me wandering around the compound in the hot sun, climbing trees and all that. I am lying there tossing and turning — sleep is out of the question. At some point my mother enters. She wanders about the room for a while searching or taking this and that, puts her silver container of betel leaves (pan) next to her pillows, loosens the tie of her sari, worn over a long slip, her 'chemise,' and lowers herself on the bed. The bed creaks. I am lying wide-eyed. She inquires — why am I not asleep? No answer follows. She does not bother to break my recalcitrant silence, lies on her side, and proceeds to chew on her pan in silence. Her breasts flop down and touch the bed. I look sideways at the dark area of her nipple visible through the chemise front. I have no breasts. My attention shifts. I look at the book lying next to her hand, which does not pick it up. I shift towards her bed — rolling on the ground — until I am just at its edge. I know the book — Kashi Das's *The Mahabharata*. It's in verse, rhymed couplets, with their neat short jingles tripping along. I already know bits of it by heart — stories of kings, queens, great wars, of children born inside a fish or springing up from the reeds, beautiful women, long wanderings through forests and other things that I don't understand and therefore ignore. I ask her if I can read the book, since I can't sleep. She is about to insist on my sleeping instead when the door opens, and my grandmother comes in. Small, lightfooted, thin, shavenheaded, fair-skinned, still not toothless, in her saffron sari, coloured with red clay. 'Let her,' says my grandmother. Turning to me she says, 'Wait until I lie down. Let's see how well you can read. All this money on a private tutor. Let's see what the result is.'

36   The book is in my hand. One of the four volumes, bound in cardboard backing and covered with little purple designs on a white base, with a navy blue spine and four triangular edges. The cardboard has become soft with handling, and the paper (newsprint from a popular press) slightly brown, here and there a corner is torn, scribbles by children on the inner sides of the binding, illustrations drawn over by children with pens, such as moustaches on the faces of the heroines and clean shaven war heroes, eyes of the wicked scratched out by my justice seeking nails, and a musty smell. I sit up, lean against the bed, my mother's rather pudgy and soft hand strokes my head, fingers running through my hair, at times the gold bangles make a thin and ringing sound as they hit each other. There is a rhythm to her hand movement, it moves to the rhythm of the verse. My grandmother has assumed a serious listening expression. I read — print, until recently only black squiggly scribbles on paper, begins to make the most wonderful sounds — words, meanings, cadences tumble out of my mouth. I am enthralled. The sound rolls, flows.

37   *Dakho dwija Manashija jinya murati*
Padmapatra jugmanetra parashaye sruti.
[See the Brahmin, who is better looking than the god of love, with lotus petal eyes that touch his ears.]

38   Understanding and not understanding, often supplying the meaning from my own mind, I read on. The palm leaf fan that my grandmother has picked up from habit hits the ground from her slack wrist. My mother's hand has stopped. Their

eyes are closed, gentle snores greet my ears. I keep reading until the end of the canto anyway.

39   *Mahabharater katha amrita saman*
    Kashram Das bhane sune punyaban
    [The words/stories of Mahabharat are as nectar
    Kashiram Das recites them, the virtuous listen.
    Or: those who listen to them acquire virtue
    (produced from good, sanctified deeds)]

40   This then for me is the world of the epic, a most humble vernacular, domestic scene, part of a child's world, which of course by definition is also the mother's world, the grandmother's world, maternal older women's world. It is interior, it is private — in afternoons when menfolk and students are at work and school — women and pre-school children, thrown together, the 'good book' playing its part between a heavy lunch and a siesta. How is Orientalist scholarship to cope with this? How is my reader of here and now in Canada, whose childhood, culture and language, [are] so far away from any of this, to grasp the essence of this experience which is not only mine, but of countless children of Bengal who are at present my age in literate, middle-class homes? This is why, not only the theme but the atmosphere, the association of Mahabharata indeed of Bengali literature, is part and parcel of what I call my mother. Today recalling her, they are dredged out of my childhood together, from the sun-soaked afternoons of East Bengal, a long time ago.

BREAKING THE CIRCLE: MOTHER-TONGUE

41 Come to think of it, this problem of reification, of English versus Bengali or the vernacular, started for me a long time ago. In the then unknown to me but lived colonial context, my mother stood for vernacular to me. Her literacy was limited but it solely consisted of Bengali. She and women of her generation, and poor rural and urban people of both sexes, namely our servants and ryots (peasant tenants), unschooled ones, only knew Bengali. In my class world, older women and servants (male and female) and small children, who did not go out to school, belonged to an interior world of home, hearth and Bengali. The public world outside held the serious business of earning money, achievement, success and English. In fact in preparation for my flight to that world, we were already being groomed in English, compulsorily, by our private tutor. But Bengali was obviously easier to learn, no sooner did we learn the alphabet and joining of consonants and vowels, we could make some sense of what was written on the page, the only limitation being vocabulary. Bengali stories and novels were what we enjoyed reading, English was our duty. We could neither understand the words, the syntax, nor the world that they portrayed. It was altogether too much to dredge out some meaning and comfort from a text in that language.

42   Bengali literature was our pleasure and those books belonged to my mother — tons and tons of novels, forbidden to us because they contained passion, romance and sexual matters, though completely unexplicit and highly mediated.

But it is from this collection of my mother and of others like her, mainly women, that I read the greatest classics of Bengali literature. In my childhood no male in my world spoke of Bengali literature as a serious and high-calibre achievement, with the exception of the romantic, abstract and spiritual literature of Rabindranath Tagore whose popularity among educated males was at least in part based on his popularity in the West, signified by being a Nobel Prize winner. Even my father encouraged me to read and memorize his poems. But in my mother's world which neither knew nor cared for English, or Europe, or the public colonial world of India, the Victorian Brahmo spiritual moralist Tagore was a distant figure. It was the Hindu nationalist novelists of Bengal, working with a familiar culture which structured our home lives, who sat on my mother's shelves uncontested by any foreign competitor. Bankim Chandra Chattyopadhyay, the father of Bengali nationalist fiction, Sarat Chandra Chattyopadhyay, rubbed shoulders with twentieth-century realists and romantics such as Manik Bandyopadhyay, Bibhuti Bhushan Bandyopadhyay, and many others. My father never read even a page of this, nor did my older learned brothers ever speak to me then or now about any of this literature. English and European literature rescued themselves by being English and European — though they were never taken very seriously compared to, let us say, 'real' subjects such as science, philosophy or economics — all of the West and all in English. My high school had no Bengali teacher. When I wanted to take it as a subject for senior Cambridge exams, a teacher came from another school to do two hours a week with me. My Bengali readings at home continued however. My mother became identified with the vernacular. '*Bengla*' (not 'Bengali,' to be accurate) was truly my *matribhasha* (mother-tongue). It is from this vernacular I learnt my nationalism — memories, history and ideology of India's independence struggle. The literature was a part of this struggle, expressing and shaping it. Mother, mother-tongue and motherland were dominant figures and themes in it. From my mother's copy of *Ananda Math*, The Temple of Joy ('the classic' of nationalist fiction), I learnt very early — Janani Janmabhumischa Swargadapi Gariasi — 'Mother and motherland are more glorious than heaven.' Naturally none of this was a conscious ideological project — nor was it noticeable to me at this time how gender- and class-organized my whole world and experiences were. Vernacular belonged to the women of the upper classes and both men and women of the middle and lower middle classes, and was spoken daily by them and the serving classes. The cultural politics of nationalism — conducted consciously in Bengali by middle-class men and women — came in indirectly or found receptive ears in upper-class households through women and young people. In pre-independence India, as in 'modern' India, the way to advancement lay through proficiency in English and collaboration with Colonial State and Western capital.

43   What I say about language, nationalism, class and gender is not merely an abstract theoretical excursion. The text I have constructed could not have been produced outside of the realm of lived experience. Much of the basis of my politics and romantic sexual emotions lies in the Bengali literature that I read stealing from my mother's collection. There they were on a shelf. I still remember the bit of newspaper she spread on the shelf and the smell of the insecticide between the pages. Summer vacations, in particular, were the more propitious times. I would devour them a few at a time, then reread slowly since the supply was often

exhausted within one or two weeks of reading. How deeply the novels of Bankim Chandra Chattyopadhyay sank into me became evident once more when lacking a voice, a form to think through my recent experiences of bereavements and confusion, Bankim's Kapalkundala came back to me offering her help to lead me through the jungle and maze of my feelings — asking the very question she once asked a shipwrecked, tired and confused man — Nabakumar — 'Traveller have you lost your way?' Literature, everyday life and politics fused into one.

My mother is kneading some dough for making sweets. They are for us and my father because he won't eat store-bought sweets. Her bangles set up a pleasant jingle, she is sitting on a low stool, with a deep bowl in front of her. It is very hot, we are both sweating, the kitchen has no fan. Occasionally a breeze brings some relief and the heady smell of nim flowers and the chirping of Shaliks who seem to speak in English saying, 'can you? can you?' in a taunting voice to each other. I am playing with a piece of dough shaping it into a human figure, putting in two cloves for eyes, an almond for the mouth and a cardamon for a nose. I am about eleven years of age, by now secretly nourished with the romantic and sentimental extravaganzas of much of nineteenth- and twentieth-century Bengali fiction. I know however that I cannot disclose much of what they call in Bengali 'untimely ripeness' to grown-ups. But I am lonely. My brothers are young and callow. We are too high up socially to mix with many people, and Hindus to boot in the Islamic Republic of Pakistan which substantially narrows socializing. I say to my mother, 'Do you think it's fair that Gobindalal should have killed Rohini like that? I don't think she alone is to blame.' My mother is not pleased. *Krishnakanter Will*, Bankim's classic fiction on lust, adultery and murder, is not her idea of a young girl's reading. A flour and dough covered hand grips my wrists. 'Don't touch those shelves, don't ever read these books without my permission. They are not meant for you.' 'What should I read then?' I ask defiantly. 'Read — read — good books. Those you have in English.' 'I don't enjoy reading in English,' I say. 'I have so much trouble figuring sentences out, that I don't even notice what they are really saying. And besides why do you have them if they are not good books?' After a short period of silence she said, 'OK, you can read some of them. Read *Ananda Math*. Read *Rajsingha*, but definitely not *Bisha Briksha* or *Krishnakanter Will*.'

I did read the books she wanted/allowed me to but with much less pleasure than the proscribed texts. And at a moment of need a vision arose from my unconscious and the inner sanctum of the Temple of Joy, where the hero sees 'the mother' in three incarnations of past, present and future. Mother, the goddess herself and the motherland had been fused for me into one, perhaps because, though a goddess and an abstraction, she was curiously susceptible to history, and non-transcendental. In her past glory, her present fall and degradation, and her future state of restored splendour, Bankim's novel implanted the abstraction into time. Today speaking of my own mother, what I have witnessed of her life and my feelings for what I have seen, unbidden by any conscious decision, Ananda Math provides me with my language, my image. How can this domestic, literary, psychological, and political fusion be seen as any more than an exercise to those who are outsiders to this world? For the lower and middle classes of Bengal it all goes without saying.

46   My present text will always remain incomplete, however, both at the level of literature and social being, fragments all, one suggesting another, and abruptly broken, or trailing off into the unknown of other moments, histories, cultures and languages. Some of this is inevitable — created by our migrations into these lands of our estrangement — but also made much more violent because of the denigration of our cultures, histories, memories and languages by this new racist-imperialist world. What we bring with us and who we are, the basis of our social being, on which our life and politics here must develop, are considered redundant. The Ministry of Multiculturalism and the various containment agencies of this country all together gesture towards and create this negation and redundancy. But curiously and interestingly this emptying out as well as blocking at the level of our social being is also present in whatever culture of resistance we have created. The difference being that it is less, or often not, by design, but more significantly through a relative and an empiricist stance regarding our lives here and now, that we leave our authentic and substantive selves unaddressed. We are other than a binary arrangement of identities, even though negatively or invertedly we are caught in a racist-imperialist definition — its ideological and institutional practices. The overwhelming preoccupation with what 'they say we are' and 'what we are not,' our 'otherization' by 'them' precludes much exploration or importance of who we actually *are*.

47   Who we are should be a historical / memorial and re-constructive excursion heralding a new content and new forms out of the very problems created by dislocation or fragmentation. Leaving this part of our lives depoliticized, dismissing it simply as 'cultural' politics, in refusing to incorporate these experiential and subjective terms into the 'world of anti-racist politics,' can lead to forms of silencing, imitative exercises, wearing masks of others' struggles.

48   A whole new story has to be told, with fragments, with disruptions, and with self-conscious and critical reflections. And one has to do it right. Creating seamless narratives, engaging in exercises in dramatic plot creating, simply make cultural brokers, propagators of Orientalism and self-reificationists out of us. My attempt here has been to develop a form which is both fragmentary and coherent in that it is both creative and critical — its self-reflexivity breaking through self-reification, moving towards a fragmented whole.

Topics for consideration:

1. In this essay Bannerji combines "creative" writing with formal academic style because she wants to produce something that is "not merely an abstract theoretical excursion." What are the difficulties of trying to combine these two kinds of writing?

2. Bannerji recalls her first experiences as a child reader. How does her account compare with the accounts of the experience of reading in the "Writing and Reading" chapter of this book?

3. Bannerji begins the "Breaking the Circle: Writing and Reading a Fragment"

section of this essay with a series of questions to the reader. How would you answer them?

Further reading:

Susie Tharu and K. Lalita, eds., *Women Writing in India, 600 B.C. to the Early Twentieth Century* (1993)

David Carpenter (1941-

David Carpenter has published several books of fiction including Jokes for the Apocalypse *(1985) and* God's Bedfellows *(1988). He is also expert at fishing and has co-written and edited a how-to book on the subject,* Fishing in the West *(1995). His essays have been published in* Saturday Night, Canadian Literature *and other periodicals in Canada and the U.S. as well as in two collections,* Writing Home *(1994) and* Courting Saskatchewan *(1997).*

This essay reconstructs in narrative form David Carpenter's discovery of the writing of Georges Bugnet, his discovery that the writer whose work he admires is still alive, and the eventual development of a friendship that leads him to become Bugnet's translator. The essay reflects on Carpenter's early infatuation with the French language and the way that Bugnet's writing fuses European sensibilities with "the feel of the West" and the "new world."

NOM DE PLUME

1 Georges Bugnet (novelist, scientist, poet, settler) was born in France in 1879, the same year as Frederick Philip Grove. When I was in graduate school I found some biographical sketches of him, but nowhere could I find a date for his death. Grove (alias Felix Paul Berthold Friederich Greve), the son of a minor official in Hamburg, reinvented himself as an aristocratic Anglo-Swede. He fooled everyone about his true identity until decades after his death. But at least he left us with a corpse, a gravesite. Bugnet's coup seemed to be that he was immortal. In 1971 or so, it didn't occur to me that he might still be alive.

2 Here is what the eminent critic E.K. Brown said in 1947 about *La Forêt*, Bugnet's masterpiece:

> Last week I was asked ... what was the finest novel of the Canadian West. I ... thought of two ... novels, Frederick Philip Grove's *Settlers of the Marsh* and Sinclair Ross's *As For Me and My House*. But the book I actually name gives ... a deeper sounding of life in the West than either of these ... The book is ... Georges Bugnet's *La Forêt* ... Bugnet ... is one of the really important Canadian writers. In him an intellect and spirit of a very high order unite with a long experience of life in the wilderness; and the result has been a literary work in which the materials of the frontier have been wrought into designs of lasting beauty, and their meaning presented with an unwavering courage ... It is a great and tragic book. We do not have many such.

3 I discovered *La Forêt* (1935) in 1971. I was a grad student writing a doctoral thesis in Edmonton. My supervisor was Mort Ross, an American literature specialist who was on a sabbatical during the time I was reading Bugnet. With Mort gone, the job fell to Dick Harrison, a Canadian specialist. When Harrison was away on research, my supervisor was Rudy Wiebe. Even then, Rudy was a writer of some repute and he noticed things about my thesis that writers would notice and scholars might not. Dick Harrison was just discovering material about settlement

narratives that he would eventually write a great deal about. He would set me straight on matters bearing on Canadian literature and history. Mort Ross had an osprey's unfaltering eye for sloppy prose, jargon-hazed thinking, and evasive arguments. So with Mort and Dick and Rudy, I had the best of three worlds. For two years they shared me like foster parents.

4 *La Forêt* hit me very hard. My own French was pretty lame, but in time I improved and reread all of Bugnet's works. I fell beneath the spell of his voice and acquired a slavish anglo respect for French. How timid these anglo writers were on the subject of love. Love. You could say the word without moving your lips. But *amour*. Now there was a doozer of a word. Watch the mouths of the francophones. *Amour.*

5 How could a bland word like "dusk" stand up to *crépuscule*? Ah, zose English, zey ave no soul. How I longed to be French!

6 And how strange to do research on a man who apparently was immortal. I must have dreamed of meeting with Bugnet and talking with him about the Big Issues. Art, Politics, and Love. I began on weekends to drive to the French communities north of Edmonton to see if there was anyone who had known Georges Bugnet. I tried St. Albert and Morinville. My third stop was Legal, about an hour's drive north of Edmonton. I drove there through a snowstorm and parked my car at the old folks' home. An elderly Sister greeted me at the door.

7 I said something like the following to her: "Have you ever heard of a man named Bugnet?"

"We have a Bugnet here," she said in French.

"Georges Bugnet?"

10 "Yes," she said.

"Is he ... all right?"

"He is very old," she said.

"Is this Georges Bugnet the writer?"

"I don't know if he writes anything," she said. "He *talks* a lot."

15 She showed me to his room, I knocked on the door, and a gravelly voice shouted, "*Entrez, entrez.*"

16 I walked into a small dim room with a bunk bed and a tiny desk. The room smelled strongly of pipe tobacco. A short man with a scraggly white beard was lying on the bed.

"Are you Georges Bugnet?" I said.

"Yes," he said.

"Georges Bugnet, the *writer*?"

20 It was the old man's turn to look incredulous. He sat up in his bunk. "You have read my books?" he said.

21 The next day I burst into Rudy Wiebe's office. It was heaped with photocopies of old newspapers. He was becoming steeped in Cree and Métis lore and the hateful propaganda in the Orange press of the 1870s and 1880s. He was writing his first draft of *The Temptations of Big Bear*. All through the winter he seemed to be visited by wave upon wave of furious inspiration. This was also one of those months when Rudy had been assigned to supervise my thesis. Alas, in 1971 he had bigger fish to fry.

22 "Georges Bugnet is alive!" I cried. "I've just spoken with him!"

23   "Hm," said Rudy. He managed to sound as though my discovery was the third or fourth most pressing thing on his mind. "That would mean that he's — what — ninety-three?"

"Something like that."

25   "So?"

"Oh, nothing. just thought you might be interested."

"I am," he said, glancing at his watch.

28   My weekly trips out to Legal began as necessary scholarship. But soon Bugnet and I strayed off the scholarly topics and onto the Big Issues. On one such occasion, he told me that I should have a wife. His exact words were, "*C'est pas bon, l'homme sans épouse.*" I still have these words on an old cassette from an interview I did with him for the *Journal of Canadian Fiction*. At the time he said this, he was well into his nineties, and I was twenty-nine. When I last came to visit him, he was 102 and still extolling the virtues of marriage in French and English. When I could still call myself a young man, Georges Bugnet came rather close, I suppose, to the human equivalent of God. He had that effect on the many people I brought out to meet him, even when he was lost and rambling.

"Carpenter, you should try for one in Beau Monde."

30   "Try for what?"

"Go to Beau Monde," he went on. "The last time I was there ... beautiful French girls. You should go soon. They want husbands and they make lovely wives."

"Beau Monde?"

"*Oui.*"

Beautiful world. A world of perfect love. She and I walking naked in some garden, God speaking to us in a stately French accent.

35   "Where is Beau Monde?"

36   "You must have approached it sometime, going to or from Edmonton." In a dreamy voice he added, "I think by now it must be not so far."

37   Can you imagine how this news must have struck me in Bugnet's rasping voice? *Elles font de belles épouses.* I suspect Bugnet had not been anywhere in twenty years, let alone to Beau Monde, Alberta, wherever that was. So naturally I thought he was talking nonsense. But somewhere else, where bushes that burn become burning bushes, I thought, *God is trying to tell me something.* And how the phrase *belles épouses* plucked melodies on the strings of my heart. All the way back to Edmonton, I probably mumbled words like *beau monde* and *belles épouses* like a rosary. (To this day I dream about that ride home from Legal. It always involves a futile search for love and always leaves the same aching residue. I'm driving fast because I've missed a rendezvous. I awaken to the memory of a woman's voice.)

38   I drove back toward Edmonton beneath a darkening winter sky, and I found myself thinking in a more familiar language. I am still young. I am only twenty-nine years old. I am not ready for six children and the paunch of a church elder even if some of my friends are. Until this time I had always opted for the woman with a sign over her head: THIS RELATIONSHIP WILL SELF-DESTRUCT IN SIXTY DAYS. A strange time in my life, if you see what I mean.

39   Somehow I managed to drive past my usual turnoff to the heart of Edmonton and instead drive south and east on an unfamiliar road. Along this road I spied the turnoff for Beaumont.

40   Of course, the village of Beaumont! I slowed, hesitated, trying to recall Bugnet's description of the old village. A gothic cathedral. Some old stone buildings, some statues of saints and virgins. But at the edge of the town, I saw none of these. Just row upon row of nearly identical pastel bungalows and duplexes on streets denuded of trees. Beaumont had become a bedroom community for commuters to Edmonton and looked determinedly Protestant to me. Protestant, perhaps even post-Christian.

41   I drove on, closer to the centre of town, past more bungalows, none of which might occasion a romantic utterance in French or in English. Past a flat pink school. But then a dip in the road, an old bridge, a slow-moving stream, and the last remnant of the old village square: a turn-of-the-century brick courthouse; facing it, an equally venerable stone cathedral; and a hotel so old in appearance, one would never mistake it for a motel. In this last little atoll of francophone culture, I parked my car.

42   Instinct led me to the coffee shop. Behind the counter was a rather plain waitress (no rings) speaking to an old man. The old man was stooped over a plate of French fries, which I suppose was appropriate, and the two of them were speaking, unmistakably, in French.

43   "*Un café, s'il vous plaît,*" I said. Perhaps teasingly.

44   All francophones in this part of the country speak English and recognize at once when an anglo is showing off his pathetic European textbook French. It's a game played by linguistic tourists: I will be French for you if you pretend that my French is acceptable.

45   "*Oui,*" she said. Not *wye* or *wa* as she might have said in a moment of low enthusiasm, but *oui*. She might just as well have said, *Je serai ta belle épouse.* Her *oui* had the same effect. Suddenly, with that one word, she was considerably less than plain.

46   All over English Canada when we WASPs affirm something, we say "yes." A terse syllable hissing from a mouth that moves almost grudgingly. This ultimate affirmation, this word that commands the blood to rush downward and release all of God's tumescence in a pledge of love. Yes? We move our lips so slightly that the word scarcely issues at all. This is not an affirmation. It is at best a furtive nod towards a workable compromise among people who want to keep their teeth warm and out of the wind.

47   But *oui*. My waitress purses her lips as if to whistle and they part in a burst that melts the snow and celebrates the whiteness of teeth and all the liquid wonder of her mouth. *Oui*. She cannot say this word without kissing the air between herself and me.

48   I was caught inside the plot of an old writer; I had become his young hero. I didn't wonder whether I'd forfeited my own language for someone else's or why my own value system seemed to have collapsed. I was taking cues from an unseen director, speaking my lines and hoping for a pleasant ending. It was clear in some unused part of my soul that God had sent me to this café — and that he wanted me married. As Bugnet would say, "You want in your body to be mated, and in your soul to be united to another."

49   My waitress brought a large cup of steaming black coffee and smiled. Her hair must have been quite long. It was black and glossy and gathered up in a fine

roll with many errant wisps behind her ears. On her uniform blouse she had sewn the letters L-M.

50 *"Que veut dire ton monogramme?"* I asked. I pronounced her letters. Their sound came back to me like an echo: *elle aime, elle aime ...*

"Louise Monpetit," she said.

"Dave Carpenter," I said.

"Salut, Dave."

54 The old man down the counter said something I didn't understand, and she returned to him. Louise Monpetit. (Note the *oui* in Louise.) No aspiring lovers hung around the counters. Perhaps all the men of the village had fled the onrush of pastel bungalows to make their fortune up north or in the city. Soon the last of the old town would fall to the anglo bulldozers. And what would happen to Louise Monpetit? The most preposterous scenario began to emerge. I saw my role clearly. I would marry her, join the Roman Catholic church, and become a champion of francophone culture in Beaumont. We would have two or three darkhaired sons and at least as many lovely daughters. They would speak perfect French, and they would repossess the town. I would become the town patriarch, coach the hockey team, and after I was gone, a statue of me in my coaching duds would stylite in front of the courthouse. I wondered whether Bugnet had ever considered such a plot.

55 I think I was glancing out the café window. The late afternoon gloom had imperceptibly turned to night. Winter. But the radiance of my scenario warmed me in my heart, and I realized that I could ask for nothing more. I turned to my waitress. Louise Monpetit, the last *belle épouse* in Beaumont, Alberta.

In English, she said, "Would you like anything more?"

57 As God is my witness, I faltered, looked down at my empty cup, and said, "No, thank you." And fled to my car.

58 There came a time, when my French had improved and I was finishing up my Ph.D., that I decided to translate *La Forêt* into English. This was the spring or summer of 1973. I approached Bugnet with the project. He said, "Your French could use some improvement, but most of all, you need to live in a forest."

"What?"

60 "You need to live in a forest. You need to watch what happens to the flora, what happens to the *saules.* You have been too long in the city, and my book is about a forest."

61 Right then and there I promised Bugnet that I would find a cabin in a forest and do his book. He agreed and we shook on it. I was awarded a post-doc at the University of Manitoba and found a small cabin near St. Norbert, a few miles south of the campus and several more from the city of Winnipeg. My cabin was part of a small forest reserve. It was surrounded by enormous ash, linden, and maple trees except where it overlooked the Red River. My cabin had no address, naturally, and I had to pick up my mail at the campus. This residence gave me a wonderful sense of disappearing from everything and everyone I had known in Edmonton. And so for two years I sank more and more deeply into French and into the silence of a forest. I chatted more on campus with botanists and horticulturalists than with English and French professors. Living as I did, so close to civilization, I acquired a sort of weekend woodsiness. Very slowly and very awkwardly Bugnet's story began to emerge in English.

62   I was lonely most of the time, and sometimes Bugnet's remembered conversations kept me company. From time to time we wrote to each other. He was more than half-blind and was forced to write and read with the help of a large magnifying glass. Following are some excerpts:

63   April 10, 1972 *This morning I met with an old idea of mine ... It deals with the origin of the universe. Today many scientists prefer the hypothesis of Georges Lemaitre: a prodigious atom that blew up and is still bursting out. My belief is that before its formation there must have been a preceding entity: motion, which produced Space, and Time, and had such velocity that, at first, it vaporized all the primitive elements. I also believe that today Motion is still the fundamental basis of our Universe.*

64   February 12,1973 *I submit to your sagacity a sentence of mine which appeared in* The American Rose Annual *in 1941. "In these times of horribly devastating wars it is a comfort to be able to work with the beneficent creative Power that some call Nature and some call God meaning after all the same thing. The same unfathomable Entity."*

65   August 21, 1973 *From the depths of my heart and the wuthering heights of my nonagenarian brain I do thank and thank you. Mainly due to you my last days are filled with public honours.*
      On a different line, my eyes are imitating the Canadian postal workers and go on rotating strikes. I can't read or write for more than 5 or 6 minutes before they want a rest. They do not hurt, they blurrrr.

66   July 27, 1974 *It is not every day that my very old eyes and fingers allow me to write. You are a very great and good part of me. Before I received your letter* [about the acceptance of the English translation of *La Forêt*] *I felt disgusted by the mismanagement of this planet ... I felt ready to depart. Your letter changed my mood. Now I want to stay and go on until I hear of your well earned victory.*

67   April 21, 1975 [This note was almost illegible.] *My long silence was due to two stages in the hospital at Westlock. The first on account of a nasal hemorrage* [sic]*, the second to an inflammation in the left foot where a clot of bad blood had lodged itself. As far as my cataracts, two doctors, my children and I decided to leave them as they are.*

68   *You seem to be a glutton for hard work ... Go to it ... If you can come and see me next month I would be delighted.*

69   *My children are taking very good care of my extremely old age.*

70   *Immensely grateful to you.*

71   The above note, quoted almost in its entirety, was his last to me. At this time he was ninety-six. The translation of *La Forêt* for which he waited with such resolve, was finished all except for minor revisions. It would appear about a year and a half after Bugnet's last note to me when he was ninety-seven.

72   The translation turned out to be much more difficult than I had imagined it could be. After each of my chapters was typed up in English, I had to take it to

Paul Savoie (a fine poet and musician then living in St. Boniface) and to Emily Denney (a French Professor at the University of Manitoba). They would go over the materials in French and English and offer variant wordings of the text. They must have realized I was not a born translator, but they were patient with me. Frequently I attempted to do more of an adaptation than a literal translation. Just as frequently I attempted to include French words for which there seemed to be only the palest of English equivalents. Almost as often my publisher, Maynard Gertler of Harvest House, would remind me that there was always a proper expression in English for a phrase in French. I am now convinced that this is not true, but at the time my knowledge of French was still too rudimentary to appreciate the subtle differences between yes and *oui*.

73   Here is a passage from Chapter XIII of *La Forêt* that illustrates the problems I was up against. The man speaking is the male protagonist, Roger Bourgouin. Like Bugnet, he is a homesteader and a writer. He is distraught over a sudden bout of sickness in his horse.

74   *Bon! Il ne manquait plus que ça. Allez donc écrire un livre avec toutes ces histoires! Maudit cheval! Qu'est-ce qu'il peut avoir? Ce doit être ce maudit froid.*

75   And here, eventually, is how I translated it.

76   *Great! That's the last straw! You try to write a book with all these delightful little things going on. GODDAMNED horse. What the HELL has he got? It's the bloody cold weather, that's what it is!*

77   Readers will note that I have taken some liberties with the word *maudit*, which means cursed, miserable, wretched. But to a modern audience alert to the fact that Bourgouin is at the end of his tether, such words carry little force. Better entirely to leave in *maudit* — which I insist has no adequate English equivalent. But no, I was not allowed to use French words, so I fiddled with other choices (darned, accursed, blasted?) and decided on goddamned and hell in upper-case letters. To my audience such words would seem mild enough, but to Christians at the turn of the century, or at the time Bugnet was writing his masterpiece, this was not considered to be a mild expression of disapproval; indeed, this was taking the name of Bourgouin's/Bugnet's Lord in vain. However, this curse would be consistent with Bourgouin's moral decline in the forest. Until this scene, he had never used such an utterance in the presence of his wife.

78   *The Forest* came out late in 1976. Early in 1977 I received a letter so outraged that it left me speechless. Twelve days later, I received a second such letter. Both were written by daughters of Bugnet. Here is a sample, word for word and letter for letter.

79   *My father for maudit or dam, in La Forêt, Its not even a word, I or any of us has ever heard him use in word of mouth, maudit which in English is dam, was used in La Forêt for one reason only, to show how Roger was loosing some of his Intellectual, Cultural Character which my Father has never lost, in any of his writings or his own Characteristic Standard of Integrity ... You were not doing this for my Father, (money)*

I was angry, it has abated, realizing you need prayers to change you and stop you doing any more damage to my Father.
Mrs. Marthe Beauchamp, March 16, 1977

80   I suppose I should thank my lucky stars that Mrs. Beauchamp's anger had abated, because if she'd really been angry with me I might have suffered a fate worse than Roger Bourgouin's horse. I can only report that her prayers have wrought little change in me.

81   In my own defence, I should say that the blasphemy on page 91 of *The Forest* is almost the only one in the book — unless you count the word "hell" as a blasphemy. When I had received these denunciations I went immediately to Bugnet to apologize for the trauma I had put him through. He was by then ninety-eight years old, nearly blind, but from all I could see that day, he was completely untraumatized. He did show some uneasiness, however, at the condition of his two daughters, who were showing their disapproval in ways that now I can only imagine.

82   "It is too bad," he said to me. "They never read very much. They grew up in a place where such things were not encouraged. The books never appealed to them. And now, they are probably looking for you with evil intentions." He laughed and his old eyes disappeared. "I told them that it was not I who uttered these words, but a character of mine."

"Did that help to ease their indignation?"

"No," he said, and we both laughed.

85   When Georges Bugnet turned one hundred, officials at the University of Alberta decided to grant him an honorary doctorate. His mind was still lucid and he was pleased with the honour. He even prepared a long anecdotal speech for the occasion, which of course he had to do in his head and commit to memory. I heard about the big event from Rudy Wiebe and was surprised that I had not been invited. After all, my articles and translations of his work had in a modest way started the Bugnet ball rolling again. Surely there had been an oversight, perhaps the fact that I was now living in another city. I phoned the organizer. He claimed that I *had* been invited, but that the Sisters had stricken my name from the guest list.

86   The Sisters. In my mind they had attained the status of Goneril and Regan. With a vanity that only a young scholar could sustain, I felt that I was much closer to Bugnet than either of them. I was determined to attend Bugnet's ceremony. I would drive to St. Albert and get inside even if I had to disguise myself. But of course I wouldn't have to do that because neither of the sisters knew what I looked like. I simply drove to St. Albert, found the hall where the ceremony was to be held, waited until a great many people had entered the church, and approached the front door. An elderly lady stood there receiving guests. For all I knew, she could have been one of the Sisters, but I would not be daunted. I held out my hand and shook hers warmly.

"And you are?" she said with a firm smile.

88   "Fred Grove," I said. The name, I thought, was appropriate. It was probably the most famous *nom de plume* in Canadian history. And Bugnet had begun his own fiction writing career with the *nom de plume* of Henri Doutremont.

89   The lady greeting me was joined by another, about the same age. "This is Fred Grove," said the first lady.

90   "I'm from the university," I said.

91   "Oh," said the second lady, "you must know these gentlemen." She ushered me into the reception hall and there to my horror stood Rudy Wiebe, Mort Ross, and Dick Harrison. My escort said to the four of them, "Do you gentlemen know Mr. Fred Grove?"

"Who?" said Rudy.

"Oh," said the lady with a knowing smile. "Perhaps it is *Doctor* Fred Grove?"

94   I turned to her just as one of my former supervisors exploded into his glass of punch. "No," I said, "Mister will do fine, thank you." I gave Rudy and Mort and Dick an imploring look and they all smiled back the way blackmailers do at the prospect of a new client.

95   I looked around for Bugnet. At the upper end of the hall I spied him sitting in a wheelchair surrounded by a quiet group of people. A quiet *watchful* group of people. Two of them were elderly women, though different from the ones who had greeted me at the front door. Were *these* the Sisters? Perhaps. They seemed to regard anyone who came too close to Bugnet with the suspicions of secret service agents.

96   Oh, Carpenter. How you *do* love to dramatize your own fears. These women were simply well wishers, and what did I have to lose by edging closer to Bugnet so that I could at least whisper my congratulations? I moved closer and closer. I could hear voices in French and English speaking about Bugnet as though he weren't there. I could almost have shouted a greeting. But he was somehow *surrounded* by these people. They were all elderly enough to be his sons and daughters, but how could I be sure? I couldn't just stride up among them, push past them, tell Georges that I was Fred Grove, and expect him to get the message. After all, he was blind and I would just confuse the man.

97   Someone at a microphone announced that the ceremony would begin. We all took our seats at the front of the hall and the chancellor announced that this was the first time the University of Alberta had ever conferred an honorary doctorate off campus. This was done, of course, to accommodate Bugnet, who was altogether too feeble and arthritic to travel more than a few blocks. After a number of people had delivered their words of praise for Bugnet and his horticultural achievements, his vigorous work for the Lac la Nonne school division, his literary accomplishments, and his courage as an early settler, Bugnet himself was asked to come and add a word or two of his own in English.

98   I had spent dozens of hours listening to Bugnet's gravelly voice, and so I was used to his rambling, his habit of going back and forth in time as if all of time were present and accessible to him, as if *the order* of things was of little consequence. He could start a story in the twentieth century and finish it in the nineteenth. And this is exactly how Georges approached his address to his audience of perhaps 150 admirers. Feeble though he was, he went on and on and on. We got scraps from his life. The days he had to walk literally all the way around his school district every summer so that he could do his enumerations of eligible students and discuss the problems of the school with the people who sent their children there. We heard about old man Majeau and about his wife who delivered all

the children in the area. We heard about his trapline, about his boyhood home in Dijon, about the farmer in Manitoba who tried to make him work for slave wages, about how he had come to know Father Lacombe without ever seeing the man, about the Métis converts who used to pray at the back of the church at Lac Majeau, about how Bugnet acquired seeds for his horticultural experiments from all over the world, about the child he and his wife lost there, about the courage and patience of his *belle épouse* ...

99   I looked around me. Something was clearly amiss. I looked at the people closest to me, academics I guessed. They seemed to be confused, whispering to one another. There were others I assumed to be relatives of Bugnet or friends from the nearby French communities, shaking their heads. What the hell was wrong with them? Didn't they know that if they *listened* they would hear the things I had been hearing for more than eight years? But no. The people were plainly confused or embarrassed that this old man was allowed to go on and on about nothing.

100   Suddenly a tall elderly woman got to her feet and with one parental gesture silenced Bugnet. In the loud voice people sometimes reserve for the hearing impaired, she said, "*You are going on too much!*"

101   Bugnet's eyes grew wild with alarm. He looked as though he had been struck. He looked, for the tiniest tick of a second, angry. But anger was useless and he was now, clearly, someone's prisoner. He went silent and the woman who interrupted his ramblings wheeled him away from the microphone.

102   I bided my time in the old church hall while the luncheon was set up and served. Always Bugnet was surrounded by these vigilant people and I couldn't get near him. But after the lunch was over and some of the well-wishers had said their piece, the sentries became fewer and fewer.

103   Sentries? Whatever was I thinking about? These were nice Godfearing folk who had greater claims of love for the man in the wheelchair than I. The Sisters were family. I was just a tourist whose encounter with French and francophones was as fleeting as a holiday in Provence. Where was this paranoia coming from? Sentries indeed.

104   I made my move. I strode up to the small clutch of people standing around Georges, smiled, and eased my way past them to the wheelchair. I knelt down so that my head was only a few inches from Bugnet's. He seemed to sense that someone was there.

105   I whispered, "Georges, *c'est moi*. Dave."

His mouth fell open. "Carpenter?" he whispered.

"Yes."

"I thought you would not have come here," he said. "They are looking for you."

109   *They are looking for you.* Such is the language of intrigue. I knew my situation was perilous, that the same woman who had silenced Bugnet could just as easily have me ejected from the church hall. But something about Bugnet at that moment made me stay. In franglais we had the sort of conversation that some boys engage in beneath a caraganna hedge when the parents are close by. We had some laughs, we made some jokes, we remained in a small way unrepentant.

110   On my last visit Bugnet said that he wanted to die. He had had a dream. He was back on his trapline near Lac Majeau. He found himself looking into the face of a coyote he had scarcely thought about for seventy-five years.

111 He told me the following story about the encounter:

You should have seen this animal. He had become trapped in one of my small devices for rodents, and to escape, he had chewed through about half of his own leg. It bothered me to see how much he had suffered and how much he had wanted to live. But when he saw me approach him, I was a young man, and with a young man's resolve to kill any animal that could be of use to me. You know. The pelt and so forth. So I picked up a thick piece of wood to strike him with. He could have snarled and fought against the chain that held him. He could have panicked, but instead he just watched me approach him with my club, and at the last moment, when I moved to the side of him and raised my club to hit him on the head … he seemed to squint with his eyes, to squint with his entire head as if anticipating the blow that would put him down. That is how he faced death. He knew it was coming. And he braced himself to face it with what some men could call courage. I dreamt of him last night. We were there again, just like the first time. That is how I want to face death.

112 Bugnet's problem was that he could not die. He had scarcely had a sick day in 102 years of life. He had made peace with his God. He knew he was declining, his strength was gone, he was completely blind, his legs were no good, and his appetite was waning. He was left with long hours to pray for death and with the hope that he would face it with the courage of his old friend the coyote.

113 I am being honest when I say I cannot find his death notice. I do know that he died *circa* 1981. Around that time, the rest of the unsold copies of *The Forest* were being remaindered. Maynard Gertler wrote me from his office at Harvest House that if I wanted to, I could buy some of the remaining copies for a pittance. The book had sold about thirty-six hundred copies in four years, then in 1981 or so the market seemed to dry up. I was sure I could sell the rest. So before too long, I received a large shipment of boxes full of *The Forest*. If I'm not mistaken, there were fourteen hundred or so. I moved them into my first house in Saskatoon and kept them in the basement. I sold some through the mail to high schools, and some to universities. I took some to readings and sold them individually. I donated some to the Saskatchewan Writers' Guild and others to university libraries. When I bought my second house, my girlfriend and some others helped me move the remaining seven hundred copies. A few years later my girlfriend and I moved in together to a larger house. Once again she and some others helped me move in the remaining five hundred or so copies of *The Forest*. They cluttered up our store room, and my girlfriend, by now my *belle épouse*, gave me an ultimatum: If I could get rid of these books, she would read the last remaining copy. I couldn't bear to throw them out, so I moved them all into my office. They are there right now, approximately four hundred hardback copies of *The Forest*. My office mate, the Métis writer Maria Campbell, has been very uncomplaining about this state of affairs.

114 The day came when my *belle épouse* made good on her promise. She read *The Forest*.

115 "How did you like it?" I said.

"It was good," she replied.

117   In our back garden we have a Thérèse Bugnet rose. Georges named it after a favourite sister and a grandchild with scholarly inclinations. He developed it himself from the wild rose of Alberta and a domestic variety from Europe. It has the hardiness of the northern wild rose and the delicacy of its European ancestors. It can grow much farther north than any other commercial variety I've encountered. Once Bugnet smiled and said about his rose, "Now I give pleasure to thousands of women."

118   Lately I've been thinking a lot about this rose.

119   Reading Bugnet is like reviewing the past two centuries of North American literature in microcosm. When I read his early work, the pieces he wrote just after he arrived in Canada, I am struck by just how much he imposed his European sensibility upon his utterly unEuropean subjects. But when I read his later works, especially his revised version of *Nipsya* (circa 1929) and of course *La Forêt*, I am struck by the many ways he allowed the new world to blow in through his window and work upon his sensibilities. The native grasses and shrubs are there, the original people begin to appear, and of course the settlers. The vast nullity of the winter proclaims itself in all its ranging emptiness. Nature reigns and culture assumes a humbler role in his last two novels. This later work has the feel of the West in it, the vigour and hardihood and mind-numbing simplicity of life in the bush. But the voice is still that of the elegant European listening to the wind and hoping to hear the voice of God. At the end, his thoughts returned to one of his favourite martyrs — not Paul or Peter or even Father Brébeuf, but the trapped coyote who grimaced, waiting for the final blow.

Topics for consideration:

1. Carpenter refers to the "slavish anglo respect for French" which he developed as a graduate student. Does this piece suggest that his attitude has changed? If so, how?

2. Carpenter tells us the name of the waitress in Beaumont whom he fantasizes marrying but not the name of his wife. Why do you think this is?

3. Carpenter gives the name Fred Grove when he shows up at the degree ceremony for Bugnet. Why did he choose that name?

4. Carpenter has written of fiction writing that "the real action is below the surface." What is "below the surface" in "nom de plume"?

Further reading:

Georges Bugnet, *La Forêt* (1935). David Carpenter's English translation, *The Forest*, was published in 1975 in the Harvest House French Writers of Canada series.

CHAPTER 3

GENDERED WORDS

The essays in the preceding chapter on "Language & Culture" explore the ways in which language both reflects and shapes culture and yet is intimately connected to the core of personal identity. Consequently, political battles about language, for example over the Quebec Bill 101 restricting the use of English on commercial signs, have been bitter and prolonged. At times, debates about gender and language have aroused a comparable level of animosity.

By the mid 1970s there was widespread discussion, particularly in North America, about the ways in which sexist aspects of the society were both reflected and perpetuated by language practices. Feminists were beginning to put up a resistance to the routine use of blatantly sexist terminology and to suggest ways in which language could be less biased and more inclusive. One of the earliest of these critiques was the 1972 essay by Casey Miller and Kate Swift, "One Small Step for Genkind," reprinted in this chapter. Such tentative critiques were greeted during the 1970s and 1980s by a mixture of outrage and derision. Institutions such as universities and colleges that tried to initiate inclusive language were often met with the angry response, "Stop messing with my language." During the same period, newspapers regularly carried letters to the editor attempting to make fun of bias-free language by suggesting such alternatives as "personhole covers" and so forth.

Since then inclusive language has become, if not the norm, widely used and routinely advocated in composition texts and the style books used by various media outlets and publishing houses. Canadian media frequently report on the activities of "fishers" rather than "fishermen," even though this still occasionally elicits the complaint that a fisher is an animal and not a person.

Much of the discussion has shifted to a comparison of the language styles of males and females in such highly popular works as Deborah Tannen's *You Just Don't Understand: Women and Men in Conversation* (1990), part of which is excerpted here. Tannen argues that women and men would have fewer difficulties communicating if they had a better understanding of one another's speech "styles." Tannen has been criticized by other linguists, such as Deborah Cameron, who argue that her approach is an essentially reactionary one, which leads to women accommodating themselves to men's more assertive "style" without either analyzing or seeking to change the disparity in power that is its source.

Although perspectives may differ at least as widely as Tannen's and Cameron's, writers are now more frequently apt to acknowledge that gender plays a significant role in the way they perceive and act in the world and that this influences the ways in which they write. More rarely, they may, like the trans-gendered Jan Morris, claim that art is "beyond gender" and that differences between how men and women experience the world are fairly trivial.

The analysis of how stereotypes about gender permeate our language has now moved far beyond the basic argument for a more inclusive language argued in 1972 by Miller and Swift. Emily Martin's essay, "How Science has Constructed a Romance Based on Stereotypical Male-Female Roles" is one such example. Martin demonstrates that biological texts purporting to be scientific and objective consistently reproduce gender stereotypes from the surrounding culture so that biological processes are actually misrepresented.

Although it has already lasted several decades, the discussion of language and gender is far from over. While Miller and Swift and their contemporaries might have thought that much would be solved once inclusive language was accepted, Susan Ehrlich's article shows that this is far from the case and that the dominant culture continues to assert itself by finding a range of ways of rendering feminist linguistic strategies meaningless.

Casey Miller (1919-1997) and Kate Swift (1923-

Casey Miller and Kate Swift acted as pioneers in publicizing sexism in language and in suggesting ways in which writers and editors could make language more inclusive. They collaborated on scores of widely read articles as well as one of the earliest comprehensive handbooks on the subject, The Handbook of Nonsexist Writing for Writers, Editors and Speakers *(1980).*

With this essay, now a classic, Miller and Swift began the exposure of the ways sexist assumptions are built into language practices. They refer to the way in which "man" and "mankind" at the time when this essay was first published (1972) were widely claimed to be generic terms, including women by default. They discuss both subtle and blatant sexism in media language and conclude by suggesting some solutions to sexist language practices.

ONE SMALL STEP FOR GENKIND

1   A riddle is making the rounds that goes like this: A man and his young son were in an automobile accident. The father was killed and the son, who was critically injured, was rushed to a hospital. As attendants wheeled the unconscious boy into the emergency room, the doctor on duty looked down at him and said, "My God, it's my son!" What was the relationship of the doctor to the injured boy?

2   If the answer doesn't jump to your mind, another riddle that has been around a lot longer might help: The blind beggar had a brother. The blind beggar's brother died. The brother who died had no brother. What relation was the blind beggar to the blind beggar's brother?

3   As with all riddles, the answers are obvious once you see them: The doctor was the boy's mother and the beggar was her brother's sister. Then why doesn't everyone solve them immediately? Mainly because our language, like the culture it reflects, is male oriented. To say that a woman in medicine is an exception is simply to confirm that statement. Thousands of doctors are women, but in order to be seen in the mind's eye, they must be called women doctors.

4   Except for words that refer to females by definition (mother, actress, Congresswoman), and words for occupations traditionally held by females (nurse, secretary, prostitute), the English language defines everyone as male. The hypothetical person ("If a man can walk 10 miles in two hours ..."), the average person ("the man in the street") and the active person ("the man on the move") are male. The assumption is that unless otherwise identified, people in general — including doctors and beggars — are men. It is a semantic mechanism that operates to keep women invisible: *man* and *mankind* represent everyone; *he* in generalized use refers to either sex; the "land where our fathers died" is also the land of our mothers — although they go unsung. As the beetle-browed and mustachioed man in a Steig cartoon says to his two male drinking companions, "When I speak of mankind, one thing I *don't* mean is womankind."

5   Semantically speaking, woman is not one with the species of man, but a distinct subspecies. "Man," says the 1971 edition of the Britannica Junior Encyclopedia, "is the highest form of life on earth. His superior intelligence, combined with

certain physical characteristics, have enabled man to achieve things that are impossible for other animals." (The prose style has something in common with the report of a research team describing its studies on "the development of the uterus in rats, guinea pigs and men.") As though quoting the Steig character, still speaking to his friends in McSorley's, the Junior Encyclopedia continues: "Man must invent most of his behavior, because he lacks the instincts of lower animals. ... Most of the things he learns have been handed down from his ancestors by language and symbols rather than by biological inheritance."

6   Considering that for the last 5,000 years society has been patriarchal, that statement explains a lot. It explains why Eve was made from Adam's rib instead of the other way around, and who invented all those Adam-rib words like *fe*male and *wo*man in the first place. It also explains why, when it is necessary to mention woman, the language makes her a lower caste, a class separate from the rest of man; why it works to "keep her in her place."

7   This inheritance through language and other symbols begins in the home (also called a man's castle) where man and wife (not husband and wife, or man and woman) live for a while with their children. It is reinforced by religious training, the educational system, the press, government, commerce and the law. As Andrew Greeley wrote not long ago in his magazine, "Man is a symbol-creating animal. He orders and interprets his reality by his symbols, and he uses the symbols to reconstruct that reality."

8   Consider some of the reconstructed realities of American history. When school children learn from their textbooks that the early colonists gained valuable experience in governing themselves, they are not told that the early colonists who were women were denied the privilege of self-government; when they learn that in the 18th century the average man had to manufacture many of the things he and his family needed, they are not told that this "average man" was often a woman who manufactured much of what she and her family needed. Young people learn that intrepid pioneers crossed the country in covered wagons with their wives, children and cattle; they do not learn that women themselves were intrepid pioneers rather than part of the baggage.

9   In a paper published this year in Los Angeles as a guide for authors and editors of social-studies textbooks, Elizabeth Burr, Susan Dunn and Norma Farquhar document unintentional skewings of this kind that occur either because women are not specifically mentioned as affecting or being affected by historical events, or because they are discussed in terms of outdated assumptions. "One never sees a picture of women captioned simply 'farmers' or 'pioneers,'" they point out. The subspecies nomenclature that requires a caption to read "women farmers" or "women pioneers" is extended to impose certain jobs on women by definition. The textbook guide gives as an example the word *housewife*, which it says not only "suggests that domestic chores are the exclusive burden of females," but gives "female students the idea that they were born to keep house and teaches male students that they are automatically entitled to laundry, cooking and housecleaning services from the women in their families."

10   Sexist language is any language that expresses such stereotyped attitudes and expectations, or that assumes the inherent superiority of one sex over the other.

When a woman says of her husband, who has drawn up plans for a new bedroom wing and left out closets, "Just like a man," her language is as sexist as the man's who says, after his wife has changed her mind about needing the new wing after all, "Just like a woman."

11   Male and female are not sexist words, but masculine and feminine almost always are. Male and female can be applied objectively to individual people and animals and, by extension, to things. When electricians and plumbers talk about male and female couplings, everyone knows or can figure out what they mean. The terms are graphic and culture free.

12   Masculine and feminine, however, are as sexist as any words can be, since it is almost impossible to use them without invoking cultural stereotypes. When people construct lists of "masculine" and "feminine" traits they almost always end up making assumptions that have nothing to do with innate differences between the sexes. We have a friend who happens to be going through the process of pinning down this very phenomenon. He is 7 years old and his question concerns why his coats and shirts button left over right while his sister's button the other way. He assumes it must have something to do with the differences between boys and girls, but he can't see how.

13   What our friend has yet to grasp is that the way you button your coat, like most sex-differentiated customs, has nothing to do with real differences but much to do with what society wants you to feel about yourself as a male or female person. Society decrees that it is appropriate for girls to dress differently from boys, to act differently, and to think differently. Boys must be masculine, whatever that means, and girls must be feminine.

14   Unabridged dictionaries are a good source for finding out what society decrees to be appropriate, though less by definition than by their choice of associations and illustrations. Words associated with males — *manly*, *virile* and *masculine*, for example — are defined through a broad range of positive attributes like strength, courage, directness and independence, and they are illustrated through such examples of contemporary usage as "a manly determination to face what comes," "a virile literary style," "a masculine love of sports." Corresponding words associated with females are defined with fewer attributes (though weakness is often one of them) and the examples given are generally negative if not clearly pejorative: "feminine wiles," "womanish tears," "a womanlike lack of promptness," "convinced that drawing was a waste of time, if not downright womanly."

15   Male-associated words are frequently applied to females to describe something that is either incongruous ("a mannish voice") or presumably commendable ("a masculine mind," "she took it like a man"), but female-associated words are unreservedly derogatory when applied to males, and are sometimes abusive to females as well. The opposite of "masculine" is "effeminate," although the opposite of "feminine" is simply "unfeminine."

16   One dictionary, after defining the word *womanish* as "suitable to or resembling a woman," further defines it as "unsuitable to a man or to a strong character of either sex." Words derived from "sister" and "brother" provide another apt example, for whereas "sissy," applied either to a male or female, conveys the message

that sisters are expected to be timid and cowardly, "buddy" makes clear that brothers are friends.

17   The subtle disparagement of females and corresponding approbation of males wrapped up in many English words is painfully illustrated by "tomboy." Here is an instance where a girl who likes sports and the out-of-doors, who is curious about how things work, who is adventurous and bold instead of passive, is defined in terms of something she is not — a boy. By denying that she can be the person she is and still be a girl, the word surreptitiously undermines her sense of identity: it says she is unnatural. A "tomboy," as defined by one dictionary, is a "girl, especially a young girl, who behaves like a spirited boy." But who makes the judgment that she is acting like a spirited boy, not a spirited girl? Can it be a coincidence that in the case of the dictionary just quoted the editor, executive editor, managing editor, general manager, all six members of the Board of Linguists, the usage editor, science editor, all six general editors of definitions, and 94 out of the 104 distinguished experts consulted on usage — are men?

18   It isn't enough to say that any invidious comparisons and stereotypes lexicographers perpetuate are already present in the culture. There are ways to define words like womanly and tomboy that don't put women down, though the tradition has been otherwise. Samuel Johnson, the lexicographer, was the same Dr. Johnson who said, "A woman preaching is like a dog's walking on his hind legs. It is not done well; but you are surprised to find it done at all."

19   Possibly because of the negative images associated with womanish and womanlike, and with expressions like "woman driver" and "woman of the street," the word woman dropped out of fashion for a time. The women at the office and the women on the assembly line and the women one first knew in school all became ladies or girls or gals. Now a countermovement, supported by the very term women's liberation, is putting back into words like woman and sister and sisterhood the meaning they were losing by default. It is as though, in the nick of time, women had seen that the language itself could destroy them.

20   Some long-standing conventions of the news media add insult to injury. When a woman or girl makes news, her sex is identified at the beginning of a story, if possible in the headline or its equivalent. The assumption, apparently, is that whatever event or action is being reported, a woman's involvement is less common and therefore more newsworthy than a man's. If the story is about achievement, the implication is: "pretty good for a woman." And because people are assumed to be male unless otherwise identified, the media have developed a special and extensive vocabulary to avoid the constant repetition of "woman." The results, "Grandmother Wins Nobel Prize," "Blonde Hijacks Airliner," "Housewife to Run for Congress," convey the kind of information that would be ludicrous in comparable headlines if the subjects were men. Why, if "Unsalaried Husband to Run for Congress" is unacceptable to editors, do women have to keep explaining that to describe them through external or superficial concerns reflects a sexist view of women as decorative objects, breeding machines and extensions of men, not real people?

21   Members of the Chicago chapter of the National Organization for Women recently studied the newspapers in their area and drew up a set of guidelines for

the press. These include cutting out descriptions of the "clothes, physical features, dating life and marital status of women where such references would be considered inappropriate if about men"; using language in such a way as to include women in copy that refers to homeowners, scientists and business people where "newspaper descriptions often convey the idea that all such persons are male"; and displaying the same discretion in printing generalizations about women as would be shown toward racial, religious and ethnic groups. "Our concern with what we are called may seem trivial to some people," the women said, "but we regard the old usages as symbolic of women's position within this society."

22   The assumption that an adult woman is flattered by being called a girl is matched by the notion that a woman in a menial or poorly paid job finds compensation in being called a lady. Ethel Strainchamps has pointed out that since lady is used as an adjective with nouns designating both high and low occupations (lady wrestler, lady barber, lady doctor, lady judge), some writers assume they can use the noun form without betraying value judgments. Not so, Strainchamps says, rolling the issue into a spitball: "You may write, 'He addressed the Republican ladies,' or 'The Democratic ladies convened' … but I have never seen 'the Communist ladies' or 'the Black Panther ladies' in print."

23   Thoughtful writers and editors have begun to repudiate some of the old usages. "Divorcée," "grandmother" and "blonde," along with "vivacious," "pert," "dimpled" and "cute," were dumped by the Washington Post in the spring of 1970 by the executive editor, Benjamin Bradlee. In a memo to his staff, Bradlee wrote, "The meaningful equality and dignity of women is properly under scrutiny today … because this equality has been less than meaningful and the dignity not always free of stereotype and condescension."

24   What women have been called in the press — or at least the part that operates above ground — is only a fraction of the infinite variety of alternatives to "women" used in the subcultures of the English-speaking world. Beyond "chicks," "dolls," "dames," "babes," "skirts" and "broads" are the words and phrases in which women are reduced to their sexuality and nothing more. It would be hard to think of another area of language in which the human mind has been so fertile in devising and borrowing abusive terms. In The Female Eunuch, Germaine Greer devotes four pages to anatomical terms and words for animals, vegetables, fruits, baked goods, implements and receptacles, all of which are used to dehumanize the female person. Jean Faust, in an article aptly called "Words That Oppress," suggests that the effort to diminish women through language is rooted in a male fear of sexual inadequacy. "Woman is made to feel guilty for and akin to natural disasters," she writes; "hurricanes and typhoons are named after her. Any negative or threatening force is given a feminine name. If a man runs into bad luck climbing up the ladder of success (a male-invented game), he refers to the 'bitch goddess' success."

25   The sexual overtones in the ancient and no doubt honorable custom of calling ships "she" have become more explicit and less honorable in an age of air travel: "I'm Karen. Fly me." Attitudes of ridicule, contempt and disgust toward female sexuality have spawned a rich glossary of insults and epithets not found in dictionaries. And the usage in which four-letter words meaning copulate are interchangeable with cheat, attack and destroy can scarcely be unrelated to the savagery of rape.

26   In her updating of Ibsen's *A Doll's House*, Clare Booth Luce has Nora tell her husband she is pregnant — "In the way only men are supposed to get pregnant." "Men, pregnant?" he says, and she nods; "With ideas. Pregnancies there [*she taps his head*] are masculine. And a very superior form of labor. Pregnancies here [*taps her tummy*] are feminine — a very inferior form of labor."

27   Public outcry followed a revised translation of the New Testament describing Mary as "pregnant" instead of "great with child." The objections were made in part on esthetic grounds: there is no attractive adjective in modern English for a woman who is about to give birth. A less obvious reason was that replacing the euphemism with a biological term undermined religious teaching. The initiative and generative power in the conception of Jesus are understood to be God's; Mary, the mother, was a vessel only.

28   Whether influenced by this teaching or not, the language of human reproduction lags several centuries behind scientific understanding. The male's contribution to procreation is still described as though it were the entire seed from which a new life grows: the initiative and generative power involved in the process are thought of as masculine, receptivity and nurturance as feminine. "Seminal" remains a synonym for "highly original," and there is no comparable word to describe the female's equivalent contribution.

29   An entire mythology has grown from this biological misunderstanding and its semantic legacy; its embodiment in laws that for centuries made women nonpersons was a key target of the 19th-century feminist movement. Today, more than 50 years after women finally won the basic democratic right to vote, the word "liberation" itself, when applied to women, means something less than when used of other groups of people. An advertisement for the N.B.C. news department listed Women's Liberation along with crime in the streets and the Vietnam war as "bad news." Asked for his views on Women's Liberation, a highly placed politician was quoted as saying, "Let me make one thing perfectly clear. I wouldn't want to wake up next to a lady pipe-fitter."

30   One of the most surprising challenges to our male-dominated culture is coming from within organized religion, where the issues are being stated, in part, by confronting the implications of traditional language. What a growing number of theologians and scholars are saying is that the myths of the Judeo-Christian tradition, being the products of patriarchy, must be reexamined, and that the concept of an exclusively male ministry and the image of a male god have become idolatrous.

31   Women are naturally in the forefront of this movement, both in their efforts to gain ordination and full equality and through their contributions to theological reform, although both these efforts are often subtly diminished. When the Rev. Barbara Anderson was ordained by the American Lutheran Church, one newspaper printed her picture over a caption headed "Happy Girl." *Newsweek*'s report of a protest staged last December by women divinity students at Harvard was jocular ("another tilt at the windmill") and sarcastic: "Every time anyone in the room lapsed into what [the students] regarded as male chauvinism — such as using the word 'mankind' to describe the human race in general — the outraged women ... drowned out the offender with earpiercing blasts from party-favor

kazoos. ... What annoyed the women most was the universal custom of referring to God as 'He.'"

32 The tone of the report was not merely unfunny; it missed the connection between increasingly outmoded theological language and the accelerating number of women (and men) who are dropping out of organized religion, both Jewish and Christian. For language, including pronouns, can be used to construct a reality that simply mirrors society's assumptions. To women who are committed to the reality of religious faith, the effect is doubly painful. Professor Harvey Cox, in whose classroom the protest took place, stated the issue directly: The women, he said, were raising the "basic theological question of whether God is more adequately thought of in personal or suprapersonal terms."

33 Toward the end of Don McLean's remarkable ballad "American Pie," a song filled with the imagery of abandonment and disillusion, there is a stanza that must strike many women to the quick. The church bells are broken, the music has died, then:

And the three men I admire most.
The Father, Son and the Holy Ghost,
They caught the last train for the Coast —
The day the music died.

34 Three men I admired most. There they go, briefcases in hand and topcoats buttoned left over right, walking down the long cold platform under the city, past the baggage wagons and the hissing steam onto the Pullman. Bye, bye God — all three of you — made in the image of male supremacy. Maybe out there in L.A. where the weather is warmer, someone can believe in you again.

35 The Roman Catholic theologian Elizabeth Farians says "the bad theology of an overmasculinized church continues to be one of the root causes of women's oppression." The definition of oppression is "to crush or burden by abuse of power or authority; burden spiritually or mentally as if by pressure."

36 When language oppresses, it does so by any means that disparage and belittle. Until well into the 20th century, one of the ways English was manipulated to disparage women was through the addition of feminine endings to nonsexual words. Thus a woman who aspired to be a poet was excluded from the company of real poets by the label poetess, and a woman who piloted an airplane was denied full status as an aviator by being called an aviatrix. At about the time poetess, aviatrix, and similar Adam-ribbisms were dropping out of use, H. W. Fowler was urging that they be revived. "With the coming expansion of women's vocations," he wrote in the first edition (1926) of *Modern English Usage*, "feminines for vocation-words are a special need of the future." There can be no doubt he subconsciously recognized the relative status implied in the -*ess* designations. His criticism of a woman who wished to be known as an author rather than an authoress was that she had no need "to raise herself to the level of the male author by asserting her right to his name."

37 Who has the prior right to a name? The question has an interesting bearing on words that were once applied to men alone, or to both men and women, but

now, having acquired abusive associations, are assigned to women exclusively. Spinster is a gentle case in point. Prostitute and many of its synonyms illustrate the phenomenon better. If Fowler had chosen to record the changing usage of harlot from hired man (in Chaucer's time) through rascal and entertainer to its present definition, would he have maintained that the female harlot is trying to raise herself to the level of the male harlot by asserting her right to his name? Or would he have plugged for harlotress?

38   The demise of most -ess endings came about before the start of the new feminist movement. In the second edition of *Modern English Usage*, published in 1965, Sir Ernest Cowers frankly admitted what his predecessors had been up to. "Feminine designations," he wrote, "seem now to be falling into disuse. Perhaps the explanation of this paradox is that it symbolizes the victory of women in their struggle for equal rights; it reflects the abandonment by men of those ideas about women in the professions that moved Dr. Johnson to his rude remark about women preachers."

39   If Sir Ernest's optimism can be justified, why is there a movement back to feminine endings in such words as chairwoman, councilwoman and congresswoman? Betty Hudson, of Madison, Conn., is campaigning for the adoption of "selectwoman" as the legal title for a female member of that town's executive body. To have to address a woman as "Selectman," she maintains, "is not only bad grammar and bad biology, but it implies that politics is still, or should be, a man's business." A valid argument, and one that was, predictably, countered by ridicule, the surefire weapon for undercutting achievement. When the head of the Federal Maritime Commission, Helen D. Bentley, was named "Man of the Year" by an association of shipping interests, she wisely refused to be drawn into light-hearted debate with interviewers who wanted to make the award's name a humorous issue. Some women, of course, have yet to learn they are invisible. An 8-year-old who visited the American Museum of Natural History with her Brownie scout troop went through the impressive exhibit on pollution and overpopulation called "Can Man Survive?" Asked afterward, "Well, can he?" she answered, "I don't know about him, but we're working on it in Brownies."

40   Nowhere are women rendered more invisible by language than in politics. The United States Constitution, in describing the qualifications for Representative, Senator and President, refers to each as *he*. No wonder Shirley Chisholm, the first woman since 1888 to make a try for the Presidential nomination of a major party, has found it difficult to be taken seriously.

41   The observation by Andrew Greeley already quoted — that "man" uses "his symbols" to reconstruct "his reality" — was not made in reference to the symbols of language but to the symbolic impact the "nomination of a black man for the Vice-Presidency" would have on race relations in the United States. Did the author assume the generic term "man" would of course be construed to include "woman"? Or did he deliberately use a semantic device to exclude Shirley Chisholm without having to be explicit?

42   Either way, his words construct a reality in which women are ignored. As much as any other factor in our language, the ambiguous meaning of *man* serves to deny women recognition as people. In a recent magazine article, we discussed the similar effect on women of the generic pronoun *he*, which we proposed to

replace by a new common gender pronoun *tey*. We were immediately told, by a number of authorities, that we were dabbling in the serious business of linguistics, and the message that reached us from these scholars was loud and clear: It - is - absolutely - impossible - for -anyone - to - introduce - a - new - word - into - the - language -just - because - there - is - a - need - for - it, so - stop -wasting - your - time.

43   When words are suggested like "herstory" (for history), "sportsoneship" (for sportsmanship) and "mistresspiece" (for the work of a Virginia Woolf) one suspects a not-too-subtle attempt to make the whole language problem look silly. But unless Alexander Pope, when he wrote "The proper study of mankind is man," meant that women should be relegated to the footnotes (or, as George Orwell might have put it, "All men are equal, but men are more equal than women"), viable new words will surely someday supersede the old.

44   Without apologies to Freud, the great majority of women do not wish in their hearts that they were men. If having grown up with a language that tells them they are at the same time men and not men raises psychic doubts for women, the doubts are not of their sexual identity but of their human identity. Perhaps the present unrest surfacing in the Women's Movement is part of an evolutionary change in our particular form of life — the one form of all in the animal and plant kingdoms that orders and interprets its reality by symbols. The achievements of the species called man have brought us to the brink of self-destruction. If the species survives into the next century with the expectation of going on, it may only be because we have become part of what Harlow Shapley calls the psychozoic kingdom, where brain overshadows brawn and rationality has replaced superstition.

45   Searching the roots of Western civilization for a word to call this new species of man and woman, someone might come up with *gen*, as in genesis and generic. With such a word, *man* could be used exclusively for males as *woman* is used for females, for gen would include both sexes. Like the words deer and bison, gen would be both plural and singular. Like progenitor, progeny, and generation, it would convey continuity. Gen would express the warmth and generalized sexuality of generous, gentle, and genuine; the specific sexuality of genital and genetic. In the new family of gen, girls and boys would grow to genhood, and to speak of genkind would be to include all the people of the earth.

Topics for consideration:

1. Inclusive rather than sexist language is now a widespread policy of publishers and media outlets. How many of the sexist practices which Miller and Swift mention can still be found? Where are they most common?

2. In a society that had freed itself of sexism the two riddles in paragraphs 1 and 2 would not be at all puzzling. Did they puzzle you at all? How typical was your experience of others in your group or class?

3. Paragraph 3 of Hugh Brody's essay "Language in the Arctic" in the "Language & Culture" chapter explains that Inuktitut names are not gender-specific — i.e., they can be applied equally aptly to a boy or a girl. Are there examples where this is true of the names of people you know? To what extent do names and forms of addressing people denote gender in North American culture?

Further reading:

Rosalie Maggio, *The Non-Sexist Word Finder: A Dictionary of Gender-Free Usage* (1988)

Deborah Tannen (1945-

Deborah Tannen holds a University Professorship in Linguistics at Georgetown University and is author of That's Not What I Meant *(1986) and the best-selling* You Just Don't Understand: Women and Men in Conversation *(1990), from which this selection is taken. She has lectured to many corporate audiences, and her* Talking 9 to 5: Women and Men in the Workplace: Language, Sex and Power *(1996) became a* New York Times Business *bestseller.*

Using a combination of personal anecdotes and published studies by linguistic researchers, Deborah Tannen describes what she calls a "constellation" of male and female speech styles. Typically, she suggests, men view conversation as an area of competition and are apt to lecture at length, while women act co-operatively and work at being "good listeners" despite being bored. She argues that this situation is unsatisfactory for both males and females and that by being aware of one another's speech styles men and women can reach a better understanding.

"I'LL EXPLAIN IT TO YOU": LECTURING AND LISTENING

1   At a reception following the publication of one of my books, I noticed a publicist listening attentively to the producer of a popular radio show. He was telling her how the studio had come to be built where it was, and why he would have preferred another site. What caught my attention was the length of time he was speaking while she was listening. He was delivering a monologue that could only be called a lecture, giving her detailed information about the radio reception at the two sites, the architecture of the station, and so on. I later asked the publicist if she had been interested in the information the producer had given her. "Oh, yes," she answered. But then she thought a moment and said, "Well, maybe he did go on a bit." The next day she told me, "I was thinking about what you asked. I couldn't have cared less about what he was saying. It's just that I'm so used to listening to men go on about things I don't care about. I didn't even realize how bored I was until you made me think about it."

2   I was chatting with a man I had just met at a party. In our conversation, it emerged that he had been posted in Greece with the RAF during 1944 and 1945. Since I had lived in Greece for several years, I asked him about his experiences: What had Greece been like then? How had the Greek villagers treated the British soldiers? What had it been *like* to be a British soldier in wartime Greece? I also offered information about how Greece had changed, what it is like now. He did not pick up on my remarks about contemporary Greece, and his replies to my questions quickly changed from accounts of his own experiences, which I found riveting, to facts about Greek history, which interested me in principle but in the actual telling left me profoundly bored. The more impersonal his talk became, the more I felt oppressed by it, pinned involuntarily in the listener position.

3   At a showing of Judy Chicago's jointly created art work *The Dinner Party*, I was struck by a couple standing in front of one of the displays. The man was earnestly explaining to the woman the meaning of symbols in the tapestry before them, pointing as he spoke. I might not have noticed this unremarkable scene, except that *The Dinner Party* was radically feminist in conception, intended to reflect women's experiences and sensibilities.

4   While taking a walk in my neighborhood on an early summer evening at twilight, I stopped to chat with a neighbor who was walking his dogs. As we stood, I noticed that the large expanse of yard in front of which we were standing was aglitter with the intermittent flickering of fireflies. I called attention to the sight, remarking on how magical it looked. "It's like the Fourth of July," I said. He agreed, and then told me he had read that the lights of fireflies are mating signals. He then explained to me details of how these signals work — for example, groups of fireflies fly at different elevations and could be seen to cluster in different parts of the yard.

5   In all these examples, the men had information to impart and they were imparting it. On the surface, there is nothing surprising or strange about that. What is strange is that there are so many situations in which men have factual information requiring lengthy explanations to impart to women, and so few in which women have comparable information to impart to men.

6   The changing times have altered many aspects of relations between women and men. Now it is unlikely, at least in many circles, for a man to say, "I am better than you because I am a man and you are a woman." But women who do not find men making such statements are nonetheless often frustrated in their dealings with them. One situation that frustrates many women is a conversation that has mysteriously turned into a lecture, with the man delivering the lecture to the woman, who has become an appreciative audience.

7   Once again, the alignment in which women and men find themselves arrayed is asymmetrical. The lecturer is framed as superior in status and expertise, cast in the role of teacher, and the listener is cast in the role of student. If women and men took turns giving and receiving lectures, there would be nothing disturbing about it. What is disturbing is the imbalance. Women and men fall into this unequal pattern so often because of the differences in their interactional habits. Since women seek to build rapport, they are inclined to play down their expertise rather than display it. Since men value the position of center stage and the feeling of knowing more, they seek opportunities to gather and disseminate factual information.

8   If men often seem to hold forth because they have the expertise, women are often frustrated and surprised to find that when they have the expertise, they don't necessarily get the floor.

FIRST ME, THEN ME

9   I was at a dinner with faculty members from other departments in my university. To my right was a woman. As the dinner began, we introduced ourselves. After we told each other what departments we were in and what subjects we taught, she asked what my research was about. We talked about my research for a little

while. Then I asked her about her research and she told me about it. Finally, we discussed the ways that our research overlapped. Later, as tends to happen at dinners, we branched out to others at the table. I asked a man across the table from me what department he was in and what he did. During the next half hour, I learned a lot about his job, his research, and his background. Shortly before the dinner ended there was a lull, and he asked me what I did. When I said I was a linguist, he became excited and told me about a research project he had conducted that was related to neurolinguistics. He was still telling me about his research when we all got up to leave the table.

10   This man and woman were my colleagues in academia. What happens when I talk to people at parties and social events, not fellow researchers? My experience is that if I mention the kind of work I do to women, they usually ask me about it. When I tell them about conversational style or gender differences, they offer their own experiences to support the patterns I describe. This is very pleasant for me. It puts me at center stage without my having to grab the spotlight myself, and I frequently gather anecdotes I can use in the future. But when I announce my line of work to men, many give me a lecture on language — for example, about how people, especially teenagers, misuse language nowadays. Others challenge me, for example questioning me about my research methods. Many others change the subject to something they know more about.

11   Of course not all men respond in this way, but over the years I have encountered many men, and very few women, who do. It is not that speaking in this way is *the* male way of doing things, but that it is *a* male way. There are women who adopt such styles, but they are perceived as speaking like men.

IF YOU'VE GOT IT, FLAUNT IT — OR HIDE IT

12   I have been observing this constellation in interaction for more than a dozen years. I did not, however, have any understanding of *why* this happens until fairly recently, when I developed the framework of status and connection. An experimental study that was pivotal in my thinking shows that expertise does not ensure women a place at center stage in conversation with men.

13   Psychologist H.M. Leet-Pellegrini set out to discover whether gender or expertise determined who would behave in what she terms a "dominant" way — for example, by talking more, interrupting, and controlling the topic. She set up pairs of women, pairs of men, and mixed pairs, and asked them to discuss the effects of television violence on children. In some cases, she made one of the partners an expert by providing relevant factual information and time to read and assimilate it before the videotaped discussion. One might expect that the conversationalist who was the expert would talk more, interrupt more, and spend less time supporting the conversational partner who knew less about the subject. But it wasn't so simple. On the average, those who had expertise did talk more, but men experts talked more than women experts.

14   Expertise also had a different effect on women and men with regard to supportive behavior. Leet-Pellegrini expected that the one who did not have expertise would spend more time offering agreement and support to the one who did. This turned out to be true — *except* in cases where a woman was the expert and

her nonexpert partner was a man. In this situation, the women experts showed support — saying things like "Yeah" and "That's right" — far *more* than the non-expert men they were talking to. Observers often rated the male nonexpert as more dominant than the female expert. In other words, the women in this experiment not only didn't wield their expertise as power, but tried to play it down and make up for it through extra assenting behavior. They acted as if their expertise were something to hide.

15   And perhaps it was. When the word *expert* was spoken in these experimental conversations, in all cases but one it was the man in the conversation who used it, saying something like "So, you're the expert." Evidence of the woman's superior knowledge sparked resentment, not respect.

16   Furthermore, when an expert man talked to an uninformed woman, he took a controlling role in structuring the conversation in the beginning *and* the end. But when an expert man talked to an uninformed man, he dominated in the beginning but not always in the end. In other words, having expertise was enough to keep a man in the controlling position if he was talking to a woman, but not if he was talking to a man. Apparently, when a woman surmised that the man she was talking to had more information on the subject than she did, she simply accepted the reactive role. But another man, despite a lack of information, might still give the expert a run for his money and possibly gain the upper hand by the end.

17   Reading these results, I suddenly understood what happens to me when I talk to women and men about language. I am assuming that my acknowledged expertise will mean I am automatically accorded authority in the conversation, and with women that is generally the case. But when I talk to men, revealing that I have acknowledged expertise in this area often invites challenges. I *might* maintain my position if I defend myself successfully against the challenges, but if I don't, I may lose ground.

18   One interpretation of the Leet-Pellegrini study is that women are getting a bum deal. They don't get credit when it's due. And in a way, this is true. But the reason is not — as it seems to many women — that men are bums who seek to deny women authority. The Leet-Pellegrini study shows that many men are inclined to jockey for status, and challenge the authority of others, when they are talking to men too. If this is so, then challenging a woman's authority as they would challenge a man's could be a sign of respect and equal treatment, rather than lack of respect and discrimination. In cases where this is so, the inequality of the treatment results not simply from the men's behavior alone but from the differences in men's and women's styles: Most women lack experience in defending themselves against challenges, which they misinterpret as personal attacks on their credibility.

19   Even when talking to men who are happy to see them in positions of status, women may have a hard time getting their due because of differences in men's and women's interactional goals. Just as boys in high school are not inclined to repeat information about popular girls because it doesn't get them what they want, women in conversation are not inclined to display their knowledge because it doesn't get them what they are after. Leet-Pellegrini suggests that the men in this study were playing a game of "Have I won?" while the women were playing

a game of "Have I been sufficiently helpful?" I am inclined to put this another way: The game women play is "Do you like me?" whereas the men play "Do you respect me?" If men, in seeking respect, are less liked by women, this is an unsought side effect, as is the effect that women, in seeking to be liked, may lose respect. When a woman has a conversation with a man, her efforts to emphasize their similarities and avoid showing off can easily be interpreted, through the lens of status, as relegating her to a one-down position, making her appear either incompetent or insecure.

A SUBTLE DEFERENCE

20 Elizabeth Aries, a professor of psychology at Amherst College, set out to show that highly intelligent, highly educated young women are no longer submissive in conversations with male peers. And indeed she found that the college women did talk more than the college men in small groups she set up. But what they said was different. The men tended to set the agenda by offering opinions, suggestions, and information. The women tended to react, offering agreement or disagreement. Furthermore, she found that body language was as different as ever: The men sat with their legs stretched out, while the women gathered themselves in. Noting that research has found that speakers using the open-bodied position are more likely to persuade their listeners, Aries points out that talking more may not ensure that women will be heard.

21 In another study, Aries found that men in all-male discussion groups spent a lot of time at the beginning finding out "who was best informed about movies, books, current events, politics, and travel" as a means of "sizing up the competition" and negotiating "where they stood in relation to each other." This glimpse of how men talk when there are no women present gives an inkling of why displaying knowledge and expertise is something that men find more worth doing than women. What the women in Aries's study spent time doing was "gaining a closeness through more intimate self-revelation."

22 It is crucial to bear in mind that both the women and the men in these studies were establishing camaraderie, and both were concerned with their relationships to each other. But different aspects of their relationships were of primary concern: their place in a hierarchical order for the men, and their place in a network of intimate connections for the women. The consequence of these disparate concerns was very different ways of speaking.

23 Thomas Fox is an English professor who was intrigued by the differences between women and men in his freshman writing classes. What he observed corresponds almost precisely to the experimental findings of Aries and Leet-Pellegrini. Fox's method of teaching writing included having all the students read their essays to each other in class and talk to each other in small groups. He also had them write papers reflecting on the essays and the discussion groups. He alone, as the teacher, read these analytical papers.

24 To exemplify the two styles he found typical of women and men, Fox chose a woman, Ms. M, and a man, Mr. H. In her speaking as well as her writing, Ms. M held back what she knew, appearing uninformed and uninterested, because she feared offending her classmates. Mr. H. spoke and wrote with authority and

apparent confidence because he was eager to persuade his peers. She did not worry about persuading; he did not worry about offending.

25   In his analytical paper, the young man described his own behavior in the mixed-gender group discussions as if he were describing the young men in Leet-Pellegrini's and Aries's studies:

> In my sub-group I am the leader. I begin every discussion by stating my opinions as facts. The other two members of the sub-group tend to sit back and agree with me. ... I need people to agree with me.

26   Fox comments that Mr. H. reveals "a sense of self, one that acts to change himself and other people, that seems entirely distinct from Ms. M's sense of self, dependent on and related to others."

27   Calling Ms. M's sense of self "dependent" suggests a negative view of her way of being in the world — and, I think, a view more typical of men. This view reflects the assumption that the alternative to independence is dependence. If this is indeed a male view, it may explain why so many men are cautious about becoming intimately involved with others: It makes sense to avoid humiliating dependence by insisting on independence. But there is another alternative: *inter*dependence.

28   The main difference between these alternatives is symmetry. Dependence is an asymmetrical involvement: One person needs the other, but not vice versa, so the needy person is one-down. Interdependence is symmetrical. Both parties rely on each other, so neither is one-up or one-down. Moreover, Mr. H's sense of self is also dependent on others. He requires others to listen, agree, and allow him to take the lead by stating his opinions first.

29   Looked at this way, the woman and man in this group are both dependent on each other. Their differing goals are complementary, although neither understands the reasons for the other's behavior. This would be a fine arrangement, except that their differing goals result in alignments that enhance his authority and undercut hers.

DIFFERENT INTERPRETATIONS — AND MISINTERPRETATIONS

30   Fox also describes differences in the way male and female students in his classes interpreted a story they read. These differences also reflect assumptions about the interdependence or independence of individuals. Fox's students wrote their responses to "The Birthmark" by Nathaniel Hawthorne. In the story, a woman's husband becomes obsessed with a birthmark on her face. Suffering from her husband's revulsion at the sight of her, the wife becomes obsessed with it too and, in a reversal of her initial impulse, agrees to undergo a treatment he has devised to remove the birthmark — a treatment that succeeds in removing the mark, but kills her in the process.

31   Ms. M interpreted the wife's complicity as a natural response to the demand of a loved one: The woman went along with her husband's lethal schemes to remove the birthmark because she wanted to please and be appealing to him. Mr. H blamed the woman's insecurity and vanity for her fate and he blamed her for voluntarily submitting to her husband's authority. Fox points out that he saw her

as individually responsible for her actions, just as he saw himself as individually responsible for his own actions. To him, the issue was independence: The weak wife voluntarily took a submissive role. To Ms. M, the issue was interdependence: The woman was inextricably bound up with her husband, so her behavior could not be separated from his.

32   Fox observes that Mr. H saw the writing of the women in the class as spontaneous — they wrote whatever popped into their heads. Nothing could be farther from Ms. M's experience as she described it: When she knew her peers would see her writing, she censored everything that popped into her head. In contrast, when she was writing something that only her professor would read, she expressed firm and articulate opinions.

33   There is a striking but paradoxical complementarity to Ms. M's and Mr. H's styles, when they are taken together. He needs someone to listen and agree. She listens and agrees. But in another sense, their dovetailing purposes are at cross-purposes. He misinterprets her agreement, intended in a spirit of connection, as a reflection of status and power: He thinks she is "indecisive" and "insecure." Her reasons for refraining from behaving as he does — firmly stating opinions as facts — have nothing to do with her attitudes toward her knowledge, as he thinks they do, but rather result from her attitudes toward her relationships with her peers.

34   These experimental studies by Leet-Pellegrini and Aries, and the observations by Fox, all indicate that, typically, men are more comfortable than women in giving information and opinions and speaking in an authoritative way to a group, whereas women are more comfortable than men in supporting others. ...

LISTENER AS UNDERLING

35   Clearly men are not always talking and women are not always listening. I have asked men whether they ever find themselves in the position of listening to another man giving them a lecture, and how they feel about it. They tell me that this does happen. They may find themselves talking to someone who presses information on them so insistently that they give in and listen. They say they don't mind too much, however, if the information is interesting. They can store it away for future use, like remembering a joke to tell others later. Factual information is of less interest to women because it is of less use to them. They are unlikely to try to pass on the gift of information, more likely to give the gift of being a good audience.

36   Men as well as women sometimes find themselves on the receiving end of a lecture they would as soon not hear. But men tell me that it is most likely to happen if the other man is in a position of higher status. They know they have to listen to lectures from fathers and bosses.

37   That men can find themselves in the position of unwilling listener is attested to by a short opinion piece in which A.R. Gurney bemoans being frequently "cornered by some self-styled expert who harangues me with his considered opinion on an interminable agenda of topics." He claims that this tendency bespeaks a peculiarly American inability to "converse" — that is, engage in a balanced give-and-take — and cites as support the French observer of American customs Alexis de Tocqueville, who wrote, "An American ... speaks to you as if

he was addressing a meeting." Gurney credits his own appreciation of conversing to his father, who "was a master at eliciting and responding enthusiastically to the views of others, though this resiliency didn't always extend to his children. Indeed, now I think about it, he spoke to us many times as if he were addressing a meeting."

38   It is not surprising that Gurney's father lectured his children. The act of giving information by definition frames one in a position of higher status, while the act of listening frames one as lower. Children instinctively sense this — as do most men. But when women listen to men, they are not thinking in terms of status. Unfortunately, their attempts to reinforce connections and establish rapport, when interpreted through the lens of status, can be misinterpreted as casting them in a subordinate position — and are likely to be taken that way by many men.

WHAT'S SO FUNNY?

39   The economy of exchanging jokes for laughter is a parallel one. In her study of college students' discussion groups, Aries found that the students in all-male groups spent a lot of time telling about times they had played jokes on others, and laughing about it. She refers to a study in which Barbara Miller Newman found that high school boys who were not "quick and clever" became the targets of jokes. Practical joking — playing a joke *on* someone — is clearly a matter of being one-up: in the know and in control. It is less obvious, but no less true, that *telling* jokes can also be a way of negotiating status.

40   Many women (certainly not all) laugh at jokes but do not later remember them. Since they are not driven to seek and hold center stage in a group, they do not need a store of jokes to whip out for this purpose. A woman I will call Bernice prided herself on her sense of humor. At a cocktail party, she met a man to whom she was drawn because he seemed at first to share this trait. He made many funny remarks, which she spontaneously laughed at. But when she made funny remarks, he seemed not to hear. What had happened to his sense of humor? Though telling jokes and laughing at them are both reflections of a sense of humor, they are very different social activities. Making others laugh gives you a fleeting power over them: As linguist Wallace Chafe points out, at the moment of laughter, a person is temporarily disabled. The man Bernice met was comfortable only when he was making her laugh, not the other way around. When Bernice laughed at his jokes, she thought she was engaging in a symmetrical activity. But he was engaging in an asymmetrical one.

41   A man told me that sometime around tenth grade he realized that he preferred the company of women to the company of men. He found that his female friends were more supportive and less competitive, whereas his male friends seemed to spend all their time joking. Considering joking an asymmetrical activity makes it clearer why it would fit in with a style he perceived as competitive. ...

MUTUAL ACCUSATIONS

42   Considering these dynamics, it is not surprising that many women complain that their partners don't listen to them. But men make the same complaint about

women, although less frequently. The accusation "You're not listening" often really means "You don't understand what I said in the way that I meant it," or "I'm not getting the response I wanted." Being listened to can become a metaphor for being understood and being valued.

43   In my earlier work I emphasized that women may get the impression men aren't listening to them even when the men really are. This happens because men have different habitual ways of showing they're listening. As anthropologists Maltz and Borker explain, women are more inclined to ask questions. They also give more listening responses — little words like *mhm*, *uh-uh*, and *yeah* — sprinkled throughout someone else's talk, providing a running feedback loop. And they respond more positively and enthusiastically, for example by agreeing and laughing.

44   All this behavior is doing the work of listening. It also creates rapport-talk by emphasizing connection and encouraging more talk. The corresponding strategies of men — giving fewer listener responses, making statements rather than asking questions, and challenging rather than agreeing — can be understood as moves in a contest by incipient speakers rather than audience members.

45   Not only do women give more listening signals, according to Maltz and Borker, but the signals they give have different meanings for men and women, consistent with the speaker/audience alignment. Women use "yeah" to mean "I'm with you, I follow," whereas men tend to say "yeah" only when they agree. The opportunity for misunderstanding is clear. When a man is confronted with a woman who has been saying "yeah," "yeah," "yeah," and then turns out not to agree, he may conclude that she has been insincere, or that she was agreeing without really listening. When a woman is confronted with a man who does *not* say "yeah" — or much of anything else — she may conclude that *he* hasn't been listening. The men's style is more literally focused on the message level of talk, while the women's is focused on the relationship or metamessage level.

46   To a man who expects a listener to be quietly attentive, a woman giving a stream of feedback and support will seem to be talking too much for a listener. To a woman who expects a listener to be active and enthusiastic in showing interest, attention, and support, a man who listens silently will seem not to be listening at all, but rather to have checked out of the conversation, taken his listening marbles, and gone mentally home.

47   Because of these patterns, women may get the impression that men aren't listening when they really are. But I have come to understand, more recently, that it is also true that men listen to women less frequently than women listen to men, because the act of listening has different meanings for them. Some men really *don't* want to listen at length because they feel it frames them as subordinate. Many women do want to listen, but they expect it to be reciprocal — I listen to you now; you listen to me later. They become frustrated when they do the listening now and now and now, and later.

MUTUAL DISSATISFACTION

48   If women are dissatisfied with always being in the listening position, the dissatisfaction may be mutual. That a woman feels she has been assigned the role of

silently listening audience does not mean that a man feels he has consigned her to that role — or that he necessarily likes the rigid alignment either.

49   During the time I was working on this book, I found myself at a book party filled with people I hardly knew. I struck up a conversation with a charming young man who turned out to be a painter. I asked him about his work and, in response to his answer, asked whether there has been a return in contemporary art to figurative painting. In response to my question, he told me a lot about the history of art — so much that when he finished and said, "That was a long answer to your question," I had long since forgotten that I had asked a question, let alone what it was. I had not minded this monologue — I had been interested in it — but I realized, with something of a jolt, that I had just experienced the dynamic that I had been writing about.

50   I decided to risk offending my congenial new acquaintance in order to learn something about his point of view. This was, after all, a book party, so I might rely on his indulgence if I broke the rules of decorum in the interest of writing a book. I asked whether he often found himself talking at length while someone else listened. He thought for a moment and said yes, he did, because he liked to explore ideas in detail. I asked if it happened equally with women and men. He thought again and said, "No, I have more trouble with men." I asked what he meant by trouble. He said, "Men interrupt. *They* want to explain to *me*."

51   Finally, having found this young man disarmingly willing to talk about the conversation we had just had and his own style, I asked which he preferred: that a woman listen silently and supportively, or that she offer opinions and ideas of her own. He said he thought he liked it better if she volunteered information, making the interchange more interesting.

52   When men begin to lecture other men, the listeners are experienced at trying to sidetrack the lecture, or match it, or derail it. In this system, making authoritative pronouncements may be a way to begin an *exchange* of information. But women are not used to responding in that way. They see little choice but to listen attentively and wait for their turn to be allotted to them rather than seizing it for themselves. If this is the case, the man may be as bored and frustrated as the woman when his attempt to begin an exchange of information ends in his giving a lecture. From his point of view, she is passively soaking up information, so she must not have any to speak of. One of the reasons men's talk to women frequently turns into lecturing is *because* women listen attentively and do not interrupt with challenges, sidetracks, or matching information.

53   In the conversations with male and female colleagues that I recounted at the outset of this chapter, this difference may have been crucial. When I talked to the woman, we each told about our own research in response to the other's encouragement. When I talked to the man, I encouraged him to talk about his work, and he obliged, but he did not encourage me to talk about mine. This may mean that he did not want to hear about it — but it also may not. In her study of college students' discussion groups, Aries found that women who did a lot of talking began to feel uncomfortable; they backed off and frequently drew out quieter members of the group. This is perfectly in keeping with women's desire to keep things balanced, so everyone is on an equal footing. Women expect their

conversational partners to encourage them to hold forth. Men who do not typically encourage quieter members to speak up, assume that anyone who has something to say will volunteer it. The men may be equally disappointed in a conversational partner who turns out to have nothing to say.

54   Similarly, men can be as bored by women's topics as women can be by men's. While I was wishing the former RAFer would tell me about his personal experiences in Greece, he was probably wondering why I was boring him with mine and marveling at my ignorance of the history of a country I had lived in. Perhaps he would have considered our conversation a success if I had challenged or topped his interpretation of Greek history rather than listening dumbly to it. When men, upon hearing the kind of work I do, challenge me about my research method, they are inviting me to give them information and show them my expertise — something I don't like to do outside of the classroom or lecture hall, but something they themselves would likely be pleased to be provoked to do.

55   The publicist who listened attentively to information about a radio station explained to me that she wanted to be nice to the manager, to smooth the way for placing her clients on his station. But men who want to ingratiate themselves with women are more likely to try to charm them by offering interesting information than by listening attentively to whatever information the women have to impart. I recall a luncheon preceding a talk I delivered to a college alumni association. My gracious host kept me entertained before my speech by regaling me with information about computers, which I politely showed interest in, while inwardly screaming from boredom and a sense of being weighed down by irrelevant information that I knew I would never remember. Yet I am sure he thought he was being interesting, and it is likely that at least some male guests would have thought that he was. I do not wish to imply that all women hosts have entertained me in the perfect way. I recall a speaking engagement before which I was taken to lunch by a group of women. They were so attentive to my expertise that they plied me with questions, prompting me to exhaust myself by giving my lecture over lunch before the formal lecture began. In comparison to this, perhaps the man who lectured to me about computers was trying to give me a rest.

56   The imbalance by which men often find themselves in the role of lecturer, and women often find themselves in the role of audience, is not the creation of only one member of an interaction. It is not something that men do to women. Neither is it something that women culpably "allow" or "ask for." The imbalance is created by the difference between women's and men's habitual styles. ...

HOPE FOR THE FUTURE

57   What is the hope for the future? Must we play out our assigned parts to the closing act? Although we tend to fall back on habitual ways of talking, repeating old refrains and familiar lines, habits can be broken. Women and men both can gain by understanding the other gender's style, and by learning to use it on occasion.

58   Women who find themselves unwillingly cast as the listener should practice propelling themselves out of that position rather than waiting patiently for the lecture to end. Perhaps they need to give up the belief that they must wait for the floor to be handed to them. If they have something to say on a subject, they

might push themselves to volunteer it. If they are bored with a subject, they can exercise some influence on the conversation and change the topic to something they would rather discuss.

59   If women are relieved to learn that they don't always have to listen, there may be some relief for men in learning that they don't always have to have interesting information on the tips of their tongues if they want to impress a woman or entertain her. A journalist once interviewed me for an article about how to strike up conversations. She told me that another expert she had interviewed, a man, had suggested that one should come up with an interesting piece of information. I found this amusing, as it seemed to typify a man's idea of a good conversationalist, but not a woman's. How much easier men might find the task of conversation if they realized that all they have to do is listen. As a woman who wrote a letter to the editor of *Psychology Today* put it, "When I find a guy who asks, 'How was your day?' and really wants to know, I'm in heaven."

Topics for consideration:

1. In this selection, Tannen uses both personal anecdotes and formal research studies to argue her case. Which evidence do you find most compelling and why?

2. Deborah Tannen suggests that the pattern of males lecturing while females listen may be unsatisfactory for both parties. What evidence does she produce for this? Do you think, judging from your own experience, that this is true?

3. Tannen suggests that men are more interested in telling jokes as well as in playing practical jokes. Do you agree? Are there exceptions?

4. Gather some of your own evidence to test Tannen's hypothesis. For example, during a set period of class discussion (preferably not one in which Tannen's article is being discussed) time the interventions of male and female students. Who talks most frequently? Who talks for the most time? Who interrupts most?

Deborah Cameron (1958-

Deborah Cameron is Senior Lecturer in the Programme in Literary Linguistics at Strathclyde University, Glasgow. She has researched and published widely in the fields of language and gender studies and sociolinguistics. She is author of Feminism and Linguistic Theory *(1992) and a co-author of* Researching Language *(1992).*

Cameron's essay was prompted by arguments among linguists about Deborah Tannen's bestselling book You Just Don't Understand. *Cameron puts the argument in perspective by sketching in trends in the developing field of feminist linguistics, beginning with the "deficit" approach propounded by Robin Lakoff in* Language and Woman's Place *(1975). Tannen, by contrast, works from a "difference" approach. Cameron points out that Tannen's work implicitly advises women to adjust to masculine norms and ignores "issues of power."*

RETHINKING LANGUAGE AND GENDER STUDIES

1 These remarks are prompted in the first instance by some interesting recent events. There has been a serious breakdown of sisterly solidarity in the field of feminist linguistics, with a recent issue of the journal *Discourse and Society* featuring a defensive piece by Deborah Tannen, responding to a hostile review of her book, *You Just Don't Understand*, by Senta Troemel-Ploetz.

2 I find the occasion for this public quarrel more than a little ironic. When I began to do feminist linguistics there was, in Britain anyway, no field more generally obscure and lacking in credibility — an interviewer once commented, about my own book *Feminism and Linguistic Theory*, 'But isn't that like writing a book on linguistics and organic gardening?'. Yet today feminist linguistics are being polarised by an issue that seems to turn precisely on the popularisation of our research. Once our credibility was threatened by obscurity; now it seems a little more obscurity would enhance it.

3 Yet perhaps this disagreement, overtly over popularisation, has the virtue of bringing to light other disagreements that were already lurking in the shadows, and forcing us to confront them. I believe the new popular linguistic advice literature, of which Deborah Tannen's book is only one example, salient to us because it happens to have been written by one of our own, raises both ethical and theoretical problems that might lead us to rethink some aspects of what we do. Certainly it has led me to clarify my own position, and here I want to present both the position I have reached and the steps by which I reached it.

4 I began by thinking about popular texts, then and now. At either end of the 1980s, a book about language and gender was published which seemed to contribute to the current state of the art, and at the same time was able to reach a sizeable popular audience. In 1980 the book was Dale Spender's *Man Made Language*: written by a radical feminist, uncompromising in its politics and broad in its scope; the book was a feminist bestseller, and the object of considerable media attention. In 1990 by contrast we had Deborah Tannen's *You Just Don't Understand*. Written by a linguist with impeccable scholarly credentials,

politically more ambiguous and more modest in its aims, this much-hyped book was a trade blockbuster of astounding proportions, spending more than a year on the *New York Times* bestseller list.

5   What happened in the ten intervening years? Perhaps feminist linguistics simply came of age intellectually, and was therefore able to speak with more authority in 1990 than in 1980. Or perhaps feminist linguistics sold out — Deborah Tannen succeeded by compromising the political principles of Dale Spender. Or perhaps, since this story is set in the 'decade of greed', it is simply about feminism's increasing commodification: Deborah Tannen's book reached a wider market than Dale Spender's because it was better packaged and more aggressively marketed. I will argue that none of these accounts is wholly without merit; but none is wholly satisfactory either.

6   As a preliminary, let me mention a few things that are not at issue here. First, and contrary to Tannen's own beliefs, the issue is not popularisation *per se*. Traditional academic snootiness about popular writing has never sat well with feminist politics, and feminist linguists from the beginning have tended to write accessibly for a non-specialist audience. Where Dale Spender, a non-linguist, was often taxed with doing this out of ignorance, Deborah Tannen, a well-respected linguist, has been charged instead with calculation: with setting out cynically to write a lucrative bestseller. But the motives of individual scholars are not the issue either. What's important is that Spender and Tannen each succeeded because they were skilful in capturing the mood of the moment. It is the change in mood from 1980 to 1990 that is really the issue.

7   I have come to believe that my initial understanding of this change was too simple. Nevertheless, I will start by putting it the way it originally appeared to me. When I first came across *You Just Don't Understand*, my reaction was to feel, as Senta Troemel-Ploetz obviously did, that feminist linguistics was being turned into a branch of the self-improvement industry. Tannen's text is actually sold in bookshops in the section labelled 'psychology', 'self-help' or 'personal growth'; it reproduces all the features of the popular advice genre; and the considerable attention it got from the media focused primarily on its potential for helping men and women to solve their problems (the US paperback edition's back cover proclaims, for instance, 'People are telling Tannen that the book is saving their marriages').

8   I think it will be obvious why this development might give cause for concern. Many feminists have criticised the self-help genre for glossing over systemic problems of gender inequality, and urging that those problems be addressed through individual adjustment rather than collective political action. Saving a woman's marriage is a far cry from producing a critique of marriage itself. What troubles me even more, though, is that in producing a self-help book about language and gender, Deborah Tannen is not just harnessing linguistics to reactionary trends outside the academy: she is carrying recent trends in feminist linguistics to what is arguably their logical conclusion.

9   A crude historical-typological account of feminist linguistic approaches since 1973 would probably distinguish between three models of language and gender. One is a *deficit* model in which women are seen as disadvantaged speakers because of their early sex-role socialisation: the obvious example is Robin Lakoff's

Language and Woman's Place. The second is a *dominance* model in which women are seen, often through an ethnomethodological frame, as negotiating their relatively powerless position in interacting with men: male social privilege is made manifest in recurrent patterns of language use. This model could be exemplified by the work of Candace West on interruptions or by Pamela Fishman's studies of heterosexual couples' talk. Finally, there is a *cultural difference* model in which analogies are made between gender and other social divisions such as ethnicity; segregation of the sexes during childhood and adolescence produces marked differences in their conversational goals and styles. A major reference point for this model is the work of Gumperz and his associates (e.g., Maltz and Borker); the work of Deborah Tannen also exemplifies it.

10   Chronologically speaking there has been considerable overlap between the three models, but during the 1980s I think it is fair to say that the difference model gained ground while the dominance and deficit approaches lost it. This development, I think, goes some way to explain why a self-help approach has recently become an option for feminist linguists. The dominance approach emphasises inequality as the root of any problems in cross-sex interaction, and suggests therefore that to solve the problems we must eliminate the underlying inequality. The difference approach, on the other hand, reinterprets the same problems as misunderstandings. Women and men are positioned not unequally, but *symmetrically*, as outsiders to each other's verbal culture. In such a situation, given good intentions on both sides, the problems can conceivably be solved by exposing the roots of misunderstanding and acting upon our new awareness of what causes it.

11   This is exactly the project of Deborah Tannen's *You Just Don't Understand*: to explain to women and men why they so often seem to be at odds when they talk. Starting from the postulate of separate cultures, the problem Tannen identifies is that each sex interprets the other's verbal strategies through the lens of their own. This gives a distorted picture: what your husband means by saying something may not be the same as what your girlfriend would mean if she said exactly the same thing.

12   For example, a much excerpted portion of Tannen's book deals with 'Eve', just out of hospital after a lumpectomy and worried that the scarring has made her unattractive. Eve's husband suggests that if it's really bothering Eve she could have plastic surgery. Eve is upset: not only does he seem to be confirming her suspicion that she is unattractive, but after all she's been through he wants her to have more surgery. Yet when she taxes him with this, he is hurt and puzzled, protesting that she has totally misunderstood what he said.

13   What's going on here, Tannen explains, is a clash of male and female norms for doing 'trouble talk'. Women bring up troubles wanting sympathy and reassurance. The commonest female response to someone's mentioning a problem is to produce 'matching troubles' — the 'I-know-just-what-you-mean-I've-had-the-same-thing-myself' syndrome. Men bring up troubles in the expectation that someone will suggest a solution — which is what Eve's husband does. Since Eve expected reassurance, however, this response strikes her as uncaring. Neither Eve nor her husband is consciously aware of violating the other's norms, and as a consequence they quarrel.

14   This is one example of a much more general difference. Men, Tannen claims, see the world as a hierarchy in which any individual may be 'one-up' or 'one-down'; the interactive task they set themselves is to gain or maintain status. They expect women to do likewise, but women have other goals. What women value is connection and intimacy, and in talking they are likely to insist on the commonality of their experience, not its uniqueness. This is one reason why men boast and women gossip. Each sex engages in the sort of talk which secures the rewards they prefer — status for men, connection for women.

15   The overall message of *You Just Don't Understand* is that both styles are valid, they are simply different. If women and men had a more explicit knowledge of the differences in question, they would not misunderstand each other so frequently and disastrously. Tannen argues that we should acknowledge gender differences without making value judgements on their content.

16   Has this line of argument been successful because of intellectual considerations, or political ones? Probably, both. The difference approach is no doubt attractive to certain people because it does not cast men as villains and feminists as anti-male. But it's only fair to point out that the difference approach gained ground among scholars for other reasons too.

17   One of these was a desire to get away from Lakoff's rather negative evaluation of women's language. In characterising women as speakers who lacked authority, Lakoff had seemed to many feminists to be accepting at face value men's own biased judgements. Another difficulty (which Tannen discusses) arose in relation to ethnicity, race and class. If men were to be criticised for their insensitive dominant behaviour, couldn't the same arguments be used against other groups with similarly combative styles, such as Jewish people and people of African descent?

18   But I think there is a deeper logic here. The gradual ascendancy of difference over dominance was almost inevitable given the ideology of twentieth-century linguistics, especially its anthropological and sociological variants. Difference, and not inequality, is what the framework of structural linguistics is designed to deal with. Indeed, for the linguist, inequality is conceived as resulting not from difference itself but from intolerance of difference. Thus linguists have insisted it is wrong to label languages 'primitive' or dialects 'substandard'; it is wrong to force people to abandon their ways of speaking, or to judge them by the yardstick of your own linguistic habits. Throughout this century, the norm in linguistics has been linguistic and cultural relativism — 'all varieties are equal'. It has always been an honorable position, and sometimes an outright radical one. In applying it to the case of male-female differences, Deborah Tannen and her colleagues have only reasserted the historical logic of the discipline they were trained in.

19   The question, of course, is whether relativism has any virtue in the case of gender difference. Applied to the speech styles of women and men in the same society, is 'all varieties are equal' a radical position? I am not persuaded that men and women are a parallel case to historically distinct nations or ethnic groups, and this is a point we must return to later on. In any event, the notion of gender as a quasi-cultural difference has caused questions of power which were fundamental to feminism to disappear almost entirely; and it is arguably because of

this that the difference paradigm has been easily co-opted to the interests of self-help in its most politically questionable form.

20 Let me try to demonstrate how relativism becomes reactionary. Deborah Tannen may say that she is trying to promote mutual understanding and tolerance between the sexes; like the women in her book, she prefers reassurance to advice. But since men and women are *not* in fact symmetrically positioned, in practice her book undermines its own aims.

21 To see this, it is only necessary to ask who the book is really addressed to. It purports to be addressing both women and men, but in reality the market for books about male-female relationships is overwhelmingly a female market (the UK rights were bought by Virago). Tannen herself argues that women care more about interpersonal relationships and invest more energy in them than men do. Avoiding or resolving cross-sex misunderstandings thus becomes women's responsibility.

22 That women do feel a need to act on what they read is borne out strongly in the reception given to Tannen's book. Over and over again, reviewers and sub-editors have used the metaphor of the phrasebook: 'a fine Berlitz guide', in the words of one reviewer; or as American *Cosmopolitan* put it with exemplary crassness, 'Here, the secrets of mantalk, and how to decode it.' One does not buy a phrasebook out of abstract interest in the language: one buys a phrasebook for the immediate purposes of basic communication. And the point is, this is not a two-way street. To be fair to Deborah Tannen, she says in her introduction that for women to do all the adjusting is 'repugnant,' and she registers some objections to the selective presentation of her thesis by the media. Yet the terms of the book's reception were surely depressingly predictable.

23 Women's magazine features based on *You Just Don't Understand* have been both very numerous and extremely prescriptive. *Glamour* ran a piece, unusual for focusing on workplace relations rather than domestic ones, which translated Tannen's arguments into a set of handy hints — for example, to avoid indirect requests to male colleagues because 'women shy away from giving blatant orders, but men find the indirect approach manipulative and confusing'. The piece repeats Tannen's view that there is nothing inherently wrong with making indirect requests; but it immediately undercuts this message by saying, in essence, that if you don't want to be misinterpreted you will do better to adopt the male norm.

24 One could argue, then, that *You Just Don't Understand* is in practice a rather reactionary self-help book which does not serve feminist ends; and that its problematic aspects arise from the shift in feminist linguistics to a difference approach. But as I warned earlier, this argument, while it is not wholly false, needs to be complicated. For it turns out that Deborah Tannen's brand of linguistic self-help is not the only one on the market. There is also a tradition based on work not in the difference framework.

25 The alternative genre of advice is mainly oriented to professional career women, and is to be found in manuals used in corporate training. A typical one is titled *Leadership Skills for Women: Achieving Impact as a Manager*. This title does not mention language explicitly, but it is full of material clearly if selectively derived from the scholarly literature on gender differences in speech. An important reference point through this genre is the work of Robin Lakoff, with its thesis that

women speakers 'lack authority'; well-known findings from the dominance per-spective are also invoked, though in conformity with the tenets of self-help they are often recuperated to a deficit model. The substance of the advice is to emu-late men: not simply in order to be understood by them, but because the male way is the best way. *Leadership Skills for Women* explains that 'men typically use less body language than women', and urges: 'Watch their body language to see how they do it'. It also admonishes, in a remarkable display of victim-blaming:

> Speak directly and stand firm when you are interrupted. Statistics show that women allow themselves to be interrupted 50% more often than men. Don't contribute to those statistics. (p. 15)

26   The same sort of thing turns up in women's magazines. US *Cosmopolitan* for instance ran an article in 1990 headed 'Why not talk like an adult?', though it should have been called 'Why not talk like a man?'. This piece informed readers that women often fail to gain respect in the workplace because of the way they talk. Certain characteristics of female speech — tag questions, ris-ing intonation, whiny, breathy or high-pitched voices — must be scrupulously avoided. Obviously, this laundry list of alleged female linguistic offences comes straight from Robin Lakoff, whose negative interpretation of them is presented as fact. *Options* magazine in 1992 included 'tentative language' — again defined in terms drawn from Lakoff — as one of the 'Ten classic career mistakes women always make'.

27   Though more overt in its sexism than *You Just Don't Understand*, this type of advice has a similar outcome, i.e. women are advised to adjust to masculine norms. Both types underline the essential limitation of self-help: by definition, it is about changing one's own behaviour, but in some cases it is other people's behaviour that really needs to change. However, 'Don't allow your husband/boyfriend/boss to contribute to those statistics' would be an idle suggestion at best.

28   I think I have said enough to make clear what I find disturbing in the pre-scriptive application of linguistic research on gender difference. It is worth pointing out, though, just how ironic the transformation is. No discipline has been more insistent than linguistics on the descriptive/prescriptive distinction, the absolute line between 'is' and 'ought'. And feminist linguists in earlier years consistently took aim at the very tendencies that are now embodied in some of their work: at massive generalizations about male and female speech, at assump-tions of all-pervading difference, at stereotypical explanations and myths of ori-gin, at the stultifying and restrictive advice with which women were bombarded. Scholars laboured long in the archives of conduct books and guides for brides, producing scathing critiques of the mythical creature they found there: a nur-turing good listener, smoothing gently over conflict and deferring to others' opinions in the interests of domestic harmony. Now this same woman steps forth from women's magazines, and peeps coyly from the pages of scholarly journals. And the question that has to be asked is how the field of language and gender studies, a field historically created by feminists in the hope that their research would empower women, has been so domesticated and depoliticised in the space of only fifteen years.

29   No doubt any research which is on a topic of public interest and reasonably accessible will sometimes get distorted and misused. But when findings on a particular subject are regularly giving rise to intellectually and politically objectionable consequences, we might begin to suspect some very basic flaw in the paradigm researchers are using. This is just what I suspect about current language and gender studies.

30   Although I find the difference approach particularly problematic, I do not think we can simply return to the good old days of the dominance approach. Both dominance and difference represented particular moments in feminism: dominance was the moment of feminist outrage, of bearing witness to oppression in all aspects of women's lives, while difference was the moment of feminist celebration, reclaiming and revaluing women's distinctive cultural traditions. It would be foolish to suggest that these responses are no longer necessary. But I do think the theories which underpinned them are no longer sufficient. Their moments have passed. And if feminist scholarship does not develop new theoretical positions in response to new conditions, it risks falling into obsolescence or hardening into reaction. That is what has happened to feminist linguistics: the monolithic notion of (male) power that informed early dominance work is now more or less obsolete, while the blithe assertion of women's difference now seems either so essentialist or else so depoliticised as to be reactionary.

31   It is not a coincidence that feminist *linguistics* finds itself in this impasse when other disciplines have managed to move on. In the study of language and gender — again, following the practice established in sociolinguistics more generally — it is *language* that is taken as the phenomenon to be explained, and gender which constitutes the explanation. Gender itself remains untheorised: it is a given, the bottom line. A linguist may seek to explain the effects of gender on language by talking about the differential socialisation of the sexes, the inequality between the sexes, the segregation of the sexes. What she cannot do is interrogate this crucial construct 'the sexes'.

32   It is hardly surprising if such an approach produces overgeneralisation (men do this, women do that) and stereotyping (men are competitive, women are cooperative). What else could it produce? In this static commonsensical worldview, there are men and there are women, bearers of the attribute we call gender: our task becomes one of simply cataloguing the ways they mark this attribute in their linguistic behaviour. Men do this, women do that — must feminist linguistics be an endless repetition of this formulaic cliché? Or can we somehow reconceptualise the terms of the debate about language and gender?

33   I would like to propose that feminist linguistics take a long hard look at two problems in particular. One is the problem of linguistic and cultural relativism; the second is the problem of conceiving gender itself.

34   Let me begin with the relativism question. What I mean by this is the assumption, traditional in linguistics, that difference itself is neutral, while inequality results from the suppression or stigmatisation of difference. Thus there is nothing 'wrong' with non-standard dialects, only with the prejudice against them. Linguistic diversity is good: only the suppression of diversity is bad.

35   This approach works well enough when the difference in question is a relatively superficial matter of linguistic form. *Aint, isn't, tomayto, tomahto*, let's call

the whole thing off. But when we are dealing with the sort of global discourse strategy that interests many language and gender researchers today, the questions become more complicated, because they relate not just to the forms but also to the functions of language.

36   Different discourse strategies arise in distinct social contexts, and they are used to accomplish different verbal tasks, rather than to do the same task in a different way. Deborah Tannen's version of this, unexceptionable as far as it goes, is that girls and boys are not engaged in the same activities, nor motivated by the same goals: therefore they evolve different norms of interaction. Another way of looking at it is to say that girls and boys already occupy different positions in the social formation, to which different activities and goals, and consequently different interactional patterns, are relevant. The question arises, then, of whether those who typically use a particular style of discourse are being excluded from (or conversely, are monopolising) not only certain verbal practices but more significantly, a range of *social* practices. If so, the issue is not so much whether X's way of speaking is as good as Y's, as whether the division of labour has significant political consequences, empowering some groups at the expense of others.

37   In the case of gender, a very good argument can be made that it does. To be sure, it makes little sense to argue about whether 'status' is better than 'intimacy', or vice versa. The position that these are both valid goals has much to recommend it, particularly if we define status as having to do with personal autonomy rather than competition for supremacy. Nevertheless, the gender specialisation whereby girls seek intimacy and boys seek status is hardly arbitrary in terms of the larger social structure. It could be characterised as a training of boys for public and girls for private life; or as a training for boys in the exercise of power and for girls in the abdication of autonomy.

38   This is not a neutral difference. The fact that it appears in single-sex peer groups in no way detracts from the important point that *this difference arises in the first place out of unequal gender relations*. To suppose that the 'problem' is intolerance of difference, and that if only we valued women's styles as highly as men's there would be no problem, is reminiscent of that brand of right-wing pseudo-feminism which enjoins us to honour the housewife and mother, glossing over the fact that her gendered occupation is itself a product of inequality and exploitation. Feminism is not about giving housewives their due, it is about changing the conditions of domestic labour altogether. Similarly, feminism cannot stop at validating the linguistic strategies typical of women; it must also ask why women find some communicative practices more relevant than others to their circumstances: a question of their social positioning, of the social practices in which they are allowed to participate.

39   This argument depends on accepting that inequality can give rise to difference, rather than vice versa. The conventional view is to see subordinated groups as oppressed *because* they are different; I am suggesting rather that many of the differences invoked to justify oppression, to the extent that they exist at all, have actually arisen historically because of it. In the case of these differences, there can be no place for cultural relativism.

40   One of the problems with *You Just Don't Understand* is that Deborah Tannen reifies gender differences. I do not accuse her of biological essentialism, but she

does practise what you might call 'social essentialism', i.e. she invokes a socially produced difference as a simple fact of life, without ever asking what it is socially produced by or socially produced for. If in fact it is produced by inequality and functions to maintain unequal relations, to accept it as a fact of life is not only theoretically naive, it is politically damaging.

41   Let me give an example. In an opinion piece for the US *Chronicle of Higher Education*, Tannen noted the discomfort many women feel with adversarial teaching methods such as requiring students to defend a position in debate. She suggested that teachers employ more single-sex small-group discussions so that women are not forced to participate (at a disadvantage) in a verbal practice for which their peer group norms do not prepare them.

42   Granted, small-group discussion has many virtues, and granted, there is a real question whether effective public discourse always needs to be adversarial. But the fact remains, there are many contexts where individuals gain autonomy and power by being able to debate and argue a case. Debate and argument are 'languages of power' in our culture. If, as Tannen claims, women experience them in the classroom as 'public humiliation', this is surely bound up with the conflicting pressures women face in that setting: for women, intellectual autonomy and academic success conflict with social and sexual acceptability to a greater degree than is true for most men.

43   A feminist solution to this very real problem involves not removing women from the context that causes discomfort, but going to the roots of their positioning as 'outsiders' to powerful language and trying to change the conditions (including male behaviour) that keep them outside. Deborah Tannen's relativism perpetuates women's exclusion from languages of power, while failing to challenge any of the masculine behaviours which reinforce that exclusion.

44   This brings me to the other question I raised: theorising gender. As I said earlier, I believe linguists can learn from scholars in other disciplines. The most important insight we need to take account of is that *gender is a problem, not a solution*. 'Men do this, women do that' is not only overgeneralised and stereotypical, it fails utterly to address the question of where 'men' and 'women' come from. Feminists must take it as axiomatic that this is indeed a question worth asking. As Simone de Beauvoir said, 'One is not born, but rather becomes a woman'. The question is, how?

45   Not only the difference theorists of language and gender but also those working in the tradition of Robin Lakoff are dependent on a view of 'becoming a woman' as something accomplished once and for all at an early stage of life — either in the pre-school years within the nuclear family or slightly later in the peer group. Thereafter, an already fixed gender identity becomes the solution to the problem of why women and men behave as they do.

46   Recent feminist theory emphasises, by contrast, that one is never finished becoming a woman, or a man. Each individual subject must constantly negotiate the norms, behaviours, discourses, that define masculinity and femininity for a particular community at a particular point in history. From this point of view, it would be desirable to reformulate notions such as 'women's language' or 'men's style'. Instead of saying simply that these styles are produced by women and men as markers of their gender affiliation, we could say that the styles themselves are

produced as masculine and feminine, and that individuals make varying accommodations to those styles in the process of producing *themselves* as gendered subjects. In other words, if I talk like a woman this is not just the inevitable outcome of the fact that I am a woman; it is one way I have of becoming a woman, producing myself *as* one. There is no such thing as 'being a woman' outside the various practices that define womanhood for my culture — practices ranging from the sort of work I do to my sexual preferences, to the clothes I wear, to the way I interact verbally.

47   Let us be clear that this way of talking about gender does not make it into something consciously and freely chosen. On the contrary, many aspects of becoming a woman (working in a suitable occupation or having certain kinds of sexual relationships) are heavily coerced, and where choice becomes possible (say I apprentice myself to a plumber, refuse to wear skirts, have affairs with women), there are real social costs. What this way of talking does, though, is problematise gender identity and leave open the possibility of challenge and change. Cooperation and competition need not be forever mutually exclusive, feminine and masculine principles of speech. We can intervene in the discourse that defines them thus. And this also allows us to account for the exceptions that exist already, the women and men who — in spite of early experiences virtually identical to what Lakoff and Tannen describe — end up outside the gender norms proposed by feminist linguists.

48   In our time and place, social science is a powerful discourse: what followers of Foucault call a 'regime of truth'. Feminist linguistics has produced a 'truth', a version of what it means to be a gendered speaker, that defines many women as deviant, while treating women's continued exclusion from important communicative practices as normal. Whereas what we need is a linguistics that can empower women — not by glossing over crucial issues about language, as Dale Spender did, and not by ignoring issues of power, as Deborah Tannen does, but by combining a more sophisticated theoretical approach with a clearer view of what's actually at stake. It is by these criteria, rather than by generic oppositions such as 'scholarly' versus 'popular' writing, that our intellectual and political credibility should be measured.

Topics for consideration:

1. Cameron is critical of both the "dominance" interpretation and of the "difference" approach argued by Tannen. What solution of her own does she suggest?

2. Cameron notes the kind of advice offered to women about both spoken language and body language in magazines and self-help books. What advice of this kind have you noticed in magazines, phone-in radio shows, or TV talk shows? Is the same sort of advice given to men?

3. Cameron suggests that Tannen's writing "purports to be addressing both women and men ... [but] in reality the market for books about male-female

relationships is overwhelmingly a female market." In your view is Tannen's work of equal interest to women and men? Was this reflected in group or class discussions of Tannen's writing?

Further reading:

Deborah Cameron, ed., *The Feminist Critique of Language: A Reader* (1990)

Jan Morris (1926-

Travel writer (or as she prefers, "travelling writer") Jan Morris began life as James Morris and served in the British Army in the Second World War before spending ten years as newspaper corespondent for The Times. *As a married man with grown-up children, with his wife's support, he "took the first steps towards a physical change of sex" later documented in* Conundrum *(1974). Jan Morris's highly respected accounts of her travels are published in newspapers and magazines throughout the English-speaking world.*

In this breezy piece written for a collection entitled The Writer on Her Work *(1992), Jan Morris argues that art is "beyond gender" and that changing gender has made only superficial differences to her experience as a traveller. She also suggests that her "peculiar sexuality" has enabled her to extend her "range of fellow-feeling" to animals and even inanimate objects and to transcend such categories as nationality.*

TRAVELLING WRITER

1 In my heart I resist the title of this book,* or rather its implication: namely that it matters whether a writer is male or female. I believe the fount of art to be beyond gender, just as I believe the human soul itself to be housed in a particular physique merely for practical purposes of reproduction — slotted along the continuum that is, in my view, the true measure of sex. The so-called war between the sexes seems to me a trumped-up conflict, presently to be resolved: and I suspect that the very distinction between masculine and feminine will one day be of purely functional significance.

2 But having lived my own life partly as a man, partly as a woman, I recognize of course how powerfully, in our own time, the circumstance of gender affects one's work as a writer: and I admit that at the core of everything I have done myself, somewhere between the lines of all my books, lies the fact of my own particular and peculiar status in the present state of sex.

3 Take for a start the workaday, humdrum aspects of the writer's life. I am a travelling writer — not a travel writer, a category I reject, but a writer who travels. That I write about place is almost incidental to my vocation. I am really an essayist, often of an all too protracted kind, but it so happens that the Second World War, by making me a traveller whether I wanted it or not, provided me with a particular range of subject matter — the matter of place, which I have manipulated ever since in works of memoir, description, history, and fiction. If chance had given me a more domestic role in life, I have no doubt that the basic material of my essays would have been altogether different, and I might have launched myself from the start into miniatures or abstractions.

4 Be that as it may, destiny made me a travelling writer, with all the addictions that such a calling implies: restless addictions, footloose addictions, a taste for

* *The Writer on Her Work*

the solitary, and an appetite for things colorful, quirky, and exciting. After the British Army and Oxford University I spent a decade as a foreign correspondent, and this soon instilled in me, as it instills in most practitioners of the trade, a cynical disregard for fame, power, and consequence: but it also disqualified me once and for all for the routines and preoccupations of life at home.

5   So I wander always, torn between the places I love the best of all, my own corner of Wales, and the kaleidoscopic variety of everywhere else: between the people I love the best, my family, and the inexhaustible allure of new faces, languages, styles, and manners of thought. It is a *wrenched* kind of life, a perpetual dichotomy, a periodical trauma, but I am certainly not complaining: if this is neurosis, you can keep your normalcy.

6   It is however a demanding existence, stressful and just occasionally dangerous, and at literary festivals especially I am often asked if it has become easier for me, or more difficult, since I made my shift along the gauge of sex. In some ways, I have to reply, more difficult, because physically it is obviously riskier, even now, for a woman to travel alone in the world with the intention of writing about it. One is more vulnerable than a man, more conspicuous too, and technically this has sometimes been a handicap to me. Aspects of life that I was once free to explore are now more generally denied me, and I have occasionally regretted it, when the dim lights and loud music of a dubious tavern beckon, or I am disbarred from entering some fascinatingly old-school club.

7   But not often. I have hated nightlife always, and seldom in fact pine for leather-backed chairs and gentlemanly tradition. Besides, I set against these lesser disadvantages the assets of travelling as a woman. The chief and most obvious of these is the fact that among the human species, as among most of the animals, the female is not generally perceived as threatening. Novelists and New Yorkers may scoff, but in general it is true, and the solitary woman traveller raises far fewer suspicions, finds far fewer doors closed against her, than does a wandering man.

8   More positively, too, the woman travelling writer can know that more than half of humanity is likely to be actually on her side — cheering her on! When Kipling wrote about "sisters under the skin," he was in his allusive way enunciating a great truth: that on the whole — and God knows, with exceptions — women are kinder to women than men are to men. You must take my word for this, as one who has experienced both relationships, and you must believe me too that for a writer especially this grand freemasonry around the world infinitely outweighs a woman's vulnerability as a traveller.

9   Twenty years ago I would have said that on the other hand the woman was hampered by male inability to take her seriously. I used to feel it myself, when I first began to travel as a woman, and found my opinions disregarded and my questions patronizingly set aside. No longer. It is the great triumph of the feminist movement that the intellectual equality of women is now all but universally recognized (if not invariably, especially when it comes to equal pay or opportunity, admitted ...).

10   Anyway all this is ancillary to the writer's craft and purpose, which is above all self-generating and internal. I don't believe a sensibility depends upon gender,

and I think I write in the way I write not because I am male, female, both, or neither, but simply because I am myself: "*le style est l'homme même*," said de Buffon long ago, but he meant *l'homme*, I do not doubt, in shorthand for humanity.

11   Sensibility however is a different thing from experience, and the experience of our gender, while it may not affect our style, certainly affects our responses. In my own case the anomalies of my sex have powerfully affected, without doubt, the way I have looked at the world, besides the way I have lived in it. I expect in some respects they have distorted or weakened my reactions, but I prefer to look upon the bright side, and contemplate their benefits instead.

12   I think they made me, from the start, one of life's outsiders. This would be a weakness for writers of other kinds, but it has been good for me. The essence of my work, whether it deals with the past or the present, whether it is fact or fiction, is detachment — not alienation or estrangement, merely standing separate. Actually detachment of a kind is endemic to the tradition of English writing to which I feel myself, though actually Anglo-Welsh, to belong: the classic detachment of the English abroad, amounting very nearly to aloofness and exemplified in the work of such masters of my own genre as Emily Eden or Alexander Kinglake. American writers about place have more generally felt the urge to get within the skin of the people they are observing: English writers have preferred to watch from a safe distance, through a screen of irony.

13   More fundamentally, and conversely, I like to think my peculiar sexuality has widened my empathies. If I feel separate from everyone, I feel close to everyone too. Starting with men and women, many of whose varied emotions I have actually shared, I have been able, as I grow older, to extend my range of fellow-feeling: to animals, for instance, to nations, even to inanimate objects. I believe in the absolute equality before God of all living things, slug to dolphin. I do not recognize the crime of treason, having long ago reached the conclusion that nationality, like loyalty, should be purely a matter of choice. I do not feel in the least foolish in apologizing to a table, if I trip over its leg, or jollying along a recalcitrant automobile with encouraging words.

14   There is a smugness to these attitudes, I know, and a sentimentality too: but then the faults of a writer, as well as the virtues, contribute for better or for worse to the nature of her art.

15   And on the whole, smug, sentimental, or just a little crazy, I feel myself to be a kind of portent. I believe the conjunction of my self and my work to be a sign of reconciliation — a minuscule sign, Heaven knows, and one apparent perhaps only to myself, but still to my mind a promise of things to come. Long ago the philosopher Teilhard de Chardin conceived the idea of "infurling," an infinitely slow, almost imperceptible coming together of the world and its beings. I see in myself and my work one all but imperceptible confirmation of his vision: and I believe that in a couple of centuries, when people read this book, they will wonder at the primitive nature of our own times, when art could still be collated with gender at all.

Topics for consideration:

1. In paragraphs 6 and 7 Morris suggests that there are few really important differences between her experiences as a male traveller and a female one. Imagine either travelling or living an ordinary day as the other sex. What practical or psychological differences would it make? Would you return to your "own" gender with relief or with regret?

2. Morris suggests (paragraph 8) that a woman travelling experiences "more than half of humanity cheering her on!" If you are female, have you found this to be the case?

3. Morris suggests that *l'homme* in the quotation from de Buffon is "shorthand for humanity." Would Casey Miller and Kate Swift, authors of "One Small Step for Genkind" earlier in this section agree? If not, what would account for the difference between their view and Morris's?

Further reading:

James Morris, *Oxford* (1965)

Jan Morris, *Conundrum* (1974)

Susan Ehrlich (1953-

Susan Ehrlich teaches in the Department of Languages, Literature and Linguistics and is Chair of the School of Women's Studies at York University. She is author of Point of View: A Linguistic Analysis of Literary Style *(1990).*

This selection introduces Ehrlich's critical linguistic study of the use of language at a university sexual harassment tribunal. Ehrlich sums up past discussions among linguists about the extent to which language shapes the consciousness of its speakers. She shows how the introduction of new terminology does not necessarily result in changes in consciousness but the dominant culture has ways of reshaping new terms to fit prevailing views.

LINGUISTICS IN ACTION

1   Advocates of non-sexist language reform have generally assumed that language is not a neutral and transparent means of representing social realities. Rather, some have argued that a particular vision of social reality is inscribed in language — a vision of reality that does not serve all of its speakers equally.

2   Susan Gal, for example, sees language as serving the interests of the dominant classes, much like other social institutions and practices;[1] in the case of sexist language, language can be said to codify an androcentric worldview. The names that a language attaches to events and activities, especially those related to sex and sexuality, often encode a male perspective. For example, Deborah Cameron discusses terms such as *penetration, fuck, screw,* and *lay,* all of which turn heterosexual sex into something men do to women.[2] (Penetration from a female perspective would be more appropriately encoded as *enclosure, surrounding,* or *engulfing.*) What becomes clear from "names" such as these is the extent to which language acts as an ideological filter on the world: language, to some extent, shapes or constructs our notions of reality rather than labelling that reality in any transparent and straightforward way.

3   The idea that language determines or in some way influences speakers' perceptions and conceptions or reality underlies much of the current work on women and language and has its origins in the work of two U.S. anthropological linguists, Edward Sapir and Benjamin Whorf.[3] The Sapir-Whorf hypothesis, as it is known within the discipline of linguistics, combines the notions of linguistic relativity and linguistic determinism. According to proponents of linguistic relativity, the grammatical properties of different languages can vary more or less without limit; linguistic determinists hold that the grammatical structure of a particular language has a powerful mediating influence on how a speaker of that language comes to view the world. Taken together, then, the two hypotheses predict that speakers of different languages will perceive the world in radically different ways. For example, Hopi (an Amerindian language investigated by Whorf) distinguishes grammatically between the hypothetical and non-hypothetical nature of an event but not between events occurring in the present or past. Therefore, according to the Sapir-Whorf hypothesis, Hopi speakers have a different

conception of time than do speakers of English, because English makes a grammatical distinction between events occurring in the present and the past. For instance, Whorf states:

> We dissect nature along lines laid down by our native languages. The categories and types that we isolate from the world of phenomena we do not find there because they stare every observer in the face; on the contrary, the world is presented in a kaleidoscopic flux of impressions which has to be organized by our minds — and this means largely by the linguistic systems in our minds. We cut nature up, organize it into concepts, and ascribe significances as we do, largely because we are parties to an agreement to organize it in this way — an agreement that holds throughout our speech community and is codified in the patterns of our language. The agreement is, of course, an implicit and unstated one, BUT ITS TERMS ARE ABSOLUTELY OBLIGATORY; we cannot talk at all except by subscribing to the organization and classification of data which the agreement decrees.
>
> The fact is very significant for modern science, for it means that no individual is free to describe nature with absolute impartiality but is constrained to certain modes of interpretation even while he [sic] thinks himself most free.[4]

4   While the Sapir-Whorf hypothesis is appealing, the strong version of the hypothesis as articulated here has few adherents today, especially because we now know that speakers of a particular language can make conceptual distinctions that their language appears not to allow. Some Australian Aboriginal languages, for instance, have few words for numbers; the number lexicon may be restricted to general words such as *all*, *many*, and *few*, and to specific words for *one* and *two*. Yet it is not the case that speakers of these languages cannot count beyond two or perform complex numerical operations, as evidenced by their mathematical abilities in second languages such as English.[5] A weaker version of the Sapir-Whorf hypothesis (which has generally come to replace the "strong" version popular in mid-century) suggests that languages predispose speakers to view the world in particular ways, but that such a worldview is not all-determining. In other words, speakers "can see through and around the settings" of their languages, but doing so may require interrogating some of the most basic commonsense assumptions encoded in those languages.[6]

5   Because individuals and speech communities are, at the least, influenced by the vision(s) of reality that get(s) inscribed in language, it becomes important for feminists to consider the extent to which language encodes a vision of social reality that may not serve the interests of certain groups of women. The tradition of critical linguistics provides a methodology well suited to these goals.[7] Rather than viewing language as a formal system at a level of abstraction that neutralizes social categories and distinctions, critical linguistics assumes that language is inextricably implicated in the socio-political systems and institutions in which it functions. Thus, the motivating principle behind critical linguistics is the investigation of the role of language in the reproduction of dominant ideologies. By highlighting the insidiousness of linguistic practices in which dominant ideologies are reflected

and constructed, critical linguistics has as its ultimate aim the demystification of such social practices.

6   Indeed, this type of linguistic analysis is critical to the feminist enterprise precisely because the ideological perspectives that languages encode often go unnoticed and are not easily foregrounded by speakers who are disposed to think about the world in a certain way. For example, Penelope Eckert and Sally McConnell-Ginet talk about the power of dominant groups being sustained by the "naturalizing" of language's ideological perspective as "neutral or 'unmarked,'" — "obscuring its status as one among many perspectives."[8] Naturalization takes place to the extent that speakers are unaware of the power relations and hierarchies influencing their social (including linguistic) behaviour.

7   This chapter looks at the value of critical linguistics to feminist analysis as a way of elucidating the non-neutrality of language. This kind of linguistic analysis allows us to "see through and around the settings" of our language, allowing for the denaturalizing of sexist and androcentric beliefs and assumptions that are often rationalized as commonsensical in our culture because of their relative "invisibility" in everyday discourse.

THE SOCIAL CONSTRUCTION OF MEANING

8   In a recent account of the social construction of meaning, McConnell-Ginet suggests some of the mechanisms by which social privilege leads to linguistic privilege.[9] Linguistic forms depend for their full interpretation or meaning on social context, including mutually accessible cultural knowledge. For example, the following sequence of sentences can be interpreted as coherent because readers and listeners have access to general cultural knowledge, including the information that picnic supplies can include beer.

9   *Mary got some picnic supplies out of the car. The beer was warm.*

10   If mutually accessible cultural knowledge is relevant to the process that endows linguistic forms with meaning, the question of whose beliefs and values inform this cultural background knowledge is crucial to a theory of meaning. McConnell-Ginet argues that the cultural knowledge that forms the background for the interpretation of linguistic utterances is not neutral: "Men (and dominant groups generally) can be expected to have made disproportionately large contributions to the generally available background beliefs and values on which speakers and writers rely in their attempts to mean."[10] Research on the linguistic behaviour of North American women and men in mixed-sex conversations has demonstrated that men control conversations in a variety of ways: they take up more air time, they interrupt women more than women interrupt men, and they are more likely than women to have their conversational topics pursued and elaborated upon.[11] This differential access to conversation has implications for those whose perspective on the world constitutes mutually accessible cultural knowledge. Thus McConnell-Ginet argues that the utterance "You think like a woman" functions as an insult in most contexts in our culture, not because all listeners adhere to the proposition that women have questionable intellectual abilities, but because listeners are aware the

proposition is prevalent and pervasive within the speech community; that is, it is part of a set of mutually accessible cultural beliefs. Likewise, Muriel Schultz traces the semantic derogation of terms designating women in English, demonstrating that words such as *mistress* and *spinster*, originally positive or neutral in interpretation, have taken on negative meanings in a way unparalleled for words designating men (such as *master*, *bachelor*).[12] The process that invests linguistic forms with sense or meaning is socially conditioned, often involving sexist (and racist) beliefs and values that are prevalent and pervasive in a culture; for example, that women are sexually wanton, that being single is an undesirable state for women. While a Humpty Dumpty theory of meaning is an attractive one (Humpty Dumpty says to Alice in *Through the Looking Glass*: "When I use a word it means what I choose it to mean, neither more nor less"), we know that meaning is not just a matter of individual will. Indeed, in response to a November 1989 "no means no" rape awareness campaign at Queen's University in Kingston, Ontario, obscene and violent messages appeared in the windows of men's dormitories. Such messages demonstrated the extent to which women's words are not their own: "no means harder," "no means dyke," "no means more beer," "no means 'tie me up.'" That is, a woman will say "no" with sincerity to a man's sexual advances, but the "no" gets filtered through a series of beliefs and attitudes that transform her "direct negative" into an "indirect affirmative": "She is playing hard to get, but of course she really means yes."[13]

11   In arguing that meanings are socially constructed and constituted, McConnell-Ginet is also saying that challenges to dominant groups' meanings are possible in the context of speech communities that endorse alternative meanings. Because meanings are authorized or codified through the social support of speech communities, alternative linguistic communities have the potential to authorize non-sexist, non-racist, and non-homophobic meanings. Consider the case of gay and lesbian communities reclaiming terms such as *queer* and *dyke* and investing those terms with in-group positive associations. At the least, a feminist critique of language challenges the absolute hegemony of meanings as constituted by racist, sexist, and androcentric social values.

12   Meanings thus become a site of ideological struggle. Here, I first examine the social construction of meanings associated with terms I call feminist linguistic innovations — such as sexual harassment or date rape. I show how such terms are often redefined and depoliticized in the print media by means of discursive strategies. Second, I show how the phenomenon of sexual harassment is socially constructed in the "talk" of a sexual harassment tribunal. The events in question, characterized as sexual harassment or date rape by the complainants, are similarly redefined and depoliticized in the discursive patterns of this institutional setting. In both cases, I am interested in how language becomes a locus of contestation: dominant ideologies are reproduced and challenged in the discursive practices of both written and spoken texts.

MEANING AS A SITE OF STRUGGLE: NON-SEXIST AND FEMINIST LINGUISTIC INNOVATIONS

13   Feminists have attempted to challenge the absolute hegemony of male-defined meanings and grammar by introducing non-sexist and feminist linguistic

innovations into English. Most attempts at linguistic reform have focused on codified instances of sexist language, that is, on those aspects of English that are in some sense intrinsic to its grammatical and lexical structure. For example, by replacing masculine generics (such as *he, man*) with neutral generics (*they, he/she, she*) advocates of non-sexist language reform challenge the claim implicit in the use of masculine generics that men are the typical case of humanity, with women constituting a deviation from this norm. Another instance of feminist linguistic resistance is the coining of new terms to express women's perceptions and experiences, phenomena previously unexpressed in a language encoding a male world-view. Dale Spender and others argue that lexical gaps are not innocent; rather, "when one group holds a monopoly on naming, its bias is embedded in the names it supplies" and the names it doesn't supply.[14] Thus, innovative terms such as *sexism* and *sexual harassment* are significant in that they give a name to the experiences of women. As Gloria Steinem says of these terms, "A few years ago, they were just called life."[15]

14 While androcentric language clearly reflects and produces sexist social structures and practices, the continuing existence of such structures and practices throws into question the possibility of successful language reform. Because linguistic meanings are, to a large extent, determined by the dominant culture's social values and attitudes — that is, they are socially constructed and constituted — terms initially introduced to be non-sexist, non-racist, or even feminist may (like a woman's response of "no" to a man's sexual advances) lose their intended meanings in the "mouths" and "ears" of a sexist, racist speech community and culture. In what follows, I report on research that I conducted with Ruth King, in which we consider the extent to which language can represent a minority ideological perspective, that is, a non-sexist and feminist one, within the social context of a dominant culture that is primarily sexist. In other words, we consider the fate of non-sexist and feminist linguistic innovations as they travel through and get integrated into the larger, often sexist, speech community.[16]

Neutral Titles and Generics

15 While non-sexist language reform has enjoyed a certain degree of success over the last decade (McConnell-Ginet, for example, points out that it is becoming harder and harder to make *he* function generically, given the debates and disputes surrounding the pronoun's so-called generic usage),[17] there are indications that this reform does not always have its intended effect.

16 For instance, the title Ms was originally popularized by feminists in the 1970s to replace Miss and Mrs and provide a parallel term to Mr in that both Ms and Mr designate gender without indicating marital status. Casey Miller and Kate Swift see the elimination of Mrs and Miss in favour of Ms as a way of allowing women to be seen as people in their own right, rather than in relation to someone else.[18] Unfortunately, while Ms was intended to parallel Mr, considerable evidence suggests that it is not always used or interpreted in this intended way. David Graddol and Joan Swann explain that Ms is not a neutral title for women in Britain, because it sometimes replaces Miss as an indicator of single marital status: "In some contexts it seems to have coalesced with Miss (official

forms sometimes distinguish only Mrs. and Ms.).”[19] Similarly, Julia Penelope maintains that speakers in the United States use and interpret Ms as referring to single women who are trying to hide the fact that they are single.[20] These two examples show that the married/single distinction continues to be marked linguistically; only the title signifying single status has changed. In addition, Francine Frank and Paula Treichler cite a directive sent to public information officers in Pennsylvania: “If you use Ms. for a female, please indicate in parentheses after the Ms. whether it's Miss or Mrs.”[21] In a Canadian study of attitudes towards the use of Ms and birthname retention among women, Donna Atkinson found that many of her respondents had a three-way distinction: they used Mrs for married women, Miss for women who had never been married, and Ms for divorced women.[22] What all of these examples demonstrate is the high premium placed on identifying women by their relationship (current or otherwise) to men. In spite of the intended neutrality associated with Ms, it seems to be used and interpreted in ways that maintain the linguistic distinction the title intended to erase.

17   In a similar way, true generics such as *chairperson* and *spokesperson*, introduced to replace masculine generics such as *chairman* and *spokesman*, seem to have lost their neutrality in that they are often only used for women. Betty Lou Dubois and Isabel Crouch cite announcements of academics changing jobs, taken from the *Chronicle of Higher Education*, demonstrating that a woman is frequently a *chairperson* but a man is a *chairman*.

18   Margarette P. Eby, *Chairperson* of Humanities at U. of Michigan at Dearborn, to Dean of the College of Humanities and Fine Arts and Professor of Music at U. of Northern Iowa.

19   David W. Hamilton, Associate Professor of Anatomy at Harvard, to *Chairman* of Anatomy at U. of Minnesota.[23]

20   As this example reveals, the attempt to replace a masculine generic with a neutral one has been somewhat unsuccessful. Rather than ridding the language of a masculine generic, the introduction of neutral generic forms such as *chairperson* or *chair* has led to a gender-based distinction between forms such as *chairperson* or *chair* (used to designate females) vs. *chairman* (used to designate males). Thus both the title Ms and these true generics are used in ways that maintain distinctions that the terms were intended to eliminate — distinctions clearly important to the speech community in question.

21   Michael Silverstein considers cases of language reform in which neutral terms such as *actor* and *waiter* are advocated as replacements for words with feminine suffixes (with demeaning connotations) such as *actress* and *waitress*.[24] In Silverstein's terms, the category of gender often gets reconstituted in these cases so that a supposedly neutral term like *server* takes on the feminine suffix that the neutral term was intended to eliminate, as in *serveress*. Again, while the terms involved in these oppositions may change (Mrs/Miss to Mrs/Ms. chairman/chairwoman to chairman/chairperson, waiter/waitress to server/serveress), what persists is the linguistic encoding of social distinctions that are clearly of ideological importance to the speech community in question (the married/single distinction among

women; the male/female distinction). We thus see the extent to which non-sexist linguistic innovations lose their intended meanings and are appropriated by a sexist speech community.

Feminist Linguistic Innovations

22   While terms designed to "name" women's experiences (such as *feminism, sexism, sexual harassment, date rape*) pervade our culture, it is not at all clear that their use is consistent with their intended, feminist-influenced, meanings. Ruth King and I identify some of the discursive strategies used systematically by the print media to redefine and depoliticize feminist linguistic innovations.[25] In the process of redefinition, phenomena such as *sexual harassment* and *date rape* are rendered non-existent at best and trivialized and delegitimized at worst. We therefore demonstrate the extent to which these kinds of feminist innovations, like the neutral titles and generics, become appropriated by a sexist speech community, in this case, non-progressive elements of the print media.

REDEFINITION AS OMISSION OR OBSCURING

23   The first kind of discursive strategy we identify involves the elimination or obscuring of crucial aspects of a term's definition. For instance, the phenomenon of sexual harassment virtually disappears when its distinguishing characteristics are omitted from its description. In an article on sexual harassment in the *National Review*, author Gretchen Morgenson reports on a *Time*/CBS sexual harassment poll in which 38 per cent of the respondents said that they had been "the object of sexual advances, propositions, or unwanted sexual discussion" with and from men who supervised them or could influence their position at work.[26] However, only 4 per cent of this group actually reported the incidents at the time that they occurred. In attempting to explain the small percentage of formal complaints, Morgenson asks: "Did *Time* offer any explanation for why so few actually reported the incident? Could it be that these women did not report their 'harassment' because they themselves did not regard a sexual advance as harassment?"

24   Notice the implication here, that without a report of sexual harassment, the harassing behaviour becomes a sexual advance. (Note also the quotation marks around harassment.) Reporting, then, becomes crucial to Morgenson's definition of sexual harassment. This kind of definition ignores the political dimension intrinsic to sexual harassment: specifically, that in the majority of cases women are harassed by male supervisors who have the power to affect the women's position at work. The question of whether to lodge a formal complaint is a complicated one, involving economic and career considerations, among others. To imply that sexual harassment only occurs when it is reported and otherwise is merely a sexual advance is to deny the political aspect of the phenomenon, and it renders the majority of sexual harassment cases non-existent. Indeed, this was one of the tactics used by Republican senators during the 1991 Clarence Thomas/Anita Hill hearings. Thomas, a Republican nominee to the U.S. Supreme Court, was accused of sexual harassment by Hill, a lawyer and his former employee. In an attempt to destroy Hill's credibility, Republican senators pointed to Hill's failure

to file a formal complaint of sexual harassment as evidence that she was not, in fact, sexually harassed.

25   While this example obscures critical aspects of the phenomenon of sexual harassment, another item from *Time* magazine redefines the prototypical case.[27] It comes from a review of the book *Step Forward: Sexual Harassment in the Workplace* by Susan Webb. The book is described as "an accessible sort of Cliffs Notes guide to the topic" and as "refreshingly free of ideology and reproach." The article offers a number of case studies from the book:

> 1) You and your boss are single and like each other a lot. You invite him to dinner, and one thing leads to another. Was someone sexually harassed? (No — though it wasn't very smart.)
>
> 2) Your boss invites you to a restaurant for dinner and — much to your surprise — spends the evening flirting with you. Just before inviting you to her house for a nightcap, she mentions that promotion you are hoping to get. (You are being sexually harassed. Whether or not you welcome her interest in you, she has implied a connection between the promotion and your response.)

26   Clearly, these types of examples are meant to help readers differentiate between behaviour that is sexual harassment and behaviour that is not. Significantly, the second case, which *does* constitute sexual harassment, involves a female supervisor and presumably a male employee. (It's difficult to imagine *Time* reporting on lesbian relations.) Thus, what is presented as the *prototypical* case of sexual harassment is a situation in which a female boss is harassing her male employee, a scenario that flies in the face of the overwhelming majority of sexual harassment cases, in which male supervisors or colleagues harass their female employees. This is not to say that women never harass their male employees, but only that this is not a typical case of sexual harassment. Here, however, the emblematic case of sexual harassment is reconfigured as females harassing males. Obscuring critical aspects of sexual harassment through redefinition only succeeds in rendering many of the actual cases non-existent.

REDEFINITION AS EXPANSION

27   The second kind of discursive strategy is employed consistently with terms such as *sexual harassment, rape,* and *sexual abuse.* It involves expanding the definition of such phenomena beyond reason (exploiting feminists' attempts to expand the definitions of these phenomena) and then imputing this expanded (unreasonable) definition to feminists. The effect of this kind of expansion strategy is to ridicule and trivialize the phenomenon in question. John Taylor quotes the journalist Stephanie Gutmann of *Reason* magazine, who states about date rape: "The real story about campus date rape is not that there's been any significant increase of rape on college campuses, at least of the acquaintance type, but that the word *rape* is being stretched to encompass *any type of sexual interaction*."[28]

28   Here Gutmann is presumably referring to feminists' attempts to expand the notion of sexual assault/rape so that it includes more than just sexual intercourse

and so that mutual consent becomes a crucial criterion in distinguishing rape from non-rape. Gutmann overstates the case by saying that rape now encompasses "any kind of sexual interaction." Later on in the same article, Taylor misrepresents a feminist revision of the notion of rape imputed to Andrea Parrot: "Any sexual intercourse without mutual desire is a form of rape." Taylor "paraphrases" Parrot — "By the definition of the radical feminists, all sexual encounters that involve any confusion or ambivalence constitute rape" — and quotes Gutmann again: "Ordinary bungled sex — the kind you regret in the morning or even during — is being classified as rape. ... Bad or confused feelings after sex becomes someone else's fault."[29]

29 This same expansion strategy is evident in an article on feminism published in the *National Review*, but this time it is sexual abuse that is redefined. Again, the author plays on feminist attempts to broaden notions such as sexual abuse, rape, and sexual harassment.

30 A raised consciousness in this area [feminism] plays with propositions of the form "X per cent of women have experienced sexual interference before the age of Y," where X is a very large number, and Y as low as you care to make it, and "sexual interference" defined so broadly that *it can include hearing an older sibling discuss his/her adolescent sexual experimentation.*[30]

31 Clearly, women's concern with issues such as date rape and sexual abuse is rendered ludicrous and misguided when date rape can refer to "any kind of sexual interaction" or "ordinary bungled sex" and when sexual abuse is defined as overhearing a sibling refer to sexual experimentation. Probably the most violent form of redefinition is the complete obliteration of a term's referent. The following examples suggest that phenomena such as date rape and sexual harassment are creations of the feminist imagination.

32 For the moment, however, there is agreement on the crime *invented* by Professor MacKinnon — sexual harassment stemming from a hostile work environment. That *invention* is only one aspect of her campaign to protect women from men.

33 By campaigning against *the thing called* "date rape," the feminist creates immense hatred and suspicion between men and women, so that the feminist advice to any woman going out on a date is to establish a virtual contract governing what will happen in the course of an evening.

34 As with the *hysteria* a few years ago over the sexual abuse of children, endless talk shows, television news stories, and magazine articles have been devoted to date rape, often describing it as "an epidemic." ... Much of this discussion starts off with *the claim that* one in four female students is raped by a date.[31]

35 The emphasized words and phrases all have a similar function: they express the degree to which the writer believes in the truth of the propositions uttered. More specifically, expressions such as *invention, the thing called,* and *the claim that*

as ways of referring to date rape and sexual harassment denote the writers' lack of confidence in the existence of such occurrences. (The use of quotation marks also calls into question "date rape" as an event in itself and certainly as "an epidemic.") Once *date rape* and *sexual harassment* become non-existent, the attention paid to the phenomena can be characterized as *hysteria*, with all of the stereotypically female connotations that this word conjures up. Invoking the spectre of "female hysteria" serves to delegitimize even further women's concern with "non-events" such as date rape and sexual harassment.

36   It is perhaps not surprising, given the current "backlash" against feminism documented so well by Susan Faludi, that feminist linguistic innovations would be redefined in ways that trivialize many of the important issues arising from the contemporary women's movement. Faludi comments on the role of language in the feminist backlash: "The backlash has succeeded in framing virtually the whole issue of women's rights in its own language. Just as Reaganism shifted political discourse far to the right and demonized liberalism, so the backlash convinced the public that women's 'liberation' was the true contemporary American scourge — the source of an endless laundry list of personal, social, and economic problems."[32] Because meanings are to a large extent socially constructed, feminist linguistic innovations become endowed with sexist-influenced meanings as they circulate within the broader, often sexist speech community. Just as words such as "no" (in the context of a woman refusing a man's sexual advances) can undergo a kind of "semantic reversal" in a sexist culture, so non-sexist and feminist linguistic innovations can also lose their intended meanings as they get infused with the sexist and androcentric social values of the larger community.[33]

Notes:

1. Susan Gal, "Language and Political Economy," *Annual Review of Anthropology* 18 (1989), pp. 345–67; Susan Gal, "Between Speech and Silence: The Problematics of Research on Language and Gender," in Michaela di Leonardo, ed. *Gender at the Crossroads of Knowledge* (Berkeley: University of California Press, 1991), pp. 175–203.

2. Deborah Cameron, *Feminism and Linguistic Theory* (London: Macmillan, 1985).

3. See, for example, Mary Daly, *Gyn/Ecology* (Boston: Beacon Press, 1978); Suzette Haden Elgin, *Native Tongue* (New York: DAW Books, 1984); Dale Spender, *Man Made Language* (London: Routledge, 1980).

4. Benjamin Lee Whorf, *Language, Thought and Reality: Selected Writings of Benjamin Lee Whorf* (Cambridge, Mass.: MIT Press, 1956), pp. 213–14; emphasis in original.

5. David Crystal, *The Cambridge Encyclopedia of Language* (Cambridge: Cambridge University Press, 1987).

6. The phrase comes from M.A.K. Halliday, "Linguistic Function and Literary Style," in Seymour Chatman, ed., *Literary Style: A Symposium* (Oxford: Oxford University Press, 1971), pp. 332–33.

7. Critical linguistics references include, for example, Gunther Kress and Robert Hodge, *Language as Ideology* (London: Routledge and Kegan Paul, 1979); Robert Hodge and Gunther Kress, *Social Semiotics* (Oxford: Polity Press, 1988); and Roger Fowler, *Language in the News* (London: Routledge, 1991).

8. Penelope Eckert and Sally McConnell-Ginet, "Think Practically and Look Locally: Language and Gender as Community-based Practice," *Annual Review of Anthropology* 21 (1992), pp. 461–90.

9. Sally McConnell-Ginet, "Language and Gender," in Frederick Newmeyer, ed., *Linguistics: The Cambridge Survey*, vol. IV (Cambridge: Cambridge University Press, 1988).

10. Ibid., p. 91.

11. See, for example, Pamela Fishman, "Interaction: The Work Women Do," and Candace West and Don Zimmerman, "Small Insults: A Study of Interruptions in Cross-sex Conversations between Unacquainted Persons," in Barrie Thorne, Cheris Kramarae, and Nancy Henley, eds., *Language, Gender and Society* (Rowley, Mass.: Newbury House, 1983). These generalizations about mixed-sex conversations are subject to qualification. Linguistic features such as interruptions or silence do not necessarily have a unitary function in conversation; that is, interruptions do not always signify power and control, and silence does not always signify lack of power. In addition, a number of contextual factors may affect the correlation of conversation features with gender.

12. Muriel Schultz, "The Semantic Derogation of Women," in Barrie Thorne and Nancy Henley, eds., *Language and Sex: Difference and Dominance* (Rowley, Mass.: Newbury House, 1975).

13. Sally McConnell-Ginet, "The Sexual (Re)production of Meaning," in Francine Frank and Paula Treichler, *Language, Gender and Professional Writing* (New York: Modern Language Association, 1989), p. 47.

14. Spender, *Man Made Language*, p. 164.

15. Gloria Steinem, *Outrageous Acts and Everyday Rebellions* (New York: Holt, Rinehart and Winston, 1983), p. 149.

16. I draw here from Susan Ehrlich and Ruth King, "Gender-based Language Reform and the Social Construction of Meaning," *Discourse and Society* 3 (1992),

pp. 151–66; and Susan Ehrlich and Ruth King, "Feminist Meanings and the (De)politicization of the Lexicon," *Language in Society* 23 (1994), pp. 59–76.

17. McConnell-Ginet, "Sexual (Re)production of Meaning."

18. Casey Miller and Kate Swift, *Words and Women* (Garden City, N.Y.: Doubleday, 1976).

19. David Graddol and Joan Swann, *Gender Voices* (Oxford: Basil Blackwell, 1989), p. 97.

20. Julia Penelope, *Speaking Freely: Unlearning the Lies of the Father's Tongue* (Oxford: Pergamon Press, 1990).

21. Francine Frank and Paula Treichler, *Language, Gender and Professional Writing* (New York: Modern Language Association, 1989), p. 218.

22. Donna Atkinson, "Names and Titles: Maiden Name Retention and the Use of Ms.," *Journal of the Atlantic Provinces Linguistic Association* 9 (1987), pp. 56–83.

23. Betty Lou Dubois and Isabel Crouch, "Linguistic Disruption: He/She, S/he, He, or She, He/She," in Joyce Penfield, ed., *Women and Language in Transition* (Albany: State University of New York Press, 1987), pp. 28–35.

24. Michael Silverstein, "Language and the Culture of Gender: At the Intersection of Structure, Usage, and Ideology," in E. Mertz and R. Parmentier, eds., *Semiotic Mediation* (New York: Academic Press, 1985), pp. 219–59.

25. Here I draw from Susan Ehrlich and Ruth King, "Feminist Meanings and the (De)politicization of the Lexicon," *Language in Society* 23 (1994), pp. 59–76.

26. Gretchen Morgenson, "May I Have the Pleasure..." *National Review*, November 18, 1991, pp. 36–41.

27. Janice Castro, "Sexual Harassment: A Guide," *Time* 139 (1992) p. 37.

28. John Taylor, "Are You Politically Correct?" *New York*, January 21, 1991, p. 39; emphasis added.

29. Ibid., p. 39.

30. Kenneth Minogue, "The Goddess That Failed," *National Review*, November 18, 1991, p. 48; emphasis added.

31. Shirley Letwin, "Law and the Unreasonable Woman," *National Review*, November 18, 1991, p. 36; Minogue, "The Goddess That Failed," p. 48;

Taylor, "Are You Politically Correct?" *New York*, January 21, 1991, pp. 38–39. All emphases added.

32. Susan Faludi, *Backlash: The Undeclared War Against American Women* (New York: Crown Publishers, 1991), p. xviii.

33. See Ehrlich and King, "Feminist Meanings and the (De)politicization of the Lexicon," for examples of similar linguistic mechanisms operative in other kinds of political and ideological disputes. I borrow the term "semantic reversal" from Gill Seidel, "The British New Right's 'Enemy Within': The Anti-racists," in Geneva Smitherman-Donaldson and Teun van Dijk, eds., *Discourse and Discrimination* (Detroit: Wayne State University Press, 1988), pp. 131–43.

34. The idea that questions accomplish ideological work comes from Sue Fisher, "A Discourse of the Social: Medical Talk/Power Talk/Oppositional Talk," *Discourse and Society* 2 (1991), pp. 157–82.

Topics for consideration:

1. Ehrlich begins by reviewing the various theories about the role language plays in shaping consciousness. Which of these views is closest to her own?

2. Compare the account Ehrlich gives from McConnell-Ginet (paragraph 8) of mixed-sex conversations with that given by Deborah Tannen earlier in this chapter.

3. Ehrlich notes that we owe such terms as "sexism" and "sexual harassment" to the feminist movement. Would sexism be more likely to go unnoticed if there were no word for it?

4. Ehrlich cites a range of examples from the media in which terms such as "feminism," "sexism," "sexual harassment," and "date rape" are redefined and trivialized. Study your community or campus newspaper for comparable examples. What are the "discursive strategies" that Ehrlich finds in her examples? Are the same ones at work in the examples you find?

Emily Martin (1944-

Emily Martin is Mary Garnett Professor of Anthropology at Johns Hopkins University. She is author of a number of books including The Woman in the Body: A Cultural Analysis of Reproduction *(1992) and* Flexible Bodies: Tacking Immunity in American Culture — From the Days of Polio to the Age of AIDS *(1995).*

Martin's essay examines standard biological texts on human reproduction and discovers that, far from giving an objective account of biological mechanisms, the descriptive language and metaphors used in such texts reproduces the gender stereotypes that prevail in the dominant culture. These texts celebrate sperm production while the role of egg cells is seen as inferior, passive and "wasteful." Even more recent texts that recognize the active role of the egg in fertilization continue to conform to cultural preconceptions.

THE EGG AND THE SPERM: HOW SCIENCE HAS CONSTRUCTED A ROMANCE BASED ON STEREOTYPICAL MALE-FEMALE ROLES

> The theory of the human body is always a part of a world-picture ... The theory of the human body is always a part of a *fantasy.*
> — James Hillman, *The Myth of Analysis*[1]

1 As an anthropologist, I am intrigued by the possibility that culture shapes how biological scientists describe what they discover about the natural world. If this were so, we would be learning about more than the natural world in high school biology class; we would be learning about cultural beliefs and practices as if they were part of nature. In the course of my research I realized that the picture of egg and sperm drawn in popular as well as scientific accounts of reproductive biology relies on stereotypes central to our cultural definitions of male and female. The stereotypes imply not only that female biological processes are less worthy than their male counterparts but also that women are less worthy than men. Part of my goal in writing this article is to shine a bright light on the gender stereotypes hidden within the scientific language of biology. Exposed in such a light, I hope they will lose much of their power to harm us.

EGG AND SPERM: A SCIENTIFIC FAIRY TALE

2 At a fundamental level, all major scientific textbooks depict male and female reproductive organs as systems for the production of valuable substances, such as eggs and sperm.[2] In the case of women, the monthly cycle is described as being designed to produce eggs and prepare a suitable place for them to be fertilized and grown — all to the end of making babies. But the enthusiasm ends there. By extolling the female cycle as a productive enterprise, menstruation must necessarily be viewed as a failure. Medical texts describe menstruation as the "debris"

of the uterine lining, the result of necrosis, or death of tissue. The descriptions imply that a system has gone awry, making products of no use, not to specification, unsalable, wasted, scrap. An illustration in a widely used medical text shows menstruation as a chaotic disintegration of form, complementing the many texts that describe it as "ceasing," "dying," "losing," "denuding," "expelling."[3]

3   Male reproductive physiology is evaluated quite differently. One of the texts that sees menstruation as failed production employs a sort of breathless prose when it describes the maturation of sperm: "The mechanisms which guide the remarkable cellular transformation from spermatid to mature sperm remain uncertain. ... Perhaps the most amazing characteristic of spermatogenesis is its sheer magnitude: the normal human male may manufacture several hundred million sperm per day."[4] In the classic text *Medical Physiology*, edited by Vernon Mountcastle, the male/female, productive/destructive comparison is more explicit: "Whereas the female *sheds* only a single gamete each month, the seminiferous tubules *produce* hundreds of millions of sperm each day" (emphasis mine).[5] The female author of another text marvels at the length of the microscopic seminiferous tubules, which, if uncoiled and placed end to end, "would span almost one-third of a mile!" She writes, "In an adult male these structures produce millions of sperm cells each day." Later she asks, "How is this feat accomplished?"[6] None of these texts expresses such intense enthusiasm for any female processes. It is surely no accident that the "remarkable" process of making sperm involves precisely what, in the medical view, menstruation does not: production of something deemed valuable.[7]

4   One could argue that menstruation and spermatogenesis are not analogous processes and, therefore, should not be expected to elicit the same kind of response. The proper female analogy to spermatogenesis, biologically, is ovulation. Yet ovulation does not merit enthusiasm in these texts either. Textbook descriptions stress that all of the ovarian follicles containing ova are already present at birth. Far from being *produced*, as sperm are, they merely sit on the shelf, slowly degenerating and aging like overstocked inventory: "At birth, normal human ovaries contain an estimated one million follicles [each], and no new ones appear after birth. Thus, in marked contrast to the male, the newborn female already has all the germ cells she will ever have. Only a few, perhaps 400, are destined to reach full maturity during her active productive life. All the others degenerate at some point in their development so that few, if any remain by the time she reaches menopause at approximately 50 years of age."[8] Note the "marked contrast" that this description sets up between male and female, who has stockpiled germ cells by birth and is faced with their degeneration.

5   Nor are the female organs spared such vivid descriptions. One scientist writes in a newspaper article that a woman's ovaries become old and worn out from ripening eggs every month, even though the woman herself is still relatively young: "When you look through a laparoscope ... at an ovary that has been through hundreds of cycles, even in a superbly healthy American female, you see a scarred, battered organ."[9]

6   To avoid the negative connotations that some people associate with the female reproductive system, scientists could begin to describe male and female processes as homologous. They might credit females with "producing" mature

ova one at a time, as they're needed each month, and describe males as having to face problems of degenerating germ cells. This degeneration would occur throughout life among spermatogonia, the undifferentiated germ cells in the testes that are the long-lived, dormant precursors of sperm.

7   But the texts have an almost dogged insistence on casting female processes in a negative light. The texts celebrate sperm production because it is continuous from puberty to senescence, while they portray egg production as inferior because it is finished at birth. This makes the female seem unproductive, but some texts will also insist that it is she who is wasteful.[10] In a section heading for *Molecular Biology of the Cell*, a best-selling text, we are told that "Oogenesis is wasteful." The text goes on to emphasize that of the seven million oogonia, or egg germ cells, in the female embryo, most degenerate in the ovary. Of those that do go on to become oocytes, or eggs, many also degenerate, so that at birth only two million eggs remain in the ovaries. Degeneration continues throughout a woman's life: by puberty 300,000 eggs remain, and only a few are present by menopause. "During the 40 or so years of a woman's reproductive life only 400 to 500 eggs will have been released," the authors write. "All the rest will have degenerated. It is still a mystery why so many eggs are formed only to die in the ovaries."[11]

8   The real mystery is why the male's vast production of sperm is not seen as wasteful.[12] Assuming that a man "produces" 100 million (10^8) sperm per day (a conservative estimate) during an average reproductive life of sixty years, he would produce well over two trillion sperm in his lifetime. Assuming that a woman "ripens" one egg per lunar month, or thirteen per year, over the course of her forty-year reproductive life, she would total five hundred eggs in her lifetime. But the word "waste" implies an excess, too much produced. Assuming two or three offspring, for every baby a woman produces, she wastes only around two hundred eggs. For every baby a man produces, he wastes more than one trillion (10^{12}) sperm.

9   How is it that positive images are denied to the bodies of women? A look at language — in this case, scientific language — provides the first clue. Take the egg and the sperm.[13] It is remarkable how "femininely" the egg behaves and "masculinely" the sperm.[14] The egg is seen as large and passive.[15] It does not *move* or *journey*, but passively "is transported," "is swept,"[16] or even "drifts"[17] along the fallopian tube. In utter contrast, sperm are small, "streamlined,"[18] and invariably active. They "deliver" their genes to the egg, "activate the developmental program of the egg,"[19] and have a "velocity" that is often remarked upon.[20] Their tails are "strong" and efficiently powered.[21] Together with the forces of ejaculation, they can "propel the semen into the deepest recesses of the vagina."[22] For this they need "energy," "fuel,"[23] so that with a "whiplashlike motion and strong lurches"[24] they can "burrow through the egg coat"[25] and "penetrate" it.[26]

10   At its extreme, the age-old relationship of the egg and the sperm takes on a royal or religious patina. The egg coat, its protective barrier, is sometimes called its "vestments," a term usually reserved for sacred, religious dress. The egg is said to have a "corona,"[27] a crown, and to be accompanied by "attendant cells."[28] It is holy, set apart and above, the queen to the sperm's king. The egg is also passive, which means it must depend on sperm for rescue. Gerald Schatten and

Helen Schatten liken the egg's role to that of Sleeping Beauty: "a dormant bride awaiting her mate's magic kiss, which instills the spirit that brings her to life."[29] Sperm, by contrast, have a "mission,"[30] which is to "move through the female genital tract in quest of the ovum."[31] One popular account has it that the sperm carry out a "perilous journey" into the "warm darkness," where some fall away "exhausted." "Survivors" "assault" the egg, the successful candidates "surrounding the prize."[32] Part of the urgency of this journey, in more scientific terms, is that "once released from the supportive environment or the ovary, an egg will die within hours unless rescued by a sperm."[33] The wording stresses the fragility and dependency of the egg, even though the same text acknowledges elsewhere that sperm also live for only a few hours.[34]

11   In 1948, in a book remarkable for its early insights into these matters, Ruth Herschberger argued that female reproductive organs are seen as biologically interdependent, while male organs are viewed as autonomous, operating independently and in isolation:

> At present the functional is stressed only in connection with women: it is in them that ovaries, tubes, uterus, and vagina have endless interdependence. In the male, reproduction would seem to involve "organs" only.
> Yet the sperm, just as much as the egg, is dependent on a great many related processes. There are secretions which mitigate the urine in the urethra before ejaculation, to protect the sperm. There is the reflex shutting off of the bladder connection, the provision of prostatic secretions, and various types of muscular propulsion. The sperm is no more independent of its milieu than the egg, and yet from a wish that it were, biologists have lent their support to the notion that the human female, beginning with the egg, is congenitally more dependent than the male.[35]

12   Bringing out another aspect of the sperm's autonomy, an article in the journal *Cell* has the sperm making an "existential decision" to penetrate the egg: "Sperm are cells with a limited behavioral repertoire, one that is directed toward fertilizing eggs. To execute the decision to abandon the haploid state, sperm swim to an egg and there acquire the ability to effect membrane fusion."[36] Is this a corporate manager's version of the sperm's activities — "executing decisions" while fraught with dismay over difficult options that bring with them very high risk?

13   There is another way that sperm, despite their small size, can be made to loom in importance over the egg. In a collection of scientific papers, an electron micrograph of an enormous egg and tiny sperm is titled "A Portrait of the Sperm."[37] This is a little like showing a photo of a dog and calling it a picture of the fleas. Granted, microscopic sperm are harder to photograph than eggs, which are just large enough to see with the naked eye. But surely the use of the term "portrait," a word associated with the powerful and wealthy, is significant. Eggs have only micrographs or pictures, not portraits.

14   One depiction of sperm as weak and timid, instead of strong and powerful — the only such representation in western civilization, so far as I know — occurs in Woody Allen's movie *Everything You Always Wanted To Know About Sex* * *But Were Afraid to Ask*. Allen, playing the part of an apprehensive sperm inside a man's

testicles, is scared of the man's approaching orgasm. He is reluctant to launch himself into the darkness, afraid of contraceptive devices, afraid of winding up on the ceiling if the man masturbates.

15   The more common picture — egg as damsel in distress, shielded only by her sacred garments; sperm as heroic warrior to the rescue — cannot be proved to be dictated by the biology of these events. While the "facts" of biology may not *always* be constructed in cultural terms, I would argue that in this case they are. The degree of metaphorical content in these descriptions, the extent to which differences between egg and sperm are emphasized, and the parallels between cultural stereotypes of male and female behavior and the character of egg and sperm all point to this conclusion.

NEW RESEARCH, OLD IMAGERY

16   As new understandings of egg and sperm emerge, textbook gender imagery is being revised. But the new research, far from escaping the stereotypical representations of egg and sperm, simply replicates elements of textbook gender imagery in a different form. The persistence of this imagery calls to mind what Ludwig Fleck termed "the self-contained" nature of scientific thought. As he described it, "the interaction between what is already known, what remains to be learned, and those who are to apprehend it, go to ensure harmony within the system. But at the same time they also preserve the harmony of illusions, which is quite secure within the confines of a given thought style."[38] We need to understand the way in which the cultural content in scientific descriptions changes as biological discoveries unfold, and whether that cultural content is solidly entrenched or easily changed.

17   In all of the texts quoted above, sperm are described as penetrating the egg, and specific substances on a sperm's head are described as binding to the egg. Recently, this description of events was rewritten in a biophysics lab at Johns Hopkins University — transforming the egg from the passive to the active party.[39]

18   Prior to this research, it was thought that the zona, the inner vestments of the egg, formed an impenetrable barrier. Sperm overcame the barrier by mechanically burrowing through, thrashing their tails and slowly working their way along. Later research showed that the sperm released digestive enzymes that chemically broke down the zona; thus, scientists presumed that the sperm used mechanical and chemical means to get through to the egg.

19   In this recent investigation, the researchers began to ask questions about the mechanical force of the sperm's tail. (The lab's goal was to develop a contraceptive that worked topically on sperm.) They discovered, to their great surprise, that the forward thrust of sperm is extremely weak, which contradicts the assumption that sperm are forceful penetrators.[40] Rather than thrusting forward, the sperm's head was now seen to move mostly back and forth. The sideways motion of the sperm's tail makes the head move sideways with a force that is ten times stronger than its forward movement. So even if the overall force of the sperm were strong enough to mechanically break the zona, most of its force would be directed sideways rather than forward. In fact, its strongest tendency, by tenfold, is to *escape* by attempting to pry itself off the egg. Sperm, then, must

be exceptionally efficient at escaping from any cell surface they contact. And the surface of the egg must be designed to trap the sperm and prevent their escape. Otherwise, few if any sperm would reach the egg.

20   The researchers at Johns Hopkins concluded that the sperm and egg stick together because of adhesive molecules on the surfaces of each. The egg traps the sperm and adheres to it so tightly that the sperm's head is forced to lie flat against the surface of the zona, a little bit, they told me, "like Br'er Rabbit getting more and more stuck to tar baby the more he wriggles." The trapped sperm continues to wiggle ineffectually side to side. The mechanical force of its tail is so weak that a sperm cannot break even one chemical bond. This is where the digestive enzymes released by the sperm come in. If they start to soften the zona just at the tip of the sperm and the sides remain stuck, then the weak, flailing sperm can get oriented in the right direction and make it through the zona — provided that its bonds to the zona dissolve as it moves in.

21   Although this new version of the saga of the egg and the sperm broke through cultural expectations, the researchers who made the discovery continued to write papers and abstracts as if the sperm were the active party who attacks, binds, penetrates, and enters the egg. The only difference was that the sperm were now seen as performing these actions weakly.[41] Not until August 1987, more than three years after the findings described above, did these researchers reconceptualize the process to give the egg a more active role. They began to describe the zona as an aggressive sperm catcher, covered with adhesive molecules that can capture a sperm with a single bond and clasp it to the zona's surface.[42] In the words of their published account: "The innermost vestment, the *zona pellucida*, is a glycoprotein shell, which captures and tethers the sperm before they penetrate it. ... The sperm is captured at the initial contact between the sperm tip and the *zona*. ... Since the thrust [of the sperm] is much smaller than the force needed to break a single affinity bond, the first bond made upon the tip-first meeting of the sperm and *zona* can result in the capture of the sperm."[43]

22   Experiments in another lab reveal similar patterns of data interpretation. Gerald Schatten and Helen Schatten set out to show that, contrary to conventional wisdom, the "egg is not merely a large, yolk-filled sphere into which the sperm burrows to endow new life. Rather, recent research suggests the almost heretical view that sperm and egg are mutually active partners."[44] This sounds like a departure from the stereotypical textbook view, but further reading reveals Schatten and Schatten's conformity to the aggressive-sperm metaphor. They describe how "the sperm and egg first touch when, from the tip of the sperm's triangular head, a long, thin filament shoots out and harpoons the egg." Then we learn that "remarkably, the harpoon is not so much fired as assembled at great speed, molecule by molecule, from a pool of protein stored in a specialized region called the acrosome. The filament may grow as much as twenty times longer than the sperm head itself before its tip reaches the egg and sticks."[45] Why not call this "making a bridge" or "throwing out a line" rather than firing a harpoon? Harpoons pierce prey and injure or kill them, while this filament only sticks. And why not focus, as the Hopkins lab did, on the stickiness of the egg, rather than the stickiness of the sperm?[46] Later in the article, the Schattens replicate the common view of the sperm's perilous journey into the warm darkness of the vagina,

this time for the purpose of explaining its journey into the egg itself: "[The sperm] still has an arduous journey ahead. It must penetrate farther into the egg's huge sphere of cytoplasm and somehow locate the nucleus, so that the two cells' chromosomes can fuse. The sperm dives down into the cytoplasm, its tail beating. But it is soon interrupted by the sudden and swift migration of the egg nucleus, which rushes toward the sperm with a velocity triple that of the movement of chromosomes during cell division, crossing the entire egg in about a minute."[47]

23   Like Schatten and Schatten and the biophysicists at Johns Hopkins, another researcher has recently made discoveries that seem to point to a more interactive view of the relationship of egg and sperm. This work, which Paul Wassarman conducted on the sperm and eggs of mice, focuses on identifying the specific molecules in the egg coal (the zona pellucida) that are involved in egg-sperm interaction. At first glance, his descriptions seem to fit the model of an egalitarian relationship. Male and female gametes "recognize one another," and "interactions … take place between sperm and egg."[48] But the article in *Scientific American* in which those descriptions appear begins with a vignette that presages the dominant motif of their presentation: "It has been more than a century since Hermann Fol, a Swiss zoologist, peered into his microscope and became the first person to see a sperm penetrate an egg, fertilize it and form the first cell of a new embryo."[49] This portrayal of the sperm as the active party — the one that *penetrates* and *fertilizes* the egg and *produces* the embryo — is not cited as an example of an earlier, now outmoded view. In fact, the author reiterates the point later in the article: "Many sperm can bind to and penetrate the zona pellucida, or outer coat, of an unfertilized mouse egg, but only one sperm will eventually fuse with the thin plasma membrane surrounding the egg proper (*inner sphere*), *fertilizing the egg and giving rise to a new embryo.*"[50]

24   The imagery of sperm as aggressor is particularly startling in this case: the main discovery being reported is isolation of a particular molecule *on the egg coat* that plays an important role in fertilization! Wassarman's choice of language sustains the picture. He calls the molecule that has been isolated, ZP3, a "sperm receptor." By allocating the passive, waiting role to the egg, Wassarman can continue to describe the sperm as the actor, the one that makes it all happen: "The basic process begins when many sperm first attach loosely and then bind tenaciously to receptors on the surface of the egg's thick outer coat, the zona pellucida. Each sperm, which has a large number of egg-binding proteins on its surface, binds to many sperm receptors on the egg. More specifically, a site on each of the egg-binding proteins fits a complementary site on a sperm receptor, much as a key fits a lock."[51] With the sperm designated as the "key" and the egg the "lock," it is obvious which one acts and which one is acted upon. Could this imagery not be reversed, letting the sperm (the lock) wait until the egg produces the key? Or could we speak of two halves of a locket matching, and regard the matching itself as the action that initiates the fertilization?

25   It is as if Wassarman were determined to make the egg the receiving partner. Usually in biological research, the protein member of the pair of binding molecules is called the receptor, and physically it has a pocket in it rather like a lock. As the diagrams that illustrate Wassarman's article show, the molecules on

the sperm are proteins and have "pockets." The small, mobile molecules that fit into these pockets are called ligands. As shown in the diagrams, ZP3 on the egg is a polymer of "keys"; many small knobs stick out. Typically, molecules in the sperm would be called receptors and molecules on the egg would be called ligands. But Wassarman chose to name ZP3 on the egg the receptor and to create a new term, "the egg-binding protein," for the molecule on the sperm that otherwise would have been called the receptor.[52]

26   Wassarman does credit the egg coat with having more functions than those of a sperm receptor. While he notes that "the zona pellucida has at times been viewed by investigators as a nuisance, a barrier to sperm and hence an impediment to fertilization," his new research reveals that the egg coat "serves as a sophisticated biological security system that screens incoming sperm, selects only those compatible with fertilization and development, prepares sperm for fusion with the egg and later protects the resulting embryo from polyspermy [a lethal condition caused by fusion of more than one sperm with a single egg]."[53] Although this description gives the egg an active role, that role is drawn in stereotypically feminine terms. The egg *selects* an appropriate mate, *prepares* him for fusion, and then *protects* the resulting offspring from harm. This is courtship and mating behavior as seen through the eyes of a sociobiologist: woman as the hard-to-get prize, who, following union with the chosen one, becomes woman as servant and mother.

27   And Wassarman does not quit there. In a review article for *Science*, he outlines the "chronology of fertilization."[54] Near the end of the article are two subject headings. One is "Sperm Penetration," in which Wassarman describes how the chemical dissolving of the zona pellucida combines with the "substantial propulsive force generated by sperm." The next heading is "Sperm-Egg Fusion." This section details what happens inside the zona after a sperm "penetrates" it. Sperm "can make contact with, adhere to, and fuse with (that is, fertilize) an egg."[55] Wassarman's word choice, again, is astonishingly skewed in favor of the sperm's activity, for in the next breath he says that sperm *lose* all motility upon fusion with the egg's surface. In mouse and sea urchin eggs, the sperm enters at the *egg's* volition, according to Wassarman's description: "Once fused with egg plasma membrane [the surface of the egg], how does a sperm enter the egg? The surface of both mouse and sea urchin eggs is covered with thousands of plasma membrane-bound projections, called microvilli [tiny 'hairs']. Evidence in sea urchins suggests that, after membrane fusion, a group of elongated microvilli cluster tightly around and interdigitate over the sperm head. As these microvilli are resorbed, the sperm is drawn into the egg. Therefore, sperm motility, which ceases at the time of fusion in both sea urchins and mice, is not required for sperm entry."[56] The section called "Sperm Penetration" more logically would be followed by a section called "The Egg Envelopes," rather than "Sperm-Egg Fusion." This would give a parallel — and more accurate — sense that both the egg and the sperm initiate action.

28   Another way that Wassarman makes less of the egg's activity is by describing components of the egg but referring to the sperm as a whole entity. Deborah Gordon has described such an approach as "atomism" ("the part is independent of and primordial to the whole") and identified it as one of the "tenacious

assumptions" of Western science and medicine.[57] Wassarman employs atomism to his advantage. When he refers to processes going on within sperm, he consistently returns to descriptions that remind us from whence these activities came: they are part of sperm that penetrate an egg or generate propulsive force. When he refers to processes going on within eggs, he stops there. As a result, any active role he grants them appears to be assigned to the parts of the egg, and not to the egg itself. In the quote above, it is the microvilli that actively cluster around the sperm. In another example, "the driving force for engulfment of a fused sperm comes from a region of cytoplasm just beneath an egg's plasma membrane."[58]

SOCIAL IMPLICATIONS

29 All three of these revisionist accounts of egg and sperm cannot seem to escape the hierarchical imagery of older accounts. Even though each new account gives the egg a larger and more active role, taken together they bring into play another cultural stereotype: woman as a dangerous and aggressive threat. In the Johns Hopkins lab's revised model, the egg ends up as the female aggressor who "captures and tethers" the sperm with her sticky zona, rather like a spider lying in wait in her web.[59] The Schatten lab has the egg's nucleus "interrupt" the sperm's dive with a "sudden and swift" rush by which she "clasps the sperm and guides its nucleus to the center."[60] Wassarman's description of the surface of the egg "covered with thousands of plasma membrane-bound projections, called microvilli" that reach out and clasp the sperm adds to the spiderlike imagery.[61]

30 These images grant the egg an active role but at the cost of appearing disturbingly aggressive. Images of woman as dangerous and aggressive, the femme fatale who victimizes men, are widespread in Western literature and culture.[62] More specific is the connection of spider imagery with the idea of an engulfing, devouring mother.[63] New data did not lead scientists to eliminate gender stereotypes in their descriptions of egg and sperm. Instead, scientists simply began to describe egg and sperm in different, but no less damaging, terms.

31 Can we envision a less stereotypical view? Biology itself provides another model that could be applied to the egg and the sperm. The cybernetic model — with its feedback loops, flexible adaptation to change, coordination of the parts within a whole, evolution over time, and changing response to the environment — is common in genetics, endocrinology, and ecology and has a growing influence in medicine in general.[64] This model has the potential to shift our imagery from the negative, in which the female reproductive system is castigated both for not producing eggs after birth and for producing (and thus wasting) too many eggs overall, to something more positive. The female reproductive system could be seen as responding to the environment (pregnancy or menopause), adjusting to monthly changes (menstruation), and flexibly changing from reproductivity after puberty to nonreproductivity later in life. The sperm and egg's interaction could also be described in cybernetic terms. J.F. Hartman's research in reproductive biology demonstrated fifteen years ago that if an egg is killed by being pricked with a needle, live sperm cannot get through the zona.[65] Clearly, this evidence shows that the egg and sperm do interact on more mutual terms, making biology's refusal to portray them that way all the more disturbing.

32   We would do well to be aware, however, that cybernetic imagery is hardly neutral. In the past, cybernetic models have played an important part in the imposition of social control. These models inherently provide a way of thinking about a "field" of interacting components. Once the field can be seen, it can become the object of new forms of knowledge, which in turn can allow new forms of social control to be exerted over the components of the field. During the 1950s, for example, medicine began to recognize the psychosocial *environment* of the patient: the patient's family and its psychodynamics. Professions such as social work began to focus on this new environment, and the resulting knowledge became one way to further control the patient. Patients began to be seen not as isolated, individual bodies, but as psychosocial entities located in an "ecological" system: management of "the patient's psychology was a new entrée to patient control."[66]

33   The models that biologists use to describe their data can have important social effects. During the nineteenth century, the social and natural sciences strongly influenced each other: the social ideas of Malthus about how to avoid the natural increase of the poor inspired Darwin's *Origin of Species*.[67] Once the *Origin* stood as a description of the natural world, complete with competition and market struggles, it could be reimported into social science as social Darwinism, in order to justify the social order of the time. What we are seeing now is similar: the importation of cultural ideas about passive females and heroic males into the "personalities" of gametes. This amounts to the "implanting of social imagery on representations of nature so as to lay a firm basis for reimporting exactly that same imagery as natural explanations of social phenomena."[68]

34   Further research would show us exactly what social effects are being wrought from the biological imagery of egg and sperm. At the very least, the imagery keeps alive some of the hoariest old stereotypes about weak damsels in distress and their strong male rescuers. That these stereotypes are now being written in at the level of the cell constitutes a powerful move to make them seem so natural as to be beyond alteration.

35   The stereotypical imagery might also encourage people to imagine that what results from the interaction of egg and sperm — a fertilized egg — is the result of deliberate "human" action at the cellular level. Whatever the intentions of the human couple, in this microscopic "culture" a cellular "bride" (or femme fatale) and a cellular "groom" (her victim) make a cellular baby. Rosalind Petchesky points out that through visual representations such as sonograms, we are given "*images* of younger and younger, and tinier and tinier, fetuses being 'saved.'" This leads to "the point of visibility being 'pushed back' *indefinitely*."[69] Endowing egg and sperm with intentional action, a key aspect of personhood in our culture, lays the foundation for the point of viability being pushed back to the moment of fertilization. This will likely lead to greater acceptance of technological developments and new forms of scrutiny and manipulation, for the benefit of these inner "persons": court-ordered restrictions on a pregnant woman's activities in order to protect her fetus, fetal surgery, amniocentesis, and rescinding of abortion rights, to name but a few examples.[70]

36   Even if we succeed in substituting more egalitarian, interactive metaphors to describe the activities of egg and sperm, and manage to avoid the pitfalls of cybernetic models, we would still be guilty of endowing cellular entities with

personhood. More crucial, then, than what *kinds* of personalities we bestow on cells is the very fact that we are doing it at all. This process could ultimately have the most disturbing social consequences.

One clear feminist challenge is to wake up sleeping metaphors in science, particularly those involved in descriptions of the egg and the sperm. Although the literary convention is to call such metaphors "dead," they are not so much dead as sleeping, hidden within the scientific content of texts — and all the more powerful for it.[71] Waking up such metaphors, by becoming aware of when we are projecting cultural imagery onto what we study, will improve our ability to investigate and understand nature. Waking up such metaphors, by becoming aware of their implications, will rob them of their power to naturalize our social conventions about gender.

Notes:

1. James Hillman, *The Myth of Analysis* (Evanston, Ill.: Northwestern University Press, 1972), 220.

2. The textbooks I consulted are the main ones used in classes for undergraduate premedical students or medical students (or those held on reserve in the library for these classes) during the past few years at Johns Hopkins University. These texts are widely used at other universities in the country as well.

3. Arthur C. Guyton, *Physiology of the Human Body*, 6th ed. (Philadelphia: Saunders College Publishing, 1984), 624.

4. Arthur J. Vander, James H. Sherman, and Dorothy S. Luciano, *Human Physiology: The Mechanisms of Body Function*, 3rd ed. (New York: McGraw-Hill, 1980), 483–84.

5. Vernon B. Mountcastle, *Medical Physiology*, 14th ed. (London: Mosby, 1980), 2:1624.

6. Eldra Pearl Solomon, *Human Anatomy and Physiology* (New York: CBS College Publishing, 1983), 678.

7. For elaboration, see Emily Martin, *The Woman in the Body: A Cultural Analysis of Reproduction* (Boston: Beacon, 1987), 27–53.

8. Vander, Sherman, and Luciano, 568.

9. Melvin Konner, "Childbearing and Age," *New York Times Magazine* (December 27, 1987), 22–23, esp. 22.

10. I have found but one exception to the opinion that the female is wasteful: "Smallpox being the nasty disease it is, one might expect nature to have designed antibody molecules with combining sites that specifically recognize the epitopes on smallpox virus. Nature differs from technology, however: it thinks nothing of wastefulness. (For example, rather than improving the chance that a spermatozoon will meet an egg cell, nature finds it easier to produce millions of spermatozoa.)" (Niels Kaj Jerne, "The Immune System," *Scientific American* 229, no. 1 [July 1973]: 53.) Thanks to a *Signs* reviewer for bringing this reference to my attention.

11. Bruce Alberts et al., *Molecular Biology of the Cell* (New York: Garland, 1983), 795.

12. In her essay "Have Only Men Evolved?" (in *Discovering Reality: Feminist Perspectives on Epistemology, Metaphysics, Methodology, and Philosophy of Science*, ed. Sandra Harding and Merrill B. Hintikka [Dordrecht: Reidel, 1983], 45–69, esp. 60–61), Ruth Hubbard points out that sociobiologists have said the female invests more energy than the male in the production of her large gametes, claiming that this explains why the female provides parental care. Hubbard questions whether it "really takes more 'energy' to generate the one or relatively few eggs than the large excess of sperms required to achieve fertilization." For further critique of how the greater size of eggs is interpreted in sociobiology, see Donna Haraway, "Investment Strategies for the Evolving Portfolio of Primate Females," in *Body/Politics*, ed. Mary Jacobus, Evelyn Fox Keller, and Sally Shuttleworth (New York: Routledge, 1990), 155–56.

13. The sources I used for this article provide compelling information on interactions among sperm. Lack of space prevents me from taking up this theme here, but the elements include competition, hierarchy, and sacrifice. For a newspaper report, see Malcolm W. Browne, "Some Thoughts on Self Sacrifice," *New York Times* (July 5, 1988), C6. For a literary rendition, see John Barth, "Night-Sea Journey," in his *Lost in the Funhouse* (Garden City, N.Y.: Doubleday, 1968), 3–13.

14. See Carol Delaney, "The Meaning of Paternity and the Virgin Birth Debate," *Man* 21, no. 3 (September 1986): 494–513. She discusses the difference between this scientific view that women contribute genetic material to the fetus and the claim of long-standing Western folk theories that the origin and identity of the fetus comes from the male, as in the metaphor of planting a seed in soil.

15. For a suggested direct link between human behavior and purportedly passive eggs and active sperm, see Erik H. Erikson, "Inner and Outer Space: Reflections on Womanhood," *Daedalus* 93, no. 2 (Spring 1964): 582–606, esp. 591.

16. Guyton (n. 3 above), 619; and Mountcastle (n. 5 above), 1609.

17. Jonathan Miller and David Pelham, *The Facts of Life* (New York: Viking Penguin, 1984), 5.

18. Alberts et al., 796.

19. Ibid., 796.

20. See, e.g., William F. Ganong, *Review of Medical Physiology*, 7th ed. (Los Altos, Calif.: Lange Medical Publications, 1975), 322.

21. Alberts et al. (n. 11 above), 796.

22. Guyton, 615.

23. Solomon (n. 6 above), 683.

24. Vander, Sherman, and Luciano (n. 4 above), 4th ed. (1985), 580.

25. Alberts et al., 796.

26. All biology texts quoted above use the word "penetrate."

27. Solomon, 700.

28. A. Beldecos et al., "The Importance of Feminist Critique for Contemporary Cell Biology," *Hypatia* 3, no. 1 (Spring 1988): 61–76.

29. Gerald Schatten and Helen Schatten, "The Energetic Egg," *Medical World News* 23 (January 23, 1984): 51–53, esp. 51.

30. Alberts et al., 796.

31. Guyton (n. 3 above), 613.

32. Miller and Pelham (n. 17 above), 7.

33. Alberts et al. (n. 11 above), 804.

34. Ibid., 801.

35. Ruth Herschberger, *Adam's Rib* (New York: Pelligrini Cudaby, 1948), esp. 84. I am indebted to Ruth Hubbard for telling me about Herschberger's work, although at a point when this paper was already in draft form.

36. Bennett M. Shapiro. "The Existential Decision of a Sperm," *Cell* 49, no. 3 (May 1987): 293–94, esp. 293.

37. Lennart Nilsson, "A Portrait of the Sperm," in *The Functional Anatomy of the Spermatozoan*, ed. Bjorn A. Afzelius (New York: Pergamon, 1975), 79–82.

38. Ludwik Fleck, *Genesis and Development of a Scientific Fact*, ed. Thaddeus J. Trenn and Robert K. Merton (Chicago: University of Chicago Press, 1979), 38.

39. Jay M. Baltz carried out the research I describe when he was a graduate student in the Thomas C. Jenkins Department of Biophysics at Johns Hopkins University.

40. Far less is known about the physiology of sperm than comparable female substances, which some feminists claim is no accident. Greater scientific scrutiny of female reproduction has long enabled the burden of birth control to be placed on women. In this case, the researchers' discovery did not depend on development of any new technology: The experiments made use of glass pipettes, a manometer, and a simple microscope, all of which have been available for more than one hundred years.

41. Jay Baltz and Richard A. Cone, "What Force Is Needed to Tether a Sperm?" (abstract for Society for the Study of Reproduction, 1985), and "Flagellar Torque on the Head Determines the Force Needed to Tether a Sperm" (abstract for Biophysical Society, 1986).

42. Jay M. Baltz, David F. Katz, and Richard A. Cone, "The Mechanics of the Sperm-Egg Interaction at the Zona Pellucida," *Biophysical Journal 54*, no. 4 (October 1988): 643–54. Lab members were somewhat familiar with work on metaphors in the biology of female reproduction. Richard Cone, who runs the lab, is my husband, and he talked with them about my earlier research on the subject from time to time. Even though my current research focuses on biological imagery and I heard about the lab's work from my husband every day, I myself did not recognize the role of imagery in the sperm research until many weeks after the period of research and writing I describe. Therefore, I assume that any awareness the lab members may have had about how underlying metaphor might be guiding this particular research was fairly inchoate.

43. Ibid., 643, 650.

44. Schatten and Schatten (n. 29 above), 51.

45. Ibid., 52.

46. Surprisingly, in an article intended for a general audience, the authors do not point out that these are sea urchin sperm and note that human sperm do not shoot out filaments at all.

47. Schatten and Schatten, 53.

48. Paul M. Wassarman, "Fertilization in Mammals," *Scientific American 259*, no. 6 (December 1988): 78–84, esp. 78, 84.

49. Ibid., 78.

50. Ibid., 79.

51. Ibid., 78.

52. Since receptor molecules are relatively *immotile* and the ligands that bind to them relatively *motile*, one might imagine the egg being called the receptor and the sperm the ligand. But the molecules in question on egg and sperm are immotile molecules. It is the sperm as a *cell* that has motility, and the egg as a cell that has relative immotility.

53. Wassarman, 78–79.

54. Paul M. Wassarman, "The Biology and Chemistry of Fertilization," *Science 235*, no. 4788 (January 30, 1987): 553–60, esp. 554.

55. Ibid., 557.

56. Ibid, 557–58. This finding throws into question Schatten and Schatten's description (n. 29 above) of the sperm, its tail beating, diving down into the egg.

57. Deborah R. Gordon, "Tenacious Assumptions in Western Medicine," in *Biomedicine Examined*, ed. Margaret Lock and Deborah Gordon (Dordrecht: Kluwer, 1988), 19–56, esp. 26.

58. Wassarman, "The Biology and Chemistry of Fertilization," 558.

59. Baltz, Katz, and Cone (n. 42 above), 643, 650.

60. Schatten and Schatten, 53.

61. Wassarman, "The Biology and Chemistry of Fertilization," 557.

62. Mary Ellman, *Thinking about Women* (New York: Harcourt Brace Jovanovich, 1968), 140; Nina Auerbach, *Woman and the Demon* (Cambridge. Mass.: Harvard University Press, 1982), esp. 186.

63. Kenneth Alan Adams, "Arachnophobia: Love American Style," *Journal of Psychoanalytic Anthropology* 4, no. 2 (1981): 157–97.

64. William Ray Arney and Bernard Bergen, *Medicine and the Management of Living* (Chicago: University of Chicago Press, 1984).

65. J.F. Hartman, R.B. Gwatkin, and C.F. Hutchison, "Early Contact Interactions between Mammalian Gametes In Vitro," *Proceedings of the National Academy of Sciences* (U.S.) 69, no. 10 (1972): 2767–69.

66. Arney and Bergen, 68.

67. Ruth Hubbard, "Have Only Men Evolved?" (n. 12 above), 51–52.

68. David Harvey, personal communication, November 1989.

69. Rosalind Petchesky, "Fetal Images: The Power of Visual Culture in the Politics of Reproduction," *Feminist Studies* 13, no. 2 (Summer 1987): 263–92, esp. 272.

70. Rita Arditti, Renate Klein, and Shelley Minden, *Test-Tube Women* (London: Pandora. 1984); Ellen Goodman, "Whose Right to Life?" *Baltimore Sun* (November 17, 1987); Tamar Lewin, "Courts Acting to Force Care of the Unborn," *New York Times* (November 23, 1987), A1 and B10; Susan Irwin and Brigitte Jordan, "Knowledge, Practice, and Power: Court Ordered Cesarean Sections," *Medical Anthropology Quarterly 1*, no. 3 (September 1987): 319–34.

71. Thanks to Elizabeth Fee and David Spain, who in February 1989 and April 1989, respectively, made points related to this.

Topics for consideration:

1. What are the different connotations of some of the terms that Martin contrasts, for example "sheds," as opposed to "produces" in paragraph 3?

2. Martin argues that the contrasting language repeatedly applied to the egg and sperm in the texts she examines echoes existing cultural stereotypes. What cultural stereotypes would account for the description of the "waste" of egg cells compared to the "production" of sperm?

3. Martin examines Wassarman's choice of language (paragraphs 24 to 28), especially his use of the lock/key metaphor. Based on the information that Martin provides about current knowledge of the physiological facts of egg/sperm interaction, what metaphor or metaphors might be more accurate?

4. Martin points out that the writers of scientific texts persist in using language so heavily influenced by cultural stereotypes that it gives a faulty impression about biological facts. Are there other fields of study in which the same sort of bias occurs?

Further reading:

Ruth Hubbard, *The Politics of Women's Biology* (1991)

Evelyn Fox Keller, *Refiguring Life: Metaphors of Twentieth Century Biology* (1995)

Barbara T. Gates and Ann B. Shteir, eds., *Natural Eloquence: Women Reinscribe Science* (1997)

CHAPTER 4

WOUNDING WORDS

"**S**ticks and stones may break my bones," goes the schoolyard chant, "But words can never hurt me." The reality, of course, is that words do hurt and that all of us at one time or another have been wounded by them. The careless remark, the deliberate insult and, most of all, the slur that marks us out as a member of a targeted group, all have the power to wound and wound deeply.

In "Heard Any Good Jews Lately," Thomas Friedmann takes the view that jokes targeting Jews, far from harmlessly letting off steam, help create an environment in which prejudice can flourish. Such jokes are, in his view, at one end of a continuum that ends in the vicious dehumanizing language of the Nazi propagandists and leads eventually to a mentality that finds mass murder acceptable. Gloria Naylor, on the other hand, in writing about one of the most explosive words in the racist lexicon, "nigger," describes a range of ways in which that word can be used to transform it from a tool of white hatred to one that signifies "varied and complex human beings."

Words intended to wound, especially those directed at groups, often carry with them the threat of physical violence. Rachel Giese's "Hating the Hate-Crimes Bill" begins with a scene in which a gay and lesbian street demonstration is harrassed by a mob of several hundred threatening to "rape our dyke and faggot asses." Despite being the target of such words and the potential victim of the violence they threaten, Giese refuses to support the hate-crimes legislation that might seem to offer protection.

For the most part when we think of words being used as weapons, the examples that spring to mind are those of hate propaganda and other material directed at particular groups. But everyday life teems with examples of both spoken and written words intended to wound. Consider, for example, the phenomenon of "flaming" on the Internet. At times the lacerating effects of such words linger long after they have been spoken or written. Lynn Crosbie's memoir of Toronto poet Daniel Jones describes the continuing ripples of distress caused by Jones's "last piece of writing," his long suicide note.

Thomas Friedmann (1947-

Thomas Friedmann is a fiction writer and author of Damaged Goods *(1985).*

Friedmann's essay traces the mass murder of Jews by the Nazis to the way in which the language used by propagandists "primed the populace to accept psychologically the annihilation of … Jews." By using words like "vermin" Hitler's propagandists spread the view that Jews were somehow subhuman. Friedmann sees the hate-propaganda that resulted in the Holocaust as the end of a continuum that begins with anti-Semitic jokes that, far from being harmless, prepare the soil "for another little seed of prejudice."

HEARD ANY GOOD JEWS LATELY?

1   The horrors of mass murder can be made bearable if the intended victim is made to appear an object that deserves extermination. The Nazis understood this. Thus, while their bureaucrats searched for the means by which the wholesale destruction of Europe's Jews could be carried out, their propagandists primed the populace to accept psychologically the annihilation of those Jews. In their manipulation of language to justify the "Final Solution," the Nazis resorted to terminology that had been utilized earlier to render Jews subhuman. Martin Luther, urging the expulsion of Jews, had written about them as "a plague and a pestilence." In 1895, three and a half centuries after Luther, a deputy in the German *Reichstag* made clear that Luther's characterization had not been forgotten. He described Jews as "parasites" and "cholera germs." Hitler's propagandists preserved the tradition. They continued to disseminate the notion that Jews were a lower species of life, designating them "vermin," "lice," and "bacilli."

2   Then, in an act that might be considered almost poetic were it not so horrifying and grotesque, the Nazi administrative apparatus captured the spirit of the metaphor its propagandists had devised. It contacted the chemical industries of the *Reich*, specifically the firms that specialized in "combating vermin." Simply, it requested that these manufacturers of insecticides produce another delousing agent, one a bit stronger than the product used for household ticks and flies, but one that would be used for essentially the same purpose. The companies complied. Thus was *Zyklon B* created. The gas, used in a milder form for occasionally fumigating the disease-ridden barracks where other victims were penned, killed millions of men, women, and children. Obscenely clinging to the metaphor they had accepted, the Nazis herded their Jewish victims into gas chambers of death that were disguised as "showers" and "disinfectant centers."

3   What the bureaucrats accomplished, the propagandists had made psychologically possible. How could anyone object when, with the whiff of invisible gas from the crackling blue crystals of *Zyklon B*, millions of Jews were exterminated? Is not extermination the deserved fate of all vermin?

4   But that was Nazi Germany, people tend to say. The mass murder of so many people was an aberration, an accident of history. That artificial, created language

that made it possible for participants to accept the horror of the Holocaust would not have the power again. Surely, that manufactured imagery, that inhuman metaphor, no matter how traditional, can never again conceal that these are Jews that are being threatened, not subhuman creatures. Call them by their name — Jew — and you could never forget that they are people. Certainly the name is an affirmation. *Jew*, by way of Middle English *Giv*, Old French *juiu*, Latin *Judæus*, and Hebrew *Yehudi*, derives from Judah, the foremost of the Twelve Tribes of Israel. Its name means "praised," its emblem is the lion, it has borne a line of kings. Surely the name itself can withstand the ravages of prejudice!

5   But the King's English has not retained the proud heritage of the name. Eric Partridge, in *A Dictionary of Slang and Unconventional English*, lists *Jew* as a verb meaning "to drive a hard bargain," or "to overreach or cheat." In addition, *Jew* as prefix yields to *Jew-down*, meaning to haggle unfairly, *Jew-bail*, meaning "worthless bail," *Jew-balance*, a name for the hammerhead shark, *Jew-food*, mockingly ham, the food forbidden to Jews, *Jew's harp*, whose French origin has nothing to do with Jews but whose sound was picked up by English dramatists to mean Jew and hence an instrument of lesser value, and finally, two astounding phrases, *worth a Jew's eye* and *a Jüdische compliment* or *a Jew's compliment*. As with the slur *sheeny*, which is probably a perversion of the flattering *shaine* (Yiddish) or *schön* (German), meaning "beautiful," both of these apparent phrases of flattery are, in fact, derogatory. To receive *a Jew's compliment* is apparently to be blessed with the misfortune of having "a large penis but little money." The great worth of *a Jew's eye* exists because that was the organ removed when a Jew failed to pay his levy or tax. Another source suggests that it was the teeth that would be threatened with removal. Because Jews invariably paid up, the expression became popular, as in, "If a Jew is willing to pay that much for his teeth, imagine the worth of a Jew's eye."

6   *Jew* also figures in the acronym JAP, applied to certain young women. A JAP, Jewish American Princess, is meant to describe a pampered, snobbish, money-conscious female who is princess in her parents' household. *Jew* is also a pejorative when used in *Jewess*. Why is there no *Protestantess*? Feminists find it doubly offensive, since the -*ess* generally reduces the worth of the noun, as in *poetess*. And, when accounting is dubbed *Jewish engineering*, a cash register a *Jewish piano*, and a dollar bill the *Jewish flag*, the term *Jew* is unmistakably being used as an insult. One thinks of the Greeks for whom anyone not Greek was a foreigner and hence primitive and uncivilized, a barbarian. Imagine the Jew whose very name is a negative term. Naming himself, he excludes himself from mankind.

7   Only the use of *Indian* comes to mind in this context. As *Jew*, *Indian* is often found as a damning prefix in such compounds as *Indian-cholera*, *Indian giver*, and *Indian tobacco*, this last the name given to a poisonous North American plant. And while the negative use of Indian is at least partially mitigated by positive (*Indian summer*) and neutral uses (*Indian pipe*, *Indian bread*), no balance exists for Jew.

8   Given the derision attached to *Jew* itself, one can imagine the multiplied power of the slur in the slang versions of *Jew*: *Jew-boy*, *geese*, *kike*, *mockie*, and *sheeny*. *Sheeny*, incidentally, is thought by some sources to have come from "shiny," a comment on the brilliantined hair of many young British Jews. The coinage of *kike*, the most familiar of these slurs, is attributed by some writers, rather gleefully perhaps and without documentation, to Jews. According to Ernest Von Den

Haag, German Jewish immigrants, the earlier arrivals to the United States, were the ones who formulated *kike* to identify their Eastern-European brethren, whom they considered their inferiors. The term is thought to have been derived from *-ki* or *-ky*, the final syllable of many Polish and Russian names. More plausible seems Leo Rosten's suggestion that *kike* comes from "kikel," the Yiddish word for circle. This was the mark with which Jewish immigrants would sign their names when they could not write, preferring it to the commonly used X which they thought resembled a cross. Whatever the origin of the term, there is no question that it is a pejorative. At Queen Victoria's court Prime Minister Disraeli wryly defined the name. "A kike," he said, "is a Jewish gentleman who has just left the room."

9   In addition to these opprobations, American English has accepted a great many Yiddish words which are used as insults. A partial list would include: *gonif* (thief), *gunsel* (catamite), *dreck* (feces, junk), *kibbitzer* (irritating bystander), and a host of *sch* words: *schnook, schmuck, schlep, schlock, schmaltzy, schlemiel, schlamazel, schwantz, schnorrer*, and possibly *shyster* (by way of *schiess* — shit). While such easy adoption of foreign words might be considered a sign of the pluralistic nature of the English language and a source of its astonishing variety, the terms cannot help but remind users of their source. Were they not, after all, insults applied by Jews to other Jews in their own tongue?

10   A few words, finally, about Jewish jokes or more precisely, jokes about Jews. One of the more bizarre aspects of Nazi propaganda was its utilization of toys, games, and jokes. German children played with "Jews Get Out," a board game produced by Fabricus Co., and their elders had the opportunity to laugh at caricatures of Jews. A typical one shows a hooknosed Jew in the form of a snake, being crushed under the boot of a National Social German Workers' Party (Nazi) member. Other cartoons, particularly political appeals, contained messages about the acquisitive nature of Jews, and hence, their exploitation of Germans. Below is an update indicating that jokes with a similar message have been reinvented in this country. Note that each of the jokes reproduced below is American, containing either an American locale or an American idiom. These are "Made in USA," not imported and translated.

11   *Question:* How was the Grand Canyon formed?
Answer: A Jew lost a nickel in a crack.

Question: Why do Jews have big noses?
Answer: Air is free.

Question: Why are few Jews in jail?
Answer: Crime doesn't pay.

12   The message in each case is clear. What is the basic nature of Jews? They are money-hungry creatures with no moral restraints who will go to great lengths for financial gain. Just jokes, right? Professor Harvey Mindess, who organized the International Conference on Humor at Antioch College, suggested that jokes are good, that laughter "lets out a little of the devil inside all of us." What

about the great big devil jokes let in, allowing people to make subtle distinctions between "them" and us, using laughter as the great divider? Jokes about Jews, about any ethnic group, communicate negative stereotypes that become just a little bit more credible with each telling.

13   A rather self-deprecating joke Israelis tell about themselves points out the increasingly secular nature of their country. The anecdote is about the immigrant Israeli mother who wanted her son to learn Yiddish so he would remember that he was Jewish. But the typical news commentator fails to see the distinction the joke makes. Israel is inevitably "the Jewish State," her neighbors "Arab countries." Why not "Moslem countries"? Why not the "Hebrew State"?

14   And it is similarly good for a laugh when the Mary Tyler Moore character in the film *Ordinary People* responds with a raised eyebrow and an unhappy face upon being informed that her son is not only seeing a psychiatrist but that this psychiatrist is named *Berger*. One of *those* people, of course. Even when they change their names, thanks to Archie Bunker their secret identities as Jews can be penetrated. It's all in the first name, Archie has explained. "They" may be named Smith or Jones, but one knows who they really are when their first names are Moe, and Iz, and Ben, unmistakably Jewish first names, right, Abe Lincoln? Oh yes, those Jewish lawyers, they're not always such smart Ginsbergs!

15   Personally, Archie, I have suffered from reverse discrimination. To this day, it is my first name that draws questions from Jew and Gentile alike. "Tom? What kind of a name is that for a Jewish boy?" And the little jokes go on with their work. Like maggots and earthworms they grind the ground in the quiet, preparing the soil for another little seed of prejudice.

Topics for consideration:

1. Compare the examples of the terminology of Nazi propagandists with the ones cited in Stephen Brockmann's essay on the Persian Gulf War ("Total Entertainment" in the "Politically Speaking" section).

2. In paragraph 7 Friedmann briefly draws a parallel between the common uses of the word "Indian" as a prefix and "Jew." What might a more extensive examination of this comparison reveal? Are there other groups whose name is used in a similar pejorative way?

3. Both the title of Friedmann's essay and much of its argument rests on his discussion of jokes. There are other groups singled out as targets of jokes. Are "Newfie" jokes, for example, harmless, or do they too prepare the soil for "another little seed of prejudice"?

Further reading:

Gordon Allport, *The Nature of Prejudice* (1954). A classic psychological examination of the roots of racial prejudice.

Gloria Naylor (1950-

Gloria Naylor is author of several novels including The Women of Brewster Place (1982), Linden Hills (1985), Mama Day (1988), Bailey's Cafe (1992) and The Men of Brewster Place (1998).

In this essay, first published in the New York Times, Gloria Naylor recalls the first time she remembers hearing the word "nigger" spoken "by a small pair of lips that had already learned it could be a way to humiliate me." She goes on to recall her earlier familiarity with the same word and the wide range of meanings and associations of which it was capable. These uses, she argues, were not "an internalization of racism," but a transformation that rendered the word impotent.

THE MEANINGS OF A WORD

1   Language is the subject. It is the written form with which I've managed to keep the wolf away from the door and, in diaries, to keep my sanity. In spite of this, I consider the written word inferior to the spoken, and much of the frustration experienced by novelists is the awareness that whatever we manage to capture in even the most transcendent passages falls far short of the richness of life. Dialogue achieves its power in the dynamics of a fleeting moment of sight, sound, smell, and touch.

2   I'm not going to enter the debate here about whether it is language that shapes reality or vice versa. That battle is doomed to be waged whenever we seek intermittent reprieve from the chicken and egg dispute. I will simply take the position that the spoken word, like the written word, amounts to a nonsensical arrangement of sounds or letters without a consensus that assigns "meaning." And building from the meanings of what we hear, we order reality. Words themselves are innocuous; it is the consensus that gives them true power.

3   I remember the first time I heard the word *nigger*. In my third-grade class, our math tests were being passed down the rows, and as I handed the papers to a little boy in back of me, I remarked that once again he had received a much lower mark than I did. He snatched his test from me and spit out that word. Had he called me a nymphomaniac or a necrophiliac, I couldn't have been more puzzled. I didn't know what a nigger was, but I knew that whatever it meant, it was something he shouldn't have called me. This was verified when I raised my hand, and in a loud voice repeated what he had said and watched the teacher scold him for using a "bad" word. I was later to go home and ask the inevitable question that every black parent must face — "Mommy, what does *nigger* mean?"

4   And what exactly did it mean? Thinking back, I realize that this could not have been the first time the word was used in my presence. I was part of a large extended family that had migrated from the rural South after World War II and formed a close-knit network that gravitated around my maternal grandparents. Their ground-floor apartment in one of the buildings they owned in Harlem was a weekend mecca for my immediate family, along with countless aunts, uncles,

and cousins who brought along assorted friends. It was a bustling and open house with assorted neighbors and tenants popping in and out to exchange bits of gossip, pick up an old quarrel, or referee the ongoing checkers game in which my grandmother cheated shamelessly. They were all there to let down their hair and put up their feet after a week of labor in the factories, laundries, and shipyards of New York.

5   Amid the clamor, which could reach deafening proportions — two or three conversations going on simultaneously, punctuated by the sound of a baby's crying somewhere in the back rooms or out on the street — there was still a rigid set of rules about what was said and how. Older children were sent out of the living room when it was time to get into the juicy details about "you-know-who" up on the third floor who had gone and gotten herself "p-r-e-g-n-a-n-t!" But my parents, knowing that I could spell well beyond my years, always demanded that I follow the others out to play. Beyond sexual misconduct and death, everything else was considered harmless for our young ears. And so among the anecdotes of the triumphs and disappointments in the various workings of their lives, the word *nigger* was used in my presence, but it was set within contexts and inflections that caused it to register in my mind as something else.

6   In the singular, the word was always applied to a man who had distinguished himself in some situation that brought their approval for his strength, intelligence, or drive:

7   "Did Johnny *really* do that?"

8   "I'm telling you, that nigger pulled in $6,000 of overtime last year. Said he got enough for a down payment on a house."

9   When used with a possessive adjective by a woman — "my nigger" — it became a term of endearment for her husband or boyfriend. But it could be more than just a term applied to a man. In their mouths it became the pure essence of manhood — a disembodied force that channeled their past history of struggle and present survival against the odds into a victorious statement of being: "Yeah, that old foreman found out quick enough — you don't mess with a nigger."

10   In the plural, it became a description of some group within the community that had overstepped the bounds of decency as my family defined it. Parents who neglected their children, a drunken couple who fought in public, people who simply refused to look for work, those with excessively dirty mouths or unkempt households were all "trifling niggers." This particular circle could forgive hard times, unemployment, the occasional bout of depression — they had gone through all of that themselves — but the unforgivable sin was a lack of self-respect.

11   A woman could never be a "nigger" in the singular, with its connotation of confirming worth. The noun *girl* was its closest equivalent in that sense, but only when used in direct address and regardless of the gender doing the addressing. *Girl* was a token of respect for a woman. The one-syllable word was drawn out to sound like three in recognition of the extra ounce of wit, nerve, or daring that the woman had shown in the situation under discussion.

12   "G-i-r-l, stop. You mean you said that to his face?"

13   But if the word was used in a third-person reference or shortened so that it almost snapped out of the mouth, it always involved some element of communal disapproval. And age became an important factor in these exchanges. It was only

between individuals of the same generation, or from any older person to a younger (but never the other way around), that *girl* would be considered a compliment.

14   I don't agree with the argument that use of the word *nigger* at this social stratum of the black community was an internalization of racism. The dynamics were the exact opposite: the people in my grandmother's living room took a word that whites used to signify worthlessness or degradation and rendered it impotent. Gathering there together, they transformed *nigger* to signify the varied and complex human beings they knew themselves to be. If the word was to disappear totally from the mouths of even the most liberal of white society, no one in that room was naive enough to believe it would disappear from white minds. Meeting the word head-on, they proved it had absolutely nothing to do with the way they were determined to live their lives.

15   So there must have been dozens of times that *nigger* was spoken in front of me before I reached the third grade. But I didn't "hear" it until it was said by a small pair of lips that had already learned it could be a way to humiliate me. That was the word I went home and asked my mother about. And since she knew that I had to grow up in America, she took me in her lap and explained.

Topics for consideration:

1. Naylor takes the position that "words themselves are innocuous: it is the consensus that gives them true power." What consensus surrounds the different early usages of the word "nigger" that she recalls?

2. Naylor points out that "nigger" would never have been applied in her community to a women "confirming worth." Why do you think this would be so? What does it tell us about the word "nigger"?

3. In paragraphs 11 to 13 Naylor describes the affectionate or admiring use of the term "girl." Have you ever come across the term used in this way? How is it usually used? What about the term "boy"?

Further reading:

http://www.lythastudios.com/gnaylor/ The unofficial Gloria Naylor home page.

Rachel Giese

Rachel Giese is features editor of Xtra!, *Toronto's lesbian and gay biweekly.*

Rachel Giese argues that including hate crimes as a special category in the Criminal Code plays into a current "hysteria about crime" which is not based on a corresponding rise in crime statistics. She suggests that such legislation ignores the societal causes of hate crimes and allows the government to avoid its real responsibilities in according full human rights protection to gays and lesbians.

HATING THE HATE-CRIMES BILL

1 I discovered gay activism in the late eighties, when it was at an intense, radical peak: "outings" of closeted celebrities, AIDS die-ins on the steps of the Ministry of Health and Queer Nation kiss-ins at family restaurants. And so, there I was, with a few dozen others marching up Toronto's Yonge Street on Hallowe'en 1990 — a night and a location notorious for harassment and beatings of gay people. We were screaming "Queers bash back!" while an angry mob, which outnumbered us by a few hundred, threw lit firecrackers at us and boys as young as 13 threatened to "rape our dyke and faggot asses." In a show of coalition-building support we stopped once, at Toronto's police headquarters, to yell our protests at a recent spate of "accidental" police shootings of blacks. But minutes later, terrified and sheepish, we sought police protection when the crowd on the sidewalk threatened to break into our group and separate us.

2 We bitterly disliked having to turn to the police. We all wanted, I suspect, to be powerful enough to combat the crowd and their hatred on our own. And, like all progressive activists, we deeply distrusted anything that smelled of police, government, or the establishment. But every one of us, I am slightly embarrassed to admit, relished watching police officers apprehend the worst offenders. From lynchings to gay-bashings, some of the worst crimes of our collective history have been motivated by hatred and bigotry. To see the bad guys get it just once — and to get it from the powers that once would have turned a blind eye — was intensely satisfying.

3 Now, the bad guys are about to get it again with Bill C-41, Canada's proposed hate-crimes law. C-41, which has already passed its first reading in Parliament, allows for stiffer penalties for criminal acts motivated by hatred toward recognizable groups. These acts include assault, harassment, hate propaganda, threats, mischief, robbery and murder. Our anger, once confined to the streets, is finally making it into the law books.

4 But now, looking at Bill C-41 more closely, I'm wondering if that's a good thing. While the bill has won enthusiastic support from both grassroots activists and human-rights lawyers, it doesn't actually do much to fight hate. It doesn't attack the root causes of prejudice, and it might even cause new human-rights abuses. Most alarmingly, the debate over Bill C-41 has pushed progressives onto

the "tough-on-crime" bandwagon — betraying longstanding ideas about crime having deep roots in socialization and inequity.

5   Bill C-41 isn't really about combating hate — it's about the government appealing to the desire of activists for revenge. And when the government gets proactive on an issue that involves all of Canada's minority groups — racial, ethnic and religious communities, gays and lesbians, women and disabled people — I get suspicious. Doesn't anyone else?

6   Traditionally, tougher penalties for crime are the purview of the right. The Reform Party, spearheaded by anti-crime zealot MP Myron Thompson, has urged that the federal government get tougher on crime — with proposals akin to California's "three strikes and you're out" policy, under which three-time offenders are automatically given a 25-year sentence, regardless of their last offence. (Ironically, the Reform Party was responsible for the most prominent opposition to C-41. They voted unanimously against the bill for its inclusion of sexual orientation, arguing that it would open the door for government protection of pedophiles and bestiality.)

7   Conservatives' hysteria about crime usually flies in the face of reality. In August 1994, Statistics Canada reported a 3-percent drop in violent crimes in Canada. This decline was the largest in the survey's 33-year history, and it applied to all categories of violent crime, including premeditated murder, sexual assault, robbery and verbal threats. Interestingly enough, despite this decline and the sense that the crime rate is fairly stable, a fear of crime and an appetite for punishment have become a national obsession. In British Columbia, for instance, several recent incidents of violent crime have initiated a petition — with close to half a million signatures — seeking the return of capital punishment.

8   It's proof of crime's pre-eminence as a political hot button. "The debates right now over criminal-justice policy are all around the crime problems getting worse and we have to make things better," said Rosemary Gartner, a sociologist at the University of Toronto's school of criminology, in a *Globe and Mail* interview. Some people have a naive optimism that changes in the justice system can make a big difference. I'm more comfortable with someone saying, 'I want to increase sentences because I feel people should be punished more.' That's more honest in my opinion."

9   Ordinarily, most progressives would balk at this conservative form of "lock-them-up-and-throw-away-the-key" justice — except, it seems, when it comes to hate crimes.

10   A gay-bashing trial in Toronto provided an interesting taste of things to come under C-41. Two young men were charged in the beating of a prominent gay man and his lover. Upon seeing a photograph of the assailants, a normally level-headed and firmly leftist, lesbian acquaintance, said to me: "They should be thrown in jail forever."

11   And she isn't the only one with such punitive thoughts. At the gay newspaper where I work, we received a letter complaining that the number of gay and lesbian observers at the trial had dropped as the case went on. The letter writer called any activist who wasn't following the trial a hypocrite. That many people's jobs did not allow them to spend all day in a courtroom was immaterial. That

observers do not have any sway over judgment or punishment was also irrelevant. In the political culture of crime and punishment, the ultimate form of activism was watching justice be done.

12 When you look behind the emotion over hate crimes, the rationale for Bill C-41 starts looking shaky indeed. That's partly because, as with Reform and its crime straw-man, there's no hard evidence that the incidence of hate crimes is going up. Statistics have only recently begun to be collected, and all reliable sources of statistics did not record a pattern. The 1994 annual report of the Metro Toronto Police hate-crime unit noted 249 crimes in 1994, as compared to 155 in 1993. However, much of the increase can be attributed to an increase in reporting — and an increasing intolerance of hate crimes. A detective with the unit, for example, said that numbers often rise slightly following mass education drives and public-service-announcement blitzes.

13 There's also the question of whether increasing punishment will stop hate. Like all hate-crime laws, C-41 only punishes acts that are already punishable under other criminal statutes. C-41 also only increases punishment based on a perpetrator's motive, not on the brutality or severity of the crime. It doesn't create any new offences. Is someone already intent on gay-bashing really going to be deterred by the possibility of a slightly stiffer sentence?

14 Even worse, the stiffer sentences probably won't even affect the most crucial demographic: youth. The most worrisome trend noted in the Metro hate-crimes report was that 61 percent of hate crimes are committed by people under 25, and that hate-crime activity in high schools is increasing due to racial, national and ethnic intolerance. And it remains to be seen if longer sentences will even be applicable to young offenders. If much of hate-crime activity can be attributed to a specific group in a specific setting, logic suggests there is a societal cause for those crimes — and, perhaps, a solution involving education and systematic reform, not punishment.

15 Even those who are in favour of the bill, such as human-rights lawyer Marvin Kurz, say C-41 is less a solution to a problem than simply an acknowledgement of the problem itself. "This is about what society deems," Kurz says. "Hate crimes are more serious than other similar crimes because they are not random crimes against individuals; they are crimes against an entire group."

16 Because Bill C-41 puts more power in the hands of the justice system — the support of community activists notwithstanding — the left finds itself curiously allied with the far right and the government. But while conservative proponents of "tough justice" may welcome more involvement from the legal system, minority communities have a much more complicated relationship with law and order. In many cases, people may want just as much protection *from* the police as *by* them. A few years back, Toronto police were under intense scrutiny for shooting blacks. Quebec police (remember Oka?) are notorious for their redneck ways. Gay men in London, Ontario, have been terrorized by police in that city's trumped-up "kiddie porn" investigation. And a detective with Metro Toronto's hate-crime unit even admits that while outreach has worked in some ethnic communities, many Asian groups don't want to cooperate with police because they don't trust them.

17   Compounding the police problem is the distinct possibility that hate-crime laws will infringe on civil liberties. And like many well-intentioned laws, C-41 may limit some of our basic rights. Well-intentioned obscenity laws have allowed for stricter censorship in art galleries and at Canada Customs, speech codes at universities have stifled dissenting voices, and anti-pornography legislation has restricted gay and lesbian magazines and books instead of straight hard-core porn. In many cases, hate crimes are straightforward, but what happens when beliefs and affiliations are scrutinized to prove bigotry or prejudice? This isn't beyond the realm of possibility. Ontario may even do C-41 one better with a proposed law that will make it illegal to belong to a hate group. This is an especially chilling thought when police — at least in Toronto — have indicated that the wearing of black-power symbols could constitute membership in a hate group.

18   Ultimately, joining the hate-crimes bandwagon has allowed the government to pretend that it's doing a lot more for minority rights than it really is. Fighting hate crimes is far sexier and far less controversial than, let's say, amending the Human Rights Act to include sexual orientation — a promise that Justice Minister Allan Rock has repeatedly made — and broken — over the last year-and-a-half. His refusal to grant basic human rights to gay and lesbian relations makes his ardent defence of the inclusion of sexual orientation in Bill C-41 downright wimpy. Gay-bashing is an important issue, but more pressing and more immediate to the lives of gay men and lesbians are same-sex spousal rights, adoption rights, the right for foreigners to immigrate through spousal sponsorships and the right to freedom from discrimination on the job.

19   On October 15, 1994, playwrights Ross Mulhearon and Steve Tait were gay-bashed by a group of young men in the heart of Toronto's gay village while several witnesses stood by and did nothing. Mulhearon and Tait brought the event to the stage this summer in their play *October 15th*. In the dramatic version, of the incident, though, the story takes a different turn: a victim of a gay-bashing turns the tables and kidnaps his assailant. "The play shows the dark reality of what victims like me really want, but are never going to get," said Mulhearon in an interview with Toronto's *Xtra* magazine. And what victims want is revenge.

20   Considering the obvious flaws of hate-crime legislation, the issue that is really driving C-41 is vengeance. What else can power a bill that even its advocates say is "not a solution"? Revenge — and punishment — provide a quick solution and temporary comfort to highly complex problems. Hate-crime legislation may institutionalize "the dark reality," but it's revenge all the same. As Wendy Kaminer writes in her book *It's All The Rage*: "One primary purpose of the criminal justice system is to replace untamed, private vendettas with more measured, less emotional acts of public retribution. The disruptive, self-destructive power of revenge is a recurrent theme in Western literature — consider the *Iliad, Medea, Hamlet* or *Moby Dick* — and it is subtext to the most ordinary criminal prosecutions."

21   As fantasy, revenge is benign, even healthy. When it's the basis of laws, however, revenge is dangerous. Support of C-41 only proves how little imagination and commitment is being used to address hate crimes. Hate-crime legislation offers nothing new — and it may even violate our civil rights. Bill C-41 will not ease suffering or allay fears. It will not make streets or schools any safer. It will

do nothing to address some of the real issues behind hate crimes: poverty, unemployment, racial animosity and distrust, an impoverished education system, social cuts and personal despair. And Bill C-41 may even obscure some possible solutions.

Topics for consideration:

1. Why does Giese begin her article with an account of a gay and lesbian demonstration being threatened by an angry mob of several hundred?

2. Why is Giese distrustful of her acquaintances having some of the same "punitive thoughts" as people with right-wing views?

3. What legal protection now exists in Canada to protect particular groups from being singled out as targets of hate crime? What sort of legislation ought to be in place?

4. Giese refers to human rights lawyer Marvin Kurz's argument that hate crimes are more serious than random crimes against individuals because "they are crimes against an entire group." Do you agree?

Further reading:

Wendy Kaminer, *It's All the Rage: Crime and Culture* (1996)

Lynn Crosbie (1963-

Lynn Crosbie is a writer, critic and editor. Her recent books include Queen Rat: Poems Selected and New *(1998) and* Paul's Case: The Kingston Letters *(1997), a highly controversial work of fictional letters based on the Bernardo murder case.*

Suicide, many psychologists tell us, is as much an act of anger and revenge as it is of despair. In this essay Lynn Crosbie describes the suicide of Toronto poet Daniel Jones and the distress created by his request that his "last piece of writing," his long suicide note, be published.

LAST WORDS: A MEMOIR

Daniel Jones, editor, publisher, fiction writer and poet, was found dead in his apartment in Toronto's Little Italy district yesterday. He was 34, and had a history of battling depression.

— *The Globe and Mail, Feb. 16, 1994*

I was on my way
home to my apartment where I would sit &
write the poems of my desperation, of loneliness,
of my ever-impending suicide. It felt good
& right somehow.

— Daniel Jones, *"Steaks"*

This is not a time for bitterness and blame, but it is a time for truth, and I think everyone would agree that Daniel wanted that.

— Moira Farr, *Jones Memorial, Feb. 20, 1994*

I owe _____ $900.00

— *Note pinned to Jones' bulletin board*

1   On the evening of Sunday, Feb. 13, 1994, Daniel Jones locked himself into his living room and lay on the couch. He had been ill all weekend, and had been attempting to outline a review of Lola Tostevin's *Frog Moon*. Beside him was a notepad, iced coffee, cigarettes, handcuffs and skeleton keys, rubber bands, plastic bags, and a lighter depicting a desert scene: pink clouds, mesas and one green cactus. Some time between 6:45 p.m. and 7 p.m., he swallowed approximately 50 1-milligram Ativan tablets (Apo-Lorazepam), and began writing a suicide note that would take him an hour and a half to complete. Addressed to "Dying with Dignity," it concludes with a request that the note be sent to "Final Exit." The EXIT Society consists of advocates of The Hemlock Society, whose literature (the now defunct Hemlock Quarterly) offers support and instruction regarding voluntary euthanasia. A popular method — used by the late novelist Jerzy Kozinski — involves a plastic garbage bag fastened over the head with rubber bands. Jones owned a copy of Hemlock founder Derek Humphry's *Final Exit*

(1991), and his note is designed after the sample holographic will outlined in this book.

2   In the note, Jones twice requests that his "letter" be published. This request, which is virtually unprecedented (suicide notes are rarely, if ever, made public), has yet to be honoured. His desire to publish the note speaks both to his Hemlock-affiliation — the society encouraged suicide testimonies, stories to share so "we can all grow" — and to his sense that truth, in writing, is imperative. In the story "A Torn Ligament," Jones writes about his struggle as a writer of autobiographical fiction, noting that if he were better able to fabricate, he knows he could write "a better story, but also that it will be a lie."

3   Jones began his career as a poet. In the early 1980s, when he was known only as "Jones" he gained infamy among Toronto's subculture, giving incendiary readings at punk clubs and, eventually, submitting a full-length, crumpled and beer-soaked manuscript to Coach House Press. By the time his book *The Brave Never Write Poetry* was published in 1985, he had been sober for several months. The book's introduction contains the standard confessional caveat: "the protagonist [of the poems] is a stranger to me, though (coincidentally) I seem to have done most of the things he's done and know most of the people he knows." The book chronicles 10 years of the writer's life as a depressive alcoholic, intellectual, "laureate of the psycho ward," and social commentator. An assiduous reader who valued poetry, Jones became involved with the Haiku Society of Canada in 1982, finding solace from his "emptiness" in "zen buddhism and the composition of haiku." Jones however, wanted to subvert the form. When reading before the conservative Haiku Society at Toronto's Harbourfront, he (in his own words) "drunkenly & somewhat pathetically lashed out at the audience: Do you really want to hear this crap?"

4   Eventually, Jones would become a prodigious writer of book reviews and essays (including an explicit account of his vasectomy), an editor, and an active member of the small-press and literary scene. He was an editor for *Border/Lines*, before dramatically quitting over a point of principle, in the late 1980s. After *The Brave*, he began to focus exclusively on fiction, a decision he recounts in the story "In Various Restaurants": "[I] had dismissed poetry as unimportant. I was going to write short stories." Between 1985 and 1994, he published five collections of short fiction, and a novel (*Obsessions*, 1992). He had also completed another novel, and a collection of short stories, *The People One Knows*, a book that attempts to inscribe Toronto and its literary denizens on the cultural map. Throughout, he never lost his capacity for subversiveness, humour, and self-irony. His novel, for example, which is an experimental account of harrowing mental illness, is referred to in *The People One Knows* in the following way:

"I think I have a fear of failure," I said to my therapist.
"But if you don't finish your novel, you will fail," my therapist said.
"Perhaps you have a fear of success."
"Not very likely," I said. "You should read my novel."

5   Jones suffered over (what he perceived to be) his failures. One of his first collections of short fiction begins with a quotation from *Frankenstein*: "I ... became

a poet ... You are well acquainted with my failure, and how heavily I bore the dis-appointment." A contradiction in terms, he was an advocate of socialism, violent social/cultural upheaval, and a self-described nihilist. At the same time he wanted (and merited) attention from the Canadian literary establishment, attention that eluded him.

6   Very little critical work exists on the writing of Daniel Jones, though much speculation has arisen over his death. His suicide note stands as his final effort to explain himself, and to offer, as context for his work and life, an account of the suicidal psyche, and the often punishing literary establishment. This document provides a significant textual coda to an unexamined life, which was, to him, not worth living.

> My eyes are unfocused. Now, it is the time.
>   — *Daniel Jones, 8:15 p.m., Feb., 13, 1994*

7   "Shaking all over but fully conscious," the note begins, a statement that may be read as a sign of a weakened mental state, or as an assertion of the validity of its contents. The note is, in fact, an extraordinary document — it contains errors of spelling and grammar; many words and phrases are illegible; and there are, at times in the text, certain temporal confusions (resulting from blurred vision). It is also a precise and cogent piece of writing, one which issues practical instruc-tions and eloquent personal testimony. Jones was a scrupulous writer and editor, one who would tirelessly research such minutiae as the bass-line of an obscure punk song, or the correct spelling of a brand of shoes (this particular fact-finding mission involved a long walk to a shoe store, if I recall correctly).

8   While the note's contents are often hazy, it is remarkably coherent. Given the amount of tranquillizers Jones had ingested, its clarity suggests an astonish-ing act of will. Perhaps the strongest (and among the most poignant) of his state-ments, is his request that the note be scrutinized by an editor, one who can "clean up the grammar and style that I would right (sic), if I had not just swallowed 45-50 Ativan ... doing this in a hurry." The 21-page note (written on small squares of paper) was written as an afterthought, "off the cuff." Jones' expressed desire to see the prose modified is in keeping with his literary meticulousness, and further, acts to reconcile the drug-addled body and "fully conscious" mind.

9   One of Jones' most forceful attempts in his note is to make amends with the women he loved. Moira Farr (Jones' lover) and Robyn Gillam (his wife, from whom he was separated at the time of his death) are the most prominent figures; they are named often, and are appointed as co-executors of his literary estate. This request was challenged in court by Gillam, who maintained that the note did not constitute a will. In a motion for direction filed in the Ontario Court, dated June 16, 1994, Gillam claims that Jones, at the time of his death, "was not in a suf-ficiently lucid mental state to draw up a will." Farr countered, in an affidavit dated June 30, 1994, that "Daniel Jones intended his suicide note to express his last wishes, and that he knew what he was doing when he wrote it." (Farr's opinion is documented as being shared by both Jones' psychiatrist and parents, Norma and Roger). This July, the note was formally honoured — though not actually pro-bated as a will — in a pre-trial agreement legally recognizing both Gillam and

Farr as executors of the estate. (His archives have been placed in The National Library of Canada, with the court's direction that some are to be sealed.)

10   In a Feb. 15. 1996 article in the Toronto weekly *Eye*, Gillam is quoted as saying Jones was "a very manipulative person," and that the note Jones affixed to the locked living room door — "Don't Come In, Call The Police" — is in fact a quotation from Martin Amis's novel *Money*. Jones' death was a theatrical act in many respects. He killed himself the night before Valentine's Day (a Valentine lottery ticket, worth $5, was left, pitifully, on his desk), a day that Farr spent with the police, most of whom amused themselves by reading Jones' letter and mocking its contents. He handcuffed himself behind his back after sealing the plastic bags, an action which horrifies because it is both pointless (legs may be slipped through handcuffed arms with minimum agility) and cruelly suggestive of the suppression of the wish to live.

11   Many artists have "staged" their suicides. The poets Stevie Smith and John Berryman both scripted their deaths in their writing. In "Henry's Understanding," Berryman (who drowned himself) writes: "& horribly unlike Bach, it occurred to me/ that one night ... I'd take off all my clothes/ & cross the damp cold lawn & down the bluff/ into the terrible water & walk forever." Sylvia Plath (who wrote of dying as "art" and theatre, for which she had a "call") left mugs of milk and bread for her sleeping children while she gassed herself, a gesture that was clearly symbolic given that one child was an infant at the time. By quoting Amis, Jones was quoting suicide itself, a well-precedented act of self-annihilation during which pain is often communicated, not by words, as suicide notes are rare, but with the props at hand.

12   When a suicide leaves a note, it is usually intended as a form of apology, and statement of intention. They are notoriously brief (Jim Morrison's note allegedly read "Last Words, Last Words, Out") and tend to augment, rather than assuage grief, as they make literal the suicide's feelings of helplessness. I knew nothing about the severity of Jones' despair in the winter of 1994. Jones and I had been close friends, but we were estranged at the time of his death. Numbed by this terrible knowledge, I went to the morgue with Gillam, and read the note, with her, for the first time, in his apartment. These actions frighten me in retrospect. They seem vampiric and wrong-minded, despite my intentions. Reconstructing these events now, I realize I wanted to look at what he had done, to face this act unflinchingly, with the acceptance he demands in his final written document. "I relish this," Jones writes, "I believe I am doing the only possible right thing."

13   The rhetoric of "right" and "wrong" is a constant in suicide discourse, as factions form precisely on this point. Jones' insistence that this is the right thing to do is based on two critical notions. As a nihilist, he held in contempt the legal obstruction of the individual's right to die (Sue Rodriguez's assisted suicide was headline news in the newspapers left on Jones' kitchen table). More significantly, Jones believed that his psychological distress was a "terminal illness," one as legitimate and painful as incurable cancer. "I have never been able to live except in the occasional brief moment," he writes, "without a sense of horror, disgust, self-loathing." In the "special language" of suicides, Jones maintains that only the "individual so-afflicted" can comprehend the horror of this condition. He continues to excoriate himself as a "petty, angry, self-obsessed ... horrible

person," stating that there was never any respite from his "guilt and extreme anger" and "hate."

14 Toward the end of his life, Jones was at odds with his Mercury Press publisher, Bev Daurio, a detail that caught *Frank* magazine's attention in March, 1994. In the Literary Review column, an anonymous writer suggests that "Beverly Daurio and Mercury Press have some serious explaining to do," citing the press' decision to pull *The People One Knows* a week before his death. Daurio, who was one of Jones' most supportive friends, was likely stunned by this accusation, one which recklessly throws cause in her corner. When I looked, with Gillam, at Jones' office, it became clear he had left an obscure narrative in the form of letters in a tray: grant rejections, a letter from Daurio pulling the book, notification of the cancellation of his Harbourfront launch. There was an angry unsigned letter as well, allegedly written by Daurio's husband and co-publisher, Don. This anger was likely caused by the letter Jones wrote to *Books in Canada*, in which he publicly resigned from editing *Paragraph* (Daurio's literary magazine). His argument in this letter involves Daurio's professional ethics, taking her to task for several points of conflict of interest (in her own work as a reviewer). Eventually, Jones contacted the publisher of *Books in Canada*, asking him to withdraw the letter.

15 Daurio's reasons for pulling the book are not fully known, although she was clearly concerned with libel. Before the book was published, Mercury Press took the unprecedented step of obtaining signed waivers from everyone named or portrayed in the stories. *The People One Knows* was Jones' "La Côte Basque" (Truman Capote's roman à clef about his high-society friends, which proved to be his social downfall). A great admirer of Capote, Jones once hired me as his stylist: to replicate the famous Truman-on-chaise-lounge photograph (gracing *Other Voices, Other Rooms*). Many of his stories were based on friends: some appear only nominally, while others are tendered in a cutting, mean-spirited way. The book was eventually published (in the fall of 1994) to a lukewarm reception. The *Globe and Mail*'s review was cold (and inaccurate); the *Toronto Star* praised two stories, lamenting "Alas, two stories do not make a satisfying book"; *Eye* published an ambivalent review written, preposterously, by one of Jones's ex-lovers.

16 Jones was a nihilist who held few lasting allegiances, a fact which prompted several people to regard his later work, and even his suicide, with malice, referring to it as a "career move." He was often more scrupulous about fact than fiction. In his note he asks that his *Books in Canada* letter (which has disappeared) and Daurio's letter be published side by side. His letter, he notes, is his "last piece of writing and I wish it to stand." By suggesting this tandem publication he is suggesting a correlation between the letters, a disturbing version of cause and effect. "I did love greatly," Jones writes, adding that his love was always undermined by his self-destructive nature. His messages of professional alliance and love to Daurio, also expressed in the note, attest to this precarious tendency.

17 Reading Jones' letter, it becomes evident that his posthumous life is of pressing significance. He asks in great detail that his work be managed properly, and makes a number of suggestions as to the presentation of his writing. His

correspondence, juvenilia, and journals are to be destroyed; his other work is to be published or republished. He suggests the title *Something Not Right* for a collection of his short fiction and his novel *1978* (which is set in the 1970s Toronto punk scene, and remains unpublished). He excludes *The Brave* from these plans, a book he despised to his death. Jones' rejection of *The Brave* has caused some consternation among those who feel it is his strongest work. In a poem about Jones in his recent book *There'll Be Another*, David McFadden conjectures, as have others, that the fiction that follows *The Brave* is disappointing, that Jones had, at some point, stopped caring about people. (Since Jones rarely spoke to McFadden, his former Coach House editor, this position is somewhat solipsistic, and wildly speculative).

18   It is difficult, as critic Jacqueline Rose has suggested, to discuss the work of people one knows. The interpretation of literature, she argues, must not be arrested "on the grounds of special, privileged, involvement or interest." My own interest is grounded in the later fiction, work I believe to be exceptional, and enviably accomplished. When I first read with Jones in the 80's, I was bored by his persona and poems, tuning out after the first scatological reference. However, my interest, or more to the point, Jones' interest, is relevant not to readers, but only to those who knew, by involvement, the meaning and value he invested in his fiction. "To plan my final publications is a bit self-centred," Jones writes in his note. "I will be dead: the work may not be any good." In this disquieting passage, Jones gestures to the subjective relationship between reader and text, how unmanageable it is. Although Jones tried to squirrel away all extant copies of his collection of poems, one of these poems ("Things That I Have Put into My Asshole") was stapled to virtually every tree in Toronto after his death, in a demonstration of unstoppered literary interpretation.

19   Jones wanted his suicide note to be published in several magazines and newspapers, a request which caused great consternation to the literary committee he appointed to oversee his works (which included myself and Bev Daurio). The note, for those closest to him, is terribly personal. His admissions of love and apology, for example, are not publicly relevant, while his contention — "I do love and care for everyone I have ever known" — stands to combat the image of Jones the "horrible person" inscribed in the note. Further, it confirms what Jones attests throughout the note, that he "look[s] forward" to death, that the thought of dying brings him "great happiness," "release," and "freedom." I will never be sure if Jones approached his death with such certainty, but his stern instruction, "I expect my last wishes to be respected fully, not matter if problems arise," merits, in my mind, obedience.

20   There were very few material clues as to the events of Jones' final days, a fact which underscores the momentousness of the suicide note. I did discover he was planning a new collection of stories, called *Something New*, which was to be an addition to what he referred to as a tetralogy, beginning with *The People One Knows* — thinly veiled autobiographical studies, some maliciously untrue, others sweetly and morbidly accurate. I had been targeted as a subject for a story that would have moved and infuriated me. I have reconstructed what I can — when Jones appointed his literary committee, he advised that they should "advise and research," but have no "final say," an appropriate description of my own role as

essayist and truth-teller. Jones' final say, however, is one, like all texts, which may and should produce multiple interpretations, and raise a number of questions.

21   The most pressing question, in this case, is the significance of the suicide note. Very few, if any, suicide notes have been published or analyzed. Jones' note, for all of its labour, is hardly an impressive exposition. Most artists who have committed suicide have either left a brief, instructive note (Plath's read "Please call Dr. ——— "), or none at all. Kurt Cobain, who also committed suicide in April, 1994, left a rambling letter in which he, bizarrely, cites Freddie Mercury. Even his liner notes contain more literary and personal substance.

22   "Suicide," Anne Sexton writes, "is the opposite of the poem." Suicidal artists create art against suicide; their work provides a way of combatting this urge, of accessing, in Julia Kristeva's words, "the secret and unreachable horizon of [their] loves and desires." In the moments preceding suicide then, artists work in the genre of the suicide note ("I'm sorry, I can't go on &c."), as their own models are no longer useful. Suicide demands closure, even banality (death's door is not the place to search for the *mot juste*). Art, which perpetuates life, must be severed upon entry.

23   It is hard to say whether such documents should be published. Jones himself was aware of the difficulties his requests would cause; after making a number of publishing demands, he writes in his note that if his wishes cannot be met, "at least you tried." Ultimately, I stand in soldierly respect beside the adamant will, that he had lost, and found in his resolution that "My affliction is my own, and has always been my own, and no one else is to blame — no one could have done anything."

24   Jones' note is dedicated to Robert Billings ("Rest in Peace"), a poet-suicide who allegedly had problems with his publisher. He very likely thought of Billings as an ally in his own illness-centred "financial and emotional suffering." If Jones' death is an object lesson in pain, penury, art and philosophy, this remains to be untangled by those concerned or devoted to the life and/or work. All of these questions wait patiently to be addressed; there is no assistance pending from the "sound mind" from which they were generated. This mind has been burned; it lies among ash and bone, and Jones surely rests in his grave, oblivious. The dead, he writes in *Obsessions*, "do not care." "What they want — even the dead do not know."

25   *With thanks to Jeffrey Canton and Moira Farr for their assistance, and to Robyn Gillam, for hers. Thanks also to David McGimpsey for his insight.*

Topics for consideration:

1. Crosbie begins her essay with a detailed account of the precise method Jones used to kill himself. Most newspapers refuse to publish such details. Is Crosbie's detailed account justified?

2. Jones' wife is quoted as saying that Jones was "a very manipulative person." Do you find evidence of this in Crosbie's account?

3. What do you make of Jones' insistence that his suicide note "be published in several newspapers and magazines"? Why would this cause "great consternation" among his former associates?

4. Crosbie describes herself in paragraph 20 as an "essayist and truth-teller." What do you think of this description?

Further reading:

Daniel Jones, *Obsession: A Novel in Parts* (1992)

_____ , *The People One Knows: Toronto Stories* (1993)

CHAPTER 5

FORBIDDEN WORDS

Almost everyone claims to be in favour of "freedom of speech." Yet nearly all of us, when faced with particular cases, say of propaganda inciting racial hatred, or the publication of false and damaging information, are apt to feel that legal limits are in order. The law as it stands already places a number of restrictions on freedom of expression. Laws relating to obscenity, libel and even forbidding "the spreading of false news" can be applied to all sorts of publications.

Much censorship throughout Canada's history has not been the result of prosecutions under the Criminal Code but rather the work of agencies such as school boards, film censors and Canada Customs, some of whose actions now seem bizarre. What can one make, for example, of the decision by the Manitoba movie censor board in 1918 to ban comedy films on the grounds that they make the audience too frivolous? While such a ruling now seems absurd, we can also interpret it as a panicky reaction having more to do with misgivings about the power of a new medium than with fear of the frivolity that might be brought on by viewing comedies. As with more recent fears about pornography on the internet, the compelling power of the new medium becomes inextricably mixed up with concern about the message.

More recent acts of censorship are often just as odd. For example, Canada Customs impounded copies of Salman Rushdie's *The Satanic Verses* for a few days during 1989, making Canada the only Western democracy to ban that novel. For several decades Canada Customs has made a practice of seizing books destined for gay and lesbian bookstores across the country, often making those seizures during Freedom to Read Week. An oddity of these seizures is that frequently the same books have been readily available in Canadian mainstream bookstores without any official intervention.

During the 1990s there were a number of complaints in colleges and universities in both Canada and the U.S. that "political correctness" was inhibiting professors and students from expressing their views. Critics pointed to the few campuses that had established "speech codes" and warned that political repression was in effect throughout the world of higher education. In the article that derives from his talk to political science students at Concordia University, Supreme Court Justice John Sopinka alludes to the self-censorship that he fears is at work among teachers and students and appeals to "the common sense of public opinion" to defend freedom of speech. In his reply to John Sopinka's piece, law professor Allan Hutchinson argues that "freedom of expression is a highly charged terrain of political contestation" where all sides ought to acknowledge their ideologies openly.

As one who has had years of work as an investigative journalist suppressed by the effects of "libel chill," Kimberley Noble writes with special insight into the ways in which Canadian libel laws allow wealthy individuals and corporations to prevent publication of any information that may show them in an unfavourable light. Typically long-drawn-out and expensive, libel cases place the burden of proof on the defendant whose financial resources and energies are generally exhausted before the case can ever come to trial.

Margaret Atwood's essay on "Pornography" also springs from direct experience — that of hours spent in the offices of the Ontario Board of Film Censors viewing "outtakes" from pornographic films as research for her novel *Bodily Harm* (1982). As a writer who has seen the work of colleagues such as Margaret Laurence and Alice Munro being banned by various school boards, Atwood is wary of censorship. She is also aware that "pornography" can mean vastly different things to different people and is acutely conscious that opposing "pornography" could lead to books she values "ending up as confetti."

The "freedom of speech" that we are so quick to defend in principle turns out, in practice, to be a complicated matter requiring not just the "common sense" that John Sopinka advocates but a scrupulous examination of our own intentions.

John Sopinka (1933-1997)

Born in Saskatchewan, John Sopinka practised law for twenty-eight years before becoming a Justice of the Supreme Court of Canada. He was also known for representing wrongfully convicted nurse Susan Nelles in the inquiry that cleared her of blame for the deaths of babies at Sick Children's Hospital in Toronto.

In this article, based on a speech given to Concordia University's Political Science Students' Association, John Sopinka argues that "political correctness" has resulted in self-censorship in university classrooms. He appeals to "the common sense of public opinion" and argues that it is up to the ordinary citizen to defend freedom of speech.

FREEDOM OF SPEECH UNDER ATTACK

1 One of the most difficult areas of the law which the Supreme Court has had to deal with is free speech. While one of the most cherished of freedoms, yet it is and has been over the centuries constantly under attack. The reason for this contradiction is that freedom for one group often poses a threat to others. As observed by Professor Isaiah Berlin, "In a lake stocked with minnows and minnow-eating pike, freedom for the pike means death to the minnow."

2 Freedom of speech is not absolute. In some circumstances the exercise of this freedom poses a threat to others that is so great that it must be curbed. To illustrate, let me cite the time-worn example of falsely crying "fire" in a crowded theatre. The freedom to do so must be curbed in order to protect the safety of others. In deciding what should be the limits on free speech, we must balance the values inherent in the freedom against the rights of others who may be affected by its exercise.

3 In the last decade there has developed a phenomenon known as the demand for political correctness. Certain segments of society who are justifiably seeking equality for their particular interests have extended their demands so far that they threaten the freedom of others. They not only criticize the expression of views that do not accord with their own but demand that contrary views be suppressed. Professor Alan M. Dershowitz, a Harvard University law professor and civil rights activist writing in the *Harvard Record*, describes the effect which this movement has had on university life. He refers to the demands for speech codes which would be enforced against politically incorrect ideas including criticism of affirmative action programs, opposition to rape-shield laws, advocacy of the criminalization of homosexuality and defence of pornography.

4 And what is the affect of all this? He states: "As a teacher, I can feel a palpable reluctance on the part of many students — particularly those with views in neither extreme and those who are anxious for peer acceptance — to experiment with unorthodox ideas, to make playful comments on serious subjects, to challenge politically correct views and to disagree with minority, feminist or gay perspectives."

5   Professor Michael Bliss of the University of Toronto has had a similar reaction to this trend of self-censorship on the part of students: "You see, especially in undergraduate papers, the new idea that nothing offensive should be said or done. But universities are places where people will be offended and should be offended. It's very, very wrong when we won't publish anything that may be construed as offensive. Free speech is offensive."

6   Many of us who may support, in general, the objectives of the groups that comprise this government cannot but be concerned about the intolerance for free speech which some of its members advocate.

7   Recently an article appeared in the University of Toronto newspaper, *The Varsity*, which was written by Glenn Sumi, himself a member of a visible minority. He decried the ban of a painting showing a black woman with a basket of bananas on her head by an art exhibitor. He concluded as follows: "Whether Robichaud's painting is racist or sexist is immaterial. What is important is that, under the stiff banner of political correctness and responsibility, the Women's Centre of Concordia has hidden from public view something with which they disagree. The issue is not art, good or bad, pleasant or offensive; the issue is censorship."

8   A further example arose out of the recent experience of an Alberta chemistry professor who wrote an article which appeared in the *Canadian Journal of Physics*. It suggested that working women are responsible for many family and social problems. This brought forth a campaign to enlist the aid of the National Research Council to recall the issue and reprint it without the offending article. This reminds one of attempts of the past to re-write history to accord with the thinking of the day.

9   This movement has had its effect on the judiciary. It has not been all negative. Judges in the past have, on occasion, been insensitive to the legitimate concerns of minority or disadvantaged groups. However, there is cause for legitimate concern that overzealous dissection of every word that drops from the bench, with a view to finding some indicia of political incorrectness which may be the basis for a complaint to the Judicial Council, may result in decisions that are politically correct but not legally and factually correct. A judge who is looking over his or her shoulder may decide a case in a way that will avoid the Judicial Council rather than accord with the material presented.

10   What may be thought to be correct today may very well be held to be incorrect tomorrow. John Stuart Mill said it this way back in 1859: "Ages are no more infallible than individuals, every age having held many opinions which subsequent ages have deemed not only false but absurd: and it is certain that many opinions, now general, will be rejected by future ages, as it is that many, once general, are rejected by the present."

11   Society should not seek to censor the speech of someone because it appears to be wrong or absurd in light of the conventional wisdom of today. It may become the conventional wisdom of tomorrow.

12   The Canadian Charter of Rights and Freedoms has provided us with the means to ward off unwarranted attacks on free speech by the state. It may also fine-tune the libel laws if it appears that they are too restrictive. With respect to demands for political correctness, we must still rely on the common sense of

public opinion to stand up for the right to say things no matter how unpalatable they may seem.

13   It is, therefore, important for all of us to defend this right, no matter that we sympathize with the ultimate goals and objectives sought to be attained by those who advocate the contrary. Because we cannot turn to the courts for redress in this regard, the greatest threat to free speech does not come from actions of the state but from ourselves.

Topics for consideration:

1. Does Alan Dershowitz's account of the repression of free speech in the classroom correspond with any of your own experiences?

2. In paragraph 3 Sopinka refers to "certain segments of society who are justifiably seeking equality for their particular interests." In paragraph 6 he refers to "the groups that comprise this government"? Presumably these are the same people. Who are they and how did they, in Sopinka's view, become "this government"?

3. Why would the *Canadian Journal of Physics* publish an article about the role of women in the workforce and "family and social problems" and why might such an article be the cause of controversy?

4. Sopinka ends his article by suggesting that it is "important for all of us to defend this right [of free speech]". What practical steps can the ordinary citizen take to "defend this right"?

Further reading:

http://insight.mcmaster.ca/org/efc/pages/chronicle/chronicle.html *A Chronicle of Freedom of Expression in Canada: Part 1, 1914–1994; Part 2, 1995–present.*

Allan C. Hutchinson (1951-

Allan C. Hutchinson is a professor at Osgoode Hall Law School and author of From Free Speech to Democratic Dialogue *(1987) and* Waiting for Coraf: A Critique of Laws and Rights *(1995).*

This article written in response to John Sopinka's "Freedom of Speech Under Attack" first appeared in University Affairs. *Hutchinson argues that Sopinka, in criticizing the "politically correct" is ignoring the political implications of his own position and that "free speech" may be a much less clearly defined concept than Sopinka is willing to believe.*

LIKE LUNCHES, SPEECH IS NEVER FREE

1 In the popular drama of contemporary democracy, Justice John Sopinka casts himself as an enemy of political correctness and a friend of free speech (In My Opinion, April 1994). With beguiling rhetoric, he chastises those who want to appropriate freedom of expression for their own political agenda. For him, freedom of expression is above partisan politics and must be kept that way — "we must still rely on the common sense of public opinion to stand up for the right to say things no matter how unpalatable they may seem."

2 Yet, like most critics of so-called political correctness, Justice Sopinka constructs an argument that is as transparent as it is disingenuous. If politics is the crime, then he is as guilty as those he so earnestly accuses. Politics is inescapable: freedom of expression is a highly charged terrain of political contestation, not a haven from such ideological engagement.

3 By labelling certain views as politically correct, Justice Sopinka and others attempt to impugn the ideological motives of their free speech opponents and, at the same time, to insulate their own views from the charge of political affiliation. However, contrary to such "apolitical" moves, the opponents of political correctness are committed to as distinct, if very different, political agenda as the politically correct.

4 Because almost all conduct qualifies as expression, it is necessary to identify what expression is to be granted constitutional protection. Murder, rape and violence generally are the most expressive and, as Justice Sopinka puts it, "unpalatable" of human acts, but they do not qualify for protection. Moreover, like lunches, speech is never free. It can only be had at the price of other competing values, like equality and dignity.

5 Consequently, the real debate is not over who is in favor of free speech, but what are to be the limits of free speech and how it is to be balanced against other values. And that is a political debate. Whereas those labelled as politically correct tend to stress a more social and egalitarian vision of justice, Justice Sopinka relies on a more individual and libertarian ideology. At least the politically correct are candid about their political commitments.

6 To suggest, as Justice Sopinka does, that professors' rights to offend always ought to take precedence over students' rights to be treated equally and with

respect is a political and obviously controversial stance. It has to be defended as such and cannot be simply paraded under the dubious rubric of "common sense", which is notoriously not always common or sensible.

7   Of course, I do not intend to defend any particular views that are held by those described as politically correct; that would be to miss the political point of my intervention. Both sides are political and neither has the lock on truth, justice or anything else. It is as problematic to see racism, sexism and homophobia in everything as it is to treat them as secondary to incursions on people's primary freedom to express themselves.

8   It is no better to accuse a black writer of being elitist because she fails to communicate with those who cannot read as it is to leap to the defence of the white supremacist. Nor is condemning Romeo and Juliet as homophobic because it deals only with heterosexual relations any better than championing the dissemination of gay-bashing material.

9   In contemporary society, the commitment to free speech is shallow. The attack on so-called political correctness diverts attention away from the profoundly unequal access to speech. Whereas some are free to share their views with millions, others can only talk to themselves. In a technological age, wealth is as much the measure of speaking as is its contribution to democratic debate.

10   If censorship is the fear, then it is already here. Although intended differently by Justice Sopinka, he is right to conclude that "the greatest threat to free speech does not come from actions of the state but from ourselves." What gets expressed and what does not is determined by those who control the means of communication. It is truly a 'marketplace of ideas' in that the haves speak and the have-nots listen.

11   The problem is not so much to do with who favors freedom of expression, but who benefits most from elevating it above other values. Put crudely, it is those who have the power to speak, not those without it. Established interests — white, male, straight, etc. — have more to gain from prioritizing free speech over equality: it serves to preserve the status quo rather than to change it.

12   Ironically, the Supreme Court of Canada, of which Justice Sopinka is a member, has engaged in exactly the kind of balancing that he rails against. It has recognized that, while freedom of expression is fundamental, it is not absolute: liberty must be balanced against other values, such as equality and harmony. In the game of constitutional cards, freedom of expression is not always the trump card that its pseudo-absolutists defenders pretend that it is.

13   Indeed, by his own definition, Justice Sopinka is a judicial proponent of political correctness. Speaking on behalf of the Court in the *Butler* case, he upheld the anti-pornography provisions of the Criminal code as constitutionally valid. It is preferable, he said, to inhibit free expression in the name of "a free and democratic society" so as to "enhance respect for all members of society, and non-violence and equality in their relations with each other."

14   In a perverse sense, the recent judicialisation of freedom of expression is the epitome of political correctness. In the name of constitutional wisdom, judges tell us what is and is not protected speech: they recast and resolve profoundly political issues as technical issues of legal doctrine. That is the abasement of democracy, not its apotheosis.

Topics for consideration:

1. Hutchinson refers in his opening paragraph to the "beguiling rhetoric" of Sopinka's article. What examples of this can you find in "Freedom of Speech Under Attack"?

2. Hutchinson is critical of Sopinka's use of the term "political correctness." Why?

3. Part of Hutchinson's argument is that "like lunches, speech is never free." What costs are associated with freedom of speech?

4. In paragraph 9 Hutchinson says that "the commitment to free speech is shallow" in contemporary society. What do you think he means by this? Do you think he is right?

5. In what ways does Hutchinson find that Sopinka's judicial decisions on the Supreme Court contradict his argument in "Freedom of Speech Under Attack"?

Kimberley Noble (1957-

Kimberley Noble is a business reporter for the Globe and Mail *and the recipient of two national newspaper awards. In 1992 Noble's book contract with Macmillan was cancelled after the publisher received threats of litigation from Hees International.*

The following selection, first published in Canadian Forum, *is excerpted from Noble's pamphlet* Bound and Gagged: Libel Chill and the Right to Publish. *Noble describes her experiences in trying to publish newspaper articles, and later a book, on the powerful Edper group of companies. Noble shows how public knowledge of corporate activities is limited by the ways in which the wealthy can use the threat of libel action to exhaust the resources and energies of writers and publishers.*

BOUND AND GAGGED

1 In this country, it is a constant fight to collect data, to distinguish what's meaningful, and then to distribute the information in any form that helps people to make some sense of their lives, without putting the writer and publisher in various sorts of peril.

2 I could tell you stories ... but then, I can't. I can tell some stories, the ones that take me years and years to piece together and construct seamlessly enough to get through the phalanx of lawyers that have to paw over every word in an effort to decide whether some poor, oppressed rich guy could possibly take offence from anything I've written. I can pass on fragments of stories that will never see the light of day because the information that I need to connect them into anything that makes sense is too well hidden or obscured to find — unless I hired my own team of lawyers or investigators, or spent all my working life chasing a handful of facts for what may or may not be a decent story.

3 I can't do this; nobody can.

• • •

4 Few organizations and individuals have the time and the inclination to research and tell stories that do not involve breaking any laws, but chart the ability of certain groups and characters to use the rules to their own advantage. These, of course, are the stories that really should be told; but just as they're the ones worth telling, they are also the ones that you have to fight for because they invariably concern matters that the people involved do not want to make public.

5 For proof, you need only look to the stories that get national recognition in this country. So often they are important stories about issues with public policy ramifications. Yet, in Canada, any successful effort to air the facts and/or a range of opinions about these matters is considered to be either extraordinary or dangerous. I think of my own work on the Edper Bronfman group of companies, the largest single corporate conglomerate in Canada, run by a small group of lawyers and accountants who, at their peak in 1989, controlled companies that represented 12 per cent of the Toronto Stock Exchange and somewhere between 5 per cent and 10 per cent of the Canadian economy. It has taken years of my life, and

months at a stretch, to research and write stories about the most rudimentary aspects of how these people do business. People in the Canadian investment community have known this stuff all along, but had either come to accept it or were too intimidated to talk.

6   As I found out last winter — when a book I had been asked to write about the Edper Bronfman group was cancelled before I had even produced a manuscript, after one of the Edper manager-lawyers had fired off a letter to my publisher that appeared to me to be threatening legal action no matter what I wrote or how carefully it was checked. Enormous courage and perseverance is required on the part of my editors at the *Globe and Mail*. It would be almost impossible for me to do this kind of work without a big, wealthy organization behind me, to pay the lawyers and foot the research bills and keep pushing me the many times when I get sick and tired of the relentless attacks on my working habits and personal character. If, for any reason, no big, wealthy organization wanted to see these stories in print, readers would simply be out of luck. There would be no way that I, or anybody else, could afford to write anything except the carefully orchestrated public relations garbage that the Edper group — and many companies like it — churn out for public consumption.

• • •

7   I was assigned to cover the Edper group of companies in late 1986. It took me a long time to get any kind of handle on the beat. For one thing, the group — which, at the time this is being written, still controls some of the oldest and best-known companies in Canada, including Brascan Ltd., Noranda Inc., MacMillan Bloedel Ltd., Royal Trustco Ltd., Hees International Bancorp Inc., Consumers Packaging Inc., John Labatt Ltd., Trizec Corp. Ltd. and, the last time I looked, Bramalea Ltd. — was in transition in 1986 and 1987, so that many of the things I'd been told to expect were not being confirmed by what I observed and the information I obtained. In addition, I have to watch something for a long, long time before I feel comfortable writing anything. So I did.

8   This meant that, with one or two lapses, I played their game for a number of years. I went to meetings, and scheduled interview sessions, and I listened to detailed "off the record" explanations of plans and circumstances that should really have been made public information, and I wrote what they wanted me to. It was hard to do anything else. The Edper managers were such a tightly knit bunch, and they had, by virtue of their size and the number of public share sales they launched, such a stranglehold on the Canadian investment community that it was next to impossible to get information not officially sanctioned by the group. At one point I called Jim Pitblado, the head of RBC Dominion Securities Inc., the country's largest and most successful investment and brokerage dealer, to ask him to talk about the relationship between the Edper group and corporate underwriters — which, it should be noted, are almost all in the business of acting as advisors and brokers to small and medium-sized investors. "Why would I make trouble for myself?" Pitblado asked. Before I could reply, he hung up the phone.

9   Investment analysts who talked to me and were identified in stories were, without exception, invited to meetings with either their corporate underwriting departments or the Edper managers themselves, and asked to account for their actions. After one experience like this, they'd either clam up or start insisting

that we meet in the most out-of-the-way place, at the oddest hours. Even then, most were circumspect. These were the brokerage industry's golden years, the hey-day of 1980s deal-making that everyone now looks back on as a period when greed ran wild and every kid with an MBA drove a Porsche or something faster and more expensive. Yet, from where I sat, I saw a small and restricted business community running scared all the time. Making deals, keeping their mouths shut, hoping for a big piece of the action or a crumb off the table, but afraid all the time to talk about what they were having to agree to in order to make their money.

• • •

10   As Bronfman group spokesman Thomas Reid — a former journalist who now makes his living teaching corporate clients how to manipulate and overwhelm the Canadian media — is fond of saying about the Edper managers, "They are not familiar with the role that the free flow of information plays in a democratic society." Did they create the atmosphere or simply cash in on it? I think the latter.

11   "The climate of fear," one of my sources called it, let up somewhat in 1989 and 1990, for a variety of reasons, including the ironic fact that as the country headed into economic recession and people really had things to worry about, they suddenly grew less frightened about what the Edper guys could do to them — maybe because the Edper guys had less to give them, I don't know. Another reason (which I was making a valiant effort to explore in my book) was that the massive 1989 reorganization of the entire $100 billion empire, the one that was to have given Edward's [Bronfman's] family a nice liquid investment they could sell on the open market, was orchestrated in such a way that it enabled the managers, the lawyers and accountants who had been hired to run the family fortune, the means to buy Edward's stake themselves. This transfer of control of the country's largest business organization was done so deftly that even people involved with it still do not know what the managers paid for their stake or where they got the money to buy it. No Canadian securities regulator has ever asked that such information be provided to any of the public investors who were affected by it because, in the words of all the regulators I attempted to interview, they did not see where the Edper managers had contravened any part of the *Ontario Securities Act* or *Canada Business Corporations Act* — and besides, they said, they had more than enough on their plates dealing with all the paper that comes across their desks without going off looking for extra work where it wasn't required.

12   Bay Street, however, saw what had gone on and didn't like it. Investment managers and securities analysts, who had been fans of the group up until that time, balked at behaviour that appeared to undermine all the principles of fair play and shared rewards that the Edper managers had been preaching for decades. This is another reason why they started to talk.

13   My real trouble started in 1990, when it became clear the country was in the middle of a major economic downturn that was going to affect everybody, the Edper group included. Real estate values started dropping, natural resource prices fell and there was widespread talk of a cash flow crunch. I began working on stories aimed at telling readers what was happening in this corporate empire that paid their dividends or their salaries, controlled companies from which they

rented office or mail space or that held their mortgages or life insurance policies. But the group had decided that it did not want any press, good or bad, until after the recession had passed and they had things under control.

14 This is where we really parted company, the Edper managers and I. I explained that, while I was prepared to write stories about how well-equipped they were to withstand a serious downturn if they agreed to provide details about their plans, I would under no condition sit by until they were ready to talk. I wrote a couple of stories they didn't like and would not agree to comment on while they were in progress. They scheduled a couple of off-the-record meetings to set the record straight on what they said were misunderstandings and misinterpretations of events. I attended a couple of these meetings, and pressed the Edper managers to go public with the numbers and explanations they provided. They refused. In the summer of 1990, they began demanding meetings with editors of other reporters who wrote stories they did not like. My editors replied by saying that they stood behind all of my stories. We told group spokesmen such as Willard (Bill) L'Heureux and Manfred Walt that we would no longer accept any information or comments that were not on the record for public consumption. We started playing hard ball. And so did they.

15 From that point on, every substantial story I have ever written about the group — as well as many of the less consequential ones — have drawn a written response, filled with complaints and threats of legal action. The word they use most often is malice: because I chose to disregard their directives, and to stop playing by their rules, I write unbalanced and biased stories that demonstrate malice and contempt toward these companies and their principles. I have thick file folders full of these letters, as well as the so-called "accuracy audits" that Reid, the PR consultant, does for his clients, which are also peppered with language about my attitude. As any lawyer will tell you — the *Globe and Mail's* lawyers informed me a long time ago — the paper trail is prepared more for the judge's benefit than the correspondent's. Every time they write to me, I have to write back, explaining that I am honest and hard-working and willing to incorporate any information they care to give me into the stories that I write. Lawyers have also told me that the charge of malice — which, like so many aspects of Canadian libel law dates from the sixteenth and seventeenth centuries — is designed to allow a plaintiff to seek aggravated damages when it can be proven that a writer has a personal vendetta resulting in salient facts being deliberately overlooked or omitted; but, in fact, is exploited to get access to all the notes and recordings and drafts used to prepare whatever story or piece of analysis leads to the libel action. What these two pieces of advice have meant is that since the summer of 1990 I have spent almost as much time responding to letters accusing me of crimes against journalism as writing and researching stories about Edper group companies.

• • •

16 It must be noted that I do not write stories about personal scandals. I have never tried to delve into the private lives of the Bronfman family, or the people who manage their companies. I write stories that are exclusively about business relationships and events: how much money companies have, where they spend it, what managers say and whether they live up to their promises, how one company

gets control of another, what people think about it, what, if anything, public reg-
ulators choose to do about controversial situations, who wins, who loses, who
benefits. That sort of thing. Essentially, it comes down to describing how people
who control a large chunk of Canada's business life get and wield power. The difficulty lies in the fact that when you get and wield enough power, you can control a great deal of how much is written about you, for two reasons. First, because
Canadian disclosure laws only require public companies to announce transactions
that are big enough to be deemed "material" to their enterprise (and the definition of material is largely left up to management), the bigger you are, the less you
disclose. Second, once you have enough cash to play with, launching a law-suit
can become part of the cost of corporate PR. A journalist might end up offending one or two thin-skinned senior managers, but the managers don't pay to keep
the lawsuit before the courts for two or three years; instead, the shareholders do,
albeit out of pretax dollars.

17   While big organizations such as the *Globe* might have the resources to fight
back against a large corporate empire with one of the best and most expensive
law firms in town, few writers can manage it. I, for one, cannot. Neither could
Macmillan of Canada, the independent publishing company that had planned to
publish my book. When Macmillan got one of L'Heureux's letters warning it to
be very careful my manuscript did not contain any mistakes that might prompt
a lawsuit — a message that, despite being couched in careful lawyerly language,
made it pretty clear that these mistakes would be in the eyes of the beholders —
owner and then-president Ron Besse reacted first and asked questions later. He
fired off a letter to Hees announcing that Macmillan was withdrawing from the
project because it could not afford to defend itself against an action from Hees.
Besse claims his intent was to get Hees to back down publicly. Hees officials
claim that they never intended to stop publication of the book, only to warn us
to be careful. Whatever the various intentions, the impact was classic libel chill:
the project sits in limbo. Macmillan has expressed interest in going ahead with
the book, but does not want to make any commitment to fight for it, in or out of
court, regardless of whether or not lawyers pronounce it fair and defensible. I am
willing to spend years in court, if necessary, explaining my research and establishing some much-needed modern common law. But I am not willing to lose my
home, a large chunk of my income and — if a publisher is persuaded to settle out
of court for economic reasons — my own reputation and ability to write about
the Edper group in the future. Under the current circumstances, this is what I
am being asked to do.

18   It's one thing for a large and fairly profitable newspaper to pay what it costs
to print material that the Edper guys do not like. It's something else for an independent publishing company — and/or an individual author — to take this sort
of battle on. When a particular newspaper story becomes the subject of a libel
suit, you are, in most cases, dealing with a limited amount of material, including notes and drafts. With a book, however, everything gets a great deal more
complicated and expensive.

19   In this country, the concern is not so much what happens to you if you get
to court (as I've been preparing for that event for years, I have no doubt about
my ability to build an airtight case), it's that the laws are so skewed toward

protecting the plaintiff that you may never get there. Under existing Canadian libel law, all a plaintiff needs to be is offended and wealthy to get a libel suit under way. This is particularly the case in Canada because there is no need to show that a writer got any facts wrong or did any tangible damage to get the whole legal show on the road. The law assumes that if someone is upset enough to sue, there must have been some real damage to pocket-book or reputation. In many cases, this is simply not true. But lack of real damage does not become an issue until you get up before the judge — if you can last long enough. So what you — or, to make this personal — what I have to worry about is the fact that the accusation of malice gives these people immediate access to years and years of research that have filled every filing drawer they'll give me at the paper and a whole bunch more at home with files full of notes. I've seen lawsuits over single newspaper stories last for years because the plaintiff can use the law ostensibly to probe the reporter's state of mind before during and after he or she wrote the offending story. This, in effect, means that the more thorough you are, and the more research you do, the easier it will be to punish you effectively if and when you are sued.

20   The vast majority of libel suits brought against Canadian journalists are settled out of court — some because the plaintiff runs out of money, some because the defendant and/or his publisher decide that it is not practical or possible to keep paying what it costs to fight the case. Libel lawyers like to tell you about the many cases where an individual of modest means engages in some justified but financially hopeless fight with a big, powerful news organization. We don't hear much about these cases because they usually involve people who do not have the money to control what's written or said about them, and the cases disappear quickly. This is worrisome, and wrong, and needs to be addressed under proposed changes to our libel laws.

21   From where I sit, however, the really scary cases are those in which valid and provocative information or commentary has been written about powerful and wealthy people who simply wish to suppress such information and commentary, and are willing to spend whatever amount of money is necessary to do so. These cases drag on and on, and, regardless of clauses in publishing contracts that are supposed to give a writer final say about an out-of-court settlement, publishing companies almost invariably seem to end up settling out of court. It is interesting how effective subtle pressure can be when someone sues a writer who would like to be published again in the future. Should Hees sue over my book, and should my publisher decide at any point that it could no longer afford to pay a small army of $250-an-hour lawyers to pick through ten filing cabinet drawers of notes and reports, and should my publisher persuade me to settle, I'd be on the hook for half the costs of our designated expenses (compared with 25 per cent if we went all the way to court, where I had no doubt of success). And the libel-related clauses in my contract started out being better than most.

22   Some people I have since talked to are persuaded to write books with no insurance at all. So what does this say about the amount of controversial material they are willing to include, however true and relevant that material might be?

Topics for consideration:

1. In paragraph 7 Noble names some of the companies controlled by the Edper group when she began her research in late 1986. Using your library and/or the Internet find out what changes may have taken place in the relationships between these companies since then.

2. Noble clearly thinks that it is in the public interest to know about the inside workings of corporations. What reasons does she give for this? Do you agree?

3. Why did Edper lawyers start threatening Noble with legal action? How did these threats hamper her work?

4. Noble describes how Canadian libel laws favour the plaintiff rather than the defendant. Do you think that this should be changed? Based on Noble's account of the law as it now stands, what changes, if any, would you recommend?

Margaret Atwood (1939-

One of Canada's foremost novelist and poets, Atwood now has an international reputation. She was awarded the Governor General's Award for her collection of poetry The Circle Game *(1964) and for her novel* The Handmaid's Tale *(1985), as well as the 1996 Giller Prize for* Alias Grace.

Atwood's response to pornography in this essay arises partly from her research for her novel Bodily Harm *(1982). She describes how people often mean vastly different things when they refer to "pornography" and focuses her own concern on violent or sadistic pornography that, since it will not "just go away on its own," will require "informed and responsible decisions about how to deal with it."*

PORNOGRAPHY

1   When I was in Finland a few years ago for an international writers' conference, I had occasion to say a few paragraphs in public on the subject of pornography. The context was a discussion of political repression, and I was suggesting the possibility of a link between the two. The immediate result was that a male journalist took several large bites out of me. Prudery and pornography are two halves of the same coin, said he, and I was clearly a prude. What could you expect from an Anglo-Canadian? Afterward, a couple of pleasant Scandinavian men asked me what I had been so worked up about. All "pornography" means, they said, is graphic depictions of whores, and what was the harm in that?

2   Not until then did it strike me that the male journalist and I had two entirely different things in mind. By "pornography," he meant naked bodies and sex. I, on the other hand, had recently been doing the research for my novel *Bodily Harm*, and was still in a state of shock from some of the material I had seen, including the Ontario Board of Film Censors' "outtakes." By "pornography," I meant women getting their nipples snipped off with garden shears, having meat hooks stuck into their vaginas, being disemboweled, little girls being raped; men (yes, there are some men) being smashed to a pulp and forcibly sodomized. The cutting edge of pornography, as far as I could see, was no longer simple old copulation, hanging from the chandelier or otherwise: it was death, messy, explicit and highly sadistic. I explained this to the nice Scandinavian men. "Oh, but that's just the United States," they said. "Everyone knows they're sick." In their country, they said, violent "pornography" of that kind was not permitted on television or in movies; indeed, excessive violence of any kind was not permitted. They had drawn a clear line between erotica, which earlier studies had shown did not incite men to more aggressive and brutal behavior toward women, and violence, which later studies indicated did.

3   Some time after that I was in Saskatchewan, where, because of the scenes in *Bodily Harm*, I found myself on an open-line radio show answering questions about "pornography." Almost no one who phoned in was in favor of it, but again they weren't talking about the same stuff I was, because they hadn't seen it. Some

of them were all set to stamp out bathing suits and negligees, and, if possible, any depictions of the female body whatsoever. God, it was implied, did not approve of female bodies, and sex of any kind, including that practised by bumblebees, should be shoved back into the dark, where it belonged. I had more than a suspicion that *Lady Chatterley's Lover*, Margaret Laurence's *The Diviners*, and indeed most books by most serious modern authors would have ended up as confetti if left in the hands of these callers.

4   For me, these two experiences illustrate the two poles of the emotionally heated debate that is now thundering around this issue. They also underline the desirability and even the necessity of defining the terms. "Pornography" is now one of those catchalls, like "Marxism" and "feminism," that have become so broad they can mean almost anything, ranging from certain verses in the Bible, ads for skin lotion and sex texts for children to the contents of *Penthouse*, Naughty '90s postcards and films with titles containing the word *Nazi* that show vicious scenes of torture and killing. It's easy to say that sensible people can tell the difference. Unfortunately, opinions on what constitutes a sensible person vary.

5   But even sensible people tend to lose their cool when they start talking about this subject. They soon stop talking and start yelling and the name-calling begins. Those in favor of censorship (which may include groups not noticeably in agreement on other issues, such as some feminists and religious fundamentalists) accuse the others of exploiting women through the use of degrading images, contributing to the corruption of children, and adding to the general climate of violence and threat in which both women and children live in this society; or, though they may not give much of a hoot about actual women and children, they invoke moral standards and God's supposed aversion to "filth," "smut" and deviated *preversion*, which may mean ankles.

6   The camp in favor of total "freedom of expression" often comes out howling as loud as the Romans would have if told they could no longer have innocent fun watching the lions eat up Christians. It too may include segments of the population who are not natural bedfellows: those who proclaim their God-given right to freedom, including the freedom to tote guns, drive when drunk, drool over chicken porn and get off on videotapes of women being raped and beaten, may be waving the same anticensorship banner as responsible liberals who fear the return of Mrs. Grundy, or gay groups for whom sexual emancipation involves the concept of "sexual theater." *Whatever turns you on* is a handy motto, as is *A man's home is his castle* (and if it includes a dungeon with beautiful maidens strung up in chains and bleeding from every pore, that's his business).

7   Meanwhile, theoreticians theorize and speculators speculate. Is today's pornography yet another indication of the hatred of the body, the deep mind-body split, which is supposed to pervade Western Christian society? Is it a backlash against the women's movement by men who are threatened by uppity female behavior in real life, so like to fantasize about women done up like outsize parcels, being turned into hamburger, kneeling at their feet in slavelike adoration or sucking off guns? Is it a sign of collective impotence, of a generation of men who can't relate to real women at all but have to make do with bits of celluloid and paper? Is the current flood just a result of smart marketing and aggressive promotion by the money men in what has now become a multibillion-dollar

industry? If they were selling movies about men getting their testicles stuck full of knitting needles by women with swastikas on their sleeves, would they do as well, or is this penchant somehow peculiarly male? If so, why? Is pornography a power trip rather than a sex one? Some say that those ropes, chains, muzzles and other restraining devices are an argument for the immense power female sexuality still wields in the male imagination: you don't put these things on dogs unless you're afraid of them. Others, more literary, wonder about the shift from the 19th-century Magic Woman or Femme Fatale image to the lollipop-licker, airhead or turkey-carcass treatment of women in porn today. The proporners don't care much about theory: they merely demand product. The antiporners don't care about it in the final analysis either: there's dirt on the street, and they want it cleaned up, now.

8   It seems to me that this conversation, with its *You're-a-prude/You're-a-pervert* dialectic, will never get anywhere as long as we continue to think of this material as just "entertainment." Possibly we're deluded by the packaging, the format: magazine, book, movie, theatrical presentation. We're used to thinking of these things as part of the "entertainment industry," and we're used to thinking of ourselves as free adult people who ought to be able to see any kind of "entertainment" we want to. That was what the First Choice pay-TV debate was all about. After all, it's only entertainment, right? Entertainment means fun, and only a killjoy would be antifun. What's the harm?

9   This is obviously the central question: *What's the harm?* If there isn't any real harm to any real people, then the antiporners can tsk-tsk and/or throw up as much as they like, but they can't rightfully expect more legal controls or sanctions. However, the no-harm position is far from being proven.

10   (For instance, there's a clear-cut case for banning — as the federal government has proposed — movies, photos and videos that depict children engaging in sex with adults: real children are used to make the movies, and hardly anybody thinks this is ethical. The possibilities for coercion are too great.)

11   To shift the viewpoint, I'd like to suggest three other models for looking at "pornography" — and here I mean the violent kind.

12   Those who find the idea of regulating pornographic materials repugnant because they think it's Fascist or Communist or otherwise not in accordance with the principles of an open democratic society should consider that Canada has made it illegal to disseminate material that may lead to hatred toward any group because of race or religion. I suggest that if pornography of the violent kind depicted these acts being done predominantly to Chinese, to blacks, to Catholics, it would be off the market immediately, under the present laws. Why is hate literature illegal? Because whoever made the law thought that such material might incite real people to do real awful things to other real people. The human brain is to a certain extent a computer: garbage in, garbage out. We only hear about the extreme cases (like that of American multimurderer Ted Bundy) in which pornography has contributed to the death and/or mutilation of women and/or men. Although pornography is not the only factor involved in the creation of such deviance, it certainly has upped the ante by suggesting both a variety of techniques and the social acceptability of such actions. Nobody knows yet what effect this stuff is having on the less psychotic.

13   Studies have shown that a large part of the market for all kinds of porn, soft and hard, is drawn from the 16-to-21-year-old population of young men. Boys used to learn about sex on the street, or (in Italy, according to Fellini movies) from friendly whores, or, in more genteel surroundings, from girls, their parents, or, once upon a time, in school, more or less. Now porn has been added, and sex education in the schools is rapidly being phased out. The buck has been passed, and boys are being taught that all women secretly like to be raped and that real men get high on scooping out women's digestive tracts.

14   Boys learn their concept of masculinity from other men: is this what most men want them to be learning? If word gets around that rapists are "normal" and even admirable men, will boys feel that in order to be normal, admirable and masculine they will have to be rapists? Human beings are enormously flexible, and how they turn out depends a lot on how they're educated, by the society in which they're immersed as well as by their teachers. In a society that advertises and glorifies rape or even implicitly condones it, more women get raped. It becomes socially acceptable. And at a time when men and the traditional male role have taken a lot of flak and men are confused and casting around for an acceptable way of being male (and, in some cases, not getting much comfort from women on that score), this must be at times a pleasing thought.

15   It would be naïve to think of violent pornography as just harmless entertainment. It's also an educational tool and a powerful propaganda device. What happens when boy educated on porn meets girl brought up on Harlequin romances? The clash of expectations can be heard around the block. She wants him to get down on his knees with a ring, he wants her to get down on all fours with a ring in her nose. Can this marriage be saved?

16   Pornography has certain things in common with such addictive substances as alcohol and drugs: for some, though by no means for all, it induces chemical changes in the body, which the user finds exciting and pleasurable. It also appears to attract a "hard core" of habitual users and a penumbra of those who use it occasionally but aren't dependent on it in any way. There are also significant numbers of men who aren't much interested in it, not because they're undersexed but because real life is satisfying their needs, which may not require as many appliances as those of users.

17   For the "hard core," pornography may function as alcohol does for the alcoholic: tolerance develops, and a little is no longer enough. This may account for the short viewing time and fast turnover in porn theatres. Mary Brown, chairwoman of the Ontario Board of Film Censors, estimates that for every one mainstream movie requesting entrance to Ontario, there is one porno flick. Not only the quantity consumed but the quality of explicitness must escalate, which may account for the growing violence: once the big deal was breasts, then it was genitals, then copulation, then that was no longer enough and the hard users had to have more. The ultimate kick is death, and after that, as the Marquis de Sade so boringly demonstrated, multiple death.

18   The existence of alcoholism has not led us to ban social drinking. On the other hand, we do have laws about drinking and driving, excessive drunkenness and other abuses of alcohol that may result in injury or death to others.

19   This leads us back to the key question: what's the harm? Nobody knows, but

this society should find out fast, before the saturation point is reached. The Scandinavian studies that showed a connection between depictions of sexual violence and increased impulse toward it on the part of male viewers would be a starting point, but many more questions remain to be raised as well as answered. What, for instance, is the crucial difference between men who are users and men who are not? Does using affect a man's relationship with actual women, and, if so, adversely? Is there a clear line between erotica and violent pornography, or are they on an escalating continuum? Is this a "men versus women" issue, with all men secretly siding with the proporners and all women secretly siding against? (I think not; there *are* lots of men who don't think that running their true love through the Cuisinart is the best way they can think of to spend a Saturday night, and they're just as nauseated by films of someone else doing it as women are.) Is pornography merely an expression of the sexual confusion of this age or an active contributor to it?

20   Nobody wants to go back to the age of official repression, when even piano legs were referred to as "limbs" and had to wear pantaloons to be decent. Neither do we want to end up in George Orwell's *1984*, in which pornography is turned out by the State to keep the proles in a state of torpor, sex itself is considered dirty and the approved practice it only for reproduction. But Rome under the emperors isn't such a good model either.

21   If all men and women respected each other, if sex were considered joyful and life-enhancing instead of a wallow in germ-filled glop, if everyone were in love all the time, if, in other words, many people's lives were more satisfactory for them than they appear to be now, pornography might just go away on its own. But since this is obviously not happening, we as a society are going to have to make some informed and responsible decisions about how to deal with it.

Topics for consideration:

1. In paragraph 7 Atwood offers a series of questions without attempting to provide answers to any of them. What answers would you give to these questions? What answers do you think Atwood would give?

2. What objection does Atwood raise to considering pornography as "entertainment"?

3. In paragraphs 17 and 18 Atwood compares pornography with alcoholism. Do you think the analogy is appropriate? Are there points where it doesn't fit?

4. Atwood mentions, without naming them, several studies on the effects of pornography. How important are such studies? What influence should they have on public policy decisions about pornography?

5. This essay was published before the Internet was in widespread use. Do you think that Atwood's arguments are more or less valid in relation to the availability of pornographic material on the Internet?

CHAPTER 6

POLITICALLY SPEAKING

We tend to consider a "politician" as an entirely separate class of human being. Even some who have repeatedly been elected to public office will frequently try to show that they are not really politicians. However, as Allan Hutchinson points out in his reply to John Sopinka in the "Forbidden Words" chapter, anyone who speaks or writes on an issue of public significance is being "political." The set of opinions and values with which we approach the world amounts to an ideology, even though the charge of expressing "political" views or "ideological" interpretations is often used as an accusation against those with whom we disagree.

Many thoughtful people develop ideologies that cannot easily be summed up with a neat political label. George Orwell, who described his own political position with the seemingly contradictory phrase "Tory anarchist," was one such person. Orwell's own experiences both as a generator of government propaganda for the BBC during World War II and as a horrified observer of the role of propaganda in misrepresenting the events of the Spanish Civil War, gave him special insight into the dynamics of the language of political debate. One of several essays he wrote on the subject, "Politics and the English Language," has become a frequently reprinted classic on the subject. Despite his now dated examples that sound quite unfamiliar to most modern readers, the general principles of clear honest writing that he outlines remain valid and useful. It is ironic that Orwell's popularity has led to his name being invoked in support of the very political views that he would find most abhorrent. One Internet website, for example, provides material on Orwell's life and writings and then a list of links to scores of sites promoting the anti-Semitic view that the Holocaust never occurred.

Brian Fawcett's response to "Politics and the English Language," written nearly fifty years after Orwell's essay was published, points out the ways in which Orwell foresaw some of the changes that would take place later in the twentieth century. Fawcett also reconsiders Orwell's guidelines for clear writing and finds them as valid as when they were first written. He adds his own practical and conceptual tools to Orwell's original writer's toolbox.

The politically manipulative language that Orwell warned against is just as pervasive as in 1946 when his essay was published. However, a whole battery of electronic media have been added to the newspapers and radio on which the politicians of Orwell's day had to rely. Stephen Brockmann, in "Total Entertainment," shows how media now report warfare as a form of entertainment and in doing so serve as effective tools of political leaders. We become "consumers" rather than "citizens" and consequently the critical skills which Orwell urged us to develop atrophy and disappear.

"Politically Speaking" closes with a classic confrontation of opposing ideologies. "Objectivity" is often presented as a goal of good journalism, but Barbara Amiel's "Backstage Mozambique: A Flagrant Violation of Rights" and Rick Salutin's "Amiel: Beyond the Fringe" show how differing ideologies can result in widely differing accounts. Amiel's Mozambique in 1981 is a police state characterized by arbitrary arrests and imprisonments, whereas Salutin's is a struggling country trying to care for its people while emerging from a brutal colonial rule. The truth is not, as we are so often urged to say, "somewhere between the two." Rather the truth lies in the reader's ability to unravel the ideology behind the words.

George Orwell (1903-1950)

George Orwell (the pen name of British writer Eric Blair) is best known for his two books reflecting his life-long distrust of authoritarian government, Animal Farm *(1945) and* Nineteen Eighty-four *(1949). After leaving school Orwell joined the Indian Imperial Police in Burma, an experience recorded in the fictional* Burmese Days *(1934). Following his return to Britain and several years of voluntary poverty, Orwell joined an anarchist unit fighting in the Spanish Civil War and was seriously wounded. During World War II he worked for the BBC, an experience that was the partial inspiration for his invention of "newspeak," the truth-denying official language in* Nineteen Eighty-four.

In this classic essay Orwell makes a direct link between threats to democracy and linguistic decay. His distrust of political propaganda arises in part from his experiences in the Spanish Civil War, one of whose "dreariest effects" was to teach him, as he wrote in Homage to Catalonia *(1938) "that the Left-wing press is every bit as spurious and dishonest as that of the Right."*

POLITICS AND THE ENGLISH LANGUAGE

1 Most people who bother with the matter at all would admit that the English language is in a bad way, but it is generally assumed that we cannot by conscious action do anything about it. Our civilization is decadent and our language — so the argument runs — must inevitably share in the general collapse. It follows that any struggle against the abuse of language is a sentimental archaism, like preferring candles to electric light or hansom cabs to aeroplanes. Underneath this lies the half-conscious belief that language is a natural growth and not an instrument which we shape for our own purposes.

2   Now, it is clear that the decline of a language must ultimately have political and economic causes: it is not due simply to the bad influence of this or that individual writer. But an effect can become a cause, reinforcing the original cause and producing the same effect in an intensified form, and so on indefinitely. A man may take to drink because he feels himself to be a failure, and then fail all the more completely because he drinks. It is rather the same thing that is happening to the English language. It becomes ugly and inaccurate because our thoughts are foolish, but the slovenliness of our language makes it easier for us to have foolish thoughts. The point is that the process is reversible. Modern English, especially written English, is full of bad habits which spread by imitation and which can be avoided if one is willing to take the necessary trouble. If one gets rid of these habits one can think more clearly, and to think clearly is a necessary first step towards political regeneration: so that the fight against bad English is not frivolous and is not the exclusive concern of professional writers. I will come back to this presently, and I hope that by that time the meaning of what I have said here will have become clearer. Meanwhile, here are five specimens of the English language as it is now habitually written.

3   These five passages have not been picked out because they are especially bad — I could have quoted far worse if I had chosen — but because they illustrate

various of the mental vices from which we now suffer. They are a little below the average, but are fairly representative samples. I number them so that I can refer back to them when necessary:

[1] I am not, indeed, sure whether it is not true to say that the Milton who once seemed not unlike a seventeenth-century Shelley had not become, out of an experience ever more bitter in each year, more alien [*sic*] to the founder of that Jesuit sect which nothing could induce him to tolerate.
PROFESSOR HAROLD LASKI
Essay in 'Freedom of Expression'

[2] Above all, we cannot play ducks and drakes with a native battery of idioms which prescribes such egregious collocations of vocables as the Basic *put up with* for *tolerate* or *put at a loss* for bewilder.
PROFESSOR LANCELOT HOGBEN
'Interglossa'

[3] On the one side we have the free personality: by definition it is not neurotic, for it has neither conflict nor dream. Its desires, such as they are, are transparent, for they are just what institutional approval keeps in the forefront of consciousness; another institutional pattern would alter their number and intensity; there is little in them that is natural, irreducible, or culturally dangerous. But *on the other side*, the social bond itself is nothing but the mutual reflection of these self-secure integrities. Recall the definition of love. Is not this the very picture of a small academic? Where is there a place in this hall of mirrors for either personality or fraternity?
Essay on psychology in 'Politics' (New York)

[4] All the 'best people' from the gentlemen's clubs, and all the frantic fascist captains, united in common hatred of Socialism and bestial horror of the rising tide of the mass revolutionary movement, have turned to acts of provocation, to foul incendiarism, to medieval legends of poisoned wells, to legalize their own destruction of proletarian organizations, and rouse the agitated petty-bourgeoisie to chauvinistic fervour on behalf of the fight against the revolutionary way out of the crises.
Communist pamphlet

[5] If a new spirit is to be infused into this old country, there is one thorny and contentious reform which must be tackled, and that is the humanization and galvanization of the B.B.C. Timidity here will bespeak canker and atrophy of the soul. The heart of Britain may be sound and of strong beat, for instance, but the British lion's roar at present is like that of Bottom in Shakespeare's *Midsummer Night's Dream* — as gentle as any sucking dove. A virile new Britain cannot continue indefinitely to be traduced in the eyes, or rather ears, of the world by the effete languors of Langham Place, brazenly masquerading as 'standard English'. When the Voice of Britain is heard at nine o'clock, better far and infinitely less ludicrous to hear aitches honestly dropped than

the present priggish, inflated, inhibited, school-ma'amish arch braying of blameless bashful mewing maidens!
Letter in 'Tribune'

4   Each of these passages has faults of its own, but, quite apart from avoidable ugliness, two qualities are common to all of them. The first is staleness of imagery: the other is lack of precision. The writer either has a meaning and cannot express it, or he inadvertently says something else, or he is almost indifferent as to whether his words mean anything or not. This mixture of vagueness and sheer incompetence is the most marked characteristic of modern English prose, and especially of any kind of political writing. As soon as certain topics are raised, the concrete melts into the abstract and no one seems able to think of turns of speech that are not hackneyed: prose consists less and less of *words* chosen for the sake of their meaning, and more and more of *phrases* tacked together like the sections of a prefabricated hen-house. I list, below, with notes and examples, various of the tricks by means of which the work of prose construction is habitually dodged:

DYING METAPHORS. A newly invented metaphor assists thought by evoking a visual image, while on the other hand a metaphor which is technically 'dead' (e.g. *iron resolution*) has in effect reverted to being an ordinary word and can generally be used without loss of vividness. But in between these two classes there is a huge dump of worn-out metaphors which have lost all evocative power and are merely used because they save people the trouble of inventing phrases for themselves. Examples are: *Ring the changes on, take up the cudgels for, toe the line, ride roughshod over, stand shoulder to shoulder with, play into the hands of, no axe to grind, grist to the mill, fishing in troubled waters, rift within the lute, on the order of the day, Achilles' heel, swan song, hotbed.* Many of these are used without knowledge of their meaning (what is a 'rift', for instance?), and incompatible metaphors are frequently mixed, a sure sign that the writer is not interested in what he is saying. Some metaphors now current have been twisted out of their original meaning without those who use them even being aware of the fact. For example, *toe the line* is sometimes written *tow the line*. Another example is *the hammer and the anvil*, now always used with the implication that the anvil gets the worst of it. In real life it is always the anvil that breaks the hammer, never the other way about: a writer who stopped to think what he was saying would be aware of this, and would avoid perverting the original phrase.

OPERATORS or VERBAL FALSE LIMBS. These save the trouble of picking out appropriate verbs and nouns, and at the same time pad each sentence with extra syllables which give it an appearance of symmetry. Characteristic phrases are: *render inoperative, militate against, make contact with, be subjected to, give rise to, give ground for, have the effect of, play a leading part (role) in, make itself felt, take effect, exhibit a tendency to, serve the purpose of,* etc., etc. The keynote is the elimination of simple verbs. Instead of being a single word, such as *break, stop, spoil, mend, kill,* a verb becomes a *phrase*, made up of a noun or adjective tacked on to some general-purpose verb such as *prove, serve, form, play, render*. In addition, the passive voice is wherever possible used in preference to the active, and noun constructions are used instead of gerunds (*by examination of* instead of *by examining*). The range of verbs is further cut down by means of the *-ize* and *de-*formations, and the banal statements are given an appearance of profundity by means of the *not un-* formation. Simple conjunctions and prepositions are replaced by such phrases as *with respect to, having regard to, the fact that, by dint of, in view of, in the interests of, on the hypothesis that,* and the ends of sentences are saved from anticlimax by such resounding commonplaces as *greatly to be desired, cannot be left out of account, a development to be expected in the near future, deserving of serious consideration, brought to a satisfactory conclusion,* and so on and so forth.

PRETENTIOUS DICTION. Words like *phenomenon, element, individual* (as noun), *objective, categorical, effective, virtual, basic, primary, promote, constitute, exhibit, exploit, utilize, eliminate, liquidate,* are used to dress up simple statements and give an air of scientific impartiality to biased judgments. Adjectives like *epoch-making, epic, historic, unforgettable, triumphant, age-old, inevitable, inexorable, veritable,* are used to dignify the sordid processes of international politics, while writing that aims at glorifying war usually takes on an archaic colour, its characteristic words being: *realm, throne, chariot, mailed fist, trident, sword, shield, buckler, banner, jackboot, clarion.* Foreign words and expressions, such as *cul de sac, ancien régime, deus ex machina, mutatis mutandis, status quo, gleichschaltung, weltanschauung,* are used to give an air of culture and elegance. Except for the useful abbreviations *i.e., e.g.,* and *etc.,* there is not real need for any of the hundreds of foreign phrases now current in English. Bad writers, and especially scientific, political and sociological writers, are nearly always haunted by the notion that Latin or Greek words are grander than Saxon ones, and unnecessary words like *expedite, ameliorate, predict, extraneous, deracinated, clandestine, subaqueous* and hundreds of others constantly gain ground from their Anglo-Saxon opposite numbers.[1] The jargon peculiar to Marxist waiting (*hyena, hangman, cannibal, petty bourgeois, these gentry, lacquey, flunkey, mad dog, White Guard,* etc.) consists largely of words and phrases translated from Russian, German or French, but the normal way of coining a new word is to use a Latin or Greek root with the appropriate affix and, where necessary, the *-ize* formation. It is often easier to make up words of this kind (*deregionalize, impermissible, extramarital, non-fragmentatory* and so forth) than to think up the English words that will cover one's meaning. The result, in general, is an increase in slovenliness and vagueness.

MEANINGLESS WORDS. In certain kinds of writing, particularly in art criticism and literary criticism, it is normal to come across long passages which are almost completely lacking in meaning.[2] Words like *romantic, plastic, values, human, dead, sentimental, natural, vitality,* as used in art criticism, are strictly meaningless in the sense that they not only do not point to any discoverable object, but are hardly ever expected to do so by the reader. When one critic writes, 'The outstanding feature of Mr. X's work is its living quality', while another writes, 'The immediately striking thing about Mr. X's work is its peculiar deadness', the reader accepts this as a simple difference of opinion. If words like *black* and *white* were involved, instead of the jargon words *dead* and *living,* he would see at once that the language was being used in an improper way. Many political words are similarly abused.

The word *Fascism* has now no meaning except in so far as it signifies 'something not desirable'. The words *democracy, socialism, freedom, patriotic, realistic, justice*, have each of them several different meanings which cannot be reconciled with one another. In the case of a word like *democracy*, not only is there no agreed definition, but the attempt to make one is resisted from all sides. It is almost universally felt that when we call a country democratic we are praising it: consequently the defenders of every kind of régime claim that it is a democracy, and fear that they might have to stop using the word if it were tied down to any one meaning. Words of this kind are often used in a consciously dishonest way. That is, the person who uses them has his own private definition, but allows his hearer to think he means something quite different. Statements like *Marshal Pétain was a true patriot, The Soviet Press is the freest in the world, The Catholic Church is opposed to persecution*, are almost always made with intent to deceive. Other words used in variable meanings, in most cases more or less dishonestly, are: *class, totalitarian, science, progressive, reactionary, bourgeois, equality.*

5   Now that I have made this catalogue of swindles and perversions, let me give another example of the kind of writing that they lead to. This time it must of its nature be an imaginary one. I am going to translate a passage of good English into modern English of the worst sort. Here is a well-known verse from *Ecclesiastes*:

'I returned and saw under the sun, that the race is not to the swift, nor the battle to the strong, neither yet bread to the wise, nor yet riches to men of understanding, nor yet favour to men of skill; but time and chance happeneth to them all.'

6   Here it is in modern English:

'Objective consideration of contemporary phenomena compels the conclusion that success or failure in competitive activities exhibits no tendency to be commensurate with innate capacity, but that a considerable element of the unpredictable must invariably be taken into account.'

7   This is a parody, but not a very gross one. Exhibit (3), above, for instance, contains several patches of the same kind of English. It will be seen that I have not made a full translation. The beginning and ending of the sentence follow the original meaning fairly closely, but in the middle the concrete illustrations — race, battle, bread — dissolve into the vague phrase 'success or failure in competitive activities'. This had to be so, because no modern writer of the kind I am discussing — no one capable of using phrases like 'objective consideration of contemporary phenomena' — would ever tabulate his thoughts in that precise and detailed way. The whole tendency of modern prose is away from concreteness. Now analyse these two sentences a little more closely. The first contains forty-nine words but only sixty syllables, and all its words are those of everyday life. The second contains thirty-eight words of ninety syllables: eighteen of its words are from Latin roots, and one from Greek. The first sentence contains six vivid images, and only one phrase ('time and chance') that could be called vague. The second contains not a single, fresh, arresting phrase, and in spite of its ninety syllables it gives only a shortened version of the meaning contained in the first. Yet without a doubt it is the second kind of sentence that is gaining ground in modern English. I do not want to exaggerate. This kind of writing is not yet universal, and outcrops of simplicity will occur here and there in the worst-written page. Still, if you or I were told to write a few lines on the uncertainty of human

fortunes, we should probably come much nearer to my sentence than to the one from *Ecclesiastes*.

8   As I have tried to show, modern writing at its worst does not consist in picking out words for the sake of their meaning and inventing images in order to make the meaning clearer. It consists in gumming together long strips of words which have already been set in order by someone else, and making the results presentable by sheer humbug. The attraction of this way of writing is that it is easy. It is easier — even quicker, once you have the habit — to say *In my opinion it is a not unjustifiable assumption that* than to say *I think*. If you use ready-made phrases, you not only don't have to hunt about for words; you also don't have to bother with the rhythms of your sentences, since these phrases are generally so arranged as to be more or less euphonious. When you are composing in a hurry — when you are dictating to a stenographer, for instance, or making a public speech — it is natural to fall into a pretentious, Latinized style. Tags like *a consideration which we should do well to bear in mind* or *a conclusion to which all of us would readily assent* will save many a sentence from coming down with a bump. By using stale metaphors, similes and idioms, you save much mental effort, at the cost of leaving your meaning vague, not only for your reader but for yourself. This is the significance of mixed metaphors. The sole aim of a metaphor is to call up a visual image. When these images clash — as in *The Fascist octopus has sung its swan song, the jackboot is thrown into the melting pot* — it can be taken as certain that the writer is not seeing a mental image of the objects he is naming; in other words he is not really thinking. Look again at the examples I gave at the beginning of this essay. Professor Laski (1) uses five negatives in fifty-three words. One of these is superfluous, making nonsense of the whole passage, and in addition there is the slip *alien* for akin, making further nonsense, and several avoidable pieces of clumsiness which increase the general vagueness. Professor Hogben (2) plays ducks and drakes with a battery which is able to write prescriptions, and, while disapproving of the everyday phrase *put up with*, is unwilling to look *egregious* up in the dictionary and see what it means. (3), if one takes an uncharitable attitude towards it, is simply meaningless: probably one could work out its intended meaning by reading the whole of the article in which it occurs. In (4), the writer knows more or less what he wants to say, but an accumulation of stale phrases chokes him like tea leaves blocking a sink. In (5), words and meaning have almost parted company. People who write in this manner usually have a general emotional meaning — they dislike one thing and want to express solidarity with another — but they are not interested in the detail of what they are saying. A scrupulous writer, in every sentence that he writes, will ask himself at least four questions, thus: What am I trying to say? What words will express it? What image or idiom will make it clearer? Is this image fresh enough to have an effect? And he will probably ask himself two more: Could I put it more shortly? Have I said anything that is avoidably ugly? But you are not obliged to go to all this trouble. You can shirk it by simply throwing your mind open and letting the ready-made phrases come crowding in. They will construct your sentences for you — even think your thoughts for you, to a certain extent — and at need they will perform the important service of partially concealing your meaning even from yourself. It is at this point that the special connection between politics and the debasement of language becomes clear.

9   In our time it is broadly true that political writing is bad writing. Where it is not true, it will generally be found that the writer is some kind of rebel, expressing his private opinions and not a 'party line'. Orthodoxy, of whatever colour, seems to demand a lifeless, imitative style. The political dialects to be found in pamphlets, leading articles, manifestos, White Papers and the speeches of Under-Secretaries do, of course, vary from party to party, but they are all alike in that one almost never finds in them a fresh, vivid, home-made turn of speech. When one watches some tired hack on the platform mechanically repeating the familiar phrases — *bestial atrocities, iron heel, bloodstained tyranny, free peoples of the world, stand shoulder to shoulder* — one often has a curious feeling that one is not watching a live human being but some kind of dummy: a feeling which suddenly becomes stronger at moments when the light catches the speaker's spectacles and turns them into blank discs which seem to have no eyes behind them. And this is not altogether fanciful. A speaker who uses that kind of phraseology has gone some distance towards turning himself into a machine. The appropriate noises are coming out of his larynx, but his brain is not involved as it would be if he were choosing his words for himself. If the speech he is making is one that he is accustomed to make over and over again, he may be almost unconscious of what he is saying, as one is when one utters the responses in church. And this reduced state of consciousness, if not indispensable, is at any rate favourable to political conformity.

10   In our time, political speech and writing are largely the defence of the indefensible.[3] Things like the continuance of British rule in India, the Russian purges and deportations, the dropping of the atom bombs on Japan, can indeed be defended, but only by arguments which are too brutal for most people to face, and which do not square with the professed aims of political parties. Thus political language has to consist largely of euphemism, question-begging and sheer cloudy vagueness. Defenceless villages are bombarded from the air, the inhabitants driven out into the countryside, the cattle machine-gunned, the huts set on fire with incendiary bullets: this is called *pacification*. Millions of peasants are robbed of their farms and sent trudging along the roads with no more than they can carry: this is called *transfer of population* or *rectification of frontiers*. People are imprisoned for years without trial, or shot in the back of the neck or sent to die of scurvy in Arctic lumber camps: this is called *elimination of unreliable elements*. Such phraseology is needed if one wants to name things without calling up mental pictures of them. Consider for instance some comfortable English professor defending Russian totalitarianism. He cannot say outright, 'I believe in killing off your opponents when you can get good results by doing so.' Probably, therefore, he will say something like this:

'While freely conceding that the Soviet régime exhibits certain features which the humanitarian may be inclined to deplore, we must, I think, agree that a curtailment of the right to political opposition is an unavoidable concomitant of transitional periods, and that the rigours which the Russian people have been called upon to undergo have been amply justified in the sphere of concrete achievement.'

11   The inflated style is itself a kind of euphemism. A mass of Latin words falls upon the facts like soft snow, blurring the outlines and covering up all the details. The great enemy of clear language is insincerity. When there is a gap between one's real and one's declared aims, one turns as it were instinctively to long words

and exhausted idioms, like a cuttlefish squirting out ink. In our age there is no such thing as 'keeping out of politics'. All issues are political issues, and politics itself is a mass of lies, evasions, folly, hatred and schizophrenia. When the general atmosphere is bad, language must suffer. I should expect to find — this is a guess which I have not sufficient knowledge to verify — that the German, Russian and Italian languages have all deteriorated in the last ten or fifteen years, as a result of dictatorship.

12   But if thought corrupts language, language can also corrupt thought. A bad usage can spread by tradition and imitation, even among people who should and do know better. The debased language that I have been discussing is in some ways very convenient. Phrases like *a not unjustifiable assumption, leaves much to be desired, would serve no good purpose, a consideration which we should do well to bear in mind,* are a continuous temptation, a packet of aspirins always at one's elbow. Look back through this essay, and for certain you will find that I have again and again committed the very faults I am protesting against. By this morning's post I have received a pamphlet dealing with conditions in Germany. The author tells me that he 'felt impelled' to write it. I open it at random, and here is almost the first sentence that I see: '[The Allies] have an opportunity not only of achieving a radical transformation of Germany's social and political structure in such a way as to avoid a nationalistic reaction in Germany itself, but at the same time of laying the foundations of a co-operative and unified Europe.' You see, he 'feels impelled' to write — feels, presumably, that he has something new to say — and yet his words, like cavalry horses answering the bugle, group themselves automatically into the familiar dreary pattern. This invasion of one's mind by ready-made phrases (*lay the foundations, achieve a radical transformation*) can only be prevented if one is constantly on guard against them, and every such phrase anaesthetizes a portion of one's brain.

13   I said earlier that the decadence of our language is probably curable. Those who deny this would argue, if they produced an argument at all, that language merely reflects existing social conditions, and that we cannot influence its development by any direct tinkering with words and constructions. So far as the general tone or spirit of a language goes, this may be true, but it is not true in detail. Silly words and expressions have often disappeared, not through any evolutionary process but owing to the conscious action of a minority. Two recent examples were *explore every avenue* and *leave no stone unturned,* which were killed by the jeers of a few journalists. There is a long list of flyblown metaphors which could similarly be got rid of if enough people would interest themselves in the job; and it should also be possible to laugh the *not un-* formation out of existence,[4] to reduce the amount of Latin and Greek in the average sentence, to drive out foreign phrases and strayed scientific words, and, in general, to make pretentiousness unfashionable. But all these are minor points. The defence of the English language implies more than this, and perhaps it is best to start by saying what it does *not* imply.

14   To begin with it has nothing to do with archaism, with the salvaging of obsolete words and turns of speech, or with the setting up of a 'standard English' which must never be departed from. On the contrary, it is especially concerned with the scrapping of every word or idiom which has outworn its usefulness. It has nothing

to do with correct and syntax, which are of no importance so long as one makes one's meaning clear, or with the avoidance of Americanisms, or with having what is called a 'good prose style'. On the other hand it is not concerned with fake simplicity and the attempt to make written English colloquial. Nor does it even imply in every case preferring the Saxon word to the Latin one, though it does imply using the fewest and shortest words that will cover one's meaning. What is above all needed is to let the meaning choose the word, and not the other way about. In prose, the worst thing one can do with words is to surrender to them. When you think of a concrete object, you think wordlessly, and then, if you want to describe the thing you have been visualizing you probably hunt about till you find the exact words that seem to fit. When you think of something abstract you are more inclined to use words from the start, and unless you make a conscious effort to prevent it, the existing dialect will come rushing in and do the job for you, at the expense of blurring or even changing your meaning. Probably it is better to put off using words as long as possible and get one's meaning as clear as one can through pictures or sensations. Afterwards one can choose — not simply *accept* — the phrases that will best cover the meaning, and then switch round and decide what impression one's words are likely to make on another person. This last effort of the mind cuts out all stale or mixed images, all prefabricated phrases, needless repetitions, and humbug and vagueness generally. But one can often be in doubt about the effect of a word or a phrase, and one needs rules that one can rely on when instinct fails. I think the following rules will cover most cases:

(i) Never use a metaphor, simile or other figure of speech which you are used to seeing in print.

(ii) Never use a long word where a short one will do.

(iii) If it is possible to cut a word out, always cut it out.

(iv) Never use the passive where you can use the active.

(v) Never use a foreign phrase, a scientific word or a jargon word if you can think of an everyday English equivalent.

(vi) Break any of these rules sooner than say anything outright barbarous.

15   These rules sound elementary, and so they are, but they demand a deep change of attitude in anyone who has grown used to writing in the style now fashionable. One could keep all of them and still write bad English, but one could not write the kind of stuff that I quoted in those five specimens at the beginning of this article.

16   I have not here been considering the literary use of language, but merely language as an instrument for expressing and not for concealing or preventing thought. Stuart Chase and others have come near to claiming that all abstract words are meaningless, and have used this as a pretext for advocating a kind of political quietism. Since you don't know what Fascism is, how can you struggle against Fascism? One need not swallow such absurdities as this, but one ought to recognize that the present political chaos is connected with the decay of language, and that one can probably bring about some improvement by starting at the verbal end. If you simplify your English, you are freed from the worst follies of orthodoxy. You cannot speak any of the necessary dialects, and when you make

a stupid remark its stupidity will be obvious, even to yourself. Political language — and with variations this is true of all political parties, from Conservatives to Anarchists — is designed to make lies sound truthful and murder respectable, and to give an appearance of solidity to pure wind. One cannot change this all in a moment, but one can at least change one's own habits, and from time to time one can even, if one jeers loudly enough, send some worn-out and useless phrase — some *jackboot, Achilles' heel, hotbed, melting pot, acid test, veritable inferno*, or other lump of verbal refuse — into the dustbin where it belongs.

Notes:

1. "An interesting illustration of this is the way in which the English flower names which were in use till very recently are being ousted by Greek ones, *snapdragon* becoming *antirrhinum, forget-me-not* becoming *myosotis*, etc. It is hard to see any practical reason for this change of fashion: it is probably due to an instinctive turning-away from the more homely word and a vague feeling that the Greek word is scientific" (Orwell's note).

2. "Example: 'Comfort's catholicity of perception and image, strangely Whitmanesque in range, almost the exact opposite in aesthetic compulsion, continues to evoke that trembling atmospheric accumulative hinting at a cruel, an inexorably serene timelessness. ... Wrey Gardiner scores by aiming at simple bullseyes with precision. Only they are not so simple, and through this contented sadness runs more than the surface bitter-sweet of resignation' (*Poetry Quarterly*)" (Orwell's note).

3. This essay was written in 1946.

4. "One can cure oneself of the *not un-* formation by memorizing this sentence: *A not unblack dog was chasing a not unsmall rabbit across a not ungreen field*" (Orwell's note).

Topics for consideration:

1. In paragraph 2 Orwell takes as his starting point the assumption that "the decline of a language must ultimately have political and economic causes." Do you agree that language is in a decline? What political and economic causes might be at work?

2. Orwell identifies "staleness of imagery" and "lack of precision" as key faults in his sample passages. Take either a recent political speech, a letter to the editor, or an editorial from your local newspaper and see to what extent these faults occur. Rewrite the example so that it is free of these faults and compare your version with the original.

3. In paragraph 10 Orwell writes that "political speech and writing are largely the defence of the indefensible." Select an indefensible public policy you are aware of and write a short speech defending it using the devices of "euphemism, question begging and ... cloudy vagueness."

4. "Politics and the English Language" was first published in 1946. What political events would most have influenced Orwell in developing the views he displays in this essay?

Further reading:

George Orwell, *Homage to Catalonia* (1938)

Bernard Crick, *George Orwell: A Life* (1980)

http://www.resort.com~prime8/Orwell/index.html Political writings of Orwell 1937 to 1949 including many newspaper columns, letters and editorials.

http://www.levity.com/corduroy/orwell.htm Biography and links.

Brian Fawcett (1944-

Brian Fawcett was born in Northern British Columbia and now lives in Vancouver. An editor of Books in Canada *and former columnist for the* Globe and Mail, *his published books combine fiction with acute social and cultural commentary. He is author of* Cambodia: A Book for People Who Find Television Too Slow *(1990).*

Fawcett's essay was written to offer guidance to students writing for their college or university newspapers. Using George Orwell's 1946 essay "Politics and the English Language," he discusses how Orwell's fundamental principles of clear thinking and honest expression are still relevant even though the political scene has changed beyond recognition. Fawcett credits Orwell with having foreseen the managerial revolution which that shape the end of the twentieth century and suggests how Orwell's principles can be applied in the society that resulted.

POLITICS AND THE ENGLISH LANGUAGE (1991)

1   Almost a half century has passed since George Orwell wrote "Politics and the English Language." For most English-speaking writers who have had a strong desire to discover and tell the truth, the essay has been a basic text. In it, Orwell argued that clear thinking and good writing are integral to the health of democracy, and that bad language can and does corrupt thought. Those ideas are almost self-evident truths today, and the detailed arguments Orwell made in the essay remain remarkably current. My renovation of the essay's contents will therefore be — as my title suggests — a bracketed and respectful addendum.

2   Since 1946, when Orwell published his essay, there have been profound changes in the way human beings speak, write, and use knowledge. Radio, television and a number of less public but powerful cybernetic technologies now occupy our days, often filling our heads with information we either haven't asked for or don't have the right equipment or the wealth to make use of. We "communicate" or "process information" through immensely powerful and fast electronic systems, but we write less, and, I suspect, think less. Certainly the critical thought going on these days concerning the crucial subjects of politics and culture is in a state of conceptual disarray. Contemporary electronic communications are a matter of fewer and fewer people speaking to (and for) more and more people.

3   Despite this, the English language itself has taken only one major turn Orwell didn't foresee. In 1946, he feared that the undefeated totalitarianisms of World War II would breed Newspeak, the official language of his novel *1984*. Newspeak made understanding impossible by truncating or outlawing all the textures and nuances of language. But instead of Newspeak, the 1990s are filled with techno-gibberish dialects that glamourize the obvious and the trivial, and obscure (or sever) connections to other fields of meaning. The intent of these dialects is to make it difficult for anyone to communicate beyond their "lifestyle" enclave. The dialects serve the same purpose as Newspeak — creating political silence — by conning us into thinking that we're somehow more fashionable and smarter than the next enclave, and by getting us to fiddle endlessly with an assortment of

disposable commodities, fake threats to our well-being, and obsessive notions of correct behaviour that border on fanaticism.

4   What that means is that politics — or maybe it is just authority — has changed. Some changes have been for the better, and some haven't. Within the industrialized nations, violent authority can no longer successfully operate indefinitely, and police states have demonstrated that they simply aren't efficient enough to compete with cybernetic economies — as witnessed by the recent economic and political collapse of the Soviet bloc. Violent authority is still the rule outside the industrialized part of the world, where, if anything, life has become more violent and arbitrary. In the privileged societies like ours, authority has merely gotten itself out of our faces and into our lowest appetites. Universal social justice, it should be noted, is as distant as it has ever been.

5   For an individual trying to think and write accurately in the intellectual and informational environments of the 1990s, politics are no longer a matter of complaining about the stupidity or corruption of the government. Politics — and they are a plural now — are the things we do to one another, or allow to be done to us by others through indifference or lust or whatever we've decided is self-interest. As the millennium nears, and as the referent ideologies that have guided and/or deluded us through the century collapse around us, politics have more to do with how we allow ourselves to be lied to and deceived than how we are imprisoned or liberated. In the industrialized democracies, most of us are free as the birds. We just happen to be turkeys and chickens, with a few aggressive but deluded raptors tossed into the mix to make the peaceful cower and to give the brainlessly ambitious something to aspire to.

6   Communists, capitalists, fascists and all the permutations in between have become meaningless epithets. Orwell himself saw that coming. Everything he wrote from *Homage to Catalonia* to his death argues against the structuring of politics by ideological claim. For us, his essay "Second Thoughts on James Burnham" (1946) ought to be read as the companion piece to "Politics and the English Language" because it reveals his characteristic skill at eluding the seductive ideological nets of his time. In that essay he summarizes Burnham's future scenario in *The Managerial Revolution* (1940) in terms that will be chillingly familiar to us: "Capitalism is disappearing, but socialism is not replacing it. What is now arising is a new kind of planned, centralized society which will be neither capitalist nor, in any accepted sense of the word, democratic. The rulers of this new society will be the people who effectively control the means of production: that is, business executives, technicians, bureaucrats and soldiers, lumped together by Burnham under the name of 'managers'." That's a fair description of the corporate oligarchy that controls the world today — an oligarchy that operates on eighteen-month financial horizons and proudly promises an end to the excesses of ideological politics. That Orwell was able to foresee and critique the weaknesses of a vast political change that contemporary analysts are just now learning to bend their minds around is typical of just how brilliant his intellectual method was.

7   Understanding how the new politics work will require a few conceptual simplifications. One of them is recognizing that there are only three kinds of political beings in the world. First, there are people who will try to see and tell the truth, and try to act on it in the interests of everyone. Second, there are — let me

put this as succinctly as possible — assholes. Third, there are people who are too weakened by poverty, disease and violence to care about being either of the first two. Good politics consists of behaviours that enlarge the numbers of type A and reduce, without violence or arrogance, the numbers of types B and C. I'm pretty sure that George Orwell would agree with this simplification.

8   In the new environment, clear political writing and thinking is perhaps more urgently needed than ever. It remains an essential component of democracy — which is, after all, not a political state but a social, intellectual and moral activity. For that activity to regain the alertness it requires to be effective, the toolbox a political writer needs to deal with the 1990s needs some additions.

9   I'm going to suggest a few tools. For the sake of convenience, I'll divide them into two categories, practical and conceptual. Most of the practical ones have to do with keeping writing direct and simple and personal, which is the only antidote I know for the poison of technogibberish. The conceptual tools I use are generally attitudinal tactics aimed at inducing and nourishing the habitual skepticism Orwell taught me. What follows isn't meant to be either an exclusive or exhaustive toolbox on its own, merely an addition to Orwell's. Intellectual tools don't work the same way for everyone, but I can at least testify that the ones I offer help me to keep my eyes open in the cyclone of lies daily life has become. And sometimes, they help me to close them with laughter.

PRACTICAL WRITING TOOLS

1. George Orwell's "Politics and the English Language" ought to be reread about every six months. Nearly everything he said remains relevant. His examples should be periodically updated with your own.

2. Write simple sentences whenever you can, and let your musicianship take care of the need for melody. If you've got a tin ear, get into another line of work.

3. Fill your writing with nouns and verbs. Naming things accurately makes them palpable, and making them move in specific ways enables them to be tested. Beware of adjectives and adverbs because they are linguistic grease. Using more than two successive adjectives in a single sentence is a reliable signal that a Mazola party is going on in the writer's head.

4. Never use a semicolon. I know I'm repeating Orwell, but this is so important it bears repeating. Semicolons are absolutely reliable signals that a sentence should be rewritten, generally to make it more direct. And incidentally, you should only use a colon if you're wearing a tuxedo or sitting on white porcelain.

5. Contemporary writers should learn how to use a word processor, and how to manipulate data systems. If you're a working writer, it is more important to own a word processor than a car. Word processors are necessary to keep up to the current speeds of information transmission and production, and because having other people decipher your lousy hand-writing is vile and exploitive political behaviour.

CONCEPTUAL TOOLS

1. Beware of sacred cattle. They are stupid, filled with inflated ideas about their importance and the unimportance of everything in their projected path, and if you let them run around inside your head they will eat or trample everything, including your intelligence. On the other hand, do not attempt to run anyone else's sacred cattle over a cliff unless you're certain you can succeed. Today's sacred cattle are a new and much more dangerous breed than the ones that emerged in the 1950s and are now dying out. The new breed are very aggressive, they're used to living in information-overloaded cities, and if you wave a red flag at them they'll pin you to the nearest concrete abutment without a qualm.

2. Good political writing always recognizes when it is running in a stampede and attempts to get out of it as quickly as possible, preferably without trying to work the herd. This is a fancy way of saying that the job of a political writer is to ask the questions that aren't being addressed by the visible agendas of authority or exclusive interest. Generally speaking, figuring out — or making up — answers is someone else's job — someone you probably won't trust or like. Never trust anyone with an answer to a question you haven't asked.

3. Recognize that everyone is sincere and that sincerity has no relationship to anything but righteousness, which is an enemy of good political writing, and usually, death to clear thinking. Accusing anyone of insincerity precludes the possibility of further political debate, and you're supposed to be writing in order to start and keep people talking to one another.

4. The language of political speeches and official communiques is never meaningless. Most of the time, speeches, press releases and official communiques are cybernetic devices meant to occupy a vital political moment or space without committing the originating speaker, institution or agency to action. They require full translation, which involves an analysis of what they both say and don't say. This is also true of commercial language, which is becoming indistinguishable from political language.

5. If you don't believe in God, don't quote Her. By this I mean that writers must try to be personal, and should not make their voices out to be more than they are — the words and gestures of a single person who has thought through and researched a subject matter. Practising this successfully involves a number of mental habits, some of which are as follows:
   a) never using the word "we" unless you know who you're collectivizing and are willing to kiss them all on the mouth — and mean it.
   b) never using the word "reality" without putting quotes around it.
   c) recognizing that there is no such thing as a rhetorical question.
   d) never dismissing a dead or older writer for not knowing what is currently fashionable around the office or inside your dopey head.

e) remembering that the surface of any important truth will more resemble the skin of a toad than an alabaster statue or brochure materials that promise to make you into a human bullet. Warts are not something that will disappear from writing and thinking just because we don't approve of bumps and lesions. They're what used to be called texture, and without texture there is no such thing as meaning. Bullets, whatever form they come in, are the opposite of meaning, and they are signals of the collapse of human intelligence.

6. Try not to contribute to the cacophony of disinformation and nonsense. In a democracy the only opinion anyone is entitled to is an informed and preferably detailed one. If all you're hearing is the sound of your own voice, silence is the right option.

7. Finally, make people laugh with your writing. Laughter disrupts narrow logic, which is the operating system for authority, cattle stampedes, and ill-conceived judgments of all sorts. People who are laughing find it hard to start wars, molest children, and are unlikely to discover that the person or persons in their immediate vicinity are in league with the devil. Orthodoxy most easily breeds where laughter is absent.

Topics for consideration:

1. Fawcett suggests that while Orwell's arguments "remain remarkably current … there have been profound changes in the way human beings speak, write, and use knowledge." Which of the examples used in Orwell's "Politics and the English Language" earlier in this section seem to you most dated and why?

2. In his list of practical writing tools Fawcett recommends rereading Orwell's essay every six months and periodically updating his examples with your own. Select one of Orwell's categories of "Dying Metaphors," Verbal False Limbs," "Pretentious Diction," and "Meaningless Words," and find current examples.

3. Fawcett's essay was written at the request of Canadian University Press for a handbook for editors of student newspapers. Look at the current issue of your student newspaper. Are the editors and writers following similar criteria to the ones Fawcett recommends? What changes do you think he would suggest?

4. Is Fawcett's own writing entirely free of the faults that Orwell names?

Stephen Brockmann

Stephen Brockmann teaches German literature at Michigan State University. His essay "Total Entertainment" was originally published in Queen's Quarterly.

The media presented the Persian Gulf War as a stunning success for coalition forces. Rejecting the equivocal language of the post-Vietnam years, allied leaders spoke of "war" and "victory" while their pilots and troops revelled in their ability to "kick butt." Television viewers were invited to marvel at "our side's" technological prowess and to welcome the return of the "good war." Brockmann examines the media fallout of the Gulf War and wonders if we are now unduly receptive to "good wars."

TOTAL ENTERTAINMENT

"Play up! play up! and play the game!"

— Henry Newbolt, *"Vitai Lampada"*

1   On the evening of 17 January 1991, between 6:30 and 7:00, the major television networks were broadcasting their news programs, and most Americans were watching to see whether the war against Saddam Hussein would finally begin. Neither the networks nor their viewers were disappointed. Fifteen minutes into the broadcasts the anchors switched to their men in Baghdad's Al-Rashid Hotel, where reporters announced that the American bombardment had started. Baghdad's anti-aircraft batteries began to go to work, lighting up the nighttime sky in a martial celebration which, many American observers noted, reminded them of the Fourth of July, New Year's Eve, or a Christmas Tree. Streaks of upward-moving light illuminated the smoke-filled city, and the explosions of incoming and outgoing shells could be heard for miles around. Two hours later, when the American president came on television to speak to the nation, consumers were watching as never before. The networks reported that the president's ten-minute speech was the most popular event in television history.

2   Finally, the unpleasant little cold war that had followed the end of the bigger Cold War was over. The uncertainty, the waiting, the feeling of impotence and isolation were at an end. The nation came together in a vast television family, and every viewer knew that he was no longer alone, that hundreds of millions of his fellow Americans were watching the very same thing at the very same time. The sense of excitement, of community, ensured that on the war's first day neither consumers nor sponsors particularly minded the disappearance of advertising or popular television game shows and sit-coms from the major television networks, all replaced by a strict regime of total news. The eight-hour time difference between the East Coast and the Persian Gulf guaranteed that operations started in the middle of the night in the Middle East would make it immediately onto prime time at home. Europeans were less lucky. Deep in sleep at the beginning of operations, they could only wake up, rub their eyes, and listen to the news from their radios or read it in their newspapers and hope to see coverage on their

evening television programs more than half a day after the events had begun. But listening to the news and reading about it were not the same thing as seeing it, live. It was not just in the United States that CNN's ratings skyrocketed 271 per cent; orders for CNN boomed in Europe, too, and many European television networks were forced to buy newsreel coverage from American suppliers. It was a video war in more ways than one. Even in the early days of the war, the French philosopher Paul Virilio declared that it had already become a "world war, the first total electronic war. No one can become a deserter." Virilio said that the war represented the triumph of total news, news as pure speed, the defeat of democracy by "dromocracy" (the rule of speed).

3   Many observers said that the war reminded them of a video game, an arcade full of pale-cheeked male adolescents pushing buttons, pulling levers, destroying the enemy. It was the "made-for-television war," "Nintendo with high explosives." Watching the war on television, the viewer became a commander or a pilot himself, zooming in on the intersection of two lines on the radar for a direct hit. The war was curiously antiseptic. It consisted of targets, flashes, bulls-eyes, missiles taking off, homing-in, exploding — all in the blueish glimmer of video light. The only human faces one saw were those of the boyish American pilots giving the thumbs-up sign as they prepared for take-off or saying, like their president, "We're gonna kick butt!" as they got into their planes. It would not be another Vietnam, Americans were assured.

4   This assurance was interpreted to mean not only that the war would be swift, successful, and relatively painless, but that it would not invade American living rooms with unpleasant details as had been the case twenty years earlier, in what reporter Tim Page called "the first and only war that could be reported openly." When, four weeks into the war, after tens of thousands of Iraqi casualties, network television finally did show brief coverage of the American bombing of an Iraqi civilian shelter on 13 February — in which hundreds of non-combatant men, women, and children were killed or wounded — shock and anger were directed not so much at the military, or even at the Iraqis, as at Peter Arnett, the CNN reporter who had first broken the story and thus, according to critics, played into the hands of Iraqi propaganda. Few made the opposite criticism, castigating reporters for their reliance on the US military for war information.

5   As for Iraqi military casualties, estimated at over 100,000 after the war, "It's almost as if you were turning on the light in the kitchen at night and the cockroaches begin to run, and we kill them," said US air force commander Dick White about Iraqi troop movements in the south of Kuwait. But the cockroaches' death agonies were not considered newsworthy, either by the military or, for the most part, by news consumers. Asked after the war what images had stuck with them from their hundreds of hours of television viewing, most consumers had forgotten any images of death and agony and remembered only the pinpoint precision of the video target.

6   In a report to the Pentagon issued many months after the war had finished, leading media organizations finally got up their courage to complain that the government's restrictions had "made it impossible for reporters and photographers to tell the public the full story of the war."[1] Covering the war for one major

newsweekly, retired Army Colonel David Hackworth, who had been the most decorated soldier in the Vietnam war, declared, "I had more guns pointed at me by Americans or Saudis who were into controlling the press than in all my years of actual combat." But such complaints were too little, too late. During the war itself there was virtually no outrage at the military's decision to censor all news at the scene of operations. Even the transport back home of the remains of dead American soldiers, euphemistically called "body bags," could not be covered; reporters were kept out of the Dover air force base where the remains were to come home. "That has no news value whatsoever, soldiers in pain and agony," said Lieutenant Colonel Angel of US central command in Dhahran. A War College textbook urged commanders to "seek out the media and try to bring them in to write stories and produce television shows or clips in support of the organization's goals."[2] Reporters were organized in pools and told never to leave the company of their military "escorts." The result was media reporting that fully served the military's aims and presented a rosy, exciting picture of the war itself.

7   By and large, the public and even most members of the media approved of these restrictions; the public did not want to hear about the war's less pleasant aspects, and the media did not want to report them. During the third week of the war, ABC polled its viewers to inquire whether they found the network's images of the war one-sided, and the viewers responded that they enjoyed the pro-American high tech videos and did not want critical journalism. Of course few media moguls were as honest as Germany's Franz Josef Wagner, editor-in-chief of the newspaper *Super!*, who declared point blank "Making newspapers is a drug." But even during the war itself few would have contested the trance-like, spaced-out, drugged states of consciousness induced by images of the war. *Ex post facto* media recrimination proved a convenient way to foist off blame for a job that appeared, in retrospect, to have been botched. During the war itself, however, television reporters took great care in their military reports to assure viewers that they were complying with military censorship and revealing nothing of value, and in general their assurances were correct. Moreover, in spite of their complaints of military censorship, the media packed up and left the theatre of war immediately after the first week of March, once the censorship was lifted and it would have been possible to present a more accurate picture of the war. "The game is over," one pilot told CNN, and that was that. The media's job was not to report on events but to create them. As one communications theorist noted in the war's aftermath, "The idea of objective reality is an illusion with a rather large potential for pleasure and therefore quite widespread."[3] The law of the media was not just the law of the land, it was the law of nature.

8   It was a vastly popular war. Before it began, Americans had been deeply divided in their opinions. In the months following the August invasion of Kuwait, it was not just Democrats, left-wingers, and representatives of most of the mainstream Christian churches in the United States who criticized the president's activist response; many in his own party and on the far right criticized the response as well, asking why the United States should be concerned at all about the invasion of a small principality, democratic or not, with which the US had no defensive treaties whatsoever. Congress had barely given the president the authority to use

military force after the expiration of the 15 January deadline. The peace movement in the United States was growing as the deadline drew near. But once the war had actually begun, a plague of yellow ribbons began infesting American oak trees and telephone poles, multiplying exponentially, filling entire neighbourhoods in a sea of yellow, and Old Glory appeared on house after house. Twenty-first century folklorists will be certain to study the transformation of Tony Orlando and Dawn's 1970s hit song about a girl tying yellow ribbons around an oak tree for her convict boyfriend into an instant tradition, first for hostages and then for the military. In some vague way, the yellow ribbon seemed to mean support for the troops, and there was no one who did not support the troops. As was reiterated again and again on network news, the men and women in the Arabian sands, well-trained professionals all, had a job to do, and they were going to do it. Some people were lawyers, some doctors, some teachers, some hit-men, some engineers, some corporate executives, some plumbers, some electricians, some computer hacks, some bureaucrats; they all had a job to do. These people's job was soldiering. No one ever inquired too closely into what that "job" was, or what the soldiers were being trained to do. Killing cockroaches was one of the more direct metaphors. Like the civilian casualties, euphemistically referred to as "collateral damage," the troops' actual mission was one of the war's taboos. Even the peace movement, which, in spite of the war's popularity, managed to pull off a large demonstration in Washington on 26 January, emphasized its support for the troops in signs and buttons that read "Support the troops! Bring them home now!," along with the *de rigueur* yellow ribbons and American flags.

9   In this war, patriotism was definitely "in"; lack of patriotism was "out." The troops, the country, the flag, the president — it all seemed to come together in one big emotional glob. T-shirts and buttons appeared that said "USA — THE BEST DAMN COUNTRY IN THE WORLD!," "USA — NUMBER ONE!," "GO, GO, GO USA!," and the like. Just as after the invasion of Panama, the president's popularity — which, due to the oncoming economic recession, various scandals involving the financial industry, and the decision in direct violation of a 1988 campaign promise to raise taxes, had been at an all-time low in the summer of 1990 — rose to new heights after the war's debut, once again demonstrating the accuracy of Machiavelli's doctrine that wars abroad always neatly deflect attention from trouble at home. Immediately after victory, news spread that the president's popularity rating was at 90 per cent, the highest level in half a century. Advertising executives expressed appreciation for the government's professional-quality marketing of the war, declaring that the government had been able to develop such refined advertising techniques by continually testing and retesting its image and its concepts in the marketplace to discover what worked.

10   Naturally, this war had its forces of darkness as well. The Prince of Darkness was the president of Iraq, referred to not as "Hussein," but rather as "Saddam," almost as if he were intimately known to those discussing him, an intimate little Satan. For some, "Saddam" was worse than Hitler; for others he was merely as bad as Hitler. But that he stood in some meaningful connection to that incarnation of evil few doubted. The good grey *New York Times* threw staid caution to the wind and published a quarter-page cartoon reminiscent of the most effective Nazi

anti-Semitic propaganda showing "The Descent of Man" from Cary Grant to ape to monkey to snake to "Saddam," emerging from a morass with flies buzzing about his head. Even those usually queasy about comparing Hitler or the Holocaust to anything actually present in the world today — afraid that such comparisons might trivialize the memory of previous events — had no trouble making the comparison now, and by the time the Scud missiles started landing in Israel, two days after the beginning of the war, the sight of Israelis in gas masks was seen as evidence of a threatened new Holocaust. No matter that not a single one of the Scuds shot at Israel carried chemical weapons, or that the Scuds proved ineffective and inaccurate, or that the Purim antics of children playing with their masks in no way resembled life and death at Treblinka or Buchenwald. This was a Holocaust we prevented; this was a Hitler we conquered before he was able to work his will.

11   Yet the comparisons with World War II and the Holocaust revealed a deep American need for repetition of and analogy with what writer Studs Terkel had accurately called "The Good War." When Captain Doug Wisnioski, an American soldier, entered Kuwait after the successful US invasion, he declared in a much-quoted turn of phrase: "I'm sure this equals what our parents saw in World War II. It makes the waiting and anticipation worth it."[4] Wisnioski's statement indicates the intense desire of a younger generation to equal or surpass the feats of its parents, but it is both exaggerated and not quite enough. Any Blitzkrieg in this war was American, not German, and it was only the Iraqi Scuds that resembled the German V-2 rockets: a weapon of retaliation by a military power already doomed to lose, they fell randomly and, for the most part, insignificantly, on civilian targets in Israel and Saudi Arabia. Their impotence was further underscored by the success of American Patriot missiles used to intercept them. The seeming terror the Scuds caused was out of all proportion to their actual effectiveness. In *Gravity's Rainbow* Thomas Pynchon pictures a London population going on with its life more or less nonchalantly while the V-2s fall around it, sometimes causing horrible damage. In the Persian Gulf war, entire populations in Dhahran, Tel Aviv, Jerusalem, Haifa, and Riyadh donned gas masks and sealed off rooms in order to prepare for a threat that never arrived. There was a quality of spectacle about the entire affair: news reporters struggling into gas masks on camera, live, while network anchors halfway around the globe told them earnestly to be more concerned with their own safety than with reporting the news. There was something safe and comfortable about the spectacle, like a horror film that sends chills down your spine, even though you know that nothing is really going to happen.

12   The impotence of the Iraqi Scud missiles contrasted poignantly with the accuracy and power of the Allied artillery. The Allies began the war with six weeks of aerial bombing, not of the World War II variety, but of a variety in which virtually every missile, from sea-launched cruise missiles to ground artillery, was reported to have hit — and often did hit — its military target precisely. There seemed little room for randomness to enter in between missile launches and "terminal orgasms," as Pynchon had referred to the landing of the V-2s. If the war was a text, then the Allied forces were far more sophisticated readers than the Iraqis. The actual ground campaign lasted for three days, and its outcome was a foregone conclusion from the very beginning. Iraqi forces surrendered in great

masses, losing almost all of their tanks and artillery. The tens of thousands of Iraqi dead compared to only a few score Allied dead. This was hardly "what our parents saw in World War II." It was vastly shorter, vastly less painful, vastly more impressive technologically. World War II became entertainment only after the fact, but the Persian Gulf war was entertainment from the very beginning. The well-trained professionals in the American infantry had little to do in this war but to march in and accept surrenders. The war was a triumph of new technology over old technology.

13 There was an inexorable quality to the war from the very first. Just as a gun that appears in the first act of a drama must, by dramaturgical consent, be used by the end of the last act, so too the appearance of such a huge contingent of the US army in the Arabian desert required its use. When, two days after the November 1990 elections, the president announced that he was increasing troop strength from two hundred thousand to half a million, it should have been clear even to the most reluctant that war really was coming. Anyone who had supported the initial two hundred thousand could hardly oppose reinforcements. The beginning of the air campaign on 16 January came with similar inevitability, as did the beginning of the short and spectacular ground campaign which brought the war to a close in the last week of February. Each step seemed preordained, inevitable, forcing viewers to remain just that: viewers observing but not influencing the course of events dictated by powers beyond them, required, as President Bush was fond of urging reporters, "to stay tuned." It was not just ordinary viewers but decision-makers themselves who claimed powerlessness. The president's repeated insistence at each stage that "the ball" was in "Saddam's court" further increased this feeling of helplessness, for the ball never seemed to be in "our" court, and "we" were always waiting for a return that never quite came. The feeling of impotence made assent to the beginning of the war all the more certain, for the potency of American technology in action gave a vicarious feeling of control, of effective activity in a world of stasis.

14 One of the most striking aspects about the Gulf war, linguistically, was that it represented a return to "normal" language. From the very beginning, this was a "war." It was not a defensive action or a conflict. American military leaders did not, for the most part, equivocate in describing what they were going to do; in spite of virtually total censorship, what information they gave referred directly to activities such as cutting off, killing, defeating, destroying. The aggressive language addressed itself specifically to an overcoming of the "Vietnam Syndrome," which the president said had been definitively "kicked" in his first victorious news conference.

15 If World War I marked the emergence of a cultural discourse of "War," then World War II marked the attempt to forge a counter-discourse of wars. If World War I, culturally, represents helplessness, loss, defeat, and uncertainty, then World War II represents the certain and triumphant resistance to evil. It is the epitome of the "good" war. Culturally, the Vietnam war and the Korean war fall into the pattern of World War I, while the Gulf war emphatically falls into the pattern of World War II. The ultimate outcome of the Gulf war represented the triumph of the WWII paradigm over the WWI paradigm. To overcome the "Vietnam Syndrome"

is to overcome the central trauma of the twentieth century: the trauma of World War I. It is to make war "fun" again.

16   To fight World War II, the paradigm of all wars, but without the trauma of World War I, without the vision of hopelessness, without the death, without the misery, is the supreme goal: a painless war in which total victory mediated by total news becomes Total Entertainment, negating recognition of Total War. The postmodern war rests on a fundament of War, the quintessential modern condition, but has returned to the residues of premodern military ideology, where wars have once again become a natural, unproblematic, weather-related occurrence. The great desire of postmodern culture, which is post-war culture, is to improve on World War II: to keep the black-and-white and the victory over absolute evil, but to do it painlessly, to transform war completely to the level of entertainment. As the First Lady declared the day after what Ted Koppel of ABC's *Nightline* called the Allied commander's successful "performance" for reporters at the "mother of all briefings," General H. Norman Schwarzkopf was more than just the World War II hero George Patton, he was also the Muppets' Fozzie Bear: triumphant warrior and cuddly toy all wrapped up in one. Entertainment had won, and would go on winning.

Notes:

1. Thomas Rosentiel, "Press asks Pentagon to Alter Wartime Curbs," *San Francisco Chronicle*, 1 July 1991, p. A6.

2. Cited by Jason DeParle, "Long Series of Military Decisions Led to Gulf War News Censorship," *The New York Times*, 5 May 1991, pp. 1 and 20. It is noteworthy that articles such as this appeared only several months after the war had ended.

3. Michael Hallev, in *Diezeit*, 5 July 1991, p.16. Haller's essay contains a useful summary of the current debate within communications theory the "radical constructivists," who hold that political reality is created by media images, and the more traditional "objectivists," who believe in an outside reality which the media report on. This debate, of course, touches on themes already covered in such earlier studies as Marshall McLuhan and Quentin Fiere, *The Medium is the Message* (New York: Random House, 1967) and Paul Watzlawick, *How Real is Real?: Confusion, Disinformation, Communication* (New York: Random House, 1976), or in William I. Thomas's 1932 declaration of the "Thomas Principle," according to which "If human beings define situations as real, then their consequences are real." See also Paul Watzlawick, ed., *The Invented Reality: How Do We Know What We Believe We Know?: Contributions to Constructivism* (New York: Norton, 1984).

4. *The New York Times*, 1 March 1991, pp. 2, 10.

Topics for consideration:

1. Brockmann refers to television viewers as news "consumers." What is the effect of this? What is Brockmann's intention?

2. What, according to Brockmann, were the key differences between the media coverage of the Gulf War and the Vietnam War?

3. The metaphor of war as a "game" is used in numerous quotations throughout this piece. What is the effect of this metaphor?

4. Brockmann refers to Nicolo Machiavelli's (1469–1527) advice to political leaders that "wars abroad always neatly deflect attention from trouble at home." What examples of this can you find in recent history?

5. Brockmann refers to the evocation of Hitler and the Holocaust in relation to Saddam Hussein. In what other contexts have you come across this comparison being used? Are these always appropriate?

6. What contrast does Brockmann make between people's experiences and behaviour during World War II and the Persian Gulf War? How can you account for these differences?

Barbara Amiel (1940-

Barbara Amiel has been a columnist for Maclean's *magazine since 1976. She was editor of* The Toronto Sun *from 1982–1984 and a columnist for* The Times *and* The Sunday Times *of London from 1986 to 1994. As Barbara Amiel Black she is Vice-President Editorial and a Director of Hollinger Inc.*

The much-discussed column from which this selection is taken described Amiel's experiences when she was imprisoned for three days in Mozambique during a trip to Southern Africa. Amiel, Toronto tour operator Sam Blyth, and American Jim Basker drove from Johannesburg to Mozambique. On entry they were waved though three checkpoints without having their passports stamped. After spending "a few days luxuriating under the African sun on the bleached beaches of the Indian Ocean," the three were arrested for not having visas when they tried to cross the border to Swaziland. Amiel told her story to Maclean's *magazine's Jane O'Hara from Johannesburg.*

[Historical note: At the time Amiel's column was written (1981) Portuguese colonial rule in Mozambique had only recently ended. South Africa was still an apartheid state, most of whose future leaders, such as Nelson Mandela, were either in jail or in exile.]

BACKSTAGE MOZAMBIQUE: A FLAGRANT VIOLATION OF RIGHTS

1 "When we were delivered to secret police headquarters, my greatest fear was that authorities would find out I was a journalist. I had been warned that Frelimo (the governing party of President Samora Machel) was wary of even Soviet-bloc journalists and was worried that it might be impossible to extricate a western journalist who had run afoul of the government. At headquarters, we were put in separate cells, and while Sam and Jim were being grilled for long periods over the next 36 hours, I began eating my notes and anything that might identify me as a journalist, including the guest list I had taken from Maputo's Palona hotel and my plastic-coated *Maclean's* I.D. card. Oddly enough, our interrogators seemed uninterested in me as a woman and directed most of their questions at the two men. It was one of the few times I had been grateful for being under the control of a male-chauvinist regime.

2 "When the secret police had finished their questioning, we were told to take only our necessities and ordered to follow two machine-gun-toting soldiers. We were not told where we were being taken. No phone calls were allowed. Mozambique is a country in which the Western concept of due process of law is unknown, and although we had been warned earlier to be careful not to break any laws — that there were no trials, no judges — the concerns had seemed foolish under the blue skies and hot yellow sun that inspired an awe of the beauty, not the terror, of Mozambique. From headquarters we were put in a vehicle with one other black man, a Mozambique-born South African, who exclaimed: 'O God. We are going to Machava.'

3   "Machava is the largest political prison in Mozambique, a vast compound surrounded by a 12-foot wall and fortified with barbed wire. There are nine cement cell blocks, each housing 20 to 30 prisoners. I was prisoner number 975 in cell block one. Sam and Jim, at times together, at times in solitary confinement, were placed in number eight. My cell mate was Tombe, a 45-year-old Mozambican woman whose crime was her suggestion of an alternate political party to Frelimo. She had been there six months, and, like most prisoners, had no idea when she would be released.

4   "Our cell was seven feet by ten feet, and specifically padlocked to keep the men from getting at us. In the daytime, it was like an oven and we would take off our clothes, although we had to suffer the indignity of having the guards peep at us through holes in the wall. The bed matting was full of lice. And most prisoners had contracted dysentery from the dirty water, a part of our dietary fixture which was supplemented twice a day with indigestible rice, bread, and two ounces of meat. Despite the appalling conditions, there was a great spirit of camaraderie among the prisoners. A prisoner in the cell next to Sam made him a pair of laces for his running shoes after the guards had taken his away so that he would not hang himself.

5   "Sam also managed to conduct a little business behind bars. During our holiday in Maputo, he had tried contacting the minister of information and tourism to discuss tour possibilities but to no avail. According to aides, the minister was either out or busy. Sam discovered how busy he really was when the minister, who happened to be imprisoned two cells down at Machava, introduced himself one day.

6   "On the third day of our imprisonment, Tombe became alarmed. Blood was coming out of my mouth while I lay sleeping. She called the guards, who looked worried that they might have an ill gringo on their hands. And so they bundled me up and prepared to take me to the military hospital in Maputo. My first instinct was to stay at the prison, thinking that our one chance was to stick together, but at the guards' insistence, I was led away.

7   "Within hours of my arrival at the hospital, I went into an intense malarial fever. Since most of the country's doctors fled the country in 1975, at the time of the Frelimo take-over, I was treated for six hours by three Bulgarian doctors who doused me with buckets of rain water to suppress my fever. Throughout, the most haunting spectacle was the faces of the armed soldiers who stood by laughing.

8   "Meanwhile, thanks to the help of the U.S. Vice-Consul, Howard Jeter, and the diligence of U.K. High Commission officials in Maputo, our release was arranged. The proper phone calls were made and Sam and Jim were told to pack their things. The car we had rented was waiting outside the prison for them. The luggage minus two pairs of men's shoes and a watch which had been stolen, was still there. When Sam and Jim came to the hospital to collect me, I was still not convinced that the ordeal was over. I had been a week without food, hooked up to an intravenous unit with unsterilized needles, and had been forced to use the most primitive of sanitary facilities. I know we have no recourse for what has happened. I can only feel sympathy for the people we have left behind in Machava."

Topics for consideration:

1. What are the implications of Amiel's title "Backstage Mozambique"?

2. Amiel gives a considerable number of factual details and measurements such as the exact height of prison walls, the dimensions of cells, the weight of the meat in prison rations. What purpose do you think these details serve?

3. What conclusions does Amiel want the reader to draw about her imprisonment?

Rick Salutin (1942-

Rick Salutin is a playwright, journalist and media critic. He has been an editor of This Magazine *and a regular columnist with the* Globe and Mail. *His best-known plays include* 1837: The Farmers' Revolt *and* Les Canadiens.

The article from which the following selection was excerpted was originally published in This Magazine *and was written as an immediate response to Barbara Amiel's account of her Mozambique experience. Salutin, who had himself visited Mozambique shortly before writing this article, casts doubt on Amiel's account and suggests that her portrayal of her experience is politically motivated.*

THE MOZAMBIQUE CAPER

1   Amiel's Mozambique Caper, a rather lazy holiday on a Mozambican beach with two companions (one a travel agent), was followed by arrest for being in the country without visas, followed by The Prison Ordeal and release. Amiel has ever since been beating this experience like a drum — as if its "I was there" quality can substitute for all the evidence she's never provided to prove her charges about "Marxism-socialism" in Southern Africa. Much of her account is, charitably speaking, implausible.

2   It is implausible, for example, that anyone, much less a travel agent, would approach such a sensitive border crossing (weeks later the South Africans sent an armed raid through) without a visa. It is however plausible that people without visas would cross the border surreptitiously if they wanted to get in but *lacked* visas. Amiel says that "barely literate Mozambican soldiers" were "confused" and simply waved them through. Amiel never tells us things like how she knew the guards were confused, or barely literate, or why anybody would post such primitives at a border point where documents are constantly being checked.

3   At any rate they spent "a few days luxuriating under the African sun on the bleached beaches of the Indian Ocean." During that time at Maputo's "Hotel Palona",* Amiel observed Cuban and Russian advisers "stuffing themselves" while outside "women and children sat on the pavement hoping for bread." Again Amiel doesn't tell us how she knew what those people were hoping for. (Assuming they were there. Truth is there *is* no pavement directly outside the Polana.) She says she found this juxtaposition "immoral and tasteless". Coming from someone who had juxtaposed jet-setters and distended bellies, this makes one pause for breath.

4   The trio were arrested for lacking visas when they tried to leave the country. Amiel says her "greatest fear was the authorities would find out I was a journalist." She'd "been warned" (naturally, we're not told by whom) that Frelimo "was wary of even Soviet-bloc journalists," and she worried "it might be impossible to extricate a Western journalist." Here we start to feel we are with Barbara in

---

*The correct name of the hotel is Polana. Graham Greene got it right in his last novel.

Wonderland. For a scant two years ago a *Maclean's* journalist, Dan Turner, made an accredited (i.e. by those same "authorities") visit to Mozambique and wrote rather positively about his trip in an issue which lists Barbara Amiel as "senior writer". Surely Amiel had read this article, given her areas of interest and her literacy. Subsequently Amiel "began eating" her notes — the ones about the Russians and Cubans gorging? — and her "plastic-coated *Maclean's* ID card". The three were taken off to Machava prison.

5   In prison, by her account, Amiel was placed in a cell "padlocked to keep the men from getting at us," and fed a diet of water plus, twice a day, "indigestible rice, bread and two ounces of meat". When she began coughing blood (that ID card?) she was taken to a military hospital where three East European doctors attended her. Now it seems to me there might have been a story were the men and women thrown *together* in jail, had she been starved (the diet is more than substantial by African standards) and had she been left to rot when she got sick. By her own account, it seems to me, the three-day prison stint fails to shock. In the hospital she tells us armed soldiers stood by laughing at her. But she doesn't explain how she knew what they were laughing at, and she also says she was in an "intense malarial fever" at the time. She spent a week in a hospital "hooked up to an intravenous unit with unsterilized needles and ... forced to use the most primitive of sanitary facilities". It isn't clear just what this last prissy phrase means, or where Amiel in her delirium thought she was — the Côte d'Azur?

6   At the end of the week, when the government was convinced the three were "bunglers" and not the kind of spies or saboteurs often uncovered in Mozambique, the three travellers returned to South Africa, which stands in a kind of counterpoint throughout Amiel's tale. Amiel had failed to heed a "conscientious warning" from the "South African authorities". They told her — Barbara, don't go! She says she was a fool to travel to Mozambique "or any other lawless country", "where political prisoners are tied in their cells with piano wire" and government practice is to "jail and torture their dissenting citizens." *And then she returns happily to South Africa??!!*

7   Has she truly not heard of Robben Island? The Pass Laws? Banning of dissident individuals and organizations, mass political trials, the murder of Steve Biko and the coverup? She must have. They're recounted in the same Amnesty International report Amiel quotes to discredit Mozambique. Not to mention the shutdown of the black press which occurred at about the time she was actually in South Africa. Or the historically unprecedented stripping of citizenship from sixteen million people as part of the Bantustan policy. The same South Africa which, along with the Khashoggi-supplied Lebanese Falange, arms and trains the right-wing terrorists of Italy? This is where I start to feel especially nonplussed.

SHEER IDEOLOGY

8   It seems to me that Amiel is pure ideologue, in the sense that her passion to propound her creed precedes just about everything else she might be doing as a writer. Standards of journalism, such as accurate reporting, argumentation, evidence, appear in her writing only occasionally and usually as mere façade for her world-view. Let me add some examples to those already given above.

9   She passes off unsubstantiated and even nonsensical claims as fact. (That she was in jail along with the Mozambican minister of Information and Tourism for example. This is ludicrous. At the most, someone *said* he was that. There is not even such a ministry as "Information and Tourism" in the Mozambican government.) She quotes sources with great selectivity and to a distorted effect. (It is true, as Amiel writes, that Amnesty International's annual report lists "detention without trial, political imprisonment and the death penalty" as concerns in Mozambique. But the three-page section is almost wholly about improvement of these conditions in Mozambique; and the far lengthier section on South Africa lists, in addition to these three concerns, banning, torture and prison conditions.)

10   She loads her language for bear. (South African border "authorities" are "conscientious", while guards at the Mozambican border are "machine-gun toting" — though machine-guns are toted all over South Africa, including the Johannesburg airport.) And she blandly presents all this as objective and reasonable.

11   More revealing however than her shoddy journalism is the cavalier way Amiel treats her own ostensible areas of humanitarian concern. In case after case they are only pretexts for ideological bashing. Starvation, for example, becomes a club with which to beat "Marxist terrorists". Or take literacy. She seems much exercised by the rate of illiteracy in Mozambique, putting it at 85%. The implication is that "Marxism-socialism" is responsible. Yet she doesn't tell us that when the Portuguese trundled off in 1974 after four hundred years the illiteracy rate was 98%, and that the dramatic decrease is solely due to the campaign Frelimo instituted.

12   I have been in Mozambican villages where virtually the entire workforce went to reading class at 5 a.m. before going to the fields. I have seen dogtired hotel workers trudge into classrooms after long hard days. (Lest Amiel guess this was staged, I saw them through a window while on a solitary stroll late at night.) I've sat in classes in northern Mozambique where peasant women lived dormitory-style all week away from their families, creating a severe drain on agricultural labour — in order to learn to read. This, in a rural Africa where traditionally women are not permitted to *speak*, much less *learn*, or leave their homes. And all of it solely due to the intense efforts of what Amiel airily calls (again no evidence) "a male-chauvinistic regime".

13   I refuse to believe Amiel does not know these basic facts about literacy in a country such as Mozambique. The literacy campaigns in third world socialist countries are renowned. At *This Mag* we sometimes feel we've printed too many such reports. The point is Amiel does not *care*. Not about illiteracy, not about starvation, not about human rights, nor about who is guilty or who is fighting back. She is out to do battle with "Marxism-socialism", that is her only real goal — and that is what lends her writing an abstract and inhuman quality even when she is ostensibly writing about humane concerns.

Topics for consideration:

1. Salutin cites numerous errors of accuracy in Amiel's account ranging from her mistaking the name of a hotel to her naming a non-existent ministry of the Mozambique government. Which errors would you consider serious and which trivial? Why?

2. Salutin says he feels "nonplussed" reading Amiel's account. Do you think that word describes his real feelings?

3. Salutin and Amiel clearly have very different political views. How are these differences shown in the perspectives they present on Southern Africa at that point in its history?

CHAPTER 7

COMMERCE & COMMUNICATION

Few people are willing to admit that their behaviour is influenced by advertising. Yet corporations spend billions every year to promote their products and in North America we inhabit an environment saturated with commercial messages. It has been calculated that college-age students are exposed to (some would say "consume") over a hundred commercials a day. Advertising takes up well over half of the space of North American newspapers and a quarter of television network prime time. Based on television viewing statistics, most people will spend a full year and a half of their lifetime watching television commercials.

The commercial messages that surround our lives have changed their form over the years. In its early days advertising generally focused on providing information about the product. A feature of such advertising tends to be extravagant or hard to verify claims about the qualities of the product. As early as 1759, Samuel Johnson, in the essay reprinted in this section, was complaining of how advertisers exploited the public appetite for news by placing their advertisements in newspapers and sought to outdo each other in the "magnificence of [their] promises."

While advertisements making inflated claims for the product are still part of the scene, advertising has now gone far beyond the "perfection" which Johnson thought it had achieved in the mid-eighteenth century. Advertisers now concentrate not so much on the intrinsic qualities of the product itself, but rather the product's image or "personality." Thus the advertisement often concentrates on promoting a particular lifestyle of which the product is shown to be an essential part. As Guy Debord wrote, "the real consumer thus becomes a consumer of illusion."*

Frank Coleman's essay, "Big Lie in Marlboro Country," examines the implications of the familiar Marlboro Country advertising on which the Philip Morris company has long relied. Coleman argues that the evocation of the "primal West" of the nineteenth century serves, not only to advertise a brand of cigarettes, but also to promote a pattern of behaviour mirroring the "unfettered exploitation" of the natural world that characterized that phase of history.

Nicole Nolan's "Isn't It Ironic?" examines the tongue-in-cheek historical "fables" presented in beer commercials and relishes the skill of an advertising

---

*The Society of the Spectacle, trans. Donald Nicholson-Smith (New York: Zone Books, 1994), p. 32.

strategy which is so closely attuned to the ironic and self-deprecating attitude to nationalism many Canadians share. Unlike Coleman, Nolan finds a good deal to admire in the "mutilations of history" that the commercials represent.

Many of the commercial messages that now surround us do not immediately proclaim themselves as advertising. For example, corporations pay large sums of money to ensure that their products are prominently displayed as part of the scene in movies and videos in an advertising practice known as "product placement." There is now also widespread corporate sponsorship of school programs and educational materials. While such sponsorships frequently enhance the sponsors' reputations, as Phil Ryan suggests in "Compromising Partnerships," they may result in major shifts in the aims of education. He alerts readers to the extensive hidden advertising in commercially sponsored health education material and suggests that such messages are not only "ethically questionable," but that they also point to a dangerous dynamic that is inherent in corporate sponsorships.

Samuel Johnson (1709-1784)

Samuel Johnson was an English essayist, poet, critic and lexicographer. Legendary in his day both for his prolific writings and his wit, many of Johnson's opinionated sayings are still frequently quoted. As well as being the author of the first dictionary of the English language, Johnson was editor of The Idler, *the journal in which this piece was originally published.*

Written in 1759, Johnson's analysis of the tactics of the newspaper advertisements of his day remain surprisingly relevant. "Promise, large promise, is the soul of an advertisement," he tells us and wryly points out the extravagant claims made by makers of cosmetics, household goods and clothing.

THE ABUSES OF ADVERTISING

1   The practice of appending to the narratives of public transactions, more minute and domestic intelligence, and filling the news-papers with advertisements, has grown up by slow degrees to its present state.

2   Genius is shewn only by invention. The man who first took advantage of the general curiosity that was excited by a siege or battle, to betray the readers of news into the knowledge of the shop where the best puffs and powder were to be sold, was undoubtedly a man of great sagacity, and profound skill in the nature of man. But when he had once shewn the way, it was easy to follow him; and every man now knows a ready method of informing the publick of all that he desires to buy or sell, whether his wares be material or intellectual; whether he makes cloaths, or teaches the mathematics; whether he be a tutor that wants a pupil, or a pupil that wants a tutor.

3   Whatever is common is despised. Advertisements are now so numerous that they are very negligently perused, and it is therefore become necessary to gain attention by magnificence of promises, and by eloquence sometimes sublime and sometimes pathetic.

4   Promise, large promise, is the soul of an advertisement. I remember a "washball" that had a quality truly wonderful, it gave "an exquisite edge to the razor." And there are now to be sold "for ready money only," some "duvets for bed-coverings, of down, beyond comparison superior to what is called otter down," and indeed such, that its "many excellencies cannot be here set forth." With one excellence we are made acquainted, "it is warmer than four or five blankets, and lighter than one."

5   There are some, however, that know the prejudice of mankind in favour of modest sincerity. The vendor of the "Beautifying Fluid" sells a lotion that repels pimples, washes away freckles, smooths the skin, and plumps the flesh; and yet, with a generous abhorrence of ostentation, confesses, that it will not "restore the bloom of fifteen to a lady of fifty."

6   The true pathos of advertisements must have sunk deep into the heart of every man that remembers the zeal shewn by the seller of the anodyne necklace, for the ease and safety "of poor toothing infants," and the affection with which

he warned every mother, that "she would never forgive herself" if her infant should perish without a necklace.

7   I cannot but remark to the celebrated author who gave, in his notifications of the camel and dromedary, so many specimens of the genuine sublime, that there is now arrived another subject yet more worthy of his pen. "A famous Mohawk Indian warrior, who took Dieskaw the French general prisoner, dressed in the same manner with the native Indians when they go to war, with his face and body painted, with his scalping knife, tom-ax, and all other implements of war: a sight worthy the curiosity of every true Briton!" This is a very powerful description; but a critic of great refinement would say that it conveys rather "horror" than "terror." An Indian, dressed as he goes to war, may bring company together; but if he carries the scalping knife and tom-ax, there are many true Britons that will never be persuaded to see him but through a grate.

8   It has been remarked by the severer judges, that the salutary sorrow of trag-ick scenes is too soon effaced by the merriment of the epilogue; the same incon-venience arises from the improper disposition of advertisements. The noblest objects may be so associated as to be made ridiculous. The camel and dromedary themselves might have lost much of their dignity between "The True Flower of Mustard" and "The Original Daffy's Elixir"; and I could not but feel some indig-nation when I found this illustrious Indian warrior immediately succeeded by "A Fresh Parcel of Dublin Butter."

9   The trade of advertising is now so near to perfection, that it is not easy to propose any improvement. But as every art ought to be exercised in due subor-dination to the publick good, I cannot but propose it as a moral question to these masters of the publick ear, whether they do not sometimes play too wantonly with our passions, as when the register of lottery tickets invites us to his shop by an account of the prize which he sold last year; and whether the advertising con-trovertists do not indulge asperity of language without any adequate provoca-tion; as in the dispute about "straps for razors," now happily subsided, and in the altercation which at present subsists concerning *Eau de Luce.*

10   In an advertisement it is allowed to every man to speak well of himself, but I know not why he should assume the privilege of censuring his neighbour. He may proclaim his own virtue or skill, but ought not to exclude others from the same pretensions.

11   Every man that advertises his own excellence, should write with some con-sciousness of a character which dares to call the attention of the publick. He should remember that his name is to stand in the same paper with those of the King of Prussia, and the Emperor of Germany, and endeavour to make himself worthy of such association.

12   Some regard is likewise to be paid to posterity. There are men of diligence and curiosity who treasure up the papers of the day merely because others neglect them, and in time they will be scarce. When these collections shall be read in another century, how will numberless contradictions be reconciled, and how shall fame be possibly distributed among the tailors and boddice-makers of the present age.

13   Surely these things deserve consideration. It is enough for me to have hinted my desire that these abuses may be rectified; but such is the state of nature, that

what all have the right of doing, many will attempt without sufficient care or due qualifications.

Topics for consideration:

1. In his opening paragraphs Johnson offers his analysis of how advertising began. Do you think that this explanation is accurate? Does the same dynamic apply to the placing of advertising today?

2. In Johnson's day advertisements appeared as newspaper displays, handbills posted on walls or as street cries. There are now many forms of and sites for advertising. How does the medium in which it appears (e.g., newspaper, billboard, radio, television, Internet) affect the substance of an advertisement?

3. Johnson suggests in paragraph 9 that "the trade of advertising" had, by 1759, come close to achieving "perfection." How do you think a modern advertising agency would rate the advertisements he quotes? What changes do you think it would make?

Frank M. Coleman

Frank Coleman works for the Environmental Protection Alliance. This essay appeared in the Vancouver-based magazine Adbusters *and is part of a forthcoming book on the subject.*

Coleman evokes the familiar image of "Marlboro Country," the mythical territory of the American "primal West" on which the Philip Morris company has based its cigarette advertising for decades. However, Coleman reminds us that an accurate history of the same "primal West" of the late nineteenth century would record a period in which the mistaken view that nature was inexhaustible would lead to "unfettered exploitation of the commons." Coleman argues that the Marlboro advertisements deliberately promote "a pattern of behavior that drives the natural world out of existence."

BIG LIE IN MARLBORO COUNTRY

1   You know the scene. A cloud of dust boiling up over the head of the cowboy, the foam-flecked horse, the mesquite and the mountains. A cowboy approaches with his message: "Come to where the flavor is. Come to Marlboro Country."

2   Current Marlboro ads picture the cowboy, the mountains, the snow-fed waters and the sleepy corral. There is no longer any consumer message. Sometimes the ads feature a bit of vintage cowboy stuff — a glinting spur, well-worn chaps, a lariat entwined around a saddle. Again, there is no message. And there is no need because this is the part for which you have been groomed all these years. You know the scene and your lines. You will utter the message, even if only to yourself, even if only at the edge of consciousness: "Come to where the flavor is. Come to Marlboro Country."

3   We may think we are being invited to America. Yet this invitation contains an unspoken thought. The America of pristine waters, undefiled skies and unfenced range is gone. It went the way of the buffalo long ago. Therefore, the cowboy is inviting us not to America as it is but to America as it should be. He is inviting us to join in recreating a vanished ideal. Or perhaps he is inviting us to create a new America. One isn't sure. It may be that he is inviting us to do both — to inhabit a particular region of the mind etched in the historical memory of the North American people and to use that as a basis for political hope. Either way the advertising industry is promoting a brand of rugged liberalism that affects the way we think, act and handle the environment.

4   The Marlboro ads make obvious use of nature, in the form of the primal West, as a "referent system" in framing ad space. A referent system incorporates two elements, a signifier — the cowboy or the mountains or the mesquite in the scene described above — and the signified — the state of affairs, cultural perspective or vision of life to which the signifier points.

5   All advertising uses referent systems taken from the surrounding culture. Thus we find such diverse examples as Egyptian pharaohs, Scottish lords, colonial masters, athletic heroes, German princes, break dancers, rock 'n roll demigods, constitutional framers, urban rappers and celebrities of all types fulfilling

this role. Such systems invest commodities with meaning. The ads say "Hey you, if you really want to be a part of this system, buy this."

6   As privileged members of the North American free-trade block, we feature a dazzling array of referent systems and we've learned to make the connection between the referent system and the commodity, which the ad industry works hard to manufacture.

7   The Marlboro Country ads celebrate the Golden West. In this period, somewhere around the second half of the nineteenth century, the West, a vast frontier, untamed (at least by Europeans) was settled by miners, shepherds, sod-busters and ranchers. In the decade following the Civil War, Congress passed the Homestead Act (1862) and the Mining Law (1872). The Union Pacific and the Central Pacific railroads were built linking the east and west coasts in 1869. Suddenly the West was accessible, and a hardworking homesteader could acquire 160 acres of land just by agreeing to put it to use.

8   The frontier closed in 1890. Shortly after, Frederick Jackson Turner claimed that the wild region's effect on the national consciousness would be lasting and decisive. In his masterwork, *The Significance of the Frontier in American Life,* Turner writes:

... to the frontier the American intellect owes its striking characteristics. That coarseness and strength combined with acuteness and inquisitiveness; that practical, inventive turn of mind, quick to find expedients; that masterful grasp of material things, lacking in the artistic but powerful to effect great ends; that restless, nervous energy; that dominant individualism, working for good and evil, and with all that buoyancy and exuberance which comes from freedom.

9   This reverent portrait of the frontiersman is a forerunner of America's love affair with the cowboy and, of course, the Marlboro Man.

10   Before we're swept away on a tide of passion here, let us remember something of the real character of the Golden West.

11   People of the primal West treated nature as a "commons" — a great storehouse of commodities from which one could take at liberty without affecting anyone else. As an example, the Mining Law of 1872, which is still on the books, confers title to public land and minerals (including oil) on those individuals and corporations who develop them. Through the combined effect of the Homestead Act and the Mining Law, about two-thirds of the country passed into private hands. In the mountain states of Utah, Wyoming, Colorado and Arizona, water law is based on the Mining Law. Colorado's constitution stresses that "the right to beneficially appropriate water shall never be denied." The reason for elevating a right of undeniable appropriation into law is that while it was imaginable that the state might seek to restrain water appropriation, it was unimaginable that water resources could be exhausted. No instance of appropriation, a dam, a hydro project, an aqueduct, could be supposed to exert a hardship on others, depriving them of water, or forcing consumption of highly saline water laden with toxic impurities. No one foresaw the problems arising from the unfettered exploitation of the commons.

12   It does not now require great insight to see the flaws in the views of the people of the primal West. The commons that once was America is gone. Domestic oil production has entered into steady decline. Exploitation of the Colorado River is threatening several endangered fish species, with extinction. Hydro power projects could wipe out the Columbia River's salmon. Public lands and national parks are over-crowded and face progressive degradation. Desertification is evident in some areas of over-grazed range.

13   All of these are the unmistakable result of the appropriation of the commons. There are many other examples that may be unrecognized as such — the fouling of the air by automobile exhaust imposes costs on use of the commons of the air, the near extinction of the blue fin tuna is an example of the reckless exploitation of the commons of the sea.

14   Against this backdrop, it is hard to believe that the makers of Marlboro commercials do not know what they are doing. They present the primal West reference material and the suburban pleasures of the shopping mall as if they were parts of a seamless whole. To "Come to Marlboro Country" is to adventure and explore solely in the area of consumer taste. It is to "enjoy the flavor," confident that your consumer taste will leave your environment as unspoiled and intact as the first day of creation. The tragedy of the commons is out of sight, out of mind, restoring us to the status quo ante of the primal West. "Come to Marlboro country," a place where the benefits of appropriation and consumption are privately enjoyed and the costs borne by others. This is probably the most self-indulgent smoke you will ever have, but then you deserve it, naturally.

15   Although Philip Morris, Marlboro's parent company, has fallen upon hard times, and the future of the cigarette brand is uncertain, the Marlboro way of life is definitely not over. It is very much alive. Ever since advertising — the driving force behind commercial broadcasting and newspaper chains — transformed North America into a mass commercial culture in the late '60s and '70s, there has been a succession of populist, anti-statist, political leaders and presidential aspirants. Ronald Reagan, George Bush and Ross Perot all came from the southwestern portion of the country. They all espouse a hands-off way of dealing with declining public resources — even in the face of mounting evidence of ecological disaster. They're all Marlboro men.

16   Ronald Reagan best exemplified the ideal. He sought to remove regulatory controls on energy and the environment. He appointed former secretary of the interior James Watt, who sought literally to restore the Golden West status quo. Watt proposed selling off public lands in the West, allegedly as a way of paying off the national debt, and he used his powers under the Mining Law to open public lands, including wilderness areas, to exploration and development. It may be pushing the argument too far to say that it was chiefly the ad industry that made Reagan electable. Nevertheless, given the power of advertising over our lives, it was probably in the cards. Reagan was our first Marlboro president.

17   The dollar value of a referent system is tied to its popularity. So if someone like basketball star Michael Jordan were to come out of retirement and shoot a few more baskets, in, say, an exhibition game, his value as a referent system would likely go up even more, if that's possible. As a referent, Jordan is in short supply and could be used to sell anything. Hence, his value as a commercial property is incalculable.

18   So it is with nature. Like Jordan, it is disappearing. As it retires, it comes to occupy the status of a distant, exotic other. Just as Jordan's value goes up now that he is in essence in scarce supply, so the value of nature as a referent system increases as the forests and wildlife are destroyed. Ads that use nature as a referent system — and Marlboro is just one of many — encourage a pattern of behavior that drives the natural world out of existence. The value of nature as a referent system is free to increase, as the industry marginalizes it, for three reasons: nature as a symbol is detached from the living thing; the living thing has become a scarce commodity; the value associated with the symbol is reassigned to a life of unfettered appropriation and consumption. Marlboro Country illuminates this perverse logic better than any other ad. It encourages us to see where we are coming from, but not where we are going.

Topics for consideration:

1. "You know the scene and your lines," writes Coleman of the way we already know the Marlboro slogan before we hear or see it. How many other phrases from commercials are apt to pop uninvited into you mind? What triggers this process? What do you think it means?

2. Coleman explains his use of the term "referent system" in paragraph 4. What other referent systems can you think of in advertisements with which you are familiar?

3. Coleman writes that "it is hard to believe that the makers of Marlboro commercials do not know what they are doing." Examine one of the advertising industry's publications such as *Advertising Age* to see how advertisers discuss their strategies among themselves.

4. Coleman points out that the Philip Morris company is not alone in using "nature" as a referent system. What other commercials can you think of that use a similar strategy? What reasoning do you think is behind that choice?

Further reading:

Ronald Collins and David Skover, *The Death of Discourse* (1996). Two American lawyers explore the way in which the commodification of American public life eliminates the possibility of genuine free speech. Excellent bibliography on the history of American advertising.

http://adage.com/site_map.html Index page for online version of *Advertising Age*.

Phil Ryan (1957-

Phil Ryan teaches in the School of Public Administration at Carleton University in Ottawa. He is author of The Rise and Fall of the Market in Sandanista Nicaragua *(1995).*

In this essay on the corporate sponsorship of educational materials, Phil Ryan focuses on Health Canada's Jr. Jays Magazine, *which claims to "promote the concepts of a positive, healthy lifestyle" to seven- to twelve-year-olds. Ryan points out that corporate sponsorship has led to the "positive lifestyle" messages being buried beneath the promotion of junk foods and electronic entertainment. In contravention of governmental policy, these messages often appear in covert form as "product placement." Ryan argues that these effects are the direct result of government/business partnerships whose dynamics inevitably work to serve commercial rather than public interests.*

COMPROMISING PARTNERSHIPS

1   Exhibit One: *The Clubhouse Kids*, published by Ontario's Ministry of Health in 1990. It has what one would expect in any effort to promote healthy habits among children: basic safety pointers, mention of the four food groups, encouragement of brushing and flossing, and cautions against watching too much TV or playing music too loud. It's sappy stuff, but my pre-school son loves it.

2   Exhibit Two: *The Jr. Jays Magazine*, published in 1995 by Health Canada. This too contains some lifestyle advice for children. But it contains much more: ads for the Batman and Power Rangers movies, Hot Wheels, Nintendo, bubble gum and YTV, among others.

3   Exhibit One hails from the bad old days when governments went it alone. Exhibit Two is a child of the new age of partnership. The magazine is the product of the Junior Jays Digest and Kids Club, initiated by Health Canada in 1992 to "promote the concepts of a positive, healthy lifestyle" to seven- to 12-year-olds. After the Toronto Blue Jays had agreed to the project, Health Canada enlisted the program's major sponsors, each of whom paid $50,000 to join. The Club's first magazine had a print run of over one million copies, delivered to schools by police officers. In the years since its debut, there have been 17 more issues of the magazine for a total circulation of seven million.

4   The *Jr. Jays Magazine*'s cartoon-format stories revolve around the adventures of "Dr. Jay" and a group of child characters. The stories and other material in the magazines offer some "positive lifestyle" messages, among them the importance of using seat-belts, the virtues of going to the dentist, the evils of cigarettes and liquor, and advice on how to deal with racist jokes.

5   But one often has to dig to detect these messages, as the publications are primarily commercial vehicles. The principal categories of advertising are snacks, fast foods and sugar products; Warner Brothers children's movies and other forms of electronic entertainment; Blue Jays merchandise; and toys. Apart from the explicit advertising, many of the articles and features are unacknowledged advertisements promoting children's movies, Super Nintendo or YTV. In one contest, Dr. Jay says, "Hey Kids! I want to hear about your greatest Hot Wheels

Adventure!" A story that purportedly teaches children how to deal with conflict uses the example of two students who both want to write school essays about Nintendo.

6   Like many modern movies, the comic-format stories come heavily laden with "product placement" advertising. One *Jr. Jay* character exchanges gifts with a Native child: pemmican for a "Crunchie Bar." A character exclaims "Let's go for lunch at McDonald's, Krystal. It must be neat to have a Mom who works for McDonald's." At the end of one story, a character suggests, "Let's go play Ken Griffey Jr. Major League Baseball on Super Nintendo, Ashley!" Dr. Jay joins children playing with Nintendo Game Boys and effuses, "Wow! This is Great!" One of the Health Canada-created characters is even named after a chocolate bar, and children are given instructions on "How to Draw Crunchie." At least 17 products and companies enjoy surreptitious advertisements in the *Jr. Jays'* comic stories.

7   The pervasive commercialism of the *Jr. Jays* publications constructs a "McPravda" world in which nothing is quite what it seems. The magazines carry movie reviews ostensibly written by real children, but every review in the magazines studied is for a Warner Brothers movie and each one gives the movie "10 out of 10."

8   The program has also tried its hand at chauvinistic propaganda: the *Jr. Jays Magazine* for Summer 1995 tells the story of an evil "Captain Cortez" who is planning to build "invisible fish nets then he plans to steal all of Canada's fish and escape!" Fortunately, "Out of the sky descends the latest in Canadian Aerospace Technology ... The Airhawk!" All ends well, of course: "We did it, Doc! We stopped those aliens from taking Canada's fish!"

HEALTHY LIFESTYLES?

9   The *Jr. Jays* program raises serious concerns, which can be divided into questions regarding content and those regarding the medium itself. First, does the program promote physical health? The nutritional message is clearly problematic: a faithful reader of the *Jr. Jays Magazine* might be forgiven for thinking that the four food groups are salt, fat, sugar and hamburger. The program, like much modern marketing, may contribute to malnutrition. Apart from its directly noxious effects, commercially stimulated consumption of junk food crowds out consumption of healthier foods. Analogously, advertising messages can drown out healthier influences on child nutrition.

10   The promotion of physical health is also undermined by the heavy concentration of explicit and hidden advertising for products that promote physical passivity, such as movies, TV shows, pop music and Nintendo. Unlike Ontario's *Clubhouse Kids*, the *Jr. Jays* program does not view the lifestyle of the "couch potato" as unhealthy.

11   The *Jr. Jays* program may also have problematic effects in areas other than physical health. Advertising to children relies on their capacity to nag, and various studies have shown links between children's exposure to advertising, the frequency of purchase requests to parents and the level of parent-child conflict. Finally, while the *Jr. Jays* magazines contain subtle messages concerning conflict resolution, these are overwhelmed by explicit and hidden advertising for violent entertainment such as the Batman and Power Rangers movies. Health Canada

promoted the latter movie *after* the Power Rangers TV show had been declared excessively violent by the Canadian Broadcast Standards Council.

THE MEDIUM HIDES THE MESSAGE

12 Many of the foregoing observations provoke questions around advertising to children in general. But there are added concerns in the case of the *Jr. Jays* program, which bypasses the oversight of parents who seek to limit their children's exposure to commercial manipulation. If we can assume that parents trust Health Canada to provide them with reliable information on health matters, then they will likely subject Health Canada material to less scrutiny than other communication aimed at their children, particularly when hand-delivered by police officers.

13   *Jr. Jays* advertising also seeks to bypass children's own perceptual defences. The rationale for hidden advertising is clear: advertisers are well aware that they can best enlist children in their cause when the latter are unaware this is happening. But what of the ethics of the practice? Hidden advertising is one of a class of practices that deceive by masking the true motivation of a communication, violating personal autonomy by preventing the target from mobilizing legitimate defences against interested persuasion. Anyone who considers this a dubious ethical criticism might simply consider the desirability of a society in which the governing party hides its advertising in the editorial columns of the local paper, or in which journalists produce purportedly "objective" articles while under hire by companies affected by those articles. (The principle that advertising should be recognizable as such has also been articulated in government regulations. In the late 1980s, the CRTC restricted "infomercials," declaring that "consumers should be protected from disguised advertising messages.")

SO WHAT?

14 Health Canada's *Jr. Jays* program promotes unhealthy practices to children and promotes them in an ethically questionable manner. But so what? Why worry about a low-visibility program costing a minuscule fraction of Health Canada's budget? As small as the program is, it raises two broad issues.

15   The first, which I will address but briefly, concerns the formation of our children. In the name of "lean government," we are apparently willing to subject future generations to an ever more intensive commercial incitement of desire. Some politicians promote the privatization of public television systems, which will end children's access to commercial-free programming. School boards raise a few dollars by turning classroom computer screens into junk food billboards and forcing students to sit through commercial-laden "news" programs. Our society has long been willing to hand over a significant portion of child socialization tasks to the makers of G.I. Joe, Barbie and Chocolate-Frosted Sugar Bombs, and we now appear intent on closing down the oases to which parents and children could once flee from such commercial bombardment.

16   A second issue arising from the *Jr. Jays* story concerns the future of our government. I am sure that no Health Canada official ever consciously set out to give

government support to the makers of junk food and junk entertainment. This odd outcome has arisen from a thick fog that has settled on Ottawa, a fog called partnership mania. Advocates of public partnerships see the practice as part of a cure for the pathologies of bureaucracy and as a response to fiscal pressures. Both claims are problematic.

17   David Osborne and Ted Gaebler, authors of *Reinventing Government*, see partnerships as one of many tools for promoting an "entrepreneurial" alternative to bureaucracy. "Classical" bureaucracy, we are told, worked well in a stable environment, when tasks were simpler and change more glacial. But bureaucracy cannot cope with our age of "breathtaking" change, with its complex and interdependent social problems, because it operates through a detailed subdivision of tasks and the constant generation of new rules. As Robert Merton argues in his famous essay "Bureaucratic Structure and Personality," ends and means get inverted and the bureaucratic obsession with rules leads to the ignoring of results. This "goal displacement" is particularly pronounced in public bureaucracies, whose official ends are often vague and ambiguous. When this pathology is addressed through quantitative measures of organizational performance, these measures suffer the same inversion of means and ends, being turned into the very goal of activity and generating perverse outcomes, as when Toronto welfare officials steer people away from gainful employment so that they can meet workfare placement targets.

18   While this type of analysis does identify some bureaucratic pathologies, its target is too narrow. Goal displacement is not a fact of bureaucracy, but a fact of life. How many people can say with confidence that their life has a clear central goal, and that their actions are always oriented towards that goal, rather than to some surrogate thereof? The Biblical tension between "letter" and "spirit," or between priest and prophet, shows that the confusion of ends and means is not a product of modern bureaucracy.

19   It is foolish to think that the advocates of "reinvented" government will solve a problem that has never been solved and can at best be mitigated. Means and ends will still be inverted, and measures of performance will still be elevated to ends-in-themselves. The persistence of such pathologies must be kept in mind when one assesses the second claim for partnerships.

20   Nearly every advocate of public partnerships expresses the hope that they will allow public sector managers to "do more with less," to which the most obvious rejoinder is: *more what?* With goal displacement always a danger, the "more" may become "more of whatever we happen to be doing at this point," rather than "more of what we originally set out to do." Success will be proclaimed on the basis of partnerships entered or total funds "leveraged," rather than actual contributions to the organization's mission: "In the last five years," trumpets one policy document, "Health Canada has entered into more than 80 partnerships which added an estimated $40,000,000 to the resources available to the department."

21   But who is "leveraging" whose resources in these partnerships? Often, those negotiating a private-public partnership do not enjoy a "level playing field." In this age of what Marylyn Collins terms "strategic" corporate philanthropy ("Global Corporate Philanthropy: Marketing Beyond the Call of Duty," *European Journal of Marketing*), when even "generosity" aims to improve bottom line performance,"

the private party has clear and measurable objectives and is willing to walk away from the partnership, as some did in the case of the *Jr. Jays*. (When companies such as Apple abandoned the program, their logos were airbrushed out of the comics, much as Trotsky retroactively disappeared from pictures during the Stalin era.)

22   Public sector managers who report increasing pressure to embrace "flavour of the month initiatives so it looks as if they're doing something," will often feel compelled to find partners one way or another. To walk away from problematic negotiations, or—horror or horrors— to abandon a partnership already in progress, will call into question a whole series of prior decisions, and the official may well be seen as someone not truly committed to the managerial realities of the '90s. Better to let the partnership forge onwards, even if it has, at best, a peripheral relation to the organization's mission. Goal displacement will then go to work on behalf of the official, who will be praised for "risk-taking" and "entrepreneurialism," whether or not the partnership has furthered the organization's mission, which no one was very clear about in any case. But when one party has clear objectives and is willing to walk away while the other has a personal incentive *not* to bargain hard on behalf of the organization's goals or abandon a partnership, it is easy to predict whose goals will prevail over time.

23   In the *Jr. Jays* case, Health Canada did the initial work developing the characters, and other preparatory work, for a total investment of some $150,000, then sold the rights to the characters for $1 to the Blue Jays, which licensed the characters to the "Community Programs Group," an organization of uncertain status whose sole *raison d'être* seems to be the *Jr. Jays* program itself. From this point on, abandoning the partnership would indicate that money had been wasted and the whole project had been misconceived and Health Canada was bound to a project fundamentally driven by commercial imperatives, as the initial agreement had stipulated that the program must operate at a profit.

24   But commercial imperatives have certain implications when children constitute the target audience: as *Children as Consumers* author James McNeal notes, "it is uncommon to see children-oriented ads for clothing, books, green beans, school supplies, or personal hygiene products!" That is, it is primarily peddlers of junk food, sugar-laden cereals and electronic pastimes that view children as a lucrative market. As a Health Canada official commented in response to my query on the *Jr. Jays* program's choice of sponsors: "These *are* the companies that sell to kids." Given the corner into which Health Canada had painted itself, it is no surprise that the same official felt that "our control of the project is limited."

25   "My point," said Foucault at one point, "is not that everything is bad, but that everything is dangerous." Public-private partnerships may sometimes serve the public interest, but they must be subject to a more critical scrutiny than has hitherto been the case. Now advocates of partnership may reply that their writings on partnership have included caveats. Checklists are available, telling the organization what it should and should not do in partnerships. The question of why the organization will in fact do what it should, however, is neglected. But if organizations did what they should, there would have been no organizational patholo-

gies in the first place. We do not need more lists of "do's and don't's," destined to be filed and forgotten, but we do need serious study of how partnerships unfold in practice, and how the public interest gets lost in the shuffle in cases such as the *Jr. Jays* program.

26   The critical scrutiny of partnerships must go well beyond a "value-for-money" approach that focuses on how many pamphlets were produced for what price and assumes that budget costs are the only cost to the public. This is the irrational rationality of Flaubert's poor Hippolyte in *Madame Bovary*, who submits to Dr. Bovary's barbaric surgery because "ça ne lui coûterait rien" [it won't cost them anything]. Indeed, since the budget costs of partnerships may be quite low, such an approach can justify the refusal to do any evaluation at all. But if healthy lifestyles are "worth" something, then *un*healthy lifestyles obviously "cost" something, however hidden and diffused those costs may be. Those costs will not be detected by evaluation procedures that refuse to look for them.

27   We might best end, then, with an image conjured by Plato: "If a cook and a physician had to dispute their claims before a group of boys, or before men as silly as boys, as to which of the two completely understood which foods are beneficial and which are harmful, the physician would starve to death." At its most literal level, the image is relevant to our story: it is astonishing that anyone should expect children to learn and act upon the basics of proper nutrition while being bombarded with commercial propaganda for junk food. But Plato's image is also pertinent at another level. How will the chef counter the physician's warnings? By declaring that the physician is a humbug bent on denying pleasure, that rich food and candy cannot hurt us, that we can eat our cake (and whatever else we desire) and have good health too.

28   At this level, Plato's image speaks to the power of our desire to have our cake and eat it too, our desire to avoid tough choices. This desire to hide from unpleasant trade-offs is a powerful force in modern-day political discourse: we find it in the Reaganites' notorious "Laffer curve," in the oft-repeated claim that we can cut taxes yet maintain government services by eliminating "waste, fraud and abuse," and in the contrary claim that we can maintain or even improve services by taxing *someone else*.

29   The claim that partnerships will allow us to "do more with less" indulges the same fantasy. It holds out the possibility that we need not pay a real price for deep cuts to government program spending. In the face of this fantasy, any responsible student of government must warn that partnerships may lead government to do, not "more with less," but something very *different* with less, something that no government has any business doing.

Topics for consideration:

1. In paragraph 7 Ryan compares the "pervasive commercialism" of the *Jr. Jays* publication with the Soviet propaganda newspaper *Pravda*. Later, in paragraph 21 he makes a passing comparison to the rewriting of Soviet history that took place in the Stalinist era. What is the point of these comparisons?

2. In paragraphs 5 to 7 Ryan points out that much of the advertising in the *Jr. Jays Magazine* is "unacknowledged," often taking the form of "product placement." What forms of unacknowledged advertising have you recently noticed?

3. Ryan's essay suggests that government/business partnerships lead to "goal displacement" or a change in aims. He is especially concerned about these changes in an educational context. What commercial influences are at work in your own educational institution and what effect does this have?

Further reading:

http://www.carleton.ca/~pryan/jj.htm Provides a wide range of references for this essay.

Nicole Nolan

Nicole Nolan is a Toronto journalist. This essay appeared in This Magazine.

Nicole Nolan examines the "witty, cosmopolitan, simultaneously proud and self-deprecating" version of nationalism presented in a series of television beer commercials. Such commercials, she suggests, appeal more strongly to young people than most government initiatives intended to encourage nationalism. Company officials, however, deny that their advertising strategies are based on political insights. Ironically, the very companies responsible for the nationalistic commercials are themselves foreign-owned.

ISN'T IT IRONIC?

1 A commercial for Labatt Blue appearing on television at the height of this summer's beer season:

2 *Opening shot:* Two scruffy-looking explorer types canoe along a river in a rocky, pine-strewn wilderness. The title tells us this is "Somewhere in Canada, 1734."

Jacques: (in a French accent and swatting at a mosquito) Such wilderness, William.

William: (in a British accent) Today, yes, Jacques, but someday ... someday it will be a *great* country.

Jacques: (swatting again at the mosquito) You think so?

William: Absolutely. You see, they shall perfect a game called hockey, invent the telephone, rescue England *and* France twice, and make one incredibly good beer. A True, Canadian Lager.

Jacques: (being bitten by a mosquito) Sacre bleu!

William: Yes! That's it!

Cut to a shot of a foaming glass of Labatt Blue, accompanied by electric guitar raunch-out.

3 An ad for Molson Canadian appearing during the same period:

A running-shoe-clad young man approaches the baggage carousel in a Canadian airport (subtly indicated by a couple of maple leaves). As the youth claims his maple-leaf emblazoned back pack, a series of funky, pencil-drawn cartoons flit across the screen — the Eiffel Tower, a tropical island, a pyramid, Big Ben, a kangaroo and, finally, a pair of eyes whose pupils metamorphose into a beaver, then a hockey puck. Meanwhile, a young male voice explains, in worldly-wise tones:

"Hell is a world where you have no home, and even though I was in heaven, something drew me back to my home. I can't put into words the things I've seen, the places I've been or what it all means.

"Because it's not so much what you look at but when you look, what you see," the voice concludes to a surge of electric guitar as the youth walks out the air-port doors into the enthusiastic embrace of a blonde babe. "And now I see that my eyes are the eyes of the world, and in my eyes" — he pauses — "I am."

Cut to a shot of a flickering image of the word "Canadian."

4   Canadian nationalism — *English* Canadian nationalism, that is — has never been renowned for its clarity of vision. This country's cultural history is so full of anguished hand-wringing over the exact nature of national identity that the angst itself might qualify as a defining feature. Possibly this is why about a half-dozen different national visions have gone down the tubes since the Second World War. The idea of Canada as "last outpost of the British empire" died during the sixties; the Somalia inquiry is putting the kibosh on the Canada-as-nonviolent-nation cliché; Canada-as-tolerant is down for the count in the embittered aftermath of the Quebec referendum; and the last gasps of Pierre Trudeau's vision of Canada as the "just society" are quickly being stifled by the likes of Mike Harris and Ralph Klein.

5   One might have expected the Quebec referendum to light a fire under our national leaders to come up with a convincing new master-narrative. After all, if they were going to convince Quebec to stick around, they had to give it a reason, didn't they? What we got instead were busloads of goons with Canadian flags painted on their faces, gyrating around the streets of Montreal in a display of such torturous pathos that it made me want to start my own separation campaign on behalf of urban youth.

6   In the aftermath, national identity has been left in the hands of Canada's gruesome TV Heritage Moments and Sheila Copps' $23-million flag giveaway campaign. "This is a good investment," Copps told *The Globe and Mail*. "One of the most visible ways to promote our country is with our flag." Both are pretty grim signs of how far the government is out of touch with Canadians. Like Bob Dole, with his white shoes and his World War II record, Copps and her flags seem trapped in an agonizingly archaic dance, recycling dusty notions in a desperate attempt to fuel national spirit. It's a scheme guaranteed to leave younger generations utterly disaffected with nationalism. They could hardly need more reason to find the emotion distasteful; after you've seen some of the atrocities committed in the name of nationalism in Bosnia, the U.S., or Burundi, the very idea of waving a flag seems offensive. No doubt Copps' flags hold strong appeal for my grandmother, but at the age of 81, she hardly represents the future of the nation.

7   In the midst of all this come the nationalist beer campaigns of Labatt and Molson: unshaven explorers who crack withering jokes as they traverse early Canada, and young urbanites who travel the world in a whirl of Gen-X hipness, then return to the Great White North to declare (with enviable taoist mystique) "I am." The companies have found the campaigns, begun in the last three years, wildly successful. They've boosted the sales of both beers and won many advertising-industry kudos.

8   It isn't hard to be cynical about the ads. Corporate shysterism is, as always, the directing principle, and playing off nationalist appeal in your advertising is a time-honoured corporate trick. But oddly enough, I have to admit that this time, the beer companies are on to something. Underneath the various chunks of cultural grot one might expect from productions aimed at twentysomething white boys, these ads are some of most compelling things I've seen in the area of national identity. Witty, cosmopolitan, simultaneously proud and self-deprecating, the

Molson and Labatt ads are the only blips on the radar that are even attempting to rethink what "Canadian" means in the late twentieth century. They're witness to an appetite for a redefined Canadian identity (particularly in the youth market) that lavishly rewards anyone who feeds it. And like any original idea, they're drawing deeply on tradition — in this case, the strain of withering, self-parodying irony and ambiguity that has long run through the country's culture. Unlike our flat-footed government, Labatt and Molson seem actually to be listening to Canadians' often ambivalent feelings about their country.

9   *Opening shot:* Jacques and William shiver over a puny fire in a snow-covered forest.
     Jacques: William! Do you know what day it is today?
     William: Yes, Jacques, today is our 243rd straight day in this cold, unforgiving wilderness.
     Jacques: No, William, today is Christmas. We are lucky my friend. Good fire, fresh snow — a true Canadian Christmas!

10   Labatt's Jacques and William are an intriguing pair. Through a series of several television ads, they gallivant about the Canadian wilderness, Jacques listening dubiously as William predicts various details of the future nation (including the GST). In the final couple of ads, the story takes on a soap-operaesque quality, as the two encounter a group of red-coated Englishmen. Apparently Jacques (true to the Pépé le Pew French stereotype) has been wooing the daughter of the commander. They end up in the Englishman's house, making passes at a couple of panier-clad beer-poster girls, and eventually swing from the chandeliers in order to escape the lovelies' sword-wielding father.

11   As might be expected, the ads' mutilations of history are truly among the most brutal ever produced. The mere fact that they can actually fly is all the proof we need that Canadian education is in deep shit. Just to point out the most obvious: the British did not manage to wrest Canada away from the French until 1763, so the presence of British armies and well-dressed English ladies is not *quite* in keeping with the state of affairs in the Canada of 1734.

12   Not that Labatt cares. Labatt Blue marketing manager Marc Solby is non-plussed when I confront him with these points. "The date is not a big deal. The ads don't strive for historical accuracy. They're kind of a fable," Solby advises me.

13   So what exactly is the 'fable' in these ads that Labatt thinks will be compelling enough to sell their mediocre ale? Of course, there's the usual nationalist boost-erism — e.g., hockey, the telephone, Canada as a haven of untouched wilder-ness. Then there's the historical fantasy of representatives from the two so-called founding nations paddling amicably around in a canoe together — a telling index of English Canadian referendum anxiety. Like the enormously popular American white guy/black guy buddy movies (think *Lethal Weapon*) the Jacques/William pairing comfortably resolves the minorities-who-hate-you problem with a homoerotic fantasy of two guys against the world.

14   But what is truly remarkable about these ads is their devastatingly ironic twist. At the same time that they forward all the clichéd "why Canada is great" dogma, they're viciously undercutting it. Sure, Canada is great and has a beautiful wilder-ness, but, hey, you know what? The wilderness *sucks*. It's full of mosquitoes. It's also fucking *cold*.

15   As for the two-founding-nations mythology, it's dubious how seriously we're supposed to take all of this, seeing as pretty well every character is a complete goof. According to Labatt (and this may actually be an impressive historical insight) Canada was created basically by a bunch of frat boys more interested in crashing parties and going after some eighteenth-century skirt than in any of the more high-minded excuses for colonialism, such as "civilizing the wilderness" or "converting the heathens." In other words, why bother with all this ethnic and national-identity stuff, seeing as we're all a bunch of idiots, anyway?

16   This summer, I spent the Canada Day weekend listening to a lot of egregious hard-rock radio while painting my apartment into an acme of urban hipness. At one point, the gravelly-voiced host felt compelled to acknowledge the occasion.

17   "Well, it's Canada Day," he intoned in between Bon Jovi's "Bad Medicine" and Rush's "Flight by Night". "So let's all head up to that Great Canadian Cottage in the Great Canadian Wilderness and fire up that Great Canadian Barbeque. Yep. Canada. The country that gave us Paul Anka, Bob and Doug MacKenzie — and poutine."

18   It was the day of national pride, and the DJ of a popular radio station — hardly the cutting edge of political radicalism — was tossing around insults. In other nations, this would be an affront. In Canada, we accept it; we like it; nay, we *need* it. Unlike other national groups, who tend to take their membership in the nation-state with the utmost solemnity, there's a delightfully strong strain in Canadian culture that just can't take the whole damn thing seriously. That's not to say Canadians aren't patriotic. But, let's face it, it's hard to forget that we live in a shit-assed little nation of 26 million, alternately dominated by the Brits and the Americans, who, of course, always do things better and bigger than we do.

19   This sort of self-deprecating irony has long been recognized by our intellectual heavyweights as the ultimate satisfaction of English Canada's perverted backlash relationship with itself. Literary critic Linda Hutcheon, in her book *Splitting Images*, argued that irony's popularity stems from its ability to say two diametrically opposed things at once. Since it means never having to decide one way or another, she wrote, it's the perfect solution to our fence-sitting predilection. Irony, and its sisters satire and self-mockery, are strategies for survival, and even a kind of celebration, in Canada. Possibly that's why we've exported so many comedians to the U.S., such as Jim Carey and the entire cast of the former SCTV comedy show.

20   In its recent poster campaign, Labatt pushed the irony button even harder than in the Jacques/William ads. One poster begins with the phrase "True Canadian …". Underneath it is a photo of a beaver with the phrase "eagle" inscribed on it; the next frame shows a picture of some pine trees, emblazoned with the phrase "air freshener."

21   There's any number of ways you could read *that* weirdness, but I figure it's a complex game of cultural one-upmanship. On the one hand, the beaver/eagle comparison reminds us of our inferiority to America. Their country's national symbol is a high-flying mountain bird, glorious in its independence and predatory ferocity; ours is a small, furry, water creature with buck teeth, renowned for biting off its own testicles when cornered. It seems pretty obvious who's superior.

On the other hand, the fact that we can acknowledge this fact and laugh about it means that we're not terribly invested in the whole stupid national-animal bullshit anyway, which, in turn, makes *us* superior.

22   The federal government, ever the straight man in this ongoing national joke, still hasn't figured out the Canadian appetite for irony. The government's Heritage Moments, promoting such Canadian high points as the Underground Railroad and the first female MP, are so smarmy and sugarcoated that they've been parodied by both *Saturday Night* magazine and *Frank*. Sheila Copps managed to ratchet the earnestness up a notch further with her flag giveaway. As Copps noted, polls regularly show that Canadians think the flag is the most important symbol of national unity; she made the logical conclusion that having a million new flags flying would be mighty popular. I venture to say that in any other country this would have been true, but not here. Only in Canada would the same people who declare the Canadian flag the most important symbol of national identity also, with equal passion, blow a gasket over spending $23-million on something so trivial and stupid.

23   "Again, I have to correct you," says Molson spokesperson Marilyn McCrae, speaking slowly, as if to a person with imperfect English. "This is *not* nationalism. If that's what people want to take away from it, that's fine. But that wasn't our intent."

24   I have just, for the third time, made the apparently egregious error of referring to Molson's "I AM" ads as a nationalist campaign. I'm initially puzzled at McCrae's defensiveness. What does she mean? I point to the "hell is a place where you have no home" commercial. What with the beavers, the hockey sticks and the maple leafs, it seems pretty clear to me. No, no, no, she insists, I've got it all wrong.

25   "When I'm talking to you and I say 'Canadian,'" explains McCrae. "I'm talking about the brand of *beer* Canadian, not the nationality."

26   I pause to ponder this stunner, admitting with a rueful admiration that McCrae has an uncanny talent for stopping journalists in their tracks. The *brand* Canadian? What is this — *L'état, c'est Molson?*

27   It isn't just semantics, though; this sort of elision is at the heart of these ads' power. I begin to realize that McCrae's right, in a weird sort of way, when she says the ads aren't nationalistic. At least, they're not simplistically so. Instead, Molson does a careful dance around national identity, playing it up wildly through the use of the blatant imagery, but posing it all in the cool rubric of contemporary individualism. In the "I AM" ads, "Canadian" isn't a static identity: it's multiple, varied, and changing. Like the multiethnic, world-beat outlook that Much Music loves to push, it's filled with nose-ringed, dancing, world-travelling hipsters. It's whatever you want it to be, whatever *you* are. It's also, as the very significant *pause* before the phrase "I AM" suggests, an identity with which you can choose to ally yourself or not. In retooling nationalism for a Gen-X audience, Molson has carried out the brilliant manoeuver of taking that boring old chestnut, the famed English-Canadian *lack* of identity, and making a virtue out of it.

28   Possibly this is because Molson, unlike the government, has actually done its research. As McCrae notes, focus groups showed them that young people were

turned on only by a subtle patriotism. "Most Canadians are not 'rah rah' but they're still proud to be Canadians," she explains. "What we found was there was a latent, quieter, not overt sense of nationalism."

29   One sure sign that the beer companies understand the game they're playing is that they keep their nationalist campaigns far, far away from Quebec. With their profit-driven instinct, Molson and Labatt have considerably less trouble than the rest of the country in recognizing Quebec's distinct-society status. Molson, for example, has never marketed its Canadian brand in Quebec, for fear it would be snubbed. And as for Labatt — pick up a bottle of Blue in Quebec and you'll find it's missing the shiny little maple leaf that peeks out from behind the brand name in the rest of the country. The company removed it in 1994.

30   Outside of Quebec, these guys' cultural radar is just as keen, because they're extremely reluctant to admit they do gymnastics around the Quebec question, "People," McCrae tells me, "came to us during the Quebec referendum and said, 'Oh, this is your nationalist campaign.' Well, I can tell you that was *not* our intent at all." Amazingly, McCrae also refuses to admit that Quebec nationalism is the reason Molson doesn't market Canadian in *la belle provence*. Instead, she tries to sell me on the notion that Quebecers just happen to prefer the taste of the less-politically-named Molson Dry. "They love the taste of Molson Dry," she says. "It is to the Quebec market what Canadian is to the Ontario market. It's not a question of politics."

31   Labatt rep Marc Solby is a bit more straightforward, although his car phone *does* suddenly hit a 'bad connection' when I bring up the subject of the missing maple leaf. "The Quebec market has its own culture, so we recognize that. Quebec has its own marketing initiatives and its own set of cultural values. I think that's a smart thing for a Canadian company to recognize."

32   No doubt there are some who would pooh-pooh my admiration of the Molson/ Labatt brand of nationalism. The patriotism they portray is, after all, completely apolitical; it's all about hanging out and having a good time, and has nothing to do with difficult notions like, say, social responsibility. There's no doubt that apoliticality is exactly what big corporations like Molson and Labatt would like to foster. The left, myself included, would say that insofar as nationalism has been a good thing for Canada, it hasn't been because it fosters any strong sense of personal chauvinism. Rather, it's been more valuable in its state-based form, giving birth to stuff like social programs and better environmental protection — all those things that the United States has fucked up royally and we've promised ourselves won't happen to us.

33   You could add in other caveats here, too. For all that Labatt and Molson are playing to Canadian identity, the banks to which they take their profits aren't, uh, Canadian. Both Labatt and Molson are foreign-owned. Labatt is 100 per cent owned by the Belgian beer company Interbrew, and Molson is 60 per cent foreign-owned (20 per cent by the U.S.'s Miller and 40 per cent by Australia's Foster's).

34   It should come as no surprise that corporate hypocrisy is as alive and well in our national (or not-so-national) beer producers as it is in the rest of corporate Canada. What *is* impressive is that regardless of what they might really believe, Molson and Labatt have done a shockingly good job of tapping into the national

zeitgeist. It's just too bad that this proven Canadian appetite for multiplicity and irony has been left in the hands of beer companies.

"We would not stay with a campaign that's not working," McCrae answers smugly when I ask her about effectiveness of the "I AM" ads. "This has been our campaign for three years."

Topics for consideration:

1. Nolan suggests that there is a difference between the generations in their attitude to nationalism. Is this true in your experience?

2. Nolan identifies a "strain of withering, self-parodying irony and ambiguity that has long run through the country's culture." Do you find that irony of this kind is particularly Canadian?

3. Nolan frequently expresses herself (e.g., "all the proof we need that Canadian education is in deep shit") in ways that many teachers of composition would find inappropriate. What do you think? What would be the effect of making the same points more formally?

4. Nolan focuses on her admiration for "the Molson/Labatt brand of nationalism." Does anything in her essay suggest that she has any reservations?

Further reading:

Linda Hutcheon, *Splitting Images: Contemporary Canadian Ironies* (1991)

CHAPTER 8

THE MEDIATED WORLD

By the time most students enter college or university they will have already spent over 15,000 hours watching television, far outstripping the mere 11,000 hours they have spent in school. Countless more hours have been spent listening to the radio, reading newspapers and magazines, or using the Internet. One consequence of this is that accents and catch phrases originating in Southern California can be heard from St. John's to Victoria, even from speakers who have never travelled beyond their home province.

We all find ourselves daily exposed to the constructions of reality produced by various media whose principal purpose is to deliver as large an audience as possible to advertisers. Canadian intellectuals have been among the earliest and most articulate analysts of the ways in which media in various forms shape our worlds. Best known among these was Marshall McLuhan (1911–1980), whose much-quoted pronouncements in such works as *Understanding Media: The Extensions of Man* (1964) represent a highly idiosyncratic development of the work of Harold Adams Innis. Innis, in *The Bias of Communication* (1951) was able to use his vast knowledge of world history to outline how different modes of communication support or erode various "monopolies on knowledge," providing a template that can be as readily applied to the age of television and the Internet as to the world of telegraph and radio on which many of his observations are based.

The essays in this section all reflect on different ways in which the various media shape our perceptions of reality and our relationship with the world around us. The excerpt from Marshall McLuhan's essay, "Television: The Timid Giant," represents an attempt to define how the television-mediated experience differs from that offered by radio, print or film. Classifying different media as either "hot" or "cool," McLuhan sees television as "cool" as opposed to "hot" media like print or radio. He argues that, while TV has an "unrivaled power" to involve the audience, "it does not excite, agitate or arouse."

Maude Barlow and James Winter, in "The Horse's Mouth," critique Conrad Black's monopoly over Canadian news media. Barlow and Winter find "something chilling and strangely medieval about one family administering its views to an entire population," and use the arguments raised by the young Conrad Black when, nearly thirty years earlier as the owner of one newspaper, he denounced the influence of media monopolies.

Not surprisingly, there is now a widespread distrust of journalists and the media. One result of this is the growth of conspiracy theories. In "We're Losing the Plot," Linda Grant gives an ironic account of her own reactions on hearing of the death of Princess Diana. Grant suggests that people's readiness to accept the most improbable conspiracy theories in preference to obvious explanations springs from a perception that governments have become powerless and are reduced to "a pathetic display of public relations."

Andrew Cash touches on another form of alienation in "Pump Up the Volume." While, as a singer and songwriter, Cash might be expected to find the karaoke fad unworthy of serious notice, he believes that people turn to this form of entertainment as a way of interacting creatively in a community rather than merely being "silenced by a mass culture that has simply stopped listening."

The comedy film *Crazy People* (1990) depicted an advertising agency CEO who insisted, "You have to drill, drill, drill that target audience until they are consuming your product, not because they love it, but because they can't escape it." In "Art by Committee" Michael Posner discusses the way in which most television series and Hollywood films are honed to reach a "target audience" by means of focus groups identical with those used in marketing toothpaste or deodorant. Before long, he warns, novels and other art works will be "developed" in much the same way, signalling "the utter triumph of the marketplace."

Marshall McLuhan (1911-1980)

One of the most widely quoted commentators on the impact of the media on our perceptions and behavior, Marshall McLuhan began his career as a literary scholar with a special interest in the fiction of James Joyce. He became an internationally known figure with the publication of Understanding Media *in 1964. His work attracted controversy throughout his career largely because of his emphatic sweeping pronouncements and his development of a "mosaic" style of writing which did not follow the customary conventions of argument.*

In this excerpt from Understanding Media *McLuhan considers television, which had only recently become a standard feature of North American homes. Using his famous classification of media into "hot" and "cool," McLuhan deems television to be a cool medium demanding absorbed audience participation. He reflects upon the impact of this new medium on political life using the example of J.F. Kennedy's electoral success and his assassination.*

TELEVISION: THE TIMID GIANT

1   Perhaps the most familiar antipathetic effect of the TV image is the posture of children in the early grades. Since TV, children — regardless of eye condition — average about six and a half inches from the printed page. Our children are striving to carry over to the printed page the all-involving sensory mandate of the TV image. With perfect psycho-mimetic skill, they carry out the commands of the TV image. They pore, they probe, they slow down and involve themselves in depth. This is what they had learned to do in the cool iconography of the comic-book medium. TV carried the process much further. Suddenly they are transferred to the hot print medium with its uniform patterns and fast lineal movement. Pointlessly they strive to read in depth. They bring to print all their senses, and print rejects them. Print asks for the isolated and stripped-down visual faculty, not for the unified sensorium.

2   The Mackworth head-camera, when worn by children watching TV, has revealed that their eyes follow, not the actions, but the reactions. The eyes scarcely deviate from the faces of the actors, even during scenes of violence. This head-camera shows by projection both the scene and the eye movement simultaneously. Such extraordinary behavior is another indication of the very cool and involving character of this medium.

• • •

3   An article by Edith Efron in *TV Guide* (May 18–24, 1969) labeled TV "The Timid Giant," because it is unsuited to hot issues and sharply defined controversial topics: "Despite official freedom from censorship, a self-imposed silence renders network documentaries almost mute on many great issues of the day." As a cool medium TV has, some feel, introduced a kind of *rigor mortis* into the body politic. It is the extraordinary degree of audience participation in the TV medium that explains its failure to tackle hot issues. Howard K. Smith observed: "The networks are delighted if you go into a controversy in a country 14,000 miles away. They don't want real controversy, real dissent, at home." For people conditioned

to the hot newspaper medium, which is concerned with the clash of *views*, rather than involvement in *depth* in a situation, the TV behavior is inexplicable.

• • •

4   An article on Perry Como bills him as "Low-pressure king of a high-pressure realm." The success of any TV performer depends on his achieving a low-pressure style of presentation, although getting his act on the air may require much high-pressure organization. Castro may be a case in point. According to Tad Szulc's story on "Cuban Television's One-man Show" (*The Eighth Art*), "in his seemingly improvised 'as-I-go-along' style he can evolve politics and govern his country — right on camera." Now, Tad Szulc is under the illusion that TV is a hot medium, and suggests that in the Congo "television might have helped Lumumba to incite the masses to even greater turmoil and bloodshed." But he is quite wrong. Radio is the medium for frenzy, and it has been the major means of hotting up the tribal blood of Africa, India, and China, alike. TV has cooled Cuba down, as it is cooling down America. What the Cubans are getting by TV is the experience of being directly engaged in the making of political decisions. Castro presents himself as a teacher, and as Szulc says, "manages to blend political guidance and education with propaganda so skillfully that it is often difficult to tell where one begins and the other ends." Exactly the same mix is used in entertainment in Europe and America alike. Seen outside the United States, any American movie looks like subtle political propaganda. Acceptable entertainment has to flatter and exploit the cultural and political assumptions of the land of its origin. These unspoken presuppositions also serve to blind people to the most obvious facts about a new medium like TV.

5   In a group of simulcasts of several media done in Toronto a few years back, TV did a strange flip. Four randomized groups of university students were given the same information at the same time about the structure of preliterate languages. One group received it via radio, one from TV, one by lecture, and one read it. For all but the reader group, the information was passed along in straight verbal flow by the same speaker without discussion or questions or use of blackboard. Each group had half an hour of exposure to the material. Each was asked to fill in the same quiz afterward. It was quite a surprise to the experimenters when the students performed better with TV-channeled information and with radio than they did with lecture and print — and the TV group stood *well* above the radio group. Since nothing had been done to give special stress to any of these four media, the experiment was repeated with other randomized groups. This time each medium was allowed full opportunity to do its stuff. For radio and TV, the material was dramatized with many auditory and visual features. The lecturer took full advantage of the blackboard and class discussion. The printed form was embellished with an imaginative use of typography and page layout to stress each point in the lecture. All of these media had been stepped up to high intensity for this repeat of the original performance. Television and radio once again showed results high above lecture and print. Unexpectedly to the testers, however, radio now stood significantly above television. It was a long time before the obvious reason declared itself, namely that TV is a cool, participant medium. When hotted up by dramatization and stingers, it performs less well because there is less opportunity for participation. Radio is a hot medium. When given additional

intensity, it performs better. It doesn't invite the same degree of participation in its users. Radio will serve as background-sound or as noise-level control, as when the ingenious teenager employs it as a means of privacy. TV will not work as background. It engages you.

• • •

6   The mode of the TV image has nothing in common with film or photo, except that it offers a nonverbal *gestalt* or posture of forms. With TV, the viewer is the screen. He is bombarded with light impulses that James Joyce called the "Charge of the Light Brigade" that imbues his "soulskin with subconscious inklings." The TV image is visually low in data. The TV image is not a *still* shot. It is not photo in any sense, but a ceaselessly forming contour of things limned by the scanning-finger. The resulting plastic contour appears by light *through*, not light *on*, and the image so formed has the quality of sculpture and icon, rather than of picture. The TV image offers some three million dots per second to the receiver. From these he accepts only a few dozen each instant, from which to make an image.

7   The film image offers many more millions of data per second, and the viewer does not have to make the same drastic reduction of items to form his impression. He tends instead to accept the full image as a package deal. In contrast, the viewer of the TV mosaic, with technical control of the image, unconsciously reconfigures the dots into an abstract work of art on the pattern of a Seurat or Rouault. If anybody were to ask whether all this would change if technology stepped up the character of the TV image to movie data level, one could only counter by inquiring, "Could we alter a cartoon by adding details of perspective and light and shade?" The answer is "Yes," only it would then no longer be a cartoon. Nor would "improved" TV be television. The TV image is *now* a mosaic mesh of light and dark spots which a movie shot never is, even when the quality of the movie image is very poor.

8   As in any other mosaic, the third dimension is alien to TV, but it can be superimposed. In TV the illusion of the third dimension is provided slightly by the stage sets in the studio; but the TV image itself is a flat two-dimensional mosaic. Most of the three-dimensional illusion is a carry-over of habitual viewing of film and photo. For the TV camera does not have a built-in angle of vision like the movie camera. Eastman Kodak now has a two-dimensional camera that can match the flat effects of the TV camera. Yet it is hard for literate people, with their habit of fixed points of view and three-dimensional vision, to understand the properties of two-dimensional vision. If it had been easy for them, they would have had no difficulties with abstract art, General Motors would not have made a mess of motorcar design, and the picture magazine would not be having difficulties now with the relationship between features and ads. The TV image requires each instant that we "close" the spaces in the mesh by a convulsive sensuous participation that is profoundly kinetic and tactile, because tactility is the interplay of the senses, rather than the isolated contact of skin and object.

• • •

9   The effect of TV, as the most recent and spectacular electric extension of our central nervous system, is hard to grasp for various reasons. Since it has affected the totality of our lives, personal and social and political, it would be quite unrealistic to attempt a "systematic" or visual presentation of such influence. Instead,

it is more feasible to "present" TV as a complex *gestalt* of data gathered almost at random.

10   The TV image is of low intensity or definition, and therefore, unlike film, it does not afford detailed information about objects. The difference is akin to that between the old manuscripts and the printed word. Print gave intensity and uniform precision, where before there had been a diffuse texture. Print brought in the taste for exact measurement and repeatability that we now associate with science and mathematics.

11   The TV producer will point out that speech on television must not have the careful precision necessary in the theater. The TV actor does not have to project either his voice or himself. Likewise, TV acting is so extremely intimate, because of the peculiar involvement of the viewer with the completion or "closing" of the TV image, that the actor must achieve a great degree of spontaneous casualness that would be irrelevant in movies and lost on stage. For the audience participates in the inner life of the TV actor as fully as in the outer life of the movie star. Technically, TV tends to be a close-up medium. The close-up that in the movie is used for shock is, on TV, a quite casual thing. And whereas a glossy photo the size of the TV screen would show a dozen faces in adequate detail, a dozen faces on the TV screen are only a blur.

12   The peculiar character of the TV image in its relation to the actor causes such familiar reactions as our not being able to recognize in real life a person whom we see every week on TV. Not many of us are as alert as the kindergartener who said to Garry Moore, "How did you get off TV?" Newscasters and actors alike report the frequency with which they are approached by people who feel they've met them before. Joanne Woodward in an interview was asked what was the difference between being a movie star and a TV actress. She replied: "When I was in the movies I heard people say, 'There goes Joanne Woodward.' Now they say, 'There goes somebody I think I know.'"

13   The owner of a Hollywood hotel in an area where many movie and TV actors reside reported that tourists had switched their allegiance to TV stars. Moreover, most TV stars are men, that is, "cool characters," while most movie stars are women, since they can be presented as "hot" characters. Men and women movie stars alike, along with the entire star system, have tended to dwindle into a more moderate status since TV. The movie is a hot, high-definition medium. Perhaps the most interesting observation of the hotel proprietor was that the tourists wanted to see Perry Mason and Wyatt Earp. They did not want to see Raymond Burr and Hugh O'Brian. The old movie-fan tourists had wanted to see their favorites as they were in *real* life, not as they were in their film roles. The fans of the cool TV medium want to see their star in *role*, whereas the movie fans want the *real thing*.

• • •

14   When Theodore White's *The Making of the President: 1960* is opened at the section on "The Television Debates," the TV student will experience dismay. White offers statistics on the number of sets in American homes and the number of hours of daily use of these sets, but not one clue as to the nature of the TV image or its effects on candidates or viewers. White considers the "content" of the debates and the deportment of the debaters, but it never occurs to him to ask

why TV would inevitably be a disaster for a sharp intense image like Nixon's, and a boon for the blurry, shaggy texture of Kennedy.

15   At the end of the debates, Philip Deane of the London *Observer* explained my idea of the coming TV impact on the election to the Toronto *Globe and Mail* under the headline of "The Sheriff and the Lawyer," October 15, 1960. It was that TV would prove so entirely in Kennedy's favor that he would win the election. Without TV, Nixon had it made. Deane, toward the end of his article, wrote:

> Now the press has tended to say that Mr. Nixon has been gaining in the last two debates and that he was bad in the first. Professor McLuhan thinks that Mr. Nixon has been sounding progressively more definite; regardless of the value of the Vice-President's views and principles, he has been defending them with too much flourish for the TV medium. Mr. Kennedy's rather sharp responses have been a mistake, but he still presents an image closer to the TV hero, Professor McLuhan says — something like the shy young Sheriff — while Mr. Nixon with his very dark eyes that tend to stare, with his slicker circumlocution, has resembled more the railway lawyer who signs leases that are not in the interests of the folks in the little town.
>
> In fact, by counterattacking and by claiming for himself, as he does in the TV debates, the same goals as the Democrats have, Mr. Nixon may be helping his opponent by blurring the Kennedy image, by confusing what exactly it is that Mr. Kennedy wants to change.
>
> Mr. Kennedy is thus not handicapped by clear-cut issues; he is visually a less well-defined image, and appears more nonchalant. He seems less anxious to sell himself than does Mr. Nixon. So far, then, Professor McLuhan gives Mr. Kennedy the lead without underestimating Mr. Nixon's formidable appeal to the vast conservative forces of the United States.

16   Another way of explaining the acceptable, as opposed to the unacceptable, TV personality is to say that anybody whose *appearance* strongly declares his role and status in life is wrong for TV. Anybody who looks as if he might be a teacher, a doctor, a businessman, or any of a dozen other things all at the same time is right for TV. When the person presented *looks* classifiable, as Nixon did, the TV viewer has nothing to fill in. He feels uncomfortable with his TV image. He says uneasily, "There's something about the guy that isn't right." The viewer feels exactly the same about an exceedingly pretty girl on TV, or about any of the intense "high definition" images and messages from the sponsors. It is not accidental that advertising has become a vast new source of comic effects since the advent of TV. Mr. Khrushchev is a very jovial comic, an entirely disarming presence. Likewise, precisely the formula that recommends anybody for a movie role disqualifies the same person for TV acceptance. For the hot movie medium needs people who look very definitely a *type* of some kind. The cool TV medium cannot abide the typical because it leaves the viewer frustrated of his job of "closure" or completion of the image. President Kennedy did not look like a rich man or like a politician. He could have been anything from a grocer or a professor to a football coach. He was not too precise or too ready of speech in such a way as to spoil his pleasantly tweedy blur of countenance and outline. He went from

palace to log cabin, from wealth to the White House, in a pattern of TV reversal and upset.

•   •   •

MURDER BY TELEVISION

17   Jack Ruby shot Lee Oswald while tightly surrounded by guards who were paralyzed by television cameras. The fascinating and involving power of television scarcely needed this additional proof of its peculiar operation upon human perceptions. The Kennedy assassination gave people an immediate sense of the television power to create depth involvement, on the one hand, and a numbing effect as deep as grief, itself, on the other hand. Most people were amazed at the depth of meaning which the event communicated to them. Many more were surprised by the coolness and calm of the mass reaction. The same event, handled by press or radio (in the absence of television), would have provided a totally different experience. The national "lid" would have "blown off." Excitement would have been enormously greater and depth participation in a common awareness very much less.

18   As explained earlier, Kennedy was an excellent TV image. He had used the medium with the same effectiveness that Roosevelt had learned to achieve by radio. With TV, Kennedy found it natural to involve the nation in the office of the Presidency, both as an operation and as an image. TV reaches out for the corporate attributes of office. Potentially, it can transform the Presidency into a monarchic dynasty. A merely elective Presidency scarcely affords the depth of dedication and commitment demanded by the TV form. Even teachers on TV seem to be endowed by the student audiences with a charismatic or mystic character that much exceeds the feelings developed in the classroom or lecture hall. In the course of many studies of audience reactions to TV teaching, there recurs this puzzling fact. The viewers feel that the teacher has a dimension almost of sacredness. This feeling does not have its basis in concepts or ideas, but seems to creep in uninvited and unexplained. It baffles both the students and the analysts of their reactions. Surely, there could be no more telling touch to tip us off to the character of TV. This is not so much a visual as a tactual-auditory medium that involves all of our senses in depth interplay. For people long accustomed to the merely visual experience of the typographic and photographic varieties, it would seem to be the *synesthesia*, or tactual depth of TV experience, that dislocates them from their usual attitudes of passivity and detachment.

19   The banal and ritual remark of the conventionally literate, that TV presents an experience for passive viewers, is wide of the mark. TV is above all a medium that demands a creatively participant response. The guards who failed to protect Lee Oswald were not passive. They were so involved by the mere sight of the TV cameras that they lost their sense of their merely practical and specialist task.

20   Perhaps it was the Kennedy funeral that most strongly impressed the audience with the power of TV to invest an occasion with the character of corporate participation. No national event except in sports has ever had such coverage or such an audience. It revealed the unrivaled power of TV to achieve the involvement of the audience in a complex *process*. The funeral as a corporate process caused even the image of sport to pale and dwindle into puny proportions. The

Kennedy funeral, in short, manifested the power of TV to involve an entire population in a ritual process. By comparison, press, movie, and even radio are mere packaging devices for consumers.

21   Most of all, the Kennedy event provides an opportunity for noting a paradoxical feature of the "cool" TV medium. It involves us in moving depth, but it does not excite, agitate or arouse. Presumably, this is a feature of all depth experience.

Topics for consideration:

1. This essay was originally published in 1964. In what ways does television now differ from the medium McLuhan describes? Which of McLuhan's pronouncements that might have been valid in 1964 have been rendered invalid by technological or social changes associated with television?

2. McLuhan classifies different media as "hot" or "cool." A hot medium in McLuhan's view is one that "extends one single sense in 'high definition'..." [i.e.] being well-filled with data." Cool media provide "a meager amount of information" and require the audience to fill in the missing information, making them "high in participation." McLuhan classes print, radio and film as hot, while television and the telephone are cool. How useful is this classification? Do you think McLuhan would class the Internet as a hot or cool medium?

Further reading:

Marshall McLuhan, *The Gutenberg Galaxy: The Making of Typographic Man* (1962). McLuhan's most lucid book, in which he examines the ways in which the printed book changed Western consciousness.

Arthur Kroker, *Technology and the Canadian Mind* (1984)

Donald F. Theall, *The Medium is the Rear-View Mirror: Understanding McLuhan* (1971)

Maude Barlow (1947-) and
James Winter (1952-)

*Maude Barlow is the National Volunteer Chairperson for the Council of Canadians and author
of ten books about Canada. James Winter is a Professor of Communications at the University
of Windsor. This essay is an excerpt from* The Big Black Book: The Essential Views of
Conrad and Barbara Amiel Black *(1997).*

*Barlow and Winter delineate the extent of Conrad Black's Hollinger Inc.'s control of Canadian
newspapers and other media news outlets. They contrast Black's present views on such monopolies
to those he expressed as a young man.*

THE HORSE'S MOUTH

1 In November 1969, a youthful but bellicose Conrad Black appeared before the
Special Senate Committee on Mass Media, chaired by Liberal senator Keith
Davey. The submission by the twenty-five-year-old Black, who at the time owned
one small daily newspaper in rural Quebec, has gained some notoriety owing to
his personal attack on journalists as, among other things, "ignorant, lazy, opinionated, and intellectually dishonest." For good measure he added that they are
"aged hacks" who are "decrepit" and "alcoholic," words which have endeared him
to the journalism profession ever since.

2   Far less attention has been paid, however, to the substance of Black's submission and presentation to the Davey Committee. Black complained to the committee that as a small-circulation independent newspaper proprietor he couldn't
reasonably be expected to own his own press, and was reliant on a competitor, Paul
Desmarais's Power Corporation, to print his paper, the Sherbrooke *Record*, thirty
miles away in Granby, Quebec. Black decried the existence of the Power Corp.
media "colossus" in Quebec as well as the development of monopolistic chains
in general. "Further consolidation" toward monopolistic situations "is reprehen-
sible," and "monopolies are undesirable," Black wrote. "Diversity of opinion and
aggressive news-gathering tend to disappear with the disappearance of competition, and public opinion could thereby become more of a hostage to private interests than a master to public policy." (When his submission was released publicly,
Power Corp. cancelled its printing agreement in response to the criticism. The
appendix to Black's submission read as follows: "So serious was the deterioration
of our relationship with our printers subsequent to the writing of this brief, that
we were obliged to transfer our business to the only other printer in our geographic area, whose place of business is in the state of Vermont. We hold the
unreasonableness of our former printers to be the total cause of the regrettable
development.")

3   By the time Black wrote his memoirs in 1993, his perception of the "total
cause" had changed. "Since the former owners' [of the Sherbrooke *Record*] press
had been repossessed, David [Radler, one of Black's partners] determined that
the most economical printer, given prevailing exchange rates, was in Newport,

Vermont. We thus became the only daily newspaper in world history to be printed in a foreign country."

4   On May 27, 1997, a greying and puffy press baron named Conrad Black looked out sleepily at the audience assembled in the Design Exchange auditorium on Bay Street in Toronto, his eyes forming little more than slits in his round face. It was just moments after 11 a.m., and Black, who dislikes rising early, may have been a little grumpy. Outside, a street demonstration sponsored by the Campaign for Press and Broadcasting Freedom greeted arriving Hollinger Inc. board members, soliciting spare change to raise $1,000 in court costs for a lost appeal of the decision by the Federal Competition Bureau allowing Black's 1996 takeover of Southam Inc. newspapers.

5   Inside, the occasion was the Hollinger annual shareholders' meeting, which Black, as chairman of the board, called to order. He resented having to slip in through a back entrance to avoid a confrontation with the protestors. Black had someone introduce the members of the board of directors, which included his wife, Barbara Amiel Black. They stood on command and were recognized. Then Black launched into a twenty-minute harangue, interrupted sporadically by applause and laughter from the mostly appreciative audience of shareholders, board members, employees, and various members of the Toronto establishment. After making it clear that comments and questions would only be accepted from shareholders, Black railed at "the politically primitive" country of Australia, which he said he was forced to exit when their foreign ownership controls wouldn't allow him to increase his stake in the Fairfax newspaper chain. He lashed out at the former Southam management, which he had recently fired. Speaking to the assembled media, he sent a warning to Southam minority shareholders that they should accept his buyout offer of $23.50 and not hold out for a better one, as "arithmetically-challenged fools and their money are soon parted." Of his attempt to make the company private by buying up 100 percent of the shares, he warned, "we are the last train leaving the station."

6   Black also ranted about the CBC, in particular the French-language network, which he described as "a house-organ of the separatist movement of Quebec." He said that endless concessions to separatists only seem to have brought separatism closer. "There is no point throwing more raw meat to constitutional cannibals," he said. And he lambasted former reporter Gail Lem, now with the Communications, Energy and Paperworkers Union, when she asked him why he didn't seek political power through public office rather than through control of the nation's press. "Her perceptions are even more deranged than I imagined," Black said, before launching into an attack on the unions which he said have "hobbled" the newspaper industry.

7   But Black reserved most of his venom for "the lords of our national media," the Toronto press such as *The Globe and Mail* and *The Toronto Star*. His complaint? That an opinion poll about Quebec separatism commissioned by his company, Southam, and presumably run in his own sixty of 105 Canadian dailies, was ignored by the Toronto papers. (*Toronto Star* publisher John Honderich said later, "When Southam buys a poll, they run it. When *The Star* buys a poll, we run it. We don't run each other's polls — and Mr. Black knows that very well.") As a result, Black told shareholders that Hollinger was contemplating starting its own

Toronto-based national newspaper, and that a decision would be made soon. Black would not be ignored. He also used the occasion to express his contempt for the Council of Canadians and its protest of his recent takeovers. He said the council would only have a case if he were buying up *The Globe and Mail* and *The Toronto Star*, or making major incursions into the television industry. "Owning Moose Jaw and the *Corner Brook Western Star* and the *Medicine Hat News*, in febrile Maude Barlow's little mind that may make me [some] kind of a Goebbels of Canada but it doesn't," he was quoted as saying.

8   In the nearly thirty years that have elapsed between these two public performances, Conrad Black has radically altered the landscape of the Canadian news media. He has gone from owning one daily newspaper to owning sixty, including all of the newspapers in the provinces of Saskatchewan, Newfoundland, and Prince Edward Island. Observers at the Senate Committee hearing in 1969 might have been amused — or perhaps taken aback — by the strong words he used at the time. In 1997, some observers were alarmed by the display of raw power, anger, and arrogance, and the blind obeisance of the assembled crowd. Even *The Toronto Star*, duly chastened, felt compelled to report on Black's Southam poll the next day in its story on Conrad Black's meeting.

• • •

9   There is something chilling and strangely medieval about one family administering its views to an entire population, yet that is exactly what is happening in Canada today. Together, Conrad Black and his wife, Barbara Amiel Black, have an astonishing influence over the Canadian news media. Barbara Amiel is arguably the most widely read columnist in the country, with a piece in *Maclean's* magazine reaching half a million families every month, and columns in (potentially) 72 out of 105 Canadian newspapers, through 60 papers in the Southam-Sterling-Hollinger chain, the 11-paper Sun chain, and *The Financial Post*. In fact, her potential newspaper audience is about three million families in Canada alone.

10   While Amiel's columns may seem to be the most obvious outlet for their views, the Blacks' true and primary influence comes through Conrad Black's corporate holdings, most importantly the newspaper/media giant, Hollinger Inc., where Barbara is vice-president editorial, and Conrad is chairman of the board and CEO, and Southam Inc., in which Black now has controlling interest. But the dozens of newspapers under his direct control extend his influence even further into the Canadian media by providing much of the material disseminated by the Canadian Press (CP) and its Broadcast News and Press News services. CP operates as a cooperative, with a relatively small newsgathering staff, and most of its employees involved in redistributing news collected by its member newspapers. Black's overwhelming membership in CP means that he reaches past his own newspapers to 9 Thomson papers, 10 in the Sun chain, those of Power Corporation and Quebecor Inc., and about a dozen independents. In all, CP is used by 86 of 105 dailies.

11   In the final analysis, then, through his own holdings and CP subscribers, *Conrad Black reaches every newspaper in Canada but four*: the *Times-Globe* and *Telegraph-Journal* of Saint John, New Brunswick, owned by the Irving family, the Sherbrooke *Record* (ironically one of Black's earliest acquisitions), now owned

by Quebecor, as well as the *Sentinel-Review* of Woodstock, Ontario, owned by Newfoundland Capital Corporation.

12   Newspapers are not the only medium in the Blacks' kingdom. CP's Broadcast News wire goes into 140 radio stations, 28 television stations, and 36 cable outlets in Ontario alone. The total across the country is: 425 radio stations, 76 television stations, and 142 cable outlets. CP's Press News service is picked up by CBC radio and television, and 110 outlets in business, government, schools, and other "non-news" outlets. So, through CP, Conrad Black reaches 753 private and public educational broadcasting outlets across the country, plus all of the CBC radio and television stations. The CBC owns 89 stations, 1,160 CBC rebroadcasters, 31 private affiliated stations, and 292 affiliated or community rebroadcasters.

13   Through Southam, Black also partially owns Coles Bookstores, which merged with SmithBooks in March 1995 to form Chapters Inc., a megachain of 430 bookstores with about 35 percent of the national book market. Such concentration is not without its effects. Jacquie McNish of *The Globe and Mail*'s Report on Business notes that "Chapters now employs one team of only nine buyers for about 400 stores. That leaves publishers with no national alternative if Chapters shows little or no interest in a book."

• • •

14   Canada is virtually alone in the industrialized world in having no legislation to prevent the concentration of newspaper ownership or cross-media concentration. This should come as no surprise, for the Competition Act, which regulates mergers and acquisitions, was drafted for the Mulroney government by the Competition Policy Task Force of the Business Council on National Issues.

15   Representing the interests of the 160 most powerful corporations in Canada (many of them branch plants of American transnationals), the BCNI is the most important corporate lobby group in the country. The mother of all special interest groups, the BCNI has been the primary influence behind government policies on trade liberalization, privatization of public assets, deregulation of environmental protection, transportation, telecommunications, investment, and corporate-friendly taxation competition practices.

16   The BCNI's recommendations were, according to its committee mandate, to "establish a cooperative and mutually supportive approach between the business community and the government on the contentious issues of competition policy in order to ensure that the public interest in having Canadian business compete vigorously in domestic and international markets can be served." Consequently, the mandate of the Competition Bureau, which administers the Competition Act, is very narrow, pitifully inadequate to protect the public interest, and skewed in favour of big business; it can only rule against a merger if the local "commercial" competitiveness of advertisers has been compromised. The Bureau refuses to examine whether editorial and news content diversity will be compromised, whether local news and the use of local reporters and columnists will be diminished, or even if a national chain will be able to control national advertising markets, thereby creating a monopoly and effectively diminishing competition at that level.

17   We can do no better than to quote once again from Conrad Black, when he was the owner of only one daily newspaper, on the need for legislative action.

"The anti-monopoly provisions of the Combines Investigations Act should be applied to the media as zealously as they have been to other industries. It is high time the media divisions of the Power Corporation group, and perhaps the Irving media interests also, had their day in court."

18 Exacerbating the problem of a weak legislative framework is the fact that public advocacy intervention in Competition Bureau proceedings is discouraged. In fact, when the bureau granted Hollinger control over Southam, it did not even hold public hearings or grant the public access to its written decision. And the Competition Bureau joined the legal counsel of Hollinger to defeat an attempt by the public interest group, the Council of Canadians, to challenge the lack of public participation in the Hollinger decision. Clearly, the federal government, through the Competition Bureau, views newspapers as being no different than widgets; newspapers are simply commercial products to be bought and sold in the open market by corporate interests.

19 There is no law to prevent Conrad Black from buying every newspaper in Canada and every private radio and television station as well. Even his current level of ownership is unacceptable to the democratic interests of Canadians. Legislation to curb the concentration of media ownership is long overdue.

Topics for consideration:

1. Barlow and Winter argue that Conrad Black's ownership of so much of Canadian news media allows him to have an undue influence. Investigate the ownership of news media in your area. Do you find evidence of similar undue influences?

2. It has been said that, "Freedom of the press belongs to the person who owns one." Barlow and Winter paint a bleak picture of one family's control of Canadian news media. What steps could be taken to ensure that news media cover a wider range of viewpoints?

Linda Grant (1951-

Linda Grant is a British journalist and author of Sexing the Millennium: Women and the Sexual Revolution (1993). Her first novel, The Cast Iron Shore, was winner of the Orange Prize for Fiction in 1997. She writes regularly for the Manchester Guardian newspaper where this piece originally appeared.

Beginning with an account of how she first heard of Princess Diana's death, Linda Grant reflects on the pervasiveness of conspiracy theories. People become more gullible, she suggests, because they themselves feel powerless and perceive governments as "unable to effect any change." As a form of "learned helplessness," conspiracy theories also reflect a yearning for meaning when "none of the big ideas have much currency any more."

WE'RE LOSING THE PLOT

1   Listen closely, because what I'm going to tell you is absolutely true. On the morning of September 1, 1997 I woke up at about 3 am and unable to get back to sleep, began to read. I turned on the radio which was playing a Prom. I read for about 45 minutes, the music in the background.

2   Then an announcement was made. There had been a car crash in Paris. Dodi Al Fayed had been killed, but Princess Diana had walked away from the wreckage with cuts to her legs. I thought two things: a) Di, darling, he wasn't good enough for you, and, b) dark, opaque tights from now on. About 20 minutes later there was a further announcement. Diana was dead. From cuts to the legs? What was going on?

3   Isn't it obvious? Diana did not die in the car crash. The coffin was empty. The island in the middle of the lake at Althorp is a vacant shrine. Longing for freedom and private life, she slipped away from us and is living quietly in the same never-never land as Lord Lucan and Elvis. And don't tell me that the first bulletin was a mistake based on a dodgy eyewitness account because if there's a choice between conspiracy and cock-up, as we are now becoming aware, conspiracy will win out every time.

4   Because I know Diana is alive, I utterly reject the rival claim that Diana was bumped off by MI5 to prevent her from marrying the Muslim son of a shady character whose Home Office file is so damning that no government has been prepared to grant him citizenship. As for the absurd nonsense that they died because the chauffeur was drunk, Diana and Dodi didn't have their seat-belts fastened and they were escaping from the paparazzi, only a brain-washed idiot would believe it.

5   Actually, I think that that's exactly what did happen. I experience deep torpor when I hear of the billions of words zooming at the speed of light around the Internet, tapped in by beings for whom the phrase get-a-life should have been invented. The United States is a nation of conspiracy theorists. Now Britain is becoming one too.

6   What's happening to us? I don't know if there were conspiracy theorists before the assassination of John F Kennedy in 1963, but it was the aftermath of

that murder which brought the breed into the full, paranoid flower of its collective madness. Conspiracy theory is a natural consequence of a self-invented country built on the foundations of a philosophy which says that anything is possible, if only you believe. Luckily for the Americans, within a few short years they had Watergate, a conspiracy actually exposed and since then much of what passes as journalistic activity in the US is devoted by hacks to the hope that they will uncover something just as amazing, for which they will collect the Pulitzer Prize.

7   Before conspiracy theorists there were harmless cranks such as the vicar in the fifties who proved by mathematics that the sun was cold, or the members of the society who believed that the earth was flat and the moon landings had been faked by the US government to divert attention from the monumental cost of the space programme. These stories seemed terribly funny at the time, fodder for end-of-page paragraphs in the *Readers' Digest*.

8   Now we have the X Files, and half the American population (or probably more) believing that aliens landed at Roswell and that their local sheriff was kidnapped for sexual experimentation by beings with three heads and the government knows but it's covering up. Hence the sick satisfaction of *Independence Day* when the alien abduction theorists are proved right at last.

9   The conspiracy theory is a product of times in which no one believes any more that governments can really effect any change, that instead of giving us the New Deal or the Welfare State, they are impotent entities, harnessed to economic forces, spinning their wheels in a pathetic display of empty public relations. And if they are doing anything, you can bet that it isn't in our interests. The world, we figure, is really run by secret cabals — bankers, Jews, aliens; forces bigger than us, otherwise why would we feel so powerless? Why would our governments seem so ineffective?

10   For 40 years, revolutions really were undermined by CIA campaigns and covert operations, but the defeat of popular movements for self-determination were never solely down to the machinations of the quiet Americans, in Graham Greene's defining phrase. I know that just because you're paranoid doesn't mean you're not being followed, but the tendency to see plots everywhere is a means of not looking at ourselves, and our own failures, of always pinning the blame on shadowy forces beyond our control. Conspiracy theories are a form of learned helplessness. Perhaps, too, the conspiracy theory is a yearning for the unified meaning in a time of fragmentation, when none of the big ideas have much currency any more.

11   Someone called me from Montreal a few days after the car crash to say that he had a friend who had a friend who was "the ambassador to Canada", and he had connections with "high-ranking policemen in Interpol" who had told him that they had been "tipped off to expect a high profile death" a week before Diana was killed. I must tell you that the individual who relayed this information is a professor of philosophy. I said, "Let's run through this again, the French ambassador to Canada said ..." No, he replied. Not the French ambassador. The Armenian ambassador to Canada. No connections to France, then? No.

12   "And how do you imagine Interpol cops?" I asked him. "A cross between James Bond and Inspector Morse perhaps? Because as I understand it, Interpol

is an office full of pen-pushers shifting files in an office in Brussels, a bit like the Motor Vehicle Licensing Centre." So the mind fills in the carefully exposed blanks, rushes towards imposing a pattern and structure on random bits of information. It's a human urge. Longing for understanding, we hate the idea that there rarely is a point to anything, particularly life. Meanwhile people are dropping dead of starvation in Sudan. No mystery about why that's happening: the usual mixture of climate and corruption. Nothing to write about on the Internet. More's the pity.

Topics for consideration:

1. What difference does Grant see between "harmless cranks" and conspiracy theorists? Why does she think the former have been replaced by the latter?

2. Who are the "we" in paragraph 9 where Grant writes "the world, we figure, is really run by secret cabals—bankers, Jews, aliens; forces bigger than us"? How does this relate to paragraph 3?

3. People who remember the assassination of John F. Kennedy generally recall where they were when they heard the news. Grant's opening paragraph implies the same sort of recall in relation to the death of Princess Diana. What events reported in the news have fused with your own experience in a similar way?

4. Grant suggests that conspiracy theories are becoming more pervasive. Do you think that this is so? What reasons does Grant offer for people's readiness to accept such theories?

5. "Urban folklore" is a broader category that includes the conspiracy theories of the kind discussed in this essay. It has been suggested that the Internet is a rich source of such folklore. What examples of this have you found?

Further reading:

Jan Harold Brunvand, *Curses! Broiled Again: The Hottest Urban Legends Going* (1989). One of several collections of urban folklore by this prominent American folklorist.

http://urban legends.miningco.com/ Links to various sites of "netlore" and urban legends.

Andrew Cash (1962-

Andrew Cash is a Toronto singer/songwriter and journalist.

*Andrew Cash's essay suggests that, while many sneer at the karaoke fad as "low-brow," peo-
ple's participation in karaoke represents "a strangely political activity." In a culture in which
most people are too repressed and self-conscious to sing, karaoke enables some to find a sense of
community and to discover a way of not being "silenced by a mass culture that has simply stopped
listening."*

PUMP UP THE VOLUME

> I'd never change the key to a Roy Orbison song. I sing it in the original. To
> change his stuff would be blasphemy.
>
> — Al, a karaoke singer

1   I'm sitting in the Eton House, one of the beer parlours that populate the east-
end working-class neighbourhood of Riverdale in Toronto. There is a couple on
stage singing a duet: Elton John and Kiki Dee's late-seventies hit "Don't Go
Breaking My Heart" (you want to say you don't know this song but you do). The
couple is in their mid-forties. They've been hanging out with their friends all
night long, mustering up the guts — with the help of hops and barley — to get
up and sing a song.

2   They finally take the plunge. The song begins, and, trading lines, they sing
into each others' eyes:

> Man: *Don't go breaking my heart*
> Woman: *I couldn't if I tried*
> Man: *Oh honey if I get restless*
> Woman: *Baby you're not that type*

3   The man sings the whole song in a monotone, coming in on all his lines
exactly one beat late. It doesn't bother his partner. She happily sings her lines in
tune and in time, no doubt listening more to the pre-recorded backing music
than to him. It also doesn't bother the audience — the song over, the couple goes
smiling back to their seats to the loud applause of the other patrons.

4   Alex Zarbo, a host with Toronto's A-to-Z Karaoke, says he sees transforma-
tions like this all the time. Karaoke draws an incredible mix of people, and Zarbo,
a veteran of the rough bars of south Riverdale, says he's seen all types. "I have seen
tough guys and ex-cons, guys who have a hard time expressing themselves. People
trapped by bad choices and yet they're not bad people. Amazingly, they get up to
sing," he says. "Karaoke seems to tap into what is best in them. It gives them a
chance to show this side of themselves to their friends. It lets down some walls."

5   The multi-million-dollar success of the karaoke industry has surprised almost
everyone, and few have been able to explain its strange allure. Maybe that's why

it has such a bad reputation in mainstream culture: even open-minded people I know think that karaoke is hokey, that it's a pastime for geeks and losers, and that it's sung only in Japanese sushi bars and obscure Vietnamese cafes.

6   I'm not so sure. My introduction to karaoke occurred one night when I unsuspectingly wandered into my local pub, one of the many working-class bars in my neighbourhood. It was karaoke night and the bar was packed with everyone from toughened factory workers and young preppie women to suburban punks and architects, all there to do one thing — sing. There was a familiarity among the people and a clear atmosphere of mutual supportiveness, which climaxed in an audience-participation performance of The Village People's timeless classic "YMCA" (yes, you know that one too — it's okay), complete with audience members dancing on the tables.

7   The fact that the working poor — that growing class of Canadians — flock to karaoke ought to be our first hint that there's more here than meets the eye. There is: beneath all the theatrics and the recycled seventies hits, karaoke is a strangely political activity.

8   In a culture driven by consumerism and celebrity-worship, karaoke is a quirky way to reclaim mass media, using it in the service of one's own creativity. It's like a pop-culture version of beating a sword into a ploughshare. What's more, it bucks the isolating trend in consumer culture, recognizing that singing is an inherently social thing — which is why singing has always been a major tool in political movements. When Zarbo says karaoke transforms its participants, I think that's what he's getting at: the rebellious act of getting together and simply singing with others.

9   Sure, you could say karaoke is a pretty compromised type of rebellion — reclaiming mass culture in some ways only reaffirms its power, and anyway, how much value is there in reclaiming Madonna? But in today's high-sell, buy-everything society, turning off the commercial faucet to entertain yourself is about as insurgent an act as you can get.

10   If this all hinges on singing, that's because it's such a neglected activity in North American society.

11   I remember a study that asked kindergarten students if they could sing. Invariably, all the children answered that yes, they could. When the same question was put to kids in grade 10, all but a few answered no. What this simple study points to is that as we get older, we receive messages about who can and who can't sing; who has a voice and who are the voiceless in our culture. As Ivan Illich pointed out in his groundbreaking work *Deschooling Society*, we live in a society that deifies the certified professional at the expense of our own collective wisdom and experience. If the toaster breaks, we have to send it to a certified toaster-fixer. If we have a cough, we have to go to a certified cough-fixer. If we want to hear music, we go to a certified, commercially-produced singer.

12   Yet what is an almost universal truth is that everybody sings. Ours is simply a culture that hides it in the shower.

13   Other cultures aren't so restrictive. I'm reminded of a ride I took on a commuter train while traveling in India. It was seven in the morning and the cramped train compartment was full of mostly young men making their daily two-hour

trek to a textile factory on the outskirts of Bombay. They were interested in the only non-Indian in their compartment. When they saw I was carrying a guitar, they asked me to sing them a song. I naturally declined. This surprised them, and they asked again, more persistently. When I still refused, they took matters into their own hands: "Okay, *we'll* sing first," one of them indicated, and they proceeded to trade songs with each other, singing back and forth for half an hour. The rug was pulled out from under me — I took my guitar out and awkwardly began to sing a tune I had written, and though they didn't speak English and didn't know the piece, they participated and sang along.

14   I was impressed by the ease with which these factory workers, so early in the morning, could sing out loud, together, in a public place — and how it was no big deal, no show, just something they did as a matter of course. Here I was, a North American singer, accustomed to performing professionally in front of people, experiencing in a very new way the liberating feelings of sharing a song with others far outside the audience/performer dynamic that dominates North America.

15   What was also amazing was that the workers knew so many of the same songs. Perhaps nowhere is the infancy of North American culture underlined as dramatically as in its canon of common songs — the songs most everyone knows and can sing together at public events like weddings, funerals, or parties.

16   Consider this story: I was once with a group of high school students on an overnight country retreat, and they were awestruck by the night sky. They were inner-city kids, so it was a new and wondrous sight for them — and they had a natural, ambiguous need to give voice to their experience, so they wanted to sing. But finding a common song was difficult — some of the kids were from Portugal, others from the Caribbean, others from Poland, Italy, the Philippines and India, and still others were third-generation Canadian. After about 15 minutes of negotiations, they decided to sing one verse from a Beatles song and one verse from a U2 song.

17   In searching for cultural common ground in North America, we inevitably land on mainstream pop culture, just as these students did. Electronic media, advertising and a decided focus on consumption are mainstream North America's defining characteristics. It's what binds us and it's what we export to the rest of the world. Just as it would be difficult to find many buildings in North America that date back a few hundred years, it would be hard to find songs that most North Americans know that pre-date pop music on the radio, a history of only about 50 years.

18 The Japanese meaning of the word *karaoke* is "empty orchestra," yet for all its low-brow qualities, karaoke delivers what the high priests of the Internet and the authors of self-help books promise but seldom deliver: community. It provides a space where the rough edges of who we are become insignificant and acceptable. For the marginalized, it affirms what mainstream culture never does: that they have a voice and a place out there where people will listen to it.

19   Al doesn't sing karaoke every night of the week — only about five times a week. He is an actor when he can find the work and a telefundraiser when he can't. "Everyone here comes to sing," he tells me as he makes his way up to the microphone to try his hand at a song recently released to the world of karaoke: "Pinball Wizard" by The Who. Al is dressed in a tank top and sweat pants. As he gets into the tune, he discovers his money belt is too encumbering, so before

he gets the second *sure plays a mean pinball* he doffs the belt for freer mobility. He tells me that he's met 90 per cent of his friends through karaoke. Tonight he has followed one of his favourite hosts out of the neighbourhood to a more upscale bar in North Toronto.

20   "These people put on a good show," he assures me. "They are good people." He's referring to Chris and Walter Henkel, who run a karaoke business called Sound Choice. In a recent issue of the fledgling publication *Karaoke News Canada*, there is a small feature on Chris and Walter. Part of it reads as follows:

> In November 1992 Chris started to attend Karaoke shows alone. She loved to sing, yet couldn't always find someone to accompany her. She was made very welcome and soon got to know numerous other devotees, one of whom introduced her to Walter, another loner. Within 2 years (they) were married, with four fellow Karaokians taking roles within the wedding ceremony. They have been hosting Karaoke for two years now and always make a big point of involving the newest. Perhaps the next time you see someone perform in their four minutes of air time, this could be your Mr. or Miss Right.

21   Carol, a secretary who has been singing karaoke for eight years, calls it "a great confidence builder. I'm a very shy person. If someone told me eight years ago that I would be singing through a microphone in front of others, I would have laughed. The first time I was so nervous. Now I can't wait until my name is called." Her specialty is jazz standards. I listen to her sultry vocalizing over Thelonious Monk's classic "Round Midnight." Later, she speaks knowledgeably about the history of the song and its composer — it turns out she combs the karaoke song book for obscure titles, and has a vast record collection.

22   Louise, a karaoke friend, finds the experience equally liberating. "This is my therapy session!" she says. "Look, I take orders all day long. This is my chance to relax." Later, she gets ready to perform: "Hey I have soul in my bones. I'm white on the outside but I'm black on the inside," she says as she goes up to the microphone and belts out a smoking version of Fontella Bass's hit of 1965 "Rescue Me." There can be little doubt that part of this transformative element lies in karaoke's vicarious thrill of stardom, or bald "ego gratification," as one singer put it. To be sure; the long walk to the stage, the tension in the gut, the grip of the microphone, others watching, then the walk back to the seat, the respectful glances, the high-fives. We have mobilized so much of our imagination around the cult of celebrity that karaoke becomes virtual reality, allowing the singer the sensation of what it must be like to cross that huge divide between audience and performer, the chosen few up *there* and the mass of commoners down in the pit.

23   But Deborah Wong, an ethnomusicologist at the University of Pennsylvania, agrees it's more than that. She has studied Vietnamese karaoke in Southern California, and in a recent article for *Drama Review* argues that "karaoke is not the latest insidious step in a long, drawn-out process of transforming consumers into dupes of transnational industries and technologies." Rather, Wong suggests, the Vietnamese community uses karaoke to try to create for itself an immigrant popular culture; having been cut off from their homeland, karaoke helps to create a contemporary sense of cultural self.

24   I think this argument applies to a majority of karaoke devotees, particularly those on the cultural margins of North America — it is an activity almost completely of the "low brow." For them, karaoke can negotiate the wasteland between the promises of consumer culture and the reality that many are excluded from these promises. It can mediate, at least momentarily, the difficulty of being silenced by a mass culture that has simply stopped listening to you.

25   If karaoke is slyly subversive because of its "reclaiming" aspect, it's doubly so when you consider the political import of people singing together.

26   Folk singer Pete Seeger, speaking on a recent CBC radio show, said that one of his main ambitions is to encourage people to sing, publicly and together, in common and in all manner of circumstances. Seeger — who has paid the price, in terms of his career, for his outspoken blend of progressive politics and music — has been an ardent supporter and nurturer of the American musical tradition of telling the stories of the lives of regular people. While the mainstream trend in popular music today is to espouse a willful lack of concern about anything, Seeger stands defiantly as one of the last great symbols of an era when music was used as a way of building community and empowering people.

27   Liberation struggles the world over have had music at their core. It reflects what the people are going through, it helps to remind them of what their vision of the future is, and it blunts the edge of their lives of toil and oppression. It's been well documented — but often conveniently forgotten — that the roots of rock and roll are in the liberation struggles of North America: the struggles of African slaves of the American South and their northern brethren that created blues, gospel and jazz; the folk songs of the depression that helped to contextualize what was happening to an agricultural America. More recently, the politics of South Africa have been immemorialized in songs like Peter Gabriel's "Biko" or Special AKA's "Free Nelson Mandela" — popular songs that mobilized opinion and drew together a community around a common goal.

28   It's when you look at this history of public song that you realize how dangerous our cultural erasure of public singing is. We live in an era of hyper-individualism, where group activity seems abnormal. Ways of participating in groups are either mediated by large corporate concerns (as in mega-sports for example) or they are frowned on as being, well, silly — like line dancing, moshing, or even the *Rocky Horror Picture Show* ritual. Part of what seems so uncool about these modes of group participation is that they require a measure of submersion of the individual into the group. They are a challenge to the cult of the individual. In that context, public singing is about as geeksville as you can get.

29   What's more, mainstream scorn for karaoke may also stem from its very insurgency, its very refusal to play by the high-brow, individualistic rules. It's accessible to everyone irrespective of class or skill; for the price of a beer or soft drink, you can participate. Perhaps the most radical aspect of karaoke is that people are entertaining each other — they aren't being passive consumers. Is it surprising that it annoys a mainstream culture that is built on denying people access to creative expression?

30   None of this is to say that karaoke doesn't have its absurdities and paradoxes. Reclaiming mass culture is always a tricky business because, in the end, you're

working with some fairly corrupted tools. At best, it is a bittersweet and ambiguous victory. It might build community, but it's a community based, ironically, on people emulating the cult of celebrity. No matter how transformative the experience is, it still reaffirms the idea that creativity is something only for specially trained "professionals." Rather than doing away with the idea of professional creators, it tries to make us all feel like professionals.

31   In a way, karaoke also illustrates how much we've lost any sense of common singing. To sing karaoke, you don't even need to know the words to the songs — like a TV anchor, you simply read from the teleprompter in front of you. What happens if the screen goes blank, as it did on one occasion at the Rio Grande bar? The unfortunate singer couldn't carry on without it. He couldn't improvise and he hadn't taken the time to learn the words to the song — he had to wait until the screen was operational again before he could continue. Meanwhile, if you're in the audience and you find that there isn't enough going on around you to hold your attention, you can watch the video vignette that runs on the TV screen along with the music on many karaoke machines. Karaoke underlines just how much we have adapted to the technological colonization of our lives.

32   If anything, these paradoxes point to the difficulty of working out our own creative niche in a commercially-driven culture. Singer Carol is philosophical about it: "Many people don't like it, they look down on karaoke. This is an underground culture." Indeed, in our search for metaphors for who we are and what we need to maintain our identity in the face of bold consumer fundamentalism, we need to look at what is brewing in all underground cultures. Who would have thought one of the things we would find down there would be karaoke?

Topics for consideration:

1. Andrew Cash points out that, while children in North America sing unselfconsciously, most adults are persuaded that they can't sing. Has this been your experience?

2. What attitudes does Cash seem to assume the reader already has about karaoke? How does he attempt to challenge them?

3. Cash regards mass culture as non-participatory and unresponsive and argues that karaoke is one way of reversing this. What other ways are there?

4. In R. Murray Schafer's essay "Dub" in chapter 11, he condemns the lack of originality in recorded as opposed to participatory "live" music. What do you think Schafer would think of Cash's argument about karaoke?

Further reading:

Gary Gumpert, *Talking Tombstones and Other Tales of the Media Age* (1987). Includes interesting reflections on the role of varieties of recorded music in our lives.

Michael Posner (1947-

Michael Posner is a Toronto-based journalist who writes for the Globe and Mail, *where this essay was originally published. He is author of* Canadian Dreams: The Making and Marketing of Independent Films *(1993).*

In this essay, Michael Posner criticizes the increasing use of market surveys, particularly focus groups, to evaluate and shape television shows and films. He concludes that this trend indicates the "triumph of the marketplace" and a value system that deems money, not art, to be the highest good.

ART BY COMMITTEE

1 Good evening, and thank you for coming.

2 It says here that my name is Ken and I'm your moderator. As you know, this focus group includes a dozen randomly chosen Canadians, all of whom have read at least one novel in the past year. Unfortunately, *Winnie-the-Pooh* does not count.

3 The soon-to-be-published work we are considering tonight is a saga of three generations of Canada's founding peoples — French, English and native. We have several topics to address. On the graphics side, we will examine such issues as cover design, paper stock, typeface, and the general feel of the book. I'm not sure what that means exactly, so I hope you do.

4 In terms of content, we want to see if consensus exists on plot. Is the story line understandable, at once accessible but not too simple-minded? Are there too many characters or too few? What about the ending? How could it be improved upon, made more upbeat, perhaps? What do you think of the title, *Three Solitudes*? Can you suggest something grabbier or less derivative? And, critically important, would you recommend this novel to your friends? Because otherwise, just between you and me, what's the point, eh?

5 A preposterous notion, of course. What publisher of sound mind would ever release a novel based on the prompted remarks, off-the-cuff asides, largely gratuitous observations (except for the $50 honorarium paid to participants), statistically irrelevant impressions, and fundamentally meaningless opinions of a focus group? You'd be surprised.

6 I've been thinking about focus groups lately because of our old friend *Seinfeld*. Amid the orgasmic convulsions that accompanied its interminable goodbye, it is worth remembering that when Jerry, George, Elaine and Kramer were first rolled out a decade ago, test audiences hated them. Too Jewish. Too New York. Not likable. Etc. The show almost never made it to air. You know the rest. Nine remarkable TV seasons later, the *Seinfeld* chorus has said sayonara, its ratings undiluted.

7 Which brings me to my point: We have been conned.

8 I mean, it's one thing to bring people together to (yawn) yak about Tide, Crest, Secret (the secret, I guess, is that but for this chemical gop, you smell) and other emanations of Madison Avenue's packaging universe. There, perhaps, focus

groups are the best thing since peanut butter (my own preference is crunchy, thank you), and helpful in determining whether the new soap box should be green with white lettering or white with green lettering.

9   But convening focus groups to deliberate artistic issues is not only an enormous waste of time, energy and money; it's a fraud. Focus groups are entirely artificial concoctions in which participants render spontaneous, ill-considered opinions on subjects they know little and care less about. In focus groups, people say things simply for the sake of saying things. What they say may be germane or absurd; it doesn't matter. The point is to say something. That's why they get the 50 bucks. Typically, in these sessions, strong voices prevail, drowning out the meek. And the entire process is tainted by a weird voyeurism, the knowledge that behind a two-way glass "the client" is watching.

10   Its purveyors call all of this "qualitative research," a dressed-up term designed to invest the exercise with the aura of quasi-scientific legitimacy. It has none. Test audiences, in general, come equipped with the artistic intelligence of a herd of bovines.

11   And yet the practice is epidemic. Virtually every big-budget Hollywood film, for example, is now market-tested (one that was not, incidentally, is *Godzilla*, its producers so cocksure of gee-whiz computer animation that they didn't bother); the consensus often determines whether the flick gets wide or narrow release, or goes directly to the video market. Focus-group flops can also spell the TV death knell for pilot sitcoms and dramas. Radio stations routinely retain market-research firms to determine their play lists. Garth Drabinsky's Broadway musical *Ragtime* should give program credits to those who attended workshop productions, answered lengthy questionnaires and helped shape its story line. At least one pop novelist, thriller writer James Patterson, rewrote an ending to conform to test readers' desires. Conrad Black's putative national daily newspaper has also been extensively focus-grouped. Even the *Globe and Mail*, I am saddened to report, has fallen for this charade. Editors, who know better but must answer to publishers, smile politely and acquiesce, praying that the results will be inconclusive.

12   Soon, perhaps, focus groups will be convened to critique painters: Too much light? Too abstract? Composers will test-market symphonies and chamber pieces: That arpeggio in the second movement is a little overdone, wouldn't you say? Poets will try out rhyme schemes: No, no, in my opinion, ABBA is thematically more apt than AABB.

13   What explains the focus-group phenomenon? The rise of the managerial class, people who have no special understanding or experience of the arts and (properly) not enough confidence in their own opinions to make artistic decisions. Seeking to insulate themselves from financial risk, film, TV and radio executives, theatre impresarios and newspaper tycoons turn to public opinion. They might as well say: "We've spent millions of dollars developing this property and hiring talent, but we basically have no faith in these people and no idea whether this show, this film, this publication is good or bad. Tell us, please." Then, if the "product" bombs, they're indemnified: Hey, it's not our fault, the research said it would work.

14   And there's something else more troubling still: Implicit in focus-group thinking is the utter triumph of the marketplace. With few exceptions, we have

essentially renounced any pretensions to producing quality. Artistry-schmartistry, will the damn thing sell? Money, not art, is the highest good. With values like these, it is hardly surprising that our society is fundamentally sick.

Topics for consideration:

1. Posner suggests that focus groups inevitably yield misleading or unhelpful results. Why does he think this is so? Is there any context in which such groups might be helpful?

2. The essay begins with Posner's imagining an absurd example of the use of focus groups. Is the example he imagines really more ridiculous than the actual uses of focus groups that he cites? If so, how?

3. Posner's essay suggests that test-marketing would almost certainly thwart anyone producing an important work of art. Take the example of a book, film, or painting that you admire and speculate on the probable views of a focus group asked to assess it.

CHAPTER 9

QUESTIONS OF TRUTH

We often use words like "unbiased," "accurate" or even "objective" when trying to identify a historical or journalistic account of events that is more or less "truthful." The essays in this chapter suggest that, as Oscar Wilde has one of his characters remark in *The Importance of Being Earnest* (1895), "The truth is rarely pure, and never simple."

Randal Marlin's "Where There's Smoke" is critical of the way journalists treat scientific evidence. Using as his example the newspaper reports misrepresenting a World Health Organization study on second-hand smoke, he shows how careless journalists working under unreasonable time constraints because of understaffing are particularly susceptible to pressure from the tobacco industry. "A lie will travel ten miles while truth is getting its boots on" goes a folk saying in Lunenburg County, Nova Scotia. Marlin's article traces a similar process when "the same distorted report" on second-hand smoke reappears throughout an entire chain of newspapers with no subsequent retraction once the inaccuracy has been pointed out.

News media regularly conduct polls of public opinion and publish their results, a process that shapes public opinion and influences public policy. A Toronto writer using the pseudonym "seeKorum," who has worked for one such polling company, reveals the very unscientific techniques of such polling in "Adventures in the Number Trade."

Just as numbers seem to offer some assurance of truth and accuracy, we tend to think of photographs as accurate records of real events. Photographic archivist Peter Robertson in "More Than Meets the Eye," demonstrates that as early as World War I photographs were being faked and manipulated for propaganda purposes. Even when the image itself has not been tampered with, our "reading" of a photograph can often be heavily influenced by how it is captioned.

While personal memoirs often have the convincing ring of truth, they may bear little resemblance to historical events. In "A Real Whopper," John Goddard examines Farley Mowat's accounts of his experiences in the Arctic. Goddard investigates both Mowat's own field journals and government records of the time, finding startling discrepancies between them and Mowat's published accounts. Mowat continues to defend his version, describing his writing as "subjective nonfiction."

Thomas King is confronted with a more profound puzzle of the relationship between "fact" and "fiction" and between "history" and "story" in "How I Spent My Summer Vacation: History, Story, and the Cant of Authenticity." The different versions of the same story that Bella tells King are history she insists, while King is tempted to call them myth. History has the distinction of being stabilized in print form, even though it may have never happened, whereas story remains fluid, able to be reshaped in each telling to offer a new "truth."

Randal Marlin (1938-

Randal Marlin is an Associate Professor of Philosophy at Carleton University. He specializes in communication ethics and is author of The David Levine Affair: Separatist Betrayal or McCarthyism North *(1998).*

Randal Marlin's "Where There's Smoke" traces the way in which an inconclusive World Health Organization study was misrepresented in newspaper reports. Through a combination of pressure from the tobacco industry, careless journalism, and understaffed newspapers, the study showing an increased *risk of lung cancer from passive smoking grabbed headlines as a story claiming, "no harm from second-hand smoke."*

WHERE THERE'S SMOKE

1 Despite the fact that the tobacco industry has, over the last few decades, been besieged by class action suits, been undermined by good science and had its customers driven from enjoying their product in most places, its lobbying remains vibrant and effective.

2 Indeed, earlier this year the industry appeared to pull off what could easily be considered a public relations coup. Here were credible newspapers trumpeting the news that second-hand smoke has been found not to cause cancer and "could even have a protective effect." Not only that, but the story supposedly came vested with the authority of one of the most credible organizations on the subject, namely the World Health Organization. The story was that the WHO's International Agency for Research on Cancer in Lyon, France, had commissioned a 12-centre, seven-country study on second-hand smoke and lung cancer and had found no connection; and furthermore, that the WHO was displeased with these results and wanted to conceal them from the public.

3 It would appear that Conrad Black's newspaper empire was the primary dupe (willing or otherwise), beginning with his London-based paper and then extending to Canada, where his recently acquired Southam chain of newspapers picked up the story.

4 The tobacco industry must have been hugely satisfied to see, screaming from the top of the *Sunday Telegraph* on March 8, 1998, the six-column headline, "Passive smoking doesn't cause cancer — official." The *Ottawa Citizen* went even further with a banner headline the same day "No harm from second-hand smoke," something even the *Telegraph* story did not support. Other Southam papers that included the same distorted report of the WHO study were the Vancouver *Province*, the Vancouver *Sun*, the *Edmonton Journal*, the *Calgary Herald*, the Kingston *Whig-Standard* and the *St. Catharine's Standard*.

5 Before explaining the nature of the deception, it is worth recounting why this kind of story is of vital importance to the tobacco industry. As long as people can be made to believe that smoking harms only the smoker and not other people exposed to the smoke, then the strongest, life-and-death part of the argument in favour of banning smoking in confined public spaces disappears.

6   The truth about passive smoking is to the contrary. A huge body of scientific evidence lends a strong weight of probability to the negative effects of passive smoking. The evidence no longer leaves room for practical doubt, which is to say that it is prudent to regard the connection as established even though, as with all sampling procedures, there is room for vestigial theoretical doubts. What is scientifically certain, though, is that a single study, involving only 650 lung cancer patients (as with the WHO study), cannot, by itself, overturn the results of numerous studies involving hundreds of thousands of subjects.

7   Journalists who know something about science treat with suspicion a study that purports to overthrow the accumulated evidence. They would certainly know that one single study involving a relatively small to medium-sized sample could not by itself establish the truth about passive smoking one way or the other. Thus, when learning that a given study involved comparing 650 lung cancer patients with 1,542 healthy people, they would know, or at least suspect, there to be something wrong with the lead paragraph in the *Telegraph* story by Victoria MacDonald: "The world's leading health organization has withheld from publication a study which shows that not only might there be no link between passive smoking and lung cancer but that it could even have a protective effect."

8   To see how deceptive this statement is, it should first be noted that the study in question actually *confirmed* the existing body of research. To quote from a WHO press release of March 9,1998: "The results of this study, which have been completely misrepresented in recent news reports, are very much in line with the results of similar studies both in Europe and elsewhere: *passive smoking causes lung cancer in nonsmokers.*

9   "The study found that there was an estimated 16 per cent increased risk of lung cancer among non-smoking spouses of smokers. For workplace exposure the estimated increase in risk was 17 per cent. However, due to small sample size, neither increased risk was statistically significant."

10 The deception consists of underlining and trumpeting, as if it were highly significant, a routine acknowledgement that the limitations of the study were such that it could not rule out the possibility of an absence of connection between second-hand smoke and lung cancer. In this way what is really the inconclusiveness of the study gets treated, falsely, as a positive and authoritative demonstration that there is no such connection.

11 For those who can appreciate the scientific terminology, the study indicated an odds ratio of increased lung cancer risk with exposure to spousal smoke of 1.16 (within a range of 0.93 to 1.44, 19 times out of 20), and with exposure to workplace smoke of 1.17 (within a range of 0.94 to 1.45, 19 times out of 20).

12 It is very easy to confuse "the study did not show that this or that connection exists" with "the study showed that this or that connection does not exist." That kind of confusion is encouraged when a scientific claim of the first kind is given the prominence that only the second kind of claim would warrant. It's not news that the study does not establish, of itself alone, a connection. It would be big news, though, if the study were somehow to establish the latter.

13 The story also claimed that the WHO was somehow "reluctant to release secret study." As the WHO explained in the March 9 news release: "In February 1998, according to usual scientific practice, a paper reporting the main study

results was sent to a reputable scientific journal for consideration and peer review. That is why the full report is not yet publicly available."

14   That the tobacco industry was behind the deception has been claimed by health officials. *The Times* of London carried a brief news item on March 10 that attributed to Karol Sikora, head of the WHO's cancer program, the charge that tobacco industry spin-doctors had "used tip-offs to the media to highlight passages in a confidential report which they considered favourable to their cause."

15   Dr. Paul Kleihues, director of the International Agency for Research on Cancer in Lyon, France, which coordinated the study for the WHO, commented on the false and misleading statements in the mass media as follows: "It is no coincidence that this misinformation originally appeared in the British press just before the No-Tobacco Day in the United Kingdom and the scheduled publication of the report of the British Scientific Committee on Tobacco and Health."

16   When Victoria MacDonald, Health Correspondent of the *Telegraph* and author of the story, was asked, pointblank, whether she had received assistance from the tobacco industry, she replied "What a peculiar question!" with an incredulous and supercilious air and begged off, saying "No journalist tells anybody where they get their stories from."

17   Whatever the source, other circumstances happened to play in favour of the tobacco industry. Indeed, part of the cleverness in this whole deception relates to the timing of the story. It took place on a weekend, when newspapers are short-staffed and do not have access to a variety of people who might have set the story straight. Further, because of the demanning of newspapers under Black, some scientifically literate people are no longer around to exercise or advise appropriate caution.

18   Given the magnitude of the error and the damage to public health that such false communication is likely to cause, one would think that newspapers that later became conscious of the error would print a retraction.

19   If the offending newspapers were intent on removing the misinformation from the public, a prompt and prominent retraction would have been in order. The Vancouver *Sun* seemed to come closest to an adequate response, with a large four-column headline at the top of its "Lower Mainland" section: "Second-hand smoke study misleading, officials say."

20   By contrast, the *Whig-Standard* didn't appear to address the issue within a week of publishing the story. And the *Edmonton Journal* carried a story on March 10 voicing scepticism regarding the original deception, but with a slant that appeared more to confirm than to deny it. The headline, "Hotels pleased with report on smoking," says it all. The *Ottawa Citizen* came out with a page one story that reflected scientific objections to its report, but the slant was towards discrediting the WHO report, and hence the WHO itself, rather than admitting the *Citizen's* and the *Sunday Telegraph's* fault in the matter.

21   Not only Southam; but another of Black's recent acquisitions, the daily Saskatoon *Star-Phoenix*, also ran MacDonald's story, though curiously three days after its first appearance and without any visible additional checking. The same paper editorialized against smoking bans on March 17, "Put smoking in perspective," in which it reported falsely that the October, 1997, *British Medical Journal* claimed that non-smokers living with smokers have a 25 per cent chance of getting

lung cancer. What the *BMJ* claimed was that there was a 25 per cent *increased risk* of getting lung cancer and cardiovascular diseases, something very different and more credible. *Star-Phoenix* readers were still in the dark about the issue as March 19 came with no correcting voice. Instead, a letter from a smoker was published that day stating that the smoking story "should have been on the front page."

22   In fairness, it should be noted that the Southam newspapers did not react as a monolith to the *Telegraph* story. The Montreal *Gazette* said that it rejected the story because *Telegraph* stories are not considered a reliable source and that the story would be checked as a matter of course.

23   For the most part, this good judgment prevailed beyond Black's papers. But even the venerable *Globe and Mail*, while avoiding the straight story, couldn't resist running a column by Spider Robinson on its opinion page. "Big Nanny's new clothes" (March 23) is an irate outburst against the health "fascists" who would restrain smokers from polluting the air in public places. Robinson adds his own hype to the mis-reporting, saying that the study "clearly and unmistakably shows (as most such studies do) that so-called second-hand smoke *does not* cause lung cancer. In fact, it seems to have a slight *protective effect.*"

24   That the tobacco industry had a hand in the deception seems unmistakable, but there were and are plenty of outside circumstances that help their cause. Black's combination of neo-liberal bias and downsizing of newspaper staff is a likely factor. But there are two other factors. One is wishful thinking among smokers and the power of addiction to warp judgment. The second is the desire to attract attention (and circulation) with a sensational news item, even when the scientific basis for the story is lacking.

Topics for consideration:

1. Randal Marlin suggests that competent journalists are likely to be sceptical of a single study which seems to contradict a large body of accumulated evidence. Does the way other scientific studies are reported in news media suggest that they are in the hands of "journalists who know something about science"?

2. Following usual journalistic practice, Victoria MacDonald, who wrote the first report misrepresenting the WHO study, refused to say if her information came from the tobacco industry. Why is it that journalists refuse to reveal their sources? Do you think there are cases where an exception should be made? If so, is this one of them?

3. Marlin points out that the timing of the story made it less likely to be checked by competent journalists. How would "scientifically literate" journalists report on the WHO study?

4. Do newspapers do a better or worse job of reporting on science stories than other news media?

Further reading:

http://www. essential.org/orgs/infact/exposed.html Web page maintained by the corporate watchdog organization INFACT analyzing deceptive statements in tobacco industry public relations statements.

seeKorum

"seeKorum" is the pseudonym of a Toronto writer who worked for a polling company. Writing pseudonymously, "seeKorum" uses his experience as a pollster to suggest that, despite politicians' trust in them, polls fail to reflect people's real views. They are, he argues, "semi-science—science with a question mark."

ADVENTURES IN THE NUMBER TRADE

1 Polls are something I know a bit about, because I am (if you will excuse the pun) low pollster on the totem poll. I work in what's euphemistically called "fielding." That is, I conduct interviews over the telephone. I'm one of the people who call you up in the evening just as you're about to sit down to supper and badger you "for a few short moments of your time."

2 The company I work for is one of the largest in Canada. Because I was sworn to secrecy when I was hired, I can't tell you which one. Or rather, I'd feel safer dropping coy hints about its identity while scrupulously guarding my own: The company I'll refer to as InfoDex; my own name ... well, let's just say I'm known as "Pete."

3 By using a *nom de téléphone*, I can at least distance myself from one of the major stresses of my job, which is, after all, attempting to monopolize other people's free time. I ask them, in tones both neutral enough to suggest the disinterest of a non-salesman and friendly enough to suggest the encouragement of a good-natured college kid, questions designed to further causes not necessarily in their own interest.

4 While the company I'm working for was referred to above as InfoDex, usually I call it "Eastbourne Research Centre" when launching into my survey. This is a sub-pseudonym; InfoDex generally prefers to hide its identity, out of the understandable fear that its name is too highly associated with the present government to be considered unbiased.

5 Like a minimum-wage Nostradamus, I can look into the future — but not too far. As befits my low earnings ($7.25 an hour), I can see only two or three weeks in advance. InfoDex is the company that did pre-referendum polling, as well as public opinion tracking for the federal government during the heat of the campaign for the Charlottetown accord. It's in this way that I witnessed first-hand how the truth is both expressed verbally and compressed numerically. I saw, too, how something was lost in the process, and this something was also the truth.

6 Most interviewers working for polling companies are people in their late teens or early twenties. Blithely disinterested in politics, they're trained to read the questions off their computer screens verbatim, like machines: When an interviewee asks a question like, "What do you mean by status? Privilege or standing?" the interviewer is technically not supposed to answer. Not because of lack of knowledge, but because the senior supervisors don't trust these kids to give their own explanations without botching it. The survey itself is treated as Holy Text:

Not to be veered from, its scientificness never to be questioned. This sometimes makes the supervisors seem insanely literal-minded, as they hector interviewers to pronounce every single word.

7   Coached in this way, interviewers, like congenitally dim bureaucrats in a Monty Python sketch, sometimes seem to hear nothing but the following magic words: "Strongly agree," "somewhat agree," "neither agree nor disagree," "somewhat disagree," "strongly disagree." Either that, or a number on a scale. The cajoling of a respondent I described above is known within the nomenclature of polling as "probing," and is considered good methodology. By keeping "don't knows" to a minimum, survey results appear to be more crisply defined than they are. These subtle inaccuracies in survey responses are multiplied by the hundreds. The resulting half-truths do not seem to the analysts — the mid-level professionals who interpret the surveys — to exist.

8   An experiment is only scientific if all the variables can be measured; social science is notoriously difficult to practise well because one of the variables — people — is so complex. A respondent population's comprehension of a series of questions may be false; unless this too is measured, the results are semi-science — science with a question mark.

9   Much has been written about the negative influence polls might have during election campaigns, but little is known about the "street reality" of polling. Pollsters point with pride at their ability to predict elections, and their results are fairly accurate. But sometimes they screw up terribly. The 1992 referendum campaign serves as a classic example of how street reality differs from its statistical cousin.

10   In mid-August of 1992, when the federal government had reached the Charlottetown accord and was considering calling a national referendum, it was already under intense pressure from two fronts: the first was the impending referendum on October 26 in Quebec, and the other was constitutional burn-out among politicians, their aides and the country at large. The feds knew that in order to sell the deal in Quebec, they needed all the leverage they could get. A national referendum seemed like just the tool. It would pressure the "No" side in Quebec while providing a focal point for patriotism in the rest of the country. This was a reasonable assumption. Theoretically at least, *this* deal made up for all the shortcomings of Meech Lake: Don Getty and the West had been placated with a triple-E Senate, Clyde Wells and Ovide Mercredi were on-side, and before that, Keith Spicer had travelled around the country with millions of dollars in video equipment to "interface" — Moses Znaimer-like — with the people.

11   Before the referendum was even announced, pollsters were already feeling the territory, attempting to calculate what margins of support existed for the accord. The federal government probably had no illusions about the nature of discontent that existed in English Canada — bitterness towards Quebec, bitterness towards Mulroney and bitterness about the economy. But its strategists didn't seem too alarmed at public anger, as long as it appeared unfocussed.

12   In mid-August, people were responding to the questions in our surveys with a degree of equanimity, although they were angry about the Meech Lake-like parts of the deal. The vast majority of them came across as being undecided,

because the survey, at this point, could not mention a vote. Misled subtly into thinking their responses were just grist for the curiosity of the polling mill, people did not speak with determination. (They would say suspiciously: "Who's this survey *for*?" And we'd respond disingenuously: "Our supervisors never tell us who the client is. This is just a survey, like the kind you read about in the paper.") Furthermore, many respondents were simply ignorant of the deal's contents. Time after time people would say, their voices almost wailing, "I don't know *anything about it!!*" Our soothing response was: "That's okay, this is just an opinion survey, you don't really have to know a lot about it, we're just trying to get people's *reactions* at this time."

13   Engaged in deep-fried questioning, we transformed doubt into little nuggets of certainty. These fast-food answers were in turn gobbled down the statistical gullet in order to satiate the hunger of the "Yes" side. But the pollsters, asking the wrong questions, misread ignorance as apathy and disagreement as mild disgruntlement. The result, for the federal government, was a national heart attack.

14   The "No" side had considerably more support in English Canada than the "Yes" side realized, and all that support was waiting for was something (somebody) to come along and galvanize it. Predictably, Preston Manning, did … and then, Judy Rebick, and then most controversially, Pierre Trudeau. At the end of a cool summer, support for the "No" side started snowballing.

15 Pollsters, like seducers, subconsciously count on a certain degree of ignorance and naive goodwill on the part of those they wish to influence. But like seducers, they also have to be sensitive to the various nuances of gesture and tone of voice that signal repulsion or attraction. It might surprise many in the general public to find that the analysts who design, interpret and defend these polls go nowhere near the phone to conduct interviews; similarly, analysts might be startled to discover people think they should have closer contact with the people whose opinions they claim to understand. Choices such as "no opinion" or "don't know" are rarely voiced by interviewers when questions are being read during a survey. And it doesn't take much acquaintance with the polling industry to figure out why this should be so: These are not responses the pollster wants to hear. The exaggeration of certainty creates ambience of knowledge. Mediocrity is best concealed by not grappling with the amorphousness of society. But because the pressures are enormous — short time lines, massive numbers of "completes" to be finished, and a grouchy population — a maybe is as good as a yes (or no), in the world of polling. And the pressures are increasing: The company I work for is starting to demand higher levels of productivity from its interviewers, and this means — all things being equal (the Canadian population not getting any more enamoured with being quizzed exhaustively) — that more corners will have to be cut, more people bullied into finishing "just the last page."

To paraphrase Nietzsche: How can so much error lead to truth? The answer is in yesterday's paper.

Topics for consideration:

1. Have you ever been polled by a company gauging public opinion? How accurate an estimate of your views do you think the pollster obtained?

2. "seeKorum" points out that interviewers are encouraged to steer people away from "don't know" or "no opinion" answers. Why is this, and how might it contribute to the unreliability of polls?

3. "seeKorum" uses different metaphors and similes to describe polling, e.g., junk food (paragraph 13) and seduction (paragraph 15). Are these effective? What other metaphors would you suggest?

4. What difference would it make if political life were conducted without opinion polls? Do you think it would be an improvement?

Further reading:

Darrell Huff, *How to Lie with Statistics* (1954). Wittily written classic work on how government and media mislead the unwary through the use of statistics.

John Allen Paulos, *A Mathematician Reads the Newspapers* (1995). Uncovers underlying mathematical concepts in newspaper stories.

Peter Robertson (1944-

Peter Robertson is an archivist with the National Photography Collection of the National Archives of Canada. He is author of Canadian Military Photographers Since 1885 *(1973).*

While photography has long enjoyed a reputation for accuracy, Peter Robertson suggests that there are a number of ways in which photographic representation can be manipulated. As a historian, Robertson is especially concerned with the ways in which faked or out-of-context photographs create a distorted view of events.

MORE THAN MEETS THE EYE

1   Somebody once said that the camera never lies. Those who support that generalisation include the many Canadians who, during the past decade, have used increasingly large numbers of photographs as historical documents. Sacrificing quality for quantity, they have overlooked the fact that photographs, for a number of reasons, can present a somewhat less than truthful image of the past. Surely it is time for archivists to understand these limitations and to moderate the undiscriminating attitude with which many of their patrons are approaching photographs.

2   Following Louis Daguerre's invention of photography in 1839, people seeing a photograph for the first time often remarked on the quality of verity. In the words of one observer, "Every object is retraced with mathematical preciseness, ... a degree of perfection that could be attained by no other means."[1] Truthfulness was a useful weapon in photography's protracted struggle for equality with, if not superiority over, traditional visual arts such as painting. What photographers were claiming was that photographs were able to depict the same subjects as paintings, and with greater truthfulness. In his definitive book *Art and Photography*, Dr. Aaron Scharf comments on the assertiveness of photographers, who "saw little reason why photography should not be considered as a Fine Art" and "conscious of the mechanical limitations of their medium ... developed new, often elaborate means for augmenting the artistic content of their work."[2] One of the most significant "mechanical limitations" was of course the inability of nineteenth-century photographic equipment to record adequately people and objects that were in motion. Partly because of this problem and partly because of their collective desire to surpass painting, photographers tended to concentrate on subjects that were both motionless *and* artistic, such as portraits, buildings, and landscapes.

3   What effect did the process of building a relationship with his clients have on the outlook of a photographer reaching for success in his profession? The client, in simplest terms, was the person who engaged the photographer to take his portrait, and who expected satisfactory results for the money thus spent. Published in 1864, the widely-used manual *The Camera and the Pencil* exhorted: "Let us never lose sight of the fact that we must, if practicable, please all who seek our services ... to secure the patronage of every visitant ... to promise compliance with their wishes."[3] Recognizing that an unflattering portrait might offend

a client, photographers routinely employed people who specialized in retouching negatives. According to a textbook entitled *The Art of Retouching*, published in 1880, the duty of the retoucher was "to make with facility any alteration taste may suggest, such as a fixed, staring and unnatural look, assumed by so many persons while sitting for a portrait, into an easy, natural smile; or to change the forced, sinister smirk into a calm and pleasing expression."[4] Retouching paid dividends, because satisfied clients were apt to return for additional portraits, and for exterior and interior views of their homes and businesses. This "portrait-home-business" sequence is present, for example, in William Topley's photographs of the prominent Ottawa lumber barons H.F. Bronson, J.R. Booth and W.C. Edwards taken between 1880 and 1920. Judging from the examples published in the book *Portrait of a Period*, similar patterns would emerge from an analysis of the photographs taken by William Notman, the shining example of the successful nineteenth-century Canadian photographer.[5]

4   Nineteenth-century photography was not only a process struggling to rise above its technical limitations and to achieve the status of art, but also a profession striving for social and economic respectability. For example, photographers in the United States and Canada often used the purely honorary title of "Professor" to impress the public with their knowledge. Furthermore, they generally displayed an acute understanding of modern advertising techniques. Consider the following typical notice, which appeared in 1888:

> There is perhaps no establishment in Port Arthur that shows more conspicuously the rapid developments and improvements in the photographic art, than that of J.F. Cooke. This studio is spacious and well arranged. The light and all other requisites for a first-class establishment are perfect. Photography, in all its branches, is here executed in the highest style of art. Mr. Cooke is an artist of rare talent and ability, and that this fact is appreciated by the public, is evinced by the large and influential patronage he now enjoys.[6]

5   Fortunate indeed was a photographer like William Topley who was able to use the title "Photographer by Appointment to His Excellency the Marquis of Lorne and Her Royal Highness the Princess Louise." The more influential the patron, the better for business.

6   Having acquired a reputation with, and made money from, clients who were influential people in their community, photographers sometimes became part of the movement known as "boosterism," a phenomenon in part manifested by the flood of illustrated brochures, pamphlets and books extolling the virtues of Canadian cities and industries during the period from 1880 to 1914. For example, Frank Micklethwaite's photographs of Toronto, widely published in periodicals and books, document a prosperous, progressive city: bustling city streets, office buildings, banks, industries, colleges and schools, churches, spacious parks, quiet residential streets. Micklethwaite's photographs, however, present an image of the city which is accurate but incomplete — incomplete because nobody commissioned him to photograph its slum housing, neglected children, and sweated labour.

7   Twentieth-century Canadian boosterism hides behind a variety of euphemistic titles: publicity, public relations, advertising, propaganda, information services,

media relations. Whatever name it assumes, the concept implies the use of certain techniques by newspapers, businesses, and by organizations such as governments, to influence people's thoughts and actions. These organizations are able to employ and train photographers, to enforce guidelines or regulations stating how the photographers are to perform their assignments and, through a number of editorial processes, to determine just which photographs the public will see.

8   One organization which has always recruited and trained its own photographers is the Department of National Defence. The reason for this policy, according to one report, is "that the fullest and most complete control over activities and personnel may be exercised by the military authorities" and thus "not only to provide an historical record but to provide informational and inspirational material for ... the maintenance of public morale and the stimulation of recruiting."7 Drawing an example from the world of business, one notes that the vice-president of Pringle and Booth, one of the largest commercial studios in Toronto, recently criticized the tendency of photography students to use "old barns and fences" as subjects, and referred approvingly to a plaque in his firm's office reading: "We do not make pictures to hang on walls. We create photographs to be reproduced in major media to sell merchandise."8

9   The manipulation of photographs may take the form of an order like the one which prohibited R.C.A.F. photographers in wartime from including in their photographs subjects like the complete aircrew of an aircraft, lest that information benefit the enemy.9 Manipulation is present too in the widespread use of photographs taken with wide-angle lenses in advertisements which convey a false and misleading impression of, say, the interior of a new car.

10   Distortion can result from the cropping or retouching of negatives and prints to delete unwanted details, such as the pennant number and radar aerials visible in a wartime negative of the destroyer H.M.C.S. *Ottawa*. Captions are another means of manipulating photographs, as these two examples will attest:

> The Canadian Corps who cracked the Hitler Line in Italy were given a well-earned rest by the shores of the blue Mediterranean.

> Academically, Indian students are considered to be as bright as any other group of youngsters. Here, a grade 8 class at Mount Elgin Indian day school at the Caradoc Agency ... are at work learning geography.

11   Whoever wrote the first caption must have been a frustrated travel agent; the colour of the Mediterranean is immaterial, but researchers will certainly want to know the names and units of the soldiers in the photograph, the exact location and date, plus the name of the photographer. Some member of the Information Division of the Department of Citizenship and Immigration wrote the second caption; perhaps that person should remove his foot from his mouth and stop perpetuating racial stereotypes.

12   The editor who makes the decision to release or not to release a photograph practises manipulation. For example, a colleague who is organizing the Montreal *Gazette* collection of some 130 000 negatives taken between 1938 and 1968 reports that an average of only one in ten of these photographs was published in

Distortion: Surely the phrase "academically, Indian students are considered to be as bright as any other group of youngsters" influences the information conveyed by this photograph.

that newspaper. There is also the example of the photograph showing the blanket-wrapped body of a Canadian soldier killed in Korea in 1951; branded with the rubber stamp "Banned," this photograph vanished into the files for the next twenty-five years. Even when released to the public, a photograph can present a distorted image. Many people have seen the well-known Canadian Press photograph of Robert Stanfield fumbling a football during the 1974 federal election campaign. Yet how many people noticed the photographer's subsequent statement that, of the many photographs he took on that occasion, the one selected for national exposure was the only time that the leader of the Progressive Conservative Party fumbled the ball? Other photographs inflicted upon the public may be described politely as re-enactments and impolitely as fakes. The most notorious examples are Captain Ivor Castle's photographs which purport to show Canadian troops in action during the Battle of the Somme in 1916. Bearing captions like "A Canadian Battalion go over the top," these photographs appeared in both official and popular histories for over fifty years, symbolizing Canadian participation in the First World War. It was one of Castle's colleagues, William Rider-Rider, who supplied the evidence which finally destroyed their credibility:

13   These alleged battle pictures were "made," or rather pieced together, from [photographs of] shell bursts taken at a British trench mortar school outside St. Pol, and those taken at rehearsal attacks of men going over the top with canvas breech covers on their rifles ... [consequently] I had a lot to live down

What the public did not see: The blanket-wrapped body of a soldier of the 2nd Battalion, Royal Canadian Regiment, killed in Korea on 3 November 1951.

SOURCE: DEPARTMENT OF NATIONAL DEFENCE/NATIONAL ARCHIVES OF CANADA/C70696

when I visited some units ... [such comments as] "Want to take us going over the top? Another faker?"[10]

14   We are now observing the proliferation of re-enacted photographs as a byproduct of the current nostalgia boom throughout North America. A number of individuals and groups in the United States are producing early photographs like daguerreotypes and tintypes showing, for example, people dressed in Civil War uniforms. There is a group in Toronto which specializes in recreating and photographing scenes characteristic of the 1940s prompting one observer to comment, "This is a possible future direction of photography ... perhaps the staged, created photograph will be the wave of the future."[11] Certainly the potential exists: so realistic were publicity photographs taken during the filming of the television documentary *The National Dream* that some have already appeared in textbooks passing as actual illustrations of the construction of the Canadian Pacific Railway.[12] Because of their careful attention to period detail, re-enacted photographs may well pose problems of authentication for archivists in the near future.

15   Those researchers who lack discrimination perpetuate the careless use of historical photographs. Far too many researchers are content to compile a sheaf of

Re-enactment or fake?: Officially captioned "A Canadian Battalion go over the top, October 1916," Captain Ivor Castle's photograph actually shows Canadian troops in training at school far behind the front line.

SOURCE: W.I. CASTLE/DEPARTMENT OF NATIONAL DEFENCE/NATIONAL ARCHIVES OF CANADA/PA648

photostatic copies of photographs already used in other publications, and then to mail these to the National Photography Collection as a request for more copies of the same. The result is further exposure of those tired old visual clichés. If only researchers would make the effort to choose from the full range of photographs available on their particular subjects, either through visits or through detailed letters asking for assistance! Other researchers, representing publishing companies or television networks, appear armed with a long list of every person, place and event mentioned in their assigned manuscript or program script. As long as they obtain one photograph matching every item on this list, regardless of its suitability, these people are satisfied. Frequently, researchers do not realize that cameras have not been on the spot recording every single event in Canadian history for the past one hundred and forty years. A classic example of this misconception was the representative of a well-known publishing company who persisted in asking for photographs of the sinking of H.M.C.S. *Fraser* in 1940, apparently unaware that the ship sank a few minutes after a collision which occurred in the middle of the night — hardly the time for a photographer to stand around recording the scene. Whenever photographs of a subject do not exist, researchers often resort to the questionable practice of using photographs taken out of context, using the rationalization that nobody will know the difference. The author of a recent British book faced the necessity of using out-of-context photographs by writing captions clearly stating that "although a photograph of such-and-such an event does not exist, this photograph taken on a different occasion shows the same conditions."[13] Canadian picture researchers should treat their audience with the same honesty.

Archivists are the people who enjoy direct contact with collections of original negatives and prints. What can we do to understand the limitations of the photographs in our custody, and to promote their intelligent use as historical documents? We can approach photographs with an ever-skeptical attitude, aware that something which is both old and a photograph is not necessarily an objective document. We can study photographs for evidence of the various types of distortion and manipulation mentioned in this article, and can check captions for accuracy and objectivity. We can learn as much as possible about the photographer who took the photographs, either through research into textual sources or through personal interviews: his qualifications, his attitudes, his economic status. We can communicate all this information to the public by stripping away the layers of misinformation from photographs, by bringing complete collections of photographs, bearing accurate and complete captions, into public view, by giving impartial advice to researchers, by making speeches to organizations and by publishing articles about our research, and by critically reviewing the use of historical photographs in all media.[14] Archivists can and should spread the message that there is more than meets the eye in a photograph.

Notes:

1. Report of Joseph-Louis Gay-Lussac, in *An Historical and Descriptive Account of the Various Processes of the Daguerreotype* (London: McLean, 1839), 35.

2. Aaron Scharf, *Art and Photography* (London: The Penguin Press, 1968), xiii.

3. M.A. Root, *The Camera and the Pencil, or the Heliographic Art* (Philadelphia: D. Appleton & Co., 1864), 90–91.

4. J.P. Ourdan, *The Art of Retouching* (New York: E. & H.T. Anthony, 1880), 12–13.

5. J. Russell Harper and Stanley Triggs, eds., *Portrait of a Period: A Collection of Notman Photographs 1856 to 1915* (Montreal: McGill University Press, 1967).

6. *The New West* (Winnipeg: Canadian Historical Publishing Co., 1888), 30. However, a contemporary mercantile directory stated that Cooke's estimated capital was less than $500 and that his credit rating was limited.

7. F.C. Badgley to W.S. Thompson, 3 January 1940, Public Archives of Canada (hereinafter PAC), Records of the Wartime Information Board, RG36, 31, vol. 16, file 9-A-6.

8. *Canadian Photography* 5 (June 1974): 23.

9. Interview of Harry Price by Peter Robertson, 23 August 1972, PAC, Sound Recordings Accession 1972-47, Henry E. Price Collection.

10. Interview of William Rider-Rider by Peter Robertson, 18–19 May 1971, PAC, Sound Recordings Accession 1972-27, William Rider-Rider Collection.

11. Robert Fulford, "A Journey in Time," *Saturday Night* 91 (March 1976): 58.

12. Statement by M. Omer Lavallée of CP Rail, Montreal, Que., March 1976.

13. Martin Middlebrook, *The Nuremberg Raid* (London: Allen Lane, 1973).

14. See for example Richard Huyda's review of the books *Macdonald: His Life and Times* and *The John A. Macdonald Album* in *Archivaria* 2 (1976).

Topics for consideration:

1. Robertson points out the role of photography in "boosterism" or public relations (paragraphs 6 and 7). Examine the photographs used in publicity material for any institution with which you are familiar. Why were they selected? What impression do you think they are intended to give?

2. Robertson points out in paragraph 10 that the caption to a photograph often shapes the way one "reads" the image. How, for example, might the photograph of Indian students be re-captioned? What difference would it make in the viewer's perception?

3. Many major events occur without anyone having the opportunity to photograph them. Survey the photographs used over the course of a week in one newspaper. What relation do they bear to the important "news" of the week?

Further reading:

Susan Sontag, *On Photography* (1990). Reflections on how photographs shape our view of the world.

John Goddard (1950-

Montreal-based journalist John Goddard has worked as a reporter and photographer for Canadian Press. He spent eight years researching the struggle of the Lubicon Cree in Northern Alberta before writing Last Stand of the Lubicon Cree *(1991).*

In "A Real Whopper," John Goddard questions the veracity of Farley Mowat's best-selling accounts of his experiences in the Arctic. Using Mowat's own journals as well as government documents, Goddard suggests that Mowat's version of events was largely shaped by his own personal difficulties at the time. The result, argues Goddard, is a misrepresentation both of Mowat's own experiences and of the government policy of the time.

A REAL WHOPPER

1 "I never invent," says Farley Mowat. "I may elaborate — Ha! Ha! — but I don't invent. I experience and observe, and then I write."

2 Mowat sounds defensive. He sits restlessly in a beige armchair at his winter home in Port Hope, Ontario, a one-hour drive east of Toronto. He and his second wife, Claire, also a writer, spend summers on the windswept east coast of Cape Breton Island and winters at Port Hope in a trim, elegant old house that he bought years ago from his mother. In a back living room, daylight from floor-to-ceiling windows washes Mowat in soft illumination. He is seventy-five years old but looks younger. He has an elfish beard, a headful of ginger-brown hair, and a small, rounded physique so full of bounce that he appears ready to stride off again — as he did nearly fifty years ago — into the Arctic Barrenlands. Visually the effect is charming, but a forcefulness in Mowat's voice signals annoyance at being asked how loosely he treats facts, a question that has dogged him throughout his long, illustrious career.

3 Asked a second time, he begins to backtrack. "The primary consideration for a writer is to entertain," he says. "Using entertainment you can then inform, you can propagandize, you can elucidate, you can do anything you want."

4 Mowat ranks with Pierre Berton and Peter C. Newman as among the country's foremost writers of nonfiction. He is a national icon. From the outset, he has drawn praise for his spirited, emphatic style, and for his ability to conjure up a scene for the reader, not only visually but also emotionally. He is part storyteller, part crusader. He is famous for the fearlessness with which he is ready to confront and ridicule established authority, and for the affinity he often shows in his books for animals, native peoples, and the natural environment.

5 Mowat also ranks as one of the best-selling Canadian authors of all time. He pays little attention to sales figures, he says, but a decade ago his secretary added print runs of his first twenty-six books. The total came to 11,300,000 copies published in thirty-five languages. Since then he has released eight more titles, which along with most of his others continue to sell in Canada and elsewhere. His publishers now put total copies printed at more than 14-million.

6 International success came with his first book, *People of the Deer*, published in 1952. In it, he tells of travelling alone into the Arctic Barrenlands, west of

Hudson Bay, to locate a little-known Inuit people said to live exclusively on caribou. He tells of living with them for two years, learning their language, and discovering that they were once a populous race of 2,000 members reduced to near-extinction through disease and starvation. Only forty-nine emaciated souls remained, he says, a fate for which he blames white trappers, missionaries, Hudson's Bay Company managers, and most particularly what he calls the "indifference and neglect" of the Canadian government.

7   Mowat's revelations were sensational at the time. As Canadians awakened to the North's resource potential and strategic importance after the war, attention was also turning to the people who lived there. American readers took an interest as well. Three excerpts from the book ran in *The Atlantic Monthly*, and the book itself appeared simultaneously from the Atlantic Monthly Press in Boston, and McClelland & Stewart in Toronto. For a new Canadian author the breakthrough was unprecedented, encouraging Mowat to build on his reputation as an Arctic authority. In 1956, he wrote a novel for young people, *Lost in the Barrens*, for which he won the Governor General's award, and in 1958 he published *Coppermine Journey*, the first of a series of books he was to edit from the journals of Arctic explorers.

8   He then returned to the field notes on which he had based *People of the Deer*. He wrote a sequel in 1959 on the Inuit starvation called *The Desperate People*, and in 1963 he produced *Never Cry Wolf*, telling of "revolutionary" discoveries he made about wolf behaviour during "two summers and a winter … as a biologist studying wolves and caribou." The wolf book became one of his all-time top sellers. Twenty years later, Walt Disney Pictures also released it as a movie. Mowat went on to write other books about whales, ships, boyhood pets, and the Second World War, but he remains best known worldwide for his startling accounts from the District of the Northwest Territories, west of Hudson Bay: *People of the Deer, The Desperate People*, and *Never Cry Wolf*.

9   The nagging question remains: how far does Mowat stretch the truth? In the Northwest Territories people openly accuse him of getting facts wrong, and call him "Hardly Know-It." Earling Porsild, an Arctic scientist who reviewed Mowat's first book for *The Beaver* magazine, conferred on him the Inuit sobriquet "Sagdlutôrssuaq," meaning "Great Teller of Tall Tales." Other reviewers, however, have tended to give Mowat the benefit of the doubt. "The reader has no way of telling whether what Mowat writes is fact or [fiction]," D.M. LeBourdais wrote in *Saturday Night* in 1952 of *People of the Deer*, while saying also that the book "cannot be ignored." Jack Batten, writing in *Maclean's* magazine in 1971, said that although he finds Mowat often gloomy and misanthropic, nobody can match him for dedication. "He dropped alone into the Keewatin as casually as you or I would drop into a neighbourhood store," Batten writes, "and, for two years, he shared his life with furious cold, storms, flies, loneliness, dull diet, a harsh landscape and plenty of danger. … Mowat really did it. He was there. And it seems wonderful and courageous of him."

10   Now it appears that Mowat did not really do it after all. Documents recently made public at the National Archives of Canada, and papers that the author himself sold years ago to McMaster University, show that Mowat did not spend two years in the Keewatin District in 1947 and 1948 as the books say. He spent two summer field seasons in the district — totalling less than six months — and

mostly in a more southerly part of the district than he describes. He did not casually drop in alone but travelled on both occasions as a junior member of well-
planned scientific expeditions. He did not once — contrary to the impression he
leaves — see a starving Inuit person. He did not once set foot in an Inuit camp.
As for the authenticity of his wolf story, he virtually abandoned his wolf-den
observations after less than four weeks.

11   In various editions of all three books, Mowat goes out of his way to portray
himself as a diligent researcher who sticks closely to the facts. "All the major
events in this book, and most of the minor ones, have been documented from
official sources," he says in a foreword to *The Desperate People*. "Other sources
which were used included published works, signed statements, and private correspondence, together with many hours of tape-recorded conversations with [Inuit
and white people] who were involved in the recorded events. To obviate the possibility of error, all Eskimo conversations were independently translated by at
least two Eskimo linguists."

12   Outside the books, he says he cares nothing for the facts. In interviews, he
has labelled his writing "subjective nonfiction," saying that he trusts what comes
from inside himself more than he trusts empirical evidence. "Truth is largely
subjective," he has also said. At home in Port Hope, pressed a third time on the
question, he says outrageously: "I never let the facts get in the way of the truth!"
And in a preface to a catalogue of his papers at McMaster University, he calls
himself "a simple saga man, a teller of tales," declaring that his motto has always
been, "on occasions when facts have particularly infuriated me, Fuck the Facts!"

13   Mowat first travelled to the Northwest Territories in the spring of 1947. He was
twenty-six years old. He had served with the infantry in Italy during the war and
felt an intense desire to escape what he recalls now as "my own kind of people,"
meaning civilized human beings who were prepared to wage mass destruction
against each other. On this point Mowat is consistent. In his first book he says,
"I wished to escape into the quiet sanctuaries where the echoes of war had never
been heard." Similarly, in an earlier letter to his parents from the battlefield, he
tells of wanting to "skedaddle to a point some five hundred or so miles northwest of Churchill in the middle of the Barren Grounds and start digging a hole."

14   What happened next is where his published books and the archival documents part company. In his books, Mowat says that after a year at the University
of Toronto (studying biology, he suggests in *Never Cry Wolf*) he headed north
by himself with only a vague idea of his destination and purpose. He says that a
bush pilot dropped him into unmapped territory, and that a half-breed trapper
led him to an Inuit camp. "I was the first outlander to come upon it in all the
centuries that tents had stood [there]," he writes in the first book, *People of the
Deer*. He goes on to describe intimate details of Inuit life — what people ate,
what they wore, what they smelled like, and how their lives were threatened by
starvation because white people were encroaching on the southern fringes of the
caribou herds.

15   Mowat's personal papers, on the other hand, show that he had been studying
for a general bachelor's degree, not one in biology, and he did not go north alone
or without plans. Through an intermediary in Toronto, he made contact with a

field scientist in Pennsylvania named Francis Harper, who engaged Mowat as a junior partner to help collect plant, bird, and animal specimens for six months in the southern Keewatin District of the Northwest Territories. Harper was well organized. Partly funded by the Arctic Institute of North America, he had arranged an air charter out of Churchill, Manitoba, and had made plans to use a set of trappers' cabins at Nueltin Lake, 250 miles farther north at the tree line (not 350 miles farther north in the Barrenlands as Mowat says in *People of the Deer*). After classes ended that spring — on May 31, 1947 — the two men flew north together in Harper's chartered plane.

16   From the beginning, they did not get along. Harper was an experienced scholar interested in cataloguing specimens; Mowat was an amateur naturalist still longing to escape into the wilds, and five weeks into the research he did escape. He met three trappers who lived in the area — brothers of mixed German and Cree parentage named Schweder. The eldest, Charles, said he would be leaving soon for Brochet, Manitoba, to buy trapping supplies for the winter, and Mowat volunteered to go with him. On July 8, over Harper's objections, he cast off with Schweder in an eighteen-foot freighter canoe heading south.

17   In his books Mowat barely mentions the trip. The books place him mostly in the Arctic Barrenlands, but he was gone a month, meaning that he spent much of that summer in northern Manitoba. When he and Schweder returned to Nueltin Lake on August 5, Harper was still angry. He said that the air charters were his, and that he would not allow Mowat to board the return plane in December. With no other option, Mowat talked Schweder into canoeing out together, and on August 15 they headed east to Hudson Bay on their way to Churchill. On a map in *People of the Deer*, Mowat shows them canoeing all the way, but in a report at the time to the Arctic Institute he says they canoed halfway, then hitched a ride on a federal-government plane.

18   Mowat next travelled to the Northwest Territories the following spring, in 1948, and most of the events he describes in his Keewatin books derive from the four months he spent there that year on a government caribou study.

19   Initially, he had planned to conduct an independent caribou study with his best friend, Andy Lawrie. The two had attended high school together at North Toronto Collegiate, and had reunited after the war. Lawrie was due to graduate that spring with a master's degree in biology. Together, they had begun soliciting funds to follow caribou along their migration routes, but when word of their interest got around, the fledgling Dominion Wildlife Service hired them for an ambitious caribou investigation of its own.

20   Few subjects appear with more distortion in the Keewatin books than the caribou investigation and Mowat's role in it is a federal-government employee. In his books, Mowat portrays Ottawa as uniformly uncaring towards the Inuit, but documents at the National Archives show federal officials responding quickly to a perception that the caribou herds, on which many Inuit groups depended, might be in danger from increased mining activity and an influx of outsiders after the war. By order-in-council, on July 3, 1947 — the summer Mowat was with Harper — the government introduced sweeping restrictions on caribou hunting in the Northwest Territories. A licensing system took effect for non-natives; sales

of caribou meat to hotels and restaurants were banned; penalties were introduced to discourage waste.

21   A short time later, the wildlife service proposed its caribou investigation. Biologists at the time knew virtually nothing about caribou — how many there were, what they ate, why they moved around the way they did. Government officials saw an urgent need for a conservation plan that would protect both the animals and the Inuit. "It is hoped that the barren-ground caribou will not follow the trail of the buffalo," one policy paper typically states.

22   Initial research was to proceed in three regions simultaneously. The chief government mammalogist, Frank Banfield, took the Back River region in the north-central Northwest Territories. A second biologist took the Great Slave Lake region in the southwest. Mowat and Lawrie were assigned for seventeen months to the Keewatin District, in the south-central part of the territories west of Hudson Bay. Lawrie, with his graduate degree, was named "leader of the Keewatin party" at a salary of $2,400. Mowat became Lawrie's assistant at $1,980.

23   Their job was to gather as much data on caribou as possible: numbers, habitat, migration routes, life expectancy, reproduction rates, and state of health. They would be based at the same cabins at Nueltin Lake that Harper had arranged to use the year before. They would be travelling to some extent, but not only by canoe as Mowat depicts in *People of the Deer*. Twenty-five hours of flight time was budgeted for the first year.

24   They were part of a well-organized government operation, but in his books Mowat barely mentions Lawrie or the study. In the first book he makes no explicit mention of a government study at all. In the second he makes a passing, sarcastic reference to it, saying, "Though no one in authority showed the least alarm about the future of the Eskimos, there was a very real alarm about the future of the northern deer." In *Never Cry Wolf*, he says, that a "predation control division" in Ottawa hired him to research wolves in an effort to justify wolf extermination. In fact, the wildlife division assigned him to watch wolves as part of the caribou study.

25   One other detail that Mowat neglects to mention in his books: he got married that winter. While he was making plans to go north with Andy Lawrie for seventeen months, Mowat fell in love with a classmate in the botany lab, and on December 20, 1947, he married her. Frances Thornhill was her name. In the books Mowat barely mentions her existence, but from the outset of the summer his feelings for her were to affect profoundly the course of events, both real and imaginary.

26   When exams ended in mid-May, Mowat and Lawrie left by government plane for Churchill, landing on the ice at Nueltin Lake on May 23. They spent their first few days hauling supplies over rotting ice and organizing their new home. Spring break-up appeared imminent. Mowat shot two caribou, adding meat to dinners of mashed potatoes, onions, tomatoes, apricots, bannock, and tea. "Good to be back in the country," he records as ice shifted loudly on the lake the third evening, "but praise God we don't have to swim for it at midnight."

27   Much of the detail of daily life that summer comes from a handwritten journal of more than 300 pages that Mowat kept in a zippered leather binder. In it he shows his playful side, so evident in *Never Cry Wolf*. "No more deer and fear

me they is gone till August," he writes of a realization that the main caribou herds have already passed. "We caribou students shall be caribouless." He also shows a tormented side not as obvious in the books.

28   Day three: "Miss Fran like the devil."

29   Day eight: "Smitten with desire for the company of my girl. This separation not good."

30   Day nine: "Little else to report except, of course, to record the growth of misery over the parting from my love."

31   To relieve his longings, Mowat tried to keep busy. He patched canoes and fixed motors. He baked bread on the wood stove, and pulled up fresh fish almost daily from nets that he and Lawrie had set in the lake. With the camp finally operational, Lawrie began his caribou-habitat studies. Mowat went looking for wolves.

32   Mowat calculates in his journal that for his study to be of value he would have to log 400 hours of den observations. At a minimum, he says, he would have to match the 195 hours logged by Adolph Murie, the American author of a standard wolf text at the time. Mowat was to complete only ninety hours, a hardcover log book now with the McMaster University collection shows, almost all between June 12 and July 6, a period of less than four weeks — far short of the "two summers and a winter" he claims in *Never Cry Wolf.*

33   The gap between Mowat's private and published writings only widens from there. In the journal, he describes commuting to his observation post each day from the cabin. Each morning he motors across a bay by canoe and hikes up an esker to a lookout two-thirds of a mile from the den. To keep off rain and mosquitoes he erects a tent, and from the doorway he peers over the ridge with periscope binoculars, allowing him to see the wolves without the wolves seeing him. "For 2 1/2 hours I lay and shivered" in a cold wind, he writes of his first sighting. "[The wolf] unaware of observation."

34   In *Never Cry Wolf* Mowat reports the experience altogether differently. He shows himself living in the tent at close quarters with the wolves, making the trip back to the cabin only occasionally. He shows himself awkwardly carrying a government-issue telescope and tripod as curious wolves approach him at such close distances that the equipment is unnecessary. He describes his first sighting on top of an esker as particularly intimate. "My head came slowly over the crest — and there was my quarry," he writes. "His nose was about six feet from mine."

35   The more the story in the book unfolds, the more outrageous the scenes become. Mowat learns to nap in short bursts like a wolf, and to mark the territory around his tent with his own urine, as a wolf might. He makes a breakthrough scientific discovery — that wolves eat mice during the summer denning period (in reality, a fact available from any standard wolf text at the time). And to prove that mice can maintain a large carnivore in good condition, he adopts an all-mouse diet himself, going so far as to reprint for readers one of many recipes he says he developed: Souris à la Crème. "Eating these small mammals presented something of a problem at first because of the numerous minute bones," he writes, "[but] I found the bones could be chewed and swallowed without much difficulty."

36   Few people who read *Never Cry Wolf* can ever view wolves the same way again. The book ripples with wit and charm, but beneath the bright writing runs

an insidious argument. Mowat contends that Ottawa views wolves as a serious menace and is committed to the wolf's "annihilation." He says that wildlife officials sent him north to prove that wolves are causing "a plunge of the caribou towards extinction," and that the officials were covertly encouraging trappers to poison wolf habitat with strychnine. "The war against wolves is kept at white heat by Provincial and Federal Governments," Mowat writes, "almost all of which offer wolf bounties ranging from ten dollars to thirty dollars per wolf." In his book, Mowat defends wolves against such policies, saying that wolves keep caribou herds strong by culling the sick and the lame.

37   Contrary to Mowat's claims, however, government documents of the period show that no anti-wolf sentiment existed in Ottawa at all. No wolf-extermination programme existed, no federal bounty existed (a provincial bounty existed in Manitoba), and federal wildlife policy already recognized that wolves benefit caribou herds by attacking mostly the weak and the lame. "The removal of diseased and abnormal individuals from the caribou herds by wolves is considered to be beneficial," the head of the Dominion Wildlife Service, Harrison Lewis, stated on December 22, 1947, five months before Mowat headed north on the caribou-wolf assignment. "This Department," Lewis also wrote, "is not prepared to use public funds for the purposes of paying wolf bounties."

38   For his book, Mowat appropriated the government position as his own rallying cry.

39   Mowat's case for the Inuit is similar to his case for the wolves. He accuses federal authorities of trying to annihilate the Inuit, not through outright extermination programmes but through indifference and neglect. "We have made a ruthless and concerted effort to dispossess them from their age-old way of life," he writes in a foreword to some editions of *People of the Deer*. "Genocide can be practiced in a variety of ways."

40   To help substantiate his thesis, Mowat tells of events at Nueltin Lake on June 4, 1948. In *The Desperate People*, he writes that all the household leaders from the Inuit camp sixty miles to the north, on the Kazan River, came to him and Lawrie looking for help. On their arrival, one of the men, Ohoto, blurted out a tale of starvation during the previous winter. "The rest of the men confirmed the grim details," Mowat writes, "and now it required only a close look at the emaciated faces of these people to know they spoke the truth." Despite their hardships, the men displayed stoic good humour, he also says. "The activities of the visitors gave no indication of what they had suffered in the flesh and in the mind."

41   In his field journal of 1948, Mowat records the events surrounding June 4 altogether differently. He says that when he and Lawrie arrived at Nueltin Lake twelve days earlier, they had encountered an Inuit hunter named Owliktuk, and Mowat had asked him, using hand signals, to bring all household leaders to the research camp. Mowat had made the request on instructions from Ottawa, other documents show. Federal officials had asked him to distribute powdered milk to each family, to distribute a supply of axes, pails, stoves, and fishing line requisitioned for the group a year earlier by a federal representative to the area, and to prepare documentation that would bring the group formally into the federal family-allowance programme.

42   "Great horseplay at the cache," Mowat writes of the men's arrival on June 4, in his most upbeat journal entry of the summer. Nowhere does he mention

starvation. "O-ho-to juggling 4 onions, while the rest played ball. ... Dished out a little loot to them and they frolicked merrily about." Mowat distributed flour, lard, tea, sugar and powdered milk to the men. Afterwards, he gave out the stoves, axes, and other equipment. "I distributed the loot to the Huskies," he says. Later that month he reported to Ottawa: "All the men that we have seen seem to be in good shape, and there are no reports of any recent epidemics or contagious diseases."

43   Another discrepancy in Mowat's versions of the June 4 encounter further explains what he means by "subjective nonfiction." A letter from Mowat to Ottawa, now in the McMaster collection, tells of being notified that 3,600 rounds of ammunition had been delivered to the Inuit group the previous fall. In the same letter, Mowat speculates that some hunters might be hoarding the ammunition rather than sharing it because of divisions within the group. In his books, however, Mowat says that the Inuit possessed almost no ammunition owing to government neglect. He says that he gave Ohoto and Owliktuk ten boxes of bullets each, a handout nowhere mentioned in the journal. Mowat describes the men's guns in the books as so old and useless that the hunters "would have been lucky to have made one kill for every ten shots fired." Interestingly, the complaints are identical to those that Mowat had voiced against the Canadian government during the war. "Even our guns were wearing out," he recalls in *My Father's Son*, an edited collection of war letters published in 1992. "Soon we would find ourselves short of ammunition."

44   Other discrepancies appear between his public and private accounts of the summer. Where the books show Mowat calling for government relief for the Inuit, his journal shows him fed up with handouts. "Gave Halo a going over," he writes on June 24, "and made it quite clear that from now on we give out tea etc. only when the Inuit produce something in return — be it only a ground squirrel tail. The happy days of milking the Kabluna [white person] [are] over ..."

45   Where the books show Mowat admiring the Inuit for being at one with nature, his journal shows him angry at the one Inuk he actually goes hunting with. "The deer were within range and [Ohoto] fired 3 times killing 3 does," Mowat says in an entry of July 31. "His oft repeated boast that he never shot does and fawns went up the spout in the face of (a) his craving for meat, and (b) his basic urge to kill deer whenever possible." Farther down in the same entry, Mowat writes, "We had trouble convincing Ohoto that when he shoots a deer he doesn't just cut off a few pounds of meat and leave the rest, trusting to shoot another on the morrow. Made him cut it all up."

46   Where the books show Mowat singularly concerned with others, the journal shows him preoccupied with his own loneliness. The more the summer dragged on, the more intensely Mowat longed for Fran. He teetered constantly on depression, able to communicate only sporadically with her through government radio messages and letters. His condition worsened on July 1, when a plane dropping fuel for a trip north also brought the first batch of mail. Fed up with distances herself, Fran was threatening to end the marriage.

47   "Won't go into this but to bed and to lie awake till dawn after tramping the hills for a while," Mowat writes that evening.

48   Throughout the journal entries of early July, Mowat's concern over Inuit starvation grows in direct proportion to his hunger for Fran. He complains constantly

of black moods and an inability to sleep, and on July 2, the day after reading Fran's letters, he describes trying to fix a canoe "to see if a little manual labour would relieve me" of depression. The same night, Ohoto, a frequent visitor, arrived at Nueltin Lake. "He without food three days and reports near-starvation at Inuit [camp]," Mowat notes briefly. "Sent him to bed at last."

49   By morning, Mowat was taking the starvation report seriously. Instead of working on the canoe that day, he threw himself into an Inuit-relief effort. He and Lawrie set aside 300 pounds of food for the group, keeping enough for themselves for several weeks, and wrote to Ottawa asking to be resupplied. "Decided today to give all possible grub on hand to the Eskimo and briefed Ohoto to act as runner to camp," he writes in the journal. "Snapped me out of it for a while — as A. intended it to!"

50   Ottawa later arranged new supplies for the researchers, and ordered an RCMP patrol to the Kazan River Inuit camp, a patrol that was to find claims of starvation to be exaggerated. In the meantime, however, unable to relieve his anguish over Fran, Mowat continued his campaign to relieve the Inuit.

51   July 9: "No sleep this night till 0400."

52   July 12-18: "Wire from Fran on the 13th did little to calm my fears, sounded both stilted and far away."

53   July 19, a surprising twist: "Got a few pages down on the starvation story, it may turn out well. Think I shall try Atlantic Monthly with it."

54   On July 20, a plane arrived to take the researchers north to Barrenlands. The day Mowat had been looking forward to since fighting in Italy had finally arrived. The plane also brought two more letters from Fran, however, plunging him even deeper into despair.

55   "Is it all over?" he asks himself. "Looks that way. ... It's your marriage as much as mine darling, and if you want to jettison it, I doubt if I can, or would, stop you."

56   For the next four weeks, Mowat and Lawrie surveyed a vast, open territory by motorized canoe. It was a pioneering journey that yielded valuable data about the caribou but which for Mowat brought only further agony. "No peace in all this peaceful land for me," he writes in his journal of a personal misery, which in his books turns into a horror for the Inuit.

57   Old tent markers detailed in his journal appear in his first book, *People of the Deer*, as ruins of a large Inuit encampment from which everybody fled in panic. Well-built burial sites from various time periods become in the book a field of plots so hastily constructed and crowded together that they resemble one mass grave. "I counted thirty-seven [bodies] in one place," Mowat writes vividly in the book. "Whole families had perished at one time." White explorers carrying disease wiped out the whole tribe, Mowat goes on to speculate, referring to the sickness as "the Great Pain" — a perfect label for his own afflictions at the time.

58   A further sign of Mowat's despair came on August 15. When a plane brought the researchers southward again, Lawrie disembarked as scheduled at Nueltin Lake, but Mowat flew all the way to Churchill. In his books, he says that he flew south to take "direct action as a private individual" to save the Inuit. He did in fact round up some army rifles and surplus clothing for the hunters, but he fails to mention that he also took the first available government flight to Toronto to

rescue his failing marriage after nearly three months away. When he rejoined Lawrie on September 9, Mowat had Fran with him.

59   For the remaining month at Nueltin Lake, Mowat devoted himself almost exclusively to the marriage-relief effort. He cancelled the planned resumption of his wolf study to clean a back room for a private bedroom. He patched the roof. He fixed the bed. He kept a stove burning all day to dry the place, and built a bathtub from an old canoe, but nothing he did could alleviate Fran of her steadfast unhappiness. The two were to stay together another twelve years and have two sons, but the journal shows that for an entire month, Fran rarely surfaced from a deep depression that is never fully explained.

60   September 30: "Fran rises not but lies in great pain and deathlike silence."
October 8: "Fran low all day."
October 10: "Fran took another dive into the dumps again."
October 11-12: "Fran extremely low."

On October 13, a plane landed to take the researchers to winter quarters at
61   Brochet. For Fran the flight could not come too soon; Brochet at least offered the comforts of a small established community. For Lawrie, however, the departure seemed premature. The fall caribou migration was still in progress. He wanted to complete the count. Lawrie elected to stay behind until December, allowing Mowat and his wife to go without him. When word of the arrangement reached Ottawa, however, the deputy commissioner of the Northwest Territories, R.A. Gibson, raised concern with the head of the wildlife service.

62   "We have had employed since May on the caribou survey a chap named Mowatt who, while greatly interested in wildlife problems, does not possess the full academic qualifications for the work that he has to do," Gibson writes on October 28, 1948. "We were not much impressed with Mr. Mowatt when we met him, but in view of his evident enthusiasm, and because there was no one else in sight, we took him on.

63   "This man has cost the Northwest Territories Administration a considerable amount of money because he made erroneous reports about the Eskimos in the district. It is now evident that these reports were based on insufficient investigation. I am told that he left the area where the caribou were congregating in order that he might bed himself down in winter quarters. His associate remained on the job. Moreover, without notifying your office, he brought his wife from Toronto to the winter quarters and is now asking us to pay rental on a building because he cannot bunk with the Signal Corps on account of having his wife with him.

64   "While I have reasonable sympathy for those who undertake tasks of this kind in remote areas, it is evident that we should replace Mr. Mowatt. ... Please arrange to bring him out, sending in a more useful man."

65   Mowat was fired effective December 31, to give him time to write his field reports. Early in the new year, he and Fran left Brochet for Palgrave, Ontario, near Toronto, where he began to write his Arctic tales.

66   Now, nearly fifty years later, Mowat admits to factual transgressions in the three Keewatin books. "*People of the Deer* is full of factual errors, lots of them, no argument about that," he says over lunch in Toronto several days after the Port Hope session. "And full of elaborations. I didn't have all the information so I elaborated

on it, and produced what I perceived to be the proper version of the way it happened." "On occasion," he also says, "I have taken something that I have heard about and I have reworked it in my own mind until I was almost sure it had happened to me."

67   Mowat justifies his approach by saying that it served a noble purpose. "As far as I'm concerned *People of the Deer* did nothing but good for individual people, the survivors" of the Kazan River group, he says. "Nobody was going to pay any attention to them unless their situation was dramatized, and I dramatized it."

68   What Mowat may not realize is that by selling fiction as nonfiction, he has broken a trust with his public. By treating facts as arbitrary and subject to whim, he has not so much served a high purpose as muddied public debate on Inuit and wildlife issues for decades. Ultimately, the Keewatin books say less about the Canadian north than they do about Mowat himself.

69   But Mowat makes no apology. "If the same situation obtained tomorrow," he says, "if I knew that a gross injustice had been done, and I didn't have all the facts to prove it, conclusively, I would still write about it and fill in the facts as need be."

Topics for consideration:

1. Goddard quotes Mowat in paragraph 12 as saying, "I never let the facts get in the way of the truth!" What do you think is the difference between truth and facts? How close is the relationship between them?

2. Which of Goddard's allegations of unreliability in Mowat's account seem most serious and which most trivial?

3. One of the main ways in which Goddard's and Mowat's versions differ is in the accounts they give of government policy towards the Inuit and towards wildlife. What are the key differences and how would you account for them?

4. Goddard ends his essay with the suggestion that "by selling fiction as nonfiction" Mowat has done lasting damage to the "public debate on Inuit and wildlife." To what extent do you think this accusation is justified?

Further reading:

Farley Mowat, *The People of the Deer* (1952)

————, *The Desperate People* (1959)

————, *Never Cry Wolf* (1963)

A.W.F. Banfield, Review of *Never Cry Wolf*, *The Canadian Field Naturalist*, 78 (1964) 52–54. The biologist who supervised Mowat's fieldwork gently chides the author for some of his inaccuracies and fictionalizing.

Thomas King (1943-

Thomas King has a heritage of Cherokee, Greek and German ancestry. He has published two novels, a collection of short stories, One Good Story, That One (1993), and edited an anthology of native writing, All My Relations (1992). He also writes and performs in the popular CBC Radio series "The Dead Dog Cafe Comedy Hour."

Presented as a personal account, King reflects on the difference between "history" and "story" through the stories told to him by a woman named Bella on the Blood reserve in Southern Alberta. Bella insists that her stories are history, while King, because of his training, is forced to see them as myth. He concludes his essay by calling these categories into question.

HOW I SPENT MY SUMMER VACATION: HISTORY, STORY, AND THE CANT OF AUTHENTICITY

1 According to the 1991 Neiman Marcus Christmas catalog, you can buy a custom carved totem pole or a painting by Rosie the Elephant. These two advertisements did not sit on opposing pages, although they should for they form a wonderful cultural diptych; the poles are carved by an authentic Native carver, and the paintings are rendered by an authentic elephant.

2 This has little to do with my essay, which is not available in the catalog, but it did suggest certain things to me about the power of advertising, the value of authenticity, and the need for essential Truths. And it reminded me of my summer vacation.

3 Last summer, I was at the Sun Dance on the Blood reserve in southern Alberta. Old friends had invited me up. I had never been to a Sun Dance before. When I told several of my neighbours in St. Paul where I was going, their eyes slowly glazed over and I imagined them conjuring up images of Catlin's romantically rendered Indians hanging about by their pectorals from poles.

4 In all honesty, I was not sure what to expect myself, but I was reasonably sure that I would have better luck seeing this kind of white-male eroticism at the theatre than I would on the Alberta prairies.

5 As it turned out, I was right. If my neighbours had gone with me that July, they probably would have been disappointed for the major activities at the Sun Dance involved an incessant coming and going: go to the store to get bread; take the kids in for a doctor's appointment; grab another load of wood; run to town for more ice; drive the bags of garbage to the dumpster in Standoff; duck home and take a shower.

6 And constant preparations. Each lodge had coffee. Food was everywhere. Not a conspicuous show of food, just its constant presence — a pot of stew, soup, a picnic ham, bread, apples and bananas. And all around, elders, adults, and children were on the move, circling the camp, visiting. You can sit in one lodge all day, and, in between the preparations, and the dances, you will be able to meet and greet many of the people in the camp, for the Sun Dance is a consummate

social ceremony as well as a religious one, and that is the way it should be. It is also an occasion for storytelling.

7   I was sitting in my friend's lodge enjoying yet another cup of coffee, minding my own business, when the flap of the teepee was pulled to one side and two elderly women and a younger man entered. We greeted each other; the women settled themselves on their side of the lodge and the man and I settled ourselves on our side. For a while, no one said a word.

8   Finally, one of the women, a woman named Bella, leaned forward, looked at me, looked at the ground, and looked back at me.

9   "I hear you're a historian," she said.

10   I quickly told her it wasn't true, that I was a writer, a novelist, a storyteller. But she waved me off.

11   "Same thing," she said, and she began to tell this story.

12   There was a young man who came to the reserve to talk to elders. He was from a university (Bella didn't say where) but when she said the word university, she slowed down and stretched out each syllable as if she were pulling on an elastic and the man sitting next to me started to laugh as if he had just heard an excellent joke. Bella waited until he stopped and then she continued.

13   The man, Bella explained, wanted to hear old stories, stories from back in the olden days, stories about how Indians used to live. So she told him about how death came into the world, how Old Man and Old Woman had argued over whether human beings should live forever or whether they should die. Old Man thought they should live. Old Woman thought they should die.

14   So they made a wager, a bet. Old Man got a buffalo chip and they agreed that if they threw the chip in the river and it sank, them human beings would live forever. If it floated, them human beings must die.

15   There are no surprises here. The chip floated, and, as Bella explained to the man, that was how death came into the world.

16   At this point in her story, Bella told me that the young man, all eager and full of sound, jumped in and said that whites had the same sort of story. And before anyone could stop him, he began a recitation of Genesis, how everything was perfect in the garden, how there was no death, how Eve found the apple, how she ate the apple, how she seduced Adam, how Adam and Eve acquired knowledge, and how, from then on, things got gloomy. He concluded by noting what a coincidence it was that women, in both cases, were responsible for these disasters.

17   After he finished, the elders thanked him for his remarks and the man from the university thanked the elders and everyone went their own way.

18   When Bella finished telling this story, she settled back in her chair and drank some coffee. Then she looked right at me, and she said, "And that's why he never heard the rest of the story."

19   The first thing that flashed through my mind was Paul Harvey. The second was to keep my mouth shut, for I understood that attached to the story Bella had just told was a caution to mind my manners and not to interrupt as the other man had done.

20   So I shut up, and I waited. Bella finished her coffee and had another cup. There was some soup in the pot and that was passed around with bread and more coffee.

21   Then Bella said, "So you see Old Woman was right. If there had been no death, there would have been so many people, the world would have sunk into the ocean. Just look at it now! Old Woman understood the need for balance."

22   I think I started to smile, but Bella cut me off quickly. "And that Eve woman was right, too," she said. "No point in being stupid all your life."

23   We sat in the lodge for a long time and talked about family and children, the price of gas, the weather, Martin's new van, Dixie's cellular telephone, and Thelma's new boyfriend from Calgary.

Finally, the three of them got up to leave and move to the next lodge.

25   "You work at a university just like that young man?" Bella asked me.

I told her that I did.

"It's real frustrating, you know, to have to keep telling that story. Maybe you can find that young man and tell him he should get it right."

"Tell him," she continued, "to remember that Eve woman of his and to use the brains she gave him."

29   I followed Bella outside. The rains had been heavier than usual that July and the prairie grass was tall. Here and there in the distance, sections of canola were in full bloom, bright gold against the deeper greens and blues, and from the camp on the Belly Buttes, you could see the sky in all directions and watch the land roll into the mountains.

30   "You write stories?" Bella asked me.

"Yes, I do."

"About us Indians?"

"Most of the time."

She smiled and shook her head. "You're kinda young to be a historian."

35   I had to leave that day to go down into eastern Oregon for a writer's conference and all the way down, I chewed on what Bella had suggested about story and history. I was, of course, able to dismiss her contention that story and history were the same, knowing that she had never studied history, knowing that she was not aware of the fine distinctions that separated the two. Of course, history was a story, and, as with all stories, it carried with it certain biases that proceeded from culture, language, race, religion, class, gender. It was burdened with the demands of nationalism, subject to the vagaries of scholarship, and wrapped up in the myth of literacy. Nonetheless, as one of my professors told me, history dealt with a series of facts rather than fictions, and, while the interpretations of those facts will vary, these small truths would remain.

I was comforted by that. I am not sure why, but I was.

37   When I finished the conference at Lake Wallowa, I headed back to the Sun Dance. I wanted to get there in time to see the men dance. But the first thing I did was to look up Bella. I found her sitting in a folding chair outside one of the lodges enjoying the panorama of the prairies and the Rockies.

"You again!" she said.

39   She motioned me to sit down beside her and I did. I did not know what to say or how to start. I wanted to tell her about history and story, but instead, we sat there and watched Chief Mountain turn blue and then purple as the light deepened.

40   "You know," Bella said, "there was this guy about your age came out to visit us. He was from Ottawa. Reporter. Wanted to know what we thought about

Meech Lake, so Florence told him about how Coyote won a bet with Old Woman and how death came into the world. You know the story?"

41   I said I thought she had told me a story like that several days ago.

But did I remember it, she wanted to know. Could I tell it, again?

I made the mistake of saying that I thought I could. Bella settled into [the] chair, waved at the mosquitoes, put her hands in her lap, and closed her eyes. I thought she was going to sleep. But she wasn't.

"You waiting for winter?"

45   So I began to tell the story, and I thought I did a pretty good job. When I finished, I settled in the grass, put my hands in my lap, and closed my eyes. As I sat there, I could hear Bella shifting her weight in the chair.

46   "Okay," said Bella. "There was this Mormon guy from Cardston came to visit us. Wilma brought him by. He was an old guy, had a bad leg, you know. He said he was collecting oral history for the church. So Francis told him about how Duck and Buffalo had a bet and how Duck won the bet and how death came into the world."

47   And Bella proceeded to tell the story once again. It was the same basic tale, but each time she told it, some of the facts changed. First it was Old Man and Old Woman who had made the bet. Then it was Old Woman and Coyote. Duck and Buffalo got into the act in a third telling. Sometimes it was a rock that was supposed to float. Once the bet involved a feather. The man from a university/ Ottawa/Cardston changed, too. First he was young, then middle-aged, and finally, old. The only thing that remained truly constant was that death came to the world.

48   "That's history," Bella told me when she had finished the fourth telling of the story. "You got any questions?"

I was dying to tell Bella that this wasn't history at all, that this was ... well ... myth. But I didn't get a chance.

50   "Some of those white people call this story myth because they figure it never happened. Is that what you're thinking?"

I was in full retreat by now and was willing to do or say anything to get out of the way.

"Maybe it's a little of both," I said.

"You think that, do you?"

54   "Well, for instance," I said, "Stanley Fish suggests that there are interpretative communities composed of groups of people who share commonalities, who agreed on how things such as history and myth are interpreted, how the universe is ordered."

55   "That so?" said Bella.

"And Adrienne Rich talks about the politics of location and how your subject position, your gender, race, class all determine what you see and how you interpret what you see."

57   "Okay," Bella said with a sigh. "There were these two guys from France came to visit us. They wanted to hear old stories, so Latisha told them about Old Man and Old Woman and how death came to the world."

It was almost dark when I left Bella.

59   I do not know exactly what Bella was trying to tell me about history and

story. Indeed, I do not know if she was trying to tell me anything at all. Perhaps, as she said, she just wanted to make sure I got the story straight.

60   But I do not believe this. The elements of her story were too well placed. The conflict too cleverly organized. The resolution too pointed and axiomatic. I even suspect that the frame of the story — the man coming to hear a story — is apocryphal. But curiously, while the supporting facts changed in each telling of the story, the essential relationships — the relationship of humans to death and the relationship of balance to chaos — remained intact. Bella had begun here and crafted a set of facts to support these relationships, to create a story, to create a history.

61   Then, too, the language itself shifted as ceremony gave way to instruction. Metaphor, imagery, the rhythmic and repetitive syntaxes, the rhetorical inter-rogatories gave way to more didactic structures that marched lockstep from beginning to end, from premise to conclusion. These shape changes were not a product of frustration, the having to tell a story again and again, making it pro-gressively simpler and simpler, but rather the concern with purpose, allowing Bella, as she told one version all full of colour and motion, to declare that this was story, and as she told another version all full of instance and example, to insist that this was history.

62   Of course, we know we cannot trust authorial intent, and you should be rightly appalled that I bring it up at all.

63   Yet in considering what Bella told me and what I know, I am struck by how thin the line between history and story is, resting as it appears to do on a single question, a single concern — did it happen/is it authentic/can it be verified/is it real — and on the assumption of the preeminence of literacy within non-Native culture. Patricia Limerick, in her fine critical study of the West, *The Legacy of Conquest*, questions this very assumption. Speaking specifically about history and anthropology and the West, Limerick says that, "human differences that hinged on literacy assumed an undeserved significance." This significance that Limerick speaks of is, I believe (and I think Limerick would agree) not merely a function of the ability to read but rather the blind belief in the efficacy of the written word.

64   As an example, let's take my own trip to Alberta. When I am famous, some bright graduate student in search of a thesis or an assistant professor in search of tenure might consider a history of my life as a writer. Chapter five might start out with several paragraphs that recount my journey in July of 1991 to the Sun Dance in Southern Alberta where I met with a Blood woman named Bella; how over a period of days, with a short break during which I went to eastern Oregon to attend a writer's conference, Bella and I discussed the relationship of history to story and how that discussion inspired a most interesting paper that I later gave at the American Studies Coffee Hour in November of 1991.

65   Ah, history. Ah, story. What if I never went to the Sun Dance? What if I made all this up? What if I went to the Sun Dance, but Bella is a fiction? What if I went to the Sun Dance and talked to a woman named Bella, but I completely made up our conversation on history and story. What if I went to the Sun Dance, met a woman named Bella, had a conversation such as I describe, and could produce trustworthy witnesses to swear that my account of that conver-sation is accurate?

66   Perhaps what really happened was that someone, say a historian, said something in passing about history that set me thinking and that during my stay at the Sun Dance and talking with some of the people and listening to the stories they told, I decided to use that particular setting as a backdrop to give my personal thoughts and remarks an authentic context.

67   We like our history to be authentic. We like our facts to be truthful. We are suspicious of ambiguity, uneasy with metaphor. We are not concerned with essential relationships. We want cultural guarantees, solid currencies that we can take to the bank.

68   I tried to explain this to Bella with one example that I knew would carry the day. As we were sitting there on the Alberta prairies, I turned to the east and said in my best matter-of-fact voice, "It's the facts that separate history from story. For instance," I droned on, "the sun rises every day in the east."

69   Bella half-turned, smiled, and nodded her head. "Has so far," she said.

70   So that is it. Bella, if she exists, believes that history and story are the same. She sees no boundaries, no borders, between what she knows and what she can imagine. Everything is story, and all the stories are true. Whereas I am forced to try to separate them. To put fancy in one pile, facts in another, so the two will not get mixed up. By training (and I am speaking here of culture and society rather than just the university) I go forth into the world, not to question the presence of God in the universe, nor to confront the mysteries of birth and death, nor to consider the complexities of being, but simply to ascertain what is authentic and what is not.

71   Harry Truman and Paul Revere for instance.

72   Harry Truman, when he was President, ordered the military to drop two atomic bombs on Japan, one on Hiroshima and one on Nagasaki. We can read about it. We can go to Hiroshima and see the monument. We can see the aftermath of the destruction.

73   Paul Revere, when he was a young silversmith in Boston, rode through the city streets to alert the citizenry to the impending British invasion. We can read about it. We can go to Boston and see the Old North Church. We can walk the path he took that fateful night, and follow the drama in Longfellow's poem.

74   Well, so much for literacy.

75   Thank God, then, for Neiman Marcus and the Christmas catalog and the certificates of authenticity they provide. While questions of history and story may continue to plague me, I can tell you I sleep easier knowing that I own a painting by a real elephant, and that the totem pole in my back yard was not chain-sawed into existence by an out-of-work lumberjack. Bella probably wouldn't care, but then she wouldn't care that Paul Revere never made his ride, either.

76   All levity aside, I want to assure you that this essay is, in the best sense of the word, authentic. In a world which believes that wisdom is, in the main, a matter of keeping facts and fictions straight, it's the least I can do.

Topics for consideration:

1. In "A Real Whopper" earlier in this chapter, John Goddard accuses Farley Mowat of recklessly mixing fiction and fact. In this essay, King teases the reader with the suggestion that some or all of the events he describes may be fictional. He does, however, claim that his essay is "in the best sense of the word, authentic." What does he mean?

2. What are the consistent features of Bella's stories and what are subject to change? Invent a story of your own that follows the same pattern as Bella's.

3. King quotes Patricia Limerick to direct the reader's attention to the role played by literacy in the non-Native culture's conception of fact and history. In what ways is an oral culture likely to interpret fact differently from a culture dominated by print?

Further reading:

Walter J. Ong, *Orality and Literacy: The Technologizing of the Word* (1982). An exploration of the differences between oral and print cultures.

http://www.radio.cbc.ca/programs/deaddog/ Website for "The Dead Dog Cafe Comedy Hour."

CHAPTER 10

CONSIDERING CONSUMPTION

In Marge Piercy's futuristic novel *Woman on the Edge of Time* (1976), the time in which we are now living is characterized as "the Age of Greed and Waste." The essays in this section dissect some of the motives and mechanisms that could lead to such a description.

Joyce Nelson, in "The Temple of Fashion," invites us to look at the shopping mall with new eyes. Our behaviour in such places, she suggests, is strongly reminiscent of religious worshippers performing rites at a shrine. Clothing, in particular, offers the promise of personal transformation and redemption through the "instantaneous magic" of the credit card. In keeping with the otherworldliness of religious faith, the fashions on display seem to have "no origin, no history of labour and creation." Nelson, however, urges her reader to be a "shopping agnostic" and to inquire "who made these things, and under what conditions?"

Typically, the answer to Nelson's "agnostic" questions reveals that the garments displayed in the malls of North America are produced under sweatshop conditions in Third World countries. Dan Robins' essay, "Third World Chic" reflects on some of the same disparities. Responding to phenomenon of the many stores that now sell clothing and household furnishings made by Third World artisans, Robins points out that, while such stores offer a soothing vision of "a stable, multi-cultural world," the reality is less reassuring. In many cases the craftspeople who produce the goods see only a tiny fraction of the profit, and, even though Alternative Trading Organizations try to establish the conditions for "fair trade," Robins holds out little hope that they can make a real difference.

McKenzie Wark explores similar contradictions in "The Postmodern Pair." He traces the way in which denim jeans, once solely work clothing, became incorporated into the lexicon of the fashion industry. The appeal of "designer jeans" owes nothing to any of their material qualities but everything to the associations accruing to the name on the seat pocket and to the marketing campaigns used to sell them.

Just as we rarely investigate the origins of our purchases, we are generally oblivious to their final destination. Lars Eighner's frequently reprinted essay "Dumpster Diving" coolly points out the ways in which other people's garbage enabled him not only to subsist but to share the attitude of the "very wealthy" to possessions—"we both know there is plenty more where

315

whatever we have came from." Cory Doctorow's "Dumpster Diving" hero Darren converts the detritus from computer companies into cash, vividly demonstrating that present bloated rates of production and consumption generate sufficient waste to support an entire shadowy underground economy.

Joyce Nelson (1943-

Canadian cultural critic Joyce Nelson has specialized since the mid-1970s in the politics of the mass-media age. She is author of Sultans of Sleaze: Public Relations and the Media *(1989) and* Sign Crimes/Road Kill: From Mediascape to Landscape *(1992), from which this essay is taken.*

In "The Temple of Fashion" Joyce Nelson elaborates on how the "religion of acquisition" is practised in North American shopping malls. With its own sacred texts, rites and saints the act of shopping mimics religious practice in which devotees "enter the ecstasy of acquisition." Nelson, however, invites the reader to become "a shopping agnostic" and to question "who made these things, and under what conditions?"

THE TEMPLE OF FASHION

1   "The act of acquiring has taken the place of all other actions, the sense of having has obliterated all other senses," the British art critic and cultural historian John Berger observed in his 1972 book *Ways of Seeing.* By the mid-1970s, acquisition had achieved the status of a new religion in the West. The appearance of a new advertising buzz-word, *spirit*, was a clear signal of this development.

2   Once Coca-Cola had merely claimed to add "life" to our lives. Now everything from a cola through a department store and a hotel chain to a fashion designer began to make even bolder assertions. In slogans such as "the Pepsi Spirit," "Simpson's Spirit," "the Spirit of Hyatt," and Yves Saint-Laurent's "New Spirit of Masculinity," advertisers proclaimed the new religion of buying. More recently, the world *soul* has entered the advertising lexicon as another religious additive to enhance acquisition.

3   In such a context, shopping malls have become the cathedrals of our time: vast horizontal-Gothic places of worship that draw the faithful together in communal rites central to the new religion. While the Prime Movers in this religion are the TV God and its consort, the advertising industry, the shopping cathedrals are themselves temples of technomagic where steps move effortlessly beneath one's feet, doors open automatically, celestial Muzak hymns permeate the atmosphere, and the wave of a credit card completes the sacred transaction. Isolated from the mundane reality of urban existence, the shopping mall is sacred space, climate-controlled and patrolled, devoted to the ease of acquisition: the meaning of life in the postwar West.

4   This religion has evolved its own holy days (such as Boxing Day solstice) and holy seasons (Back-To-School octave). It also has its important sites of pilgrimage (in Canada, the West Edmonton Mall and Toronto's Eaton Centre), although every North American city has its lesser malls where the same litany of brand names holds out the promise of salvation. Nevertheless, this is a religion in which both faith and good works are necessary. This facet of the religion is nowhere more apparent than in the domain of Fashion, whose side chapels in each shopping cathedral remind us that last season's profession of faith is up for renewal.

5   According to the arcane hermeneutics of the Fashion Bible, one risks damnation by last year's colour or the slightest oversight of tie, lapel, or faux nail. Thus, the Gospels according to Armani and Alfred Sung, Ralph Lauren and Christian Dior are continually being reinterpreted for our edification and enlightenment. While slogans such as Calvin Klein's "Eternity for Men" and Alfred Sung's "Timeless" collection evoke an eschatological promise signifying the end-time of shopping, it is a central tenet within the religion (and certainly dogma in Fashion) that our indulgences are never plenary. "Shop Till You Drop" is the vulgar — but correct — grasp of this aspect of consumer theology.

6   Fortunately, the high priests of Fashion (particularly the college of ecclesiastics gathered at *Women's Wear Daily*) continually disseminate guidance on each chapter and verse of the Fashion Bible. Their perennial lists of "Best Dressed" and "Worst Dressed" remind us that even those not banished to the purgatory of obscurity risk hellfire by sinning against Fashion commandments that are perpetually under revision.

7   For this reason, there exists a wealth of inspirational literature and illustrated texts to assist us in our salvific efforts. *Vogue, Esquire, Gentleman's Quarterly,* and *Flare* provide not only the necessary iconography for the consumer aspirant's meditation but also details on those Fashion sins (venial and mortal) that can impede our progress. The pages of such inspirational texts also offer devotional readings on the lives of the Fashion saints: popular saints of the past like St. Marilyn and St. James Dean; current beatified exemplars like Madonna and Billy Idol; and our living martyr to Fashion, Elizabeth Taylor. But such devotional reading and contemplation are only preparations for the greater liturgies of the mall.

8   Window shopping brings the congregation into closer proximity to the Fashion priesthood and the means of redemption, but before we enter any of the mall's side chapels there is usually an impressive form of statuary to mediate our passage. Modern mannequins have evolved with the mall itself, becoming increasingly elaborate, detailed, and even startling in their effect.

9   The old form of mannequin (like the old form of storefront) was, for the most part, simply uninspiring; its wig askew, its coiffure outmoded, its facial expression vague and nondescript, its limbs akimbo or missing, its stand ridiculous or pathetic. Only by the greatest leap of faith could the consumer attain the proper buying spirit through a glance at such a guardian of the portals.

10   The new mannequins, on the other hand, are appropriate statuary for the impressive cathedrals that surround them. Figures of anatomical perfection, these statues with their erect nipples, painted fingernails, detailed eye makeup, stunning hairdos, high cheekbones, and long sinewy legs remind us at a glance just what it is that we, as mundane Fashion consumers, aspire to. While the male statuary is somewhat less intimidating, it too bespeaks the contemporary codes of the Fashion cult: chiselled jaws, muscled but sleek torsos, long-legged figures of power.

11   But it is the faces of the new statuary that are most significant in their religious function: aloof, haughty, disdaining, beyond appeal. Inspiring neither solace nor prayer, these figures at the portals are part of the shrines of envy and are meant to inspire a certain measure of fear.

12   To gaze at one of these detailed figures is an oddly unsettling experience (though in truth they are meant to be only glimpsed in passing). Typically, the

statue is posed so that its haughty gaze is directed above or away from us, as though we were quite obviously beneath contempt. At the same time, the statue's fetish of forever-perfect and hyperrealistic detail cruelly reminds us of our own imperfections. Whether we are fully conscious of the effect or not, we enter the chapels of Fashion subtly diminished and suitably envious.

13   Such feelings enhance the redemptive power of the array of apparel within. Each article of clothing promises to increase our status and transform us in turn into objects of envy, in our own eyes and the imagined eyes of others. Here, the numinous brand name confers its accretion of socially envious connotations, religiosity, and sacred trust. This veneer laid upon mere cloth by the high priests of Fashion is necessary for passing through the challenging ritual of the changing room.

14   Within this confessional enclosure, one is confronted by the attendant mirror revealing all the sins of the flesh that mar one's progress: the cellulite thighs, the body hair, the paunch, the girth, the less-than-perfect contours reminding us that the spirit is willing but the flesh is weak. Making promises to join the modern-day *flagellantes* in a daily workout routine, we proceed to put on the desired article of clothing that promises to miraculously transform our lives.

15   The moment of beholding ourselves dressed in the desired brand name has also been prefigured and prepared by the statue at the chapel's portal. Like it, we must harden our gaze, overlook that small inner voice of protest about the price, and focus on a future vision of ourselves as the envied possessor of this article of apparel that most of the faithful will have already seen (and desired) in the inspirational Fashion texts. We know that the envious others will recognize at a glance that we have joined the elect.

16   Where once it was possible for the faithful to identify, from a momentary glimpse, the habit of a Franciscan friar or Benedictine nun, so now the congregation is steeped in the familiar cut and style of various designer looks. Indeed, one can dress oneself entirely from head to foot in Ralph Lauren or YSL, Lee or Esprit. As the most dedicated of the Fashion faithful realize, it is the brand, not the cloth, that clothes us. So the slogan says, "Life's Necessities: Food, Shelter and Lee Jeans."

17   As we become the objects of our own devotion, the high point in the shopping mall liturgy approaches: the transforming ritual of the credit card. Through its instantaneous magic, we momentarily redeem ourselves and enter the ecstasy of acquisition, consuming and consumed by the bliss of possession.

18   It is precisely this ease of acquisition that is fundamental to the new religion. The technomagic of the credit card is in keeping with the whole aura of effortlessness that pervades the mall. Indeed, the many objects on display seem magically conjured out of nothing to fulfil the promise of advertising images' sleight-of-hand. For all intents and purposes, these millions of objects seem to have no origin, no history of labour and creation. Only the shopping agnostic would think to consider such questions as: who made these things, and under what conditions?

19   For example, most of our brand-name clothing is made by Third World garment workers, primarily women, who are grossly underpaid and exploited by North American contractors paying as little as ten cents an hour for the labour.

In the export-processing zones of the Philippines, Thailand, Hong Kong, Mexico, Indonesia, and dozens of other countries, non-unionized workers typically work sixteen-hour days for the most meagre of wages, assembling the host of products that fill our malls. Even Canada's high priest of Fashion, Alfred Sung, employs Hong Kong labour to work at a fraction of Canadian wages in sewing the apparel of the elect.

20   But the religion of acquisition excludes any knowledge of the actual work that goes into the making of our products. For most of the consumer faithful, these millions of objects simply appear "as seen on TV" or in the photo magazines: as though untouched by human hands, as though the image itself (like an idea in the mind of God) had somehow spawned its progeny, as it were, "in the flesh." Like Doubting Thomases, we touch and buy their tangibility to reaffirm our faith. Thus, while some have dubbed this new religion the Church of Perpetual Indulgence, it may more accurately be described as the Church of the Wholly Innocent: wilfully apolitical, purposely unknowing, steeped in the mystification and technomagic of our time.

Topics for consideration:

1. How serious is Nelson in her comparison of fashion to a religion? How can you tell?

2. In paragraph 2, Nelson points out that advertising now incorporates religious words such as "spirit" and "soul." What current examples can you add to those Nelson gives?

3. In paragraphs 11 to 13 Nelson discusses the way in which "the haughty gaze" of the store mannequins is "meant to inspire a certain measure of fear." Is the same true of illustrations in fashion magazines? Examine the "gaze" of the models in a current magazine. What feelings does such a gaze incite?

4. At the end of the essay Nelson alludes to the circumstances in which much of North American clothing is produced. What difference would it make to people's "worship" of fashion if they were more aware of these conditions?

Further reading:

Andrew Ross, ed., *No Sweat: Fashion, Free Trade and the Rights of Garment Workers* (1997). A popular anthology of articles on the garment industry.

Daniel Miller, *A Theory of Shopping* (1998). A social anthropologist looks at shopping.

Dan Robins

Dan Robins writes for This Magazine, *from which this essay is taken.*

In "Third World Chic" Dan Robins observes the "trade in fashions from the world's poorest areas." Not only are such goods inauthentic in that they cater to the fickle tastes of North American consumers, but they are also often created in exploitative conditions. Robins suggests that Alternative Trading Organizations (ATOs) may hold out some hope for fairer trade practices, but warns that such organizations may do no more than offer the world's poor "better pimps for their products."

THIRD WORLD CHIC

1   Along one wall were small laughing Buddhas. Opposite them, some Indonesian embroideries. I was in the back, browsing through shelves of handmade paper from Nepal, and wood carvings from Africa and Thailand. To get there I'd had to pass racks of beeswax candles, incense and pro-hemp knapsacks. I had entered the land of Third World Chic.

2   The store is called One World, and you can find it on Montreal's trendy boulevard Saint-Laurent. There are others like it in all of Canada's major cities, shops where you can flip through the world's cultures like baseball cards. I guess you could call it multiculturalism: Welcome To My Mall.

3   The trade in fashions from the world's poorest areas is immense, targeted mostly to professionals (especially women and couples setting up house) and their university-aged progeny. It ranges from small shops like One World to importers like Pier One, with 30 stores in Canada and over 600 in the U.S., all selling their favourite brands of Third World Chic.

4   Maybe it seems petty to complain about fashion statements in a world where maquiladoras are fast becoming the model of progress, but Third World Chic is more than a metaphor. It expresses and reinforces an image of GATT-happy globalization, a picture of a world where nattily dressed brown people dance to funky music, all available for mass consumption.

5   In this world, Jamaica appears as a country where everyone wears red, gold and green tams, says Montreal black activist Moji Anderson. She suggests that by going "multicultural," white liberals try to excuse themselves from their privilege, to prove an anti-racist stance just by wearing a sweater. Few Third World Chic products involve expressing any commitment to the political interests of the people who make them ("Free Tibet" t-shirts and Palestinian *kafiyehs* are the only exceptions I can think of). The code word, it seems, is "authenticity," not "solidarity."

6   But the artisans aren't involved so much to express their own cultures as to produce commodities for an exterior market. "They're responding to contemporary fashion demands," says Ted Macdonald of Massachusetts-based Cultural Survival International, an indigenous peoples' advocacy group.

7   For example, Pier One buyers regularly provide artisans with designs that are in demand, and "alternative" trade organizations give producer groups marketing seminars on what's in style on the other side of the globe. "This is created for fucking gringos," says Kevin McGrath, who owns Poncho Villa in Old Montreal. Dillon Maxwell, who runs a shop called New Earth, says he's tried selling the kind of clothing actually worn by rural Guatemalans, but no one was interested.

8   This reminds me of a town I once visited in southwest China, called Dali. That's Mandarin for "great principle," not a surrealist reference, but it may as well be one. I remember it as a place where I could eat hot burritos and oatmeal cookies, rent a copy of *Love in the Time of Cholera* and giggle at the (mostly English) graffiti. Though I haven't been back in three years, the last I heard the Coca-Cola Restaurant was still going strong. Other diners included Salvador's and Jim's Peace Cafe, most of them serving pizza. My souvenir is a batik pullover, complete with Chinese-style collar.

9   There was a debate raging among the tourists there, the kind who call themselves Travellers and carry backpacks instead of suitcases: Was this the authentic China they were experiencing? Or were they allowing those inscrutable Chinese to cheat them with a clever fake? (Perhaps they would rather have been shot by People's Liberation Army soldiers alongside the area's farmers, whose very realistic uprisings never seem to make the local papers.)

10   With Third World Chic, we can get that Dali feeling without even leaving home, spending our money to tell ourselves lies about a stable, multicultural world — One World, it seems, where colonialism never happened.

11   What's more, the ethnic clothing trade is far from ideal for Third World artisans. "It's capricious. It's not something we would ever encourage anyone to become deeply involved in," says Ted Macdonald. The most common problem is a lack of diversity in both products and markets. Artisans depend on consumers in only a few countries staying interested in a small range of crafts. Even a minor change in tastes can be disastrous.

12   With the more popular products — like Indian carpets, Javan batiks and Filipino rattan furniture — makers move away from a subsistence farming base to work in urban factories. But more commonly, agents based in rural areas buy crafts produced in workshops and family homes, then sell them to urban merchants, who have access to exporters. Artisans often don't know what their work is worth on the world market, so middlemen get most of the profit.

13   Often, labour is divided and craftspeople don't even see the finished product. In Thailand, for example, an eight-step weaving process is often subcontracted to eight different households. This helps exporters circumvent government regulation and prevent unionizing. According to Ann Weston, one of the authors of a 1986 study by the Indian Council for Research on International Economic Relations, rural artisans often come down with respiratory problems; child labour is common; and dyes and other pollutants make their way into local water sources.

14   Trade policies in Canada and the U.S. don't help. Enterprises in developing countries compete for shares of our import quotas, doled out by local governments. Large-scale urban businesses are more likely to have pull, so smaller (and likely less exploitative) producers have a hard time reaching an export market.

15   Enter the Alternative Trading Organizations (ATOs), groups that try to work more directly with producers and offer them "fair trade." In Canada the largest are Bridgehead, owned by OXFAM-Canada, and Self-Help Crafts, a wing of a U.S. company run by the Mennonite Central Committee. ATOs deal in crafts and clothing, as well as cash crops like sugar and coffee, which they sell through independent shops and mail-order catalogues distributed in publications like *This Magazine*. Alternative traders usually try to choose their trading partners according to social interests, dealing with cooperatives and other community-based enterprises.

16   But does this really make a difference? "It's a hard question because at a superficial level everybody agrees it's great," says Tim Broadhead, former director-general of the Canadian Council for International Cooperation. "But there are a lot of alternative trading organizations now, and my experience is that not all those using the rhetoric are following through." Paul Leatherman of the International Federation for Alternative Trade (an umbrella group of about 60 organizations) acknowledges that some of the producer groups that advertise themselves as co-ops aren't really anything of the sort.

17   ATOs are often branches of non-governmental organizations with broader political aims, but those messages seldom make it into their catalogues or their "consumer education." Still, ATOs that provide higher wages to people with definite political interests can strengthen local struggles. For example, I like to think that Bridgehead money paid to the UCIRI coffee-growers' collective in Oaxaca, Mexico found its way into Zapatista pockets. "It's one of the few ways that's been found to bring money into these rural areas," Ann Weston says.

18   Perhaps unfairly, it all reminds me of Bryan Johnson, the *Globe and Mail* reporter who shocked Canadians with a 1980 front-page story giving an in-depth account of the lives of teen prostitutes in the Philippines. In December 1991, an article in *Saturday Night* revealed that Johnson was now running his own strip club in Manila. He told reporter Sean O'Malley that years of trying to get kids off the streets had failed, and all he could do for them was run a better bar. And so it is with Third World Chic: Maybe it's true that the best the world's poor can hope for is better pimps for their products. But it's not a heartening thought.

Topics for consideration:

1. Robins uses two autobiographical examples in this essay. What function does each of them serve?

2. In paragraph 5 Robins refers to the way in which clothing can be selected with the intention of conveying a political message. What other examples of this use of clothing have you observed? Is it usually as shallow as Robins suggests? Are there ways in which it can be made meaningful?

3. Robins ends his essay by implying that fair trade with "the world's poor" is still a distant goal. What would bring this goal nearer?

4. Both Joyce Nelson in "The Temple of Fashion" and Dan Robins refer to the exploitative conditions in which much of our clothing is produced. Select an article of your own clothing and investigate where, how and by whom it was made.

Further reading:

http://www.clc-ctc/news/bstoc.html Canadian Labour Congress website giving information on global sweatshop conditions.

http://www.sweatshopwatch.org/ U.S.-based corporate watchdog specializing in the garment industry.

http://trfn.clpgh.org/Environment/altrade.html A list of Alternative Trade Organizations.

McKenzie Wark (1961-

McKenzie Wark teaches media studies at Macquarie University, Sydney, Australia and is author of Virtual Geography: Living with Global Media Events (1994) and The Virtual Republic: Australia's Culture Wars of the 1990s (1997).

McKenzie Wark traces the origins of "designer" jeans to the mass production techniques required to supply troops in the American Civil War and shows how their image has been manipulated to fit the needs of garment industry production and marketing.

THE POSTMODERN PAIR

1   It's strange how an idea as contradictory as 'designer jeans' comes, after a while, to seem quite normal. Jeans are a practical garment that made their way into the quite impractical world of the post-war fashion system. Right alongside Tiffanys and other designer brands on New York's classy Fifth Avenue sits an outlet for Levi's jeans. In this paradox lies one of the most striking changes in the shape of the fashion industry.

2   Jeans are a garment that puts together the ingenuity and resources available in the US at the time of the civil war. This very large-scale conflict was the incentive for the industrialization of a good many work processes. The first example of what we would now recognize as mass-production techniques was for civil-war firearms. The need for military uniforms led to similar techniques being used for clothing, and to a system of standard sizes that is still with us today.

3   Fashion and clothing were — and to some extent still are — a modern, industrialized system with two distinctive rhythms of production and consumption. Whatever people wear until it wears out is clothing. Whatever people wear until a new style comes along is fashion. Jeans were once clothing rather than a fashion garment, until something happened to them that was part of a whole shift in the workings of the fashion system. Where a style would usually pass down the fashion system, jeans were one garment style that moved up.

4   Think of a classic image from the US of the 1950s in which jeans figure. James Dean or Marilyn Monroe are likely to come to mind. Actually, these Hollywood stars were not the first to borrow this lowly garment and use it as a sign of style rather than as a practical garment. The fashion career of jeans probably starts with subcultures on the fringes of American society such as the 'rough trade' side of male homosexual life and the demobilized wartime pilots who took up the motorcycle as recreation.

5   In the 1960s, jeans proliferated as a garment that could appear to its wearer to be a statement against the whole hierarchy of fashion, while in the end fitting quite well into a new kind of fashion order.

6   Easy Rider was a low-budget film, made on the fringes of the Hollywood system, and it indicated that much the same thing was happening to the movie industry as to the fashion industry. The orderly mass production of cultural artefacts and signs gave way to a much less stable pattern of culture industries without

as definite a hierarchy of price and quality. An idea or an image could come out of nowhere and pass into mass popularity.

7   The cut and colour of denim jeans started to vary seasonally, just like a fashion garment. Here is the beginning of the paradox of the 'postmodern' fashion system. Jeans are functional and cheap to assemble. Yet, in spite of their basic cuts and exposed seams, they can support an elaborate range of meanings.

8   With 'modern' fashions, the material quality of the garment and its ability to signify fashion and stylishness went together. With 'postmodern' fashion there need be no such connection. What the garment signifies might be quite at odds with its material qualities — as it is in the archetypal case of the blue jean. Much the same garment can support quite a wide variety of meanings with a few minor variations in its appearance.

9   The 1960s saw a great proliferation of pop culture, as incomes rose throughout the developed world and more and more people went looking for something on which to spend their disposable income. This was both a good time and a bad time for mass manufacturers of a clothing item like blue jeans. Rising incomes meant more purchasing power and a bigger market, but it also meant rising costs. While the production of the fabric lends itself to automation and to economies of scale, some parts of the cutting and assembling of garments do not.

10   To make matters worse, the 1960s also saw an explosion of small-scale manufacturers and retailers who took advantage of the vast expansion of pop culture to market a bewildering array of ever-changing styles. Big manufacturers often found it hard to keep up. The aura of style created around the blue jean by Hollywood and Western pop culture did not end at the borders of the US. The names Levi Strauss and Wrangler found their way onto the behinds of people living far from the badlands of American life from which the garments allegedly arose.

11   The proliferation of pop culture, with its unpredictable style shifts, its valuing of cheap materials, its multiple-entry points for new expressions of style, was a difficult time for the mass manufacturers. Such a basic garment was easily copied, even counterfeited, in the developing world. Moving production there might have lowered costs, but it also created an industry that could quickly duplicate such a basic commodity.

12   One response was to absorb jeans fully into the bottom end of the fashion system, with annual variations in styles, with decorative stitching, choice of colour, distinctive ranges for men and women, extremes of cut such as the flare and even the zipper on the back — a shortlived innovation of the 1970s. The point of these changes was the effort by the big manufacturers to stay one jump ahead of imitators. Ironically, just as big firms like Levi Strauss benefited from the circulation of images, so their imitators benefited from the advertising campaigns, which promoted the idea of the garment as much as any particular brand. Hence the continual efforts to distinguish products made by the leading brands.

13   Another change ushered in during the 1970s was the adoption of the garment by formerly high-status designers much further up the old fashion chain. The mass manufacturers had trouble adapting to the unpredictable tastes of pop culture before cheaper imitators caught up. But things were getting just as hard for the more up-market designers, who once had a secure lock on élite tastes.

14   The high-fashion houses responded by licensing their own names to less-

than-the-best-quality goods, including designer jeans. And so, in the 1980s, jeans appeared with the names of European design houses on them. These garments often had little to do with the designers who owned the trade mark, which would simply be licensed to a mass manufacturer. The design houses came to depend on licensing fees — particularly for perfumes but also for products like jeans — to offset the rising cost of exclusive lines and the extravagant marketing they required. The production of élite-design products became less a business in itself and more a way of generating a mass market for the brand. One might not be able to afford an Armani suit or Versace dress, but there might be a subsidiary line marketed as a cheaper alternative.

15   While the élite brands cashed in on the value of the sign that is their label by moving it discreetly down market, pop culture was also throwing up its own kind of style élite. It isn't just the subcultural credibility of Levi Strauss that can be copied: so too can the aura of style of a high-fashion house. Designers such as Calvin Klein and Donna Karan built names for themselves in ready-to-wear clothing that could then be marketed as a sign of a certain kind of style and taste, which in turn could be branded onto the seat of a pair of jeans.

16   The designer jean also incorporates a third phenomena — the mass marketers who decided to differentiate their product by setting up several apparently distinct labels, each with their own house style and target market, but sharing the same manufacturing, distribution and accounting systems. So besides the high-class label moving down market and the streetwise label moving up in the world, there is the mass-market label moving sideways. The Gap and Banana Republic are basically variations on the same corporate structure, but tailored to different niches in the world of brands.

17   In all of these cases, what you will find are basic garments that all meet at least minimum standards of quality and durability, but are in many ways interchangeable. What distinguishes them is not their material qualities, but the signs stitched onto the back pocket, the environments in which they might be sold, and the marketing campaigns that define the range of possible meanings for the sign. This is the paradox of the 'postmodern' fashion world.

18   The same proliferation of communication that made possible the pop-media world of culture and consumption also enables a fragmented production system. The cotton might come from wherever the exchange rate and the weather is favourable this season. The fabric might be made in a newly industrializing country with high levels of capital and skilled labour, if perhaps rather fewer environmental constraints. The cutting and stitching might be relegated to sweatshops in a less-developed part of the world. The designers, on the other hand, might be close to the New York garment district, where you can also find skilled garment makers who can run up experimental batches for the new-season range. The advertising firm who has the company's account might be nearby on Madison Avenue where suppliers of image-making skills, from hair stylists to photographers, are clustered.

19   The point of the whole process is to make a basic garment as cheaply as possible and attach it to a sign that conveys just exactly the right range of meanings to just exactly the right range of consumers, who will be happy to walk around with that sign on their backsides.

Topics for consideration:

1. In paragraph 3 Wark distinguishes between "fashion" and "clothing": "Whatever people wear until it wears out is clothing. Whatever people wear until a new style comes along is fashion." Which items in your wardrobe are clothing and which are fashion?

2. Wark describes the process by which elite fashion design houses license their labels to mass-produced products such as perfume and jeans in order to subsidize their exclusive lines of clothing. What is the "range of meanings" associated with labels such as Armani and Versace?

Further reading:

Susan Willis, *A Primer for Daily Life: Studies in Culture and Communication* (1991). An examination of the cultural meanings of familiar consumer products.

Lars Eighner (1948-

Lars Eighner's writing first attracted national attention in the U.S. when his essay on "dumpster diving" was published in 1991. Since then he has published a book-length account of his experience of being homeless in Texas and California in Travels with Lizbeth (1993).

Lars Eighner's personal essay marks the stages of the career of a scavenger showing how he is able to clothe and feed himself largely from what others throw away.

DUMPSTER DIVING

1   I began Dumpster diving about a year before I became homeless.

2   I prefer the term "scavenging" and use the word "scrounging" when I mean to be obscure. I have heard people, evidently meaning to be polite, use the word "foraging," but I prefer to reserve that word for gathering nuts and berries and such, which I do also, according to the season and opportunity.

3   I like the frankness of the word "scavenging." I live from the refuse of others. I am a scavenger. I think it a sound and honorable niche, although if I could I would naturally prefer to live the comfortable consumer life, perhaps — and only perhaps — as a slightly less wasteful consumer owing to what I have learned as a scavenger.

4   Except for jeans, all my clothes come from Dumpsters. Boom boxes, candies, bedding, toilet paper, medicine, books, a typewriter, a virgin male love doll, change sometimes amounting to many dollars: All came from Dumpsters. And, yes, I eat from Dumpsters too.

5   There are a predictable series of stages that a person goes through in learning to scavenge. At first the new scavenger is filled with disgust and self-loathing. He is ashamed of being seen and may lurk around trying to duck behind things, or he may try to dive at night. (In fact, this is unnecessary, since most people instinctively look away from scavengers.)

6   Every grain of rice seems to be a maggot. Everything seems to stink. The scavenger can wipe the egg yolk off the found can, but he cannot erase the stigma of eating garbage from his mind.

7   This stage passes with experience. The scavenger finds a pair of running shoes that fit and look and smell brand-new. He finds a pocket calculator in perfect working order. He finds pristine ice cream, still frozen, more than he can eat or keep. He begins to understand: People do throw away perfectly good stuff, a lot of perfectly good stuff.

8   At this stage he may become lost and never recover. All the Dumpster divers I have known come to the point of trying to acquire everything they touch. Why not take it, they reason, it is all free. This is, of course, hopeless, and most divers come to realize that they must restrict themselves to items of relatively immediate utility.

• • •

9   The finding of objects is becoming something of an urban art. Even respectable, employed people will sometimes find something tempting sticking out of a Dumpster or standing beside one. Quite a number of people, not all of them of the bohemian type, are willing to brag that they found this or that piece in the trash.

10   But eating from Dumpsters is the thing that separates the dilettanti from the professionals. Eating safely involves three principles: using the senses and common sense to evaluate the condition of the found materials; knowing the Dumpsters of a given area and checking them regularly; and seeking always to answer the question, Why was this discarded?

11   Perhaps everyone who has a kitchen and a regular supply of groceries has, at one time or another, eaten half a sandwich before discovering mold on the bread, or has gotten a mouthful of milk before realizing the milk had turned. Nothing of the sort is likely to happen to a Dumpster diver because he is constantly reminded that most food is discarded for a reason.

12   Yet perfectly good food can be found in Dumpsters. Canned goods, for example, turn up fairly often in the Dumpsters I frequent. All except the most phobic people would be willing to eat from a can even if it came from a Dumpster. I have few qualms about dry foods such as crackers, cookies, cereal, chips, and pasta if they are free of visible contaminates and still dry and crisp. Raw fruits and vegetables with intact skins seem perfectly safe to me, excluding, of course, the obviously rotten. Many are discarded for minor imperfections that can be pared away. Chocolate is often discarded only because it has become discolored as the cocoa butter de-emulsified.

13   I began scavenging by pulling pizzas out of the Dumpster behind a pizza delivery shop. In general, prepared food requires caution, but in this case I knew what time the shop closed and went to the Dumpster as soon as the last of the help left.

14   Because the workers at these places are usually inexperienced, pizzas are often made with the wrong topping, baked incorrectly, or refused on delivery for being cold. The products to be discarded are boxed up because inventory is kept by counting boxes: A boxed pizza can be written off, an unboxed pizza does not exist. So I had a steady supply of fresh, sometimes warm pizza.

15   The area I frequent is inhabited by many affluent college students. I am not here by chance; the Dumpsters are very rich. Students throw out many good things, including food, particularly at the end of the semester and before and after breaks. I find it advantageous to keep an eye on the academic calendar.

16   A typical discard is a half jar of peanut butter — though non-organic peanut butter does not require refrigeration and is unlikely to spoil in any reasonable time. Occasionally I find a cheese with a spot of mold, which, of course, I just pare off, and because it is obvious why the cheese was discarded, I treat it with less suspicion than an apparently perfect cheese found in similar circumstances. One of my favorite finds is yogurt — often discarded, still sealed, when the expiration date has passed — because it will keep for several days, even in warm weather.

17   I avoid ethnic foods I am unfamiliar with. If I do not know what it is supposed to look or smell like when it is good, I cannot be certain I will be able to tell if it is bad.

18   No matter how careful I am I still get dysentery at least once a month, oftener in warm weather. I do not want to paint too romantic a picture. Dumpster diving has serious drawbacks as a way of life.

19   Though I have a proprietary feeling about my Dumpsters, I don't mind my direct competitors, other scavengers, as much as I hate the soda-can scroungers.

20   I have tried scrounging aluminum cans with an able-bodied companion, and afoot we could make no more than a few dollars a day. I can extract the necessities of life from the Dumpsters directly with far less effort than would be required to accumulate the equivalent value in aluminum. Can scroungers, then, are people who *must* have small amounts of cash — mostly drug addicts and winos.

21   I do not begrudge them the cans, but can scroungers tend to tear up the Dumpsters, littering the area and mixing the contents. There are precious few courtesies among scavengers, but it is a common practice to set aside surplus items: pairs of shoes, clothing, canned goods, and such. A true scavenger hates to see good stuff go to waste, and what he cannot use he leaves in good condition in plain sight. Can scroungers lay waste to everything in their path and will stir one of a pair of good shoes to the bottom of a Dumpster to be lost or ruined in the muck. They become so specialized that they can see only cans and earn my contempt by passing up change, canned goods, and readily hockable items.

22   Can scroungers will even go through individual garbage cans, something I have never seen a scavenger do. Going through individual garbage cans without spreading litter is almost impossible, and litter is likely to reduce the public's tolerance of scavenging. But my strongest reservation about going through individual garbage cans is that this seems to me a very personal kind of invasion, one to which I would object if I were a homeowner.

23   Though Dumpsters seem somehow less personal than garbage cans, they still contain bank statements, bills, correspondence, pill bottles, and other sensitive information. I avoid trying to draw conclusions about the people who dump in the Dumpsters I frequent. I think it would be unethical to do so, although I know many people will find the idea of scavenger ethics too funny for words.

24   Occasionally a find tells a story. I once found a small paper bag containing some unused condoms, several partial tubes of flavored sexual lubricant, a partially used compact of birth control pills, and the torn pieces of a picture of a young man. Clearly, the woman was through with him and planning to give up sex altogether.

25   Dumpster things are often sad — abandoned teddy bears, shredded wedding albums, despaired-of sales kits. I find diaries and journals. College students also discard their papers; I am horrified to discover the kind of paper that now merits an A in an undergraduate course.

26   Dumpster diving is outdoor work, often surprisingly pleasant. It is not entirely predictable; things of interest turn up every day, and some days there are finds of great value. I am always very pleased when I can turn up exactly the thing I most wanted to find. Yet in spite of the element of chance, scavenging, more than most other pursuits, tends to yield returns in some proportion to the effort and intelligence brought to bear.

27   I think of scavenging as a modern form of self-reliance. After ten years of government service, where everything is geared to the lowest common denominator, I find work that rewards initiative and effort refreshing. Certainly I would be happy to have a sinecure again, but I am not heartbroken to be without one.

28   I find from the experience of scavenging two rather deep lessons. The first is to take what I can use and let the rest go. I have come to think that there is no value in the abstract. A thing I cannot use or make useful, perhaps by trading, has no value, however fine or rare it may be. (I mean useful in the broad sense — some art, for example, I would think valuable.)

29   The second lesson is the transience of material being. I do not suppose that ideas are immortal, but certainly they are longer-lived than material objects.

30   The things I find in Dumpsters, the love letters and rag dolls of so many lives, remind me of this lesson. Many times in my travels I have lost everything but the clothes on my back. Now I hardly pick up a thing without envisioning the time I will cast it away. This, I think, is a healthy state of mind. Almost everything I have now has already been cast out at least once, proving that what I own is valueless to someone.

31   I find that my desire to grab for the gaudy bauble has been largely sated. I think this is an attitude I share with the very wealthy — we both know there is plenty more where whatever we have came from. Between us are the rat-race millions who have confounded their selves with the objects they grasp and who nightly scavenge the cable channels looking for they know not what.

32   I am sorry for them.

Topics for consideration:

1. Eighner notes that, although he is prepared to eat discarded food he finds in dumpsters, others find this repellent. What is your own reaction to the prospect of eating what others have thrown away? Do you have the same attitude towards wearing clothes that other people have discarded?

2. Where do Eighner's views parallel those of the ordinary "consumer" and where do they diverge?

3. Eighner writes that he has reached the point when, "I hardly pick up a thing without envisioning the time I will cast it away," noting that he finds this a "healthy state of mind." Which of the things you now own are most difficult to imagine discarding?

Cory Doctorow (1971-

Cory Doctorow is a science fiction writer, columnist and multimedia developer.

Originally published in Wired *magazine, Cory Doctorow's essay recounts his nighttime expeditions with Darren, a professional dumpster diver who scavenges high-tech components from industrial sites.*

DUMPSTER DIVING

1 When my grandfather came to Toronto after the war, arriving via Halifax on a refugee boat from Hamburg, he went into business as a rag-and-bone man, riding a horse-drawn cart through the streets, salvaging scrap metal, fabric, paper — trash. Eventually, the business grew into a scrap yard and produced the money for a split-level ranch home in the burbs, university educations for his kids, and a condo in Fort Lauderdale for his retirement years. He built his house on garbage, but that fact never struck home for me until I met Darren.

2 Tonight, Darren, Mike, and I are cruising through the self-same suburb in Darren's police-auction paddy wagon. Darren handles the armored truck like my grandfather drove his Caddy — fast enough to make a committed cyclist like myself flinch, but with a great deal of precision as he weaves in and out of late-night traffic on the icy streets.

3 We're whipping through sprawling, one-story industrial plazas, slowing only to take a closer look at the dumpsters. We're all bitheads, but we're not looking for unshredded hard copy — that's old news. We're after tastier trash.

4 Finally, we spy a likely-looking site, a strip mall where the lone restaurant is perpetually going out of business. Mike puts on the superwarm jester's hat his mom made for him the year before he dropped out of electrical engineering at Ryerson Polytech. Darren pulls into the driveway, past the circling minivans of parents waiting to pick up kids from swimming lessons at the strip mall, and pulls up around back, along a row of dumpsters. He tugs a woolly toque over his long hair, zips up his army-surplus jacket, and puts on his heavy leather gloves.

5 I grab my own gloves and scramble to catch up. Darren's already headfirst in a dumpster, and a minivan is pulling up 20 yards from us, switching on its high beams. Darren looks at it. "A fucking vigilante. Thinks I'm here to *steal*" — like it's a dirty word. "Let him sit there. It's working light."

5 Darren dives back into the dumpster, flashlight clenched between his teeth. He tosses something onto the ice at my feet. It's a 3/4-inch Beta cassette, labeled "*Bonanza* Episode 87-5654." I peer cautiously over the dumpster's edge. Hundreds of broadcast-quality tapes. Darren pushes them aside, looking for something with a higher dollar-to-dimensions ratio. The paddy wagon's already half-full of spent laser toner cartridges and 386s, which occupy a lot of volume in a cargo space designed, after all, to transport humans in shackles, not the high tech detritus of Toronto's profligate industrial parks.

6 There's nothing but reruns in the first dumpster, so Darren moves on. He casts long, weird shadows in the minivan's headlights. I stare into their glare and try to

imagine what the guy behind the wheel is thinking. What must he make of three guys in their 20s, jumping in and out of the trash? What if he calls the cops? It makes me nervous. I mean, what we're doing isn't actually *illegal* or anything. Trash is a strange legal gray zone in Canada. The Trespass to Property Act — a hunk of legislation dating back to the British North America Act of 1867 — grants property owners and their rent-a-cops the power to ban anyone from the premises, for any reason, forever. The catch is, they have to actually ask you to leave — serve you with a notice prohibiting entry — then you have to return for it to be trespassing. And ever since a cop dug through a curbside trash can, looking for a ditched weapon used in a holdup, and the judge ruled that he needed no search warrant to do so, Canada's garbage has become fair game. So as long as we don't make a mess — that would be littering — we're on the warm and fuzzy side of the law.

7   Darren hits pay dirt in dumpster number two. "Active-matrix LCDs!" he says, and starts frisbeeing the displays to Mike, who stacks them, dozens of them, on one of the prisoner benches inside the truck.

8   Then suddenly Darren stops, holds one up, and his five o'clock shadow splits in a wide grin. He smashes the LCD against the frozen corner of the dumpster. "I got 500 of these things back home," he exclaims. "It's a fuckin' clown show!"

9   He's right — it's all absurd. In less than an hour, I've seen literally tens of thousands of dollars' worth of equipment, most of it too low on the dollars-to-volume graph to bother with. All of it in the trash. Darren's got a quarter-million-dollar recording studio, built entirely out of garbage, in a warehouse a couple blocks from my own studio. Upstairs, in a soundproofed mezzanine, is a room completely jammed with baroque computer trash: old SGI servers, NT boxes, 21-inch monitors, cables from here to Hong Kong, shrink-wrapped software, bookcases overflowing with manuals. That's just the stuff he didn't sell. Ten Darrens couldn't even make a dent.

10   The vigilante behind the headlights apparently decides he's not going to be a hero tonight. He switches back to low beams and pulls away.

11 We knock off early. It's *cold* out, a vicious icy windy bastard of a Toronto night. Out in the burbs, there's nothing to cut the gales, and they find the chinks in your long underwear and scarves.

12   We head downtown for Vietnamese salad rolls. I'm mentally cataloging tonight's haul: a bushel of gold-tipped RCA cables for Darren, 20-some PCM-CIA modems, the LCDs, some old 386s, laser toner cartridges — to buy it all new would cost thousands. Darren will sell it for less than a grand. Still, it's pretty good money for three or four hours' work.

13   Cruising through Chinatown, looking for a parking spot, we pass an electronics store with a sign in the window: "16MB SIMMs — $800!" This sparks a story from Darren.

14   "Yeah, I was at this distributor out in Mississauga, and they had a dumpster filled with little cardboard boxes, like so" — he takes both hands off the wheel to form an 8-inch square — "and they each had a sticker that said 'Empty Box, Do Not Open.' You get that a lot, empty boxes they stick in packing crates so the stuff won't shift around. I see one of these boxes, sealed, but with no label. I think, well, maybe someone in Japan just forgot to put a sticker on it, and maybe someone in Toronto didn't bother to look inside, and I open it, and there's 10 16-meg

SIMMs inside. Eight thousand dollars' worth of RAM! And people wonder why RAM costs so much. Sold it for five grand."

15   Over green tea, Darren starts to get philosophical. It's an occupational hazard. You can't spend half your time alone in dumpsters without formulating trash cosmologies.

16   "Those guys who go after tin cans and pop bottles, those *garbage pickers*, they're fuckin' nuts! Why waste your time on a nickel bottle, when you can sell an empty toner cartridge for 10 or 20 bucks? They're nuts, man." He looks genuinely upset. He gets upset when he talks trash. But he also swells with pride, describing this strange little niche he's carved for himself.

17   "I got caught in somebody's trash one night, and the next time I went back, I found 10 CD-ROM drives, and they'd smashed 'em up with hammers, so I couldn't sell 'em." He grimaces. "It's criminal. This is useful stuff! Why would they want it to end up in a landfill?"

18   Good question.

19   Darren takes me out again, just the two of us in his landlady's ancient Buick. The night starts slowly, as we cruise past empty dumpsters.

20   We're in Motorola country, but that dumpster — source of hundreds of flip phones and batteries — is off-limits these days. Darren, it seems, dropped in one night and found someone else already in the trash. Two guys, in fact, pulling out featureless black boxes, the likes of which he'd never seen. The guys became, well, aggressive, and chased him off. Darren figures they were pros, industrial spies working with someone on the inside to spirit out top-secret tech via the trash.

21   It turns out some dumpster divers come from the other side of the thin blue line as well. "The cops around here like to pull me over," Darren explains, "just to see what kind of stuff I've got tonight. A couple months ago, I got some sports cards from this place, and they pull me over, and the cop says, 'Are you kidding me? You found these in the trash? My kid spends a fortune on these.' So I come back a couple nights later and bam, there's the cop, headfirst in the trash. Hell, I don't care. Plenty more where that came from."

22   "Speaking of which," Darren says, "there's another place I want to check out. They moved a couple months ago, but they still haven't put a dumpster out at the old site. There's got to be tons of stuff, just waiting to be trashed."

23   And there is. Acer America Corporation has a big old 40-cubic-yard dumpster out. It's about a third full. Darren smiles and sticks the end of his flashlight between his teeth.

24   This dumpster is the night's big score. We find 400 laptop batteries, five 15-inch Trinitron tubes, half a dozen laptop hard drives, most of a carton of shrink-wrapped PowerPC monitor adapters — I wince thinking of the 60 bucks I shelled out for one a few weeks back — voltmeters, multitesters, and enough miscellaneous monitor hardware to fill the whole backseat of the Buick. Cash value? Ten thousand Canadian (around US$7,150).

25   Of course, it's going to take some effort to turn this garbage into money. There's a guy who takes in the monitor trash, and for every two units he can build from it, Darren gets one. Only half the laptop batteries can be salvaged, by cannibalizing what good cells remain from the other half. The salvage guy will keep half of those. That leaves Darren with 100 power packs, retail C$200 — if he can find a buyer at $75 a pop, that's $7,500 right there.

26   After a good two hours sorting the trash and loading the car, Darren carefully restores the dumpster to its original state, making sure that the same kinds of trash are back on top, that there are no suspicious holes or visible bootprints. With luck, Acer will refill the dumpster over the next week; once the trash is up to the rim, Darren can start tunneling, building corridors shored up with cardboard flats from the recycling bin a few yards off.

27   Around 2 a.m., Darren drops me off at home, a couple blocks from his multimedia studio, then heads home to unpack the haul. I'd offer to help, but I'm freezing, and my stomach is one big bruise from using it as the fulcrum to lever myself into the dumpster. Darren, on the other hand, is as graceful as a gymnast, vaulting dumpster lips, making impossible twists in tight corners, stooping double for long stretches while he burrows.

28   Acer America Corporation doesn't know what to make of my phone call: "Hi, I'm a freelancer writing a piece about a guy who made 10 grand off stuff you threw out when you moved."

29   I end up being transferred to Marc DeNola, head of security and safety.

30   "Every product," he intones, "has a product life. In a high tech field, the product life can be quite short. At some point, a decision has to be made as to whether there is any salvage value. When something is discarded, it means that the storage costs are greater than the value of the item."

31   Why not donate the discards to charity, or hold a yard sale, or give them to schools?

32   Karen Grant, of Acer's PR company Editorial Edge Inc., insists that schools aren't interested in salvage — they want complete, working systems. As for yard sales, "It's something we'll have to look into."

33   So then why are the dumpsters at the new Acer site kept indoors, behind locked doors?

34   "It's part of the comprehensive security program," DeNola explains. "These days, we take security much more seriously."

Topics for consideration:

1. Doctorow refers to Darren's "philosophical" approach to trash. How does Darren's philosophy differ from Lars Eighner's in the previous essay with the same title?

2. When one company deliberately destroys valuable CD-ROM drives before putting them in the dumpster, Darren describes their action as "criminal." What do you think?

Further reading:

John Hoffman, *The Art and Science of Dumpster Diving* (1993). A practical guide.

http://www.craphound.com/ Cory Doctorow's home page.

CHAPTER 11

THE HOUSE OF TECHNOLOGY

We are often told that we are living in the midst of a technological revolution, an age in which medical, military, biological and, most of all, communications, technologies are being developed at a faster rate than ever before. The essays in this section all reflect on the various electronic technologies that are so rapidly altering our everyday experience of the world. Although politicians and corporate managers are apt to see these new technologies as irresistible evidence of "progress," most of the writers here treat them with more thoughtful scepticism.

Although our word "technology" owes its origins to the Greek word *tekhne*, which means art, craft or skill, the introduction of new technology often means that people either lose or never acquire a particular skill. Known as "de-skilling," this has been observed as an unintended effect of automation and computerization in the workplace. Ursula Franklin, in "All Is Not Well in the House of Technology," alerts members of the Royal Society of Canada to this process and argues for an analysis of technology that uses similar tools to those employed in studying literature.

In a survey of some of the global effects of computer technology, Wayne Ellwood also notes the unintended effects of technological innovation. Foreseeing widespread unemployment, he urges "democratizing the process of introducing new technologies into society and into the workplace" and restructuring our economy to guarantee a livelihood for those whose paid work has been eliminated by technology.

In "Digital Diploma Mills," David Noble examines the impact of the mandatory use of computer technology in higher education. The brainchild of a partnership between university administrators and large corporations, computer-based instruction signals the commoditization of education. Noble shows how this process destroys the autonomy and independence of teachers and replaces face-to-face education with a "cyber-counterfeit."

The new communications technologies are also reshaping our lives beyond the workplace. In "The New Nature," Tony Leighton shows that digital imaging has now transformed the photograph from a stable record of an event to an image infinitely manipulable to bear no relation to "reality."

The rise of electronic information technologies has led to speculation about the future of the printed book. Robert Fulford admits "we are right to be nervous," then argues that the book represents not just a particular technology but an ideology, carrying with it a whole range of humane values that may lie beyond the scope of the new (and more expensive) technologies.

Just as photography has conferred the power to reproduce visual images, ever more sophisticated recording technology allows for the re-creation of sound far away from the voice or musical instrument that produced it. In "Dub," R. Murray Schafer urges his audience to reject the world of "dubs, clones, simulacra" and to seek instead a life of "diverse experiences, memories … that will never be repeated."

Ursula M. Franklin (1921–

Born in Germany, where she and her family were incarcerated in a labour camp by the Nazis, Ursula Franklin emigrated to Canada as a graduate student in experimental physics. Following a distinguished scientific career she was made University Professor Emeritus at the University of Toronto and a Fellow of Massey College. A former board member of the National Research Council and the Science Council of Canada, she is known as an activist for peace and social justice. Her 1989 Massey Lectures were published as a book under the title The Real World of Technology *(1990).*

Originally given as a lecture to members of the Royal Society of Canada at a symposium entitled "The Well-Being of Canada," Ursula Franklin's essay discusses ways in which technology can be best analyzed and understood. She argues that since technological innovations do not exist as isolated phenomena, they may only be fully understood by using some of the analytical tools used in the humanities for the study of literary texts.

ALL IS NOT WELL IN THE HOUSE OF TECHNOLOGY

1 My notion of the well-being of Canada is not expressed by the GNP or international credit ratings, much as these measures may have their place in the scheme of things. Even employment data, infant mortality statistics, income distributions or levels of pollution can convey to me only part of the picture of the well-being of a country. My indicator of the well-being of my country is the degree of real hope and range of opportunity among the least powerful members of our society.

2 I was asked to "examine how well Canada is doing in the area of technology." Some might begin such a lecture with statistics on the number of computers, telephones, or television sets in Canadian homes, or with the number and areas of high tech patents filed by Canadian inventors — and maybe the fate of such intellectual resources.

3 However, I do not intend to hand out merit or demerit points. Rather, I would like to look at "the area of technology" as both a field of specific knowledge and a field of general interest, because I want to emphasize those facets of the question to which we, as members of the Royal Society of Canada, might be able to make a contribution. We are, after all, intellectuals and academics for whom the temptation of analyzing problems and coming to the conclusion that someone else — not us — must do a. or b. and c. is always present. Yet, we do not need to yield to this temptation since there is something specific for us to do. I am convinced that the problems in what I call The House of Technology are not all "other people's problems."

4 I have always defined technology as *practice*, i.e., as "the way things are done around here."[1] Technology is not the sum of inventions or of pieces of hardware. Technology is a *system*. It entails far more than its individual material components.

It involves organization, procedures, symbols, new terminology, and, most of all, a mindset.

5   This definition, while including all the elements of design, of devices and systems, of purpose and control, emphasizes that technology is a social phenomenon, not confined to the application of modern scientific knowledge. Technology, defined as culturally and socially rooted practice, is thus an integral part of every society. As a social activity it is interactive and involves the structures of the whole society. You cannot have technology alone, just as you cannot have literature alone—the very act of writing assumes a reader, separated from the writer in space and/or time.

6   Technologies have always been important to the well-being of societies, and yet there is a stunning discrepancy between the amount of intellectual attention, the level of methodological scrutiny, the extent of care and scholarly work devoted to what people have done and how they have done it, compared to what was *said* and *written*.

7   Let me illustrate what I am trying to argue with the help of two drawings created a century apart. The first one comes from a series of cards, commissioned by a French publishing house[2] in 1898 in order to illustrate life in the year 2000. The illustrator was asked to depict the changes in society under the impact of new and anticipated technologies. In this particular card, we see "airmail" showing how the artist expects the new way of getting a letter from here to there to be implemented in the year 2000.

8   He thought that this new way of doing something, this new technology, would not change anything else within the social fabric and that it would be done by direct home delivery as usual, probably twice a day.

9   The second drawing is a cartoon from a flyer advertising a public meeting on technological unemployment in Toronto in November 1997.[3] A librarian, presiding over a room full of readers, each sitting in front of an individual video display terminal, answers an inquiry with, "Sir, this is a library; if you want a book, go to a book store."

10   Here, again, is a new technology applied to an established activity ... but can we assume that "there will be public libraries as usual" in the manner in which a hundred years ago an artist assumed that there would be home delivery of letters in the year 2000? If we believe that one social practice, one technology, cannot be changed without affecting other social practices, how do we study, describe or assess the interplay of technologies in general and in systemic terms?

11   If we were to imagine the interdependent technologies as rooms in a house, connected by doorways and corridors, then I suggest that this House of Technology is not well lit. It seems to be full of trap doors, lacking exits and windows, and, most of all, signs or direction indicators.

12   Although we live in a country, and in a world, that is increasingly and rapidly restructured by new practices, by new technologies, we have few if any intellectual tools to address technology as a social force — not in terms of good, bad or indifferent, but in terms of its attributes, statements and internal consistencies or inconsistencies. Yet without analytical tools and methodologies, it is almost impossible to contemplate an answer to the question "How well is Canada doing with respect to technology?"

13   In other words, I would argue that nothing has had a greater impact on the events of the past hundred years than changes in technology. There have been dramatically novel and different practices used to accomplish what one might call the basic tasks of civilization. These tasks have really not changed profoundly over the millennia. Human communities have always tried to provide food and shelter for their members, direction and instruction for the young, myths and signposts that validate their traditions, safety, care and room for change and growth within the society.

14   What has changed profoundly over time is *how* these tasks have been and are being carried out. Advances in knowledge or access to new resources have been translated into new practices, new ways of doing the task at hand. Yet where do we turn for an analysis of these technologies? It seems to me that we cannot as easily inform ourselves on technology as technology as we can, for instance on literature as literature, on language as language.

15   The domain of "doing" — its context and its actors — has not had the degree of intellectual illumination that the domain of "declaring" — the world of the spoken and written word, with its context, rules and meanings has had.

16   There may be historical reasons for this lack of systematic scholarship of technology as a field of inquiry. The Euro-centred emphasis on *literacy* in education rather than *conduct* and *action*, may have something to do with it. But whatever the roots of this imbalance, it needs to be addressed.

17   There is, I would suggest to you, a new and major field of scholarship in the making, a field that is transdisciplinary more than interdisciplinary, because it will cut across the traditional boundaries of disciplines and academic faculties. Its new knowledge, while building on scholarship and insights of existing fields, will transform and extend in scope and method the inquiry into the nature of technology.

18   I am conscious of the contributions made already. No one will labour in this area of study without being influenced and stimulated by Lewis Mumford,[4] Michel Foucault,[5] Ludwig von Bertalanffy,[6] Jacques Ellul[7] and many others. Particularly the notions of technology as a system, or Ellul's concepts of technology as "milieu," have influenced thinkers and practitioners alike.

19   But we are still, I feel, without adequate methodologies to analyze technology in general terms. I would like to indicate how the mapping strategies of other disciplines might provide fruitful morphological parallels for the work of those concerned about the structure of technology.

20   Why not look at technology as text?

21   We are all aware of the simultaneous presence of declaring and doing, of word and deed in our lives. We have the artifacts of the word as well as the scholarship to evaluate and critique the written record. But we also have the artifacts of the deed, the physical, social and institutional evidence of technologies past and present, though only a much less developed scholarship of analysis and critique.

22   Think, for a moment, of the introduction of a new technology as *doing a text*. Looked upon as a text, does a given technology, a particular practice, not have substantative and/or relational components in its "language"? Surely there are also subtexts and assumptions here, just as there is context, meaning, consistency or inconsistency to be discerned in any technological process or activity.

23   In my own work, I have put forward the general distinction between holistic and prescriptive technologies, but there is so much more to be done to discern the recurring elements, the words and the vocabulary of technology. We need grammar, syntax, and structure as well as the signs and the symbolic components of technology as text and/or language.

24   In the past, technology has been "read" by those who commented on it, including myself, mainly as social instruction, the how-to manual that outlines a task and its context. Now it is to time to read and interpret technology as literature, as text per se. It is no longer solely a matter of content, but also one of analysis of the constituent elements, both visible and implied.

25   In the examples that follow I have tried to indicate how one might approach a textual analysis of technology. Carrying out such a new methodological work is obviously beyond the reach of my own scholarship. The examples and their discussion are intended mainly to stimulate my colleagues, who master different intellectual instruments, to look again at the discourse about technology.

26   Let me assure you that I am not trying to revisit the debates about structures in literature and science,[8] or the discussions on ways of knowing.[9] What I am wrestling with is the need for an anatomy of technology that could stand in a point-counterpoint relationship to the anatomy of literature — in the broadest sense of the term.

27   As I try to understand the world of technology, I am grappling with the lack of intellectual tools and look to the humanities for help. The domain of doing requires the mapping and orienteering instruments that the world of *declaring* generally takes for granted. It may, in the end, turn out to be a quest for an appropriate taxonomy.

28   My first example relates to the ski lift. When I came to Canada I was astonished to see the effects of rather serious skiing accidents among my fellow students. Though I had skied in Germany, I had never known ski lifts and it took me a while to see the link between the availability of a lift and the severity of the accidents encountered. Quite simply, the process of getting up a slope without mechanical help seems to develop skills that are adequate to getting down again reasonably safely. Mechanizing the "up" part of the practice increased the risks of the "down" part.

29   How might one analyze this simple change in technology as a *doing text?*

30   There is a task, the plot, the story: to get up to a certain point on a mountain and down again. There is an *activity* associated with the task, i.e., to do the climb and descend on skis. The prerequisite for the activity, in addition to the trivial ones such as having skis, a mountain, snow, etc., are skiing skills as well as some skills of informed observation, assessment, collaboration.

31   The text may be divided into two parts, Chapter 1, the ascent, Chapter 2, the descent and we have two versions before us: the Pedestrian version, in which the task is carried out without mechanical assistance, and the Ski Lift version in which the ascent is mechanized.

32   The task remains the same in both versions, but in the Ski Lift version the ascent is accomplished externally. Something different, another actor, another voice, tense or language has come into the Ski Lift version. This change does not affect the task level of the text; the ascent is readily accomplished. The change in

technology, though, does affect the activity and skill level of the text. It becomes clear that although the task in Chapter 1 can be more readily completed with the help of the new technology, the very use of an external mechanism diminishes the activity and skill content of Chapter 1 in the Ski Lift version.

33   Chapter 2, the descent, is the same in both versions as far as task and activity are concerned. Yet in terms of context and form, there is a significant discontinuity (might it be in vocabulary, language, grammar, or syntax?) between Chapter 1 and Chapter 2 of the Ski Lift version, a discontinuity that is not apparent in the Pedestrian version, where Chapter 1 and Chapter 2 seem to flow without a break (pardon the pun) in either the skill or the activity levels (subtexts?).

34   Actually *doing* Chapter 1 in the Pedestrian version confers skills required to do Chapter 2. The Ski Lift version, though lacking the activity that allows the acquisition of the necessary skills, implicitly assumes their presence.

35   A textual analysis would notice the changes as well as the new, unstated, and possibly unwarranted, assumptions. One could request clarification through footnotes or other editorial devices in order to draw attention to the significant changes between apparently identical texts (plots).

36   This discussion is not intended as an argument against ski lifts but a plea for clarity, using as a case in point a simple and transparent illustration. Yet any good analysis of a simple situation ought to identify structural elements, signifiers of discontinuities or conceptual gaps, that could be transferred to more general and complex considerations.

37   In my second example, I would like to extend the ski lift analysis to the much more complex situation of external aids to teaching and learning; i.e., to the realm of the development and transfer of knowledge and understanding.

38   Of course, there have always been external aids to teaching and learning: books and dictionaries, mathematical tables, charts and slide rules. But the scope and capacity of modern computers and their linking must be seen as much more than a vast increase in the number of standard aids and their uses. The structure of teaching and learning has so changed that we may want to examine the new text of education and compare it to the previous version.

39   For the sake of transparency, I would like to confine myself to certain aspects of education in a school setting, in particular the introduction of electronic spellers and calculators or their equivalents into the classroom.

40   Looking at the situation as a *text*, one can again discern a specific task: the mastery of spelling or the competency to carry out a mathematical operation. As before, the tasks involve an activity level (i.e., learning) and a skill component (i.e., applying what has been learned).

41   The specific tasks arise within a larger context, be it writing and composition, be it setting and solving numerical or mathematical problems. As in the ski lift case, part of the larger task can be accomplished today by external devices. Therefore, the consequences of the task-related skills (spelling and calculating correctly) are presumed to be present in spite of by-passing the task-related activities of how to do these things.

42   One of the questions arising from the new technological possibilities is this: how is the overall text, its content, its internal logic and consistency, its credibility, and conclusions, affected by the external task substitutions and transpositions?

To answer these questions, we will have to go back to the main text of education in which the specific tasks are embedded.

43   In the context of this analysis I will define the purpose of classroom education as the growth of the student's knowledge and understanding. Thus, the tasks of spelling and calculating correctly are only part of the plot/story of the text.

44   In the ski lift case, mechanizing the ascent may leave the skier with inadequate skills for a safe descent. The classroom case is similar, though less transparent. The activities related to learning how to spell and calculate teach more than mastering the tasks at hand. They include implicit lessons for the student on how to work in a group and to learn how to learn, as well as lessons in tolerance and anger management, in inventiveness and response. Such implicit social learning has to be accomplished, even if the explicit tasks of spelling and calculating can be relegated forever to external devices.

45   Physical injuries resulting from the imprudent use of ski lifts can be identified relatively easily and remedial measures can be undertaken. But do we have to await potential social injuries and their tracing back to changes in explicit and implicit learning, before discussing the new teaching technologies or supplementing them with new sources of skills? Can one not analyze the changes in "syntax" of the new text of education — as text — to illuminate its structure, gaps or discontinuities and compare this text to other texts with similar plots/stories?

46   Other examples that I could give you, such as the use of electronic communications and transactions,[10] are of greater complexity, but I could see them being analyzed and discussed in terms of elements and motives identifiable in the simpler cases.

47   Here again comes my plea to colleagues in the humanities for their help. Serious methodological research into technology as text would be brain intensive, but not capital intensive. It would promote a new kind of inter- and transdisciplinarity and encourage a fundamental approach to our most relevant problems.

48   Canada, as a country, could provide many examples for such a textual analysis of technology: examples of new practices, novel ways of doing things as well as of their structuring impacts. Such examples might range from roads vs. railways to radio, telephone, fax, and internet penetration of both the North and the southern parts of our country. Both the French and the English language analysis of the realm of "declaring" is well represented among our colleagues and I am confident that they will be able to adapt their scholarship to the realm of "doing."

Notes:

1. Franklin, U.M. *The Real World of Technology*. Toronto: House of Anansi Press, 1990.

2. Azimov, Isaac. (illustrations by Jean Mark Cote) *Futuredays*. London: Virgin Books, 1986.

3. Coalition against Technological Unemployment. Toronto, 1997.

4. Mumford, Lewis. *The Myth of the Machine: Technics and Human Development*. New York: Harcourt Brace Jovanovich, 1967.

5. Foucault, Michel. *The Order of Things*. New York: Random House, 1970.

6. Bertalanffy, Ludwig von. *General System Theory*. New York: Braziller, rev. 1973.

7. Ellul, Jacques. *The Technological Society*. New York: Knopf, 1964.
   ———. *The Technological System*. New York: Continuum, 1980.

8. See for instance, *Chaos and Order: Complex Dynamics of Literature and Science*, ed. N. Katherine Hayes. Chicago: University of Chicago Press, 1991, particularly the editor's introduction.
   Latour, Bruno, *Science in Action*. Milton Keynes, U.K.: Open University Press, 1988.

9. Bateson, Gregory. *Steps to an Ecology of Mind*. New York: Ballantine, 1972.
   Poulson, William R. *The Noise of Culture*. Ithaca: Cornell University Press, 1988.

10. Franklin, U.M. *Every Tool Shapes Its Task*. Vancouver: Chapbooks, 1997.
    ———. "Beyond the Hype," *Leadership in Health Services* July/August, 1996, 14–18.

Topics for consideration:

1. Franklin's analogy of the ski lift and her examples of spell-checks and pocket calculators point to the phenomenon of "de-skilling" as a result of technological innovations. What other examples of de-skilling induced by new technology can you think of?

2. In this essay and in *The Real World of Technology*, Franklin uses the analogy of technology as "the house in which we all live." Continually under reconstruction, "more and more of human life takes place within its walls, so that today there is hardly any human activity that does not occur within this house." How appropriate do you find this analogy? How far can it be extended?

Further reading:

Heather Menzies, *Whose Brave New World? The Information Highway and the New Economy* (1995). An investigation into the impact of technology in everyday life and work experience.

Langdon Winner, *The Whale and the Reactor: A Search for Limits in an Age of High Technology* (1988). An analysis of the social impact of technology.

Wayne Ellwood

Wayne Ellwood is Canadian editor of New Internationalist, *where this essay originally appeared.*

Despite their association with "progress," and however seductive their appeal, computers are changing our world in unintended ways, argues Wayne Ellwood in this essay. They promote unfettered financial speculation, they desensitize us to the reality of war, and they centralize power. Most alarmingly, the fully computerized workplace is one without workers.

SEDUCED BY TECHNOLOGY

1   My neighbour, Nick, is a soft-spoken, easy-going fellow who owns a big, ungainly hound named Duffy and has a passion for music. He's been a freelance musician all his adult life and plays the double bass for a living — an imposing, upright, stringed instrument that's virtually the same size as he is. But things have changed in the music business: it's not as easy to earn a living as a freelance musician today as it was a few years ago.

2   A lot of the well-paid 'session work' (making commercials and advertising jingles) has disappeared and been replaced by pre-programed, computerized synthesizers. Nick still plays in the 'pit' when he can — in splashy, touring musicals like *Miss Saigon* or *Phantom of the Opera*. But today he also works part-time in a music store, helping to ship out trumpets and French horns to school bands and re-stocking inventory when new shipments arrive.

3   Nick is not untypical these days. In fact his story is just one of millions that unveil the other side of the computer revolution — the human costs and consequences of the new 'wired world' which receive little attention from government bureaucrats or industry boosters.

4   Fantastic, science-fiction tinged claims about the benefits of the coming 'information age' are hard to escape. The press is full of hacks extolling the liberating virtues of electronic mail and tub-thumping about how the Internet will unite the masses in a sort of electronic, Jeffersonian democracy (at least those with a personal computer, modem and enough spare cash to pay the monthly hook-up fee).

5   'If you snooze, you lose' is the underlying message. Jump on board now or be brushed aside as the new high-tech era reshapes the contours of modern life. This is not the first time that technology has been packaged as a panacea for social progress. I can still recall a youthful Ronald Reagan touting for General Electric on American television back in the 1950s: 'Progress is our most important product,' the future President intoned.

6   That ideology of progress is welded as firmly to computers in the 1990s as it was to the power-loom in the early nineteenth century, the automobile in the 1920s or nuclear power in the 1960s. Yet the introduction of all these technologies had disastrous side effects. The power-loom promised cheap clothing and a wealthier Britain but produced catastrophic social dislocation and job loss. The

car promised independence and freedom and delivered expressways choked with traffic, suburbanization, air pollution and destructive wars fought over oil supplies. Nuclear power promised energy 'too cheap to meter' and produced Chernobyl and Three Mile Island.

7   There is a lesson here that can and should be applied to all new technologies — and none more so than computers. One of the century's more astute analysts of communications technologies, Marshall McLuhan, said it best: 'We shape our tools and thereafter our tools shape us.' In his cryptic way McLuhan was simply summing up what a small band of dogged critics have been saying for decades. Technology is not just hardware — whether it's a hammer, an axe or a desk-top PC with muscular RAM and a pentium chip. Limiting it in this way wrenches technology from its social roots. The conclusion? It's not 'things' that are the problem, it's people.

8   This has the simple attraction of common sense. Yet the more complex truth is that technologies carry the imprint of the cultures from which they issue. They arise out of a system, a social structure: 'They are grafted on to it,' argues Canadian scientist Ursula Franklin, 'and they may reinforce or destroy it, often in ways that are neither foreseen or foreseeable.'[1] What this means is that technology is never neutral. Even seemingly benign technologies can have earth-shaking, unintended, social consequences.

9   The American writer Richard Sclove outlines what happened when water was piped into the homes of villagers in Ibieca in north-eastern Spain in the early 1970s. The village fountain soon disappeared as the centre of community life when families gradually bought washing machines and women were released from scrubbing laundry by hand. But at the same time the village's social bonds began to fray. Women no longer shared grievances and gossip together; when men stopped using their donkeys to haul water the animals were seen as uneconomical. Tractors began to replace donkeys for field work, thus increasing the villagers' dependence on outside jobs to earn cash needed to pay for their new machines. The villagers opted for convenience and productivity. But, concludes Sclove: 'They didn't reckon on the hidden costs of deepening inequality, social alienation and community dissolution.'[2]

10   When it comes to introducing new technologies we need to look less at how they influence our lives as individuals and more at how they impact on society as a whole. Let's consider computers for a moment. Over the last decade new technologies based on micro-electronics and digitized data have completely changed the way information is transmitted and stored. And word processors and electronic mail have made writing and sending messages around the globe both cheap and quick. 'Surfing the net' (clicking around the Internet in a random fashion for fun and entertainment) has become the fashionable way to spend your leisure time. But these are benefits filtered through the narrow prism of personal gain.

11   What happens when we step back and examine the broad social impact? How else are computers used? Let's look at just four examples:

The money maze: The computer that allows us to withdraw cash from an automatic teller, day or night, is the same technology that makes possible the international capital market. Freed from the shackles of government regulation corporate money managers now shift billions of dollars a day around the globe. 'Surfing the yield curve,' big money speculators can move funds at lightning speed, day and night — destabilizing national economies and sucking millions out of productive long-term investment. The global foreign-exchange trade alone is now estimated at more than $1.3 billion a day.

Computer games: They come in all shapes and sizes and you can find them as easily in Kuala Lumpur as in Santiago or Harare. They vary from the jolt-a-second, shoot-'em-up games (often offensively sexist) to the mesmerizing hand-held and usually more innocuous variety. Now think of 'Desert Storm', the world's first (and certainly not the last) electronic war. Lethal firepower as colourful blips on our TV screens, charred bodies reduced to the arcing trail of an explosive starburst.

The ability to kill and maim large numbers of our fellow human beings is not a new skill. We've been able to destroy human life many times over for more than half a century and computers have not changed that reality. What they have done is sideline human decision-making in favour of computer programs — making catastrophe ever more likely. As one software engineer has pointed out, complex computer programs require maintenance just like mechanical systems. The problem is that 'every feature that is added and every bug that is fixed adds the possibility of some new interaction between parts of the program' — thus making the software less rather than more reliable.[3]

Information as power: This is the mantra of those who suggest that both the Internet and the World Wide Web will establish a new on-line paradigm of decentralized power, placing real tools for liberation into the hands of the marginalized and the poor. That's a tall order but it is nonetheless true that the new communications technologies can be used positively by political dissidents and human-rights activists. Examples abound. At the 1995 UN Conference on Women in Beijing the proceedings were posted instantaneously over the Net thus bringing thousands of women, who would have otherwise been left out, into the discussions.

This 'high-tech jujitsu', as critic Jerry Mander calls it is both valiant and necessary. But it doesn't change the key fact that computers contribute more to centralization than to decentralization. They help activists, but they help the centralizing forces of corporate globalization even more. This is what the communications theorist Harold Innis described as the 'bias' of technology in the modern era. Computers, as the most powerful of modern communications tools, reflect their commercial and military origins.

Efficiency and employment: Technology has always destroyed jobs. In the economy of industrial society that is its main purpose — to replace labour with machines, thereby reducing the unit cost of production while increasing both productivity and efficiency. In theory this spurs growth: producing more and better jobs, higher wages and an increased standard of living. This is the credo of orthodox economics and there are still many true believers.

12   But evidence to support this view in the real world of technology is fading fast. More widespread is the pattern detailed in a recent Statistics Canada report which underlined the growth of a 'two-tiered' labour market in that country. On the top tier: long hours of overtime by educated, experienced and relatively well-paid workers. And on the bottom: a large group of low-paid, unskilled and part-time workers 'who can be treated as roughly interchangeable'.[4] And then there are those who miss out altogether — the chronic jobless, the socially marginalized who form a permanent and troubling underclass.

13   This same trend is repeated throughout the industrialized world. In the US, author Jeremy Rifkin says less than 12 per cent of Americans will work in factories within a decade and less than two per cent of the global work force will be engaged in factory work by the year 2020. 'Near-workerless factories and virtual companies' are already looming on the horizon, Rifkin claims. The result? 'Every nation will have to grapple with the question of what to do with the millions of people whose labour is needed less or not at all in an ever-more-automated economy.'[5]

14   Computerization is at the core of the slimmed down, re-engineered workplace that free-market boosters claim is necessary to survive the lean-and-mean global competition of the 1990s. Even factory jobs that have relocated to the Third World are being automated quickly. In the long run machines will do little to absorb the millions of young people in Asia, Africa and Latin America who will be searching for work in the coming decades. Slowly, that sobering fact is beginning to strike home. A Chinese government official recently warned that unemployment in the world's most populous nation could leap to 268 million by the turn of the century as Chinese industries modernize and automate.

15   In the long run computers don't eliminate work, they eliminate workers. But in a social system based on the buying and selling of commodities this may have an even more pernicious effect. With fewer jobs there is less money in circulation; market demand slackens, re-inforcing recession and sending the economy into a tailspin. The impact of automation on jobs is a dilemma which can no longer be ignored.

16   Though thinkers in the green movement have been grappling with this issue for over a decade, most governments and even fewer business people are prepared to grasp the nettle. Both cling to the increasingly flimsy belief that economic growth spurred by an increasing consumption of the earth's finite resources will solve the problem. It won't. And serious questions need now to be raised about alternatives.

17   First, we need to think about democratizing the process of introducing new technologies into society and into the workplace. At the moment these decisions are left typically in the hands of bureaucrats and corporations who base their decisions on the narrow criteria of profit and loss. This blinkered mindset that equates technological innovation with social progress needs to be challenged.

18   But there is also the critical issue of the distribution of work and income in a world where waged labour is in a steady, inexorable decline. We can't continue to punish and stigmatize those who are unable to find jobs just because there aren't enough to go around. Instead, we need to think creatively about how to redefine work so that people can find self-esteem and social acceptance outside

of wage labour. This may mean redesigning jobs so that workers have more control and input into decisions about which technologies to adopt and what products to make. Up to now this has been exclusively a management prerogative. But it also means developing strategies to cut the average work week — without cutting pay. This would be one way of sharing the wealth created by new technology and of creating jobs at the same time. The Canadian Paperworkers Union has been a leader in this area. Hard work also needs to go into designing a plan for a guaranteed annual social wage. This is a radical (some would say outrageous) idea for societies like ours that have anchored their value systems on the bedrock of wage labour.

19   But how can we deny people the basic rights of citizenship and physical wellbeing simply because the economic system is no longer capable of providing for them?

Notes:

1. *The Real World of Technology*, Ursula Franklin, Anansi Press, Toronto, 1990.

2. 'Making Technology Democratic', Richard Sclove, from *Resisting the Virtual Life*, ed. James Brook and Iain Boal, City Lights, San Francisco, 1995.

3. *Why Things Bite Back: Technology and the Revenge of Unintended Consequences*, Edward Tenner, Knopf, New York, 1996.

4. *Canadian Economic Observer*, Statistics Canada, July/96.

5. *The End of Work*, Jeremy Rifkin, Putnam Publishers, New York, 1995.

Topics for consideration:

1. Ellwood suggests that the computer is to our time what the power loom was to the early nineteenth century, what the car was to the 1920s and what nuclear power was to the 1960s. In what ways are the consequences of these technologies similar and how do they differ?

2. "We shape our tools, and thereafter our tools shape us," wrote Marshall McLuhan. In what ways does the computer as tool shape our experience of the world?

3. Ellwood cites the example of the many unforeseen results of providing piped water to a village in northeast Spain. What other examples can you think of where the introduction of a single technological innovation led to a chain of unintended consequences?

4. Ellwood predicts that mass unemployment is only one of the likeliest effects of the computer revolution. What is the scenario on which this prediction is based? How likely is it?

Further reading:

James Brook and Iain Boal, eds., *Resisting the Virtual Life* (1995)

Edward Tenner, *Why Things Bite Back* (1996)

David Noble (1945-

David Noble is a historian who teaches in the Department of Social Sciences at York University. He is author of Progress Without People: New Technology, Unemployment, and the Message of Resistance *(1995) and* The Religion of Technology: The Divinity of Man and the Spirit of Invention *(1998).*

More extensive use of computers and on-line course materials in universities and colleges is often assumed to enhance learning and offer wider access. In practice, however, David Noble argues, this form of automation is being forced on students and faculty by commercial interests who profit from the sale of "educational products."

DIGITAL DIPLOMA MILLS: THE AUTOMATION OF HIGHER EDUCATION

1   Recent events at two large North American universities signal dramatically that we have entered a new era in higher education, one which is rapidly drawing the halls of academe into the age of automation. In mid-summer of 1997 the UCLA administration launched its historic "Instructional Enhancement Initiative" requiring computer Web sites for all of its arts and sciences courses by the start of the Fall term, the first time that a major university has made mandatory the use of computer telecommunications technology in the delivery of higher education. In partnership with several private corporations (including the Times Mirror Company, parent of the Los Angeles *Times*), moreover, UCLA has spawned its own for-profit company, headed by a former UCLA vice chancellor, to peddle online education (the Home Education Network).

2   In the spring of 1997 in Toronto, meanwhile, the full-time faculty of York University, Canada's third largest, ended an historic two-month strike having secured for the first time anywhere formal contractual protection against precisely the kind of administrative action being taken by UCLA. The unprecedented faculty job action, the longest university strike in English Canadian history, was taken partly in response to unilateral administrative initiatives in the implementation of instructional technology, the most egregious example of which was an official solicitation to private corporations inviting them to permanently place their logo on a university online course in return for a $10,000 contribution to courseware development. As at UCLA, the York University administration has spawned its own subsidiary (Cultech), directed by the vice president for research and several deans and dedicated, in collaboration with a consortium of private sector firms, to the commercial development and exploitation of online education.

3   Significantly, at both UCLA and York, the presumably cyber-happy students have given clear indication that they are not exactly enthusiastic about the prospect of a high-tech academic future, recommending against the Initiative at UCLA and at York lending their support to striking faculty and launching their

own independent investigation of the commercial, pedagogical, and ethical implications of online educational technology. The student handbook distributed annually to all students by the York Federation of Students contained a warning about the dangers of online education.   —

THE CLASSROOM VS THE BOARDROOM

4   Thus, at the very outset of this new age of higher education, the lines have already been drawn in the struggle which will ultimately determine its shape. On the one side university administrators and their myriad commercial partners, on the other those who constitute the core relation of education: students and teachers. (The chief slogan of the York faculty during the strike was "the classroom vs the boardroom"). It is no accident, then, that the high-tech transformation of higher education is being initiated and implemented from the top down, either without any student and faculty involvement in the decision-making or despite it. At UCLA the administration launched their Initiative during the summer when many faculty are away and there was little possibility of faculty oversight or governance; faculty were thus left out of the loop and kept in the dark about the new web requirement until the last moment.

5   UCLA administrators also went ahead with its Initiative, which is funded by a new compulsory student fee, despite the formal student recommendation against it. Similarly the initiatives of the York administration in the deployment of computer technology in education were taken without faculty oversight and deliberation much less student involvement. What is driving this headlong rush to implement new technology with so little regard for deliberation of the pedagogical and economic costs and at the risk of student and faculty alienation and opposition? A short answer might be the fear of getting left behind, the incessant pressures of "progress." But there is more to it. For the universities are not simply undergoing a technological transformation. Beneath that change, and camouflaged by it, lies another: the commercialization of higher education. For here as elsewhere technology is but a vehicle and a disarming disguise.

6   The major change to befall the universities over the last two decades has been the identification of the campus as a significant site of capital accumulation, a change in social perception which has resulted in the systematic conversion of intellectual activity into intellectual capital and, hence, intellectual property. There have been two general phases of this transformation. The first, which began twenty years ago and is still underway, entailed the commoditization of the research function of the university, transforming scientific and engineering knowledge into commercially viable proprietary products that could be owned and bought and sold in the market. The second, which we are now witnessing, entails the commoditization of the educational function of the university, transforming courses into courseware, the activity of instruction itself into commercially viable proprietary products that can be owned and bought and sold in the market. In the first phase the universities became the site of production and sale of patents and exclusive licenses. In the second, they are becoming the site of production of — as well as the chief market for — copyrighted videos, courseware, CD-ROMs, and Web sites.

7   The first phase began in the mid-1970s when, in the wake of the oil crisis and intensifying international competition, corporate and political leaders of the major industrialized countries of the world recognized that they were losing their monopoly over the world's heavy industries and that, in the future, their supremacy would depend upon their monopoly over the knowledge which had become the lifeblood of the new so-called "knowledge-based" industries (space, electronics, computers, materials, telecommunications, and bioengineering). This focus upon "intellectual capital" turned their attention to the universities as its chief source, implicating the universities as never before in the economic machinery. In the view of capital, the universities had become too important to be left to the universities. Within a decade there was a proliferation of industrial partnerships and new proprietary arrangements, as industrialists and their campus counterparts invented ways to socialize the risks and costs of creating this knowledge while privatizing the benefits. This unprecedented collaboration gave rise to an elaborate web of interlocking directorates between corporate and academic boardrooms and the foundation of joint lobbying efforts epitomized by the work of the Business-Higher Education Forum. The chief accomplishment of the combined effort, in addition to a relaxation of anti-trust regulations and greater tax incentives for corporate funding of university research, was the 1980 reform of the patent law which for the first time gave the universities automatic ownership of patents resulting from federal government grants. Laboratory knowledge now became patents, that is Intellectual capital and intellectual property. As patent holding companies, the universities set about at once to codify their intellectual property policies, develop the infrastructure for the conduct of commercially-viable research, cultivate their corporate ties, and create the mechanisms for marketing their new commodity, exclusive licenses to their patents. The result of this first phase of university commoditization was a wholesale reallocation of university resources toward its research function at the expense of its educational function.

8   Class sizes swelled, teaching staffs and instructional resources were reduced, salaries were frozen, and curricular offerings were cut to the bone. At the same time, tuition soared to subsidize the creation and maintenance of the commercial infrastructure (and correspondingly bloated administration) that has never really paid off. In the end students were paying more for their education and getting less, and the campuses were in crisis.[1]

9   The second phase of the commercialization of academia, the commoditization of instruction, is touted as the solution to the crisis engendered by the first. Ignoring the true sources of the financial debacle — an expensive and low-yielding commercial infrastructure and greatly expanded administrative costs — the champions of computer-based instruction focus their attention rather upon increasing the efficiencies of already overextended teachers. And they ignore as well the fact that their high-tech remedies are bound only to compound the problem, increasing further, rather then reducing, the costs of higher education. (Experience to date demonstrates clearly that computer-based teaching, with its limitless demands upon instructor time and vastly expanded overhead requirements — equipment, upgrades, maintenance, and technical and administrative support staff — costs more not less than traditional education, whatever the reductions in direct labor, hence the need for outside funding and student technology fees).

Little wonder, then, that teachers and students are reluctant to embrace this new panacea. Their hesitation reflects not fear but wisdom.[2]

THE BIRTH OF EDUCATIONAL MAINTENANCE ORGANIZATIONS

10 But this second transformation of higher education is not the work of teachers or students, the presumed beneficiaries of improved education, because it is not really about education at all. That's just the name of the market. The foremost promoters of this transformation are rather the vendors of the network hardware, software, and "content" — Apple, IBM, Bell, the cable companies, Microsoft, and the edutainment and publishing companies Disney, Simon and Schuster, Prentice-Hall, et al. — who view education as a market for their wares, a market estimated by the Lehman Brothers investment firm potentially to be worth several hundred billion dollars. "Investment opportunity in the education industry has never been better," one of their reports proclaimed, indicating that this will be "the focus industry" for lucrative investment in the future, replacing the health care industry. (The report also forecasts that the educational market will eventually become dominated by EMOs — education maintenance organizations — just like HMO's in the health care market). It is important to emphasize that, for all the democratic rhetoric about extending educational access to those unable to get to the campus, the campus remains the real market for these products, where students outnumber their distance learning counterparts six-to-one.

11   In addition to the vendors, corporate training advocates view online education as yet another way of bringing their problem-solving, information-processing, "just-in-time" educated employees up to profit-making speed. Beyond their ambitious in-house training programs, which have incorporated computer-based instructional methods pioneered by the military, they envision the transformation of the delivery of higher education as a means of supplying their properly-prepared personnel at public expense.

12   The third major promoters of this transformation are the university administrators, who see it as a way of giving their institutions a fashionably forward-looking image. More importantly, they view computer-based instruction as a means of reducing their direct labor and plant maintenance costs — fewer teachers and classrooms — while at the same time undermining the autonomy and independence of faculty. At the same time, they are hoping to get a piece of the commercial action for their institutions or themselves, as vendors in their own right of software and content. University administrators are supported in this enterprise by a number of private foundations, trade associations, and academic-corporate consortia which are promoting the use of the new technologies with increasing intensity. Among these are the Sloan, Mellon, Pew, and Culpeper Foundations, the American Council on Education, and, above all, Educom, a consortium representing the management of 600 colleges and universities and a hundred private corporations.

13   Last but not least, behind this effort are the ubiquitous technozealots who simply view computers as the panacea for everything, because they like to play with them. With the avid encouragement of their private sector and university patrons, they forge ahead, without support for their pedagogical claims about the alleged

enhancement of education, without any real evidence of productivity improvement, and without any effective demand from either students or teachers.

14   In addition to York and UCLA, universities throughout North America are rapidly being overtaken by this second phase of commercialization. There are the stand-alone virtual institutions like University of Phoenix, the wired private institutions like the New School for Social Research, the campuses of state universities like the University of Maryland and the new Gulf-Coast campus of the University of Florida (which boasts no tenure). On the state level, the states of Arizona and California have initiated their own state-wide virtual university projects, while a consortia of western "Smart States" have launched their own ambitious effort to wire all of their campuses into an online educational network. In Canada, a national effort has been undertaken, spearheaded by the Telelearning Research Network centered at Simon Fraser University in Vancouver, to bring most of the nation's higher education institutions into a "Virtual U" network.

15   The overriding commercial intent and market orientation behind these initiatives is explicit, as is illustrated by the most ambitious U. S. effort to date, the Western Governors' Virtual University Project, whose stated goals are to "expand the marketplace for instructions materials, courseware, and programs utilizing advanced technology," "expand the marketplace for demonstrated competence," and "identify and remove barriers to the free functioning of these markets, particularly barriers posed by statutes, policies, and administrative rules and regulations."

16   "In the future," Utah governor Mike Leavitt proclaimed, "an institution of higher education will become a little like a local television station." Start up funds for the project come from the private sector, specifically from Educational Management Group, the educational arm of the world's largest educational publisher Simon and Schuster and the proprietary impulse behind their largesse is made clear by Simon and Schuster CEO Jonathan Newcomb: "The use of interactive technology is causing a fundamental shift away from the physical classroom toward anytime, anywhere learning — the model for post secondary education in the twenty-first century." This transformation is being made possible by "advances in digital technology, coupled with the protection of copyright in cyberspace."

17   Similarly, the national effort to develop the "Virtual U" customized educational software platform in Canada is directed by an industrial consortium which includes Kodak, IBM, Microsoft, McGraw-Hill, Prentice-Hall, Rogers Cablesystems, Unitel, Novasys, Nortel, Bell Canada, and MPR Teltech, a research subsidiary of GTE. The commercial thrust behind the project is explicit here too. Predicting a potential fifty billion dollar Canadian market, the project proposal emphasizes the adoption of "an intellectual property policy that will encourage researchers and industry to commercialize their innovations" and anticipates the development of "a number of commercially marketable hardware and software products and services," including "courseware and other learning products." The two directors of the project, Simon Fraser University professors, have formed their own company to peddle these products in collaboration with the university. At the same time, the nearby University of British Columbia has recently spun off the private WEB-CT company to peddle its own educational Web site software, WEB-CT, the software designed by one of its computer science professors and now being used by UCLA. In recent months, WEB-CT has entered into

production and distribution relationships with Silicon Graphics and Prentice-Hall and is fast becoming a major player in the American as well as Canadian higher education market. As of the beginning of the Fall term, WEB-CT licensees now include, in addition to UCLA and California State University, the Universities of Georgia, Minnesota, Illinois, North Carolina, and Indiana, as well as such private institutions as Syracuse, Brandeis, and Duquesne.

EDUCATION AS A COMMODITY

18 The implications of the commoditization of university instruction are two-fold in nature, those relating to the university as a site of the production of the commodities and those relating to the university as a market for them. The first raises for the faculty traditional labor issues about the introduction of new technologies of production. The second raises for students major questions about costs, coercion, privacy, equity, and the quality of education.

19 With the commoditization of instruction, teachers as labor are drawn into a production process designed for the efficient creation of instructional commodities, and hence become subject to all the pressures that have befallen production workers in other industries undergoing rapid technological transformation from above. In this context faculty have much more in common with the historic plight of other skilled workers than they care to acknowledge. Like these others, their activity is being restructured, via the technology, in order to reduce their autonomy, independence, and control over their work and to place workplace knowledge and control as much as possible into the hands of the administration. As in other industries, the technology is being deployed by management primarily to discipline, de-skill, and displace labor.

20 Once faculty and courses go online, administrators gain much greater direct control over faculty performance and course content than ever before and the potential for administrative scrutiny, supervision, regimentation, discipline and even censorship increase dramatically. At the same time, the use of the technology entails an inevitable extension of working time and an intensification of work as faculty struggle at all hours of the day and night to stay on top of the technology and respond, via chat rooms, virtual office hours, and e-mail, to both students and administrators to whom they have now become instantly and continuously accessible. The technology also allows for much more careful administrative monitoring of faculty availability, activities, and responsiveness.

21 Once faculty put their course material online, moreover, the knowledge and course design skill embodied in that material is taken out of their possession, transferred to the machinery and placed in the hands of the administration. The administration is now in a position to hire less skilled, and hence cheaper, workers to deliver the technologically prepackaged course. It also allows the administration, which claims ownership of this commodity, to peddle the course elsewhere without the original designer's involvement or even knowledge, much less financial interest. The buyers of this packaged commodity, meanwhile, other academic institutions, are able thereby to contract out, and hence outsource, the work of their own employees and thus reduce their reliance upon their in-house teaching staff.

22   Skeptical faculty insist that what they do cannot possibly be automated, and they are right. But it will be automated anyway, whatever the loss in educational quality. Because education, again, is not what all this is about; it's about making money. In short, the new technology of education, like the automation of other industries, robs faculty of their knowledge and skills, their control over their working lives, the product of their labor, and, ultimately, their means of livelihood.

23   None of this is speculation. This Fall the UCLA faculty, at administration request, have dutifully or grudgingly (it doesn't really matter which) placed their course work — ranging from just syllabi and assignments to the entire body of course lectures and notes — at the disposal of their administration, to be used online, without asking who will own it much less how it will eventually be used and with what consequences. At York University, untenured faculty have been required to put their courses on video, CD-ROM or the Internet or lose their job. They have then been hired to teach their own now automated course at a fraction of their former compensation. The New School in New York now routinely hires outside contractors from around the country, mostly unemployed PhDs, to design online courses. The designers are not hired as employees but are simply paid a modest flat fee and are required to surrender to the university all rights to their course. The New School then offers the course without having to employ anyone. And this is just the beginning.

24   Educom, the academic-corporate consortium, has recently established their Learning Infrastructure Initiative which includes the detailed study of what professors do, breaking the faculty job down in classic Tayloristic fashion into discrete tasks, and determining what parts can be automated or outsourced. Educom believes that course design, lectures, and even evaluation can all be standardized, mechanized, and consigned to outside commercial vendors. "Today you're looking at a highly personal human-mediated environment," Educom president Robert Heterich observed. "The potential to remove the human mediation in some areas and replace it with automation — smart, computer-based, network-based systems is tremendous. It's gotta happen."

25   Toward this end, university administrators are coercing or enticing faculty into compliance, placing the greatest pressures on the most vulnerable untenured and part-time faculty, and entry-level and prospective employees. They are using the academic incentive and promotion structure to reward cooperation and discourage dissent. At the same time they are mounting an intensifying propaganda campaign to portray faculty as incompetent, hide-bound, recalcitrant, inefficient, ineffective, and expensive — in short, in need of improvement or replacement through instructional technologies. Faculty are portrayed above all as obstructionist, as standing in the way of progress and forestalling the panacea of virtual education allegedly demanded by students, their parents, and the public.

26   The York University faculty had heard it all. Yet still they fought vigorously and ultimately successfully to preserve quality education and protect themselves from administrative assault. During their long strike they countered such administration propaganda with the truth about what was happening to higher education and eventually won the support of students, the media, and the public. Most important, they secured a new contract containing unique and unprecedented provisions which, if effectively enforced, give faculty members direct and

unambiguous control over all decisions relating to the automation of instruction, including veto power. According to the contract, all decisions regarding the use of technology as a supplement to classroom instruction or as a means of alternative delivery (including the use of video, CD-ROM's, Internet Web sites, computer-mediated conferencing, etc.) "shall be consistent with the pedagogic and academic judgments and principles of the faculty member employee as to the appropriateness of the use of technology in the circumstances." The contract also guarantees that "a faculty member will not be required to convert a course without his or her agreement." Thus, the York faculty will be able to ensure that the new technology, if and when used, will contribute to a genuine enhancement rather than a degradation of the quality of education, while at the same time preserving their positions, their autonomy, and their academic freedom. The battle is far from won, but it is a start.

STUDENT REACTIONS

27 The second set of implications stemming from the commoditization of instruction involves the transformation of the university into a market for the commodities being produced. Administrative propaganda routinely alludes to an alleged student demand for the new instructional products. At UCLA officials are betting that their high-tech agenda will be "student driven," as students insist that faculty make fuller use of the Web site technology in their courses. To date, however, there has been no such demand on the part of students, no serious study of it, and no evidence for it. Indeed, the few times students have been given a voice, they have rejected the initiatives hands down, especially when they were required to pay for it (the definition of effective demand, i.e. a market).

28 At UCLA, students recommended against the Instructional Enhancement Initiative. At the University of British Columbia, home of the WEB-CT software being used at UCLA, students voted in a referendum four-to-one against a similar initiative, despite a lengthy administration campaign promising them a more secure place in the high tech future. Administrators at both institutions have tended to dismiss, ignore, or explain away these negative student decisions, but there is a message here: students want the genuine face-to-face education they paid for not a cyber-counterfeit. Nevertheless, administrators at both UCLA and UBC decided to proceed with their agenda anyway, desperate to create a market and secure some return on their investment in the information technology infrastructure. Thus, they are creating a market by fiat, compelling students (and faculty) to become users and hence consumers of the hardware, software, and content products as a condition of getting an education, whatever their interest or ability to pay. Can all students equally afford this capital-intensive education?

29 Another key ethical issue relates to the use of student online activities. Few students realize that their computer-based courses are often thinly-veiled field trials for product and market development, that while they are studying their courses, their courses are studying them. In Canada, for example, universities have been given royalty-free licenses to Virtual U software in return for providing data on its use to the vendors. Thus, all online activity including communications between students and professors and among students are monitored,

automatically logged and archived by the system for use by the vendor. Students enrolled in courses using Virtual U software are in fact formally designated "experimental subjects." Because federal monies were used to develop the software and underwrite the field trials, vendors were compelled to comply with ethical guidelines on the experimental use of human subjects. Thus, all students once enrolled are required to sign forms releasing ownership and control of their online activities to the vendors. The form states "as a student using Virtual U in a course, I give my permission to have the computer-generated usage data, conference transcript data, and virtual artifacts data collected by the Virtual U software ... used for research, development, and demonstration purposes."

30   According to UCLA's Home Education Network president John Korbara, all of their distance learning courses are likewise monitored and archived for use by company officials. On the UCLA campus, according to Harlan Lebo of the Provost's office, student use of the course Web sites will be routinely audited and evaluated by the administration. Marvin Goldberg, designer of the UCLA WEB-CT software acknowledges that the system allows for "lurking" and automatic storage and retrieval of all online activities. How this capability will be used and by whom is not altogether clear, especially since Web sites are typically being constructed by people other than the instructors. What third parties (besides students and faculty in the course) will have access to the student's communications? Who will own student online contributions? What rights, if any, do students have to privacy and proprietary control of their work? Are they given prior notification as to the ultimate status of their online activities, so that they might be in a position to give, or withhold, their informed consent? If students are taking courses which are just experiments, and hence of unproven pedagogical value, should students be paying full tuition for them? And if students are being used as guinea pigs in product trials masquerading as courses, should they be paying for these courses or be paid to take them? More to the point, should students be content with a degraded, shadow cyber-education? In Canada student organizations have begun to confront these issues head on, and there are some signs of similar student concern emerging also in the U. S.

CONCLUSION

31   In his classic 1959 study of diploma mills for the American Council on Education, Robert Reid described the typical diploma mill as having the following characteristics: "no classrooms," "faculties are often untrained or nonexistent," and "the officers are unethical self-seekers whose qualifications are no better than their offerings." It is an apt description of the digital diploma mills now in the making. Quality higher education will not disappear entirely, but it will soon become the exclusive preserve of the privileged, available only to children of the rich and the powerful. For the rest of us a dismal new era of higher education has dawned. In ten years, we will look upon the wired remains of our once great democratic higher education system and wonder how we let it happen. That is, unless we decide now not to let it happen.

Notes:

1. Tuition began to outpace inflation in the early 1980's, at precisely the moment when changes in the patent system enabled the universities to become major vendors of patent licenses. According to data compiled by the National Center for Educational Statistics, between 1976 and 1994 expenditures on research increased 21.7% at public research universities while expenditure on instruction decreased 9.5%. Faculty salaries, which had peaked in 1972, fell precipitously during the next decade and have since recovered only half the loss.

2. Recent surveys of the instructional use of information technology in higher education clearly indicate that there have been no significant gains in either productivity improvement or pedagogical enhancement. Kenneth C. Green, Director of the Campus Computing Project, which conducts annual surveys of information technology use in higher education, noted that "the campus experience over the past decade reveals that the dollars can be daunting, the return on investment highly uncertain." "We have yet to hear of an instance where the total costs (including all realistically amortized capital investments and development expenses, plus reasonable estimates for faculty and support staff time) associated with teaching some unit to some group of students actually decline while maintaining the quality of learning," Green wrote. On the matter of pedagogical effectiveness, Green noted that "the research literature offers, at best, a mixed review of often inconclusive results, at least when searching for traditional measures of statistical significance in learning outcomes."

Topics for consideration:

1. Noble quotes one enthusiast who looks forward to the university or college of the future being "like a television studio." What would be gained or lost by this?

2. Noble devotes most of his attention in this essay to the impact of computerization on the work experience of the faculty. What changes does it bring about in the experience of the students. Do these seem to you to be benefits or disadvantages?

3. The title of Noble's essay alludes to the radical changes in people's work experience during the Industrial Revolution of the nineteenth century. What parallels exist between the changes in higher education forced by computerization and the changes to production brought about in the "age of steam"?

4. One of Noble's headings is "The Classroom vs The Boardroom." Do corporate interests and "the market" have a place within universities and colleges? In what ways do corporate interests alter the ways in which teaching and learning take place?

Tony Leighton (1954-

Tony Leighton has written for Harrowsmith, Canadian Geographic *and* Equinox, *where this essay was first published in 1994.*

Digital imaging is rapidly replacing traditional photography in advertising and even in news coverage. Tony Leighton's essay explores the impact that this has on our confidence in the veracity of photographs. The infinitely manipulable image provided by digital photography, argues Leighton, is part of a profound shift in what our culture is prepared to accept as "real."

THE NEW NATURE

1   Of all the media coverage that has whirled around O.J. Simpson's indictment for murder, one image has had lingering impact. Shortly after Simpson's arrest on June 17, the Los Angeles Police Department released a now infamous photograph that appeared on the covers of both *Time* and *Newsweek*. It's not a particularly striking image. Simpson is being arraigned at a courthouse. He is obviously tired and shaken. What's significant is what *Time* did to it. The magazine's art department used a computer to "process" the image digitally, darkening Simpson's features and his day-old beard and making the background details appear indistinct and shadowy. The result is unmistakably sinister. *Time*'s Simpson looked more threatening than *Newsweek*'s.

2   Once discovered, *Time*'s use of computer manipulation was hotly criticized as a cheat on an unsuspecting public. But it's more than that. The Simpson episode reflects a broad trend in contemporary media that's giving rise to a new ethical debate. Thanks to the revolution of digital technology, the original source materials of many cultural media, including photographs, films, and recordings, can now be reshaped with amazing — and some say alarming — felicity. Reality can be transfigured with a few swift strokes of a keyboard. And it can be done with such skill that the difference between an authentic image or sound and a digitized fake is no longer recognizable.

3   For those who work in the fantasy business producing movies, commercials, pop records, or fine art, digital manipulation offers cost savings and enhanced creative power. But when it is used to alter, say, news photography, it has much darker implications. It can be argued that for every advancement of technology, there is a price to pay. With the digitization of photography, the price is veracity. We can no longer believe what we see.

4   "It's that old thing about 'photography never lies,'" says Doug Smith, a computer-support specialist at The Banff Centre for the Arts in Alberta, where resident artists are taught digital photography. "We know that photography lies, but we still rely on newspapers, television, and magazines for truthful information. I guess we have to trust somebody. If we know they are manipulating images, it becomes just another of the many things we have to mistrust."

5   Learning to mistrust may soon be a survival skill for the customers of media, one that forces us to break some very old habits of mind. "For a century and a

half ... photographs appeared to be reliably manufactured commodities, readily distinguishable from other types of depictions," wrote William J. Mitchell, a professor of architecture and media arts at the Massachusetts Institute of Technology (MIT), in the February 1994 issue of *Scientific American*. "The emergence of digital imaging has irrevocably subverted these certainties, forcing us all to adopt a far more wary and vigilant interpretive stance. ... We will have to take great care to sift the facts from the fictions and falsehoods."

6   Anyone who doubts the urgency of the issue need only consider a handful of classic digital ploys. Last February, *New York Newsday* showed Olympians Tonya Harding and Nancy Kerrigan skating "together" shortly after the famous bashed-knee incident. The photo was a composite, with the skaters stitched in place electronically. In the musical realm, Frank Sinatra sang "duets" on a recent compact disc with artists he never met, their voices recorded digitally, some transmitted with flawless clarity over telephone lines. In Hollywood, John Candy's last movie, *Wagons East*, unfinished at the time of his death, was completed with digitally cloned images of the actor inserted into essential scenes.

7   Historically, of course, the media have always been able to manipulate source materials one way or another. American Civil War battlefields were rigged with "dead" bodies by photographers drumming up sympathy for the Union's cause. Trying to rewrite history, Stalin had Trotsky expunged from a 1920 photograph that showed him at Lenin's side. What's the difference today? Those who altered photographs in the '20s used knives, light, silver-halide paper, and darkrooms, and only a handful of skilled specialists could work such magic. Today, with an hour of practice, you and I could do a much better job in a few minutes on a desktop computer.

8   Of all media, photography provides the most instructive look at both the seductive power and the haunting price of the new digital technology. When the content of a conventional photograph is stored as digital code, it is transformed from a static reflection of reality frozen on film and paper to a fluid bit stream that is as alterable as a fantasy. In fact, most of what you see in newspapers, magazines, and books these days are no longer photographs at all. They are digital images.

9   Put most simply, digital code is a binary, or "on-off" language, a kind of simplified alphabet with only two characters, O and I. Any computer program is a huge script of these two characters strung together into large, meaningful patterns that ultimately command a word-processing program to place letters on a screen, a spreadsheet to calculate, or a design program to display an automobile part in three dimensions.

10   Photographs enter the digital realm by way of a tool called a scanner. With a bar of intense light, it moves across a photograph, reading colours and details, breaking down the original image into thousands of tiny "picture elements," or "pixels," that are like the dots that make up a television screen. Pack together enough dots in sufficient density, and you have a picture. Once digitized, an image can be redescribed at will. In other words, it can be copied, transmitted, or altered with utter mathematical precision.

11   Working conventionally, a photographer must labour for hours in a darkroom to alter what a camera and film captured in the field. It is fussy, messy work to isolate certain elements in a photograph and then "dodge" them (deny

them light) to darken them in the final print or "burn" them (expose them to more light) to lighten them. Elaborate composites or montages used to require multiple exposures and manual contrivances, to say nothing of all the paper and caustic chemicals devoured in the process. "Now," says Doug Smith, "you can do and undo experimental changes ad infinitum without being in a dark-room, without expending materials, and without standing on your feet for hours and hours."

12   If you pay any attention to the popular media, you've probably seen the products of digital imaging. Practised photo manipulators have worked some cheeky digital deceptions: Hillary Rodham Clinton's head on the barely dressed body of a voluptuous young model (on the cover of *Spy* magazine). Arnold Schwarzenegger and Queen Elizabeth as black people and black director Spike Lee with white skin and green eyes (in *Colors*, a magazine published by Italian clothier Benetton). And Marilyn Monroe flirting arm-in-arm with Abraham Lincoln (on the cover of *Scientific American*). These images are astonishing and stand as the comic beginning of revolution in image control.

13   No organization has been quite as engaged in this technological leap as pho-tographic giant Eastman Kodak Company of Rochester, New York. Kodak recently hired chief executive officer George Fisher, who aims to find a new way for the company synonymous with the old way of taking pictures, the analogue way. Fisher's strategy is to focus Kodak's energies on the highly competitive fray of consumer electronics (copiers, printers, Photo CD players) and, of course, to transform Kodak into the company synonymous with digital imaging. In the lobby of Kodak Canada's corporate offices in Toronto's west end, the writing is liter-ally on the wall. The company's business lines are inscribed proudly on several mounted plaques: Printing and Publishing Imaging, Office Imaging, Professional Imaging, Consumer Imaging, Motion Picture and Television Imaging. Nowhere is the word "photography" used.

14   When asked whether photography is as good as dead, Neil Buchanan, the national sales manager of Kodak Canada's Digital Imaging Group, says no, con-ventional silver-halide photography will coexist with digital imaging for many years to come. "Technologies don't get displaced," he says. "They just reinvent themselves."

15   But at the very moment Buchanan is explaining film's importance, one of his colleagues in the same room is downloading an image that was captured moments ago on perhaps the single most subversive tool of the digital age: the filmless camera. Kodak's DCF 420 camera looks like a normal 35 mm model that a professional photographer might use. (And indeed, the main part of the body is a standard Nikon N90.) But inside it is the future of photography — a "charge-coupled device," or CCD array. A CCD is a chip composed of millions of micro-scopic light-sensing cells that generate millions of little electrical charges in proportion to the intensity of light that strikes them through the camera's lens. The charges are converted to numbers. The numbers describe pixels. In essence, the CCD snatches an image straight from the ether. The electronic image is then stored on a credit-card-sized cartridge that fits in an extension at the base of the camera. It can be downloaded directly to a computer or stored for later use.

16   The DCF 420 is not for you and me. It costs around $15,000. The image it

currently produces is not quite as sharp as a photograph, but it's not far off. And it's getting better with each new version of the camera.

17 The CCD is a key component in a whole digital desktop system contained in Kodak's demonstration room that can, in minutes, convert what we see around us into a finished colour print. No film. No chemicals. No monopolistic middlemen. No waiting. The system includes a Macintosh computer loaded with Adobe Photoshop software for altering digital images, a "continuous-tone digital-output device" for printing colour images straight from the computer, and if you want to store the images for later retrieval, Kodak's remarkable Photo CD technology that digitally encodes dozens of pictures on a compact disc.

18 Products such as Kodak's Photo CD and Adobe System's Photoshop are technological watersheds. They have, within the past five years or so, vaulted the entire field of image capture and manipulation through a critical barrier. Granted, not many photographers are working extensively in the medium just yet, considering the cost factors and the leap of faith involved in leaving silver and celluloid behind. But those who have gone digital are proving its huge potential.

19 "This is about creative control," says Burton Robson, Canadian director of Adobe Systems. "It's putting creative control in a photographer's hands or a designer's hands. Photographers can now provide concepts in advertising and promotions that couldn't be done before."

20 Toronto photographer Philip Rostron's advertising work is a case in point. He estimates that about 70 percent of his photography is now altered with digital-imaging software, gaining him a creative and financial edge. His work on a Chrysler Canada ad for instance, featured a photograph of a car apparently roaring around a turn in an attractive rural landscape. But it is a landscape of deception. The grassy fields in the background, originally a limp grey-green, were warmed up in Photoshop with the roasted autumnal tones of a chaparral. The sky, in reality a blue, was dramatized with beguiling purple. The car, actually photographed when stationary but jacked up on one side to suggest motion, was touched up with a slight digital blur at its back end to create the illusion of speed. Its paint job was raised to the high lustre of polished lacquer. And to finish things off, an intrusive-looking lamp post was simply vaporized. "You could stay on location for two years and not see that landscape," says Rostron. "And it's very hard to justify $20,000 of location photography with no guarantee that God will cooperate."

21 Rostron says he still works hard to take the best possible photographs. "The stronger the image that goes into the system," he says, "the better the final product that comes out." But he can rest a lot easier these days if a sky is pale or a model has a pimple. The computer will forgive the imperfections.

22 Digital technology has had a similar effect on Louis Fishauf, a partner in Reactor Art & Design, one of Toronto's best-known graphic-design studios. Fishauf works exclusively on a Macintosh, frequently in Photoshop, and increasingly with Kodak's Photo CD. "The major change," says Fishauf, "has been that the whole process of design can now be telescoped into days, even hours, and be accomplished by one person."

23 Canada Post Corporation recently hired Reactor to create a stamp and commemorative booklet to honour the 125th anniversary of The T. Eaton Company

Limited. With access to a vast trove of Eaton's memorabilia from the Archives of Ontario, Fishauf and his associate, Stephanie Power, decided to do both the stamp and booklet in collage style, displaying as many old photos and illustrations as possible. They selected more than 300 items from the archives and had them photographed on 35 mm slides. All 300 images were then digitized onto Photo CDs.

24   "It was a great way of organizing so many images," says Fishauf. "With an electronic collage, if you make a mistake or change your mind, you can reuse the same source elements, go back and make it bigger or smaller, change the colour balance, make it transparent, change the brightness or the contrast. You have all kinds of capabilities for manipulating imagery that don't exist in the real world."

25   The enthusiasm of users such as Rostron and Fishauf is not universally shared. Some critics worry that the greater ease offered by digital technology will seduce us into modifying images without due reflection on a variety of ethical questions. This was a theme at a conference called Ethics, Copyright, and the Bottom Line: A Symposium on Digital Technologies and Professional Photography, held in 1992 at the Center for Creative Imaging in Camden, Maine. One of the speakers, Fred Ritchin, director of photography at *The New York Times Magazine*, summarized the double-edged nature of digital imagery. "As we applaud the technology — as we should," he said, "I think we have to simultaneously ask, 'Is this helping us to see, to understand the world?' You have this impulse to make it bigger, make it smaller, make it pink, because it is so easy. This is what some people have called the God Complex."

26   The God Complex may be harmless enough in the hands of an artist retouching a mole on the cheek of a *Vogue* cover model, but what about when it crosses over into photography that we are conditioned to trust as documentary evidence? Ritchin gave the example of a Swedish plane that crashed in Finland. No photographer was present, so a newspaper interviewed three eyewitnesses and created a composite image of a plane crash, which it ran as a "news photo."

27   As Ritchin and others point out, historically we have relied on the accuracy of photography (and film and video) to get the truth — about Tiananmen Square, the Rodney King incident, Gary Hart, and Marion Barry. Or for that matter, about the Civil War, Auschwitz, Hiroshima, and the assassination of JFK. But when truth can so easily be falsified and news travels so rapidly and completely around the world through huge, centralized news organizations or courtesy of the Pentagon, can we believe what we see any more? Will photography ever be taken seriously as evidence again? Will powerful people still need to be "afraid of photographs," as Ritchin puts it?

28   All of this is good cause for soul-searching among professional image makers. "I think there is a moral decision we have to make," says Nancy Shanoff, another Toronto-based commercial photographer. "We have to think about what engages our minds. If I want to create a photographic illusion, that's one thing, but manipulating a photograph in a news context, that seems to me totally void of morality. Just because we have the technological ability to do something, does that exonerate people from moral obligation? I don't think so."

29   Olusegun Olaniyan, a Montreal graphic designer who teaches digital imaging to photographers, gives a qualified endorsement to photo manipulation. "I

personally have no problem with it, as long as I'm told. As humans, we have a need to know what reality is. When our reality is being played around with, it puts us in a shaky position. It's a state of mind."

30   If the ethics of current digital developments are difficult to wrestle with, the future looks even more unsettling. As Ritchin said in his conference talk: "We now have something called a range-camera, which is a 360-degree scan that is being developed at the MIT Media Lab. So you could basically encode George Bush's data from any angle, and then you could reconstruct the image from any angle you want any time you wanted, with any stop, with any depth of field, any focus, any lighting, any people next to him that you want. Basically what you end up with is that you no longer need the photographer there."

31   There's also a persuasive argument to be made that computer images have retarded creativity at least as much as they have advanced it. If ad agencies are now content with digital cut-and-pastes that avoid the high cost of putting a photographer in front of the Eiffel Tower or the Grand Canyon, will professionals become lastingly complacent? "Will we any longer be the originators of images?" asks Shanoff. "Or will we be reduced to image makers who supply pieces of images? This background, this person — like sampling music or actors?"

32   Shanoff is not an unschooled technophobe. Like Rostron, she has spent hundreds of hours working with Photoshop. For clients who prefer their images in digital format, she now delivers her work on magnetic disk. Yet she is a reluctant participant. She doesn't alter her own images. She has hired an operator to use the computer in her studio. "I am a middle-aged woman, and I decided a long time ago I wasn't going to be left behind. [But conventional photography] is the craft I have spent my life training for, and there is an intrinsic human thing that doesn't want to let go of that."

33   In the long run, the impact of digital imaging on our culture may be profound. The cognitive consequence of altering reality is dissonance, the uncomfortable befuddlement we feel when our anchor points are uprooted and there's nothing left to hang onto. News as entertainment does this to us. Television does it in general. Digitally altered photographs do it. As Marshall McLuhan said, "We become what we behold," and "We shape our tools, and afterwards, our tools shape us."

34   Lewis H. Lapham, the editor of Harper's, recounted these words of McLuhan's in a recent editorial. Lapham believes that in the here-there-and-everywhere universe of modern media, "a world in which the stars of daytime soap opera receive 10,000 letters a week from fans who confess secrets of the heart that they dare not tell their husbands, their mothers, or their wives," our perceptions are being perilously reshuffled. As he argues it, we are moving intractably from the pre-electronic straight lines of intellectual cause and effect to nonlinear ways of thinking based on emotions, impressions, sensations — things that invite manipulation. When we allow our tools to shape us, he concludes, we "deconstruct the texts of a civilization" and "nothing necessarily follows from anything else."

35   The same can be said very specifically for rearranging photographic reality. If all things are digitally fluid, nothing necessarily follows from anything else. A photograph no longer tells the truth. It only suggests a possibility.

Topics for consideration:

1. Leighton cites examples of misleading presentations of images current during 1994 when the article was written, such as O.J. Simpson and figure-skaters Tonya Harding and Nancy Kerrigan. What more recent examples spring to mind?

2. Compare the techniques Leighton describes for altering photographs with those outlined by Peter Robertson in "More Than Meets the Eye" in the "Questions of Truth" chapter. What use do you imagine might have been made of digital imaging photography in the historical contexts Robertson cites?

3. A Kodak Canada sales manager is quoted in paragraph 14 as saying, "Technologies don't get displaced. They just reinvent themselves." Do you think that this is true? What examples can you think of?

Robert Fulford (1932-

Robert Fulford is a nationally respected journalist whose columns appear regularly in the Globe and Mail. *He has devoted much of his writing life to exploring the relationship of culture and society.*

Robert Fulford's essay speculates on the future of books in "the order of daily life" and notes his own changing perceptions of electronic communications technologies. He defines his own attachment to books as an "ideology," driven, in part, by the democratic values represented by print culture. By contrast, the cost of "digitalized information" may keep it "beyond the range of those who are not affluent."

THE IDEOLOGY OF THE BOOK

1   Memories of Marshall McLuhan should make us permanently sceptical of any attempt to explain the shape of things to come through technological determinism. McLuhan was brilliant, but just as often wrong as right. Three decades ago, around the time *Understanding Media* appeared, he told me during an interview on the TV program *This Hour Has Seven Days* that we would all soon be designing our own cars, because computer-aided design would be universal throughout the industry: automakers would function like "bespoke tailors," as he put it. Earlier, he remarked that nationalism had no future at all, having been killed by television. In the mid-1960s, McLuhan's generation introduced the term "futurist," and a new profession of soothsayers sprang up. Its practitioners have shown themselves to be no more reliable than economists or art critics, but they are everywhere around us. The future has become one of those topics, like education, on which everyone pontificates. Today, in a sense, we are all futurists.

2   On the future of books, and the particular ideology that enshrouds and protects books, I can claim no more than that these are subjects I have thought about over some decades. And if the beginning of wisdom lies in the acknowledgment of ignorance, then I'm on the way to becoming wise. I've read a great deal about new forms of information, and used some of them, from CD-ROM to virtual reality, but I admit that I'm as ignorant as anyone of their most profound implications. Moreover, my ignorance is progressive: I know less about this subject than I did ten years ago. My guess is that ten years from now, if I'm spared, I will know even less. Like most people, I sit on a small life raft of knowledge surrounded by a constantly growing ocean of information. The ocean expands under the pressure of human intelligence, energy, and greed, none of which shows any sign of abating. Engineers and entrepreneurs are creating new techniques so quickly that even people working in the business of information need only look away for a year or two in order to feel obsolete. Few of us can keep up, so our ignorance continues to grow. Ignorance has become a major byproduct of the knowledge industry.

3   A fear for the future of books has been a persistent theme in our culture for decades. The publishing business, here and elsewhere, is more or less always on the brink of collapse, though the possible causes of disaster vary from time to

time. Sometimes it seems that no one wants to invest in book publishing, which leaves the business in poverty. At other moments it becomes so attractive to investors that gigantic conglomerates buy up all the publishers, and even the bookstores, which is also dangerous. Writers are sometimes said to make so little money that there's a danger they won't be able to write at all, but we also read that some writers are getting *too much* money — so much that gigantic advances become a danger to the health of the business.

4   Those are minor problems when set beside the dark fantasies about the future of books that creative artists have produced. A famous example is *Fahrenheit 451*, the Ray Bradbury novel from the 1950s that became the basis for a film by François Truffaut in 1966. *Fahrenheit 451* imagines a future society in which the state regards individualism as the root of all evil and correctly identifies books as promoters of individualism. The authorities burn all books, not for being pornographic or revolutionary but simply for being books. Truffaut made his film an elegy for book culture. He depicted a group of isolated rebels who have despaired of preserving physical books and instead have re-invented the ancient art of memorizing. They dedicate themselves to committing whole volumes to memory, so that the classics can be transmitted to succeeding generations by word of mouth. His film's most vivid image has a group of volunteers walking in circles in the snow, reciting their books aloud, playing in this dystopian future the role that medieval monks played when they preserved ancient wisdom by copying Aristotle in their monastic libraries. The film and the book both left us with a troubling question. Was this repression brutally imposed by a small totalitarian élite seeking to reshape humanity, or did it express the wish of the people themselves, who wanted to be free of the ambiguities that are a necessary part of literary culture?

5   A more recent tribute to the power of the printed word appears in Peter Greenaway's 1991 film, *Prospero's Books*. This hysterical version of *The Tempest*, with John Gielgud as the philosopher-magician, drowns most of the poetry in overwrought images and a cluttered sound track. What's interesting about it is Greenaway's peculiar treatment of the books Prospero possesses on the island; it implies a kind of nostalgic spirituality related to paper and binding. For Shakespeare the possibility that books contained certain keys to magic was natural, but he allowed the books themselves a relatively minor role. In Greenaway's hands the books fill the screen and overpower the story, so that we forget about Miranda and most of the others. By computer animation, Greenaway makes the books come to life — for instance, when someone turns to a chapter on frogs, frogs jump out of the pages, and in a section on human anatomy the page comes alive with a pulsing heart. Greenaway makes the books the stars of his drama. His flamboyant effects imply a genuinely nightmarish prospect — not the political nightmare of book-banning, as in *Fahrenheit 451*, but something even more dangerous, the movement of the book out of ordinary life and into an exalted realm of magic. Since the Enlightenment, Western civilization has made the book the shrine of modernity, the place where we store and locate our ideals. It now stands in some danger of becoming *only* a shrine, a place for occasional worship.

6   In fact, something like this has been happening. McLuhan became notorious for suggesting that books were dead, but what he meant was that books were no

longer central to the shaping of the public imagination. They had been supplanted in this role by other media, and the process of supplanting them at the centre of consciousness would continue. In that sense, subsequent events have supported McLuhan.

7   In any imaginable future, books will not entirely disappear. For the most part, methods of communication do not disappear. Instead, the passage of time re-arranges their position in the order of daily life, sometimes pushing them from the centre to the margins. The distant ancestors of our book — the rolled-up scrolls of Egyptian and Roman antiquity made from papyrus, the rolled sheets of silk in China or palm leaves in India — became technologically obsolete 2,000 years ago with the invention of the codex, the binding of pages into something that looked roughly like what we call a book. But for many centuries the scroll retained its emblematic power as priestly or government document, and even today it lives among us as the Torah that is ceremonially rolled and unrolled in synagogues. In the twenty-first century, this could be the fate of paper books. If the book as a form is merely a convenience, and if other forms are more conve-nient, then most of humanity will adopt the more convenient format. Books will survive as art objects and icons.

8   A decade ago I felt much more confident about books and their future. In 1984 I wrote a piece in the *Toronto Star* satirizing the boasts of the knowledge industry while upholding the permanent value of books. I imagined an alterna-tive history: what if the Renaissance and the Enlightenment failed to invent books, and they became the latest rather than the earliest means of mass educa-tion? What if humanity had somehow progressed from hand-copied documents to television and computers? I further imagined that in the 1980s a team led by a brilliant engineer at Texas Instruments, Jack Gutenberg, invented the book, putting together the whole package (type, paper, binding, high-speed printing, the lot) and rushing it to market.

9   My theory was that this invention would break the communications indus-try wide open. Books would be recognized instantly as a technological revolution of unprecedented scope, the most exciting concept in the history of mass media. Sales people would recite the advantages: a book is so light you can carry it on plane, train, or subway; you can read it in the bath or in bed; you don't have to plug it in, and it never needs to be repaired. And then there's the unique turn-back facility: you can flip back if you've missed something. And for people who have spent all their lives staring at computer screens, a book is easy on the eyes. Because the ink is solid on the page, rather than a shadow on a screen, it looks much like the concrete objects for which evolution designed human eyes.

10   We can imagine the slow-dawning astonishment with which the world would greet this invention — first, as always, the scoffing laughter, then curios-ity, then respect. Soon a media guru would make his reputation with a brave announcement: "The book renders all previous forms of communication, such as television, obsolete." Old-fashioned schoolteachers would stick with TV and com-puters for a while, but eventually some visionary would announce the obvious truth: "As a learning tool, the book is so revolutionary that it will surpass anything previously available in classrooms."

11   I wrote that in a more innocent time, when it was easier for the bookish to
scorn cheeky newcomers. Now we know that certain kinds of paper books are
moving swiftly toward obsolescence. The clearest case is the reference book. The
complete OED has shrunk to a little CD-ROM package that costs a third of the price
of the 20-volume set and is incomparably easier to use. In CD-ROM we can now
buy Shakespeare, five versions of the Bible, and the entire canon of British poetry,
all of them scannable at inhuman speed. Those who have read the first important
new book issued in both formats, H.R. Haldeman's diaries, claim the CD-ROM
version is much better: it contains every word Haldeman set down, and can be
scanned with ease. And the classicists at the University of California at Irvine
have put every available word of ancient Greek literature onto CD-ROM — 3,000
authors, every one of them searchable and accessible in libraries across the world.

12   Academics having helped generate much of this change, we can read some of
the history of it in the ways universities define their activities. The succession of
names given to the library school at the University of Toronto could in itself
inspire a little essay on the nomenclature of the information age. In 1928 the university founded something humbly described as the Library School, tucked into
the education faculty. In 1965, when librarians were elevating the status of their
profession, it became the School of Library Science, the word "science" indicating the relatively new sense that handling knowledge was becoming a profession
in itself. Later the curriculum expanded to encompass more technology, and the
word "information" began appearing in the names of library schools across the
continent. In 1972 the University of Toronto's school became the Faculty of
Library and Information Science. In June 1994, the word "library" disappeared
entirely and the school became the Faculty of Information Studies. As one of the
people working there told me, "We took out what we call 'the L-word.'"

13   That was one more recognition of a titanic change in the way we study and
learn. What's especially interesting is that this change has been accomplished
within relatively narrow professional worlds, with relatively small markets. As
similar ingenuity is applied to general reading, computers will certainly become
small enough to carry on the subway, they won't have to be plugged in, and we'll
be able to flip the pages of what we're reading with the greatest ease. My ten-
year-old piece in the *Toronto Star* now seems vaguely Luddite and far too self-
assured. Before long it will sound almost medieval. Years ago Jack McClelland,
the publisher, told me that in the not distant future a published book would be
roughly the size of an aspirin. I thought he was crazy, but I think so no longer.

14   For example, when McClelland made that prediction I pointed out that light
on a screen can never be as easy to read as type on paper. Today that's still the
truth: it's much harder to read a video display terminal than a book. As an article
in *The Economist* recently put it, "A computer screen ... as easy to read as a black-
on-white printed page would need to have three times the contrast ratio, 20 times
the pixels and twice the refresh-rate that a typical screen has today." But computer
designers are well aware that the screen we use now is primitive. The Xerox
Corporation has recently developed a screen that's as easy to read as a book. If
marketed now it would sell for US $200,000 or so, but one educated prediction
is that it can come down to a reasonable price in five years or so. Given the pace
of miniaturization, it's not inconceivable that ten years from now someone will be

lying in bed reading the new Michael Ondaatje novel on a viewer that weighs no more than the 1994 paperback version of *The English Patient.*

15   Those of us for whom what we might call *bookism* has long been unquestioned orthodoxy continue to clutch at whatever straws we can. When contemplating change it's sometimes hard for us to banish malice and *schadenfreude* from our souls. We tend to greet news of technological failure with a certain pleasure. We who have always lived by books are delighted to discover gigantic flaws in computerized library catalogues. When I first used Metrocat, the computerized catalogue of the Metropolitan Toronto Central Reference Library, I was reassured to find that it was much slower than a card-file. I imagined clerks at the other end of the wire in the basement shouting to each other, "Hey, Fred, we got anything here on movies by, uh, Kurosawa." (It's since become faster.) When using a university catalogue I'm not at all displeased to discover that computers have trouble pulling into one place records that belong together and keeping apart records that should be separate — they confuse, for instance, the philosopher Francis Bacon with the painter Francis Bacon, and they mix Samuel Butler the poet with Samuel Butler the novelist. Similarly, until I began using a computer, I loved collecting stories of friends who had lost whole chapters of their books in the course of lightning storms.

16   The truth is that bookish people believe like ideologues in what the computer business calls *hard copy*, and we harbour a deep atavistic suspicion of anything else. In the *Village Voice*, Peter Givler recently wrote that he found it a cheerless prospect to

> imagine a world full of books made without ink and paper, books without the sweet musty smell of the hands that have held them. ... For centuries books have ... quickened us to knowledge, given us charms against despair, taught us to speak of love, sung us to sleep. I cannot imagine a future in which they are replaced by the electronic ghosts of books, locked inside a machine ...

17   Eloquent. But then Givler confessed: "Before I go any further, though, I have to tell you that I'm writing this on my new, unspeakably cool Macintosh PowerBook 520, a gadget that in our short acquaintance I have come to love ..." The truth is that writers like Givler contemplate an entirely electronic future with trepidation while preparing to embrace it, if necessary.

18   We are right to be nervous. For one thing, the technological imagination traditionally suffers from over-confidence, typified by C.P. Snow's famous remark about engineers and scientists: "They have the future in their bones." There's a tone of manifest destiny in that sort of utterance, and a wrongheaded belief that a new technology not only can but should automatically supersede the old. Once I heard a man who teaches computers at an art college describe government support for oil painting and string-quartet playing as reactionary and harmful. As he put it, "I don't know how long we can go on, carrying the burden of an obsolete culture."

19   The servants of technology, because they know so many of its possibilities so well, sometimes assume that they own the future and can manipulate it. They can't. What we know of technology is that we should not trust it because we should

not trust our civilization to use it well, and we don't need to wander away from the history of modern culture in order to see that point graphically illustrated. We live at the end of the first great century of museums and libraries, and we are better at preserving the past than we have ever been. And yet we know by experience that we cannot trust ourselves with our culture. We can be vandals, too.

20   The history of silent cinema provides a chilling cautionary tale. Between 1910 and 1930, around the world, the movies developed into a magnificent art form with their own intricate conventions and their own superb artists. Then sound was added, and immediately two startling things happened. First, just about everyone quickly agreed that no more silent movies would be made. That was understandable, since the money appeared to be in talkies. But the other development was not so understandable: people who owned prints of silent films decided they were worthless and threw them in the garbage; among the prints that were kept, many were allowed to rot, the nitrate film slowly decomposing in the vaults. And this wasn't the failing of one national culture or one region. It apparently happened that way everywhere in the world, from Copenhagen to Shanghai.

21   The result is that a large part of the accomplishment of the artists of that period disappeared from the face of the earth. Today no more than ten per cent of these silent films exist. This was a major act of vandalism, like the sacking of a great library, but on an international scale, and it happened not through malice but through carelessness. It was carried out by people who saw themselves as progressive and intelligent, people who were eagerly meeting the future on its own terms.

22   It now seems bizarre that Shakespeare's plays survived their first 400 years on earth in much better shape than D.W. Griffith's films survived their first four decades. When we contemplate that fact, we understand that we have learned to treat the paper book in a way we don't treat technological culture. While publishing of books is faddish, the preservation of books is not — but so far we have no reason to invest any similar confidence in the handling of digitalized information. Because of its cost, technology may never be able to avoid the fashions that dominate the market. Information systems come and go, as the history of sound reproduction demonstrates. It's hard now to find a machine that will play a 78 rpm record, and the lp record was transformed in only 40 years from Peter Goldmark's brilliant, world-conquering system of the late 1940s to a nostalgia item of the late 1980s. If we publish on CD-ROM, we can't even be sure that, a century from now, someone will have a machine to play the disc. Moreover, we have only a vague idea of how permanent CD-ROM discs are, or for that matter the hard discs in our computers and the diskettes on which we confidently store our memories. Permanence is proven only by time, not advance tests in a lab.

23   The social implications of the new technology are even more troubling. It seems obvious that if we replace books with digitalized information, we will change the economics of reading and the place of knowledge in society. Many librarians understand what can happen, but I have no sense that in all the discussions of "the information highway" there is any wide understanding, either among the public or among policymakers, of the darker possibilities.

24   My great fear is that we are moving in the wrong direction: we may be at a

moment when history reverses itself. We are all beneficiaries of a great historical movement, the gradual broadening of knowledge, outward from its original
owners, the princes and priests, toward all of humanity. As Harriet Taylor and
J.S. Mill once wrote, "when we take all history into view we find that its whole
course is a getting rid of privileges and exclusions." That noble, optimistic nineteenth-century liberal view may not apply to every aspect of society, but certainly
it applies to knowledge. The impulse to make it universally available was born
uncounted centuries ago, but we can mark the events that gave it shape within
our world of information: Johannes Gutenberg's invention in the fifteenth century, the commercialization of books in the Enlightenment, the industrialization
of publishing in the nineteenth century, the development of linotype by Ottmar
Mergenthaler in 1885, and then the free library movement, which we can date
from 1901, when Andrew Carnegie began his career as a philanthropist.

25   This movement has been based on a persistent magnanimity. It has been driven by a belief in the inherent value of making information available, the belief
that now drives several professions, notably the profession of librarians. This is
the spirit that animates our best instincts. It is at the centre of the ideology of the
book. Unlike many ideologies, this one can claim unqualified successes.

26   Since Gutenberg, it has been focused on the paper book. Now it confronts a
new problem. Digitalized information is costly, and may well be beyond the range
of those who are not affluent. We should be concerned about making it as available as books have been made available, since it will be equally important. Given
that all governments agree on the central place that the information revolution
will play in our lives, given that all of them insist that only an educated population will be able to maintain itself in the future, we might expect that public
libraries would now be receiving vastly enhanced budgets, so that they can help
the citizens deal with these new challenges. In fact, anyone associated with
public libraries knows this isn't true. As it stands now, new forms of information are likely to be costly, and likely to be restricted in many cases to those with
economic power or connections to power.

27   What we need in the near future is vision something like Carnegie's. He made
it his practice to provide a community with a library in return for the promise to
staff it and fill it with books. He invented seed money and matching grants, two
ideas that are with us still. Clearly, he *shamed* many of the cities of the English-
speaking world into creating public libraries.

28   The information revolution awaits a visionary on the Carnegie scale, someone who can dream of places where citizens can use information networks and
CD-ROMS at low cost. Without intervention on some such scale, it's hard to imagine how we can prevent knowledge from becoming once again the possession of
the powerful. Bill Gates, who has made billions at Microsoft, would be the ideal
candidate to become the new Carnegie — but so far he seems to believe, like most
computer entrepreneurs, that his only role is to make better devices that will
make more billions.

29   When I read about what Gates and his competitors are preparing for us, I
sometimes think about those pioneers of information technology, the monks
who preserved part of the wisdom of antiquity during the centuries when hardly
anyone else seemed to care about it. They were successful partly because they

understood that this work was central to their existence. The American historian Daniel Boorstin, in his wonderful book, *The Discoverers*, quoted some lines set down by a monk in Normandy in the year 1170. "A monastery without a library is like a castle without an armoury," the monk wrote. "Our library is our armoury. Thence it is that we bring forth the sentences of the Divine Law like sharp arrows to attack the enemy. Thence we take the armour of righteousness, the helmet of salvation, the shield of faith, and the sword of the spirit ..."

30 In the environment created by onrushing technology, scholars, librarians, teachers, writers — all those who take responsibility for generating and spreading knowledge — may well find themselves called to a similar battle. They will need to be shielded by faith in the value of their endeavours, and by the sword of the spirit.

Topics for consideration:

1. In paragraphs 8 and 9 Fulford recounts his earlier fantasy in which the invention of electronic communications technologies precedes that of the book, so that the book is hailed as a miraculous innovation. How credible do you find this fantasy?

2. In "All Is Not Well in the House of Technology" earlier in this chapter, Ursula Franklin quotes a cartoon caption suggesting a possible future bookless library. In paragraphs 10 and 11, Fulford hints at a similar trend. Do you think that this is probable?

3. Fulford sees book culture as being driven "by a belief in the inherent value of making information available." Is book culture as fundamentally democratic as Fulford suggests?

Further reading:

Sven Birkerts, *The Gutenberg Elegies: The Fate of Reading in an Electronic Age* (1994). Provocative personal essays on the decline of book culture.

R. Murray Schafer (1933-

R. Murray Schafer is a renowned Canadian musician and composer. He is the author of numerous books, including On Canadian Music *(1984) and* The Thinking Ear *(1986), and he is the publisher of Arcana Editions. This essay is taken from a lecture he delivered in 1994 at Brandon University, where he was Stanley Knowles Visiting Professor in Public Policy.*

Although we live in an age of duplicates, in which the handmade has totally disappeared from many people's lives, R. Murray Schafer makes a strong argument for the value of the original in art, music and in our everyday lives. He investigates the way in which our sense of sound is shaped by recording and broadcasting technologies and urges his audience to attend to the unrepeatable and unique experiences of their lives.

DUB: DEFENDING THE VALUE OF THE ORIGINAL IN AN AGE OF DUPLICATES

1 We live in a world of dubs — manufactured multiples of originals. The social effects of this distinguishing feature of modern life have been widely discussed but the often hostile commentaries have in no way impeded the production or acquisition of copied material, so that by now it is quite common to enter a home and see not a single original object in it. Disappearing are the sewn quilts, the embroidered tablecloths and the hand-carved corner cabinets. The only hand-made objects are a few children's drawings stuck to the refrigerator door. Everything else on the floor or walls has been seen before: every stick of furniture and gew-gaw comes from Eaton's or K-Mart; even the bagatelles on the mantelpiece are from Disneyland. And, of course, the devices for making music are identical all the way up the street — radios, tape recorders, CD players, VCRs — so that the piano, still lingering in the odd house, out of tune and pushed into a corner, begins to look like a decorated hearse. In earlier times, the piano, together with the family Bible, stood at the centre of domestic social life in those very homes — the prayers and readings alternating with the sing-songs.

2 The subject of this article is the original versus the duplicate, and I will say at once that I am about to defend the value of the original. You may consider this old-fashioned. Today it is fashionable to defend reproduction, but fashion, as Jean Cocteau once said, is what goes out of fashion; we might therefore conceive of another era in which the original is upwardly revalued. My main concern is with music, but my thoughts may spill into other areas.

3 Let's begin with the suggestion that all recording is cultural misappropriation. The notion that recording involves transposition, taking something away to place it in a different context, has to some extent occurred to everyone; but that this taking is a form of theft has scarcely been considered until recently. Who loses as a result of recording?

4 Fifty years ago there was a lot of excitement about recording folk songs before they were forgotten. Perhaps at first we didn't understand that by recording them

we were helping them to become forgotten. The repetitive singing of songs was the means of retaining them in the pre-electroacoustic era, and the first societies to stop singing were those, like our own, that became spellbound by the microphone and recorder. Today the folk songs of the world, once regarded as universally anonymous, are beginning to acquire owners — either the people who recorded them and in whose favour the copyright laws will work to bestow royalties, or, on the other side, people claiming to represent the cultures from which they were taken, who are also usually seeking compensation for what they regard as the theft of ethnic or tribal property. The case of Paul Simon using backup material from a black South African group made the news a few years ago, and I can only imagine that as the song soared on the record charts, the lawyers settled the claims to everyone's satisfaction.

5   The microphone is the instrument by which we are allowed to make sound copies of events and preserve them or move them to other environments. What the microphone preserves, the loudspeaker broadcasts. Together they introduce what I have elsewhere called *schizophonia* — split sound, sound separated from its origin. I intended the word to have a nervous connotation, bearing in mind what is accomplished here: the de-contextualization of sound objects and their huge proliferation. But this procedure has long since ceased to seem unnatural; today we accept recorded and broadcast sound as perfectly normal, even though it has differentiated us from all listeners before us on this earth.

6   Though many intellectuals in the early part of the century hated radios and recorded music, philosophers of the media such as Marshall McLuhan were more welcoming in their assessments of the electroacoustic revolution — or that, at least, is the tone of McLuhan's influential book *Understanding Media*. Privately McLuhan said he intended the book as a warning, but it was picked up so enthusiastically that he declined to stress this until later in his life. In his last book, *Laws of Media*, McLuhan poses the following four questions, which, he says, are the only four worth asking of any medium:

1. What does it enhance or intensify?
2. What does it render obsolete?
3. What does it retrieve that was previously obsolesced?
4. What does it produce or become when pressed to an extreme?

7   The microphone, says McLuhan, enhances the private or individual voice. Whether a Caruso or a pop singer, a politician or a bystander at the scene of a crime, anyone can be transformed into a celebrity by the microphone, at least for a time. The concern with the human vocal tract has, in fact, been so obsessive that all recording instruments have been shaped to interface with the human voice to the extent that it is still difficult if not impossible to transduce other natural sounds such as thunderstorms, fire, wind or distant panoramas effectively onto disc or tape. Technology is never neutral and recording technology has, since its invention, discriminated in favour of the human voice and against the sounds of nature.

8   The result has been a shrinking of the audio field, a "silencing" of certain sound objects and a magnifying of voices into the cult of personality — literally *per sonare* from the ancient Greek, meaning to speak through the trumpet of the

actor's mask. The private or individual voice is "enhanced" to become the media voice: lively, brash, confident, fixed on the topic without pauses or loitering. It is the voice of the radio or TV host; but it is also our voice whenever we step before the microphone, for the microphone frames us like a camera. We pose for it.

9   What, then, does the microphone render obsolete? Nature. Acoustic space. Distant listening and "phantom sounds", as when one listens to the voice of conscience, to the voices of spirits, of the dead or the unborn, or to the Music of the Spheres, or to the blooming of the lotus. (In the early Showa period in Japan — c. 1925 — people gathered at Sinobazu-no-ike Pond in Ueno Park, Tokyo, to listen to the blooming of the lotus. Could such a sound be heard, or was it merely a communal auditory hallucination?)

10   Among the first environmental recordings were those produced by *The World Soundscape Project*, which I directed, dating from the mid-sixties and early seventies. Among other things, we prepared 10 one-hour broadcasts for the CBC entitled "Soundscapes of Canada". Although many of them were broadcast in several countries (Australia, Sweden, Germany, France), the CBC didn't like them because the needle of the VU meter rarely ticked up high enough (they said) to engage the listener's conscious attention. They didn't understand that acoustic environments are overheard, not heard; they bring into play what I would call peripheral or oblique listening, revealing other aspects of sound or sound constellations than those sensible to the hard focus.

11   Other early environmental recordings were those produced commercially by Irv Triebel, simply called "Environments". Triebel had the notion, which sounds credible, that a recording of a rainforest could suggest a cooling effect, so that, if played in offices or hotel lobbies, the actual temperature could be somewhat higher than normal, thereby saving wattage on air conditioners. The best recordings of tropical rainforests are those made by Steve Feld in Papua New Guinea; they have been assiduously mixed down and enhanced in Mickey Hart's California studio.

12   Then what does the microphone retrieve? McLuhan says it retrieves the "close group" and gives the example of the "cozy night club". He also adds the phrase "tribal mode", which is somewhat stronger. Elsewhere he had spoken of the "tribal drum of radio", to emphasize the way radio gathers people up into a unified social group. Although they may be isolated or performing different tasks, their feet tap and their heads bob to the same songs and commercials.

13   Demagogues and dictators of all persuasions adore the microphone. "Without the loudspeaker we never would have been able to conquer Germany," declared Hitler. McLuhan asserts that the microphone reverts into "closed collective space" — territoriality, based on shared speech or shared songs, replacing the old territoriality of fences, maps or nation-states. Broadcasting becomes narrowcasting; reinforcement for special interest groups in which both the music and the messages are propaganda. As the nation-state gives way to the more partisan proclamations, national broadcasting systems wither. The CBC is the network of the nation-state, of an identity called Canada, now threatened by retribalization.

14   A microphone is a gatherer of information for broadcast or storage. In either case an original sound is duplicated. This duplication is taking place at an ever-increasing pace, according to manufacturing and sales statistics. In 1993 Canadian consumers spent an all-time record of $2.8 billion on videotapes, films, CDs and

cassettes, according to Canadian Press. That was $400 million more than in 1992 and represents about $93 for every man, woman and child in the country. Of the total, $825 million was spent on sound recordings, almost all of it on CDs. In slightly over 10 years the CD has triumphed over the LP and the cassette, proving the ability of the industry to force everybody to jettison a good deal of usable equipment, which immediately becomes trash. So does the antique record collection, even though it contained much material that will never be reissued — for instance, music by Canadian composers. The media hype promoting the conversion has, of course, been domineering.

There's still something intoxicating about cradling a brand new CD in your hands.

Tear off the cellophane wrapper. Pop the shiny medallion out of its protective shell. Admire the iridescent sheen of its playing surface.

Press the button on your CD player that brings out the carrying tray with a precise, satisfying "Kechunnuk".

Tenderly place your treasure on the tray. Press the button again and watch it disappear into the dark interior of the machine. Hit the PLAY button and enjoy. Pure music, no noise, no distortion.

(David Howell, *The Ottawa Citizen*, Oct. 31, 1993)

15   I don't need to go on with this. Everyone knows the newspapers and magazines are full of it. No one gets ahead in music today without a handful of CDs and the acknowledged leaders in the field are those who sell the most of them. The individual concert has undergone a devaluation, not necessarily in popularity, but in the media's evaluation of its significance, or even acknowledgment of its existence. The reviews it receives in the local newspaper will be pushed further onto the back pages to make way for press releases with the Hollywood or New York dateline — the manufacturing centres of the entertainment industry. The same thing happens to local theatre as it gets shoved out by the latest movie. In the era of the International Growth Society we are entertained by clones, by echoes, by dubs.

16   In ancient Greece philosophers argued the problem of the original versus duplication in a debate known as "Theseus's Boat". Theseus had returned to Greece after defeating the Cretan Minotaur to become the King of Athens. As a memorial to his triumph, his boat was preserved. In time, however, it needed repairs. First one plank, then another, was substituted until eventually every part of the boat had been replaced. And so the question: Is this still Theseus's boat? Can one thing be transformed faithfully into another? Can an idea outlive its original form, and if so, for how long? Is a thing less valid when copied? Or does duplication make it more valuable? Can we truthfully say reproductions bring nothing but unblemished goodness into the world?

17   Try to forget the media hype and answer these questions.

18   The answers I've come up with have made me increasingly suspicious of reproductions.

19   Of course I live in a world in which the reproduction of my work is inevitable, and without which it would be unknown. I even participate in this by operating my own publishing company, Arcana Editions, to print my books and music. But there are very significant differences between what I am doing and what the big

publishers of the past attempted to do. I intend to remain small, publishing only my own works and in small quantities, or at least the smallest quantity that keeps the price competitive. I also want the works to look beautiful.

20   Arcana Editions has been operating since 1978, usually in the black. We have never applied for financial assistance from the government and we have survived the various ways they have tried to kill us: GST on books, elimination of special postal rates for small publishers, etc. In other words, we are operating an anachronistic business in a country without the infrastructure to encourage or support it. Arcana Editions is called a "vanity press" by people who don't realize that there is no other way to publish our kind of music in Canada. This means also that there is little technical support and no subsidized job-training programs to create the necessary skills; so I have become my own engraver, editor, proofreader, publicist, promoter and salesman. All my musical publications are reproduced from the manuscript; some of my books are even in my handwriting. This is how I am trying to give them a unique appearance, by comparison with copycat computer imagery.

21   How long can this continue? My house is already full of unsold books and scores, and each new work I write, if it is to be printed, poses a real storage problem. I have thought of hauling everything out into a field on my eightieth birthday and setting fire to it, considering that by then the world will have had enough time to get acquainted with my work. If they want anything after that, they'll have to deal with it themselves. All this, as I say, is very different from the aspirations of the big publishers of the past. They were interested in the big scene, potentially the world, and it worked for them as long as European classical music was in vogue. Many publishers and a few composers became rich in the era of printed music. Songbooks and piano music were in particular demand, but also string quartets and reductions of operas and symphonies. The service network behind the industry was intricate and well managed; its directors also lobbied governments for special concessions that would make them richer — the formation of performing rights societies being just one example.

22   Today everything has shifted to the electronic media. An enormous fleet of trained professionals oils the industry and lobbies for its advancement: producers, managers, lawyers, publicists, engineers. It would be difficult to imagine anyone building a reputation in music today without entering this world, either to exploit it or to be screwed by it.

23   Draw a line. On one side place all the repeatable pleasures of your life, on the other the unique events, uncounterfeit and uncounterfeitable. On the one side you will find your personal tape and record collection. You will also find your radio, with a repertoire selected for you. Even when it brings novelties, it does so always in the same format, imparting a uniformity of tone and texture. On the other side you will find a collection of diverse experiences, memories really, that will never be repeated.

24   Right now I am thinking of the last recital of my piano teacher, Alberto Guerrero — who, incidentally, was also Glenn Gould's teacher. There were fistfuls of wrong notes in the Ravel but there was a sense of line and contour that took us right to the composer himself, for Guerrero had known him. We knew we would never hear Ravel played so authoritatively again and we were spellbound. Should the recital have been recorded? Why? Its power as a memory far exceeds any

documentary value it might have. To hear Guerrero on recording would have impressed no one who had not known him or studied with him. And I am thinking now of the premieres of certain important works of my own, works I shall probably never hear again before I die: *Lustro, Ra, Apocalypsis* — I could go on, for Canada is not very generous when it comes to remounting the more ambitious works, even of its better known composers. Would a recording be useful in generating a remount of any of these works? I don't know. Would it assuage my wounded vanity by allowing me the pleasure of secretly reliving the experience in my music room? Certainly not. Equating the pale fire of a recording with the explosion of a production would be like mistaking a passport photograph for a human being.

25   Every kind of experience has value. Even carrying a pail of sand from one end of the beach to the other could have value if performed in a certain state of mind. The value of a record collection is that it allows a piece to be heard many times, revealing new aspects of it, deepening your appreciation. There is another side: it can bore you. The unique experience doesn't do that. If you remember it at all, each recollection will refresh you.

26   We tend to think of education as a plodding up the steps to higher achievement, higher rewards. But suppose education was really a history of the most memorable experiences in your life, dramatically imprinted on your brain so as never to be forgotten. Some cultures teach by means of high drama: circumcision or menstruation ceremonies: initiation into adulthood, the self-torture of the Sun Dance ritual ... here the single experience is intended to elevate you suddenly to a new state of existence.

27   E.E. Cummings had something similar in mind when he said that a man is a poet maybe three times in his life. That is how infrequently you touch the ultimate, even if you spend every day of your life trying. But when you have had such an experience you know you've been changed forever. It need not be dramatic to be profound. Sometimes such experiences can be very simple. I'll tell you about one that happened to me not long ago.

28   Every summer I go with a group of people into the wilderness forest where together we are creating a work entitled *And Wolf Shall Inherit the Moon*, intended to be the last part of my Patria cycle of music dramas. There are no roads or habitation anywhere near us. We are cutting our own trails and creating the work in virgin forest. Of course we are very sensitive ecologically and everything we take in comes out with us when we leave. I can't tell you the nature of the work except to say that it is quite dramatic, also very spiritual, and contains a number of rituals that we all perform together. One of these is the Opening of the Great Wheel of Life, which we do every morning. Everyone has their place in the Great Wheel of Life and throughout the week they decorate it in a very personal way. We have a chant that we sing together as we walk to the Wheel of Life each morning to open it. Each evening we perform a similar ceremony to close the Wheel. It was one night as we were closing the Wheel that I had an uncanny experience. We had been chanting the Iroquois words for the four directions, which also stand for the four stages of life:

OYANDONEH
NEHOGAH

DAJOJI
YAOGAH

29   The chanting faded away, but not to silence. I had the distinct impression that it was continuing softly from somewhere. I looked around the circle. No one was singing now. Yet the singing was continuing from somewhere. It seemed to be coming from the lake which lay before us, or from under the lake. When I tried to locate it more precisely, it slipped away and now seemed to be coming from the forest behind us. Eventually, after many minutes, it ceased.

30   From the Wheel of Life we walked silently back to the campsite. When we got there I asked whether others had heard the singing. Two people had, one of them that night with me, and one of them on another occasion.

31   Reflecting on the experience I began to be convinced that the music had an existence independent of us, that in fact it was not really ours but belonged to the land. The more I thought about this the more I felt convinced that even the music I had composed for *And Wolf Shall Inherit the Moon* did not belong to us, but had sprung up to us out of the land itself. Perhaps each piece belonged to the site where we performed it, for certainly we knew the place where each piece sounded best and we performed it there. But the notion that each site had chosen us and had loaned us the music to perform there was overwhelming.

32   I had written a little *Aubade* for trumpet and voice. Each morning our wake-up call was an *Aubade*, played across the water. There is no talking in the camp at this time. We just listen to the music and then rise, wash and dress in silence. Stuart Langdon, for whom (I thought) I had written the *Aubade*, wanted to record it with Wendy Humphries. They are both in the Wolf Project and had performed it many mornings across the lake at sunrise.

33   This was a really big decision. Should I prohibit it? But if I believed the piece belonged to the lake, only the lake could tell Stuart whether or not it was right to record it. He and Wendy did record it. It's a good recording, but everyone who knows the original setting in the Haliburton Forest knows it has no power in the recorded form. The piece belongs to the forest and only once a year, when they perform it, does it have power.

34   I have been drawn back to some very old ideas as I struggle (now with about 40 co-workers) to create the week-long forest event we are calling *And Wolf Shall Inherit the Moon*. I am even approaching a point in my thinking where we might consider special rituals or ritual music deliberately kept secret. Nothing like this exists at the moment, but why shouldn't it have its place, as it has had in many cultures before us? Imagine a piece of music heard only once a year, or once every five years, on a special day at a special place exclusively for an initiated group who are sworn to keep it secret. I had something like this in mind when I wrote *In Search of Zoraster* in 1970, but the Wolf Project gives us a context in which the idea could be more favourably developed. The instinct for secrecy is as naturally human as is sharing. I am not just referring to cabalistic occultism or Hermetic magic; your bank account is secret and what you do in bed at night is also secret.

35   It is absurd to think that culture can only manifest itself under searchlights or appear to us through the light screen of television. The current notion that if it isn't recorded, it isn't worthwhile — though obstinately upheld by the media —

is false, and I hope you are beginning to appreciate that. During the recent New Music Festival in Winnipeg we were even reminded from the podium of how well a certain composer's CD was selling, as if his merit should rise accordingly even before we heard his music. We witness the same techniques used for selling country and western hits every night on TV.

36   The media produce dubs, clones, simulacra — everybody's driving cars advertised last year on television, listening to the same 10 tunes over and over and being told in the commercials where to shop next and what to buy in order to keep on looking like everyone else. All manufactured articles are copies. All recordings are dubs. Talk like a rock star; walk like a cowboy or a TV *vedette*; eat at McDonald's, Burger King; drink Pepsi or Coke — and you've lost yourself as an original creation on this earth. Yet that life you live is still more fascinating than any novel you'll ever read or any film you'll ever see, even if that fact is being withheld from you. Your life is still your own. It won't be repeated and it can't be passed on.

37   Final advice: Be yourself. Live your own lifestyle. Make your own music.

Topics for consideration:

1. Schafer toys with the idea of destroying all his books and musical compositions on his 80th birthday on the principle that "by then the world will have had enough time to get acquainted with my work." Would you consider such an act a destructive or a creative one?

2. In paragraph 16 Schafer recalls the Greek philosophers' debate over Theseus's Boat in order to ask the question whether a reproduction can ever be the "same" as an original. Consider a work of music, performance or art whose original you have seen or heard compared with any reproductions you have encountered. In what sense can the reproduction be considered the "same"?

3. Schafer points out that broadcasting and recording technologies favour the human voice over other subtler sounds in the environment. Pay attention to the soundscape around you for a set period of time. Is it a soundscape in which the "distant listening" described in paragraph 9 can take place? What interferes with this?

Further reading:

R. Murray Schafer, *The Soundscape: Our Sonic Environment and the Turning of the World* (1993)

http://interact.uoregon.edu/MediaLit.WFAEHomePage Website for the "World Forum for Acoustic Ecology," an association that studies natural and human-made soundscapes.

CHAPTER 12

FINDING OUT

"**a**ll ignorance toboggans into know
and trudges up to ignorance again,"

writes ee cummings. Anyone who has been involved in research is familiar
with the experience of alternating between moments of insight and the
daunting awareness of the vastness of the field to be studied. Recently the
process of research has been altered so radically by the introduction of new
technologies that the see-sawing between ignorance and knowledge now
takes place at a dizzying rate. The comparatively straightforward tests of
authority that could be applied to print sources are difficult to utilize in the
vast ephemeral world of the Internet. In this world without gatekeepers or
security guards, a source that today offers apparently sound information can
disappear without trace or explanation tomorrow.

Yet the mental state required to pursue effective research remains the
same whatever the tools employed. Timothy Findley describes the essential
"magnet effect" that comes into play once one has become fully engaged with
a topic. Suddenly relevant information begins to pop up everywhere. Findley,
as a novelist, finds himself searching for a different range of material than
that which either an historian or a journalist would seek. He needs to establish the sights, smells and sounds of the historical period in his imagination
and to see that world through the eyes of his characters. Findley also reminds
us that conversations with friends can be among the most valuable sources
of information and gives examples of nuances supplied by his friends which
he could not have derived from formal research.

Librarians now find themselves on the leading edge of the technological
revolution that is reshaping how we receive information. In "Ten Internet
Myths" Mark Jordan debunks some of the popular misconceptions about
the Internet that have gained prominence because of media coverage. He
points out that the Internet is still struggling to achieve a standard of
accessibility and organization approaching that attained by libraries many
decades ago.

Joyce Thomson in "Scholarly Surfing" begins by challenging the belief
that many student researchers cherish—that the Internet can readily supply

everything they need to complete a research paper on any topic. She points out the many hazards that lie in wait for the unwary and advises that the researcher approach the Internet in a mood of scepticism and with the mind-set of a detective.

Stephen Overbury
An Interview with Timothy Findley (1930-

Noted Canadian novelist Timothy Findley, a former actor, is author of eight novels including The Wars *(1977),* Famous Last Words *(1981),* Not Wanted on the Voyage *(1986) and* The Piano Man's Daughter *(1995) as well as a memoir,* Inside Memory *(1990). The* Wars *was winner of the Governor General's Award for Fiction.*

In "The Magnet Effect" Timothy Findley describes the combination of rational and intuitive processes that guided his research for Famous Last Words, *a novel that reveals the activities of an international cabal supporting the Nazis before and during the Second World War.*

THE MAGNET EFFECT

1   At a writer's conference, I had a wonderful talk with the author E.L. Doctorow. He wrote what I would call the definitive metafiction book, *Ragtime.* When I asked him how he did his research, he answered this way: "I discovered that once I had really stated my subject, I became a magnet." That is a very good definition of what happens when you have staked out your territory. Doctorow's territory was pre-First World War. My territory was 1943 back to wherever it was going to lead as far as the Duke and Duchess of Windsor were concerned.

2   The magnet phenomenon works as follows: you pick up a book of basic history, you read, and you discover a sequence of names. Let us pretend that Doctorow and I have picked up the same book. Doctorow does not write or think like me, and I do not write or think like him; therefore, he and I are not going to follow the same line in reading this book. As Doctorow reads — and this is the magnet at work — his eye hits on a particular sequence, and he follows it. He picks up on names, personality traits, the recurrence of links between people and events. A whole other set of magnetic episodes are going to happen with me.

3   My subject dictated a sequence that followed fascist thinking from one set of people to another. I had to begin with something basic, so I used W.L. Shirer's *Rise and Fall of the Third Reich* — an invaluable guide to fascism and the Second World War. Where did it take me? For one thing, its bibliography gave me a reading list. I discovered an alarming consistency in the cast of characters from one piece of reading to another. Here's a good example: in one book I discovered that the wedding of the Duke and Duchess of Windsor had taken place at the Château du Conde in France, which was owned by a man named Charles Eugène Bedaux. The information was a mere mention of the wedding — just a sentence — but I had never heard of Bedaux and was intrigued. In another book, however, I had read that prior to the wedding the Duchess was staying with friends in their villa in the south of France and the Duke was with friends at a castle in Austria. That led to the question, "Why did they get married at Bedaux's villa — seemingly, the home of a stranger — when they could have been married where they already had friends whom they knew were willing to perform the ceremony?"

4 Reading newspaper accounts of the wedding, I learned that Bedaux had offered the Windsors his villa absolutely out of the blue — he did not even know them. And I still knew very little about him; he was a mystery and a challenge. What helped me understand this man was a series of columns written by Janet Flanner in the *New Yorker.* Sure enough, my instinct had been correct. I had made the right connection, and Bedaux had been worth tracking, because it turned out that he had been pivotal to the Windsors' fascist connections.

5 Bedaux was the inventor of the concept of *time study.* He would walk into factories and say, "Get rid of those people — they're stopping you. Bring in other people and make use of them." He worked out a system that to me is highly fascist: he would extract the most from labourers, making them work very hard for four minutes, then relax for one minute. In other words, he advocated turning people into machines to make them more productive. The carrot to reward them was the one minute of rest. He made a fortune. And, not incidentally, some Canadian firms adopted his methods.

6 I read through all the books I could find on the Windsors to discover any further connections with Bedaux. I had to do a lot of scrutinizing, because some books were very sympathetic and others were overly damning. A good researcher has to learn to recognize an author's bias.

7 The real starting point for me was to determine what was to be the circle of events and who were to be the people involved in this cabal I was imagining — and then to discover what might have been real. By reading through material I had borrowed from libraries and purchased at bookstores, I discovered that at its widest, the circle included people like Ezra Pound, the Duke and Duchess of Windsor, Bedaux, Walter Schellenberg (who was the top SS counterintelligence officer), Ribbentrop, and Rudolf Hess. The magnet in me took over once I had that overview. As, soon as I saw any of those names, I would mentally reach out to collect data. I could be walking down the street and out of the corner of my eye see Hess's face staring out of a bookstore window from the dust jacket of a book. It's an eclectic process.

8 I also read the *bibliographies* of every book I used and followed them up, ultimately reading nearly everything written about some of these key figures. By reading and rereading material I acquired, over time, a deeper understanding of the characters I had found.

9 Another thing that paid off for me was to tell friends what I was writing about. One of these friends, the writer Charles Taylor, was especially helpful. His father, E.P. Taylor, lives in Nassau, and the Taylors inevitably got to know some of the people in the circle around the Duke of Windsor during his tenure there as governor during the Second World War. This connection turned out to be invaluable for me. In my novel I used a real-life incident involving Sydney Oakes and his father, Sir Harry Oakes, but I gave my own interpretation of the circumstances in which it had taken place. It is a pertinent scene that develops the character of Sir Harry and, I think, forms a part, however small, of the explanation of why he was murdered.

10 When I had finished *Famous Last Words,* the lawyers for my publisher, Clarke Irwin, were worried that Sydney might still be alive and sue. My memory told me he had died in a car accident. Charles Taylor helped me confirm this by telephon-

ing his father's secretary in Nassau. The secretary made a few calls to relatives of the Oakeses, who confirmed that, indeed, he was dead.

11   There were other areas where Charles Taylor helped me. A number of places mentioned in my book — Spain, Vienna, Rome, Venice, and Nassau — were places I had never been. Quite deliberately, I avoided visiting them, because I wanted to maintain a kind of mythic view of them, so that they would be "written" places, not real. I read a lot about them and asked a lot of questions. For instance, I mentioned to Charles Taylor that I had placed the governor's mansion in Nassau at the top of a hill. He remarked, "Yes, it's at the top of a sort of hill. It's actually just a slight rise in the land." He was greatly amused. I also asked him other questions: "What do the trees smell like?" "What does the land smell like at night?" By researching the setting in this way, I was getting a mythic, distanced, very "writerly" interpretation of the place. Don't forget: the book was being written by a writer, Mauberley, who was a failed romantic. I had to serve his style.

12   I also studied maps in the library to get the geography and street connections right. Studying the photographs was also helpful to make sure I was correctly describing the clothing, cars, and things like that. There were the kinds of details Mauberley thrived on: dress, appearance, atmosphere.

13   This process is, of course, different than a journalistic reportage of a place. That is a valid type of approach, but it would destroy a book like mine, which requires a different kind of shape to make it succeed.

14   I didn't do all the research in one fell swoop. I would research, then write, then repeat the process. I might suddenly say to myself, "Okay, now I need everything I can get about Ezra Pound," then plunge into that and place the material into my Pound file.

15   I used four filing boxes for my novel, each of them measuring two-and-a-half-feet deep. I would file material under names, places, clothing, photographic material, and songs.

16   Songs were very important. I had to find the words to various songs, and that's not as easy as it might appear. There is a moment in *Famous Last Words* when Edward and Mrs. Simpson are experiencing the sort of romance where they have to hold hands under the table. They couldn't touch one another openly, because the whole world was staring. I thought it was appropriate to have music in the background that would recreate the atmosphere of this scene. I cross-referenced songs at a special library at the Canadian Broadcasting Corporation and came up with Jerome Kern's 1936 hit, "A Fine Romance," with the words, "… A fine romance, my friend, this is; a fine romance, with no kisses …" Perfect.

17   I never made a trip to the reference library in Toronto to research just one point. I would make a list of ten points to research, and this made the trip worthwhile.

18   You have to be very careful when you research a novel. I made a few embarrassing mistakes. For one thing, I created a non-existent rank in the Royal Air Force. Somebody picked it up early enough, so that by the time the book was published in the United States, it had been corrected.

19   Here's a story to explain how I could have avoided a few other major errors. Every year in mid-August, I visit a wonderful old hotel along the coast of Maine. Some very interesting people stay there. On this particular visit, I met an

Englishwoman, Diana Marler, and told her about my novel, which was then in progress. She told me that her best friend was the daughter of Sir Edward Peacock, who had been the Duke of Windsor's lawyer. Diana even had a desk that Peacock had once owned and that the Duke himself had used when signing legal papers.

20   I lent Diana all of the manuscript dealing with Ned Allenby, whom I had created as the British Undersecretary of State for Foreign Affairs. The Allenby home is set in Kent, England, where Charles Lindbergh turns up and Allenby is murdered. I had, in fact, made Allenby up by modelling him on a conglomerate of several people, some of them well known. The portrait of Allenby was apparently so effective that people told me after they had read the book that they had known him! Some had even known him "very well."

21   Diana Marler told me she had found two *glaring* mistakes. I was alarmed. The first one concerned a scene I had written in which a gardener is pushing a wheelbarrow full of dead marigolds. She pointed out that people of Allenby's station would never have grown marigolds — marigolds were "cottage" flowers. My flowers would have to be some other kind, like roses. That may sound silly, but it was terribly important. The garden had to be right; it was key material.

22   She also pointed out where I had used an improper phrase. In the scene where Lindbergh is trying to sell Allenby on fascism and the Nazis, Allenby becomes so angry that he says: "I don't want to hear about this, you goddamn son of a bitch." Diana said Allenby would never have used the term "son of a bitch." He might have called Lindbergh a bloody idiot, or a bastard, but no Englishman of that class would have used the North American term I had given him. Like a fool I said, "Thank you, Diana, I'll think about that." I thought that "bastard" wasn't strong enough and left my original term in.

23   I shouldn't have. A dozen people have come up to me since the book was published and told me, "I really loved the book, but — in *England* — why did Ned Allenby call Lindbergh a son of a bitch? He would never have said that." Readers pick up on these things, and Diana was right. It sounds almost trite, but, you see, it isn't; using the wrong phrase destroyed the veracity of that scene.

24   The lesson here is that you have to learn to be a good listener. Your will has to bow to the research, and you have to accommodate information. I didn't, and it had a jarring effect on a significant number of readers. They lost the thread of the moment when they read that sentence and thought, "Oh, that's wrong!"

25   Coming back to where I began, the personality searching for any given information dictates how that research proceeds. If you handed five writers the same subject and said, "All five of you are going to research and write about this topic," they would write five totally different books. This is so because each writer has his or her own magnet, a completely unique way of interpreting things, guided by personal imagination.

Topics for consideration:

1. In paragraph 13 Findley distinguishes between the kinds of research a journalist would do and his own method. How would a journalist's research differ?

2. Findley's file headings were "names, clothing, photographic material and songs." What headings would a historian use? How do they differ?

3. Findley conducted his research for *Famous Last Words* before the Internet came into being. If he were researching the novel now, do you think he would use the Internet? How would it change the way he did his research and affect the type of material he found?

Further Reading:

Timothy Findley, *Famous Last Words* (1981)

Mark Jordan

Mark Jordan is Manager of the Information Technology Lab at the University of British Columbia School of Library, Archival and Information Studies.

Mark Jordan itemizes ten popular misconceptions about the Internet that have been promulgated in the popular media.

TEN INTERNET MYTHS

1 The media, especially popular television and movies, mainstream news magazines, and syndicated newspapers, very often misrepresent the Internet by oversimplifying it, over-reporting certain aspects of it, or just plain getting things wrong. The following are ten "myths" or misconceptions about the Internet that popular media (and others) would have you believe.

2 If you're interested in how the media misrepresents the Net, see the archives of the alt.internet.media-coverage Usenet group. The best-documented example of the popular media's misrepresentation of the Net is *Time* Magazine's 1995 coverage of "cyberporn."

1. By now everyone has access to the Net.
   Most statistics emphasize how many people have access to the Internet; a more significant figure is how many do not have access. A generally accepted rule of thumb is that each year the number of people using the Net doubles; using this rule, less than 2% of the world's population is now using the Net. Even if people have access to the Net they may have only limited access. For example, an analyst at the Electronic Library Network, a group of academic and public libraries in British Columbia, reports that nearly 75% of B.C. post-secondary students don't have easy access to a graphical Web browser.

   Access is improving, with government commitment to connect all public libraries and public schools to the Net by the year 2000, but many people, especially people who can't afford luxuries like a computer and an online account, don't have access.

2. You have to be "good at computers" to be good at using the Net.
   Learning to install software is simple. Learning to find the information you need is complex. Technology is getting easier to use, and it's easier to get connected to the Net than ever before, but the explosive increase in the amount of information available on the Net is making the Net harder to use effectively.

   More than ever there is a need for people who can use the Internet to solve problems and to find information, and to teach others to find, evaluate, and organize information using the Net.

3. Cool Web sites are the best Web sites.

If you're using the Net for recreational purposes, cool Web sites are ... cool. However, many of these sites are difficult to navigate, slow, and make finding what you're looking for difficult (or impossible, if the computer you're using isn't ultra modern).

The best "informational" sites are simple, well organized, and accessible to as many people as possible. Many people don't have the latest multimedia gadgetry or super-fast connections to the Net, so to them, most cool sites are inaccessible anyway. If you want to know more about Web sites that are cool and accessible to a lot of people, see Best Viewed With Any Browser at http://www.anybrowser/org/campaign/

4. The Web is the entire Net.

The World Wide Web is probably the fastest-growing part of the Internet, but email remains the most-used part. Usenet News is thriving, and can be an excellent source of information on almost any topic, especially if you search accumulated postings using services such as DejaNews at http://www.dejanews.com

5. Things you find on the Net are free to use.

If people put information or software up on the Net for downloading, they're giving it away, right? Not true. The Internet is just like any other medium people use to distribute information and products, with one important difference: it makes theft of intellectual property very easy. But then again, so do VCRs, blank audio tapes, and photocopiers.

If you're interested in finding out more about copyright and the Internet, information is available at http://www.templteons.com/brad//copymyths. html

6. You are anonymous on the Net.

Not really. A recent article in Internet World documents some of the ways your privacy is being invaded while you use the Net and offers suggestions on how to guard your privacy. For example, when you fill in a form on a Web site, that information is often sold to people who compile junk-mailing lists. Also, your web browser can give up information about you to Web sites that ask for it, without your consent.

7. The Net contains the information you need.

The Internet is a valuable source of information, and it may be the best medium for certain types of material such as software updates and up-to-the-minute news stories. For an impressive outline of the kinds of information you can find on the Web, see Choosing the Best Search Engine for Your Information Needs at http://www.nueva.pvt.ka12.ca.us/

However, the Net does not provide access to many types of information. No matter how hard you look, you still can't find the full text of many local newspapers, the full text of (or even reviews of) most books, and the full text of most magazines. The best encyclopedias are on the Net, but they often aren't free (like *Britannica*). Some media, like CDs and video tapes, can't be found on the Net. All of these things are available in libraries.

8. If you found something once on the Net, you can find it again.
One of the biggest problems with using the Internet as a source of information is that addresses on the Net are unstable. URLs (the addresses of Web pages) and other addresses on the Net change frequently, leaving behind broken links and error messages. There are tools to help overcome this problem (like URL Minder), but they can't track down every changed address on the Net.

When an item in a library is given an address (usually in the form of a call number), it stays at that address indefinitely and is therefore always retrievable.

9. Information you find on the Net is reliable, complete, and current.
Since anyone can publish on the Net, it's difficult to decide what information is worth using and what is not. All information must be evaluated to determine if it's reliable, complete, and current. If you'd like to learn more about evaluating information you find on the Net, see Evaluating Internet Research Sources at http://www.sccu.edu/faculty/R_Harris/evalu8it.htm Another useful site, How to Critically Analyze Information Sources at http://www.library.cornell.edu/okuref/research/skill26.htm deals with evaluating information sources in general, not only material found on the Net.

The Net is good for distributing very current information, but just because something is on the Net doesn't mean it's current. Many organizations put up a Web site, for example, and find out they can't afford to keep it current. Also, don't be fooled by "Last updated" tags on Web pages that indicate today's date — these can be automatically generated to display the current date even though the text of the page may not have been changed for months.

10. The Net will replace libraries.
Not likely. The Net is disorganized, libraries are organized. Search engines that look for keywords in the text of a Web page are only so useful and directories such as Yahoo are reinventing versions of the standard, proven classification schemes that libraries have always used. Some people are even adopting the Dewey system to organize Web sites (see the Expanding Universe site for example at http://www.mtrl.toronto.on.ca/centres/bsd/astronomy/ Most noticeably, the Net doesn't use standardized subject headings, an important tool for accessing information in libraries.

Also, the whole Net can be accessed from within a library, but an entire library can't be accessed from the Net.

Topics for consideration:

1. Which of the "myths" that Jordan names are most likely to hamper good research?

2. Many misconceptions about the Internet originate with media reports. Survey news media for a week and note the way in which material concerning the Internet is handled. What patterns emerge?

Further reading:

http://www.slais.ubc.ca/users/jordan/myths/index.htm Web version of "Ten Internet Myths" with links.

http://www.cybernothing.org/cno/reports/cyberporn.html A large site documenting the misleading elements in the sensational 1995 *Time* Magazine story about pornography on the Internet.

Joyce Thomson (1962-

Joyce Thomson has been Head of User Education at the Patrick Power Library, Saint Mary's University, since 1992. She also serves as an elected member of the Librarians' Committee of the Canadian Association of University Teachers.

Based on her experience of the problems confronting students using the Internet for research, Thomson suggests strategies for finding useful information on the Internet and offers advice on how to make discriminating choices between the types of material to be found on different sites.

SCHOLARLY SURFING: SMART STRATEGIES FOR INTERNET RESEARCH

1   So, what's so hard about using the Internet to research a term paper? Everything's on the Internet, right? Well, maybe, but do you really want everything? Sure, the Internet expands your research possibilities, but those vast resources really can be too much of a good thing.

2   If you've spent even a little time using the World-Wide-Web, you know how much useless and irrelevant information you can find on the Net. It's common to retrieve thousands or even millions of items in an Internet search, and still not be able to locate anything truly useful. Imagine: Among the first 60 sites you look at, 17 are not really about your topic at all, 11 are written for elementary school students, 9 have links that say "Error: file-not-found", 7 want you to pay for the information, 5 have data that's outdated, 2 don't respond at all, 6 don't identify who wrote the stuff, 4 are still under construction and contain almost no data, 3 have information, but you need extra software to access it, 2 contain information that's just plain wrong, and 1 turns out to be a pornographic site (How did *that* happen?!). By then it's time for supper, and you still haven't started that term-paper!

3   Sifting through the garbage to find the really great stuff is a huge challenge, but there's no need to settle for such fuzzy results. It is possible to find reliable information, quickly, without drowning in a sea of information. All it takes is a determined attitude and a suspicious mind.

4   Before rushing to the Web to research your next paper, stop and ask yourself: "Is the Internet the best place to look for the information I need?" Often the answer to that question will be, "No." Remember that reliable information may be available quickly and easily from print sources in your local library. Do not underestimate the value of print-based information resources in favour of fancy-computer, Internet-derived information.

5   However, the World-Wide-Web does provide access to a considerable array of resources for research purposes. Many large organizations, including universities, governments, corporations and non-profit groups, use the Web to disseminate information. This makes it a valuable *addition* to traditional, print-based information resources. However, information published on the Web is different from traditional print-based information in significant ways. These differences

will affect the ways in which you think about and use the Internet for information gathering.

6   Think about any useful book you have used in the past for information. How many people do you think were involved in the production of that book? There was the writer, the publisher, the editors, the book reviewers, the booksellers, the professors and the librarians, all of whom had a hand in making this book available to you. Along the way these people exercised considerable judgment regarding the accuracy and usefulness of the content of that book.

7   That's a lot of people helping you get useful information for your assignment. In theory, this publishing system for traditional print-based research limits the volume of totally erroneous and unreliable information available to researchers. Each person still has to judge the value of a given book for their particular needs, but nevertheless, everyone, unconsciously, tends to rely on a certain level of quality from anything they find published in a print source.

8   This is NOT the situation with web-published information. *Anyone can, and will, publish anything they like on the Internet!* That is the utopian, democratic promise of Internet technology — that it enables anyone to speak their mind on the global stage. And, believe it or not, some people out there don't know what they're talking about!

9   So, it's up to you to use your head, to evaluate what's reliable and what's not, based on some smart strategies we'll talk about here.

STRATEGY #1: OUTSMART THE SEARCH ENGINE!

10   As Mark Jordan point out succinctly in his essay "Ten Internet Myths," the Net is disorganized; libraries are organized. Librarians organize information in indexes and physically within libraries, using sophisticated subject classification systems, while information made available via the Web has no corresponding structure imposed upon it. The Web is a lot like the world's biggest flea market: all kinds of stuff might be available there, but how are you going to find the table selling the tennis racquets when you need it?

11   The first step to outsmarting a search engine is two-fold: Analyze your topic thoroughly, so that you have lots of alternative words and phrases to search, and learn to use the advanced search commands of your chosen search engine.

12   There are many different search engines available on the web, designed and run by organizations with various objectives. Points to remember about all search engines:

- Each one works differently from another — searching methods learned on one system probably will not work on another system.
- No one search engine searches the entire Web! Some will concentrate on recreational information, some may emphasize scholarly information, and many will fall somewhere between these two extremes. One-stop shopping does not exist on the Internet.
- Search engines index millions of webpages. These pages are not selected by a person, based on quality, but are collected automatically by the search engine, using software called a "spider" or "robot".

- The commands you learned to use yesterday may not work today — search engine software is constantly evolving, making today's search methods obsolete tomorrow.
- Your best results will depend upon how accurately you can define your topic and how well you can express that topic using the search engine's query commands. For example, a search for *'training dolphins'* might retrieve training camp reports for the Miami Dolphins football team; *'marine mammals training'* may find what you really want.

13   Whichever search engine you choose to use, take some time now to become familiar with the details of its operation. This will save you a lot of time later. All search engines provide some explanation of their search software. It's always a good idea, to read the help files provided by the search engine authors. Learning a few precision search commands, such as Boolean logic, phrase searching or truncation, will go a long way to reducing the labour of searching the Net.

14   Yes, I know, reading those help screens and practicing good search technique slows you down, and all you really want to do is zip onto the Net, get the answers and be done with research before lunchtime. Let's face it, you don't have to construct a very sophisticated search to get some kind of result out of a search engine. Even if you get a million hits, the first ten are likely to give you something useful, right?

15   Think again. Think about how a no-brainer search strategy might waste your time: Your psych professor asks you to research anxiety among workers in computer-intensive professions. You search "computers, stress" in your favorite search engine. Your results: a "stress-free" chat page for computer programmers, a handful of sales pitches for stress management software, computer-assisted engineering sites describing component stress testing, lots of suggestions on computer workstation designs to relieve physical stress, and a news article on how computers have relieved the stress of registration at universities.

16   Smarter strategies: Before starting your search on the Internet, do some background reading on your topic, perhaps in a traditional print source. Browsing encyclopedia articles, newspaper articles, or essays assigned in class will give you a wealth of alternative words and phrases to try for your computer searches. In this example, you might discover and search for the more specific word *"technophobia"*. You might also try to construct a clearer search statement, using both alternate words and the search engine's advanced search commands, *employee AND "new technology" AND (anxiety OR stress)*. A third strategy might be to repeat your search, using a different, more scholarly search engine.

17   One of the best ways to improve your use of a search engine is to take it for a test-drive, that is, analyze its performance using variations on a specific topic.

18   At each step in the test, write down the number of retrieved hits, then compare your results to see what works well and what doesn't. Here's an example:

- Start with a very simple search e.g. *language inuit* (No fancy commands, no capitals, no symbols)
- Repeat the search, changing it slightly each time:
  - capitalize a term, e.g. *language Inuit*;

- insert "AND" between the terms, e.g. *language AND Inuit*;
- insert plus signs in front of all words, e.g. *+language +Inuit*;
- turn the search into a phrase, using quotes, e.g. *"language of the Inuit"* or *"Inuit language"*.
- Try the same test on a different search engine to see how different the results can be from one search service to another.

19   It won't take long for you to see which search structures work best with your favorite search engine. Time invested now to learn this will be paid back handsomely in time saved down the road.

STRATEGY #2: CHECK THE SIGNS ON THE INFORMATION HIGHWAY!

20   The first order of business when you visit a new webpage is to figure out where the heck you've just landed. Often you will find yourself in the middle rather than at the beginning of a resource, so get oriented as soon as possible. A quality website will provide some overt clues to help you identify the source of the webpage. Look for a link referring you to the main page, a site map, or a table of contents for the website. If this is not evident, look for any other information about the author and source of the information.

21   Understanding the qualifications, expertise and bias of the author or sponsoring organization will help you evaluate whether this information is reliable and relevant to your research project. Authors on the Internet use this unfiltered, uncensored medium to broadcast an extreme range of opinion, often presented as unquestionable fact. You will find the Internet to be the ideal publishing medium for extreme points of view and beliefs. It is common for people to disguise their biases, in an attempt to "sell you" their ideas as the only "truth" about a topic.

22   Be prepared to do some digging to determine hidden agendas in web publications. Of course, a specific bias or particular viewpoint is not necessarily a bad thing, especially if it is openly stated and acknowledged by the author. However, always anticipate that a web author may have hidden intentions. More often than not, extreme bias may be cloaked by innocuous sweet-talk.

23   For example, how might you evaluate a webpage devoted to the legal abortion issue if the information was sponsored by a pro-choice organization, versus a right-to-life organization? What if the article you've used for your paper on immigrant contributions to the Canadian economy was written by the Canada-for-Canadians anti-immigration lobby group? How would you categorize an article on the health dangers of second-hand smoke written by a cigar smokers club?

24   Commercial sites also call for critical evaluation. Many for-profit organizations use the Web to distribute information that will sell their product or service. For example, would you expect to get a balanced picture on the health benefits and risks of taking a certain herbal supplement from a company that sells that product by mail order over the web? Although some corporations on the web do provide useful information as a service to their public, commercial information can sometimes be shallow, incomplete or misleading.

25   Always consider the implications of an author's association with a particular group, such as a university, government office, social organization, or private business.

26   Sometimes the origin of the webpage and the source of the author's expertise will not be evident from the content of the webpage. Don't lose hope. A great deal of source information can be gleaned by a resourceful researcher from the URL (Uniform Resource Locator), or web address of the page.

27   The basic structure of a URL is: protocol://server-name.domain-name/ directory/filename The protocol indicates what type of Internet software is used to access the resource. "http://" indicates a world-wide-web page. The server-name may be any word assigned to identify a particular computer holding internet files. The domain-name will often indicate the name of the organization and either the type of organization or the geographic location of the organization. "www.shark.stmarys.ca" would indicate a server called shark at an organization called St. Mary's in Canada. The following suffixes are often used to indicate the type of organization: .edu or .ac (educational or academic site), .com or .co (commercial site), .gov (government site), .org (non-government, or non-profit organization site).

28   Domain and server names are not always good clues to the origin of a document. There are few rules governing what a domain and server may be called, so don't assume you know from this evidence alone what the site is all about. For example, it is possible that the URL "www.roots.ca" does not point to the site of the Canadian clothing company by that name, but instead points to a Canadian genealogical supply shop. Some groups will deliberately mislead you with the construction of their URL. At first glance the well-known American site, "www.whitehouse.com", looks like the real thing, but a closer inspection reveals a spoof of the American presidential page, designed to market a company's considerable webpage construction skills.

29   Following the server-domain name, the URL indicates the name of the directory within which the displayed file resides. Names of directories, subdirectories and files can sometimes inform you about your resource. Directory or file names beginning with the character ~ often indicate the personal directory of an individual. This is a hint to check the credentials of the author carefully, even if the domain-name indicates a reliable resource such as a university. Remember, the organization hosting a page does not necessarily claim any responsibility regarding the authenticity or authority of information placed on their site by an individual.

30   So, if you're lost in cyberspace, pick up the trail of clues left to you by the site's URL. Starting from the right-hand side, delete the part of the URL following the last slash mark (/), then follow the new, shorter URL. By repeating this you can move up through the directory tree within which the file resides, until you discover the homepage of the information.

31   This is an especially useful trick to escape from those "Error: File-Not-Found" or "Error-Access-Denied" messages you often run into on the Web. Often the filename of a specific page may be changed by the authors, or the file structure may be rearranged. By tracing back to the central homepage, you may find a new link to get you to the file you need.

STRATEGY #3: LET OTHER PEOPLE FIND THE GOOD STUFF FOR YOU!

32   Not all Internet sites contain actual information on a topic. Some consist solely of links to other websites, chosen for their relevance to a particular topic. Such a website may be assembled by an expert in a particular field, or may be compiled by an amateur enthusiast.

33   Competently compiled internet subject directories are designed to help you find useful information quickly, working in a way similar to a traditional library. A subject directory lists a small, selected number of websites, all of which are evaluated and organized by a real person, using a logical subject scheme and certain criteria of excellence. Often the listings include a review or summary of each site.

34   Browsing through sites identified as useful by someone else can give you a clear sense of the characteristics common to a reliable and authoritative website. However, it can be frustrating to look for information on a very specific topic by browsing through the categories of an Internet subject directory, since such lists are often constructed using very broad subject categories. To further complicate your search, these subject categories are not standardized between different directories. Ultimately, your success with such a resource depends on the organizational talent of the directory editors, and on your persistence trying alternate searches to locate your topic.

35   Most subject directories include some kind of search software, so some of the tricks you have learned for effective searching on regular search engines, such as plus signs, quotation marks or Boolean commands, may also work when searching a subject directory. A subject directory indexes far fewer sites than a search engine, because all the indexed sites have been hand-picked by human editors. This increases your chances of finding quality resources from the start.

36   However, not all subject directories are reliable. Certain criteria are essential to help you judge the usefulness of a particular Internet subject directory. In addition to evaluating the search software and the subject structure by browsing, you should also try to determine the following details:

- Who selects the sites and who writes the comments for the included sites? What are their credentials?
- How useful are the review comments? Does the review identify such things as the scope, accuracy, or currency of the reviewed site?
- If you used the directory's search feature to find sources on a specific topic, do most of the retrieved sites seem relevant to your search?

37   Consider these types of questions to determine whether you should rely on a particular subject directory for your Internet information needs.

STRATEGY #4: BECOME A SURFING SUPER-SLEUTH!

38   Sooner or later, it all comes down to you. No one else's definition of quality will replace your own best judgment about a particular source for your particular research requirements. Your best bet is to cultivate the skills of a super-sleuth:

Look for clues, ask lots of questions, consider everybody's motive, and trust no one, until you're sure of the evidence!

39 Once you evaluate what you find on the Web against some basic quality guidelines, you can then weigh the value of the website against your particular information needs. Here are some of the most important criteria to consider:

Accuracy

40 How accurate and reliable is the information presented? Web documents are seldom subjected to the kind of editorial double-checking common in the print publishing world. Remember, anyone can publish on the Web, even if they have very little expertise about their subject. Authors can easily lie about their data and their credentials.

41 *Super-Sleuth Strategy:* Always start out by being suspicious! Try to double-check the facts against alternate resources. Has the document also been published in traditional print format? That may indicate that third-party fact-checkers helped out along the way.

42 This double-checking goes for such sources of Internet information as discussion-lists and newsgroups, as well as webpages. Just because someone thinks they are an expert on a certain topic does NOT actually mean they know what they are talking about!

Authority

43 What are the author's qualifications for writing on this subject? What organization is sponsoring the publication of this webpage? It is often very difficult to determine the authorship of a web document. Remember too, that the organization hosting the webpage may claim no responsibility for the content of the page.

44 *Super-Sleuth Strategy:* Try to determine the author's name and their qualifications. Can the author be reached other than by e-mail, such as through a regular mail address or telephone number? How did the author gather his information? Does he cite his research methods, or document his research through a quality bibliography?

45 Examine the URL, or web-address for the site, to determine the host organization of the webpage. A page sponsored by a university or other accredited organization may have more credibility than a personal webpage published by a commercial Internet supplier.

Viewpoint

46 What perspective is being offered by the author? Is there an attempt to persuade the audience of a particular opinion, or are several sides of the issue explored in a balanced, well-researched manner? If there is a perceived bias to the work, is that bias openly admitted by the author?

47 The Web often functions as a virtual soapbox, where anyone can express their opinions about any issue. The motivations of individuals who create webpages are varied and may be skillfully disguised.

48 *Super-Sleuth Strategy:* Identify the purpose of the webpage — is it trying to inform, persuade, or sell something? Does the author honestly address various

aspects of the topic, building on the scholarship of others? Weigh the effect of the author's stated or perceived bias against your information needs. Is this information, advertising or propaganda?

Currency

49 Is the content of the work up-to-date? Has the date of publication clearly been stated? There are at least three important dates relating to webpages: the date the information was first written, the date the information was placed on the web, and the date the information was last revised.

50   *Super-Sleuth Strategy:* Identify all available date information relating to a page, either stated overtly or implied by the text. Check the links on the page: are they still working, or are they outdated? Is the page updated on a regular basis, only occasionally, or never?

Coverage

51 Does the page provide in-depth or superficial coverage of the topic? Does the page contain primary information and original ideas, or is it merely a compilation of secondary links to other people's webpages? Do the graphics contribute to the information value of the page? Is there a reasonable balance between the amount of graphics and text?

52   Hypertext documents further confuse the coverage issue. It is difficult to know where one author's coverage ends and another begins. If an article is available in both print and electronic format, such as a newspaper item, it is possible that the coverage and content will differ between the versions.

53   *Super-Sleuth Strategy:* Explore web document and associated links thoroughly. Search backward, through the URL, for related files. Compare content with printed versions if possible. Always record an electronic version of a document separately from its printed counterpart in your list of works consulted. The print and electronic versions are considered to be two, separate sources.

54   The unique character of web documents adds complexity to this evaluation process. Consider these additional problems:

55   Webpages are unstable and impermanent. What is here today may be gone tomorrow. Always thoroughly document the source of your web document. Print a copy of the page, as it exists at the time you use it, and keep it on file for the duration of your project. This will ensure you can reproduce your source, just in case the item disappears from the web in the meantime.

56   Software problems can limit your access to data. Not all browsers will give you full access to all webpages. They may display only parts of the information, or they may be unable to display any of the information. Pages you may be able to access from your computer may not be accessible by others who want to follow up on your research.

57   Webpages are easily altered. Webpage data does not have the permanence of printed data formats. Pages may be rewritten and changed easily, either by the authors, or by eager hackers. Double-check with other sources when necessary.

58   Pages are often retrieved out of context. Always track down the homepage of a document, to verify the context in which the data is being published.

59   The quality of webpages may vary, even within a single website. Evaluate the quality of each webpage separately. Do not assume the entire website to be of equal reliability and quality.

SCHOLARLY SURFING CHECKLIST

60 It takes time to develop the critical thinking skills necessary to identify the relative value of different webpages. Improve your evaluation skills using a checklist such as the one below:

61   Answer Yes or No to the following questions, to help you quickly determine the merits of a webpage. The greater number of "yes" answers below, the more likely the item is of higher quality.

Authority and Accuracy
- Can you determine who is the author of this page?
- Is it clear what person or group is sponsoring this page?
- Are the background credentials supporting the authority of the author provided?
- Is any information provided to help you verify the legitimacy of the page's author/sponsor? (e.g. phone number, postal address or additional contact information? An e-mail address is not enough!)
- Are there sources for any factual information clearly listed so they may be verified in another source? (i.e. is there a bibliography?)
- Are there any editors or fact checkers who may have verified this information before it was published here?

Viewpoint
- Do the author(s) present the information as fact or opinion or conjecture?
- Are the organization's or individual's biases clearly stated?
- Does this page present more than one side of an issue?
- If there is any advertising on this page, is it clearly differentiated from the information content?
- Try to determine who or what group sponsors this webpage. Do they hold a particular view or opinion?
- Is the organization's motivation for presenting the information clearly expressed?

Currency and Coverage
- What does "up-to-date" or "current" mean for this site? (Hint: what is the latest date you can find on the site?)
- Are there dates on the page to indicate when it was written, when it was first placed on the Web, and/or when it was last revised?
- Does the site really provide information on all the aspects it claims to cover?
- If there is a print equivalent of this webpage, is there a clear indication of whether the entire work is available on the Web, or only parts of it?

ESSENTIAL INTERNET RESOURCES FOR SCHOLARLY SURFERS

Electronic Discussion Forums
The Directory of Scholarly and Professional E-Conferences
http://www.n2h2.com/KOVACS/

DejaNews
(Newsgroup Archive Search Engine)
http://www.dejanews.com/

World-Wide-Web Subject Directories
Canadian Information By Subject
http://www.nlc-bnc.ca/caninfo/ecaninfo.htm

Clearinghouse for Subject-Oriented Internet Resource Guides
http://www.lib.umich.edu/chhome.html

Digital Librarian: a librarian's choice of the best of the web
http://www.servtech.com/~mvail/home.html

Internet Public Library
http://ipl.sils.umich.edu/

Librarian's Index to the Internet
http://sunsite.berkeley.edu/InternetIndex/index.html

Lycos to 5% of the Web
http://point.lycos.com/categories/

Magellan: McKinley's Internet Directory (Click on Reviewed Sites only)
http://www.mckinley.com

WWW Virtual Library
http://vlib.stanford.edu/overview.html

Yahoo —subject directory, not search engine
http://www.yahoo.com

World-Wide-Web Search Engines
Alta Vista
http://www.altavista.digital.com

Excite
http://www.excite.com/

Infoseek
http://www.infoseek.com/

Northern Light
http://www.northernlight.com/

Open Text
http://pinstripe.opentext.com/

Lycos
http://www.lycos.com/

GoTo.com (formerly "World-Wide-Web-Worm")
http://www.goto.com/

Webcrawler
http://webcrawler.com/

Meta-Search Engines (Searches multiple search engines)
Inference Find
http://www.infind.com/

Metacrawler
http://www.metacrawler.com/

Internet Sleuth
http://www.isleuth.com/

Citing the Internet

Electronic References & Scholarly Citations of Internet Sources
http://www.gu.edu.au/gint/WWWVL/OnlineRefs.html

Karla's Guide to Citation Style Guides
http://bailiwick.lib.uiowa.edu/journalism/cite.html

Topics for consideration:

1. Searches on the Internet frequently turn up material differing wildly from the searcher's intention. What does your own experience of surprisingly irrelevant results tell you about how the Internet functions?

2. Thomson warns readers against websites that function as "virtual soapboxes" for writers whose motivations are "often not clearly professed." Analyze the content of and possible motivation for one such site you have come across.

3. The URLs given in the "Further reading" sections throughout this text were all up-to-date at the time of publication. How many of these have since disappeared? How many of these "disappeared" sites can you find using the technique Thomson suggests?

Further reading:

http://home.ptd.net/~everhart/schoolmedia.html A Web page evaluation worksheet.